SHAKESPEARE'S PROVERBIAL LANGUAGE

An Index

SHAKESPEARE'S PROVERBIAL LANGUAGE
AN INDEX

R. W. DENT

UNIVERSITY OF CALIFORNIA PRESS
Berkeley   Los Angeles   London

University of California Press
Berkeley and Los Angeles, California

University of California Press, Ltd.
London, England

Library of Congress Cataloging in Publication Data

Dent, Robert William.
    Shakespeare's proverbial language.

    Bibliography
    1. Shakespeare, William, 1564–1616—
Dictionaries, indexes, etc.   2. Shakespeare,
William, 1564–1616—Language.   3. Proverbs,
English—Indexes.   I. Title.
PR2892.D43   1981   822.3'3   80-19673
ISBN 0-520-03894-0

Printed in the United States of America

To the Memory of
JOHN CROW, J. C. MAXWELL, AND F. P. WILSON

ACKNOWLEDGMENTS

I wish to express my gratitude for the good-humored patience of my wife and children, for the able and gracious staffs of the Huntington and UCLA Libraries and of the University of California Press, and for the encouragement and counsel of such friends as Albert Braunmuller, Thomas Clayton, William Elton, Catherine Gannon, Paul Jorgensen, Richard Lanham, Richard Levin, and Paul Zall.

CONTENTS

ROMANCES

POEMS

APPENDIXES

INTRODUCTION

In 1950 a major contribution to students of English Renaissance literature appeared: Morris Palmer Tilley's *A Dictionary of the Proverbs in England in the Sixteenth and Seventeenth Centuries*.[1] It was made especially valuable for students of Shakespeare by the provision of a "Shakespeare Index" (pp. 803–808), a work-by-work, line-by-line cross-reference to almost 3,000 Shakespeare citations within the collection. One may not agree with all the citations, and one may discover that many additional passages might similarly have been recorded, but the index has been an extremely useful starting point for many editors and students of Shakespeare's language, although it has been ignored or badly misused in a surprising number of recent major editions. Two decades after Tilley, two additional proverb collections of major importance appeared: *Proverbs, Sentences, and Proverbial Phrases from English Writings mainly before 1500*, edited by B. J. and H. W. Whiting,[2] and F. P. Wilson's Shakespeare-and-Tilley-minded revision of *The Oxford Dictionary of English Proverbs*.[3] Both have been largely ignored by Shakespeare scholarship.

The present work, composed in the light of post-Tilley scholarship, including that by Whiting and Wilson, is primarily a revision and expansion of Tilley's "Shakespeare Index." To make it as useful as possible without recourse to its principal sources, the resulting index is accompanied by three separately paginated appendixes. Their purpose and relationship to the index itself are described on pp. 1–3 below.

For reasons there explained, this index should prove far less subject to misuse than its predecessor, but it needs to be employed with a comparable wariness. The next few pages, although focused upon difficulties in using Tilley and its "Shakespeare Index," suggest precautions necessary in working with this volume as well. Where possible, I use *1 Henry IV* for illustration, partly because it is a play especially rich in proverbial elements, but mainly because it has an old Arden edition full of notes relevant to proverbs (ed. R. P. Cowl and A. E. Morgan, 1914+), a new Arden edition much better than several in its use of Tilley, though not

1. Ann Arbor: University of Michigan Press.
2. Cambridge, Mass.: The Belknap Press of Harvard University Press, 1968. Referred to as Whiting below, or as Wh when with an entry number.

Whiting, pp. x–xvii, provides an illuminating discussion of his own principles of inclusion. As he implies on p. xvi, many of his entries are supported by only a single quotation and are only tentatively proverbial. This inclusiveness is one great value of his collection for any student of Elizabethan literature, but it must be used with common sense. For an entry supported only by a line from Chaucer, for example, it would be extremely perilous to assume that a recurrence in an Elizabethan author is necessarily the reflection of something proverbial. But the present index will indicate frequently how a single instance in Whiting can provide us just such assurance as we need. See, for example, on *The Two Gentlemen of Verona* 2.3.10–12.
3. Oxford: Clarendon Press, 1970.

ideal (ed. A. R. Humphreys, 1960), and a Variorum *Supplement* employing Tilley (ed. G. B. Evans, 1956). I refer to these as OA, Arden, and Variorum.

Precautions[4]

Tilley's *Dictionary*, referred to as Tilley, has been and will remain an immensely useful tool. It is the careful and thoughtful product of a man who devoted his entire scholarly career to the study of proverbs, especially Elizabethan proverbs. Nothing in the following pages intends to imply anything to the contrary. This volume is intended to replace Tilley's "Shakespeare Index" in a format usable without access to Tilley (or Wilson or Whiting); it is nothing more than a Shakespeare-oriented supplement to Tilley's *Dictionary*. But that *Dictionary*, like my own Appendix A to a lesser degree, remains a tool to be used with caution. These present pages are wholly concerned with clarifying some of the reasons for that caution, especially in defining what may be called "proverbial" in Shakespeare.

Paradoxically, I shall attempt no definition of the word "proverb," and I know of no existing definition that will embrace all acknowledged examples. I would agree with James Howell, in the preface to his 1659 collection, that "the chief Ingredients that go to make a true Proverb [are] *Sense, shortnesse* and *Salt*" (although some of Howell's own examples are neither short nor salty), and I would agree that many, although far fewer than Howell implies, are "in point of Generation . . . a kind of Naturall Children, and of an unknown birth . . . legitimated by Prescription and long Trace of Ancestriall Time." Tilley's own solution, or rather the principal part of that solution, begins his "Foreword":

> There is no agreement on what constitutes a proverb. In this collection of proverbs, proverbial phrases, and proverbial similes I have entered such material as the writers in the period from 1500 to 1700 included in their elastic conception of what was proverbial. Obviously this contemporary conception transcends the limited definition of a proverb as a saying of the folk.[5] The proverb collections from these two centuries, which are the basis of our Dictionary, admitted material that seemed to their compilers to be proverbial or at least of sufficient currency to be entitled to that term.

---

4. This section of the Introduction is adapted from my "Shakespeare and the use of Tilley's *Dictionary*," an as yet unpublished essay written for *SRO: Shakespearean Research Opportunities*, ed. W. R. Elton. Even in references to other editions, Shakespeare lineation throughout is that of *The Riverside Shakespeare*, edited by G. Blakemore Evans, et al. (Boston: Houghton Mifflin, 1974).

5. Archer Taylor's still authoritative *The Proverb* (Cambridge, Mass.: Harvard University Press, 1931) begins: "The definition of a proverb is too difficult to repay the undertaking. . . . Let us be content with recognizing that a proverb is a saying current among the folk. At least so much of a definition is indisputable . . ." (p. 3).

Usually, despite some complications to be discussed later, this collection-based principle of selections is a satisfactory one. By it, however, one can get such an entry as M475 (A man's mind often gives him warning of evil to come), supported only by a half dozen Shakespearean reflections of this familiar belief and by the 1616 proverb collection of Thomas Draxe, from whom Tilley took the drab wording used for his entry form (i.e., heading). The collection of passages from Shakespeare is useful, perhaps well worth citing in editions, but I for one, despite Draxe, would not willingly call either his formulation or any of the Shakespearean passages "proverbial."[6]

In addition, Tilley includes passages whose context indicates they are proverbial, whether or not they appear in any proverb collections. Once again, the principle of selection is undoubtedly sound, although it may be suspected that not every writer who called something a "proverb" did so legitimately. Thus, in Henry Porter's proverb-saturated *The Two Angry Women of Abingdon*,[7] Philip Barnes speaks disparagingly of his father's servant, Nicholas Proverbes:

> This formall foole your man speakes nought but proverbs,
> And speake men what they can to him, hee'l answere
> With some rime, rotten sentence, or olde saying,
> Such spokes as the ancient of the parish use,
> With neighbour tis an olde proverbe and a true,
> Goose giblets are good meate, old sacke better than new.
>   [MSR, lines 848–853]

Line 853 is Tilley's unique example, predictably, for G93, a proverb entry that almost certainly should be deleted. For Philip's "olde proverbe" is a parody, goose giblets being proverbially worthless (cf. G364: To steal a goose and give the giblets in alms), "stinking garbage" in Nashe's terms,[8]

---

6. This index excludes extreme instances of this kind, especially when there is no corresponding entry in Wilson (OW below), but records more marginal ones. The latter are preceded by a question mark in Appendix A. Concurrence in OW, however, need not imply F. P. Wilson's intentional agreement, although in some cases it may do so. Since one of Wilson's principal purposes was to provide earlier examples for entries where Tilley began misleadingly late, and since revising the ODEP did not allow him the luxury of footnotes, some Tilley-derived entries and citations obviously result from this aim. Others, one infers, must have been the result of some clerical process—for example, S150 (identical in OW705a), which consists merely of a line from *The Two Gentlemen of Verona* used as an entry form and supported by two passages in Lyly, both verbally dissimilar, and at least one expressing a very different idea. The present index, of course, excludes this entry (cf. Appendix C), although Arden includes a "cf. Tilley, S150."
H305 (A good heart conquers ill fortune [overcomes all]) presents a rather frustrating and puzzling instance of such concurrence. In addition to examples verifying the existence of such a proverb, Tilley cites *2 Henry IV* 2.4.31 f. and *Othello* 1.3.206 f. I exclude both, since the first is not concerned with conquering ill fortune, and the second is not concerned with a good heart. But OW320a not only includes both but adds passages from *2* and *3 Henry VI* which seem to me even more remote.
7. Published in 1599, but a 1590 allusion appears to date it at least a decade earlier. Anyone interested in Elizabethan proverbs and their use in the drama will wish we could be more certain.
8. Ed. McKerrow, I, 239.

and an old sack (not Falstaff's species of sack) proverbially a source of trouble (e.g., S8: An old sack asks much patching).

In this connection, it may be profitable to observe Shakespeare's own use of the word *proverb*. Most frequently the referent is a familiar sententious proverb (e.g., "A staff is quickly found to beat a dog" in *2 Henry VI* 3.1.170 f.), sometimes explicitly stated, sometimes not, and with its identity occasionally open to debate.[9] But all usages are not of this kind. In *The Comedy of Errors* 3.1.51 f., a "proverb" exchange appears to consist merely of an allusion to "To set up one's staff" (S804) answered by a newly popular rejoinder, "When? can you tell?" (T88). Especially interesting is the proverb-capping battle of *Henry V* 3.7.113–124:

	Orl. "Ill will never said well."	(I41)
	Con. I will cap that proverb with "There is flattery	
115	in friendship."	(cf. F349, T562)
	Orl. And I will take up that with "Give the devil	
	his due."	(D273)
	Con. Well plac'd. There stands your friend for the	
	devil; have at the very eye of that proverb with "A	
120	pox of the devil."	
	Orl. You are the better at proverbs, by how much	
	"A fool's bolt is soon shot."	(F515)
	Con. You have shot over.	
124	*Orl.* 'Tis not the first time you were overshot.	

As noted, the sequence includes four common sententious proverbs, all in Tilley and in his index.[10] But the context implies, in addition, that there *must* be something proverbial about "A pox of the devil" (119 f.), and very possibly about "shot over" and "overshot." Let us begin with the last. Compare the 1616 Draxe mentioned on p. xiii (one of Tilley's principal sources, but one he employed with some puzzling inclusions and omissions), s.v. Wisdome, no. 2438: "A wise man may sometimes overshoot himselfe." In the present index, keyed to Tilley, this becomes M427.1; in Appendix A, it is supported by earlier instances. It seems clear that line 124 alludes to this conventional sententious proverb.

The same proverb might seem to account for line 123, although it would be awkward for two speakers in a contest to use the same proverb. They do not, even though the two are closely related, and the non-sententious one for 123 must precede the other. Because *tongue-tied*, for example, occurs in John Heywood's famous dialogue of proverbs, and hence "To be tongue-tied" in Tilley, OW, and Whiting, this present index

9. See on *A Midsummer Night's Dream* 3.2.463, *The Merry Wives of Windsor* 3.5.152, *Romeo and Juliet* 1.4.37 f., and *Coriolanus* 1.1.207.
10. I am somewhat misleading. Tilley, followed by OW243b, enters 114 f. under F41, inserting a parenthetical "(flattery)" into the common "There is falsehood in friendship," although giving no other example with *flattery*. My index instead excludes F41 and cites two alternate proverbs that parallel the idea but not the precise wording.

nervously but dutifully records every instance of the word in Shakespeare. *Henry V* makes clear that Shakespeare would have expected an equally simple entry for "To overshoot oneself (be overshot)." 091.1 in Appendix A cites instances from c1530, including 1546 Heywood and three other passages in Shakespeare.

As for "A pox of the devil," which appears in context more necessarily proverbial than the two passages just examined (if that is indeed what is "proverbial" in lines 118–120), I have nothing helpful to suggest. *OED* s.v. *Pox* sb. 3 gives various examples of *A pox on* or *of* (I should probably have included the expression in my Appendix B), but only this with *devil*. Nor have I noted the expression elsewhere. We can scarcely assume, despite the context, that there should be an entry for "A pox of the devil," although *proverb* is used broadly enough in Shakespeare to include such a phrase. Nor can we assume, conversely, that every context-determined entry in Tilley reflects what Shakespeare had in mind. In *The Two Gentlemen of Verona* 3.1.304 f., for example, despite B450/OW85a (Blessing of your heart, you brew good ale), I suspect the "proverb" may be no more than the phrase "Blessing of your heart."

Nevertheless, Tilley's first two criteria for determining entries are generally beyond cavil. A third principle of inclusion, although it contributes greatly to Tilley's usefulness, is more questionable in a dictionary of proverbs:

> In addition to recording admitted proverbs, I have, where I found recurring independent instances of the same thought in printed works of the period, included such sayings as well, preferring to err on the side of inclusiveness rather than on the side of exclusiveness. I have entered pithy expressions of old truths or of accepted facts, the observations of generations, warnings, admonitions, guides to conduct, accumulated wisdom that has stood the test of time.

Thus, even when supported with a proverb collection, a good deal of Tilley's informative data can be described as "proverbial" only with reservation, if at all. This is probably true of G449/OW338b (Grief pent up will break the heart), a recurrent idea never given any characteristic verbal formulation such as one tends to expect of full-fledged proverbs; it may well be true both for the entry form and for most of Tilley's examples under Biblically based C23/OW230b (Everyone must walk [labor] in his own calling [vocation]), although a few examples suggest that Falstaff's wording in 1.2.104 f. intentionally perverts a formulation that could be called proverbial (neither Variorum nor Arden cites Tilley);[11] it is cer-

---

11. Some editors are inclined to reject the claim for "proverbial" on passages whose ultimate origins are Biblical. For such an entry as L250/OW461b (Life is a shuttle), which consists merely of a quotation from Job and one from *The Merry Wives of Windsor*, they would undoubtedly be correct. But Falstaff abundantly illustrates that many Biblical entries are legitimately "proverbial." When he and Prince Hal play upon "wisdom cries out in the streets, and no man regards it" (1.2.81–89), nothing "proverbial" from an Elizabethan point of view is involved, even though the origin is in Proverbs 1.24. But when Falstaff Euphuizes

tainly true for N307, Tilley's first entry for *1 Henry IV*. This last I exclude from my index, instead recording it in Appendix C with the explanation "Not a proverb." Here Arden's note, warning that the idea reflected in 1.1.106 f. is only "quasi-proverbial," is considerably more satisfactory than Variorum's noncommittal "TILLEY" (1950) N307: Nothing is well said or done in a passion (in anger)." One could give further instances by the score (cf. Appendix C)—for example, the entry on vengeance belonging only to God (V24),[12] or on the dangers of fresh air for a diseased or wounded man (A93)—especially if one included all instances of folklore lacking proverbial formulations.

A Tilley-like *Dictionary* devoted to folklore and superstition would be a useful tool. Such an entry as the following could remove the puzzlement of OA and could replace the silence of Arden:

D623.1 DROWSINESS is ominous
c1591 (1592) *Arden of Feversham* v.17: This drowsiness in me bodes little good.
c1592 (1594) Marlowe *Edward II* 4.6.44 f.: Drowsiness Betides no good. 1620
Melton *Astrologaster* G3ᵛ: If a man be drowsie, it is a signe of ill lucke.
Shakespeare: *Tit.* 2.3.195−197 (just before catastrophe for both)
[My sight is very dull, what e'er it bodes. / And mine, I promise you;
were it not for shame, Well could I leave our sport to sleep a while.]

No such entry appears in Tilley, but analogous entries do. Probably not one out of every dozen Elizabethan superstitions receives an entry, and anyone interested in Shakespeare's use of proverbs should realize that, with rare exceptions, those that do appear are no more "proverbial" than those that do not. One of Tilley's two Shakespeare citations under T259/OW818b (To stumble at the threshold)[13] illustrates the point. It alludes to

---

on the defiling effect of touching pitch (2.4.410−414), or defends his "frailty" (3.3.167 f.), he is playing with what was incontestably proverbial (P358, F363; Arden acknowledges the latter). One further instance is somewhat interesting. For Falstaff's "If then the tree may be known by the fruit, as the fruit by the tree" (2.4.428 f.), Arden cites Scripture and Lyly (as it does for 2.4.410−414 above); both undeniably contain the first half of Falstaff's line. Both halves are proverbial, however, as T497 makes evident; Whiting gives each a separate entry (T472, 465, the latter varied).

12. A very inadequate entry, incidentally, both in its Biblical and its Elizabethan citations. OW673a revises to a legitimate proverb (Revenge is a morsel for God), but retains Tilley's citation of *Richard II* 1.2.6−8, which has no hint of this blasphemy. John of Gaunt was no speaker of what were called "Satan's proverbs." See on S300.

13. This is a proverb only when used figuratively; cf. fn. 22. Somewhat inconsistently, I retain R33/OW665a (with a question mark in Appendix A) on the ominous raven, but exclude B99/OW31b (The basilisk's eye is fatal) and C495 (The cockatrice slays by sight only). These I replace with more legitimate entries, proverbial similes: "To kill like a basilisk" (B99.1) and "To kill like a cockatrice" (C496.2).

Although all the following seem to me more folklore than proverb (each accordingly gets a question mark in Appendix A), the index for *A Midsummer Night's Dream* retains S66/OW696b/Wh S26 (On Saint Valentine's day all the birds in couples do join), S490/OW817a/Wh S353 (The three sisters ["the Sisters Three" by proverb-loving Launce in *The Merchant of Venice* 2.2.63 suggests my question mark may be a mistake]), even M240/OW504a/Wh M138 (The man in the moon), but with a protesting footnote on the latter. Supported by Whiting, the index courageously excludes R147/OW681a (Robin Goodfellow).

a wholly different superstition, but one that might with equal justice be called "proverbial": "Three times to-day my foot-cloth horse did stumble" (*Richard III* 3.4.84). On dying Hotspur's "O, I could prophesy" (5.4.83), Arden provides what seems to me an appropriate note, one that makes Tilley's information available without any implication of its being proverbial: "cf. Tilley, M514—'Dying men speak true (prophesy)';[14] an allusion to the belief that a dying man can foretell the future . . ."; here the Variorum is sensibly silent, since Tilley's nonproverb adds nothing to earlier Variorum notes.

So much for the need for caution as it relates to Tilley's three principles of inclusion. Another source of difficulty, as with any comparable dictionary of proverbs, is the entry form. Here the resulting danger, as obvious as it is inescapable, is often ignored. A group of passages gathered together under an entry form that sounds proverbial may or may not support the legitimacy of the entry. H292 (To drink health is to drink sickness) sounds very like a proverb; instead, it is simply a slight misquotation from Dekker (who has *healths*), and the examples supporting it are merely variously worded warnings on the physical and financial consequences of drinking excessive toasts. The Arden *Timon of Athens*, misled by the entry form, in turn misleads its users by describing 1.2.56 f. as "A variation on the proverb"; there is no evidence that any such proverb ever existed. The most easily misused entries of this kind, of course, are those where the entry form is verbatim, or nearly verbatim, Shakespeare (a fact noted where pertinent in my Appendix A). For example, D354/OW189b (Discretion is the better part of valor) takes its entry form from a slight reordering of Falstaff's famous rationalization. That discretion is an essential component of true valor is an ancient idea, as OW makes evident, and its formulation by Falstaff has long been proverbial, with echoes beginning as far back as Fletcher; but our present evidence does not warrant Arden's simple description of 5.4.119 f.: "Proverbial; Tilley, D354."[15]

---

14. M514 muddles together two quite different elements—the superstition specified by Arden (which I exclude) and the more rational conviction, perhaps proverbial, that dying men speak true. Several of Tilley's entries for thoroughly legitimate proverbs similarly, but more seriously, need division: for example, E116, which fails to distinguish between the end as triumph and as judge (a distinction clear in OW and Whiting); F585, which equates our desire for the forbidden with our desire for the self-destructive (OW excludes the latter); and F604, which combines the abhorrent blindness of Fortune with the admirable blindness requisite for Justice (OW mistakenly has no entry for the latter). Less important are the instances where entries might well be combined without loss (almost always they are cross-referenced to one another). Thus S574, under which Tilley cites Hotspur's "O, he is as tedious / As a tired horse, a railing wife, / Worse than a smoky house" (3.1.157–159), is merely a minor variant of H781. While Arden cites both, Variorum cities neither, presumably satisfied by the single quotation from Chaucer provided ever since Steevens. This is misleading.

15. Akin to the misleading H292 are L568 (merely *The Merchant of Venice* 2.6.4 and a wholly nonverbal analogue in *The Two Gentlemen of Verona*; the Arden *Two Gentlemen*, nevertheless, says "cf. Tilley, L568"), and C918 (*Troilus and Cressida* 1.3.389 with a paren-

If an entry form can mislead us into calling something proverbial that is not, it can similarly encourage our missing something actually proverbial. Take the 1530 citation under C706 (Oft counting makes good friends): "The commune proverbe is that ofte rekenynge holdeth longe felawshyp." For me, at least, this clarifies the jest in what has otherwise seemed a pointless line: Falstaff's "Well, thou hast call'd her to a reckoning many a time and oft" (1.2.49 f.). The entry form obscures it completely. Troublesome in a slightly different way is D148/OW174a (Death pays all debts), undeniably a proverb of the period, although our earliest known unmistakable example is Tilley's third citation from Shakespeare: *The Tempest* 3.2.131. The wording of the earliest citation, however—Prince Hal's "the end of life cancels all bands" (3.2.157)—so closely resembles the "common saying" cited for 1603 and the following citation of 1609 that the three should perhaps have been given a separate entry.[16] Arden is misleading: "The sentiment is proverbial: 'Death pays all debts' (Tilley, D148)"; Variorum is silent. Just such an additional entry OW186b provides for Tilley's second Shakespeare citation under D148: *2 Henry IV* 3.2.238. Citing 1578 Thomas White, but not Shakespeare, it nevertheless informs us that Feeble's "He that dies this year is quit for the next" had been disapproved a generation earlier as a "Heathen proverb . . . too common among Christians" (D326.1 in this index and Appendix A). Only the chance survival of a single sermon assures us that proverb-mouthing Feeble was not, on one occasion, surprisingly original. Rather than the mere entry form for D148, apparently, there were at least two—perhaps three—closely related but verbally distinct proverbs, with Shakespeare providing an example of each of them. These illustrations are enough, I trust, to show the danger of ever assuming that an entry form adequately represents the content of the entry as a whole.[17] It would be easy to provide more, especially since a

---

thetical ["bite"] to allow two late instances of an actual proverb, a proverb differently worded and with a wholly different sense). Both are relegated to Appendix C.

A bit more defensible, and hence included with a question mark, is M1050. The entry form is *The Merry Wives of Windsor* 2.2.168 f., with *do* omitted. Arden calls it "a popular maxim," but the four supporting entries have verbally nothing in common beyond the word *money*, and they share only a very widespread and ancient idea.

16. Because the 1609 entry may be a mere echo, I decided against making a separate entry.

17. Some proverbs admit so many variations that they defy any adequate entry form. An extreme example is B607: "His old brass (cloak) will buy you a new pan (kirtle)," under which, along with many other variations, one finds "An old cloak makes a new jerkin" (*The Merry Wives of Windsor* 1.3.17) and "your old smock brings forth a new petticoat" (*Antony and Cleopatra* 1.2.168 f. The present index amends the entry form to "His old brass (etc.) will buy (make) you a new pan (etc.)," which scarcely helps much. Thanks to Tilley's "Shakespeare Index," it has long been easy to correlate these two passages with B607. Had he missed either of them, things would be more difficult. For Tilley's terminal "Index of Significant Words," unlike that in Whiting, limits itself to words in the entry forms. The *Wives* passage could eventually be found among the thirty entries under *Cloak*, and the *Antony* passage, theoretically, after looking in vain under *Smock* and *Petticoat*, amid the hundred or so entries under *Old* (except that B607 is not listed under *Old*, although the index is an exceptionally full and accurate one). As for Hal's "The end of life cancels all bands," discussed above, one could find it in Tilley's index only by guessing that "the end of life" might, in the entry form, prove to be "death."

favorite source for Tilley's entry forms is the proverb collections of the late 17th and early 18th centuries, those of John Ray and Thomas Fuller, M.D., most of all. Early citations under these forms, if any, may be of most interest for Shakespeare when least like the form.

Mention of Ray and Fuller can introduce the problem of dates, a problem ignored or slighted by many Arden editors (grossly by a few). Although Hilda Hulme is partly right in assuming "a proverb will take root in the spoken language before it finds a place in the printed collections,"[18] the fact that Tilley records a passage from a late collection need not mean it was proverbial in Shakespeare's day; frequently it may not mean that the passage was proverbial ever. Near the conclusion of Howell's 1659 "English Proverbs," for example, are two passages for which Tilley's only earlier examples are from Bacon's 1612 *Essays* (M547, W379). Both then reappear, just as we would expect, in 1670 Ray and in 1732 Fuller. Should we then infer that they were proverbs when Bacon wrote them? Or even by the time of 1732 Fuller? I doubt it, and I am glad that OW excludes both.[19] Equally dubious are many entries where the proverbial quality of a passage from Lyly is supported mainly by 1732 Fuller (in at least twenty-five instances only by him), for it would be easy to prove that Fuller (or some contributor to his collection) worked directly from copies of *Euphues* and *Euphues and his England*, sometimes even for common proverbs.[20] Fuller's title page, we must realize, does not promise that all "witty sayings" in the collection can be called "proverbs." Thus, when a passage in Shakespeare is only analogous to one in Lyly, we need more than Fuller before calling the Shakespeare "a variation on [or 'an expansion of'] the proverb." And I would be at least as hesitant so to describe (as does the Arden *Comedy of Errors* 2.1.34−37) a passage with nothing outside Shakespeare except Fuller. (In this instance, I should concede, analogues preceding Shakespeare can be found under M182.)

For *1 Henry IV* 3.1.58, 61, Variorum omits T566 (Speak the truth and shame the devil), presumably considering the earlier Variorum's reference to 1678 Ray quite enough. Tilley's entry reassures us that the proverb was indeed common even before Shakespeare was born. But for Falstaff's "Hang thyself in thine own . . . garters" (2.2.43 f.)—where, pre-

18. *Explorations in Shakespeare's Language* (London: Longman, 1962), p. 49.
19. In *John Webster's Borrowing* (Berkeley: University of California Press, 1960), p. 285, concerning a passage in "A Divellish Usurer," I glibly wrote: "James Howell, probably with no awareness of the present passage, offers an almost verbatim version in his 1659 collection of proverbs. . . . Tilley, U28, begins with Howell." On the matter of awareness I was demonstrably wrong. The same page (with both Bacon passages nearby) includes "A Drunkard is doubly divorced from himself, for when he is got sober, he is scarce his own man, and being in drink, he cometh short by many degrees." This makes better sense in Burleigh's *Certaine Precepts* (c1598 [1617]), sig. A6 f., for it there concerns a drunken *servant*. This particular section of Howell, clearly, has plenty of nonproverbial borrowings in it.
20. For example, Fuller's unusual version of the very common H160 (You shall as soon catch a hare with a tabor) is verbatim from an uncited passage in *Euphues and his England* (ed. Bond, II, 99).

sumably for the same reason, Variorum does not cite G42—Tilley has no examples prior to Shakespeare, and only Harington's 1591 Ariosto has since been discovered (OW349b).

It is similarly perilous to assume something is proverbial where the only cited examples outside Shakespeare may merely be echoes. Conceivably this is true of Hal's "the devil rides upon a fiddle-stick" (2.4.487 f.), which Arden unquestioningly annotates with "Proverbial; Tilley D263," although the three other known instances are in later plays by Fletcher and Brome-Heywood. (Characteristically, and, in this instance, probably correctly, OA is similarly positive, pre-Tilley, on the basis of the same evidence.)

Closely related to the problem of "echoes," if not identical with it, are difficulties caused by the extensive borrowing from one another practiced in widely varying degrees by virtually every author of Shakespeare's day. Until proved mistaken (which may well happen), I shall continue to think Sidney's Astrophil the originator of "I am no pickpurse of another's wit." But I have seen the same claim, verbatim in its essentials, in translator Sir John Harington (1591), astrology-defender Sir Christopher Heydon (1603), epigrammatist Henry Parrot (1608), preacher George Benson (1609), and poet William Drummond (1615)—more evidence of currency than Tilley provides for at least half its entries. The expression should probably be added to Tilley, but we have at present no reason to think it was proverbial when Sidney used it, or even when Harington did so.

In such an age of pickpurses it is frequently difficult, or impossible, to identify what Tilley called "independent instances of the same thought" (see above, p. xv); a good many Tilley entries, certainly, provide more evidence of borrowing than of anything one can call genuinely proverbial. Let me illustrate the problem, however, with four passages *not* cited by Tilley:

1579 S. Gosson, *The Schoole of Abuse*, sig. A2: "The *Syrens* songe is the Saylers wracke: the Fowlers whistle, the birdes death: the wholesome baite, the fishes bane: The Harpies have Virgins faces, & vulturs Talents [cf. H176.1]: *Hyena* speakes like a friend, & devours like a Foe: The calmest Seas hide dangerous rockes: the Woolfe iettes in weathers felles [cf. 1575 Gascoigne under W614 (A wolf in a lamb's skin): Wolves do walke in wethers felles].

1595 R. Turner, *The Garland of a greene Witte*, sig. B4ᵛ: "the Siren sweetly sings yᵉ Saylers wracke"; sig. C1: "the Scarabe flyes over many a sweet flower, and lights on a Cowshard [B221; Gosson, sig. A1ᵛ] . . . the Sirens song is the Saylers wracke, the Fowlers whistle the birds death, the wholesome bayte the Fishes bane, the Harpies have virgines faces, the vultures talents. Hienna speakes like a friend, and devours like a foe, the calmest seas hides dangerous rocks, the Woolfe iets in Weathers fells."

1601 A. Dent, *The Plaine Mans Path-Way to Heaven*, sig. M6: "These men are like . . . a daungerous rocke hid under a calme sea. Or as the Heathen say: Like the *Syrens* song, which is the Saylers wracke. Like the Fowlers whistle, which is the birds death. Like the hid baite, which is the fishes bane. Like the Harpies, which have virgins faces, and Vultures talents. Or like *Hyena*, which speaketh like a friend, and devoureth like a foe."

1609 D. Tuvil, *Essayes, Morall and Theologicall*, sig. G3ᵛ: "Saith the Italian Proverb. Every mans looke is not the mappe of his meaning. The Syrens song is the sailors wrack; the Fowlers whistle the birds death; and the wholesome baite the fishes bane."

The Gosson passage (like several others in this little work) could easily introduce several additional entries for Tilley (cf. H176.1), and the degree of their interrelationship would be hidden by their being scattered throughout the *Dictionary*. What is true for these potential entries is equally true for many actual entries, as I have suggested by the bracketed notes above. But some of these potential entries, despite the particular evidence of borrowing indicated above, may have been, or have become, legitimate proverbs.

If Tilley's inclusiveness in his almost 12,000 "proverb" entries is one source of difficulty, so, too, is his inclusiveness in Shakespeare citations. Although the Foreword never explicitly says so, many of these must surely have been intended as suggestions for consideration rather than as declarations of supposed fact (just as are many citations with a question mark in the present index). Despite its title, Tilley is by no means a dictionary in the sense that the *OED* is one, and its compiler must have endlessly regretted a format that precluded his explaining the rationale underlying some of his inclusions. It is no surprise to see that many such suggestions are rejected by editors (never, one hopes, without due consideration of Tilley's possible reason for citing).[21] Of the nine Shakespeare passages under F3 (Fair face, foul heart), for example, only two seem to me similar enough verbally to be worth mention (the clearest is Lady Macbeth's "False face must hide what the false heart doth know"); the others might just as easily have been included under F29 (Fair without but foul within), or merely omitted, as sharing no more than an extremely common idea. The present index excludes them (although my F3 has six Shakespeare citations). It similarly excludes citations that are literal applications of some-

---

21. I doubt that either Variorum or Arden so considered what seems to me the clear relevance to *1 Henry IV* 4.4.34 f. of W912 (It is good to fear the worst), an unmistakable proverb reflected several times in Shakespeare, as Tilley and the present index indicate. Had Arden done so, it would not have preferred Capell's semicolon after *fear* to Pope's deletion of a comma in the original text. Arden reads: "yet needful 'tis to fear; / And to prevent the worst, Sir Michael, speed." The retention of the original comma in the Riverside text is somewhat less objectionable. Probably both should have heavier punctuation after *worst*.

thing proverbial only when figurative. There is nothing proverbial about literally kissing the ground, or dancing barefoot, or blowing one's nails, or putting one's finger to one's lips.[22] Even so, given the implied intention of citing every relevant passage, Tilley entries are sometimes surprisingly incomplete. One aim of the present index and of Appendix A is to compensate not only for this shortcoming, but for that discussed next.

What is true for individual entries is true for individual works; for some, the number of Shakespeare citations seems relatively excessive (although, in every instance, my own index adds at least as many Tilley entries as it excludes);[23] for some, it seems much too spare. The late J. C. Maxwell, an expert on Elizabethan proverbs, tacitly rejected 27 of Tilley's 62 entries for the Arden *Titus Andronicus*, at least 8 because he must have considered them too common or too trivial to mention (this index excludes 10); Clifford Leech's *The Two Gentlemen of Verona*, in contrast, cites so many of Tilley's 75 entries that I suspect the two omissions (P326, U22) may have been accidental (I exclude 7, but neither of the pair just named). As for *1 Henry IV*, I would expect an ideal edition to cite at least 61 of Tilley's 111 citations, frequently on the basis of additional evidence not available to Arden or Variorum. Arden cites only 41, Variorum only 38, partly because rarely willing to mention Tilley for passages called proverbial by previous editors, however slight their evidence. The present index excludes 19, but it adds enough from Tilley and elsewhere to end up with 187. Admittedly, many of these I would totally ignore were I an Arden or Variorum editor.

In this connection, one further word can be said about such fully annotated editions as the Arden and Variorum. Some of the OAs spend a depressing proportion of their available space citing parallels from Shakespeare's predecessors, contemporaries, and successors. Tilley, or the present index, often allows extensive space saving. For Hotspur's repeated "tell truth, and shame the devil" (3.1.58, 61), Arden's "Proverbial; Tilley, T566) adequately replaces eleven lines in OA and assures the reader, as OA's examples do not, that the proverb was indeed current prior to Shakespeare.[24] Arden itself could have replaced most of 36 lines on "Saint Nicholas' clerks" (2.1.61 f.) with a mere "cf. Tilley, S54." But unless the editor employs such condensation with care, he may mislead

22. I have excluded, for example, literal references to thumb-biting in *Romeo and Juliet* 1.1.42–51 (T273 OW62a), to looking to one's water in *2 Henry IV* 1.2.1 f., (W109/OW483b), to stumbling at the threshold (T259 OW818b; see p. xvi above), and to means of recognizing the devil in *Othello* 5.2.286 (D252/OW182a). 1611 Cotgrave s.v. Diable (on the last named) well illustrates the distinction: "On cognoit le diable a ses gristes: Pro. *The divell is knowne by his clawes; a covetous heart discerned by catching hands.*" Othello's "I look down at his feet; but that's a fable" is literal.
23. See "Principles of Inclusion" below and p. 3 f.
24. In composing Appendix A, I have drawn frequently upon OA annotations that have wholly or partly disappeared in Arden. Admittedly, some OA suggestions did not merit survival. See, for example, on *1 Henry IV* 2.1.43.

the reader. Thus, for the first half of Falstaff's "happy man be his dole, say I—every man to his business" (2.2.76 f.), Arden's unsupported "Proverbial" needs only "Tilley, M158" to replace adequately twenty-seven lines in OA. But for the second half, on which OA is silent, Arden's "Proverbial: 'Every man as his business lies' (Tilley, M104)" is overly simple. M104 consists of 1678 Ray, which provides the entry form, Falstaff's words, and a repetition of Falstaff's words in 1682 Aphra Behn, very possibly an echo.

One final problem should be noted, with which the present index attempts to deal. Tilley sometimes cites Shakespeare for one relevant entry when another may be of considerably greater interest. Such seems to me to have occurred with the following dialogue:

Prince. Did I ever call for thee to pay thy part?
Falstaff. No, I'll give thee thy due, thou hast paid all there.

[1.2.52 f.]

Arden (like OA) has nothing. Tilley suggests D634, an approximation of Romans 13.7: "Render therefore to all their dues." Variorum, even though Tilley had not suggested it, supplements with the more demonstrably common D273 (Give the devil his due), explicitly used sixty-five lines later. This suggestion seems to me correct, but bettered by the addition of still another: the almost equally common D288 (Let the devil pay the maltman). As in line 49 f. (on which see p. xviii above), we recognize the jest or barb only if we know the pertinent proverbs.

Problems of Completeness

Appendix A allows brevity in this portion of the Introduction on the need for a supplement to Tilley's entries, and even to those added by OW. Roughly one-fourth of the entries in Appendix A (all decimaled) do not appear in Tilley, and, of these, a great many do not appear in OW either. This is not a criticism but merely a statement of fact.

Any dictionary of proverbs, or index to Shakespeare's use of proverbial language, is bound to be incomplete. This is partly because of blind spots in the compiler and partly because of pertinent evidence not yet seen. Were I to continue working on the present index a few more years— checking in detail the many 17th-century proverb collections I have not even looked at, or reading every extant play to 1700—no doubt this index would grow longer by at least a hundred entries, possibly by far more than that. A revised *Dictionary*, not restricted to "Shakespearean" entries, would certainly expand by hundreds.

It should be no surprise that Wilson and Whiting found pertinent proverbs unknown to Tilley, or that I have found some unknown to

Wilson and Whiting. It was a surprise to me, I confess, to discover how much in Lyly and Pettie (most of it irrelevant to Shakespeare) escaped Tilley's *Dictionary*, for Tilley's first major publication was *Elizabethan Proverb Lore in Lyly's* Euphues *and in Pettie's* Petite Pallace;[25] it was also surprising to discover how much Nashe was not in OW, since a supplement to McKerrow's Nashe was one of Wilson's best-known contributions to scholarship. It was again a surprise to discover how frequently pertinent passages in Heywood's *Dialogue*,[26] or in such compilations as I did examine with care (1530 Palsgrave, c1580 Conybeare, 1616 Draxe, 1639 Clarke), appeared in neither Tilley nor OW. Others may be comparably surprised by gaps in the present volume.

Some degree of incompleteness, however, is irremediable. As already illustrated by Freeble's "He that dies this year is quit for the next" (p.xviii), sometimes we learn only by a stroke of luck that something in Shakespeare was unmistakably proverbial at the time he used it. With some of Freeble's cousins, we can feel almost as certain even without such evidence. No one imagines that Dogberry could have originated "And two men ride of a horse one must ride behind," nor would we do so if a single c1640 recurrence had not allowed the proverb entry in Tilley (T638). For largely the same reason, we may be willing to accept Arden's "a popular tag (Tilley, T518)" for the First Carrier's "I know a trick worth two of that" (*1 Henry IV* 2.1.36 f.), although Tilley's other examples are all from plays more than a decade later (which OW839a supplements only with instances from the 18th and 19th centuries). Here we may feel little need for the reassurance of Wh G24, with its single example from a1400: "I con a game worthe thei twoo," although only the Whiting entry allows Appendix A to use no question mark. Within the same First Carrier context, I would be willing to accept the carrier's "as good deed as drink" (2.1.29) as "proverbial" (OA), or at least as "a popular tag" (Arden)—perhaps modified by an "apparently" or "almost surely." The expression is not in Tilley, and there are no known instances outside Shakespeare until Sir Wilfull Witwood in Congreve. It is difficult otherwise to account for Falstaff's sharing the whole of an expression with the First Carrier, and the bulk of it with Sir Andrew Aguecheek. Hence Appendix A's unquestioning entry: D183.1.

The First Carrier can introduce a different species of incompleteness in Tilley, almost certainly intentional, and usually thoroughly defensible. In the following passage (2.1.22−31), all the italicized expressions other than

25. New York: Macmillan, 1926.
26. Predictably, given the popularity of Shakespeare and the care of scholars, little has escaped attention beyond a few phrases or influences upon Shakespeare's diction. But they can be called "proverbial" as legitimately as those treated in fn. 28 below. See on F672.1, T456.1, and in Appendix B BB4, PP13, SS19, SS26, WW34. More interesting are entries involving the question of what, in Heywood's verse dialogue, he intended to be recognized as proverbial (e.g., O91.1, discussed above, p. xv). See on A211.1, B450, B686.1, P73, S97, W257.

the one just discussed were common colloquialisms, obviously a major aspect of Shakespeare's characterization; but Tilley cites nothing below in his "Shakespeare Index," nor does the present index cite any Tilley entries. What it does cite, and what it ignores, is indicated below:

> 1. *Car. What*, ostler! *come away and be hang'd* [H130.1, with fn]! *come away.*
> 2. *Car.* I have a gammon of bacon and two razes of ginger, to be deliver'd as far as Charing-cross.
> *1 Car. God's body*, the turkeys in my pannier are quite starv'd. *What*, ostler! *A plague on thee* [App. B]! *hast thou never an eye in thy head* [cf. E248.1, with fn]? Canst not hear? *And* twere not *as good deed as drink* [D183.1] to break the pate on thee, *I am a very villain* [J49.1]. Come, and be hang'd [H130.1]!

Why Tilley (and OW) excluded "as good deed as drink" I am not sure, perhaps because neither was aware of any instance outside Shakespeare (but both have entries consisting exclusively of Shakespeare). The rest Tilley undoubtedly excluded on the ground that oaths, imprecations, and the like should be ignored (although L374 [As sure as you live—one of Kate's three reported oaths in 3.1.249 f.] and G266 [God's blessing on your heart for it] are minor departures from this principle). Fifteen years before the publication of his *Dictionary*, Tilley had noted that "Come away and be hang'd" appears in Merbury's proverb-laden *Marriage Between Wit and Wisdom*;[27] nevertheless, he denied it an entry. One cannot call Tilley's decision on oaths mistaken, but given his extreme inclusiveness in other respects,[28] one can wish he had been a little less exclusive in this one. An awareness of such colloquial elements, whether or not they can be called "proverbial," is very useful when examining dialogue in Shakespeare. My own not very systematic solution is suggested by the brackets above, and by

27. *Shakespeare Association Bulletin*, 10 (1935), 91. But, as noted in Appendix A, a version appears in at least one of the 17th-century collections used by Tilley.
Wilson somewhat muddies Tilley's distinction by adding two more oaths of Shakespearean interest: "God save the mark" (cf. G179.1) and "By this fire, that's God's angel" (G264.1). He also adds another variant on "Come away and be hang'd (OW245a: Farewell and be hanged), almost certainly because he objected to Tilley's using 1670 Ray for F733's entry form (Farewell and be hanged, friends must part), thereby submerging a legitimate proverb, for which Wilson had several earlier examples (OW290b: Friends must part). As a consequence, "Farewell and be hanged" appears as a proverb in OW, although "Come (away) and be hanged" does not. H130.1 combines the two.
28. What follows serves to supplement earlier references to Tilley's inclusiveness. It concerns entries that basically involve merely a single word (in which case I have simply listed that word, the key to Tilley's entry) or an extremely simple phrase. All but one appear in OW as well as Tilley. I retain them in Appendix A with a parenthetical "cf. Appendix B": carpet knight, catercousins, cockney, cold comfort, come what will, to be dog at something, eyesore (in *Wh*, not OW), a fig for him (it), that's flat, right hand, hob nob, at an inch, to play the jack (but not knave, fool, etc.) with one, Jack-a-lent, true lover's-knot, merry Greek, Monmouth caps, mumbudget, laced mutton, nightwork, in a pickle, pissing-while, in print (under *Man*), to pocket up (under *Injury*), in a quandary, to pick a quarrel, saving your reverence, smoke, tag and rag, trencherman, in a trice, utterly undone, vease, with a witness, go whistle.

sporadic explanatory footnotes in Appendix A. Most oaths I exclude, but I retain those in Tilley and OW and I add a few, usually for reasons explained in footnotes. Some colloquialisms I ignore as simply too common to note, some I relegate to Appendix B, and some I enter in Appendix A. Whenever uncomfortably aware of my inconsistencies, I have comforted myself with a proverb created by Emerson.

Principles of Inclusion

In the preceding sections and their footnotes I have said a good deal about principles of inclusion and exclusion for the following index. A bit more needs to be said.

To begin with, it is not the business of such an index as this to be selective. The present index is intended to be as complete a cross-reference as possible to relevant entries in Tilley, to OW and Whiting where these usefully supplement Tilley, and to any additional evidence of which I am aware. Undoubtedly there are some obvious omissions, especially in recording the most common colloquialisms and proverbial similes (with some plays—*Hamlet*, for example—the ratio between significant citations and trivia is already embarrassing). But failure to cite sententious proverbs should be rare. If a proverb-sounding piece of sententiousness by Friar Laurence, or Gaunt, or Polonius, or the Duke of Venice (none of whom uses proverbs to any degree) fails to be cited, it fails because I know nothing worth citing. With Polonius, certainly, I have erred on the side of inclusiveness.[29]

I have said "as complete as possible," and in a sense that is true. But, as explained in footnote 2 on *Sonnets*, nearly one-fourth of my citations in that index are included only because their relevance is defended in the commentary of Stephen Booth's invaluable edition.[30] I rely on that commentary as my defense for these inclusions. On the other hand, to be equally full on Shakespeare's other works would require an endless commentary of my own. For most users this would prove more a distraction than a help.

A few illustrations of inclusions and exclusions may be helpful, although some may imply no high degree of consistency in my decisions. Take Lysander's rejection of Hermia in *A Midsummer Night's Dream*. Because of a possible, barely possible, link between "you Ethiop" and "thou

29. See on *Hamlet* 1.3.69. Although I have excluded six of Tilley's entries for 1.3.20−80 (the dialogue ending with Polonius's counsel to Laertes), I have added three, and my index thus includes fourteen (i.e., almost 8 percent of the entire *Hamlet* index for far less than 2 percent of the play). But a glance at Appendix A shows that very little in these lines can legitimately be called proverbial.
30. New Haven: Yale University Press, 1977.

cat" (3.2.257–260), the index cites without comment two expressions based on a single Biblical passage. Conversely, the index ignores "you acorn" (line 330), although A22 (From acorns come oaks) indicates their proverbial smallness, and two closely related proverbs in OW32 (To esteem acorns better than corn; Acorns were good till bread was found) employ *acorns* contemptuously. As for the "you bead" that precedes "acorn," I wish there were textual warrant, even from a Pope or Theobald, allowing the index to cite B118 (Not worth a bean; cf. Wh B82–92, all antibean). Shakespeare nowhere else uses *bead* with comparable implications.

Earlier in the same scene (lines 138–143) Demetrius adores Helena with a series of what are essentially very conventional images:

> To what, my love, shall I compare thine eyne?
> Crystal is muddy. O, how ripe in show
> Thy lips, those kissing cherries, tempting grow!
> That pure congealed white, high Taurus snow
> Fann'd with the eastern wind, turns to a crow
> When thou hold'st up thy hand.

For such a passage it may seem ridiculous to cite three "proverbial" similes, a proverbial phrase,[31] and then Appendix B for "cherry lips." But completeness and consistency require inclusion, although even a Variorum editor may think none worth the mention. For "What's in a name? That which we call a rose / By any other word would smell as sweet," one must be steeled to accept "cf. R178" (As sweet as a rose)—my most humiliating inclusion.

But a line, however shadowy, must be drawn somewhere. For Othello's "flinty and steel couch of war" (1.3.230), it seemed superfluous to cite the centuries old "hard as flint" and "hard as steel," although each phrase, when used in full, gets cited. Analogously, the even older and commoner "sweet as honey" and "honey-sweet" are dutifully acknowledged time after time after time. And here comes a surprise, I suspect. I, for one, would have expected "sweet as sugar" to be almost as common. But there is nothing in Tilley or OW, only five examples in Whiting, and I have myself recorded nothing between Tottel and Shakespeare. Accordingly, the index cites S957.1 for mere allusions to sugar's sweetness in *The Merchant of Venice*, and *Richard II*, and, of course (along with H544 and M930.1 [Wh M544]), for *Love's Labor's Lost* 5.2.230 f.:

> *Ber.* White-handed mistress, one sweet word with thee.
> *Prin.* Honey, and milk, and sugar: there is three.

31. I added C853 (He will say the crow is white) while in the process of writing this paragraph. Surely the commonness of making the crow white has something to do with making the white a crow.

Slightly more than one-sixth of the citations in Tilley's "Shakespeare Index" are excluded from mine,[32] but never merely because they seem too minor to be worth retaining.[33] For example, since Tilley cites I66 (Ingratitude comprehends [is the worst of] all faults [vices]) for Viola's protestation against the charge of ingratitude (*Twelfth Night* 3.4.354–357), this index retains that citation (the proverb is undeniably relevant to some degree, although neither used nor alluded to), but it does not make the same citation for several other anti-ingratitude passages (three of which encouraged my adding a questionable entry: I66.1 [Ingratitude is monstrous (a monster)]).

I have mentioned the use of a question mark, both in Appendix A for entries I think dubiously legitimate and in the index for citations whose relevance seems to me extremely marginal. Although no distinction can be apparent on the printed page, any user can readily distinguish between the question mark employed for near rejections and that used for some of the most interesting entries and citations in the volume—including those for several of the Falstaff passages discussed above, under "Precautions."

Neither the index nor Appendix A employs a question mark if the validity and relevance of an entry, no matter how trivial, seem certain to me. In many cases, especially in the late plays (some of which are predominantly allusive in their use of proverbs), there is little or no verbal resemblance between the passage in question and any examples of the proverb cited. But frequently there is no reason to doubt the allusion. Take "our stomachs / Will make what's homely savory" (*Cymbeline* 3.6.32 f.). Although Tilley does not cite it, this seems to me an unmistakable allusion to H819 (Hunger is the best sauce). Or Macbeth's "Whole as the marble, founded as the rock, / As broad and general as the casing air" (3.4.21 f.). Again Tilley ignores, but this seems to me a good example of Shakespeare's increasing tendency to retain the noun and the sense of a proverbial simile while varying the adjective. Hence the index cites without question M638.1 (As hard as marble), R151 (As fixed [firm] as a rock), and even the less indisputable A88 (As free as the air). I can conclude with an example in both Tilley's index and mine, one that allows me to make a final plea against misuse of our indexes. In *Henry VIII* 1.1.52 f., Buckingham says of Wolsey: "no man's pie is freed / From his ambitious finger." Obviously, he alludes to F228 (To have a finger in the pie). But merely to call his statement "proverbial," as Arden does, is a distortion of fact.

---

32. See "Precautions" and p. 3 f.
33. Where some particular word or words are essential to the entry, this index normally excludes Tilley citations lacking that essential. See p. xxi on "Fair face, foul heart" (F3), for example. Four of Tilley's citations for this proverb lack all four words; two others have but one. This index excludes all six.

INDEX

Shakespeare's Proverbial Language: An Index

The following index is a revision and expansion of that provided on pp. 803–808 of M. P. Tilley's *A Dictionary of the Proverbs in England in the Sixteenth and Seventeenth Centuries.*[1] It is based principally upon evidence in Tilley and in two later proverb collections: F. P. Wilson's revision of *The Oxford Dictionary of English Proverbs* (OW below) and B. J. Whiting's *Proverbs, Sentences, and Proverbial Phrases from English Writings mainly before 1500* (Wh below),[2] all duly acknowledged. Entries originating in these two later collections have been given decimaled numbers corresponding to where they would appear in Tilley. Many of the new decimaled entries, however, are wholly new and are based upon miscellaneous Shakespeare studies (acknowledged) or editions—especially the old Ardens (OA below)—(usually unacknowledged), or upon my own research. I have not cluttered the index with efforts to indicate the frequency of the latter. Where there is reason to doubt whether an entry can be legitimately called "proverbial," or whether an acknowledged proverb was current when Shakespeare employed the expression, the entry number is preceded by a (?). The index retains without question such colloquial expressions as "Take it as thou wilt" (T27), and adds whatever ones could not be relegated to Appendix B (see below). Numbers for new entries follow Tilley's system of ordering, except where this would result in listing under an unimportant, nonessential, or variable word (e.g., Tilley's F180: A white-livered FELLOW, or M226: A MAN cannot live on air like a chameleon, or B376: An ill [evil] BIRD [crow] lays an ill [evil] egg).

The index is followed by three appendixes. Appendix A lists all entries in the index itself, with enough accompanying information to make the index usable for most purposes, obviously not all, without recourse to Tilley, Wilson, or Whiting. Appendix B lists phrases as "proverbial" as a good many in Tilley, entries I have headed with a parenthetical "cf. Appendix B" (cf. Introduction, fn. 28). Appendix B lists the phrase, its OED location and earliest date, and instances in Shakespeare. Occasionally, where the *OED* is inadequate, I have myself originated "cf. Appendix B" entries (e.g., A208.1: To set ALL on hazard). Pertinent Appendix B

---

1. Ann Arbor: University of Michigan Press, 1950.
2. 3d ed. (Oxford: Clarendon Press, 1970); Cambridge, Mass.: The Belknap Press of Harvard University Press, 1968. It must be remembered that many entries in Whiting are supported by only a single example (often Chaucer) and with no supplementary evidence from other collections. A large number of these may indeed have been proverbial, but none can be assumed so. See Introduction, fn. 2. For reasons provided in J. C. Maxwell's review, Appendix B does not attempt cross-references to Charles G. Smith, *Shakespeare's Proverb Lore* (Cambridge, Mass.: Harvard University Press, 1963). See *Notes and Queries*, n.s., 5 (1965), 357–359.

entries are listed in the index's terminal footnote for each work. For the content of Appendix C, see below.

Rather than employ Tilley's alphabetical-by-genre order, this index follows the roughly chronological-by-genre order of *The Riverside Shakespeare*,[3] whose lineation it uses throughout. Act, scene, and line are all in arabics (i.e., 1.2.13 rather than I.ii.13). Unlike Tilley, this index employs "cf." before the entry number for citations whose pertinence may not be immediately evident from the entry form (i.e., from the entry heading chosen by the editor; frequently the most relevant examples have little verbal resemblance to the entry form), for citations whose relationship to both entry form and examples is largely or wholly nonverbal, and when for any other reason more than the entry form needs looking at. When a single example is especially relevant, its date is added parenthetically to the entry number and the example is included in Appendix A. In addition, the index employs the following symbols:

A question mark preceding the citation: the relevance of the passage to the cited entry is questionable.

An italicized line number: the passage is sententious.

An italicized entry number: the passage in question is the earliest known example.

An asterisk after an undecimaled entry: the citation does not appear in Tilley's "Shakespeare Index."

For reasons explained more fully in the Introduction, this index excludes more than one-sixth of the citations in Tilley's. It does so for entries I think either irrelevant or too peripherally relevant to warrant retention, and for entries I consider impossible to classify as proverbial expressions (e.g., A93: Fresh air is ill for the diseased or wounded man), even when the examples cited may be useful as data relevant to the passage in Shakespeare. Since others may disagree, these exclusions are recorded in the initial footnote for each work, with the entry number italicized if "useful." To make this footnote intelligible without recourse to Tilley, Appendix C lists any of the excluded entries that cannot be found in Appendix A, briefly noting why each has been excluded.

It will be obvious to any user that this index intentionally errs on the side of fullness. My principle has been: when in doubt, include, but with a (?).[4] This was clearly Whiting's principle, except that he used no question

---

3. Edited by G. Blakemore Evans, et al. (Boston: Houghton Mifflin, 1974).

4. Some questioned entries, especially if retained from Tilley's original index, are extremely marginal. Others, conversely, are of far greater interest than many unquestioned ones, for reasons discussed in the Introduction. Hackneyed "white as snow" and "snow-white," for example, need no question mark, and must appear in such an index as this not only for the sake of completeness but also because a good many images that now sound equally familiar are *not* in Tilley, Whiting, or Wilson, and frequently are not in the present index as well.

mark (cf. fn. 2), and its fruitfulness is evident in several of my entries. Undoubtedly this index has lacunae resulting from blindness rather than from lack of evidence, but my hope has been to keep these at a minimum.[5]

The above paragraphs suggest why comparing works in mere terms of total citations is not very meaningful. *1 Henry IV* and *Hamlet* have almost identical totals, but the former and shorter play is infinitely the more interesting with regard to Shakespeare's use of proverbial language. Nevertheless, in a crude way, the totals are of sufficient interest to make an appropriate conclusion to this preface. (When citing alternative entries, incidentally, I have counted them as a single entry.)

	Total in Tilley	My exclusions	Total in this index
The Comedy of Errors	53	11	64
The Taming of the Shrew	75	11	123
The Two Gentlemen of Verona	75	7	108
Love's Labor's Lost	137	21	189
A Midsummer Night's Dream	53	8	98
The Merchant of Venice	85	23	117
The Merry Wives of Windsor	102	17	136
Much Ado about Nothing	96	15	145
As You Like It	100	23	135
Twelfth Night	107	19	150
Troilus and Cressida	78	16	138
All's Well that Ends Well	65	15	96
Measure for Measure	68	13	110
Total	1,094	199	1,609
King Henry the Sixth, Part One	35	8	51
King Henry the Sixth, Part Two	74	6	109
King Henry the Sixth, Part Three	68	6	106
King Richard the Third	77	17	124
King John	55	5	99
King Richard the Second	72	11	122
King Henry the Fourth, Part One	111	19	187
King Henry the Fourth, Part Two	86	10	169
King Henry the Fifth	80	8	136
King Henry the Eighth	29	2	80
Total	687	92	1,183

5. See Introduction, p. xxvi f.

Titus Andronicus	62	10	92
Romeo and Juliet	120	25	223
Julius Caesar	47	9	71
Hamlet, Prince of Denmark	140	35	185
Othello, the Moor of Venice	90	22	158
King Lear	82	14	197
Macbeth	71	21	102
Antony and Cleopatra	52	18	85
Coriolanus	60	11	98
Timon of Athens	43	10	69
Total	767	175	1,280
Pericles, Prince of Tyre	26	7	56
Cymbeline	46	12	77
The Winter's Tale	49	12	89
The Tempest	60	9	87
The Two Noble Kinsmen	39	2	70
Total	220	42	379
Venus and Adonis	37	13	59
The Rape of Lucrece	52	9	82
Sonnets	48	6	92
Total	137	28	233
Grand total	2,905	536	4,684

COMEDIES

The Comedy of Errors.[1]

1.2.35−8 (cf. D613), 66 (cf. S872) (2)
2.1.15* (? cf. L225), *34−7* (cf. *A124*),
41 (cf. F496), 57 (H628), 93 (cf.
M638.1), *110−2* (? cf. I92);[2]
2.2.22 (cf. T429), 24 (cf. J46), *43f.*
(cf. W331), 48* (cf. W332), 48
(R98), 51f.* (cf. S623), *65* (T314),
69f. (cf. T311), 82f. (cf. B736),
106 (cf. T311), 125−7 (cf. D613),
130 (Q13), 152 (W892.1), 174* (cf.
V61), 192 (cf. B160), 194 (?cf.
S579), 204 (F229) (23)
3.1.11 (K173), 21−6 (cf. W258), 35
(O62.1), 37* (cf. F579a), 39* (?cf.
T88), 51 (S804), 52 (T88), 55
(T225), 56 (B471.1), 69 (S621), 72
(cf. B692), 72 (B787), *75* (W833),
83 (cf. C855); 3.2.13 (cf. F3), 61*
(cf. H49), 91* (R93), 103f. (cf.
S380),   145   (H310.1),   153
(T307.1) (20)
4.1.46 (cf. T323), 50f. (cf. C579), 57
(cf. B641);[3] 4.2.18* (cf. W723), *27*
(cf. L68), *60* (T334.1); 4.3.27
(R86.1), 51* (?cf. D225), 55f. (cf.
D231), *63f.* (S771), 80 (cf. P157);
4.4.19f. (cf. A42.1), 29f.* (cf.
A355), *41* (cf. E125), 42f. (cf.
R172.1), 85f. (cf. H338.1, R6.1),[4]
150 (S21.1) (18)

1. Exclusions from Tilley's 53 "Shakespeare Index" citations: 1.1.31f.
   (R89); 1.2.45 (S872), 46 (N210);
   2.2.38f. (W548), 88 (M360); 3.1.39
   (W331), 79 (F766), 105f. (E172);
   3.2.9f.   (T140),   119−21   (*H86*);
   4.3.71−4 (S616) (11)
2. I92 is relevant only if one accepts
   Theobald's *Wear* for *Where.* Riverside
   does not.
3. As the 1608 entry suggests, Anti-
   pholus's entire phrase was probably
   proverbial. Cf. L555.1 fn.
4. Whether the similarity between Nashe
   and Shakespeare is a sign of either's
   indebtedness, or instead a proverbial
   combination of two familiar phrases, is

5.1.97*(cf. L9)(1)   (64)[5]

The Taming of the Shrew.[1]

Induction, i.1 (V22), 4f. (C594), 5f.* (cf.
W879), 9f. (B186.1), 14 (I52), 21
(P516.1), 34* (cf. B152.1, S1042),
35* (cf. S527), 41f. (cf. B247),
122* (Y25), 125f. (cf. O67); ii.9f.
(cf. W61), 48 (cf. R158), 127f.* (cf.
F367), 133 (cf. M866), 143 (cf.
W879), 143f. (Y36) (18)
1.1.3f. (cf. L414), 64 (cf. H270), 79
(F229), 105* (?cf. D225), 106
(*M328*), 107f.* (N10.1), 108f.
(C12), *134f. (C358)*, 139f. (M158),
140 (cf. R130), 144 (W731), 151
(cf. L513.1), 190 (?cf. *W578*), 212
(cf. B354), 222f. (cf. W295.1);
1.2.32f. (cf. O64), 48f. (cf. W441),
50−2* (cf. *N274*), 56 (cf. T264),
65f. (cf. W796), 72f. (cf. E57.1),
112 (W280.1), 139* (H280), 140
(L427.1), 185 (cf. S117), 196
(*L374.1*), 210 (cf. B703), 247
(J29.2), 265 (I3) (29)
2.1.33 (?cf. *D22*), 34 (M37), 66 (S724),
73 (cf. M1183), *134f.* (cf. W424),
152 (F672.1), 199 (A371.1), 209*
(cf. W76), 213−5* (?cf. B211), 224
(B534), 246* (cf. F389, 389.1),
254f.* (cf. N360),[2] 257 (cf. C245),

still unknown. Each phrase by itself
clearly had some currency.
5. Cf. Appendix B: BB8, 18, CC22,
   DD15, GG12, HH3, 14, 19, LL1, 7,
   MM25, NN2, OO3, SS16, TT16, 18,
   WW2 (17)

1. Exclusions from Tilley's 75 "Shakespeare Index" citations: Induction,
   ii.68−72 (S212); 1.2.160 (W746);
   2.1.209 (W705), 213f. (S858), 390f.
   (M609); 3.2.115−7 (S451); 4.1.9f.
   (C460), 127f. (F488), 190−2 (T298);
   4.2.53 (T89), 5.1.150 (L85) (11)
2. Cf. 1579 Lyly, *Eupheus* (I, 254): "If she
   be well sette, then call hir a Bosse, if
   slender, a Hasill twigge, If Nut-
   browne, as blacke as a coale." A version of T632 (Best to bend while it is a
   TWIG) further clarifies Petruchio's

The Two Gentlemen of Verona.[1]

W576), *47f.** (cf. B702), *74f.* (cf. S312), 97 (cf. M1338), 108* (cf. P334), 116f.* (cf. L1), 140f. (S839), 148–50 (cf. B139); 1.2.23f. (cf. B179), *30* (cf. F265), *32* (cf. L165), *55f.* (cf. W660), 59 (R156), 67–9 (?cf. *M187, 846**),[2] 134 (M1109), 136 (cf. W500); 1.3.65 (E113.1), 78f.* (cf. e.g., F784) (22)

2.1.28f. (?cf. B289), 56f. (*C704.1*), *70* (L506), 135f. (cf. N215), 141–4 (cf. R98.1), 161f. (E113.1), 169 (M239), 172–4 (cf. M226, L505.1); 2.2.1f.* (cf. R71), 14* (?cf. T323), *17* (cf. L165), *18** (cf. W820); 2.3.10f.* (cf. H311), 10f.* (cf. D510.1), 11f.* (cf. J50.1), 15–7* (cf. W709), 20 (L296), 20f. (W23), 31f. (D650.1), 35f. (?cf. T323), 44f. (M1264); 2.4.23–6 (cf. C222), 25–8 (cf. M226), 29 (S118.1), 29f. (cf. S117), *96* (cf. L506), *136** (cf. e.g., L509.1), 149f. (cf. P327), *177* (cf. L510), *192* (cf. F277), *193* (N17), 203–6* (cf. L549); 2.5.19 (F301); 2.6.*11* (cf. O7), *13* (cf. B26), 23 (cf. N57); 2.7.19 (cf. *F284*), *25f.* (cf. S929), 46 (L571), 55 (P334), 69 (T82.1), 75 (cf. M458), 78 (cf. E27.3) (44)

3.1.1 (L167.1), 51 (W316.1), 88 (cf. S968.1), 89* (?cf. W704), 156 (cf. S825), 172* (cf. F696), 243* (cf. G453), 243f.* (cf. M999a), 252 (M931.1), 267 (?cf. H717.1), 288 (I73), 304f. (cf. B450), 315 (cf. W893), 327 (?cf. T420), 353, 358f. (B736), *362* (cf. G437), *369f.* (cf. N298.1);[3] 3.2.14f. (cf. T322) (18)

4.1.60 (V73); 4.2.14f. (cf. S705), *19f.* (cf. K49), 26–9 (?cf. S14), 46f.* (cf. L506), 51f. (cf. E27.2); 4.3.33

---

irony. Cf. 1590 C. Gibbon, *Not so new, as True*, p. 11: "the hasell must be bent in the twigge."

3. Cf. Hulme, *Explorations*, pp. 47 f.

4. Cf. Appendix B: AA4, 6, BB5, 10, CC9, 11, 17, 21, DD14, FF2, 9, GG6, HH4, 7, 16, JJ1, 2, MM2, 10, 23, OO2, SS1, 7, 16, 19, TT3, 8, 16, 25, UU1, VV2, WW7, 10, 13, 22, 27, 34 (37)

1. Exclusions from Tilley's 75 "Shakespeare Index" citations: 1.1.111–5 (N199); 1.3.84–7 (L92a); 2.2.1f. (C922); 3.1.95 (S150 [OW705a]), 293–7 (*M1193*); 5.1.4f. (L568); 5.4.71 (W930) (7)

2. These two late (?) proverbs are probably related to the proverbial threat not to eat until taking some vengeful action. Cf. B627.2.

3. Given the centuries-old popularity of N299 (Nothing is impossible to a willing heart), Rowe's generally accepted substitution of a dash for F1's period may be warranted. It scarcely appears necessary, however.

Love's Labor's Lost.[1]

4. Cf. Appendix B: AA2, BB2, 18, GG7, HH7, MM10, 13, OO2, SS13, 17, 25, TT16, 25, 27, UU1, VV2, WW8, 23, 28 (19)

1. Exclusions from Tilley's 137 "Shakespeare Index" citations: 1.2.73f. (S85); 2.1.15f. (P546), 201f. (*M1193* [OW20b]), 238f. (H198); 3.1.153–8 (M283), 198f. (E254); 4.1.23 (F24), 131f. (P571), 138f. (B569); 4.3.47 (C571), 70f. (B26 [OW26a]), 125f. (C571), 332f. (F134), 357 (W692), 360–2 (W873), 368f. (W731), 380 (T228); 5.2.70–2 (M321), 412f. (T593), 581f. (D42), 581f. (M148) (21)

2. Cf. 1571 R. Edwards, *Damon and Pithias* xiv (MSR 1393): "you haue so much mother wit, that you lacke your fathers wisdome."

A Midsummer Night's Dream.¹

3. *Titus Andronicus* 2.3.123 may imply that Armado's vow concerns sexual activity, not farming. Cf. B89.1.
4. Cf. Appendix B: AA8, BB18, CC20, DD15, 16, EE7, FF4, 10, GG7, 14, HH4, 10, 16, 18, 20, JJ2, KK2, MM2, 18, NN1, OO2, PP3, 4, 8, 14, TT11, 24, 25, WW6, 10, 28, 30, 31, YY2 (34)

1. Exclusions from Tilley's 53 "Shakespeare Index" citations: 2.1.34 (*R147*); 2.2.115 (R43 [OW666b]); 3.2.48 (S380), 85, 435 (S662); 5.1.52f. (*M1316*), 91f. (W393), 372 (D449) (8). Cf. Introduction, pp. 000f.
2. Unlike all other citations for this play, this was almost surely not proverbial in Shakespeare's day.

3. Cf. Introduction, fn. 31.
4. The "country proverb" may well be the entire 461–463, although extant examples would lead one to expect "country proverbs."
5. The cited proverb (which McKerrow's Nashe traces through Renaissance and ancient sources) is not very relevant; the ancestry of "Furor Poeticus" would be far more so.
6. Cf. Appendix B: BB18, CC10, HH18, MM1, 12, 13, 16, 20, NN5, OO2, PP16, RR3, SS3, 16, TT25, WW7, 22 (17)

The Merchant of Venice.[1]

1.1.7 (?cf. K175), 17f. (*G422*), 42 (cf. A209), 47f. (cf. S14), 49 (L92a.1), *77f.* (cf. W882), 89 (cf. P465), 94 (cf. D526), 95–7 (cf. F531), 97–102* (?cf. F300, G473),[2] 106* (cf. F531), 140–3 (cf. *A325*); 1.2.*14f.* (cf. P537a), 19f.* (cf. H148), 50–2* (B517), 56f. (cf. M162), 61f. (S262), 71 (?cf. P219.1), 89 (cf. B152.1), 89f. (cf. W911), 95 (cf. W912); 1.3.22 (?cf. M502, 541*), 46 (H474), *98* (cf. D230), 101 (cf. A291.1), 113 (cf. O99), 160–2* (?cf. F117) (28)

2.1.29 (cf. S292), 36 (cf. F604); 2.2.2f. (D243.1), 5f.* (?cf. L195), 9 (*H393.1*), 24 (G179.1), 26 (R93), 52 (cf. S114), 63 (S490), 66f. (S803.1), *76f.* (cf. C309 [1617]), *79f.* (T591), 79 (M1315), 92f. (F366), 102f. (R86.1), 110f. (G252.1), 112f. (J49.1), 127 (L419), 130f. (R93), 130f. (C191), 139* (cf. S114), 149–51 (G393), 156f. (cf. T402), 165 (E56a.1), 168 (T635), 179f. (cf. M1331), 197 (cf. T558.1); 2.5.17 (B657.1), 24 (*N282.1*), 43 (cf. J53),[3] 47 (cf. S579), *54* (B352); 2.6.16 (?cf. A88), *36* (L506), 41* (?cf. C40); 2.7.44f.* (cf. H355), *65* (A146), 73

---

1. Exclusions from Tilley's 85 "Shakespeare Index" citations: 1.1.50 (J37); 1.2.7f. (V80), 27f. (*M514*), 1.3.32–7 (J50), 95f. (U28), 101 (A300), 179 (F3); 2.1.1.2 (M1130); 2.2.106f. (R100), 135f. (M472); 2.6.4 (L568); 2.7.69 (S225); 3.2.313 (D12); 3.4.22f. (M476), 35f. (W155); 4.1.163f. (M500 [OW589bf.]), 200–2 (M895); 5.1.90f. (S713), 92f. (S988), 102f. (L70), 112f. (B365), 230 (E254), 242f. (B8) (23)
2. Hulme, *Explorations*, p. 172, suggests the possible relevance of the first (although she is unaware of its currency in English) and Arden, the second.
3. If J53 was indeed proverbial—and G96 supports the probability—Arden rightly takes the original *Iewes* to mean *Jew's*, with Pope's popular *Jewess'* an unwarranted emendation. Riverside has *Jewess'* without brackets.

(S960.1), 74* (cf. L9), 75 (F769); 2.9.59* (?cf. C582), *61f.* (cf. M341), 79 (cf. F394), *83* (cf. W232) (43)

3.1.34,* 37f. (cf. F366), 39f. (cf. B438,* J49,* I109), 77f. (?cf. W910); 3.2 (cf. J55), *8* (?cf. M14.1, 45), 16–8 (cf. M980), 30f.* (cf. F284), 35 (?cf. C587), 44f. (cf. S1028), *67* (cf. L501), 86 (cf. M931, F180*), 106* (cf. L135),[4] 110 (cf. *J38.2*), 111f. (?cf. L559), 119 (cf. S957.1), 160f. (cf. L153.1), 237 (cf. S914.1), 248* (cf. H49), 302 (H26.1); 3.4.22f. (cf. M476), 52* (cf. T240), 79 (Q11.1); 3.5.16f. (cf. S169), 22f. (O62.2), 34f. (M868.1) (28)

4.1.31 (cf. B605.1), 31 (H311), 47 (cf. P310), 97f.* (cf. O99), 114f.* (cf. S308), *188–97* (cf. M898), 216 (?cf. E112, 203*), 283 (L244.1), 334 (H474), 440* (cf. B247, A345)[5] (11)

5.1.87* (cf. H397), 92f. (cf. S826.2), *95–7* (cf. R140), *130* (cf. W351, G7*), 157 (G198.1), 220 (cf. C49.1) (7)   (117)[6]

The Merry Wives of Windsor.[1]

1.1.19–21 (cf. L471), 25f. (cf. M701), 60f. (P189), 77 (cf. T49), 104 (?cf.

---

4. The proverbial simile supports *paleness* over Theobald's frequently accepted *plainness*. Nonetheless, it is hard to account for *pale* in line 103, since silver was proverbially bright (Wh S320f., S453).
5. Cf. Hulme, *Explorations,* p. 170.
6. Cf. Appendix B: AA3, CC11, GG7, HH7, 15, 16, 21, MM10, OO3, PP3, 10, RR1, SS16, 26, TT8, 11, 17, 19, WW5, 10, 11, 25, 34 (23)

---

1. Exclusions from Tilley's 102 "Shakespeare Index" citations: 1.1.174–7 (W583), 181f. (D129), 196f. (F732), 266–8 (*A93*), 294–6 (B134); 2.1.4–6 (L517); 2.2.3f. (M777 [OW519b]), 60–3 (Q1 [OW658af.]); 3.1.37–9 (F351), 104f. (W761); 3.2.13 (H128); 4.4.11 (E223); 4.5.59–62 (W545), 97f. (D616); 5.1.23 (*L250* [OW461b]); 5.2.13f. (*D252* [OW182a]); Q1 5.5.144 (T200) (17)

2. One can only guess from context
which of several "few words" proverbs
Evans alludes to, if indeed he alludes
to any. Nym's more belligerent "*Pauca,
Pauca*" at 132 may reflect W797, or
even W781 (Few words to the wise
suffice).

3. Arden and Riverside justifiably reject
Theobald's emendation of *contempt*
for *content*.

4. Given the speaker, Arden is probably
right to call Shallow's greeting "of
course a cliché," despite the slender
external evidence. The same principle
holds true for several citations where
Mistress Quickly provides the earliest
known example. See Introduction, p.
xxiv.

5. Cf. 1599 (1600) Dekker, *The Shoemaker's Holiday* 5.2.60f.: "the law's on
our side, he that sowes in another
mans ground forfets his harvest."

6. Although Arden may be right to dis-
miss it, OA's note has not yet been
proved wrong: "Caius must have the
credit for this common saying. If it had
been in use previously it would not
have escaped Nashe, who collected
herring sayings in *Lenten Stuffe*."

7. Ford's "let the proverb go with me"
probably alludes to line 150 rather
than 152.

8. OA cites c1589 (1592) Lyly, *Midas*
4.1.47 f.: "Love made *Iupiter* a goose,
and *Neptune* a swine, and both for love
of an earthlie mistresse."

9. Cf. Appendix B: AA1, 3, BB6, 18,
CC11, 15, DD11, 14, EE1, 4, GG7, 10,
11, 14, HH4, 9, 10, 14, 16, JJ2, MM2,

Much Ado about Nothing.[1]

10, 13, 23, OO2, 3, PP3, 4, RR2, 3, SS1, 21, TT16, 25, VV2, WW5, 7, 10, 27, 28, YY1, 2 (42)

1. Exclusions from Tilley's 96 "Shakespeare Index" citations: 1.1.96f. (T532), 238 (W637); 2.1.94f. (V92), 150−2 (W155); 2.3.44f. (S482); 3.1.61 (P559); 3.3.99 (E98); 3.4.24f. (*M475*), 33f. (L65), 60f. (C582); 4.2.60 (M1160); 5.1.1−3 (D126), 39f. (D125 [OW171a]), 90 (W603); 5.2.96 (C505) (15)

2. Dogberry is of course muddled. Cf. *As You Like It* 1.2.40−2.

3. Perhaps a version, scarcely original with Dogberry, of 1581 Guazzo (Pettie), *Civile Conversation* III (II, 43): "as a little childe riding behind his father, sayde simply unto him, Father, when you are dead, I shal ride in the Saddle."

4. Cf. Appendix B: BB8, 14, DD10, 16, EE5, FF1, GG7, 11, HH4, 12, 14, 16, JJ2, MM10, 13, OO2, 3, PP3, 8, TT6, 12, 27, UU1, WW20, 23, 28, 29, 32 (28)

As You Like It.[1]

1.1.30f. (cf. M48), 32f.* (cf. M162), 34f.* (cf. I7), 35f. (N51.1), 53f.* (cf. B686), 57−9,* 61f.* (cf. F92), 81* (?cf. D506); 1.2.*37−9* (cf. B163), 44* (cf. S570), *54f.* (cf. W298.1, 299), 56 (cf. W570), 104* (cf. W560), 106 (*T539*), 175* (cf. E232), 176* (cf. K175), 201 (cf. E28.1), 208f. (cf. V50, M1031*), 287 (cf. S570); 1.3.2f. (cf. W762), *12** (?cf. B673), 13 (?cf. B724), 19f. (*H413.1*), 97* (cf. F696) (23)

2.1.2f. (?cf. C933), *12* (cf. A42), 33−5 (cf. D189), *51f.* (?cf. P529); 2.3.14 (W889.1), 50 (cf. F590.1), 76 (cf. D165); 2.4.6 (cf. W655), 16 (F505.1), 57 (cf. M1158), 58f. (cf. *F543*, S342.1), 71 (cf. L479.1); 2.5.20 (W280.5), 36f. (B487.1); 2.6.9f. (A317); 2.7.9 (cf. W889.1), 13* (cf. W896), 19 (cf. G220), 23* (cf. W879), 28 (T48), 39 (cf. *B404*), 47f.* (?cf. A88), 64f. (?cf. F107), 72f. (cf. S182.1), *139f.* (cf. W882), 146 (cf. S579), 152 (cf. *B691.1*), *165* (cf. M570), 186 (cf. B309) (29)

3.2.21* (S874), 65* (cf. M253), 88 (cf. E43.1), *103* (C135), *109* (cf. N360), *111f.* (cf. R182), 113 (cf. G14.1), 115−8 (cf. *F546*), 118−20 (cf. M863, ?R133*), 121 (S118.1), *129f.* (cf. L249), *131f.* (cf. L251), 174 (cf. W728), 176f. (?cf. D158), *184−6* (cf. F738), 193* (?C871.1), 204f. (M162), 249f. (?cf. H334),

255* (?cf. F76), 289f.* (?cf. C391), 306* (?cf. T327), 317* (cf. Y25), 328 (F560), 358f. (cf. P271), 398 (R98), *400−4* (L505.2), 415 (?cf. *H665*); 3.3.2f. (cf. I88), 30f. (?cf. B163, M839*), *35−7* (cf. M834), 41f. (cf. B65), *51f.** (cf. C889), *52f.* (cf. E122); 3.4.17* (cf. *I1*), 30 (?cf. T98.1); 3.5.39f.* (cf. C50, J57), 54 (cf. G132.1), 57 (K175), 60 (cf. M670), *82* (?cf. L426), *133* (cf. F584) (41)

4.1.8f.* (cf. P490), 54f. (cf. S579,* 580), *57−9** (cf. C889), 66 (P407.1), 123f. (cf. T142, 158),[2] 142 (cf. T240), 145 (D74), 151f.* (cf. C854), 153−6 (cf. H839), 155f. (cf. H844), 166 (cf. W570), 172 (cf. W670), *173−5* (cf. C579), 188f. (G173.1), 199f. (cf. T336), 200 (T308.2), 203f. (cf. B377); 4.2.13 (cf. H625); 4.3.4f. (B564.1), 14 (A172), 17 (P256), 19* (cf. W269), *128* (?cf. H170, R92*), 173f. (H328.1) (24)

5.1.10 (M842), *31f.* (cf. W522),[3] *40* (cf. H215), 43f. (cf. I88); 5.2.29 (W295.1), 31f. (C540), 109f. (cf. D449); 5.3.4f. (W637.4), 28 (cf. L248.1), *30* (cf. T312); 5.4.56 (S1030.1), 57f. (?cf. M131, T141.1), *59−61* (cf. P166.1), 64 (cf. F515), 90 (M239), 106 (cf. R63,* S816), 149 (W825) (17)

Epilogue, *3f.* (W462) (1)   (135)[4]

---

1. Exclusions from Tilley's 100 "Shakespeare Index" citations: 1.2.77f. (M326), 115 (B318); 1.3.54 (T560), 102f. (G447); 2.1.13 (T360); 2.4.55 (M502); 2.5.15 (*S482*); 2.7.50−5 (J42), 79−82 (O99); 3.2.299−301 (O9a); 3.3.79 (T303), 99−101 (*O40*); 3.4.7f. (*B143* [OW668a]), 9 (J92), 30f. (*L570*); 4.1.148 (M44); 4.3.11f. (*M905*); 5.1.31f. (M425); 5.3.11−3 (S482), 28 (B165); 5.4.57f. (B389), 108ff. (M688), 119 (S212) (23)

2. Although a misinterpretation of T142 supports Rosalind, a right interpretation of an even commoner proverb refutes her.
3. W522 contains the only evidence that Touchstone's "saying" may have existed in much the same form he presents it. Therefore, I exclude Tilley's M425 (The wise man knows himself to be a fool, the fool thinks he is wise).
4. Cf. Appendix B: AA3, BB1, 18, CC24, DD11, GG3, 7, HH2, 10, 14, 16, JJ2, KK2, LL1, MM10, 12, 13, 16, OO2, PP3, 8, RR4, SS13, 17, TT12, 25, WW7, 10, 14 (29)

1. Exclusions from Tilley's 107 "Shakespeare Index" citations: 1.2.33 (F422), 1.3.7 (C579), 20 (M163); 1.4.37f. (A228); 1.5.19f. (H130), 33–5 (M425), 70f. (H347); 2.2.40f. (T333), 116 (C211); 2.4.110–2 (G449), 98f. (C581); 3.2.29–31 (P462), 53–5 (F711); 3.4.143 (cf. V63), 367–9 (D410); 4.3.2 (S212), 4.3.2 (T446); 5.1.6f. (T129), 12–20 (G212) (19)

Troilus and Cressida.[1]

2. Cf. Appendix B: AA3, BB6, 8, 17, 18, CC11, DD2, 6, GG7, 12, HH15, JJ1, MM2, 10, OO1, 2, PP8, 11, RR3, SS16, 22, TT3, WW7, 10, 19, 20, 22, 24 (28)

1. Exclusions from Tilley's 78 "Shakespeare Index" citations: 1.1.39f.

(L277); 1.2.66 (M243); 1.3.33f. (C715), 116−8 (M922), 389 (C918); 2.1.43f., 73f. (W548); 2.2.14f. (W152); 2.3.155−7 (A26); 3.1.101 (T640); 3.2.84f. (*L570*), 90f. (P83), 95 (W828); 3.3.151ff. (W866); 5.2.129−34 (W637); 5.3.27f. (H565); 5.10.41−4 (S858) (16)

2. I suppose we must continue to reject the emendation proposed by Grey in 1754: *'s words* (cf. e.g., 3.1.90's *'s excuse*). It makes excellent sense in context, nevertheless, and eliminates the question of why Ajax should say *swords* rather than use the customary singular. Possibly Shakespeare—scarcely Ajax—intentionally played on both nouns. Cf. c1599 (1610) Marston, *Histriomastix* 5.1 (III, 287): Swallow those words or thou shalt eat my sword." For such wordplay on the similarity of

sound cf. e.g., 1639 Clarke, s.v. Fortitudinis, p. 121: "Better at swords than words"; Garrulitas, p. 132: "Words are swords"; Iactantia, p. 143: "He's good at words, is he so at swords?"

3. Riverside rejects the emendation *but* for *not*, and apparently denies the pertinence of the proverb.

4. Cf. Appendix B: AA3, BB18, CC11, 17, 18, DD11, FF2, GG7, 10, HH4, 6, 10, 16, 17, 18, MM10, 24, NN3, OO2, PP3, 7, 10, 11, RR3, SS3, TT12, 21, 25, 26, VV2, WW7, 8, 10 (33)

*Measure for Measure.*¹

---

1. Exclusions from Tilley's 65 "Shakespeare Index" citations: 1.1.40−5
(B456), 66 (F752, L407); 1.3.25f.
(C331); 2.2.58f. (G58); 2.4.28−31
(C828); 2.5.48 (G318), 84−6 (U13);
3.2.37−40 (D79); 4.1.16f. (M100);
4.2.46 (V79); 4.3.259−64 (D383);
4.4.31−3 (R182); 5.1.42−5 (F224);
5.3.105f. (K175)(15)
2. Given Lavatch's speech habits in this
scene, a proverb appears very probable. Arden follows Tilley in citing
C331 (Children are poor men's riches
[*varied*]), a common enough proverb
but with no examples using *blessings*.

3. Cf. Appendix B: BB6, CC11, DD3, 6,
12, GG7, HH5, 16, LL3, 4, MM10,
OO2, 3, PP3, 11, 18, RR2, SS1, 2, 11,
26, TT8, 16, 25, WW7, 12, 14, 29, 35
(29)

1. Exclusions from Tilley's 68 "Shake-
speare Index" citations: 2.2.75−9
(M895), 136−8 (I27); 2.4.76−9
(N276); 3.1.2f. (H602), 39f. (C774),
40f. (D143), 54−60 (H347), 133−5
(N41); 3.2.38f. (S214); 4.2.153f. (F5),
205f. (D418); 5.1.411 (L286), 439
(M116) (13)

HISTORIES

King Henry the Sixth, Part One.[1]

King Henry the Sixth, Part Two.[1]

1. Exclusions from Tilley's 35 "Shakespeare Index" citations: 1.1.34 (T249); 2.1.58f. (W83); 2.4.31–3 (R182); 2.5.5 (H31); 3.2.80 (L374); 4.2.35–8 (G132 [OW305b]); 5.3.107 (F295); 5.5.62 (L499) (8)

2. Cf. Appendix B: AA6, DD9, GG3, 5, 7, HH1, 8, 10, 16, 17, 18, KK2, LL1, MM7, 13, 14, PP11, 13, RR2, SS3, 5, TT10 (22)

1. Exclusions from Tilley's 74 "Shakespeare Index" citations: 1.1.21f. (B168); 1.3.152f. (N307); 2.1.96–8

King Henry the Sixth, Part Three.[1]

2. Cf. Appendix B: AA4, BB18, CC9, 14, DD9, 13, EE2, FF4, 8, 9, GG7, HH11, 18, II2, KK4, MM3, 5, 8, 9, 13, OO2, PP3, 10, 11, SS5, 10, 16, 27, TT1, 7, 8, 11, 14, 15, 17, VV2, WW10, 13, 22 (39)

1. Exclusions from Tilley's 68 "Shakespeare Index" citations: 1.4.145f. (R16); 2.1.171 (W135); 2.2.138 (T360); 2.6.27 (*A93*); 3.3.77 (T325 [OW823a]); 5.7.31f. (C312) (6)

King Richard the Third.[1]

C601), 280 (cf. *D88*), 281−7* (cf.
S985), 305 (B787) (15)   (124)²

King John.¹

1.1.19 (cf. B458), 24−6* (cf. L281),
60−2* (cf. M1193), 63* (cf. C309),
105 (T581), 123f. (cf. C765), 145
(*S861*), 154−6 (cf. P89), 158f. (cf.
L30.1), 171 (W456), *173* (*H215*),
181* (cf. W155), 184* (cf. J57),
187 (cf. H583), 213 (cf. F349.1),
213 (?cf. T420), 218f.* (cf. H618),
230 (L167.1), 234f. (cf. P75) (19)
2.1.70 cf. W61,* L452), *82* (?cf. *C715*,
N70.1), 127f.* (cf. D225), 137f.
(cf. H165), 143f. (cf. S366,²
A351*), 162* (cf. F213), 194* (cf.
W723), 288f. (cf. S42), 293 (cf.
C876.2), 315 (S453.1), 329 (cf.
B458), 335−40 (cf. S929), 351
(F287.1), 352−4* (cf. *W47*,
D138.1), 439f.* (cf. W718), 451
(S169.2), 452 (cf. e.g., L307.1),
452f. (cf. M1214.1, R151) (20)
3.1.61 (*F603.1*), 94 (?cf. B261), 128f.
(cf. A351), 174f. (cf. F33), 200
(I70), 235 (cf. H109.1), 242
(P401), 242* (cf. *J45.1*), 258
(S228.1), *270ff.* (cf. O7), 277 (cf.
D174), 277f. (cf. F277), 298
(B112.2), 299 (M1264), 324 (cf.
T311), 324f.* (cf. *R198*),³ 340−3

2. Cf. Appendix B: AA4, CC10, 11,
EE5, FF9, GG2, 5, 7, 9, HH3, 16, KK1,
MM3, 10, 13, OO2, 3, PP1, 3, 4, 11,
SS3, 5, 16, 20, 23, TT3, 8, 15, 16,
WW8, 32 (32)

1. Exclusions from Tilley's 55 "Shakespeare Index" citations: 2.1.446f.
(U12); 3.1.258−60 (W603), 277
(L237); 4.3.32 (L458); 5.2.12−5
(S647) (5)
2. Arden, unlike Riverside in retaining
Fl's *shooes* (*shoes*) rather than Theobald's *shews* (*shows*), justly argues that
both meanings are present.
3. Arden thinks the same proverb and
time/thyme pun apparent in the final
sentence of Greene's *Mamillia: The
second part* (1583 [1593]; II, 297):
"Choose not *Modesta* so that thy

(cf. B465.1); 3.3.12 (cf. B276), 53
(B546.2); 3.4.17−9* (cf. B497),
48f. (cf. F480), 82* (cf. C56), 91
(?cf. C341), *108* (cf. T53.1), 167f.*
(F244), 176f.* (cf. *S595*) (26)
4.1.18 (D57), 40 (M1330.1), 55f. (cf.
M1331), 76 (S879.1), 79 (cf. L34),
115f. (?cf. M258), 119f.* (cf. F254,
H310.1); 4.2.13f. (cf. C519), 14f.
(cf. S988), 18f. (cf. T53.1), *28f.**
(cf. W260), *30f.* (cf. *E215*), 99f.*
(cf. F582), 135f. (cf. W912), 163
(cf. F248), 170 (F570), 175 (cf.
T240); 4.3.27 (cf. W915), *32*
(P595.1), 32f.* (cf. A247) (20)
5.1.21* (W221), 48* (cf. F277); 5.2.64
(cf. A242), 83−7 (?cf. W424),
176−8* (cf. W47); 5.4.10 (B787),
24f. (cf. W137.1), 26−9 (cf.
M514); 5.6.4 (W280.4); 5.7.21f.
(cf. S1028), 28 (cf. E104), 42
(C542), 53f.* (cf. T250), 117f.
(L54.1)⁴ (14)   (99)⁵

King Richard the Second.¹

1.1.19 (S169.2, F246.1), 48f.* (cf.
W675), 55* (cf. B671), 125 (cf.
T268), 156 (cf. F597), *174f.* (cf.

friends shall like the choice and thou
mislike the chaunce, least time and
triall make thee account Rue a most
bitter hearbe."
4. Cf. 1595 W. Burton, *The Rowsing of the
Sluggard* (1602 *Wks.*, p. 467) versus
"secure sluggards," who claim "one
English man will be too hard for ten
Spaniards: and if we all be true
amongst our selves and hold together,
we neede not care how many or how
mightie they be. Thus we see how fool-
ishly foolish men talke."
5. Cf. Appendix B: AA1, CC13, 16,
DD9, 12, FF9, HH16, MM19, OO3,
PP6, 11, 13, RR2, SS6, 18, 19, TT1,
UU1 (18)

1. Exclusions from Tilley's 72 "Shakespeare Index" citations: 1.2.6−8 (V24
[OW673a]); 1.3.280f., 292f. (I72);
2.1.91−3 (H285), 153 (R133), 174
(L34); 3.2.103 (M505); 3.3.68f. (E6),
164−8 (D618), 207 (B354); 3.4.3f.
(B569) (11)

King Henry the Fourth, Part One.[1]

2. Cf. Appendix B: AA3, BB10, 18, CC1, 7, DD11, FF9, HH16, 18, KK2, MM8, SS10, 16, 20, 26, 28, TT8, 25, WW6, 12 (20).

1. Exclusions from Tilley's 111 "Shakespeare Index" citations: 1.2.31–3 (M1111), 33–5 (G91), 52 (D634); 2.2.86 (U8), 108f. (D616); 2.3.9f. (D28); 2.4.17 (D649), 153f. (L329), 427f. (F5); 3.1.157–9 (S574); 3.2.55–7 (M20), 71f. (S1011); 3.3.31 (F248), 170 (F116); 4.1.103 (G167); 5.3.46f. (A206), 5.4.83 (*M514*; cf. Introduction, pp. p. 000), 125 (A206), 136f. (S212) (19)

2. I list D634 (Give everyone his due) among the exclusions, not because it is necessarily irrelevant but because, in this proverb-rich context, it appears probable that Falstaff is playing upon two more derogatory proverbs, the first of them used explicitly at line 119. Cf. Introduction, p. xxiii.

3. The pertinence of S962 seems extremely dubious. OA compared analogous word play on "obtaining of suits" in later Dekker and Brome, but nothing proverbial appears to have been involved.

4. Arden wisely rejects OA's evidence for "A proverbial saying," although I am uncertain what it means to imply by its replacement: "Evasive rustic wit." Because of the speaker and the proverbial density of the scene, however, like OA, I suspect a proverb. My candidate is B197, as reflected in 1546 Heywood: "And whan ye have made me a loute in all these, / It semeth ye wolde make me go to bed at noone." The second carrier would then, in effect, be saying, "You'll not make a fool of me, Gadshill."

5. Arden follows the Variorum and Tilley in instead citing D28 (cf. Appendix C), which seems to me very different in meaning.

6. Whether Falstaff originated this simile or not, he is surely responsible for its later popularity. Given, on the one hand, Falstaff's fondness for proverbial expressions, and, on the other, the obvious popularity and influence of his role, it is frequently impossible to tell whether later parallels, especially in plays, are legitimate signs of anything actually proverbial. Tom

Brown, however, has several Falstaff echoes.

7. Strictly, only half this passage is Biblical, but both halves are proverbial.

8. Riverside's comma after "fear" obscures the proverb less than the semicolon found in many editions. Cf. Introduction, fn. 21.

9. OA quoted from an anonymous poem attributed by Bond to Lyly (III, 451): "Who yongest dies he doth [but] pay / a debt (he owes) before the daye." For youth-minded Falstaff this seems much more relevant than T290, even if there were evidence of the latter's currency. There is no evidence, however, that the "Lyly" was proverbial.

King Henry the Fourth, Part Two.¹

10. See fn. 6 above. Although the basic idea here is ancient, I suspect Falstaff's famous formulation is his own. Cf. Paul Jorgensen, "Valor's Better Parts: Backgrounds and Meanings of Shakespeare's Most Difficult Proverb," *Shakespeare Studies*, 9 (1976), 141–158.
11. Cf. Appendix B: AA8, BB7, 10, 18, CC2, 4, 5, 8, 11, DD2, 6, 10, 11, 12, 18, 19, EE7, FF6, GG7, 9, 13, 15, HH4, 8, 13, 14, 16, LL4, MM1, 2, 10, 13, 15, 16, OO2, 3, PP3, 5, 8, 11, 12, 15, SS3, 17, 29, TT1, 8, 12, 22, 28, WW7, 10, 18, 27 (54)

1. Exclusions from Tilley's 86 "Shakespeare Index" citations: 1.1.161 (N307); 1.2.1f. (W109 [OW483b]); 2.2.103–5 (H285); 2.4.31f. (H305 [OW320a]), 240f. (M1333 [OW809a]); 3.1.88–90 (D180); 3.2.126f. (*M1193*), 238 (D148); 5.1.64–8 (M536); 5.5.85 (M184) (10)
2. Had the Chief Justice used *lion*, he would have referred to himself. In using *wolf*, presumably as an intensification of *dog*, he apparently refers to Falstaff's pre-Shrewsbury behavior.

3. Cf. Hulme, *Explorations*, pp. 48f. I am sceptical, but her explanation seems more plausible than that in Arden.
4. Arden rightly interprets in terms of E116.1, but wrongly labels as a version of E125.

5. Both Arden and Riverside follow Sisson in preferring Q's *time*. A case can be made for either reading.
6. Cf. Appendix B: AA3, BB10, 12, CC11, 15, 22, 24, DD2, 6, 12, EE5, GG2, 7, 11, HH4, 7, MM6, 10, 15, 16, OO1, PP2, 3, 6, 13, SS16, 23, TT8, 15, WW10, 12, 15, 23, 35, YY2 (35)

1. Exclusions from Tilley's 80 "Shakespeare Index" citations: 3.6.47f. (T249); 3.7.20 (H646), 64 (D455), 114f. (F41 [OW243b]), 145f. (M1231); 4.7.106f. (W85), 141f. (M66); 4.8.31f. (M184) (8)
2. One wonders if Hal's seeming nonce word can have been a misprint. I find neither in *OED*.

3. Cf. Hulme, *Explorations*, pp. 53 ff.
4. See Introduction, p. xivf.

5 Chorus, 15 (cf. T240); 5.1.*3f.* (cf. W332), 14f. *(T612)*, 31−3 (?cf. N311), 80 (cf. F603.1); 5.2.14−7 (cf. B99.1), 34f. (cf. P139), 36 (cf. L414 [1604]), 41* (cf. W460), 129f. (H109.1), 148f. (E242.1), 155−8 (R98.1), 175f. (cf. M980), 209 (B143.1f.), 234f. (B479.1), 242f.* (cf. K66), 272−5* (cf. M1264f.), *300f.* (L506), 359* (cf. M688) (20)

Epilogue, 7 (cf. L414) (1)   (136)[5]

King Henry the Eighth.[1]

1.1.52f. (cf. F228), 83f. (cf. B16, L452), 109−11 (cf. K87), 120 (cf. B764.1), 121f. (cf. W7), 123−5* (cf. G189, P107), 128* (cf. N229), *131f.** (cf. C413), *133f.** (cf. H642), 134−6* (?cf. C688), *140f.** (cf. e.g., P356),[2] 141−3* (cf. e.g., H198), 158−60* (cf. F629), 159 (cf. W601.2, 601), 191f.* (cf. B787), 208f. (cf. B440), 223* (cf. L251); 1.2.123f.* (cf. H397); 1.3.24f. (F451.1), 41 (F181.1), 48 (cf. C525); 1.4.*22** (?cf. W221), 27−9 (cf. L505.2, M2.1 [c1620], 2.2) (26)

2.1.1 (W316.1), 37f. (cf. W724.1), 65 (cf. B112.1), 153f. (cf. S520); 2.2.8f.* (cf. M1264), 22 (cf. K175), 66 (W318.1), 78* (cf. T64), 142f. (cf. C598); 2.3.15f. (S666.1), *22f.**

5. Cf. Appendix B: AA4, BB16, 18, CC20, DD8, 11, 18, EE3, GG2, 4, 7, 8, HH13, II1, KK2, MM10, 17, 21, OO2, PP2, 3, SS3, 17, 23, TT8, 10, 15, 20, 27, WW25 (30)

1. Exclusions from Tilley's 29 "Shake-speare Index" citations: 1.1.157f. (S878); 3.2.366 (M170) (2)

2. Whiting's abundant cross-references indicate how commonplace is the general idea, but I have seen nothing at all close to Norfolk's specific image (except, in context, 5.2.148 below). Arden says "based on proverbs," but those suggested seem too remotely akin even for this portion of *Henry VIII.* See Introduction, p. xxviii.

(cf. e.g., C624), 23 (cf. M45.1), *28f.* (cf. W707.2), 32 (C608); 2.4.79,* 94* (C465), 160f. (cf. D539), 171 (cf. C598) (17)

3.1.*23* (cf. H586), 25 (?cf. W912), 30f.* (cf. T587), *39* (cf. e.g., T587, P383*), 100 (H348), 145* (cf. F3); 3.2.40f. (cf. D133), 96f.* (?cf. C49), 140 (?cf. L251), 149−52 (cf. S119), 153f. (cf. e.g., D402, W820), 233 *(C554.1)*, 244* (?cf. W947), 259* (cf. H19), 270* (cf. W813.1), 371f. (cf. H604.1), 378* (K175), 424 (cf. H310.1), 429−31 (W637.2) (19)

4.2.41f.* (cf. P602), *45* (cf. B607.1, I71), *45f.** (cf. W114) (4)

5.1.86 (S118.1), 104f. (cf. H328.1 [c1569]), 168f. *(C276.1)*, 176 (cf. I94); 5.2.31 (A392), *45−7** (cf. F363, M544), 58 (?M1264), 73 (H330.1), 138−40 (?cf. S889),[3] 148* (cf. C465), 161f. (cf. S704); 5.3.70 (cf. H99), 75 (cf. M541) (14)   (80)[4]

TRAGEDIES

Titus Andronicus.[1]

1.1.83 (cf. H533), *117f. (cf. M898, K64.1)*, *176f.* (cf. M333), 201 (cf.

3. As Arden rightly notes, far more pertinent is Prov. 26.27 (1560 Geneva: He that diggeth a pit, shal fall therein [P356, Wh P232], and he that rolleth a stone, it shal returne unto him). Neither Tilley nor Whiting has any entry for this latter half, or for its variant in Ecclus. 27.26.

4. Cf. Appendix B: BB6, 11, 12, DD5, GG7, HH4, MM9, 13, OO3, PP11, SS11, 13, 15, TT4, 8, 9, WW7, 10, 28 (19)

1. Exclusions from Tilley's 62 "Shake-speare Index" citations (1.2.90 belongs under *Troilus and Cressida*): 1.1.93 (V85), 314 (T405); 2.3.150−2 (L316); 3.1.45 (W135), 267 (C84); 3.2.66f. (M1130), 4.2.144 (T257);

4.4.82f. (E1); 5.1.13−5 (M738); Q2F 5.3.169 (C571) (10)
2. Cf. Appendix B: AA2, 7, BB18, CC14, DD5, 9, HH1, 16, II1, JJ2, KK2, LL2, MM8, 10, OO3, SS16, 25, 29, TT25, UU1, WW2, 7 (22)

Romeo and Juliet.[1]

1. Exclusions from Tilley's 120 "Shakespeare Index" citations (* marks those rejected despite expert J. C. Maxwell's having included them in the New Cambridge edition): 1.1.42−51 (T273 [OW62a]), 126f. [Q1] (A228), 179−81 (L505a); 1.2.32 (O52); 1.4.106f. (*M475*); 2.2.156 (L514*); 165 (S458), 2.3.1f. (E32),* 9 (E31)*; 2.4.107f. (V92); 2.5.23f. (S1038); 3.1.96f. (B93),* 189 (A159); 3.2.84f. (F3), 116 (C571)*; 3.3.22 (G19), 62 (W683),* 92 M505); 3.4.4 (M505); 3.5.240 (T640); 4.1.27f. (P548); 4.2.46 (L277)*; 4.5.28f. (F391); 5.1.22f. (M905), 294 (F123)* (25) The New Cambridge adds two further references I have excluded: 3.3.30−2 (C141); 4.5.100f. (C111).

2. Tilley appears to have omitted these lines accidentally. Wilson records them under both C40 (OW921a) and C51 (OW100b): A good candleholder proves a good gamester [collections from 1659]. The latter, frequently cited by editors, seems to me contrary to Romeo's intent; we have, moreover, no evidence of its currency in Shakespeare's day. Ending line 38 with a colon, as the Riverside text does, appears unwarranted.

3. A pause before "house" would recall this common derisive expression. Recorded instances with "house" rather than "head" begin with the present passage. Rightly or wrongly, *OED* 5c equates the two expressions.

4. Although possibly an echo, the Heywood passage is spoken by a lover of proverbial expressions (like Mercutio), and in a proverbial context. Even so, I am unable to follow Tilley and New Cambridge in accepting the relevance of B93 (As broad as a barn door [unique in Heywood's *Four PP*]) for Mercutio's accompanying "church door" simile.

5. I doubt there is sufficient evidence to warrant OW717b's distinguishing between Nurse's "set up his rest" in 4.5.6 and Romeo's usage here.

6. Cf. Appendix B: AA3, 7, BB4, 9, 15, 18, CC6, 11, 23, DD1, 12, 17, EE6, FF6, GG7, HH4, 16, LL7, MM7, 9, 10, 13, OO2, 3, PP8, 11, RR4, SS1, 9, 12, 16, 17, TT8, 16, 26, WW1, 7, 10, 17, 22, 28 (40)

Julius Caesar.[1]

1.1.25 (cf. M66), 35* (cf. B453, S878, 866.1), 62* (T416); 1.2.*52f.* (*E231a*, 232*), 122 (cf. C773), 130 (S828), 131 (P37.1), 171* (cf. C896), 186 (cf. E255), 192 (cf. *F419*), 194, *208f.* (cf. M96), 213* (?cf. E11, 13),[2] 258 (cf. T10), 284 (G439), 300−2 (?cf. S96.1); 1.3.26−8 (cf. R33), 65 (cf. F526.1), 104f.* (cf. S300) (20)

2.1.22−7 (cf. *L25.1*), 32−4* (cf. C496), 274, 282 (cf. F696,* H49), 291−7* (cf. S196); 2.2.*26f.* (cf. F83), *32f.* (cf. C774), *36f.* (cf. N311), 69−71* (?cf. B179, W723), 128 (cf. A167); 2.3.7 (L427.1); 2.4.9 (cf. W706.1),[3] 39f. (cf. W703.1) (14)

3.1.*42* (cf. W794), 42f. (S704), *67* (cf. F367), 74 (cf. M1214.1), *99f.* (cf. N311), *171* (cf. F277, P369.1), 189 (L82), 254 (P290.1); 3.2.73 (E18), *75f.** (cf. I71), 111 (cf. B332), 115 (F248), 142f.* (cf. 1.1.35, S877), 150 (O91.1), 252 (A250) (16)

4.1.21−7 (cf. A360), 26 (cf. E16), 48 (S813.1); 4.2.8f. (cf. T200); 4.3.27 (cf. D449), 92 (cf. O40.1), 99 (T429), 111−3 (cf. F371), 117f.* (cf. H339), *190* (cf. M505), *218−24* (cf. T283, 323*), 222 (?A54) (12)

5.1.34f. (?cf. H544), 41* (cf. 3.1.42f.),

---

1. Exclusions from Tilley's 47 "Shakespeare Index" citations: 1.1.21 (A406); 2.1.81−5 (F3), 147−9 (M533), 175−8 (K64), 224−8 (F16); 3.2.75f. (T619); 4.1.50 (F16); 4.2.20f. (C732); 4.3.158f. (F732) (9)
2. Cf. Douglas Peterson, "Wisdom Consumed in Confidence: An Examination of Shakespeare's *Julius Caesar*," *Shakespeare Quarterly*, 16 (1965), 19−28.
3. In 2.1.291 ff. Portia convinces Brutus she has the strength to transcend a proverb, one she does not explicitly mention (S196). She here recognizes her weakness in the language of a kindred proverb (perhaps thereby implying Shakespeare's acceptance of its truth?).

64* (cf. T429), 95f. (cf. W912), *124* (?cf. D70, 59*); 5.3.19 (cf. T240), 93 (cf. F15.1); 5.5.20 (cf. H741.1), 22 (cf. W884.1) (9) (71)[4]

Hamlet, Prince of Denmark.[1]

1.1.10 (M1236.1), 16 (?cf. G185.1), 56−8* (cf. E264.1, B268), 112 (?cf. M1189); 1.2.6f.* (cf. W532, R72.1),[2] 11 (?cf. E248), 65 (?cf. K38), 67* (?cf. G272), *72−4* (cf. D142), 135−7 (?cf. W241), 144f. (?cf. A286), *146* (cf. W700.1), 159* (cf. G449), 161 (cf. F696), 200 (T436.1), 220f.* (cf. S914, L374), 227f. (T436), *256f.* (?cf. M1315);[3] 1.3.10 (M1158.1), 20 (cf.

---

4. Cf. Appendix B: BB8, 18, FF9, GG5, 7, HH16, 18, II3, MM10, PP3, RR5, SS14, 23, TT16, 17, WW8, 24, 28 (18)
1. Exclusions from Tilley's 140 "Shakespeare Index" citations: 1.1.162 (P389); 1.2.92−104 (D126), 106f. (C921), 120 (W155), 146 (W674); 1.3.25−7 (S121), 47−51 (W160), 59 (T219 [OW263a]), 61 (F741), 70 (E217), 79 (N164); 1.4.36−8 (W240); 1.5.43 (W588); 2.1.100 (N321); 2.2.95 (T575), 174 (G473), 206 (*A93*); 3.1.131f. (A67), 153 (K70); 3.2.65−8 (P613), 167f. (W651), (cf. M81 for a proverb peculiar to Q1); 3.4.33 (T534), 85 (G433), 95 (T405); 4.1.10 (R31); 4.2.17f. (N363 [OW583b]); 4.4.39−44 (D571), 40f. (T183); 4.7.187 (C934); 5.1.57 (A369), 203f. (B549), 286 (D573); 5.2.133−5 (D383), 212f. (*M475*), 271−83 (P166) (35)
2. As R72.1 indicates, Claudius has in mind a more secular sense than would occur to many Elizabethans.
3. Of course, Hamlet need not here be thinking of murder. Cf. e.g., c1330 *Gregorius* 129 A. 709 f.: "There nis non so dern dede That sum tyme it schal be sene" [Wh D134], a1420 Lydgate *Troy* III 709.4955−4960: "For the peple which that is rual Seith that secres, whiche be nat kouthe at al, the erthe wil, as thei make mynde, Discuren hen of his owne kynde, And of nature up casten and disclose The thing that men ar wont in it to close"

C110), 25−7* (cf. S119), 35 (cf. G482), 38 (?cf. E175), *39f.** (?cf. C56), 47−51* (cf. P537a),[4] 59* (cf. e.g. M602), *62−5* (cf. e.g., F752, T595), *64f.* (cf. H68), *68* (cf. M1277), *69* (cf. M299),[5] *70f.* (cf. C541), *72* (cf. A283), *76* (cf. F725), 85f. (K24.1), 115 (cf. S788), 117−20* (cf. B107); 1.4.15f. (cf. *C931*), 19* (cf. S1042), *36−8* (cf. C585), 57 (?cf. W332), 65 (cf. P334), 88f. (H218.1); 1.5.29f. (cf. T240), 40 (*S666.2*), 43−5 (cf. W704), 66 (cf. Q14.1), *108* (cf. F16), 128−30 (?cf. M104), 165* (cf. R213, S914.1), 187 (cf. F239), 188 (J75), 188f. (B140.1) (53)
2.1.60* (cf. L237), 63 (?cf. L237)[6] 78

(?cf. C446); 2.2.10 (cf. D592), 67* (H94), *90* (*B652*),[7] 141* (?cf. E107), 178 (W884.1 [c1553]), 179 (cf. M217), 184f.* (?cf. G272), 187 (cf. S936), 235f. (F603.1), 237 (cf. W893.1), *249f.* (cf. M254), 267 (M754.1), 274 (cf. H50.1), 360 (C100.1), 379 (cf. *H226*), 382f. (S1021.1), *385* (M570), 427f. (R130.1), 478* (cf. M931), 486 (cf. D133.1), 493 (F603.1), 568 (*J64*), 574 (cf. T268), 577 (cf. D574), *593f.* (cf. M1315), 597 (cf. Q13), 599f. (?cf. D231) (30)
3.1.58 (S177.1), 64 (*R196*), 74 (cf. Q16), *80f.* (cf. H166), *82* (cf. C606), 97−*100* (cf. G97), 102−4 (cf. B163), 135f. (cf. I1), 138f. (cf. C876.2), 158 (T598.1);[8] 3.2.33−5 (?cf. M162), 70* (?cf. W560, F611), 93f. (cf. M226), 97f. (cf. W776), 106 (cf. C16.1), *167−72** (cf. L507), 193* (cf. P603), *196f.** (cf. N321, E222), *200** (cf. *W884*), *207−9* (cf. T301), 230 (?cf. *P614*), 242f. (cf. H700), 249f. (E57.1), 251 (cf. B333), 251f. (cf. M65), 254 (cf. R33), 266 (cf. F40.1), 271 (cf. D189), *273f.* (cf. W884.1),[9] 276 (T609), 286f. (T248.1), 333f. (cf. T343.1), *338f.** (?cf. G447), *343f.* (G423), 396 (D8.1); 3.3.45f.* (?cf. W85, H122), 46 (S591), 50 (L431.1), 68f. (cf. B380), 81 (cf. M763, F389*), 93* (?cf. H392), 94f. (H397); 3.4.24 (?cf. R31,

---

[Wh E23], a1440 Burgh *Cato* 3.4.443 f.: "Thouh wykkydnesse for tyme be kept secre, Yitt att the laste will it discurid be" [Wh W237].
4. Cf. 1605 E. Philips, *Certaine Godly and Learned Sermons*, p. 52: "Thus may Preachers be as *Mercuriales statui*, set up as directors to others, shewing the way to heaven, and yet go themselves to hell."
5. Tilley's citing M299 for line 68 rather than 69 was surely a slip, although neither line has much in common verbally with either the entry form or any of the examples. Since this is generally true for Polonius's entire speech, and since several of the pertinent entries are more reflections of common ideas than actual proverbs, it is difficult to know how many this index should include. Every idea in the speech is a commonplace, but only lines 72 and 76 have much verbal resemblance to any legitimate proverb. Cf. Introduction, fn. 29.
6. The following is almost surely the clearest of several *Hamlet* echoes rather than the sign of any proverb: "onely of the deepe discerning politician it must be saide, *tam cernit acutim quam aut aquila aut serpens Epidaurius*, such as have such insight into the State as by indirections they can finde directions out, though they were hid fathome deepe" (J. Melton, *A Sixefolde Politician* [1609], sigs. E5ᵛf.).
 Incidentally, a fainter Melton echo, sig. C8ᵛ, on the "frensie of poetasting," supports the F1 reading for 3.1.158 rather than the Q2 retained by Riverside: "they may be compared to instru-

---

ments alwaies out of tune, which yeeld but harsh and iangling accents." Cf. T598.1, especially the c1564 citation.
7. Even if earlier analogues are discovered, "brevity is the soul of wit" almost surely begins with Polonius. The same can be said for Hamlet's "there's the rub" (R196), "Hoist with his own petar" (P243.1), "speak by the card" (C75.1), and very possibly for "know a hawk from a handsaw" (H226).
8. Cf. end of fn. 6 above.
9. The Q1 reading for line 273 ("Some must laugh while some must weep") better fits the typical examples from Whiting—and, of course, better fits lines 271 f.

30.1), 33 (cf. B759.1), 35−8 (cf. C934, B605.1), 87 (cf. F283.1), 89 (cf. B546.1), 95 (cf. D8.1), 156f. (H329.1), *161−5* (cf. C934, 932.1), *168* (cf. C932), *179* (cf. W918, B261*), 206f. (cf. e.g., F626, W204, *P243.1*), 216 (E128.1) (56)

4.1.7 (cf. S170), 9f. (?cf. R30.1); 4.2.11f. (cf. C682); 4.3.*9f.* (cf. D357), 23−5 (?cf. D143); 4.4.26* (cf. S918), 53* (cf. E95), 55* (cf. S918), 55f. (S813.2), 62 (B192.1); 4.5.36 (S591), 43 (?B54.1), *78f.* (cf. M1012), 84 (H805), 88f. (?cf. C443.1, 444), 136 (cf. C529), 152f.* (cf. D56), 158 (cf. F389), 185f. (E133.1), 195 (S591); 4.6.20−2 (cf. T616); 4.7.*111−3* (?cf. T340), *118−21* (?cf. N54), 134−6 (cf. T221), 163 (cf. M1012f.*) (25)

5.1.17 (W401), 39* (?cf. C587),[10] 56 (cf. B602), *57* (cf. A348.1), 67f. (cf. C933), 71 (?cf. A70), 116f. (cf. S295.1, C16.1), 137f. (*C75.1*), 251−3 (cf. O81), *292* (D464); 5.2.*10f.** (?cf. M298), 74 (?cf. O50.1), 105 (E35.1), *139f.* (?cf. K175), 183f. (cf. P545.1), 185f. (L69), 234f. (O64.1), 256f. (cf. *S826.1*), 306 (cf. F626, S788*), 336 (D142.2) (21)   (185)[11]

Othello, the Moor of Venice.[1]

1.1.5 (?cf. D592), 21* (?cf. e.g., H657), 26 (cf. *P550.1*), 33

10. I include only because Dover Wilson so suggested in his edition. The suggestion seems far less plausible than that for 2.2.184 f. above.
11. Cf. Appendix B: AA4, BB6, 18, CC11, 22, DD6, 9, 11, 15, 18, FF2, 4, 9, 10, GG7, HH3, 15, 16, JJ1, MM3, 10, 20, NN4, PP1, 3, 7, 9, 13, SS8, 20, 26, TT4, 8, 9, 16, 25, WW7, 10 (38)

1. Exclusions from Tilley's 90 "Shake-speare Index" citations: 1.1.21 (W377); 1.3.67−70 (L111), 202f. (G453), 206f. (H305), 289f. (D410),

(G179.1), *43* (cf. M107), 53 (?cf. P664), 59 (G198.1), 64 (?cf. F32), 105f. (cf. *T455.1*), 116f. (cf. B151); 1.2.17* (cf. W914); 1.3.55−8 (cf. G446), 106 (cf. S1019), 173 (?cf. *B326*), *202f.* (cf. e.g., R71.1), *218** (cf. W832), 229 (C932.2), 229−31 (?cf. C933), 293 (?cf. D180), 300 (T340.2), 309f. (D142.3), 313f.* (cf. C251),[2] 319 (cf. F210), 339ff. (*M1090*; cf. M1038.1), 344f. (cf. B262, N321*), 358f. (W165.1), 399f. (cf. T221), 401f. (N233) (30)

2.1.*109−12* (cf. W702), 114 (cf. J49.1), 129ff. (cf. F28), 132f. (cf. W314.1), 155* (?cf. e.g., H259),[3] 185 (cf. S908), 187f. (cf. O40.1), *214−7** (?cf. D216), 221 (cf. F239), 251f.* (cf. W466 [1580], 470.1), 253* (?cf. P620 [*AWW*]), 305 (H474), 309 (A379.1); 2.3.52 (S431.1), 63* (cf. W429),[4] *72* (cf. L251), 101f. (P375.1), *102* (H348), 114f.* (cf. H74), 170 (T609), 173 (cf. C110), 202* (cf. C251), 219 (cf. T590), *241* (cf. M541), *241* (cf. M335, B316.1), 247 (M755), 251 (*E212.1*), 262−4 (cf. C817), *270f.* (cf. M254), 274f. (cf. D443), 279* (cf. P60), 304 (cf. H278), 304f.* (M1264), 305f. (cf. B152.1), 322−5 (cf. B515), *351f.* (cf. D231), 366f.* (cf. L1), *370** (cf. *P103*), *379** (cf. H747) (39)

389f. (F135); 2.1.112 (B486), 155 (H161), 253f. (*H86*); 2.3.182 (P389), 305f. (V60), 172 (W194), 268−77 (M682), 329−33 (*J101*); 3.4.38f. (*H86*); 4.3.46 (D618); 5.1.104 (A93); 5.2.21f. (G251), 94 (D135), 205f. (T249), 286f. (*D252*), 303 (K173) (22)

2. Iago characteristically perverts a Christian commonplace. Cf. Leeds Barroll, *Artificial Persons* (University of South Carolina Press, 1974), p. 61.
3. I have seen nothing involving "cod" or "salmon," although conceivably the 1603 citation for S620.1 is remotely pertinent.
4. Cf. 1563 E. Ferrers "Edmund duke of Somerset" 13 f. *Mirror for Magistrates* 388: "who so wyth force wil worke agaynst kynde, Sayleth as who sayeth, agaynst the stream & wynde."

*King Lear.*¹

Philip's unrestrained complaint about having been stripped to "not a crust" with " 'Twil out, 'twil out, but now for the apparel." Cf. Emilia's "No, I will speak. . . ."

9. Cf. Appendix B: AA3, 4, BB17, 18, CC1, 9, 19, EE5, GG7, HH4, 10, 16, 17, JJ1, MM1, 11, 13, OO2, PP3, 17, RR1, 3, SS13, 24, TT5, 10, 16, 25, VV1, WW6, 9, 10, 26, 28 (34)

1. Exclusions from Tilley's 82 "Shakespeare Index" citations: 1.4.257 (M875); 2.2.4f. (D643), 74f. (M1235 [OW548a]); 3.1.26 (S598); 3.2.1 (W446); 3.4.19−21 (M866); 3.6.18f. (T551); 4.2.38f. (F219); 4.6.73f. (M471 [OW507a]), 80 (T244), 118−23 (M553 [OW911af.]), 164f. (A284), 182f. (D82), 259f. (B637) (14)

2. More pertinent, of course, with the text of Q1−2. Riverside follows F1. Cf. also 1.1.90, 1.4.166, 2.2.77, 3.4.48, 5.3.155.

3. Cf. Wh W237 cited on *Hamlet* 1.2.256 f.

4. Cf. Hulme, *Explorations*, pp. 73 ff.

---

5. For monkeys, cf. *2 Henry IV* 3.2.314, and the implications of "like apes in bed" in many versions of W702.

6. Cf. *2 Henry VI* 5.2.50.

7. "Rash as fire" may itself have been proverbial, as the context here suggests, and as some editors assert.

8. Cf. on *Hamlet* 1.2.256 f. Emilia may not be alluding to any proverb, however. In Heywood and Rowley's *Fortune by Land and Sea* (c1609 [1655]) 1.3 (VI, 384) the clown punctuates

6. For a pre-*Lear* version of Tilley's 1683 citation cf. e.g., 1580 C. Carlile, *A Discourse of Peters life*, sig. P4: "*Severus* said that a woman was the worke of the devil, and the upper part of a man of God, but from the navell downe of sathan: and therefore they that marrie doe fulfill the works of the devill." Neither passage can rightly be called proverbial.

7. Some of the examples suggest that Shakespeare may have intended ominous overtones of which Lear is unaware.

8. Cf. Appendix B: CC1, 12, DD3, 5, FF5, GG1, 7, HH16, JJ1, LL5, MM10, 12, 13, PP3, 11, SS4, 13, TT2, 13, 16, VV2, WW7, 33 (23)

5. Because the two cited examples include analogues to "a whore's oath," they strengthen the emendation *heels* for *health*. Riverside retains *health*. For the first member of Fool's trio, cf. Dennis R. Klinck, "Shakespeare's 'Tameness of a wolf,' " *Notes and Queries*, n.s., 24 (April, 1977), 113 f.

Macbeth.[1]

1.1.4 (W408.1; cf. M337,* W43.1), *11* (cf. F29); 1.2.14f. (cf. F603.1), 35 (cf. e.g., H147,* L307.1), 67 (cf. M337); 1.3.6 (?cf. W584), 18 (H231.1), 38 (?cf. F29), 97 (?H11),[2] 107 (cf. D266), 117 (cf. B318), 123f. (cf. D266), 146 (C529), *147* (cf. D90); 1.4.*11f.* (cf. F1.1), 22f. (?cf. V81); 1.5.17f. (?cf. *W142.1*), 38−40 (cf. R33), 42 (C864.1),[3] 62f. (cf. B531.1), 63 (T340.1),[4] 65f. (cf. S585); 1.6.22−4 (cf. *L481*); 1.7.1 (cf. T149, 200*), 25* (cf. R16 [1586]), 45 (cf. C144), 67 (cf. S1042), *82* (cf. F3) (28)

2.1.4f. (cf. C49.1), 57f. (cf. S895.1); 2.2.3f. (cf. R33), *51f.** (cf. B703),[5] 57f. (cf. W85), 70* (?cf. K175); 2.3.32 (cf. M48), 37f. (cf. T268), *50* (?cf. D407), 76 (cf. S527); 2.4.21 (W884.1), 40f. (cf. *E140.1*) (12)

3.1.80* (H94), 81−3* (cf. H47), 90 (cf. M541), 113 (cf. M874); 3.2.*11f.* (cf. R71.1), *12** (cf. T200),[6] 24* (cf. W914), 34f. (?cf. F3), *55* (cf. C826); 3.4.20 (cf. A82.1), 21 (cf. M638.1), 21* (cf. R151), 22* (cf. A88), *32−6** (cf. W258), 54* (cf. T240), 66f. (A211.1), 73 (cf. S818), 79 (E113.1), *121* (B458), 133f. (cf. W915, 912*), 135−7 (cf. F565.1, S379*), 141f.* (?cf. U24, C934); 3.5.*32f.* (cf. W152) (25)

4.1.85f. (cf. T275.1), 98f.* (cf. M327), 149 (cf. S117); 4.2.19* (?cf. K175), *24f.* (cf. T216), 41* (cf. B787), 83 (cf. B376); 4.3.12 (cf. R84), 16 (cf. L34.1), 52f. (cf. B440,*S591), 53* (cf. I1), 54 (cf. L34.1), 81f. (cf. M1144), 176−9 (cf. H347), *209f.* (cf. G449), 213 (S118.1), 214f. (?cf. D125,* 357), 216 (cf. C341), 219 (*S1046.1*), 230 (W637.2), 235 (?cf. T343),[7] *239f.* (cf. N164) (23)

5.1.*68* (T200), 79 (cf. *T220*, L367*); 5.3.15 (cf. F180, L296*), 16 (cf. L32.1, 306.1), 50f. (?cf. W109); 5.5.6 (cf. B143.1), *24* (L249.1), *24f.* (cf. W882); 5.7.1 (cf. S813.1); 5.8.8* (cf. L9), 28 (?cf. D651); 5.9.5 (cf. D148, 168*), 14 (cf. H30) (14) (102)[8]

1. Exclusions from Tilley's 71 "Shakespeare Index" citations: 1.2.19 (C110); 1.3.44f. (F239); 1.4.33−5 (J87); 1.5.5−8 (W758), 42 (T436), 62−6 (F3); 1.7.21 (B137), 25−8 (A235); 2.2.50f. (S527), 64 (W91); 2.3.136f. (F3), 140f. (K38); 3.2.4 (S742); 3.4.77f. (B597), 135−7 (G152), 140 (S80); 4.1.39f. (P24 [OW572bf.]), 52f. (W418), 85f. (C609 [OW660af.]); 5.1.72f. (C696); 5.5.27f. (P619) (21)
2. Pertinent only if, like Rowe, one emends to *hail*. Riverside does not.
3. Tilley instead cites the infinitely more popular T436 ("From top to toe"), but Lady Macbeth has an understandable preference for *crown*.
4. Despite such glosses as Arden's or Riverside's, I doubt that Lady Macbeth intended any meaning other than the normal one, or that an Elizabethan audience might so have interpreted her. "To look like the time," however, may have been proverbial also. The parallel in the 1609 version of Daniel's *Civil Wars*, noted since Steevens, implies at the very least that Daniel would have interpreted 1.5.64 as some editors interpret 63. Cf. VIII.89.3−6: "But, being arriv'd at Cort, / He drawes a Traverse 'twixt his greevances; / Looks like the time: his eye made not report / Of what he felt within."
5. Cf. my *John Webster's Borrowing*, p. 107.

Antony and Cleopatra.[1]

1.1.42f. (O64.1); 1.2.40* (?cf. *W585*), 57 (S118.1), 109f. (cf. W241),[2]

6. Strictly speaking, Lady Macbeth will not give this idea a proverbial formulation until she is sleepwalking (5.1.68).
7. Pertinent only if, unlike Arden or Riverside, one rejects Rowe and retains *time*. May *time* be used as is *world* in the familiar "Thus goes the world" (W884.1), or "The world goes on wheels" (W893)? Cf. 1602 Marston, *Antonio and Mellida* 3.1.101: "How goes the time?"
8. Cf. Appendix B: AA3, CC1, DD7, FF3, GG7, LL1, MM3, 15, SS6, TT18, WW34 (11)

1. Exclusions from Tilley's 52 "Shakespeare Index" citations: 1.2.41f. (C696), 52f. (*H86*), 59−61 (155), 105 (M755), 185−7 (S244); 2.5.67 (M905);

126(cf. W924, G298.1), 129f. (?cf. I13), 165f. (?cf. W631), 168f. (cf. B607), 169f. (cf. O67, P391*); 1.3.3−5 (cf. H839), *12** (cf. *L556*), 13 (?cf. S964); 1.4.*43*f. (cf. 1.2.126, M1015); 1.5.26f. (cf. P456.1) (15)

2.1.3 (cf. D198.1 [1907]), 5* (cf. K175), *43* (cf. G446); 2.2.90f. (?cf. K175), 108 (cf. T594), 110* (cf. S879), 172(B503.1), 177* (cf. C705), 181* (?cf. E1), 216−8* (cf. N42), 234 (?cf. C930), 234f. (cf. V18); 2.5.8f. (cf. W393), 32f. (cf. H347), 58 (cf. T616), 80 (M2.2); 2.6.23* (cf. T312), 42f.* (cf. M476, P547), 107 (S118.1); 2.7.30f. (?cf. C486.1), 49 (cf. C831), 53 (cf. H130.1), *83f.* (cf. N54), 90−2 (W893), 117f. (W885.1) (25)

3.2.28f. (P291.1), 34 (S118.1), 43f. (cf. S411); 3.4.10 (cf. T423); 3.6.84f. (cf. e.g., G453); 3.7.66 (cf. W269); 3.10.14f.* (cf. B651), 24* (cf. B641), 25f. (cf. 064.1); 3.11.65* (cf. M48), 70* (cf. M337, W43.1, 408.1), 72 (cf. L134); 3.12.3 (cf. P441.1); 3.13.47 (F743.1), 63−5 (?cf. M1243), 89* (cf. K116), *94f.* (cf. L321.1), *111−3* (cf. G257), 142 (cf. S936), 176, 191 (cf. L265) (21)

4.2.8 (cf. A192.1), 35 (cf. O67); 4.4.33 (?cf. S842, *M545**); 4.6.34* (cf. T240); 4.9.15f.* (cf. H311); 4.12.21 (cf. S704), 28 (cf. P401); 4.14.9* (cf. T240), *27* (cf. M219) 99−101 (cf. B192.1); 4.15.44 (cf. F603.1), 46f.* (cf. D35) (12)

5.1.*32f.** (cf. M116); 5.2.3 (?cf. F617.1), 7 (cf. D645.1), 122−4 (cf. W700.1), 235 (cf. F211), 240* (cf. H311), 240f.* (cf. M1111), 277*

2.6.99f. (F3); 2.7.122−5 (D362); 3.2.20 (B221); 3.4.19f. (E223); 4.1.9f. (N307); 4.4.20f. (D407); 4.9.13 (*A93*); 4.14.120f. (*M475*), 136−8 (E136); 4.15.37 (W539); 5.2.151f. (M980), 235 (F213) (18)

2. The proverb supports Warburton's commonly accepted emendation, *minds*. Riverside retains *winds*.

(cf. M48), 289f. (cf. A94.1), 311 (B63.1, A91.1, *88.1*) (12)   (85)[3]

Coriolanus.[1]

1.1.23 (cf. R22), 171 (cf. L307.1, H147), 172* (cf. F629, G348), 202f. (cf. D354), *206* (cf. H811), *206* (cf. D487,* 538,* *533*), *207* (*M828*),[2] 212f. (?cf. *C60*), 233 (cf. E23); 1.3.57 (cf. F97); 1.4.38 (cf. A82.1), 47 (cf. P504); 1.5.20−2* (?cf. F601); 1.9.45 (cf. S449, 839*), 89 (?cf. A88); 1.10.11 (cf. B143.1), 31f. (W884.1) (20)

2.1.12 (?cf. L311), 27* (cf. W269), 30* (cf. B671), 46 (cf. K171.1), 53* (cf. H334), 65f. (K171.1), 67 (cf. K175), 114f.* (?cf. Y25), 175 (?cf. S447), *190* (?cf. S699); 2.2.108 (cf. T436), 113f. (cf. P389), 126 (M1298), 127f. (cf. V81); 2.3.9−11 (cf. I66.1), 16f. (cf. M1308), 233 (*G404*), 252 (cf. S936) (18)

3.1.92f. (cf. H278, M1308*), 152f.* (cf. L378), 154f.* (cf. D357), 155−7 (cf. R32.1), 176* (cf. G169), 178f. (?cf. B528.1), 196 (cf. F251), *198f.* (cf. M555), 217 (cf. S214), *219−21** (cf. D357), 246f.

3. Cf. Appendix B: BB6, 18, CC1, 3, 17, DD15, FF7, GG7, 9, JJ2, KK2, 3, LL7, MM4, 10, OO1, PP3, SS6, 20, 26, TT8, WW4, 10, 13, 25, 31 (26)

1. Exclusions from Tilley's 60 "Shakespeare Index" citations: 1.1.144−6 (M875), 177−9 (M211), 259−61 (S989); 1.3.82−4 (P186); 1.8.3f. (A56); 2.3.117−9 (C933); 3.1.70f. (T228), 152f. (L386), 256 (H312); 3.3.129−31 (E220); 4.5.150f. (S451) (11)

2. Although most proverbs allow considerable variance in formulation, Arden may be right in thinking only H811 an actual proverb. But OW522a's 1607 citation for M810 (All meat pleases not all mouths), although probably not an example of the proverb under which it appears, intriguingly suggests the contrary: "Everie meate was not made for everie mouth; only bread was made for all."

3. Cf. Appendix B: BB6, 9, 18, CC11,
EE3, FF6, HH4, 10, JJ2, MM10, 24,
PP3, 11, 13, RR2, 3, SS3, 16, 20,
TT16, 25, WW10, 13, 16, 19, 23, YY1
(27)
1. Exclusions from Tilley's 43 "Shakespeare Index" citations: 1.1.24f.
(S929), 170f. (W923); 1.2.13 (F24),
15−8 (C732), 56f. (*H292*);
2.2.169−71 (F762); 3.3.41 (H246);
3.5.103f. (A67); 5.1.26 (W820), 50
(S184) (10)
2. So Hulme, *Explorations*, pp. 81 ff., ar-
guing for the retention of F1's *Gowne*
and *uses*. The argument seems strained.
Riverside makes the conventional
emendations.

3. Although Arden and Riverside disagree in interpreting this passage,
neither thinks F562 relevant. The
1563 addition suggests it is.
4. Riverside argues that P382 gives
"some support" to F1's *cast*, which it
retains. As OW193b implies by using
cost, P382 seems rather to support F3's
cost. Cf. *The Tempest* 2.2.31 f.
5. I include only as the closest I know to
what Arden, following Malone, calls a
"common expression": "he has wit in
his anger."
6. Cf. Appendix B: BB6, 12, 13, CC2,
11, GG7, HH15, 16, MM10, 23, PP3,
11, SS13, TT15, 17, 25 (16)

ROMANCES

Pericles, Prince of Tyre.[1]

1 Chorus, *10** (cf. O38 [1587]), 15f. (cf. C39), 29f. (cf. C934); 1.1.41f.* (cf. K175), *46* (B641.1), 97* (cf. D650), *103* (G275.1), *103** (cf. K72), *132f.** (?cf. B208), *137* (S467.1), *138** (cf. S569);[2] 1.2.7f. (cf. K87), 43 (cf. E179); 1.4.4 (cf. F251), *63f.* (cf. e.g., M1012), 78 (cf. G464), 108 (cf. F598.1) (17)
2 Chorus, 12* (cf. A147), 18f. (cf. D612.1); 2.1.*28f.* (F311), 46f. (cf. D612.1); 71f.* (cf. K175), *113* (T202); 2.2.32f. (cf. T443); 2.3.12 (?cf. G337), 36 (?cf. D323.1), 37−42 (cf. S826), 43f. (cf. G142.1); 2.5.29f. (cf. G337, P407.1), 35f. (S966.1), 55f.* (cf. T268) (15)
3.1.7f. (cf. V28); 3.2.22f. (cf. S525.1) (2)
4 Chorus, 22 (M931), 31−3 (cf. D573.2, C844, B435); 4.1.9f. (cf. G251), 51 (?cf. N213); 4.2.24f.* (cf. M253), 70* (G188), 87f.* (cf. T632), 110 (cf. W269), 142f. (cf. T276.1); 4.3.1 (cf. T200), 19 (cf. W269), 46−8 (cf. H176.1); 4.6.29 (D184.1), 35f.* (cf. R182), 111 (P291.1), 142 (cf. W646), 150 (M699.2), 171* (cf. Y25) (20
5.1.109 (W23.1), 5.2.9f. (cf. T264) (2) (56)[3]

---

1. Exclusions from Tilley's 26 "Shakespeare Index" citations: 1.1.137 (E196); 1.2.108 (T249); 1.4.75 (C732); 2.1.23f. (*P483*); 2.2.37f. (T448); 4 Chorus, 32f. (C853); 4.6.150 (C740) (7)
2. Concerning the first half of this line, cf. my *John Webster's Borrowing*, pp. 105 f., on *The White Devil* 3.2.112 f. I have seen no formulation that appears proverbial.
3. Cf. Appendix B: BB6, FF4, GG7, HH16, JJ2, MM2, 9, PP11, SS23, 29, TT10, 15, WW3, 7, 10, 28, 34 (17)

Cymbeline.[1]

1.1.57* (cf. H300), 71* (cf. H374, S848.1), 135f.* (cf. G446); 1.2.29f. (cf. B164); 1.3.19* (N95), 36 (?cf. N213); 1.4.11−3*((cf. E3), 91 (cf. W700.1); 1.6.16f. (cf. P256), 19 (cf. T436.1), 20 (cf. P80), 39−41 (cf. A273.1), *96f.* (R71.1), 113* (?cf. F480), 125f. (?cf. P457), 186 (cf. F156) (16)
2.1.3−5 (?O99), 20 (B306, F215.1); 2.2.15f.* (cf. L295.2, 296), 16 (?cf. C446),[2] 31 (cf. S527); 2.3.42−4 (?cf. T340), 67f. (?cf. M1050, A356*), 72f.* (cf. M1102), 94 (cf. S446); 2.4.27 (cf. H181.1), 107f. (cf. B99.1); 2.5.13 (cf. I1), 34* (cf. W723) (15)
3.1.23f. (cf. C540), 31 (cf. F603.1), 82 (E113.1); 3.2.20 (cf. I73); 3.3.2−7 (cf. H346.1), 30* (cf. Q15, *L244*), 40* (cf. F629), 42−4 (cf. B387.1); 3.4.*33f.* (cf. *S521.1*, W839), 136 (?cf. S985), 159* (cf. W211.1); 3.5.162 (cf. L1); 3.6.9−11* (cf. A53), 32f.* (cf. H819) (14)
4.1.5 (cf. R93); 4.2.*4f.* (cf. A119), *22* (cf. L517), 81−3 (cf. T17, A283*), 134 (cf. B27), 144f. (cf. S152.1), 201 (cf. L295.4, 295.1), *243* (cf. G446), *246f.* (cf. A119), *252f.* (?cf. D143), 261* (cf. H533, W3.1), *262ff.** (cf. E30), 267* (cf. O3), 372 (cf. E43.1); 4.3.45* (cf. T324); 4.4.37 (cf. H147, G167) (19)
5.3.57* (cf. M570); 5.4.7 (D142.3), 157−9 (cf. D148), 167 (T517); 5.5.41f. (cf. M514), 43 (H94), 50−2 (cf. I60.1), 58f. (D216.1), 75

---

1. Exclusions from Tilley's 46 "Shakespeare Index" citations: 1.2.12f. (H246); 1.4.77 (W923); 1.6.39−41 (M1030); 2.2.34 (G375); 2.3.66f. (P664); 3.2.33 (A53); 3.3.1−4 (D555); 45−8 (C412); 5.1.6 (W155), 29−33 (A285); 5.4.196f. (D554); 5.5.29f. (S47) (12)
2. Though allusions to the whiteness of sheets were common, *OED* s.v. White *a.* gives no instance of *white as a sheet* until 1866. OW608a has 1841.

(cf. C223), *106f.* (?cf. L526, C318.1), 168 (cf. F287.1), 232 (cf. W885.1), 418f. (cf. H170) (13)
(77)[3]

The Winter's Tale.[1]

Title (W513.1) (1)
1.2.6f.* (cf. C391), 27* (T416), 67−9* (cf. L33), 110f. (cf. H331.1), 126 (cf. W38.1), 130 (E66), 131f.* (cf. W412), 131f. (cf. W86.1), 137 (cf. C517), 161 (E90), 163 (M158), 180f. (L304.1), 186* (H268), 190−8 (cf. C571), 218f. (cf. C877), 388 (cf. B99.1), 447 (cf. F1) (17)
2.1.25 (cf. W513.1), 45 (S749.1), 73f. (?cf. E175), 121f. (cf. A53); 2.2.27* (cf. B4), 31* (cf. e.g., H547), 31 (cf. R84); 2.3.73 (cf. W884.1),[2] *86f.* (cf. S521.1, W839*), 97f. (cf. *L290*), 154* (cf. F162), 183 (?cf. M874) (12)
3.1.14f. (cf. G227.1); 3.2.92* (cf. B703), 110 (cf. S917), 192f. (?cf. W107), *222f.* (cf. e.g., G453, C921*), 231f. (cf. H328.1 [c1569]); 3.3.69 (W280.2), 81 (D126.1) (8)
4.1.*1* (cf. T336); 4.3.7 (cf. T431), 8 (D363.1), 50 (B140.1), 125* (cf. H320a); 4.4.154f.* (cf. T624), 177f.* (cf. S114), 204f. (C519), 218 (S591), 219 (cf. C844), 220 (cf. R178), 227* (T436), 317 (cf. D630.1), 319 (?cf. T456.1), 363 (cf. D576.1, 573.2), 363f. (cf.

S591), 383 (cf. H109.1), *444−6* (cf. S985), 554 (cf. T240), *573−5* (?cf. P611, T301*), 578* (Y25), 585 (T239), 595 (cf. H539.1), 623 (W280.2), 638f. (K171.1), 642f.* (?cf. S558), 667 (L421.1), 678f. (C426.1), 689−95 (cf. F366), 698 (W313), 728* (M633), 760 (cf. L9), 801f. (cf. N233), 836* (cf. M1034) (35)
5.1.29f. (cf. H347), 94 (P289.1, 290.1), 151f. (cf. F390), 215 (L431.1); 5.2.49f. (cf. S507), 74−6 (?cf. E248), 89f.* (cf. H311), 128−32 (?cf. *S451*, G58.1), 164−8 (cf. M163), 170−2 (T558.1); 5.3.4 (H535.1), 20 (cf. S527), 37f. (cf. H310.1, 311*), 39−42 (cf. S893.1), 132−5 (cf. T624) (16)
(89)[3]

The Tempest.[1]

1.1.15f.* (cf. S170), 20 (cf. N57), 28−33 (cf. B139), 53 (cf. M1248,* 1260.1), 58−60 (cf. B139); 1.2.30 (cf. H26.1), 55−7 (?cf. M1193), 56 (P291.1), 93−5 (cf. T555, E137.1, T549*), 106 (?cf. T51), *120* (?cf. C761), 201f.* (cf. L281), 214f. (cf. H403), 217 (cf. H26.1), 416 (cf. C56), 441f. (?cf. L426), 470 (cf. F562), 499f. (?cf. A88) (18)
2.1.27 (T64.1), 28−31* (cf. C491), 32−7 (cf. L93), 68 (cf. I70), 139 (cf. S649), 155f.* (cf. I9, 13), 160f. (cf. S1031), 167 (cf. 2.1.155f.), 221−3 (cf. E56.1), 249 (M240),[2]

---

3. Cf. Appendix B: BB6, DD4, FF9, GG3, HH3, 4, 10, 16, MM12, PP3, 8, RR3, 5, SS28, TT13, WW21, 23, 25 (18)

1. Exclusions from Tilley's 49 "Shakespeare Index" citations: 1.2.295f. (N285), 304−6 (H285), 305f. (G132 [OW305b]); 3.2.30f. (C597 [OW140a]), 104−6 (*A93*); 3.3.80f. (M562), 138f. (D60); 4.3.125 (M71); 4.4.10−3 (C934), 736 (T436); 5.1.119f. (R89), 199 (D651) (12)
2. Cf. *Hamlet* 2.2.178 f.

---

3. Cf. Appendix B: BB1, 10, 12, GG7, 9, KK2, MM1, 11, 25, OO2, PP13, 15, RR2, 3, TT12, 25, 27, WW6, 11, 19 (20)

1. Exclusions from Tilley's 60 "Shakespeare Index" citations: 1.2.147f. (*M1243*), 180−4 (T313); 2.2.53 (M49), 100f. (T446); 3.1.14f. (A228); 3.3.51 (B318); 4.1.9−14 (P546); 5.1.39 (*M1319*); Epilogue 15−8 (P557) (9)
2. I have not indexed subsequent instances of this nonproverb.

The Two Noble Kinsmen.[1]

3. Antonio may mean he is no such fool as to have a conscience.
4. I include only because in OW.
5. Lines 60 f. and 70 are obviously akin, but formulations verbally so different should perhaps have been given separate entries.
6. Although Shakespeare's source is Montaigne, the proverbial idea underlying both is worth citing.
7. Cf. Appendix B: BB12, 18, CC11, DD11, 12, FF4, GG7, HH4, 14, MM5, 10, 24, PP3, 11, 13, 18, SS13, TT8, 16, WW28, 31 (21)

1. Exclusions from Tilley's 39 "Shakespeare Index" citations: 1.3.6 (S903); 1.4.37f. (*A93*) (2)

POEMS

Venus and Adonis.[1]

2. Cf. Appendix B: AA7, DD10, GG7, 9, HH4, MM1, 10, OO2, 3, TT23, WW7 (11)

1. Exclusions from Tilley's 37 "Shakespeare Index" citations: 35 (F248), 220 (M341), 302 (W5), 329f. (G449), 331 (F265), 527 (R133), 567f. (N299), 569f. (H302), 707f. (P468), 773 (O70), 909 (H198), 987 (W651), 1032 (S826) (13)

The Rape of Lucrece.[1]

2. Cf. Appendix B: AA5, BB2, 18, CC11, DD4, 6, HH20, RR5, WW34 (9)

1. Exclusions from Tilley's 52 "Shakespeare Index" citations: 29f. (B177), 87f. (I82), 268 (B177), 588−91 (D618), 638f. (P252), 1337 (D357), 1342f. (F117), 1774 (K23), 1821f. (G446 [OW338a]) (9)

2. S477 may be too peripherally related to be worth citing. For what is probably simply a borrowing cf. 1599 R. Roche, *Eustathia*, sig. E8: "*And deeds unknowne, are ev'n as thoughtes unacted.*"

Sonnets.[1]

3. Some common origin, possibly proverbial, probably underlies the present passage, *Henry V* 1.2.209, and *Twelfth Night* 1.1.9−14, 2.4.100 f. Cf. 1601 Jonson, *Cynthia's Revels* 5.1.13−6: "good men, like the sea, should still maintaine / Their noble taste, in midst of all fresh humours, / That flow about them, to corrupt their streames, / Bearing no season, much lesse salt of goodnesse."

4. Cf. Appendix B: CC14, KK1, SS4, TT8 (4)

1. Exclusions from Tilley's 48 "Shakespeare Index" citations: 18.5f. (S978), 43.1 (W500), 66.1f. (D206), 73.1f. (N124), 102.12 (F47), 121.1f. (T140) (6)

2. I am indebted to the persuasive commentary in Stephen Booth's edition (Yale University Press, 1977) for

nearly one-fourth of the Tilley citations in this index (although some I have prefaced with a question mark): 8.14, 18.1, 34.1−4, 48.14, 52.3, 54.3f., 61.10−3, 93.13 (but substituting A291.1 for Tilley's more limited A300), 94.13, 103.3f., 105.13f., 118.5−8, 126.11, 135.1, 137.12, 144.14, 147.10. On the other hand, I exclude many Booth citations as inappropriate for this index, although useful for his purposes: 4h, 19.13f., 30h, 33h, 41.1−14, 43.1, 46.12, 47.3−8, 48.1, 49.6, 50.5−12, 51.2, 58.2, 60.9−12, 74.7, 76.12−14, 95.14, 100.9, 101.8, 103.9−12, 104.2, 8, 110.10f., 116.12, 118.5, 119h, 13, 121.4, 124.8−11, 125.8, 129h, 11, 130.1, 132h, 135h, 13f., 144.14, 151.1. A few others I exclude, either because I think the evidence too weak that the Tilley entry was a recognizable proverb in Shakespeare's day or because its relevance seems to me too slight: 14.14, 48h, 50.9f., 14, 70.2, 98.13f., 121.1.

In my index, but not in Booth, are the following Tilley citations: 15.3,* 17.10, 19.13,* 23.13,* 24.9, 26.13,* 39.2,* 44.7f.,* 47.2, 66.9,* 70.2, 74.6,* 7,* 77.7f.,* 85.1,* 90.7,* 94.3f.,* 98.10f.,* 126.14, 127.9,* 135f.,* 140.2,* 143.13,* 146.5,* 147.14,* 152.5f. Most of these are as trivial as the three involving "tongue-tied" (a word regarded as proverbial by Heywood, Howell, and Torriano, and therefore given an entry by Tilley).

A Lover's Complaint

The Passionate Pilgrim

The Phoenix and Turtle

3. Cf. Appendix B: BB3, MM15, RR3, TT8, 26, WW30 (6)

APPENDIXES

APPENDIX A

Entries Cited

As explained on p. 1, this appendix lists all entries cited in the preceding index. Each entry's brevity is governed by avoidance of the dangers discussed in the Introduction. If an entry originates in Tilley, has no complications in its entry form, and is supported there with adequate evidence of currency, the non-Shakespeare portion of the entry can be as simple as the Shakespeare portion:

> J49   As black as JET (From 1549)
>   Shakespeare: *MV* 3.1.39f., *2H6* 2.1.110, *Tit.* 5.2.50

More often than not, however, the entry form and/or the parenthetical indication of currency—and of origin, if of interest—require supplementation, the latter usually from Whiting (Wh) or Wilson (OW). Where Whiting has only a single example, its date is indicated. Where Whiting has more than one but fewer than five, the number is indicated in brackets. Entries based on Tilley, Whiting, or Wilson are supported by examples only where necessary or useful. Such examples are frequently cited because they are especially akin to Shakespeare in phrasing; they are not necessarily typical. Any wholly new entry, whether based on my own research or that of others, includes supporting evidence, from the earliest known instance through demonstration of currency (if possible). First performance dates for plays, often extremely conjectural, normally follow Harbage and Schoenbaum's *Annals of English Drama 975–1700*.

A question mark preceding an entry indicates doubtful legitimacy. Sometimes the supporting evidence in English is thin (in only such cases do I follow Tilley in citing Erasmus's Latin, if any); sometimes the evidence is abundant, but the phrase itself is of the "cf. Appendix B" kind; sometimes the entry reflects a commonplace idea or belief on the borderline between this appendix and Appendix C.

Parenthetical comment following the entry form sometimes includes "not in OW," usually either for entries where Shakespeare provides the earliest example in Tilley or where I question the legitimacy of Tilley's entry. In the former instance, OW's silence is significant (cf. Introduction, fn. 6); in the latter, it need not be. Understandably, hundreds of legitimate Tilley entries are not allowed space within the limits of OW.

Two speakers are occasionally noted parenthetically, the first for reasons his name indicates (Nicholas Proverbes of Porter's *Two Angry Women of Abingdon*), the second for characterization by cliché responses, especially sarcastic ones (Silena of Lyly's *Mother Bombie*).

Abbreviations other than OW, Wh, MSR (Malone Society Reprint), and OA (Old Arden edition) are conventional. In embarrassingly obvious cases (e.g., "He holds a wet eel by the tail" or "Make not the wolf your shepherd") I have omitted "(fig.)."

This appendix provides occasional cross-references to analogous entries, especially in connection with new (i.e., decimaled) entries. But in this respect it is no substitute for the valuable fullness of both Tilley and Whiting.

A

(?) A8 ABRAHAM's bosom (Luke
16.22; from *R3*; OW1a from c1533;
Wh A15 from a893)
   Shakespeare: *R3*   4.3.38,   *R2*
4.1.103f., *H5* 2.3.9f.

A29 The old ADAM (From 1537)
   Shakespeare: *H5* 1.1.29

A30 When ADAM delved and Eve
span who was then the gentleman?
(From 1530; Wh A38 from 1374)
   Shakespeare: *2H6* 4.2.134

A30.1 We are all come from ADAM
and Eve (Wh A37 *varied* from a1396;
OW3b "We are all Adam's children"
to parallel A31 [from 1659]: We are
all Adam's children but silk makes
the difference; includes *Ado* but has
nothing closely resembling entry
form or *Ado*)
Add: 1607 Sharpham *Cupid's Whirligig* ed. Nicoll 11: Are we not all
Adams Offspring?
   Shakespeare: *Ado* 2.1.63f.

A31.1 As the ADAMANT draws
iron (Wh A39 a1400)
1577 Grange *Golden Aphroditis* O2ᵛ:
As Adamant stones do the Iron,
plucke them to: So amorous lookes,
hath force the like to do. 1579 Lyly
Euphues I,212: Ye Adamant draweth the heavy yron. 1580 Lyly *Euphues
and his England* II,56: Wine . . . alwayes drew with it, as the Adamant
doth the yron, a desire of women.
c1592 Kyd *Soliman and Perseda*
2.1.198f.: Perseda, whom my heart
No more can flie then iron can
Adamant.
   Shakespeare: *MND* 2.1.195f., *Tro.*
3.2.179

A31.2 As hard as ADAMANT (Often of hearts) (Wh A40 from c1200)
   Shakespeare: *MND* 2.1.195f.

A32 As deaf as an ADDER (Cf. Ps.
58.4; from *2H6*; OW172a from
1590)
   Shakespeare: *Tro.* 2.2.172, *2H6*
3.2.76, *Son.* 112.10f.

A38 Much ADO about nothing (Ver-
batim from *Ado*, idea from 1529;
OW549a supplements)
Add: 1579 J. Stockwood *Sermon*
(STC 23284) 48: I have not made
much ado about nothing.
   Shakespeare: *Ado* (title)

A42 ADVERSITY makes men wise
(From *3H6*; OW4b adds analogues
from 1574)
Add: 1550 O. Werdmuller (M. Coverdale) *Spirituall . . . Pearle* I.viii ed.
1593 88–94 (chapter title): Trouble
and affliction doe helpe & further us
to the knowledge of our selves and of
God also, and specially to wisdome.
1563 L. Bruni (A. Golding) *Historie
of Leonard Aretine* 47: Adversitie
maketh men wise. 1601 A. Dent
Plaine Mans Path-Way I6ᵛ: Afflictions
are their scoolings, and Adversitie,
their best Universitie.
   Shakespeare: *AYL* 2.1.12, *3H6*
3.1.24f.

(?) A42.1 He is wise that can be
patient in ADVERSITY (Wh A57
1504 [1])ⁿ
I.e., 1504 Hawes *Example* 2C1(6f.):
For evermore right wyse is he That
can be pacyent in adversyte.
   Shakespeare: *Err.* 4.4.19f., *3H6*
3.1.24f.

ⁿI have not cluttered the index with
nonverbal reflections of this commonplace idea.

(?) A53 AFFLICTIONS are sent
us by God for our good (1659 N.R.,
variant 1675, cf. *Cym.* [excluded],

WT; OW5a *varied* from 1541)[n]
Shakespeare: *Oth.* 4.2.47f., *Cym.*
3.6.9–11, *WT* 2.1.121f.

[n]Wilson probably included this to correct the misleading impression of Tilley's entry. He establishes the currency of a Christian commonplace, but one never given any proverbial formulation. Cf. Introduction, fn. 6.

A54 To be AFLOAT (fig.) (Cf. Appendix B) (From 1546 Heywood)
Shakespeare: *JC* 4.3.222

A55 More AFRAID than hurt
(From 1530; Wh A64, OW543a supplement)
E.g., 1639 CL. 310 (More feared).
Shakespeare: *H5* 1.2.155

A64 AGE (Winter) and wedlock tame both man and beast (*Varied*; *winter* from *Shr.*, collections from 1639 CL.)
Shakespeare: *Shr.*4.1.23f.

A70 OLD AGE comes stealing on (upon us) (Collections from 1616; *varied* from 1577, OW587b from 1530)
Shakespeare: *Ham.* 5.1.71

(?) A72 Old AGE is full of infirmities (1616 DR., cf. *Lr.*)
Shakespeare: *Lr.*1.1.293

(?) A82.1 To have an AGUE FIT of fear (Cf. Appendix B)
1679 Dryden *Troilus and Cressida* 4.2 VI,373: This ague fit of fear is o'er.
Shakespeare: *R2* 3.2.190, *Mac.* 3.4.20, *Cor.* 1.4.38

A88 As free as the AIR (wind) (Shak., 1607ff.; OW286a adds c1592 analogue; *wind* only in Shak.)
Shakespeare: *LLL* 4.3.102, *MV* 2.6.16, *AYL* 2.7.48, *Tro.* 1.3.253, *H5* 1.1.48, *Oth.* 4.2.78, 5.2.220, *Mac.* 3.4.22, *Cor.* 1.9.89, *Tmp.* 1.2.499f.

A88.1 As gentle as AIR
c1620 (1647) Fletcher & Massinger *Custom of the Country* 3.2.156–8: I will . . . not long to kiss ye, But gently as the air. c1625 (1647) Fletcher *Chances* 2.2.23f. (to Love): Thou art young and fair, Thy mother soft and gentle as the air.
Shakespeare: *3H6* 2.6.21, *Ant.* 5.2.311

A90 As light as AIR (wind) (*Wind* c1530 [Wh W293 from a1200], *air Oth.*; not in OW)
Add e.g.: 1596 (1598) Chapman *Blind Beggar of Alexandria* iii.80: Thus can I lift my love as light as ayre. 1601 (1607) Marston *What You Will* II II,252: Lett's be as light as aire.
Shakespeare: *Oth.* 3.3.322, *Lr.* 4.6.49

(?) A91.1 As soft as AIR
Cf. on A88.1, W135.1
Shakespeare: *Ant.* 5.2.311

A92 As subtle (clear, thin) as AIR (*Thin* from 1558)
Shakespeare: *Rom* 1.4.99

A94.1 To be AIR and fire
1607 R. Turner *Nosce Te* D2[v]: Susanne's all mettle, onely aire and fire. ?1621 (1652) Fletcher *Wild Goose Chase* 2.2.110–2: Sometimes too Our lighter, airy, and our fiery metals Break out and show themselves. 1673 Dryden *Assignation* 1.1.163: I am not all Ayr and Fire, as you are.
Shakespeare: *H5* 3.7.21f., *Ant.* 5.2.289f.

A94.2 To trust the AIR
?1596 (1640 Jonson *Tale of a Tub* 1.1.65f.: I will not trust the ayre with it: Or scarce my Shirt [S357]. a1623 Dekker *Welsh Ambassador* 2.1.203f.:

No more, trust not the ayre With our proiections. 1629 Massinger *Roman Actor* 2.1.206f.: The pleasure of her bed I dare not trust the winds or air with.
Shakespeare: *Tit.* 4.2.169f.

(?) A95   As mad as AJAX (who killed sheep) (*LLL.* 1607, 1732; OW498a *LLL,* 1607)[n]
I.e., c1604 (c1607) Chapman *Bussy D'Ambois* 3.2.432f.: Quarrel with sheep, And run as mad as Ajax.
Shakespeare: *LLL* 4.3.6f.

[n]OW rightly omits "who killed sheep" and the 1732 Fuller entry. As Arden observes, the latter is one of three unmistakable borrowings from *Love's Labor Lost* (cf. 4.3.88, 5.2.643).

(?)   A95.1   As smooth as ALA-BASTER
1621 Burton *Anatomy of Melancholy* III.ii.ii.2 III,90: An high brow like unto the bright heavens . . . white and smooth like the polished Alabaster.
Shakespeare: *Oth.* 5.2.5

A95.2   As white as ALABASTER
1580 Lyly *Euphues and his England* II,20: Hee espyed an olde man . . . with a head as white as Alabaster. 1621 (cf. A95.1).
Shakespeare: *Ven.* 362, *Luc.* 419

A99   ALE (Liquor) that would make a cat speak (From 1585–1616; OW8b supplements)
Shakespeare: *Tmp.* 2.2.82f.

A119   ALL are of the same dust (Cf. Eccl. 3.20; *varied* from 1552; cf. Wh E22 from c1395)
Shakespeare: *Cym.* 4.2.4f., 246f.
Cf. E30: Earth must go to earth (Dust to dust).

(?) A124   ALL commend patience but none can endure to suffer (*Err., Ado,* 1732 Fuller)[n]
Shakespeare: *Err.* 2.1.34–7, *Ado* 3.2.28f., 5.1.27–31

[n]See Introduction, p. xix; also 1565 Sackville & Norton, *Gorboduc* 4.2.159–64 (scarcely formulated as a proverb): Many can yelde right sage and grave advise Of pacient sprite to others wrapped in woe, And can in speche both rule and conquere kinde, Who, if by proofe they might feele natures force, Would shew them-selves men, as they are in-dede,Which now wil nedes be gods.

A127   ALL covet all lose (From a1536)
Shakespeare: *1H6* 5.4.144–6

A133   ALL in all and all in every part (From 1596; *all in all* from 1583)
Add: 1583 Melbancke *Philotimus* 2E2[v].
Shakespeare: *2H4* 5.5.29
Cf. Appendix B: ALL in all.

A136.1   ALL is for the best (Wh A93.1 from c1390)
Add: 1678 Dryden *All for Love* 5.1.228: All for the best; go on.
Shakespeare: *3H6* 3.3.170, *Rom.* 3.1.104

A146   ALL is not gold that glisters (glitters, glares) (From a1536; Wh G282 from c1200)
E.g., 1578 Florio *First F.* XIX 32: Al that glistreth is not gold.
Shakespeare: *MV* 2.7.65

A147   ALL is not gospel that comes out of his mouth (*Varied* from 1546; cf. Wh G401 [To be (Not to be) gospel] from c1250)
Shakespeare: *Per.* 2 Chor. 12

A153   ALL is well and the man has his mare again (From *MND*; OW504a

a1548 analogue)
I.e., a1548 R. Copland *Jyl of Brentford's Testament* 62: The poore mare shal have his man agayn.
Shakespeare: *MND* 3.2.463

A154   ALL is well that ends well (Collections from a1536)
Shakespeare: *AWW* title, 4.4.35, 5.1.25, Epilogue 2

A164   (ALL shall be well) and Jack shall have Jill (*Jack* from c1517, whole from 1546)
Shakespeare: *LLL* 5.2.875, *MND* 3.2.458, 461f., *Wiv.* 1.4.120f.

A167   ALL that is alike is not the same (1639 CL., *JC*; OW464b combines with L288, from 1587)
I.e., 1587 Bridges *Defence* 1387: It is an old and a true proverbe, Nullum simile est idem, Nothing that is the like is the same.
Add: c1591 (1595) Peele *Old Wives Tale* 160, 169, 413: Things that seeme are not the same.
Shakespeare: *JC* 2.2.128
Cf. L288: No like is the same [from 1600].

A172   Bear (Take, Suffer) this, bear (take, suffer) ALL (From c1590 [1598]; ditto OW35a)
Shakespeare: *AYL* 4.3.14

A187   He that gives ALL before he dies provides to suffer (is a fool) (Collections *varied* from 1623, cf. *Lr*; ditto OW304af., which combines with G308 [Who gives away his goods before he is dead take a beetle and knock him on the head], *varied* from 1641)
Shakespeare: *Lr.* 1.4.105−8

A192.1   He that wins shall take ALL (Wh A105 c1330; cf. Wh A109 [Win all or lose all] from a1338 [4])
Shakespeare: *Lr.* 3.1.15, *Ant.* 4.2.8
Cf. L395: Let the longer liver take all.

A192.2   He will kill ALL he sees (meets), and eat all he kills.[n]
1611 COT. s.v. Charrette: Mangeur de charrettes ferrées. A terrible cutter, swaggerer, bugbeare, swashbuckler; one that will kill all he sees, and eat all he kils. Cf. Mangeur: a notable kill-cow, monstrous huffsnuff, terrible swaggerer; one that will kill all he meets, and eat all he kills.
Shakespeare: *Ado* 1.1.42−5, *H5* 3.7.92

[n]Editors at least since Steevens have called "eat all he kills" a proverbial turn of phrase, but without providing evidence other than the two passages in Shakespeare.

A202   Speak not ALL you know, do not all you can, believe not all you hear (*Varied* from 1576)
E.g., 1598 Barckley *Fel. Man* V 535: Beleeve not all thou hearest: doe not all thou maiest: nor speake all that thou knowest.
Shakespeare: *Lr.* 1.4.118ff.

A203   Take ALL and pay all (From *Wiv.*; ditto OW798b)
Shakespeare: *Wiv.* 2.2.118

A205.1   To make (let) ALL split (Cf. Appendix B)
1611 Middleton & Dekker *Roaring Girl* 4.2.68f.: If I sayle not with you both till all split, hang mee up at the maine yard. c1613 (1616) Beaumont & Fletcher *Scornful Lady* 2.3.113: Two roring boyes of Rome that made all split. c1615 Middleton *Witch* 2.2.44: I'll make you eat your word; I'll make all split else. ?1621 (1652) Fletcher *Wild Goose Chase* 5.6.36f.: I love a sea-voyage, and a blustering tempest; And let all split.
Shakespeare: *MND* 1.2.29f., *Lr.* 3.1.15

A207   To set ALL a going if it were a mile to the bottom (1666 TOR., cf. *2H4)*
I.e., 1666 TOR. *Prov. Phr.* s.v. Sughero 208: (Prodigally to sink all one hath; the English says, To set).
Shakespeare: *2H4* 5.3.54

A208   To set ALL at six and seven (From 1542)
Shakespeare: *R2* 2.2.122

(?) A208.1   To set ALL on hazard (Cf. Appendix B)
c1589 (1594) Lyly *Mother Bombie* 3.4.9f.: Nay, if you set all on hazard, though I be a pore wench I am as hardie as you both.
Shakespeare: *Tro.* Prologue 22

A209   Venture not ALL in one bottom (*Varied* from 1580; OW859a from 1513)
Shakespeare: *MV* 1.1.42, *1H6* 4.6.32f.

A211   When ALL is consumed repentance comes too late (*Varied* from 1481; = OW672a [Repentance comes too late] from c1440)
E.g., 1575 Gascoigne *Posies* I,66 (the normal secular sense): Bought witte is deare [W546], and drest with sower salte, Repentaunce commes to late. 1601 J. Manningham *Diary* 26 Jan. 17 (the rare religious sense): All our life wee have tyme to repent, but at death, it is too late.
Shakespeare: *Oth.* 5.2.83, *Lr.* 1.4.257
Cf. R80: Repentance never comes too late.

A211.1   When ALL is done (said and done)[n]
E.g., 1546 Heywood *Dialogue* I.vii B4: Ye there was god (quoth he) when all is doone. c1569 T. Ingeland *Disobedient Child* A3: Whan all is saide and all is done . . . none under the Sonne Bryngeth to children so much heavynesse. 1583 Melbancke

Philotimus S3: It must be as ye woman will, when all is said & done.
Shakespeare: *Ado* 2.3.61, *TN* 2.3.29f., *Mac.* 3.4.66f.

[n]Tilley and Whiting were probably mistaken in taking the Heywood proverb to be a unique example of "There is God when all is done" (G250, Wh G263). Cf. Introduction, fn 26.

A214.1   Win ALL or lose all (Wh A109 from a1338)
E.g.,c1450 *Merlin* II 598(15–6): Ffor this day be ye come all for to lese or all for to wynne.
Shakespeare: *1H4* 5.3.16

A220   An ALMOND for parrot (From c1517)
Shakespeare: *Tro.* 5.2.193

A225   It were ALMS (almsdeed) to punish (etc.) him (From c1497)
E.g., 1533 Elyot *Of Know.* IV 67b: Nay I trowe, than were it almes to hang me.
Shakespeare: *Ado* 2.3.158f.

(?) A231   What cannot be ALTERED must be borne not blamed (1575 [belongs in G453], 1580, 1592 [both Lyly], 1732 FUL., cf *Cor.*; not in OW)[n]
Shakespeare: *Cor.* 4.7.11f.

[n]Cf. Introduction, fn. 6.

(?) A231.1   Not ALTOGETHER (a) fool (ass)
c1561 (1595) *Pedlar's Prophecy* i (MSR 479): What man thinke not that I am altogither a foole.
Shakespeare: *Wiv.* 1.1.172, *Lr.* 1.4.151, *Tim.* 2.2.115

A242   There spoke an ANGEL (From c1588 [1599]; OW767af. supplements)
Shakespeare: *Jn.* 5.2.64

A246 ANGER is short madness
(From 1615, variants from 1477;
OW13bf. Horace, from 1539)
Shakespeare: *Tim.* 1.2.28

(?) A247 ANGER punishes itself
(1732 FUL., 1580; ditto OW14a)
I.e., [ERAS. *Similia* 588c: Ita
iracundia sibi nocet saepenumero,
cum aliis nocere studet.] 1580 Lyly
Euphues and his England II,66: It fell
out with him as it doth commonly,
with all those that are cholaricke,
that he hurt no man but himself.
Shakespeare: *Jn.* 4.3.32f.

A249.1 As well (soon) as AN-
OTHER
1598 (1601) Jonson *Every Man In*
3.1.151f: Nay I have my rewme, and
I be angrie, as well as another. c1604
(1605) Marston *Dutch Courtesan*
3.3.25f.: I ha' wit and can see my
good as soon as another.
Shakespeare: *Wiv.* 1.4.164

A250 (You are) such ANOTHER
(Cf. Appendix B; *OED* lc from
c1300) (From c1517)
Shakespeare: *Wiv.* 1.4.150, *Ado*
3.4.87, *Tro.* 1.2.271, *2H4* 2.4.253, *JC*
3.2.252

A273.1 To mow like an APE (Wh
A149 [3])
Shakespeare: *Cym.* 1.6.39–41

A275 A PER SE (Cf. Appendix B)
(From a1511; Wh A3 from c1475)
Shakespeare: *Tro.* 1.2.15

A283 APPAREL makes (Clothes
make) the man (*Varied* from a1500;
OW16b supplements)
Shakespeare: *AWW* 2.5.43f., *Ham.*
1.3.72, *Lr.* 2.2.54f., *Cym.* 4.2.81–3

A286 APPETITE (Stomach) comes
with eating (French from c1594,
stomach collections from 1623, *appetite* 1666 TOR., cf. *Ham.*; OW16b
adds Rabelais and later instances)

E.g., a1721 Prior *Dialog. of Dead*
(1907) 227: But as we say in France,
the appetite comes in eating.
Shakespeare: *Ham.* 1.2.144f.

A290 As dear as the APPLE of my
eye (*Varied* from 1562; *OED* Apple
7b from c885)
Shakespeare: *LLL* 5.2.475

(?) A290.1 As like as an APPLE to an
apple (crab) (OW17a, as below)
1579 Lyly *Euphues* I,258: The sowre
crab hath the shew of an apple as well
as the sweet pyppin. 1654 Gayton 35.
1705 11 Aug. Defoe *Review*: As like a
brat of their own begetting, that like
two apples, they could not know
them asunder.
Shakespeare: *Lr.* 1.5.15f.

A291 As like as an APPLE is to an
oyster (nut) (*Nut* from 1559, *oyster*
from *Shr.*; OW17a *oyster* from 1532)
Shakespeare: *Shr.* 4.2.100–2

A291.1 An APPLE may be fair without and bad within (Wh A155 *varied*
from a1225)
Shakespeare: *MV* 1.3.101, *Son.*
93.13f.

A310 In the APRIL of one's age
(From c1583 [1590])
Add e.g.: 1582 (1589) *Rare Triumphs*
(MSR 583). 1588 ?Lyly in Munday
Banquet III,458.
Shakespeare: *Son.* 3.10

A317 To keep (hold) one at ARM'S
end (From 1592)
E.g., 1592 Nashe *Pierce Penilesse*
I,185: Onely poore England gives
him bread for his cake [B633], and
holdes him out at the armes end.
Shakespeare: *TGV* 5.4.57, *AYL*
2.6.9f.
Cf. G122: I shall give you (you
shall have) as good as you bring
[from 1542].

A318   He that fights with silver ARMS is sure to overcome (1611 COT., 1664 COD., cf. *PP*)
Shakespeare: *PP* 18.17f.

A322   As swift as an ARROW (From 1563; Wh A186 from 1340)
Shakespeare: *LLL* 5.2.261, *MND* 3.2.101, *2H4* 1.1.123, 4.3.32f.

A325   Shoot one ARROW after another (1559 German, English from *MV*; OW726a supplements)
Shakespeare: *MV* 1.1.140–3

A332   ART is long, life short (From 1552; Wh L245 from c1380)
E.g., 1594 Huarte Navarro (R. Carew) *Exam. Men's Wits* I 7: Mans life is very short, and the arts long and toilsome.
Shakespeare: *1H4* 5.2.81

A339   As pale as Ashes (From c1475)
Shakespeare: *R3* 1.2.6, *Rom.* 3.2.55, 4.1.99f., *Ven.* 76, *Luc.* 1512

A343   ASK and have (From 1535; OW20a from c1475)
Shakespeare: *Tit.* 1.1.201

A345   A good ASKER (shameless beggar) should have a good naysayer (shameless denial) (*Asker* from 1611 COT., *Shameless beggar* from 1616 WITHALS)
Shakespeare: *MV* 4.1.440

A347.1   Between ASLEEP and awake (OW21a, from 1591)
Shakespeare: *MND* 4.1.147, *Lr.* 1.2.15.

(?) A347.2   I think X is ASLEEP c1570 *Misogonus* 4.2.50: The devils asleape, I thinke.
Shakespeare: *1H6* 3.2.122, *Lr.* 1.4.48, *Cor.* 4.5.2

A348.1   A dull ASS must have a sharp spur.
1602 (French 1557) G. Corrozet

Memorable Conceits C1: The common saying is: A dull Asse must have a sharpe spurre.
Shakespeare: *Ham.* 5.1.57
Cf. H684: A resty (boisterous) horse must have a sharp spur (a rough bridle) (from 1539).

A351   An ASS in a lion's skin (From 1484) Cf. on S366.
Shakespeare: *LLL* 5.2.624f. *Jn.* 2.1.143f., 3.1.128f.

A355   An ASS is known by his ears (*Varied* from 1538)
Shakespeare: *Err.* 4.4.29f.

A356   An ASS laden with gold climbs to the top of the castle (*Varied* from 1542; OW21bf. Plutarch, supplements from 1539)
Shakespeare: *Cym.* 2.3.67f., *PP* 18.17f.

A360   The ASS though laden with gold still eats thistles (From 1611, cf. *JC*; OW22a from 1581)
Shakespeare: *JC* 4.1.21–7

(?) A371.1   ASSES are born to bear 1593 Harvey *Pierces Supererogation* II,236: Asses are borne to beare; and Birdes to soare aloft.
Shakespeare: *Shr.* 2.1.199

A379.1   To make an ASS of (OW22a; *MND*, then 1605 Marston) Add: 1579 Lyly *Euphues* I,180: He would make himselfe an Asse. 1604 Dekker & Middleton *1 Honest Whore* 3.1.35. 1607 Dekker & Webster *Westward Hoe* 1.2.106f. 1611 Dekker & Middleton *Roaring Girl* 3.2.53. 1630 (c1605) Dekker *2 Honest Whore* 2.2.64. 1652(?1621) Fletcher *Wild Goose Chase* 2.1.125f.
Shakespeare: *MND* 3.1.120f., *Wiv.* 5.5.119f., *TN* 2.3.168f., 3.2.13, 5.1.17f., *Tro.* 5.1.56–60, *2H4* 2.1.37, *Oth.* 2.1.309

A388 An ASSHEAD of your own
(*MND*, c1605, 1636)
  Shakespeare: *MND* 3.1.116f.
  Cf. F519: A fool's head of your
own.

A392 To dance ATTENDANCE
(From c1522)
  Shakespeare: *2H6* 1.3.171, *R3*
3.7.56, *H8* 5.2.31

A402 AUTHORITY (Honor, Office) shows what a man is (*Varied*
from a1500)
  E.g., 1549 Latimer *Serm.* 11 177: It is
a proverb that Magistratus virum
commonstrat, Office and authority
sheweth what a man is.
  Shakespeare: *MM* 1.3.53f.,
2.2.117ff.

A411.1 To saye AYE and no (Cf.
Appendix B)
  1594 Drayton *Idea* 57: Nothing but
No and I, and I and No [in *OED* 1].
1602 J. Nichols *Plea of the Innocent*
203 (on conflicts between *Book of
Common Prayer* and the *Articles*): For
we are commaunded: To speak the
trueth everie man to his neighbour
[Zach. 8.16]. Which we can not doe,
if we say, I and no, in one & the same
particuler.
  Shakespeare: *Lr.* 4.6.98−100

A411.2 As blue as AZURE (Wh
A260 from a1400 [2])
  Shakespeare: *Luc.* 419

B

B4 As innocent (clear) as a newborn
BABE (child, chrisom-child) (*Varied*
from 1538; OW404b supplements)
  Shakespeare: *Wiv.* 2.2.36−8, *WT*
2.2.27
  Cf C363.1: To die like a chrisom
child.

B8 To look BABIES in another's
eyes (From c1565)
  Shakespeare: *Tim.* 1.2.110f.

B16 To break one's BACK (fig.)
(From *Tim.*; *OED* 24a from *H8*)
  Add: c1613 (1630) Middleton *Chaste
Maid in Cheapside* 3.2.65f.: I heard a
citizen complain once That his wife's
belly only broke his back. 9 Feb. 1615
J. Chamberlain 576: He hath under-
taken a business, which . . . may
chaunce breake his backe.
  Shakespeare: *H8* 1.1.83f., *Tim.*
2.1.24

B26 To change (the BAD) for the
better (From 1576; *bad TGV*)
  E.g., 1591 STEP. 156: It is alwayes
good to change for a better.
  Shakespeare: *TGV* 2.6.13

B27 (To go) from BAD (ill, evil) to
worse (From 1546; Wh E181 1492)
  Add e.g.: 1578 J. Rogers *Displaying*
E3: As the olde proverbe is, he is
gone, A malo in peius, from evil to
worse.
  Shakespeare: *Cym.* 4.2.134

B35 Lincolnshire BAGPIPES (Cf.
Appendix B) (From 1590; OW466a
from c1545)
  Shakespeare: *1H4* 1.2.76

(?) B54.1 BAKER'S daughter[n] (Cf.
Appendix B)
  ?1555 J. Bradford *Copye of a Letter*
(STC 3480) F6[v]: Peradventure his
maiestie after he were crowned
would be content with one woman,
but in this meane time his grace wil
every night, have v. or vi. to see
whiche of them pleaseth him best. If
thei wer ladies or gentle wemen, it
were more tolerable, but bakers
daughters and such other poore
whores, is abominable. [margin:
Poore bakers daughters of brussels.]
F7[v]: But know ye their reportes: they
saye the good bakers daughter is

more worth in her goun then Quene Mary without her croun.
Shakespeare: *Ham.* 4.5.43

"See Robert Tracy, "The Owl and the Baker's Daughter," *Shakespeare Quarterly*, 17 (1966), 83–86. It is at present impossible to tell whether Bradford originated the rhyme he claimed "they saye," but he does imply a current implication for "baker's daughter." Possibly the following does so also. 1589 *Hay any worke* (STC 17456), sig. H1: I am travelling towards Banbury / for I here say that there hath bin old adoe. For bakers daughters wold have knights whether they would or no.

B62   He has struck the BALL under the line (fig.) (From 1562 [c1549]; OW78la supplements; both include *Tmp.*)
Shakespeare: *Tmp.* 4.1.236

B63.1   As sweet as BALM (Wh B34 from a 1405)
Shakespeare: *Ant.* 5.2.311

B65   Be as be may (is no BANNING) (*Be as be maye* from 1530; Wh B74 from c1386)
Shakespeare: *AYL* 3.3.41f., *3H6* 1.1.194

B73   As common as a BARBER'S chair (From 1554)
Shakespeare: *AWW* 2.2.17

B74   Like a BARBER'S chair, fit for every buttock (*AWW*, 1678 Ray, 1732 FUL.; OW137b combines with B73)
Shakespeare; *AWW* 2.2.17

B80   To sell one a BARGAIN (Cf. Appendix B) (From 1666)
Add: 1611 Cotgrave s.v. Foin: Bailler foin en corne. To deceive, gull, cousen, sell a bargaine, give a gudgeon.

Shakespeare: *LLL* 3.1.101–3
Cf. B537: To give one the boots.

B83   As near as BARK to tree (1580 analogue, *LLL*, 1633, 1639)
I.e., 1580 Lyly *Euphues and his England* II,87: As neere is Fancie to Beautie . . . as the stalke to the rynde. 1633 Marmion *Fine Companion* 5.2 191: Master Dotario, and my daughter Aemilia, hand in hand, and married together! . . . Well, there they are bark and tree. 1639 CL. 286.
Shakespeare: *LLL* 5.2.285
Cf. H88: Put not your hand between the bark and the tree [from 1546].

(?) B89.1   To thrash in (*a woman's*) BARN (Wh 850 a1500)
I.e., a1500 *Ragman Roll* 72.53: And whoo so lyst may thressyn in youre berne. Apperson 627.
Shakespeare: *Tit.* 2.3.123

B99.1   To kill like a BASILISK (*Varied*) (Wh B56 [As mortal as a basilisk] 1512; cf. Appendix C: B99)
E.g., c1400 Mandeville ch. 28 285: Thei sleu him anon with the beholdynge, as dothe the Basilisk. [in OW31b].
Shakespeare: *2H6* 3.2.52f., *3H6* 3.2.187, *R3* 1.2.150, *H5* 5.2.14–7, *Cym.* 2.4.107f., *WT* 1.2.388
Cf. C496.2: To kill like a cockatrice.

B104   BASTARDS by chance are good, by nature bad (French c1594, English from 1611 COT.)
Shakespeare: *Lr.* 5.3.244f.

B107   The BAVIN burns bright but it is but a blaze (*Varied* from 1579; OW33a supplements)
Add e.g.: 1557 *Tottel* 237: Then doth the baven blase, that flames and fleteth by and by.
Shakespeare: *1H4* 3.2.6lf., *Ham.* 1.3.117–20

B109   At a BAY (Cf. Appendix B)
(Collections from 1546)
Shakespeare: *Tit.* 4.2.42

B112.1   BE it as it is (Let it be as [what] it will)
c1553 (1575) Stevenson *Gammer Gurtons Nedle* 5.2.33: What, woman! let it be what it wil, tis neither felony nor treason. 1578 T. Blenerhasset "Cadwallader, Induction" 7 *2 Mirror for Magistrates* 441: But let it be as it wil, warned folkes may live. Ibid. "Sigebert, Induction" 27. 450: Truely (quoth *Memory*) let it be as it is, you shall see good sport shortly. 1594 *Knack to Know a Knave* xii (MSR 1429): Well, be it as it is.
Shakespeare: *R2* 2.1.146, *2H4* 1.2.114, *H8* 2.1.65

B112.2   Will it (It will) not BE?
c1554 (1568) *Jacob and Esau* 1.1 (MSR 13): Why when? Up, will it not be? Up. c1591 (1593) Peele *Edward I* vi (MSR 1221): It will not be.
Shakespeare: *1H6* 1.5.33, *Jn.* 3.1.298, *Rom.* 4.5.11

(?) B125.1   As fouly (*ugly*) as a BEAR (Wh B96 a1400)
Shakespeare: *MND* 2.2.94

B132   Sell not the BEAR'S skin before you have caught him (*Bear* from 1616, *beast* 1580; OW713b *beast* 1578)
Shakespeare: *H5* 4.3.93f.

B139   He that is BORN to be hanged (drowned) shall never be drowned (hanged) (*Varied* from c1503)
Shakespeare: *TGV* 1.1.148–50, *Tmp.* 1.1.28–33, 58–60

B140.1   (Alas) that ever I was BORN (the day that I was born)
a1460 *Herod* (Wakefield) 343: Alas that I was borne! c1490 (c1530) *Everyman* 348: Alas that ever I was bore! c1508 (1522) *World and the Child* 765, 783: Alas the day that I was born. 1533 Udall *Floures* D6, N6ᵛ, R2, V5ᵛ: Alas that ever I was borne. c1552 (c1567) Udall *Ralph Roister Doister* 4.8.8: That ever I was borne! 1566 (1575) Gascoigne *Jocasta* 3 Chorus I, 294: Happy were he that never had bin borne.
Shakespeare: *Tro.* 4.2.85f., *Rom.* 4.5.15, *Ham.* 1.5.188f., *Oth.* 4.2.69, *WT* 4.3.50

B140.2   We are BORN to die
1566 (1575) Gascoigne *Jocasta* 3.2 I,290: Being borne (as all men are) to dye. 1576 Pettie *Petite Pallace* 49: Wee are borne to die. 1579 E. K., on Spenser *Shepheardes Calender* Nov. Embleme: By course of nature we be borne to dye. 1587 Churchyard "Wolsey" 420 *Mirror for Magistrates* 509: All are borne to die.
Shakespeare: *Rom.* 3.4.4

B141   We are not BORN for ourselves (*Varied* from c1523; OW75b supplements)
Shakespeare: *MM* 1.1.29–40, *Tim.* 1.2.101f., *Ven.* 166

B143.1   To meet (etc.) in the BEARD (Wh B117 from a1338)
Shakespeare: *H5* 3.2.70f., 5.2.209, *Mac.* 5.5.6, *Cor.* 1.10.11

B143.2   To shake one by (play with one's) BEARD (fig.) (Wh B118 from c1330 [3])
Add: 1571 Edwards *Damon and Pithias* i (MSR 138): I have played with his beard in knitting this knot. 1631 Jonson *Bartholomew Fair* 4.4.144: How, Rascall? are you playing with my beard?
Shakespeare: *H5* 5.2.209

B151   The BEAST with two backs (*Oth.*, 1650ff.: OW36a adds Italian, French)
I.e., 1591 Florio *Giardino di Ricreatione* 105: Far la bestia a due dossi. 1611 Cotgrave s.v. Dos (also s.v.

Beste): Faire ensemble la beste a deux dos. To leacher.
Shakespeare: *Oth.* 1.1.116f.

B152.1 A drunken man is a BEAST (*Varied*)
E.g., 1547 W. Baldwin *Treatise of Morall Phylosophie* 05: Wrathe maketh man a beast, but dronkennes maketh hym worse. ?c1588 (1599) Porter *Two Angry Women of Abingdon* iv (MSR 989): Drunke: hees a beast and he be drunke. 1601 A. Dent *Plaine Mans Path-Way* N3[v]: Drunkennesse . . . is a most swinish thing. It maketh of a man, a beast. c1605 (1606) Marston *Fawn* 5.1.161−3 (of drunkenness): It makes the king and peasant equal, for if they are both drunk alike, they are both beasts alike.
Shakespeare: *Shr.* Induction i.34, *MV* 1.2.89, *Oth.* 2.3.305f.

B160 To BEAT (pinch) one black and blue (*Beat* from c1550; *pinch* from *Err.*)
Add: 1588 (1591) Lyly *Endymion* 4.3.29: Pinch him, pinch him, blacke and blue.
Shakespeare: *Err.* 2.2.192, *Wiv.* 4.5.111f., *TN* 2.5.10

B163 BEAUTY and chastity (honesty) seldom meet (*Varied* from 1576; Wh B150 from a1400)
Shakespeare: *AYL* 1.2.37−9, 3.3.30f., *Tro.* 5.2.67, *Ham.* 3.1.102−4, *Son.* 105.13f.

B164 BEAUTY and folly are often matched together (Collections *varied* from 1611; Wh B151 1532)
E.g., 1532 Berners *Golden Boke* 246.4225: For beautie and foly alway gothe to gyther.
Shakespeare: *Cym.* 1.2.29f.

B165 BEAUTY does fade (like a flower) (*Fade* from 1563, *flower* from 1579)
Add e.g., 1588 Greene *Pandosto* ed.

Bullough VIII,185: Be not proud of beauties painting, for it is a flower that fadeth in the blossome.
Shakespeare: *TN* 1.5.52, *PP* 13.1−3
Cf. B169: Beauty is but a blossom [from c1589 (1592)].

B170.1 BEAUTY is made for use 1601 (1602) Dekker *Satiromastix* 1.1.7: Beauty is made for use. c1604 (1605) Marston *Dutch Courtesan* 1.2.131: Beauty's for use; 5.1.62−4: That things of beauty created for sweet use . . . Custom should make so unutterably hellish!
Shakespeare: *Ven.* 164

B179 BECAUSE is woman's reason (*Varied* from 1551)
Shakespeare: *TGV* 1.2.23f., *Tro.* 1.1.106f., *JC* 2.2.69−71

B184 Early to BED and early to rise makes a man healthy, wealthy, and wise (Collections from 1659; analogues from 1523; OW211b from 1496)
E.g., 1602 ?T. Heywood *How a Man May Choose* 653−5(B) (echoing Lily's *Grammar*): *Ladie Willowby.* Shall teach him that Diliculo surgere, Est saluberrimum.
Shakespeare: *TN* 2.3.2f.

B186 Go to BED with the lamb and rise with the lark (From 1580; OW38b *lark* from c1555)
Shakespeare: *R3* 5.3.56, *H5* 3.7.31f.

(?) B186.1 Go to thy cold BED and warm thee[n]
Shakespeare: *Shr.* Ind. i.9f., *Lr.* 3.4.48

[n]Cf. Introduction, p. xxivf.

(?) B192.1 To go to one's grave (death) like a BED
1570 (1583) J. Jewel *Exposition . . . Thessalonians* M1[v]f.: The death of a

godly man, is nothing else, but a sleepe. . . . Who soever dyeth in the peace of conscience, hee maye saye, I wyl lie downe and take my rest. . . . He goeth into his grave, as into a bed. c1604 (1607) Dekker & Webster *Sir Thomas Wyatt* 4.4.37: Death frights my spirit, no more then can my bed. 1606 (1608) W. Perkins *Cases of Conscience* K2: Death . . . qualified by Christ . . . is a blessing . . . And the grave a resting chamber, yea a bed perfumed by the death of Christ, for the bodies of all the Elect. c1613 (1616) Beaumont & Fletcher *Scornful Lady* 2.1.40−4: To sleepe to die, to die to sleepe: a very Figure Sir. / Cannot you cast another for the Gentleweomen? / Not till the man bee in his bed, his grave; his grave, his bed; the very same againe Sir. 1619 J. de L'Espine *Treatise Tending to take away the feare of death* 64: In dying our spirit returneth into heaven, and our body into the earth, as into a bed there to rest and repose.
Shakespeare: *MM* 2.4.101f., *Ham.* 4.4.62, *Ant.* 4.14.99−101

B195 Who goes drunk to BED begets but a girl (*Varied* from 1606)
Shakespeare: *2H4* 4.3.93f.

B197 Ye would make me go to BED at noon (From 1546)
Shakespeare: *1H4* 2.1.43, *Lr.* 3.6.85

(?) B197.1 Misery (Adversity) makes (acquaints men with) strange BED-FELLOWS (OW535a; *Tmp.*, 1837−9, 1861, 1927)
Shakespeare: *Tmp.* 2.2.39f.

B205 The BEE sucks honey out of the bitterest flowers (thyme) (*Varied* from 1579; Wh B169 a1450)
E.g., 1579 Lyly *Euphues* I,206: The Bee . . . gathereth Honny out of the weede. Add e.g., 1578 Whetstone *Promos and Cassandra* Ep. Ded.

II,443: The Bee suckes honny from weedes.
Shakespeare: *H5* 4.1.11

B208 Where the BEE sucks honey the spider sucks poison (*Varied* from a1542)
Shakespeare: *Per.* 1.1.132f.

B211 BEES that have honey in their mouths have stings in their tails (tongues) (*Tail* from 1579; Wh B170 from a900, *tongue* a1420)
I.e., a1420 Lydgate *Troy* III 717.5218−9: And as a be, that stingeth with the tonge Whan he hath shad oute his hony sote.
Shakespeare: *Shr.* 2.1.213−5, *Luc.* 493

(?) B215.1 To be BEEF-witted (-brained) (*OED* 5 from *Tro.*)
Add: 1593 Nashe *Christs Teares* II,122: For shame, bury not your Spyrits in Biefe-pots. Let not the Italians call you dul-headed Tramontani. 1594 *Terrors of the night* I,370: Lives there anie such slowe yce-braind beefe-witted gull. 1611 COT. s.v. Boeuf: Teste de boeuf: A ioulthead, iobernoll, cods-head, grouthead, logerhead; one whose wit is as little as his head is great.
Shakespeare: *TN* 1.3.85f., *Tro.* 2.1.12f.

B229 The BEGGAR may sing before the thief (*Varied* from 1546; Wh M266 from c1380)
E.g., c1395 Chaucer *CT* III(D) 1191−4: Verray poverte, it syngeth proprely; Juvenal seith of poverte myrily: "The povre man, whan he goth by the weye, Bifore the theves he may synge and pleye." a1439 Lydgate *Fall* II 344−5.582−5: The poore man affor the theeff doth synge Under the wodis with fresh notis shrille; The riche man, ful feerful of robbynge, Quakyng for dreed(e), rideth foorth ful stille.

Shakespeare: *2H6* 4.2.54f.
Cf. N331: They that have nothing
need fear to lose nothing.

B238   Set a BEGGAR on horseback
and he will ride a gallop (run his
horse out of breath) (*Varied* from
1576; OW41b supplements)
Add e.g., 1591 A. Colynet *Civill
Warres of France* B1ᵛ: As the Proverbe is, Set a begger on horsebacke,
and he will ride until he break his
necke.
Shakespeare: *3H6* 1.4.127

B247   BEGGARS should be no
choosers (From 1546)
Shakespeare: *Shr.* Ind. i.41f., *MV*
4.1.440

B261   An ill (bad) BEGINNING has
an ill (bad) ending (*Varied* from
1580; Wh B199 from c1300)
Shakespeare: *Jn.* 3.1.94, *R2*
2.1.213f., *Ham.* 3.4.179

B262   Such BEGINNING such end
(From 1546)
Shakespeare: *Rom.* 2.6.9, *Oth.*
1.3.344f.

B268   I will BELIEVE it when I see it
(1616 Withals; Wh B220 c1330)
Add: 1519 Horman *Vulgaria* 287:
Thou canst not make me beleve it tyl
I se it. 30 April 1616 J. Chamberlain
626: For my part I shall beleve yt
when I see yt.
Shakespeare: *Ham.* 1.1.56−8

B269   We soon BELIEVE what we
desire (Collections from 1596; *varied*
from 1576; OW43b Caesar, Ovid; cf.
Wh T126 1509)
Shakespeare: *2H4* 4.5.92

B272   As sound as a BELL (From *Ado*;
OW755a from 1576)
Shakespeare: *Ado* 3.2.12

B276   To curse with BELL, book, and
candle (From c1470)
Shakespeare: *Jn.* 3.3.12

B289   The BELLY that is full may
well fast (*Varied* from 1586)
E.g., 1586 WITHALS M1: The
man whose belly filled is, com-
mendeth fasting much iwis.
Shakespeare: *TGV* 2.1.28f., *LLL*
1.2.148f.

B299   I wish it were in your BELLY
(for me) (From c1589 [1594])
Add e.g.: 1599 (1600) Jonson *Every
Man Out* 5.7.59f.: Would this pot,
cup, and all were in my belly, if I
have a crosse about me. 1600 (1601)
Jonson *Cynthia's Revels* 4.4.5: Take
your bottle, and put it in your guts
for me.
Shakespeare: *1H4* 3.3.49

B306   To have a BELLYFUL (Cf. Appendix B) (From c1475)
Shakespeare: *Wiv.* 3.5.36 *Cym.*
2.1.20
Cf. F215.1: To have one's fill of
fighting.

B309   BENEFITS are soon forgotten
(*AYL*, 1630, 1732)
Add: 1595 G. Babington *Funeral Sermon* C4: Common saying . . . Nihil
citius senescit quam gratia. Nothing
so soon wexeth olde, as dooth the
remembrance of a benefit. 1603 R.
Allen *Oderifferous Garden of Charitie*
Ii1ᵛ: Beneficis memoria brevissima:
at iniuriae solet esse tenacissima.
The remembrance of a benefite is
verie short: but an iniurie is kept
very long in mind.
Shakespeare: *AYL* 2.7.186

B316   Bad is the BEST (From 1564;
OW26a adds 1587, *3H6*)
Shakespeare: *3H6* 5.6.91, *Son.*
114.7, *PP* 7.18

B316.1   The BEST go astray

c1570 *Misogonus* 1.1.111: The best of us all before god goeth astraye. 1600 Drayton et al. *1 Sir John Oldcastle* 4.1.182: Once in their lives the best may goe astray. c1616 (1652) Middleton *Widow* 4.2.203: The best have their mistakings.
Shakespeare: *Oth.* 2.3.241

B318 The BEST (?greatest) is behind (*Best* from c1500 [Wh B265 supplements]; *greatest* 1579, *Mac.*)
I.e., 1579 Lyly *Euphues* I,279f. (with context): Lette them also be admonished that when they shall speake, they speake nothing but truth.... But the greatest thinge is yet behinde, whether that those are to bee admitted as cockemates with children which love them entirely.
Shakespeare: *Mac.* 1.3.117
Cf. W918: The worst is behind.

B326 Make the BEST of a bad bargain (market) (etc.) (?From 1622, cf. *Oth.*, *Cor.*; Tilley and OW48b include an irrelevant 1589)
I.e., 1589 Puttenham *Art Eng. Poesy* III.xvii 184: The figure diastole ... we call the Curry-favell, as when we make the best of a bad thing.
Shakespeare: *Oth.* 1.3.173, *Cor.* 5.6.146

B332 Seldom comes the BETTER (From c1515)
Shakespeare: *R3* 2.3.4, *JC* 3.2.111

B332.1 The BETTER for you (your asking) (OW20bf.; Chaucer analogue, then from 1598)
I.e., c1380 Chaucer *Troilus* III 1562: And ner he [Pandarus] com, and seyde, 'how stant it now This mury morwe, nece, how kan ye far?' Criseyde answerde, 'never the bet for yow.'
Add: a1460 *Annunciation* (Wakefield) 180f.: What chere with the(e)? The better, sir, for you. c1520 *Youth* 423f.: I do well enow, And the better that you will wit. 1594 Lyly *Mother*

Bombie 2.3.53: The better for you, sir.
Shakespeare: *Wiv.* 1.4.135f., *R3* 3.2.97

B333 The BETTER the worse (From 1582; OW56a from 1542)
Shakespeare: *LLL* 1.1.281, *Ham.* 3.2.251

B338 He turns (falls) to his old BIAS (again) (From 1580; OW58a from 1573)
Shakespeare: *TN* 5.1.260

B339 To run against (Out of) the BIAS (Cf. Appendix B) (From *R2*; OW58b *against* c1580)
Shakespeare: *Shr.* 4.5.24f., *LLL* 4.2.109, *R2* 3.4.5, *Lr.* 1.2.111, *PP* 5.5

B352 Fast (Sure) BIND fast (sure) find (*Fast* from 1546)
Shakespeare: *MV* 2.5.54

B354 They that are BOUND must obey (From 1525)
Shakespeare: *Shr.* 1.1.212, *Lr.* 3.7.54

B359 As blithe (light, merry) as BIRD on bough (brier) (Wh B289, 294, 296)
Shakespeare: *MND* 5.1.394, *H5* 3.2.18f.

B365a A BIRD (egg) of the same nest (egg, brood) (From *AWW*; OW60a from 1553 [= E81])
Shakespeare: *AWW* 4.3.286
Cf. E81: To come of the same egg (nest) [*nest* from 1553].

B374 I heard a BIRD sing (A little bird said so) (*Heard* from 1546, *little bird* from 1583)
Shakespeare: *2H4* 5.5.107

B375 If every Bird had (should take) his own feathers he should be as rich as a new-shorn sheep (you would be

naked) (*Varied* from c1580; ditto OW60af.)
Shakespeare: *Tim.* 2.1.30f.

B376   An ill (evil) BIRD (crow) lays an ill (evil) egg (*Varied* from 1536)
E.g., 1539 TAV. 18ᵛ: Of an evyll ravyn an evyll egge.
Shakespeare: *Tit.* 2.3.149, *Mac.* 4.2.83

B377   It is a foul (etc.) BIRD that defiles his own nest (From 1509; OW397b from a1250)
Shakespeare: *AYL* 4.1.203f., *2H6* 2.1.184

B380   The more the BIRD caught in the lime strives the faster he sticks (*Varied* from 1576; OW59b from 1557)
Shakespeare: *Ham.* 3.3.68f.

B387.1   To sing like BIRD(S) in the cage (*Varied*)
1575 Gascoigne "Hearbes" I,335: Much like the seely Byrd, which close in Cage is pent, So sing I now, not notes of joye, but layes of deep lament. 1580 Churchyard *Charge* D1ᵛ: God knowes what care the bird doeth feele, in cage that swetly sings. 1590 Sidney *Arcadia* I Eclogues I,139: The house is made a very lothsome cage, Wherein the birde doth never sing but cry. 1607 W. Alexander *Alexandraean Tragedy* 4.2 2389f.: As Birds, whose cage of golde the sight deceives, Do seeme to sing whilst they but waile their state. c1611 (1631) Dekker *Match Me in London* 5.1.23f.: Birds in Cages mourne At first, but at last sing. 1612 Webster *White Devil* 5.4.117: Wee thinke cag'd birds sing, when indeed they crie.
Shakespeare: *Lr.* 5.3.9, *Cym.* 3.3.42−4

B393   BIRDS of a feather will flock (fly) together (From 1578)

Shakespeare: *3H6*   2.1.170, 3.3.161, *2H4* 5.1.70f., *Tim.* 1.1.100f.

(?) B394   BIRDS once snared (limed) fear all bushes (c1579, *3H6*, *Luc.*, *varied*; OW61a adds c1590 [1596])
I.e., c1579 F. Merbury *Marriage between Wit and Wisdom* viii (MSR 1278-81): The silly bird once caught in net if she ascape alive will come no more so ny the snare her fredome to deprive. c1590 (1596) *Edward III* 4.3.21f.: What bird that hath escapt the fowlers gin, Will not beware how shees insnared againe?
Shakespeare: *3H6* 5.6.13f., *Luc.* 88

B397   Small BIRDS must have meat (1639 CL., variants from *Wiv.*; OW744b cf. Job 38.41, Ps. 147.9)
Add: c1604 (1605) Marston *Dutch Courtesan* 2.3.71f.: Sparrows must peck and Cocledemoy munch.
Shakespeare: *Wiv.* 1.3.35

B404   As dry as a BISCUIT (*AYL*, 1620; OW206b; adds 1599 [1600])
Shakespeare: *AYL* 2.7.39

B435   BLACK best sets forth white (*Varied* from 1523; cf. Wh W231 from a1333)
Shakespeare: *Rom.* 1.1.231, 1.5.48, *3.2.19, Per.* 4 Chor. 31−3

B436   BLACK will take no other hue (From 1546)
Shakespeare: *Tit.* 4.2.99f.

B438   No more like than BLACK is to white (*Varied* from c1570; Wh B331 from 1513)
E.g., 1587 Rankins *Mirr. Monsters* 14: Easily then is white discerned from blacke, a vile offence from a godly pretence.
Shakespeare: *MV* 5.1.39f., *H5* 2.2.103f.

B439   (To have it) in BLACK and white (white and black) (From

c1570; Wh B328 from c1385)
Shakespeare: *Ado* 5.1.304f.

B440 To make BLACK white (From 1582; Wh B330 from a1393; OW884b Juvenal)
Shakespeare: *Tro.* 1.1.56, *H8* 1.1.208f., *Mac.* 4.3.52f., *Tim.* 4.3.28f.

(?) B441.1 Not set a BLACKBERRY (Wh B333 c1412)
Shakespeare: *Tro.* 5.4.11f., *2H4* 1.2.173

(?) B442 As plentiful (cheap) as BLACKBERRIES (*1H4*, 1690; OW634a adds Carlyle, Gaskell)
E.g., 1690 T. Brown *Chang. Rel.* II: *Bay's Reasons* 35: Were Reasons as cheap as Black-berries.
Shakespeare: *1H4* 2.4.239

B445 He that BLAMES would buy (*Varied* from 1590; cf. Prov. 20.14)
Add: 1578 J. Yver (H. Wotton) *Courtlie controversie* Fl: But You use the trade of suttle marchants, who ever dispraise the wares they determine to buy, to the ende thy may bargaine at their owne price.
Shakespeare: *Tro.* 4.1.76f.

B448.1 BLEEDING new (Cf. Appendix B)
1639 CL., s.v. Novitas p. 228: Bleeding new.
Shakespeare: *Tim.* 1.2.78.

(?) B450 BLESSING of your heart, you brew good ale (c1515, TGV, 1622; ditto OW85a)[n]
I.e., c1515 (1530) Barclay *Eclog.* II 17: God blesse the brewer well cooled is my throate. 1622 Jonson *Masque Augurs* 181 *Masques at Court* VII,635: Our Ale's o' the best, And each good guest Prayes for their souls that brew it.
Shakespeare: *TGV* 3.1.304f.

[n]Tilley's citations other than that from Shakespeare suggest that only

"Blessing of your heart" was proverbial (cf. G266), but that good brewers were frequently so blessed. Cf. Introduction, fn. 26.

(?) B450.1 Children (Bairns) are BLESSINGS
1613 (1630) Middleton *Chaste Maid in Cheapside* 3.2.33f.: Children are blessings, If they be got with zeal by the brethren.
Shakespeare: *AWW* 1.3.25f.

B452 If the BLIND lead the blind they both fall into the ditch (Luke 6.39; from 1509; Wh B350 from a900)
E.g., 1580 Baret C−270: *A Proverbe to be used towardes those, which want the gift of reason, and yet will seeme to give counsayle.
Shakespeare: *Lr.* 4.1.46

B453 As dull (senseless) as a BLOCK (*Dull* from 1565; OW68b *insensible* 1549, *senseless* 1590)
Shakespeare: *Ado* 2.1.239f., *JC* 1.1.35

B455 As red as BLOOD (From c1470)
Shakespeare: *2H6* 2.1.108, *LC* 198

B458 BLOOD will have blood (*Varied* from c1560; Wh B361 from c1395; cf. Gen. 9.6)
Shakespeare: *Jn.* 1.1.19, 2.1.329, *Mac.* 3.4.121

(?) B461.1 He has not so much BLOOD as will feed a flea (*Varied*)
1614 (1631) Jonson *Bartholomew Fair* 4.2.57f.: In his blood? hee has not so much to'ard it in his whole body, as will maintaine a good Flea. 1679 Dryden *Troilus and Cressida* 2.2 VI,312: She has no blood of mine in her, not so much as will fill a flea.
Shakespeare: *LLL* 5.2.691f., *TN* 3.2.60−2

B465 Like BLOOD, like good, and

like age make the happiest (best) marriage (Collections from 1639 [OW464a adds 1579, Wh B363 a1450], *TN*)

Shakespeare: *TN* 1.3.109f.

B465.1   Only BLOOD can quench the fire (*Varied*)

c1591 R. Wilmot *Tancred and Gismund* E4: This heart hath felt the fire That cannot els be quencht but with his bloud. 1593 (?1594) Marlowe *Massacre at Paris* ii.35f.: Those neverdying flames Which cannot be extinguished but by blood. 1608 Chapman *Byron's Tragedy* 5.2.296: We must quench the wild-fire with his blood. c1613 (1623) Webster *Duchess of Malfi* 2.5.63f.: 'Tis not your whores milke, that shall quench my wild-fire, But your whores blood.

Shakespeare: *Jn.* 3.1.340−3, *Rom.* 1.1.83−5

B466.1   To have one's BLOOD boil (*Boil* 10b begins 1675)

1606 Marston *Sophonisba* 3.1 II,33: My strong blood boiles. 1620 Boccaccio *Decameron* (Bullough VIII,53): Bernardoes blood now began to boyle. ?1625 (1637) Fletcher *Elder Brother* 4.4 II,46: How my Blood boils, as if't were o're a Furnace!

Shakespeare: *Ven.* 555

B471.1   BLOW for blow (Cf. Appendix B)

1578 G. Whetstone *1 Promos and Cassandra* 2.4 II,454: No harme is done; here is but blow for blow.

Shakespeare: *Err.* 3.1.56

B479.1   A maiden BLUSH (Cf. Appendix B)

1639 CL. s.v. Pudor 268: A maiden-blush.

Shakespeare: *H5* 5.2.234f., *Rom.* 2.2.86

B480   BLUSHING (Bashfulness) is virtue's color (is a sign of grace)

(*Varied* from 1562; OW71a from 1519)

E.g., 1539 Taverner *Garden* ii F3: Blusshynge is token of an honest nature. 1562 Heywood *Epigrammes* 64: [Red is] a token of grace: they blushe for shame.

Shakespeare: *TGV* 5.4.165, *Ado* 4.1.34−8, *2H4* 2.2.75f.

B483   He feeds like a BOAR in a frank (1678 Ray, *varied* from *2H4;* ditto OW252b)

Shakespeare: *2H4* 2.2.146f.

(?)   B487.1   Give God (Heaven) thanks and make no BOAST of it

Cf. 1601 Dent *Plaine Mans Path-Way* D6: They are worthy to bee Chronicled for fooles, which are proud of Gods gifts which are none of their owne.

Shakespeare: *Ado* 3.3.19f., 3.5.43, *AYL* 2.5.36f., *H5* 4.8.114−6

B497   The BODY is the prison of the soul (1584, 1732 only)

Add e.g.: 1547 W. Baldwin *Treatise of Morall Phylosophie* I6: Suche as have lyved more godlye than other, beyng by deathe delivered from the pryson of the bodye, shall ascend. c1587 (c1592) Kyd *Spanish Tragedy* 1.1.1f.: When this eternall substance of my soule Did live imprisoned in my wanton flesh. c1588 (1590) Marlowe *2 Tamburlaine* 4.3.33−5: Draw your sword, Making a passage for my troubled soul, Which beats against this prison to get out. c1589 (1594) Peele *Battle of Alcazar* 5.1 (MSR 1445f.): Weapons have made passage for my soule That breakes from out the prison of my brest. c1591 (1593) Peele *Edward I* xxv (MSR 2678): In this painfull prison of my soule.

Shakespeare: *3H6* 2.1.74, *Jn.* 3.4.17−9

B501   A little BODY does often harbor a great soul (heart) (*H5*, col-

lections from 1611; OW469b supplements)
E.g., 1611 COT. s.v. Buisson: A little bodie (oft) harbours a great heart; and a small head much wit [H261]; s.v. Lievre: A little bush may hold a great Hare; a little bodie a great heart.
Shakespeare: *H5* 2 Chorus 17

B503.1 One soul (heart, mind) in BODIES twain (*Varied*) OW289af. (A friend is another self [F696]) includes 1539 Taverner I *Garden* F1ᵛ: Demaunded, what a frend is, One soule, quoth he [Aristotle], in two bodyes. 1542 Erasmus tr. Udall *Apoph.* (1877) 233 The prouerbe *amicus alter ipse* . . . two frendes are one soul and one body. 1579 *Proverbs* of Sir James Lopez de Mendoza tr. B. Googe 101ᵛ We reade in the Cronicle of the Philosophers that Aristotle beeing demaunded what hee accounted a friend to be; made answere, that it was one minde in two bodyes.
Add e.g., 1557 ?Grimald "Of frendship" *Tottel* 01ᵛ: Behold thy frend, and of thy self the pattern see: One soull, a wonder shall it seem, in bodies twain to bee. c1569 *Marriage of Wit and Science* (MSR 1547) (of title marriage): Wee twaine hence forth one soule, in bodyes twayne must dwell. 1571 Edwards *Damon & Pithias* (MSR 1834): In two bodies they have but one heart. c1592 ?Kyd *Soliman and Perseda* 4.1.30: What are friends but one minde in two bodies?
Shakespeare: *MND* 3.2.212, *Ant.* 2.2.172, *Cor.* 4.4.13

B515 A broken BONE (leg) is the stronger when it is well set (fig.) (*Varied* from 1579)
Shakespeare: *2H4* 4.1.220f., *Oth.* 2.3.322–5

B517 He has a BONE in his mouth (throat) (*Throat* from 1542; *mouth* from 1623)
Add: 1603 S. Harsnet *Declaration*

P1ᵛ: Stands like a mute . . . with a bone in his mouth, and dares not speake one word.
Shakespeare: *MV* 1.2.50–2

B528.1 To make the BONES rattle (in someone's skin)
E.g., c1560 (c1569) T. Ingeland *Disobedient Child* Fl: By Coxe bones I wyll make thy skyn to rattell. c1564 (1571) Edwards *Damon and Pithias* xiii (MSR 1214): I wyll so pay thee, that thy bones shall rattell in thy skinne. 1566 (1575) Gascoigne *Supposes* 5.6.8f.: I wil make those old bones rattle in your skin. 1578 Lupset *All for Money* 1273f.: Oh, it doth Mother Croote much good to have her bones rattled, And especially by her lover.
Shakespeare: *Cor.* 3.1.178f.

(?) B531.1 To read one like a BOOK (OW665b; *Tro.* and 1874)
Cf. a1415 *Lanterne* 134.34f.: Her owene conscience as open as a book in the whiche thei schal rede here owene dampnacioun [Wh B454: As open as a book].
Add: c1593 (1598) Marlowe *Hero and Leander* II.129f.: Therefore even as an index to a book, So to his mind was young Leander's look [in F1]
Shakespeare: *Tro.* 4.5.239, *Mac.* 1.5.62f.

B532 To speak (etc.) without BOOK (From 1579; OW762a from 1551; in *TN* sense from 1575)
Shakespeare: *TN* 1.3.26f., 2.3.149, *Tro.* 2.1.17f., *Rom.* 1.2.59, 1.4.7

B534 To be in (out of) one's BOOKS (From 1547)
Shakespeare: *Shr.* 2.1.224, *Ado* 1.1.78f., *2H4* 4.2.16f.

(?) B536 Be jogging while your BOOTS are green (*Shr.*, *OEP*; OW412a, 1777)
I.e., 1777 C. Dibdin *Quaker* 1.1: You

may as well be jogging, Sir, While yet
your boots are green.
Shakespeare: *Shr.* 3.2.211

B537   To give one the BOOTS (Cf.
Appendix B) (From c1589)
E.g., 1611 Cotgrave s.v. Bailler: To
give one the boots, to sell him a
bargaine.
Shakespeare: *TGV* 1.1.27
Cf. B80: To sell one a bargain.

B540   To play BOPEEP (Cf. Appendix B) (From 1528; OW75b supplements)
Shakespeare: *Lr.* 1.4.177

B546   He will (To) creep into your
(one's) BOSOM (From 1546)
Add e.g.: c1542 (1557) Wyatt "Of
the fained frend" 5 *Tottel* Fl: Yet
know it well, that in thy bosome
crepeth. 1581 Guazzo (Pettie) *Civile
Conversation* I I,79: They teach men
to insinuate, and by coloured wordes
to creepe into mens boosomes.
Shakespeare: *2H6* 4.1.1f., *1H4*
1.3.266

(?) B546.1   To go into one's own
BOSOM (turn one's eyes inward)
(Cf. Appendix B)
c1554 (1574) O. Werdmuller (M.
Coverdale) *Hope of the Faithfull* A2ᵛ:
If we goe into our owne bosomes, we
finde that we . . . frame oure lives
after the world. 1599 (1600) Dekker
Old Fortunatus 1.2.128: Turne your
eyes inward, and behold your soule.
c1604 (1605) Chapman *All Fools*
3.1.185–7: Turne your eye into
your selfe . . . and weygh your owne
imperfections with hers. c1621
(1662) Middleton *Anything for a Quiet
Life* 5.1.148f.: Turn your eyes into
your own bosom.
Shakespeare: *MM* 2.2.136–41,
Ham. 3.4.89

B546.2   To pour into someone's
BOSOM (Cf. Appendix B)
1582 Guevara (Fenton) *Golden
Epistles* T1ᵛ: So simple ought we to

be towards our friende, as in his
bosome to powre our secretes. c1602
(1608) *Merry Devil of Edmonton*
3.2.22f.: Good sir Arthur . . . Hath
even powrd himselfe into my
bosome. 1612 Webster *White Devil*
1.2.195f.: Let me into your bosome
happy Ladie, Powre out in stead of
eloquence my vowes. c1613 (1623)
Webster, *Duchess of Malfi* 3.1.62: I
powre it in your bosome.
Shakespeare: *Jn.* 3.3.53

(?) B564.1   To take one's BOW and
arrows and go to bed (OW78b;
Greene, Nashe, *AYL*)
Shakespeare: *AYL* 4.3.4f.

B567   Wide at (of) the BOW HAND
(From *LLL*; OW887b supplements)
Shakespeare: *LLL* 4.1.133

B568.1   To lack but a BOWL and a
besom (*broom*) of being an honest
man (Wh B489 1520)
I.e., 1520 Whittinton *Vulgaria* 96.3f.:
Ye behave you lyke an honest man,
ye lak but a bolle and a besom.
Shakespeare: *LLL* 5.2.581–3

B583   Jest with BOYS and leave the
saints (holy things) alone (Non bonus
est, ludere cum sanctis [from 1578])
Shakespeare: *MM* 2.2.127

B588   BRAG is good dog but Hold-
fast is a better (Collections from
1709, cf. *H5*; OW80a adds possible
1583 analogue)
I.e., 1583 Melbancke *Philotimus* Fl:
As to have is good happ, so to hould
fast is a great vertue [merely a version of H513: Hold fast when you
have it].
Shakespeare: *H5* 2.3.52
Cf. B587: Brag is a good dog
[from 1580].

B596   To bear a BRAIN (From
c1517)
Shakespeare: *Rom.* 1.3.29

B597   You will not believe he is bald (dead) till you see his BRAIN (From 1580)
Shakespeare: *TN* 4.2.116f.

B602   To beat one's BRAINS (From c1579; OW160a [To cudgel (beat) one's brains] *beat* from 1560, *cudgel Ham.*, 1849)
Shakespeare: *Ham.* 5.1.56

(?) B602.1   To have one's BRAINS buttered
?1621 (1647) Fletcher *Pilgrim* 4.2 V,201: The thing's mad, Abominably mad, her brains are butter'd. 1669 Dryden *Wild Gallant* 4.2: He has not brains enough, if they were buttered, to feed a blackbird.
Shakespeare: *Wiv.* 3.5.7f.

B605.1   As hard as (any) BRASS (Wh B511 from 1300 [3])
E.g., a1325 *Cursor* II 342.5903: The king(s) hert wex herd as bras.
Shakespeare: *MV* 4.1.31, *Ham.* 3.4.35−8

B607   His old BRASS (etc.) will buy (make) you a new pan (etc.)[n](*Varied* from 1580)
Shakespeare: *Wiv.* 1.3.17, *Ant.* 1.2.168f.

[n]Cf. Introduction, fn. 17.

(?) B607.1   To live in BRASS
Shakespeare: *H5* 4.3.97, *H8* 4.2.45

(?) B627.1   To bake bitter BREAD (Wh B517 a1450; cf. 1 Kings 22.27)
Shakespeare: *R2* 3.1.21

B627.2   To eat no more BREAD (not dine) (Wh B520 *varied* from c1400)
E.g., a1450 *Generydes* A 96.3067f.: I shuld for Anazaree be awreke, and elles brede mot I never breke.
Add: 1537 (c1561) ?Udall *Thersites* B3: I make an othe That yer I eate any breade I wyll dryve a wayne ye

for neede twayne Betwene your bodye and your heade. c1550 (c1565) R. Wever *Lusty Juventus* (MSR 809f.): I wyll never eate meate that shal do me good Tyl I have cut his fleshe. c1553 (1575) W. Stevenson *Gammer Gurton's Needle* 4.4.55f.:I will surely neither byte nor suppe Till I fetch him hether. c1591 (1593) *Jack Straw* 3.2 (MSR 933f.):By him that dide for me, I wil not dine, Till I have seene thee hangd or made away. 1596 Spenser *Faerie Queene* 6.1.31.3−5: The dwarfe ... Brought aunswere backe, that ere he tasted bread He would her succour.
Shakespeare: *R3* 3.4.76f., *Lr.* 5.3.94

(?) B636.1   To give a hot BREAKFAST (fig.) (*Varied*) (Cf. Appendix B)
c1591 (1593) Peele *Edward I* ix (MSR 1700f.): Ere many daies be past, England shall giue this Robin Hood his breakfast; xviii (2389f.): Many a whot breakefast have wee beene at together. 1594 Nashe *Unfortunate Traveller* II,215: The King hath vowed to give Turwin one hot breakfast.
Shakespeare: *2H6* 1.4.75

B640   He can laugh and cry both with a BREATH (*Ven.*, Collections *varied* from 1616; ditto OW444af., which combines with L92a)
E.g., 1616 DR., s.v. Dissimulation 515: He doeth laugh and weepe with one breath.
Add: 1600 Bodenham *Bel-vedere* ed. 1875 31 [from *Ven.*]: Love well is said, to be a life in death, That laughes and weepes, and all but with a breath.
Shakespeare: *Ven.* 413f.

B641   He runs himself (To run) out of BREATH (fig.) (From 1599)
Add: 1588 R. Some *Godly Treatise* T2: You have runne your selfe out of breath. You had dealt more

wisely, if you had gone with lesse haste and better speede [cf. H198]. c1590 (1598) Greene *James IV* 4.2 1689: Feare not, ile run all danger out of breath. 1608 J. Day *Humour out of Breath*.

Shakespeare: *Err.* 4.1.57, *Ant.* 3.10.24

B641.1 Life (Man) is but a BREATH (Wh L240 c1400)
1592 Nashe *Pierce Penilesse* I,201: A man is but his breath. c1615 (1657) Middleton *More Dissemblers besides Women* 2.1.49f.: You see, my lords, what all earth's glory is, Rightly defin'd in me, uncertain breath.

Shakespeare: *MM* 3.1.8, *R3* 4.4.90, *Per.* 1.1.46

B642 You but spend your BREATH (wind) in vain (*Wind* 1578 [= W81.1]; *breath* 1639 CL.)
Add e.g.: 1537 (c1561) ?Udall *Thersites* B3: They dyd theyr wind but in vaine spente. c1572 (1581) N. Woodes *Conflict of Conscience* 5.3 1860: You do your labor lose [L9], and spend your breath in vain.

Shakespeare: *R2* 2.1.30
Cf. W81.1: To waste one's wind (breath, words).

B645 She wears the BREECHES (From 1567−8)
Shakespeare: *3H6* 5.5.23f.

B651 To have a BREEZE in his breech (From c1615, *tail* 1612; ditto OW84b)
Add e.g.: c1553 (1575) W. Stevenson *Gammer Gurton's Needle* 1.2.31 −3: Tome Tannkards cow . . . she set me up her saile, And flynging about his halfe-aker, fysking with her taile, As though there had ben in her ars a swarme of bees. 1578 G. Whetstone *Promos and Cassandra* 3.5.2: He fryskes abought as byrdes ware in his breech.

Shakespeare: *Ant.* 3.10.14f.

(?) B652 BREVITY is the soul of wit (*Ham.*, 1612; OW84b adds faint 1647 analogue and 19th-century *Ham.* echoes)
E.g., 1612 J. Taylor *Laugh and Be Fat: Wks.* F 237: Shortest writ, the greatest wit affoords, And greatest wit, consists in fewest words.

Shakespeare: *Ham.* 2.2.90

B657.1 There is something BREW-ING (Cf. Appendix B)
1553 ?Udall *Respublica* 5.2 1371: Something breweth? 1599 J. Chamberlain 1 Aug. 79: We are not without suspicion of some tempest brewing in Scotland. 1600 Ibid. 22 Dec. 113: We listen still for newes from thence as yf there were some tempest abrewing. 1616 DR. s.v. Danger, or perill, no. 424: Somewhat is in brewing.

Shakespeare: *MV* 2.5.17

B663 Happy is the BRIDE the sun shines on and the corpse the rain rains on (1678 Ray, *corpse* 1607, *sun* 1632, cf. *TN*)
E.g. 1648 Herrick *Hesperides: Poet. Wks.* 113: Blest is the Bride, on whom the Sun doth shine.

Shakespeare: *TN* 4.3.34f.

B664.1 Fresh as a BRIDEGROOM
1590 Spenser *Faerie Queene* 1.5.2.3: Phoebus, fresh as brydegrome to his mate. 1601 (1607) Marston *What You Will* 2.1 II, 245: He is . . . neate as a Bride-groome, fresh as a new-minted six-pence. c1604 (1630) Dekker & Middleton *1 Honest Whore* 4.4.67f.: Go, attire yourself Fresh as a bridegroom, when he meets his bride.

Shakespeare: *Tro.* 4.4.145, *1H4* 1.3.34, *Lr.* 4.6.198

B671 To give one the BRIDLE (reins) (From 1546 Heywood, like OW86a, but neither with instances using *reins*)
Add: 1568 Grafton *Chron.* II 927: A

larger reyne of mischiefe geven to the vulgare people [*OED Rein* 2b]. c1597 (1609) Jonson *Case is Altered* 2.3.24: Give me the reines and spare not.

Shakespeare: *LLL* 5.2.657, *MM* 2.4.160, *R2* 1.1.55, *Cor.* 2.1.30

B673 (To leave one) (To be) in the BRIERS (From 1520; Wh B544 from c1450)

Shakespeare: *AYL* 1.3.12

B686 He has made a younger BROTHER of him (1597, 1678 Ray; OW928b adds *AYL* 3.2.372−8)

Add: c1585 (1592) Lyly *Gallathea* 5.2.67−71: Hee hath gotten a Maister nowe, that will teach him to make you both his younger brothers. . . . Nay he will teach him to cozen you both. 1588 Martin Marprelate *Epistle* (STC 17453) C2: Thus you see Brother Bridges M. Marprelate an please him is able to make a yonger brother of you.

Shakespeare: *AYL* 1.1.53f.

B686.1 And (Though) he were my BROTHER[n]

a1450 *Castle of Per severance* 3282−6: That sinne, Lord, thou wilt not reles In this werld nor in the tother . . . Thou[gh] he were my brother. c1475 *Mankind* 588: I shall slepe full my bely, and he were my brother. 1546 Heywood *Dialogue* I.xi E1[v]: I will not trust hym though he were my brother. 1573 *New Custom* 2.3 C3: I would not misse him, no if hee were mine owne brother. c1576 *Common Conditions* 266: I cannot hold my hands & if hee were my brother; 276: Ile breake your noddell if you were my brother.

Shakespeare: *MM* 2.2.81, 4.2.61f.

[n]Whiting was probably mistaken to take the whole of the Heywood citation as his unique example of Wh B568. Cf. Introduction, fn. 26.

B691.1 Honor (Reputation) is a BUBBLE

1624 (?1625) Middleton *Game at Chess* 2.1.139f.: Art thou so cruel, for an honour's bubble T'undo a whole fraternity? c1625 (1647) Fletcher *Elder Brother* 5.1.34: Honour is nothing with you? / A mere bubble. 1629 (1630) Massinger *Picture* 1.2.17f.: This bubble honour, (Which is indeede the nothing souldiers fight for).

Shakespeare: *AYL* 2.7.152

B692 As wild as a BUCK (From 1618; OW889a from 1530; Wh B573 from 1509)

Shakespeare: *Err.* 3.1.72

B695 Like two BUCKETS of a well, if one go up the other must go down (*Varied* from 1484)

Shakespeare: *R2* 4.1.184−7

B698 (If you be angry you may) turn the BUCKLE of your girdle behind you (From *Ado*; ditto OW14b)

E.g., 1600 ?R. Armin *Quips upon Questions* C4[v]: But for to quiet this distempered elfe, The next way is, to let him please him selfe. Or as the proverbe is, no man to minde him, But turne the buckle of his belt behind him. 1639 CL., s.v. Contemptus 68: Turne the buckle of your girdle behind you.

Shakespeare: *Ado* 5.1.141f.

B700.1 To give (one) the BUCKLERS (i.e., to yield) (OW89af. from 1589)

Shakespeare: *Ado* 5.2.17

B702 To nip (blast) in the BUD (blossom) (From *2H6;* OW567b *blade* 1590)

Shakespeare: *TGV* 1.1.47f., *LLL* 5.2.802, *2H6* 3.1.89

Cf. H272.1: To nip in the HEAD.

B703 BUGBEARS (Bugs) to scare

babes (*Varied* from 1582; OW89b from 1530)
Shakespeare: *Shr.* 1.2.210, *3H6* 5.2.2, *Mac.* 2.2.51f., *WT* 3.2.92

B715   To roar like a BULL (From 1545; Wh B590 from c1300)
Shakespeare: *1H4* 2.4.260f., *2H4* 3.2.175f.

B716   The town BULL is as much a bachelor as he (*Varied* in collections from 1666, cf. *2H4*; OW834b adds 1591)
I.e., 1591 Harington (Ariosto) *Orl. Fur.* XXXVIII Moral: Imagine some man so chast (as Caesar was called), Omnium mulierum vir, or to use our homely English phrase (as the towne Bull of the Parish).
Shakespeare: *2H4* 2.2.157f.

B719   He looks as big as if he had eaten BULL BEEF (*Varied*)
E.g., 1580 Baret T-270: Titanicus aspectus. A Proverbe applied unto such as have a terrible and frowning countenance, and (as our common byword saith) which looke as though they had eaten Bulbeefe.
Shakespeare: *1H6* 1.2.9

B719.1   As swift as a BULLET
1593 (1600) Marlowe *Lucan* 231: Swifter than bullets thrown from Spanish slings. 1595 Peele *Anglorum Feriae* 291: This lusty runner . . . Flies like a bullet from a cannon's mouth.
Shakespeare: *LLL* 3.1.57−62, 5.2.261, *2H4* 4.3.32f.

(?) B720.1   Paper BULLETS (*OED Paper* 10c fig. misc. from 1592)
1601 (1602) Dekker *Satiromastix* 5.2.201: Fashion-mongers quake at your paper Bullets. 1604 ?Dekker *Newes from Graves-end* (STC 12199) B1: The Goose-quill should never more gull me, to make me shoote paper-pullets into any Stationers

shop. 1613 T. Sutton *Englands Summons* 17 (of Noah's futile efforts): All these painefull Sermons proved but like paper bullets shot against a brasen wall.
Shakespeare: *Ado* 2.3.240f.

B722   To take a BUNTING for a lark (From 1600; OW91a adds 1589 analogue)
Shakespeare: *AWW* 2.5.6f.

B724   To stick like BURS (*Varied* from 1534)
Shakespeare: *MND* 3.2.260, *AYL* 1.3.13, *Tro.* 3.2.111f., *MM* 4.3.179

B736   (BUSH natural,) more hair than wit (*Varied* from 1562)
E.g., 1601 (1602) Dekker *Satiromastix* 4.3.55f.: Haire? It's the basest stubble; in scorne of it, This Proverbe sprung, he has more haire then wit.
Shakespeare: *Err.* 2.2.82f., *TGV* 3.1.353, 358f.

B738   He thinks every BUSH a bugbear (bear, thief, etc.) (*Thief* from 1584 [OW813a from 1534, *monster* 1579])
Add: 1563 J. Dolman "Lord Hastings" 122−4 *Mirror for Magistrates* 272: We then the realme a pryson deemed. / Ech bush a barre, eche spray a banner splayed, / Eche house a fort our passage to have stayed.
Shakespeare: *MND* 5.1.21f., *Luc.* 972f.

(?) B759.1   To be too BUSY is dangerous
1559 G. Ferrers "Thomas of Woodstock" 91 *Mirror for Magistrates* 95: By beyng to busy I caught a sore checke.
Shakespeare: *Ham.* 3.4.33
Cf. C621: To be too busy gets contempt [from 1640].

B764.1   A BUTCHER'S CUR (dog, mastiff)

c1523 Barclay *Mirrour* 78(24): Grinning and gnarring as doth a butchers curre [Wh C639]. 1581 Field *Caveat for Parsons Howlet* A5: You faune upon her [Elizabeth] like gentle Spaniels, and yet most cruelly you bite her, (tanquam canes clanculo mordentes, as the proverbe is [)], like butchers curres. 1583 Melbancke *Philotimus* G1ᵛ: A butcher's curre doth never alter his nature. 1602 Darrell *Survey of certaine dialogical discourses* A4: And herein you lay about you mightely, bragging your selves like butchers mastives with their collers of iron pykes, & daring any to set upon you. 1678 Ray 208: As surly as a butcher's dog [B764].
Shakespeare: *R3* 1.3.289, *H8* 1.1.120

B767 As fat as BUTTER (From 1584; OW247a supplements)
Shakespeare: *1H4* 2.4.511

B780 To melt like BUTTER before the sun (From 1592; OW94a from 1562)
Wiv. 3.5.115f., *1H4* 2.4.120−2

B781 To scold like BUTTER-WIVES (butterwhores) (From 1639 CL.; OW 704b adds 1611, 1621)
Shakespeare: *AWW* 4.1.41

B783 Better to BUY than to borrow (beg, beg or borrow) (From 1539)
E.g., 1639 CL. 59: Better buy then beg or borrow. Ibid. 220.
Shakespeare: *TN* 3.4.3

B787 To be BOUGHT and sold (buy and sell) (i.e., be deceived, deceive) From c1497; Wh B637 from c1325)
Shakespeare: *Err.* 3.1.72, *LLL* 3.1.142, *Tro.* 2.1.46, *1H6* 4.4.13, *R3* 5.3.305, *Jn.* 5.4.10, *H8* 1.1.191f, *Mac.* 4.2.41

C

C12 His (etc.) CAKE is dough (From 1559)
Shakespeare: *Shr.* 1.1.108f., 5.1.140

C15a CALAMITY (Extremity) is the touchstone of a brave mind (unto wit) (*Varied* from 1607; OW98a adds 1602)
E.g., c1606 (1607) Jonson *Volpone* 5.2.6: Good Wits are greatest in extremities.
Add: 1603 Daniel "To . . . Southampton" 7f. ed. Sprague 122: Only men shew their abilities, And what they are, in their extremities.
Shakespeare: *Cor.* 4.1.3f., *TNK* 1.1.118

C16.1 As wise as a CALF (Wh C8 1533 [2]; OW899a adds 1562 [under W22: As wise as Waltham's calf].
Shakespeare: *Ham.* 3.2.106, 5.1.116f.

(?) C23 Everyone must walk (labor) in his own CALLING (vocation)[n] (*Varied* from 1539; cf. 1 Cor. 7.20)
E.g., 1549 Latimer *Serm.* 12 215: Labour in they vocation.
Shakespeare: *2H6* 4.2.16, *1H4* 1.2.105

[n]Cf. Introduction, p. xv.

C24 After a CALM comes a storm (*Varied* from 1576; Wh C12 from a1420)
Shakespeare: *Ven.* 458

C26 As hard as for a CAMEL to pass through a needle's eye (Mark 10.25; from 1534)
Shakespeare: *R2* 5.5.16f.

C34 The more CAMOMILE is trodden down the more it spreads (*Varied* from 1567)
Shakespeare: *1H4* 2.4.400f.

C39   A CANDLE (torch) lights others and consumes itself (From 1584; OW100a adds 1599)
Add e.g., 1604 W. Alexander *Alexandraean Tragedy* 5.1 2743f.: Good kings are like the fire which (flaming bright) Doth waste it selfe to serve anothers turne.
Shakespeare: *MM* 1.1.32f. *Lr.* 1.4.217, *Per.* 1 Chorus 15f., *Ven.* 163, 755f.

C40   He that worst may must hold the CANDLE (From 1546)
Shakespeare: *MV* 2.6.41, *Rom.* 1.4.37f.

C49   To go out like a CANDLE in a snuff (*Varied* from a1535)
E.g., a1535 (1553) T. More *Dial. Comf.* II.iii: *Wks.* (1557) 1172: I cannot licken my life more metely now than to the snuffe of a candle that burneth within the candlestickes nose.
Shakespeare: *2H4* 1.2.156f. *H8* 3.2.96f., *Lr.* 4.6.39f.
Cf. Appendix B: The CANDLE [of life].

C49.1   Night's CANDLES (Cf. Appendix B)
1598 (1616) W. Haughton *Englishmen for My Money* vi (MSR 1324): Nights Candles burne obscure. 1604 J. Hanson *Time is a Turne-Coate* K3: Even as the Sun with his transcendent Light Tiends [sic] all the twinkling Candles of the Night. 1612 Dekker *Troia-Nova Triumphans* 570: Nights Candles lighted are and burne amaine.
Shakespeare: *MV* 5.1.220, *Rom.* 3.5.9, *Mac.* 2.1.4f.

C50   When CANDLES be out (At night) all cats be gray (From 1562)
Add e.g., 1595 S. du Bartas *First Day* (STC 21658) E1ᵛ: Master and slave: foule maukyn and faire may: Daies candle out, the night maks all things gray.
Shakespeare: *AYL* 3.5.39f., *Lr.* 3.6.45
Cf. M39: There are more maids than Malkin [from 1546]; J57: Joan is as good as my lady in the dark.

C56   The CANKER soonest eats the fairest rose (*Varied* from 1576)
Shakespeare: *TGV* 1.1.42f., *Jn.* 3.4.82, *2H4* 2.2.94f., *Rom.* 2.3.30, *Ham.* 1.3.39f., *Tmp.* 1.2.416, *Son.* 35.4, 70.7

C60   Cast your CAP at the moon (1639 CL., cf. *Cor.*, 1609)
I.e., 1609 R. Armin *Ital. Tailor* To Rdr.: *Wks.* 143: Every Pen and inckhorne Boy, will throw vp his Cap at the hornes of the Moone in censure.
Shakespeare: *Cor.* 1.1.212f.

C62   He may cast his CAP after him for ever overtaking him (*Varied* from 1606; OW101b from 1592)
Shakespeare: *Tim.* 3.4.100f.

C63.1   My CAP (hat) to a noble (etc.) c1553 (1575) W. Stevenson *Gammer Gurton's Needle* 1.2.27: I durst have layd my cap to a crowne. Ibid. 5.2.144f.: I durst aventure wel the price of my best cap. c1590 (1594) Creene & Lodge *Looking Glass for London* 2.2 684: I hold my cap to a noble. c1592 (1594) *Knack to Know a Knave* i (MSR 90): My cap to a noble. 1596 Lodge *Wits Miserie* I4: It is his hat to a halfepenny but hee will be drunke. 1598 (1616) Haughton *Englishmen for My Money* xi (MSR 2331): Ile lay my Cappe to two Pence.
Shakespeare: *LLL* 1.1.308, 5.2.560

C74   (He has) a sure CARD (Cf. Appendix B) (From c1537)
Shakespeare: *2H4* 3.2.86, *Tit.* 5.1.100

C75 To outface with a CARD of ten (From c1510)
Shakespeare: *Shr.* 2.1.405

(?) C75.1 To speak by the CARD (OW760a; *Ham.*, 1875)
Shakespeare: *Ham.* 5.1.137f.

C82.1 CARE is a corrosive
1576 Gascoigne *Steele Glas* II,135: The corrosyve of care woulde quickely confounde me. 1588 Green *Pandosto* ed. Bullough VIII,172: In things past cure, care is a corrosive [OW102b for C83].
Shakespeare: *1H6* 3.3.3f.

C83 CARE is no cure (*1H6*, 1678 Ray)
Shakespeare: *1H6* 3.3.3
Cf. C82.1: Care is a corrosive; C921: Past cure past care.

C83.1 CARE (Sorrow, Grief) shortens life
1560 Ecclus. 30.23f.(Geneva): Sorow hathe slaine many, and there is no profite therein. Envie and wrath shorten the life, and carefulnes bringeth age before the time. 1583 G. Babington *Expos"* *of the Command"* 270: Often . . . have I hard men say that sorow and care wil shorten our time [in OW102b (C82: Care brings grey hair)]. 1602 ?T. *Heywood How a Man May Choose* B2: They say griefe often shortens life [in C84].
Shakespeare: *TN* 1.3.2f., *AWW* 1.1.56

C84 CARE will kill a cat (*Varied* from 1585–1616, 1597 [1601])
Shakespeare: *Ado* 5.1.132f., *TN* 1.3.2f.

C85 Hang CARE (sorrow) (*Care* 1639 CL., *sorrow* from c1600; ditto OW349a)
E.g., 1666 TOR. *It. Prov.* note 24 162: As the English say, Hang sorrow, cast away care.
Shakespeare: *R3* 2.2.99f.

(?) C98 A CARPET KNIGHT (Cf. Appendix B) (From 1580; OW103b from 1574)
Shakespeare: *Ado* 5.2.32f., *TN* 3.4.235f.

C100.1 To CARRY it away (Cf. Appendix B)
1594 Nashe *Unfortunate Traveller* II,251: From all the world he caries it awaie. 1598 (1601) Jonson *Every Man In* 1.3.171: He thinkes to carrie it away with his manhood. c1602 (1611) Chapman *May-Day* 2.4.153: They do in earnest to carry it away so.
Shakespeare: *Rom.* 3.1.74, *Ham.* 2.2.360

C103 To set the CART before the Horse (*Varied* from 1520)
E.g., 1529 T. More *Dial. Diverse Mat.* I: *Wks.* (1557) 154: Muche like as if we woulde go make the carte to drawe the horse.
Shakespeare: *Lr.* 1.4.223f.

C109 As common as the CART-WAY (etc.) (*Cartway* 1493, 1566; Wh C64 from a1376, *way* c1475; OW137b combines with H457, *highway* from 1671)
Shakespeare: *2H4* 2.2.167

(?) C109.1 A dry CART-WHEEL cries the loudest (Wh C66 c1450)
Shakespeare: *1H4* 3.1.130

C110 To be one's own CARVER (From 1573; OW105a from c1558)
Shakespeare; *R2* 2.3.144, *Ham.* 1.3.20, *Oth.* 2.3.173

C111 The CASE is altered (quoth Plowden) (Without *Plowden* from 1578, Wh C67 a1500)
Shakespeare: *3H6* 4.3.31

C112.1 In (a) heavy CASE (Cf. Appendix B)
c1587 (c1592) Kyd *Spanish Tragedy* 2.6.11: Ile shew thee Balthazar in

heavy case. 1596 Spenser *Faerie Queene* 4.7.38.4: Full of sad anguish and in heavy case. 1604 E. Grymeston *Miscelanea* F3: Turne not from me thy favourable face, What day or houre I am in heavie case. 1615 Bretnor (Crow e 322 Feb.): In a heavy case.
Shakespeare: *Lr.* 4.6.146f.

(?) C122.1 (As safe) as in a CASTLE
c1619 Fletcher & Massinger *Little French Lawyer* 1.2.81f.: We Shall fight as in a castle; 4.6.11: We may do't, as safe as in a castle.
Shakespeare: *1H4* 2.1.86

C124.1 (Old) lad (Dick) of the CASTLE
1592 G. Harvey *Foure Letters* I,225: Never childe so delighted in his ratling baby; as some old Lads of the Castle have sported themselves with their rapping bable. 1593 G. Harvey *Pierces Supererogation* II,44: Heere is a lusty ladd of the Castell, that will bind Beares, and ride golden Asses to death. 1596 Nashe *Saffron-Walden* Ep. Ded. III,5: A Cute & amiable Dick, not *Dic mihi* . . . nor old Dick of the Castle.
Shakespeare: *1H4* 1.2.41f.

C127 As a CAT plays with a mouse (From 1566; Wh C80 from 1340)
Shakespeare: *Luc.* 554f.

C129 As melancholy as a (gibbed) CAT (From 1592, *gibbed 1H4*; OW524a [no *gibbed*] cf. c1580)
Shakespeare: *1H4* 1.2.73f.

C135 CAT (Kit) after kind (*Varied* from 1578; OW107b from 1559)
E.g., 1559 ?T. Phaer "Owen Glendower" 11 *Mirror for Magistrates* 11: Though it be true that Cat wil after kinde.
Shakespeare: *AYL* 3.2.103

C136 CAT after kind, good mouse

hunt (From 1546; OW107b from 1540)
Shakespeare: *Rom.* 4.4.11

C144 The CAT would eat fish but she will not wet her feet (From a1500; Wh C93 from a1300)
Shakespeare: *Mac.* 1.7.45

C154 Like a CAT, to have nine lives (From 1570)
Shakespeare: *Rom.* 3.1.77f.

C167 That CAT is out of kind that sweet milk (cream) will not lap (lick, steal) (*Varied* from c1547; cf. Wh C109 from c1492)
Shakespeare: *1H4* 4.2.58f., *Tmp.* 2.1.288

C171.1 To tear a CAT (Cf. Appendix B) (*Tear* v..[1] ld MND, 1610; *Tear-2* 1606, 1611)
I.e., c1599 (1610) Marston *Histriomastix 5.1* III,291: Sirha is this you would rend and teare the Cat Upon a Stage, and now march like a drown'd rat [M1237]? 1606 Day *Isle of Gulls* Prologue 6: I had rather heare two good baudie iests then a whole play of such teare-cat thunderclaps. 1611 Dekker & Middleton *Roaring Girl* 5.1.118: I am cal'd by those that have seen my valour, Tear-Cat.
Shakespeare: *MND* 1.2.29f.

C175 When the CAT'S away the mice will play (*Varied* from a1536)
Shakespeare: *H5* 1.2.172

C187.1 To tickle someone's CATASTROPHE (etc.) (i.e., to beat or whip someone [usually])
E.g., c1595 A. Munday et al. *Sir Thomas More* 2.2.1f.: Wele tickle ther turnips, wele butter ther boxes. c1602 (1608) *Merry Devil of Edmonton* 2.1.9f.: A plague of this winde; O, it tickles our Catastrophe; 5.2.13f. (different speaker): Ile tickle his Catastrophe for this. c1606 *Nobody and*

Somebody C1: They tickled my Collifodium.
Shakespeare: *2H4* 2.1.60

(?) C191 They are (not) CATER-COUSINS (Cf. Appendix B) (From 1519; ditto OW111b)
Shakespeare: *MV* 2.2.130f.

(?) C207 As straight (tall) as a CEDAR (1585 [OW112b adds c1580]; *tall* 1611)
Shakespeare: *LLL* 4.3.87

C208 High CEDARS fall (are shaken) when low shrubs remain (are scarcely moved) (*Varied* from c1592; OW112b *cedars* from 1570, *cedars* and *shrubs* from 1588)
E.g., 1570 F. Thynne *Debate betw. Pride & Lowliness* ed. Collier 76: And bring full lowe their cedars high and tall. 1576 ?W. Hunnis *Paradise of Dainty Devises* no. 88: The higher the Ceder tree unto the heavens doe growe, The more in danger at the top, when sturdie winde gan blowe.
Shakespeare: *R3* 1.3.263f., *Tit.* 4.3.46

C212.1 As light as CHAFF (Wh C127 c1200)[n]
1608 Middleton *Family of Love* 1.2.59f.: They are windy turning vanes; Love light as chaff.
Shakespeare: *2H4* 4.1.193

[n]A surprisingly infrequent simile, although the lightness of chaff is often alluded to.

C222 The CHAMELEON can change to all colors save white (From 1547)
Shakespeare: *TGV* 2.4.23–6, *3H6* 3.2.191

C223 The CHANCE of war is uncertain (*Varied* from 1551; cf. Wh B65 [Battles are ever in doubt], *varied* from c1395, Wh F533 [The fortune of fighters (etc.) is uncertain], *varied*

from a1400, Wh W39 [In war some win and some lose], *varied* from a1300).
Shakespeare: *LLL* 5.2.530f., *Tro.* Prologue 31, *1H4* 1.3.95, *2H4* 1.1.166f., *Tit.* 1.1.264, *Cor.* 5.3.141, *Cym.* 5.5.75, *TNK* 2.2.3

C234 To be no CHANGELING (From 1563; OW114b from 1551)
Shakespeare: *Cor.* 4.7.10f.

(?) C245 Thou dost not bear my CHARGES that thou shouldst command me (*Varied*; ?c1588, *Shr.*, 1666 TOR.)
E.g. c1588 (1599) Porter *Two Angry Women of Abingdon* iii (MSR 900f.) (Nicholas Proverbes): I need not except I list, you shall not commaund me, you give me neither meate, drinke, nor wages.
Shakespeare: *Shr.* 2.1.257

C251 CHARITY begins at home (*Varied* from 1509; Wh C153 [Charity begins with oneself] from c1400)
E.g., 1509 Barclay *Ship Fools* I 277: For perfyte love and also charite Begynneth with hym selfe for to be charitable.
Shakespeare: *Oth.* 1.3.313f., 2.3.202

C263 CHEEK by jowl (cheek) (From c1530)
Shakespeare: *MND* 3.2.338

C268 As thin as Banbury CHEESE (*Varied* from 1562)
Shakespeare: *Wiv.* 1.1.128

(?) C276.1 As alike as CHERRY to cherry
?1619 (1647) Fletcher *Humorous Lieutenant* 5.5.30: A cherry to a cherry is not liker.
Shakespeare: *H8* 5.1.168f.

(?) C290.1 To eat a CHICKEN (chickens) in the shell

1623 (1653) Middleton & Rowley
Spanish Gypsy 2.1.250f.: Marry me?
eat a chicken ere it be out o' th' shell?
Shakespeare: *Tro.* 1.2.134

C305 Happy is the CHILD whose
father goes to the devil (From 1549)
Shakespeare: *3H6* 2.2.47f.

C309 It is a wise CHILD that knows
his own father (English from 1586;
OW899b adds Homer, 1589)
E.g., 1617 B. Rich *Irish Hubbub* 16:
We were wont to say, it was a wise
childe that did know the owne
Father, but now we may say, it is a
wise Father that doth know his owne
childe.
Shakespeare: *MV* 2.2.76f, *Jn.*
1.1.63

C318.1 Trust no CHILD (etc.)
1460 Paston III 213f.: Et est commune et vulgare dictum: A man
schuld not trusty on a broke swerd,
ne on a fool, ne on a chylde, ne on a
dobyl man, ne on a drunke man [Wh
M174]. 1483 Caxton *Cato* G5(26f.):
The chylde (for an apple one leseth
his love) [Wh C207; cf. A295: Won
with an apple and lost with a nut].
a1500 *Salamon sat and sayde* 291.7−9:
Tyl riche men hetynges trayst thou
ryth noght, And of womannis
wepynges charge thou never noght,
A chyldis love is sone done for a
thynges of noght [Wh M297].
Shakespeare: *Lr.* 3.6.18f., *Cym.*
5.5.106f.

C324 (It is) no CHILD's play (From
c1517; Wh C221 from a1325)
Shakespeare: *1H4* 5.4.75f.

(?) C333 CHILDREN pick up words
as pigeons peas and utter them again
as God shall please (*LLL*, 1678 Ray;
ditto OW120b)
Add: 1616 Unsigned verses in T.
Coryate *Traveller for the English Wits*
H3: He picks up wit, as Pigeons
pease, And utters it when God doth

please: O who can hold from
Laughter?
Shakespeare: *LLL* 5.2.315f.

C341 He that has no CHILDREN
knows not what love is (1666 TOR.,
1639 analogue, cf. *3H6*, *Jn.*, *Mac.*;
OW120b supplements slightly)
E.g., 1639 CL. 240: None knowes the
affection of Parents but they that
have children.
Shakespeare: *3H6* 5.5.63f., *Jn.*
3.4.91, *Mac.* 4.3.216

(?) C358 There is small CHOICE in
rotten apples (*Shr.*, a1667)[n]
Cf. 1622 J. de Luna (I. W.) *Gram.
Span. & Eng.* 263: Ther's but small
choyce where the whole flocke is bad
[OW121b].
Shakespeare: *Shr.* 1.1.134f.

[n]Tilley's only supporting evidence is
Lacy's *Sauny the Scot*, the subtitle of
which, after all, is *The Taming of the
Shrew*. But OW suggests that some
species of "small choice" proverb did
exist.

C363.1 To die like a CHRISOM
CHILD[1] (OW186a *H5*, 1680)
I.e., 1680 Bunyan *Life Badman* 566:
Mr. Badman died like a lamb; or as
they call it, like a chrisom-child,
quietly and without fear [in B4]. [[1] a
child newly baptized, still wearing
the chrisomer, or christening robe.
In the bills of mortality children
dying within a month of birth were
called *chrisoms*.]
Shakespeare: *H5* 2.3.10−2
Cf. B4: As innocent (clear) as a
newborn babe (child, chrisom-child).

C375.1 To be one's own
CHRONICLE
1600 (1601) Jonson *Cynthia's Revels*
3.4.12−18: A proud, and spangled
sir ... Is his owne chronicle. 1607
Dekker *Knights Coniuring* 14[v]:
Skorning to be his owne Chronicle.
1612 Webster *White Devil* 5.1.100f.:

'Tis a ridiculous thing for a man to bee his owne Chronicle. c1613 (1623) Webster *Duchess of Malfi* 3.1.110f.: You Are your owne Chronicle too much.
Shakespeare: *Tro.* 2.3. 155f.

C383 CHURCH WORK goes on slowly (*Varied* from 1629; ditto OW123b)
Shakespeare: *2H4* 2.4.230

C389.1 As dark as the blackness of CIMMERIA
1548 Elyot s.v. Cimerii: Cimmeriis tenebris atrior, blacker than the darkenesse of Cimmeria, applyed to muche darknesse, dulnesse of wit, or lack of wisedom. Again c1580 Conybeare 36. E.g., c1588 (1590) Marlowe *2 Tamburlaine* 5.3.7–9: Hell and Darkness pitch their pitchy tents, And Death, with armies of Cimmerian spirits, Gives battle 'gainst the heart of Tamburlaine. 1591 Spenser *Teares of the Muses* 256: Darknesse more than Cymerians daylie night.
Shakespeare: *Tit.* 2.3.72

C391 He is a CIPHER among numbers (Cf. Appendix B) (*Varied* from 1547; OW124a from 1399)
Add e.g.: 1579 Lyly *Euphues* I,195: If one bee harde in conceiuing, they pronounce him a dowlte. . . . if without speach, a Cypher.
Shakespeare: *LLL* 1.2.56, *AYL* 3.2.289f., *MM* 2.2.39, *H5* Pro. 15–7, *Lr.* 1.4.192f., *WT* 1.2.6f.

(?) C410.1 To wind a (goodly) CLEW (fig.) (*OED* 2 fig. begins with *AWW*)
1588 R. Some *Godly Treatise* Cc1: I have your booke by me: and it is a fault in extremo actu deficere, that is, to resemble the slouthful poet in the winding up of the clewe.
Shakespeare: *AWW* 1.3.182
Cf. T252: You have spun a fine (fair) thread [from 1546]

C413 Hasty CLIMBERS have sudden falls (Collections from 1616; *varied* from 1592; OW357a from 1563)
Shakespeare: *H8* 1.1.131f.

C421 To have a CLOAK (To be) for all waters (for any weather) (*Cloak for all waters* 1666 TOR., *waters* from *TN*)
Add: c1554 (1568) *Jacob and Esau* 4.8 (MSR 1288): Mine owne poore homely geare will serve for all wethers. c1639 *Telltale* 3.1 (MSR 1068–71): Notable rogue . . . thow art dyed in graine [cf. K28]. / Try mee in all waters weare mee in all wethers, yf I Change Coulor hang mee.
Shakespeare: *TN* 4.2.63

C426.1 To have a CLOG at one's heel(s)
c1540 (1557) Wyatt "Of the courtier's life" 86 *Tottel* L4: A clogge doth hang yet at my heele. 1557 ?Grimald *Tottel* S2: I had no clogge tied at my hele. 1597 G. Harvey *Trimming of T. Nashe* E2ᵛ: Now thou hast a clog at thy heele as the proverbe is.
Shakespeare: *AWW* 2.5.53, *WT* 4.4.678f.
Cf. J10: Can jackanapes (an ape) be merry when his clog is at his heel (Wh A146: To be like an ape tied with a clog).

C432 Like Northern CLOTH, shrunk in the wetting (From 1594; ditto OW577b)
Shakespeare: *1H4* 5.4.88

C442 After black CLOUDS clear weather (From 1546)
Shakespeare: *AWW* 5.3.34f.

C443 All CLOUDS bring not rain (storms) (1666 TOR., cf. *3H6*; OW128a adds 1584)
E.g., 1584 Withals A4: Non stillant omnes quas cernis in aëre nubes, All

the clowdes which thou seast in the ayre do not yeeld rayne.
Shakespeare: *3H6* 5.3.13

C443.1   To carry (convey, walk) in a CLOUD (clouds)
1585 ?Munday *Fedele and Fortunio* III (MSR 1006): I can play the knave and convay it in the clowdes. 1616 DR. s.v. Dissimulation 519: Hee would carry the matter invisibly in a cloud. (c1624) Massinger *Unnatural Combat* 3.4.88: He shall walke in clouds, but I'll discover him. c1625 (1633) Massinger *New Way to Pay Old Debts* 1.1.125: You thinke you walke in clouds, but are transparent.
Shakespeare: *Ham.* 4.5.89, *Tim.* 3.4.42

C444   To speak in the CLOUDS (From 1602; OW128b from 1560)
E.g., 1581 C. T. *Inventory* A6ᵛ: If by chance they write or speake, it is alwayes in clowds, in libel manner, and to the defamation, and discredite of some one . . . man. 1587 J. Bridges *Defence* 101: Raysing of mystes, dazeling of eyes, walking in cloudes [cf. C443.1].
Shakespeare: *Ham.* 4.5.89

C446   As pale (white) as a CLOUT (*Pale* from *Rom.*, *white cloth* c1489; OW608a *clout* from 1563)
Add: 1557 *Tottel* 222.35f.: No life I fele in fote nor hand, As pale as any clout and ded.
Shakespeare: *Rom.*   2.4.205f., *Ham.*   2.1.78,   *Oth.*   5.2.273,   *Cym.* 2.2.16

C462   As hot as COALS (From 1540; Wh C327 from a1349)
Shakespeare: *Ven.* 35

C462.1   As red as (a) COAL(S) (Wh C329 from c1350)
Shakespeare: *Ven.* 35

C464   He   will   carry   (bear)   (no) COALS (From c1522)
Shakespeare: *H5* 3.2.46f., *Rom.* 1.1.1

C465   To blow the COAL(S) (From 1485; *fire* from 1576)
Shakespeare: *H8*   2.4.79,   94, 5.2.148

C469   The COAST is (is not) clear (From a1525)
Shakespeare: *1H6* 1.3.89

C473   I would not be in your COAT (skin) for anything (*Varied* from 1520)
Shakespeare: *TN* 4.1.30f.

C480   Let not the COBBLER (shoemaker) go beyond his last (*Varied* from 1539)
E.g., 1579 Lyly *Euphues* I,180: The Shomaker must not go aboue his latchet, nor the hedger meddle with anye thing but his bill. It is unsemely for the Paynter to feather a shaft, or the Fletcher to handle the pensill. 1616 Withals 293: Cobler keepe your last.
Shakespeare: *Rom.* 1.2.39−41

C486.1   A good COCK will never out.
Shakespeare: *2H4* 5.3.66, *Ant.* 2.7.30f.

C491   The young COCK crows as he the old hears (*Varied* from 1509)
E.g., 1573 G. Harvey *Let. Bk.* 31: The yung cockerels, hearing thes ould cocks to crow so lustely, followid after with a cockaloodletoo.
Shakespeare: *Tmp.* 2.1.28−31

C492.1   To wear a COCK'S-COMB (Wh C357 from 1522 [2]) (fig.)
E.g., 1546 Heywood *Dialogue* II.v H2: Ye bryng him to weare a cocks combe at ende.
Add: 1599 (1600)Dekker *Old Fortu-*

natus 4.2.107f.: Whilst wee strive to make others fooles, we shall weare the Coxcombes our selves. 1604 (1605) Chapman *All Fools* 3.1.336f.: Youle set a badge on the ielous fooles head, sir; Now set a Coxcombe on your owne.
Shakespeare: *Lr.* 1.4.95ff.

C493   He sets (To set) COCK on the hoop (From 1519)
Shakespeare: *Rom.* 1.5.81

C496   Crush   (Kill)   the   COCKA-TRICE in the egg (From 1656)
Add: c1592 R. Southwell "losse in Delaies" 25f. *Poems* 59: Crush the Serpent in the head, Breake ill egges ere they be hatched. (Repeated in 1604 E. Grymeston *Miscelanea* A4.) 1598 Meres *Palladis Tamia* 2P2ᵛ: Kill a cockatrice when he is an egge. 1612 C. Richardson *Repentance of Peter and Iudas* 89: Men are careful to kill serpents in the shell.
Shakespeare: *JC* 2.1.32−4

C496.1   To   hatch   the   COCKA-TRICE egg
1572 H. Bedel *Sermon* 25 Nov. 1571 C2: Ye gather together even the devil and al, and why? because ye wil hatch the Cockatrice egge. 1583 (1593) Greene *2 Mamillia* I,233: Have I hatched up the egge that wil prove a Cockatrice? 1589 ?Nashe *Return Pasquil* I,77: You see howe foule a Cockatrice may be hatcht of so small an egge.
Shakespeare: *R3* 4.1.54

C496.2   To kill like a COCKATRICE (*Varied*) (Cf. Appendix C: C495)
E.g. c1548 Brinkelow *Compl. Rod.* XXIV 69: What a cockatryse syght was it to se such an abhomynable sort of pompos bisshops in lordly parlament robys. 1595 Spenser *Amoretti* 49.9f.: Let them feele th'utmost of your crueltyes, And kill with looks, as cockatrices doo.
Shakespeare: *TN* 3.4.195f., *R3*

4.1.54f., *Rom.* 3.2.47, *Luc.* 540
Cf. B99.1: To kill like a basilisk.

C499   As close as COCKLES (a cockle) (*TNK*, 1631; OW127b from 1601)
Shakespeare: *TNK* 4.1.131

(?) C501   A (London) COCKNEY (Cf. Appendix B) (From 1557; OW478a from 1552)
Shakespeare: *TN* 4.1.15

(?) C501.1   Not worth a COD (*seed pod*) (Wh C362 a1338)
Shakespeare: *Lr.* 1.4.200
Cf. P138.1: Not give two peascods.

(?) C502   Hold or cut CODPIECE POINT (1678 Ray, cf. *MND*; *ditto* OW377b)
Shakespeare; *MND* 1.2.111

C505   To keep a (foul) COIL (Cf. Appendix B) (From 1571; OW132a [To keep a coil] from 1566)
Add: c1587 (c1592) Kyd *Spanish Tragedy* 3.13.45: How now, what noise? what coile is that you keepe? c1588 (1590) Marlowe *2 Tamburlaine* 4.1.72: What a coil they keep!
Shakespeare: *AWW* 2.1.27, *TNK* 2.4.18

C511   COLEWORTS   (Cabbage) twice sodden (From 1552)
E.g., 1559 Morwyng *Treas. Evon.* 8 47: Theese repetycions move ircke-somenesse to the reader, yea even if it be but meanly learned, never a whit les then colewortes twise sod.
Shakespeare: *LLL* 4.2.22

C513   After a COLLAR comes a halter (From 1583; OW5b supplements)
Shakespeare: *1H4* 2.4.324f., *Rom.* 1.1.3−5

C517   It is a dear COLLOP that is taken (cut) out of the flesh (*Varied* from 1546)

E.g., 1569 J. Rogers *Glass Godly Love* 186: For they dye not all together, that leave collops of their owne flesh alive behinde them.
Shakespeare: *1H6* 5.4.18, *WT* 1.2.137

C519   As many COLORS as there are in the rainbow (*Varied* from c1590; OW133b from 1562)
Shakespeare: *Wiv.* 4.5.115f., *Jn.* 4.2.13f., *WT* 4.4.204f.

C520   To fear no COLORS (From 1594; OW843af. from 1592)
Shakespeare: *LLL* 4.2.149f., *TN* 1.5.6, 10, *2H4* 5.5.88

C520.1   To show oneself in one's COLORS
1616 DR. s.v. Malice no. 1341: He sheweth himselfe in his colours.
Shakespeare: *2H4* 2.2.169f.

C525   He has a COLT'S tooth in his head (*Varied* from c1565)
Shakespeare: *H8* 1.3.48

C529   Come (Hap, Befall) what come (hap, befall) may (*Hap* from c1495; *Come* from 1546; *Befall* from *2H6*)
Add: 1562 A. Brooke *Romeus and Juliet* 1678: I will returne to you (mine owne) befall what may befall.
Shakespeare: *Shr.* 4.4.107, *LLL* 5.2.112, 870, *TN* 2.1.47, *2H6* 3.2.402, *1H4* 1.2.145, *Tit.* 5.1.57, *Ham.* 4.5.136, *Lr.* 4.1.50, *Mac.* 1.3.146, *TNK* 2.3.17, 3.6.127

C540   I CAME, saw, and overcame (*Varied* from 1587; OW99b from 1542)
Shakespeare: *LLL* 4.1.67–70, *AYL* 5.2.31f., *2H4* 4.3.40–2, *Cym.* 3.1.23f.

(?) C541   COMELY not gaudy (*Gaudy Ham.*, 1631, *gorgeous* 1615; OW557b adds *neat* 1850)
Shakespeare: *Ham.* 1.3.70f.

C542   Cold COMFORT (Cf. Appendix B) (From 1571)
Shakespeare: *Shr.* 4.1.31, *Jn.* 5.7.42

C547   It is better COMING to the beginning of a feast than the end of a fray (*Varied* from 1590; OW52b combines with C548 [It is ill coming to the end of a feast and beginning of a fray (from 1546)] and E114 [Better come at the latter end of a feast than the beginning of a fray (from 1616)])
Shakespeare: *1H4* 4.2.79f.

C553   The ten COMMANDMENTS (fig.) (From a1521)
Shakespeare: *2H6* 1.3.142
Cf. Appendix B: By these TEN bones.

(?) C554.1   Where is your COMMISSION?
1639 CL s.v. Aliena curantis 20: Where is your commission Sir.
Shakespeare: *H8* 3.2.233

C565.1   Draw to such COMPANY as you would be like (Wh C395 *varied* from a1325 = OW138af. [As a man is, so is his company], from 1541)
Shakespeare: *2H4* 5.1.75–7

C566   Good COMPANY makes short miles (*Varied* from 1580; Wh C394 a1500)
E.g., c1590 (1605) *King Leir* 1.4 390: Thy pleasant company will make the way seeme short. 1653 Walton *Complete Angler* I,2: Good company makes the way seem the shorter.
Shakespeare: *R2* 2.3.16–8, *Luc.* 791

C571   It is good to have COMPANY in trouble (misery) (*Varied* from 1509; Wh W715 from c1385)
E.g., 1549 Latimer *Serm.* 9 136: It is comfort of the wretched to have company. 1576 Pettie *Petite Pallace* 98: Not withstandinge the comfort by other mens calamitie be miser-

able, yet it doth me good to thinke that others have been as sluttishly served by women as my selfe. 1579 Lyly *Euphues* I, 238: In miserie Euphues it is a great comfort to have a companion.
Shakespeare: *Lr.* 3.6.104−7, *WT* 1.2.190−8, *Luc.* 790, 1111

C575.1 There's no COMPARISON (Cf. Appendix B)
1481 Caxton *Mirrour of the World* III.xxxi.181: So moche a debonayer lorde ... that ther is no comparison to hym [in *OED* 2]. 1600 (1657) Dekker et al. *Lust's Dominion* 3.3.80: S'blood, there's no comparison between them. 1639 CL s.v. Excellentia & aequalitas 105.
Shakespeare: *Tro.* 1.1.41−3, 1.2.62

C576 COMPARISONS are odious (From 1573; Wh C400 from c1440)
Shakespeare: *Ado* 3.5.16

C577 Live within COMPASS (From 1596: OW139a from 1579)
Shakespeare: *1H4* 3.3.19

C577.1 Out of all COMPASS (Cf. Appendix B)
1605 (1607) Dekker & Webster *Northward Ho* 2.2.31−3: I was in doubt I should have growne fat of late: and it were not for law suites: and feare of our wives: we rich men should grow out of all compasse. 1611 Cotgrave s.v. Desordonné: Disorderlie ... unbridled, out of all good compasse.
Shakespeare: *1H4* 3.3.21−3.

C578 Compare not with thy COMPEERS (betters) (*Compeers* 1659, *betters* 1520, *TN*)
Add: 1519 Horman *Vulgaria* M2: Compare nat with thy betters. / Certare noli cum maioribus.
Shakespeare: *TN* 1.3.117f.

(?) C579 Some complain to prevent

COMPLAINT (*Varied* from 1580)
E.g., 1580 Lyly *Euphues and his England* II,95: Pretily to cloake thine own folly, thou callest me theefe first [OW98bf.], not unlike unto a curst wife, who deserving a check, beginneth first to scolde.
Add: c1589 (1594) Lyly *Mother Bombie* 5.3.139f.: This is your olde tricke, to pick ones purse & then to picke quarrels.
Shakespeare: *Err.* 4.1.50f., *AYL* 4.1.173−5, *R3* 1.3.323−5, *1H4* 3.3.67

C582 He that is wise in his own CONCEIT is a fool (*Varied* from 1573; cf. Prov. 26.5, etc.)
E.g., 1573 SANF. 51[v]: The greatest token of a foole is to accounte him selfe wise.
Shakespeare: *MV* 2.9.59, *Ado* 4.2.80, *TN* 1.5.33f.

C585 One ill CONDITION mars all the good (1616, *varied* from 1546)
E.g., 1546 Heywood *Dialogue* II.vi I2: With many condicions good, one that is yll Defaceth the floure of all, and dothe all spyll.
Shakespeare: *Ham.* 1.4.36−8

C587 CONFESS and be hanged (From c1589 [1633]; OW139b from 1589)
Shakespeare: *MV* 3.2.35, *Ham.* 5.1.39, *Oth.* 4.1.38, *Tim.* 1.2.22, 5.1.131

C589 CONFESSION of a fault is half amends[n] (From 1592; OW248b adds 1558 analogue)
Shakespeare: *Wiv.* 1.1.104
Cf. D590: Confession of a fault pardons it [*Varied* from 1606]

[n] The entry form in OW248b has "redressed" rather than "amends," but with only the following to support it: 1822 Scott *Nigel* ch. 29: Indeed, to confess is, in this case, in some slight sort to redress.

C594　He came in with the CON-QUEROR (*Shr.*, 1639; OW139b from 1593)
Add: 1573 (1586) R. Curteys *Sermon preached at Greenewiche* C8ᵛ: I am a Gentleman, a noble man, I came in with the conqueror.
Shakespeare: *Shr.* Ind. i.4f.

C598　The CONSCIENCE and the eye are tender parts (1639 only)
Add: 1578 T. White *Sermon at Paul's Cross* 3 Nov. 1577 E8: Tenera res conscientia est, qua nec tangi nec angi debet, Conscience is a tender thing, and maye not bee touched nor troubled.
Shakespeare: *H8* 2.2.142f., 2.4.171

C601　CONSCIENCE is a thousand witnesses (From 1539; OW140af. supplements)
Shakespeare: *R3* 5.2.17, 5.3.193−5

C601.1　CONSCIENCE is for beggars (*Varied*)
c1588 (1590) Robert Wilson *Three Lords and Three Ladies of London* D4: Who cares for Conscience but dies a beggar? c1589 Marlowe *Jew of Malta* 1.1.117f.: Haply some hapless man hath conscience, And for his conscience lives in beggary. c1606 (1607) Jonson *Volpone* 3.7.211: If you haue conscience— / 'Tis the beggers vertue.
Shakespeare: *R3* 1.4.141

C606　A guilty CONSCIENCE is a self-accuser (feels continual fear) (*Varied* from 1598; OW340b from 1545 [= Wh G492 from c1390])
E.g., c1390 *Cato* (*Vernon*) 567:179−80: The wikked mon weneth that alle men Have him in heore thought. 1590 H. Roberts *Defiance to Fortune* Pl: Guiltie consciences be timorous. 1597 *Politeuphuia* 10ᵛ: A guiltie conscience is never without feare.
Shakespeare: *R3* 1.4.134f., 5.3.179, *Ham.* 3.1.82

C608　He has a CONSCIENCE like a cheverel's skin (cheverel conscience) (From 1583)
Add: 1576 R. Curteys *Two Sermons* C8: Most men now a dayes have Cheverel consciences, if the matter touch their own profit or pleasure.
Shakespeare: *TN* 3.1.11f., *H8* 2.3.32, *Rom.* 2.4.83f.

C616　You might be a CONSTABLE for your wit (*Varied* from *Ado*; ditto OW140b)
Add: a1570 *Misogonus* 3.1.18: I have bin lected for my scretion five times constable. 1588 (1591) Lyly *Endymion* 4.2.99f.: Let Maister Constable speake: I thinke hee is the wisest among you.
Shakespeare: *Ado* 3.3.22f., *MM* 2.1.258−68

(?) C618　CONSTANCY has one foot on land and another on sea (1664 COD., cf. *Ado*)
Shakespeare: *Ado* 2.3.64f.

C623　CONTENT (A mind content) is a kingdom (crown) (*Varied* from 1591; OW142a from c1560)
Shakespeare: *3H6* 3.1.64

C624　CONTENT is happiness (pleased) (*Varied* from 1580; OW141b from 1579)
Shakespeare: *H8* 2.3.22f.

C629　CONTENTMENT (A contented mind) is great riches (*Varied* from c1565; OW873b from 1550)
Shakespeare: *Oth.* 3.3.172

C636　He is an ill COOK that cannot lick his own fingers (From 1520)
Shakespeare: *Rom.* 4.2.6f.

C644　A COOLING CARD (Cf.Appendix B) (From c1570; ditto OW143b)
Shakespeare: *1H6* 5.3.84

(?) C648.1 As red as CORAL (Wh C423 c1390)
Shakespeare: *Ven.* 542, *Luc.* 420, 1234

C668 The CORRUPTION of the best is worst (From 1630 [1618]; OW145b adds *Son.* and a 1579 version of N317)
E.g., 1618 T. Adams *Happiness of the Church* ed. 1861−2 I, 85: But it is ever true, optimi corruptio pessima,—the fairest flowers putrefied, stink worse than weeds.
Shakespeare: *Son.* 94.13f.
Cf. N317: Nothing so good but it (The best things, Everything) may be abused.

C682 The COUNSEL thou wouldst have another keep first keep thyself (*Varied* from 1566; Wh C462 from c1390)
Shakespeare: *Ado* 3.3.86, *Ham.* 4.2.11f.

(?) C684.1 Good COUNSEL is good to hear (lere) (Wh C457f., a1393, c1380)
Shakespeare: *Rom.* 3.3.159f.

C688 He can give others good COUNSEL but will take none himself (From 1616 DR.; OW304a *varied* from 1533−4)
E.g., 1533−4 N. Udall *Flowers* 189: Thou canst gyve counsaylle vnto others, and . . . be wyse in other mennes mattiers, and not . . . be able to helpe or ease thyne owne selfe.
Shakespeare: *H8* 1.1.134−6

C704.1 Out of all COUNT (*OED* 1 *Out of count TGV*, 1768)
1598 W. Haughton *Englishmen for My Money* v (MSR 901): It was out of all count; vi (1268f.): Out of all scotch and notch [S160] glad, out of all count glad.
Shakespeare: *TGV* 2.1.56f.

C705 (To be put) out of COUN-

TENANCE (From *LLL*; OW147b from 1544)
Shakespeare: *LLL* 5.2.272, 607, 621, *Ant.* 2.2.177

C706 Oft COUNTING makes good friends (*Varied* from 1530)
E.g., 1530 Whitforde *Wk. Householder* A4: The commune proverbe is that ofte rekenynge holdeth longe felawshyp.
Shakespeare: *1H4* 1.2.47−50
Cf. R54: Even reckoning makes long friends [from 1546].

C715 Great COURAGE is in greatest dangers tried (1611 COT., analogues from *Jn.*)
Shakespeare: *Jn.* 2.1.82

(?) C716.1 The COURSE of true love never did run smooth (OW148b; *MND*, Scott)
Shakespeare: *MND* 1.1.134

C739 Call me COUSIN but cozen me not (1648 Ray, with puns on *cousin-cozen* from *R3*; OW149a has pun from c1552)
Shakespeare: *Wiv.* 4.5.77f., *R3* 4.4.223, *1H4* 1.3.254f., *TNK* 3.1.43f.

C761 Many a good COW has an ill (evil) calf (From 1520)
Shakespeare: *Tmp.* 1.2.120

C765 Who bulls the COW must keep the calf (*Varied* from 1550; Wh C505 1304)
Shakespeare: *Jn.* 1.1.123f.

C773 A COWARD changes color (Collections from 1552)
Shakespeare: *JC* 1.2.122

C774 A COWARD dies many deaths, a brave man but one (*Varied* from *JC*; OW151b adds 1596)
I.e., 1596 Drayton *Mortimeriados* 2723: Every houre he dyes, which ever feares.
Add: 1596 (1633) R. Devereux *Pro-*

fitable Instructions 44: As he which dieth Nobly, doth live for ever; so hee that doth live in feare, doth die continueally.
Shakespeare: *JC* 2.2.32f.

C817   He that has lost his CREDIT is dead to the world (Some collections from 1640; *varied*, including other collections, from 1519)
E.g., 1590 Greene *Francesco's Fortunes* VIII,154: She which hath crackt her credite is hanged.
Add: 1596 Lodge *Wits Miserie* D2: Hee that looseth his credite, hath nought els to loose.
Shakespeare: *1H4* 1.2.55−8, *Oth.* 2.3.262−4
Cf. N25: He that has an ill name is half hanged [from 1546].

C825   As merry as a CRICKET (From 1546)
Shakespeare: *1H4* 2.4.89

C826   CRIMES (Mischiefs) are made secure by greater crimes (mischiefs) (*Varied* from c1592; OW154b from 1566 Seneca)
Shakespeare: *Mac.* 3.2.55
Cf. S467.1: (Every) SIN brings in another.

C831   CROCODILE TEARS (From 1548)
Shakespeare: *2H6* 3.1.226f., *Oth.* 4.1.245f., *Ant.* 2.7.49

C832   As rich as CROESUS (a king) (From 1577; Wh K39 *king* from a1500)
Shakespeare: *Ado* 3.5.21

C843   He has CROTCHETS in his head (Cf. Appendix B) (*Varied* from 1577)
Shakespeare: *Wiv.* 2.1.154f.

C844   As black as a CROW (From 1538; Wh C565 from c1330)
Shakespeare: *MND* 3.2.141f.,

Rom. 1.5.48, *Per.* 4 Chorus 31−3, *WT* 4.4.219

C853   He will say the CROW is white (From 1529)
Shakespeare: *MND* 3.2.141f.

C854   The hoarse CROW croaks before the rain (Collections from 1616; OW156b adds 1615)
Add: 1557 *Tottel* Aa4: Thou dunghyll crowe that crokest agaynst the rayne. 1575 Gascoigne "Flowers" I,57: The caryon Crowe, that lothsome beast . . . cryes agaynst the rayne.
Shakespeare: *AYL* 4.1.151f.

C855   I have a CROW to pluck (pull) with you (To have a crow to pull, pluck) (From c1517)
Shakespeare: *Err.* 3.1.83

C860   You look as if you would make the CROW a pudding (1678 Ray, *varied* from *1H4*: OW502a c1598)
E.g., c1598 (1639) Deloney *2 Gentle Craft* iii 163: Let no man . . . say thou gavest the Crow a pudding, because love would let thee live no longer.
Shakespeare: *H5* 2.1.87

C863   CROWNS have cares (*Varied* from 1576; ditto OW157b)
Shakespeare: *R2* 4.1.194, *2H4* 3.1.31, 4.5.23

C864   From the CROWN of the head to the sole of the foot (From 1533)
Shakespeare: *Ado* 3.2.8f., *Tmp.* 4.1.233

C864.1   From the CROWN to the toe (Wh C575 c1300)
Add: 1596 Nashe *Saffron-Walden* III,123: From the crowne to the little toe.
Shakespeare: *Mac.* 1.5.42
Cf. T436: From top (head) to toe (heel).

C871.1   Out of all CRY (ho, whoop-

ing) (OW601b; *cry* from 1581, *ho* in a1593, *whooping* only *AYL*)
Shakespeare: *AYL* 3.2.193
Cf. H477: He has (There is) no ho with him (Beyond all ho).

C875 As clear as CRYSTAL (From 1509; Wh C589 from a1350)
E.g., a1350 *Ywain* 25.900: Hir yghen clere als es cristall. a1500 *The Beauty of his Mistress* II in Robbins 124.16: With eyes clere as crystall stoune [in Wh C589]. 1520 Whittington *Vulgaria* 36: His eyes be clere as crystall.
Shakespeare: *MND* 3.2.138f.

C876.1 A CUCKOLD has no gall (Wh C595 *varied* from a1439)
Shakespeare: *Wiv.* 3.5.149f.

C876.2 A CUCKOLD is a beast (monster)
1622 (1647) Fletcher & Massinger *Spanish Curate* 4.2.7f.: I would have him horn'd For a most precious beast. c1626 (1633) Dekker ?& Rowley *Noble Spanish Soldier* 2.2.45f.: A shee-cuckold is an untameable monster. c1632 (1633) Ford *'Tis Pity She's a Whore* 5.2.7: A cuckold is a goodly tame beast, my lord.
Shakespeare: *Jn.* 2.1,293, *Ham.* 3.1.138f., *Oth.* 4.1.62

C877 The CUCKOLD is the last that knows of it (Collections *varied* from 1636, cf. *WT;* OW159b adds 1604)
Shakespeare: *WT* 1.2.218f.

C889 CUCKOLDS come by destiny (1577, *Wiv.*, *Oth.*)
I.e., 1577 Grange *Golden Aphroditis* R2: As Cuckoldes come by destinie, so Cuckowes sing by kinde.
Add: c1590 (1595) Peele *Old Wives Tale* 682f.: Lobb be your comfort, and Cuckold bee your destenie. 1605 Jonson et al. *Eastward Ho* 4.1.296f.: Farewell thou Horne of Destinie, th'ensigne of the married man.
Shakespeare: *Wiv.* 3.5.104f., 149f., *AYL* 3.3.51f., 4.1.57−9, *AWW* 1.3.63, *Oth.* 3.3.275−7

(?) C894.1 No one regards the June (summer) CUCKOO'S song (*Varied*)
c1400 *Femina* 61(13−4): Song of kokkow in somer we have To preyse that take we non hede [in Wh C603 Cuckoos and cuckolds (*varied*)]. 1562 Heywood *Epigrammes* Sixth Hundred 95: In Apryll the Kookoo can syng hir song by rote, In Iune out of tune she can not syng a note [= A309]. 1575 Gascoigne *Master F. J.* I,436: Dame Pergo heard a Cuckoe chaunt, who (because the pride of the spring was now past) cried Cuck cuck Cuckoe in hir stamering voyce. 1604 Drayton *Owle* 1023−5: No Month regards him but lascivious May, Wherein whil'st Youth is dallying with the Day; His Song still tends to Vanitie and Lust.
Shakespeare: *1H4* 3.2.75f.

C896 To chew the CUD upon a thing (From 1547)
Shakespeare: *JC* 1.2.171

C909 To kiss the CUP (From 1579; Wh C629 from a1400)
Shakespeare: *Tmp.* 2.2.130

C911 To be in one's CUPS (Cf. Appendix B) (From *H5*; analogues from 1562)
Add: 1611 1 Esdras 3.22: And when they are in their cups, they forget their love both to friends and brethen.
Shakespeare: *H5* 4.7.45f.

C915 A CUR will bite before he bark (Collections from 1623)
Add: 1601 A. Dent *Plaine Mans Path-Way* M6: These fawning curres will not barke til they bite.
Shakespeare: *R3* 1.3.289

C917.1 CURS fight with each other but show all their might against a stranger (Wh C638 c1515)
Add: 1589 Charles Emanuel I (E. Aggas) *Admonition* (STC 5043) A4f.: Too common a proverbe . . . That dogges do often fight together, yet

so soone as they spye the wolfe, they leave their brawles, and together runne against the common enimie.
Shakespeare: *R3* 1.3.187−9

C921   Past CURE past care (From 1593, *varied* from 1567)
Add e.g.: 1559 "Lord Clifford" 11 *Mirror for Magistrates* 192: All care is bootles in a cureles case.
Shakespeare: *LLL* 5.2.28, *1H6* 3.3.3f., *R2* 2.3.171, *WT* 3.2.222f., *Son.* 147.9

C922   What cannot be CURED must be endured (*Varied* from 1579; Wh T179 from c1450)
E.g., c1489 Caxton *Aymon* I 202.17f.: A thyng that can not be amended, must be suffred and borne as well as men may. 1579 Spenser *Shep. Cal.* "Sept." 138f.: And cleanly cover that cannot be cured: Such il as is forced mought nedes be endured.
Shakespeare: *Wiv.* 5.5.237, *3H6* 5.4.37f.
Cf. e.g., R71: There is no remedy but patience.

(?)   C930   As stale as CUSTOM (c1595, cf. *Ant.*; not in OW)
I.e., c1595 Munday et al. *Sir Thomas More* 2.4.249: To urge my imperfections in excuse, Were all as stale as custome.
Shakespeare: *Ant.* 2.2.234

C931   A bad CUSTOM is like a good cake (A bad custom is), better broken than kept (From 1622, analogues from *Ham.*; ditto OW25b)
Shakespeare: *Ham.* 1.4.15f.

C932   CUSTOM (Use) is another (a second) nature (*Varied* from 1547; Wh C646 *custom* from a1387, *usage* from a1393)
Shakespeare: *Ham.* 3.4.168

C932.1   CUSTOM is overcome with custom (Wh C644 from a1500 [2])
E.g., 1502 *Imitatione* (2) 170.14f.: For

evyll custome may be overcome by good custome.
Add: 1616 DR. 415: A good custom must root out that which an ill has brought in, or up [C936].
Shakespeare: *Ham.* 3.4.161−5

C932.2   CUSTOM is a tyrant
1581 Guazzo (Pettie) *Civile Conversation* I 1,62: Doubtlesse custome is a great Tyrant. 1606 Daniel *Queen's Arcadia* 5.4 2563f.: That universall Tyrant of the earth, Custome.
Shakespeare: *Oth.* 1.3.229

C933   CUSTOM (Use) makes all things easy (*Varied* from *AYL*; not in OW)[n]
Add: c1585 (1592) Lyly *Gallathea* 1.3.22: Use will make it easie. 1666 TOR. *It. Prov.* 4 318: Use makes any thing that is difficult, easie [in U24].
Shakespeare: *AYL* 2.1.2f., *Ham.* 5.1.67f., *Oth.* 1.3.229−31
Cf. U24: Use (Practice) makes mastery (perfectness) [Wh U8 from 1340].

[n]Cf. my *John Webster's Borrowing*, p. 235, on *The Duchess of Malfi* 4.2.29−32.

C934   CUSTOM makes sin no sin (*Varied* from 1576)
E.g., 1576 Pettie *Petite Pallace* 124 (cf. 7): Use of evill maketh us thinke it no abuse, sinnes oft assayed are thought to bee no sinne.
Add e.g.: 1559 "King James the First" 111f. *Mirror for Magistrates* 159: Sinnes ofte assayed are thought to be no sinne, So sinne doth soyle, the soule it sinketh in. 1592 Nashe *Pierce Penilesse* I,216: Consuetudo peccandi tollit sensum peccati.
Shakespeare: *Ham.* 3.4.35−8, 161−5, *Mac.* 3.4.141f., *Per.* 1 Chor. 29f.

C938   Come CUT and longtail (*Wiv.*, 1605ff.; OW134b from 1590)
Shakespeare: *Wiv.* 3.4.46, *TNK* 5.2.49

C940 (Then) call me CUT (From c1495)

Shakespeare: *TN* 2.3.187, 2.5.86−9, *1H4* 2.4.194

D

D8.1 To speak DAGGERS (poinards) (Cf. Appendix B) (*Varied*) 1602 ?T. Heywood *How a Man May Choose* 2573f.: Every word thou speakst, Is a sharpe dagger thrust quite through my heart. c1621 (1623) Massinger *Duke of Milan* 2.1.377f.: Everie word's a Poynard, And reaches to my Heart. 1623 (1624) Massinger *Bondman* 1.3.266f.: I am sicke, the man Speakes poniards, and diseases.

Shakespeare: *Ado* 2.1.247f., *Ham.* 3.2.396, 3.4.94f.

(?) D22 To DANCE barefoot (fig.) (*Shr.*, 1742; ditto OW166a) Add: 1706 ?S. Butler *Dildoides* B2 (of poxed lechers): Such . . . Might fill the lusty Fore-man's Place, And make our elder Girls ne'er care for't, Tho 'twere their Fortune to dance bare-foot.

Shakespeare: *Shr.* 2.1.33

D30 DANGER itself the best remedy for danger (*Varied* from 1651 HERB.; OW167a from c1526) Shakespeare: *1H4* 2.3.9f.

D35 The more DANGER the more honor (*Varied* from c1534) Shakespeare: *3H6* 4.3.15, 5.1.70, *H5* 4.3.22, *Ant.* 4.15.46f.

D41.1 At first DASH (Cf. Appendix B) (OW168a from 1525−40) Shakespeare: *1H6* 1.2.71 Cf. D42: He is out at first DASH [from 1639].

D42.1 The DATE is out (OW168af., from 1587) Shakespeare: *Tro.* 1.2.257, *1H4* 2.4.503, *Rom.* 1.4.3

(?) D49.1 To choke a DAW (Cf. Appendix B) 1627 (1636) Massinger *Great Duke of Florence* 4.2.192: Gape wider yet, this is Court-like. / To choke Dawes with.

Shakespeare: *Ado* 2.3.254f.

D50 As wise as a DAW (From c1525; OW899a adds 1609) Shakespeare: *1H6* 2.4.18

D56 As clear as (the) DAY (noonday) (From 1566; Wh D34 c1460) Shakespeare: *2H6* 2.1.105, *Ham.* 4.5.152f.

(?) D56.1 As Fair as DAY 1624 Fletcher *Wife for a Month* 4.1 V,47: Fair as the day, and clear as innocence.

Shakespeare: *LLL* 4.3.88 Cf. Wh D35 [1]: As doughty as the day is fair.

D57 As merry as the DAY is long (From 1594; OW527b adds 1566) Shakespeare: *Ado* 2.1.49, *Jn.* 4.1.18

D57.1 As sure as DAY c1592 (1594) ?Green *Selimus* xiv (MSR 1410): As sure as day, mine eyes shall nere tast sleepe. 1618 (1647) Fletcher *Loyal Subject* 4.2 III,138: Sure as 'tis day. c1625 (1647) *Chances* 1.2 IV,178: As certain As day must coame again.

Shakespeare: *1H4* 3.1.250

D59 Be the DAY never so long, at last (at length) comes (it rings to) evensong (From 1508; Wh D40 from a1393 *varied*) Shakespeare: *JC* 5.1.124

D68 Every DAY is not holiday (Sunday) (Collections from 1611, cf. *1H4*) Shakespeare: *1H4* 1.2.204 Cf. S548: With sluggards every day is holiday.

D70   Every DAY the night comes (*Varied* from 1573)
Shakespeare: *JC* 5.1.124
Cf. D90: The longest day has an end.

D74   For ever and a DAY (From 1540; OW227b from c1528)
Shakespeare: *Shr.* 4.4.97, *AYL* 4.1.145

D81.1   I have seen the DAY
E.g., 1533 J. Heywood *Johan Johan* 588: I have seen the day when I was a little one. ?c1588 (1599) Porter *Two Angry Women of Abingdon* x (MSR 2382): I have seene the day, I could have daunst in my sight. c1590 (1595) Peele *Old Wives Tale* 88f.: I have seene the day when I was a little one. c1604 (1607) Middleton *Phoenix* 3.1.59f.: I ha' seen the day I could have told money out of other men's purses.
Shakespeare: *Wiv.* 2.1.227–9, *Tro.* 4.5.210, *Rom.* 1.5.21, *Oth.* 5.2.261ff., *Lr.*5.3.277f.

D88   To be (make) a black (bloody) DAY to somebody (fig.) (*Black* from *R3*, *bloody* from *2H4*)
Add: 1596 Nashe *Saffron-Walden* III,130: He would make a bloodie day in Poules Church-yard.
Shakespeare: *3H6* 5.6.85, *R3* 5.3.280, *2H4* 5.4.11f.

D90   The longest DAY has an end (evening) (fig.) (*Evening* from 1580, *end* from 1611)
Shakespeare: *Mac.* 1.3.147
Cf. D70: Every day the night comes.

D92   No DAY so clear but has dark clouds (fig.) (*Varied* from *2H6*; ditto OW169bf.)
Add e.g.: 1575 Gascoigne "Flowers" I,77: What sunne can shine so cleare & bright but cloudes may ryse among? 1576 Pettie *Petite Pallace*

142: No sunne shineth so bright but that cloudes may over cast it.
Shakespeare: *2H6* 2.4.1

D99   One may see DAY at a little hole (fig.) (From 1546)
Shakespeare: *LLL* 5.2.723f.

(?) D113.1   To do a good DAY'S work (*Varied*) (*OED Day's-work* begins with *R3*)
c1553 (1575) W. Stevenson *Gammer Gurton's Needle* 1.3.43 (sarcastic): Ye have made a fayre daies worke, have you not?
Shakespeare: *R3* 2.1.1, *Cor.* 4.6.80f., 5.1.15
Cf. D113: He does an excellent day's work who rids himself of a fool [from 1611]; H99: To make a hand (fair hand) of a thing.

D116   Halcyon DAYS (Cf. Appendix B) (From 1580; OW343bf. from 1540)
Shakespeare: *1H6* 1.2.131

D118   My dancing DAYS are done (From 1604, cf *Rom.*; OW166b from 1573)
Shakespeare: *Rom.* 1.5.31

D121.1   To be mad once in one's DAYS
1596 Nashe *Saffron-Walden* III,79: Semel insanivimus omnes, once in our dayes there is none of us but have plaid the ideots. 1607 Dekker & Webster *Northward Ho* 4.3.33: Come a spurt and away, lets bee mad once in our dayes. c1616 (1652) Middleton *Widow* 5.1.347f.: I'll be mad Once in my days.
Shakespeare: *1H4* 1.2.142f.

D121.2   To have seen better DAYS (*OED* 13a from 1806)
c1595 Munday et al. *Sir Thomas More* 4.5.86: Having seene better dayes; 90: Sir, we have seene farre better

dayes then these. 1639 CL. 132: Our best dayes are gone [in D115].
Shakespeare: *Tim.* 4.2.27

D123 You (To) burn DAYLIGHT (From c1565; OW91b from c1560)
Shakespeare: *Wiv.* 2.1.54, *Rom.* 1.4.43

D124 Speak well of the DEAD (*Varied* from 1648; OW761b Greek, Latin, 1540ff.)
E.g., 1540 Erasm. tr. Taverner *Flores sententiarum* A6: Rayle not upon him that is dead.
Shakespeare: *LLL* 5.2.661

D124.1 To belie the DEAD is a sin 1591 Greene *Maidens Dreame* 287 II,232: Tis sin and shame for to bely the dead. 1606 Dekker *Seven deadlie Sinns* ed. Brett-Smith 18: He is asham'd to belye the dead. c1606 (1607) Middleton *Michaelmas Term* 4.4.37f.: 'Tis the scurviest thing . . . to belie the dead so. ?c1610 (1631) Heywood *1 Fair Maid of the West* 3.1.24: 'Tis more then sinne thus to belye the dead.
Shakespeare: *2H4* 1.1.98

D125 To lament the DEAD avails not and revenge vents hatred (*Ado* [excluded], 1666 TOR.; OW171a adds 1591)
I.e., 1591 Ariosto (Harington) *Orl. Fur.* IX.41: By teares no good the dead is done, And sharpe revenge asswageth malice cheefe.
Shakespeare: *Mac.* 4.3.214f., *Luc.* 1821ff.

D126 To lament the DEAD avails not and to the living it is hurtful (*Varied* from 1530−60)
E.g., 1599 (1600) Dekker *Shoemakers' Holiday* 3.4.98f.: Come, weepe not: mourning though it rise from love Helpes not the mourned, yet hurtes them that mourne.
Add: 1602 ?T. Heywood *How a Man May Choose* B2: They say griefe often

shortens life [in C84].
Shakespeare: *TN* 1.3.1−3, *AWW* 1.1.56, *R3* 2.2.36f., *Rom.* 3.5.71−3, 4.5.82f.

D126.1 DEAD and rotten (Cf. Appendix B: DEAD and gone)
E.g., c1475 *Herod* (Wakefield) 492−5: It shuld have bene spokyn How I had me wrokyn, Were I dede and rotyn, With many a tong. 1533 N. Udall *Floures* S2: But this acte shal be hadde in memorie, when that I am deed & rotten. 1578 T. Lupset *All for Money* (MSR 1108): When I am dead and rotten. 1596 Nashe *Saffron-Walden* III,106: But this I will say for him, though hee bee dead and rotten.
Shakespeare: *LLL* 5.2.660, *Lr.* 5.3.286, *WT* 3.3.80f.

D133 After DEATH the doctor (physician) (From 1566; *physic* variant from 1611)
I.e., 1611 *Second Maiden's Tragedy* 2.2 29: This comes like phisick when the parties dead, flowes kindnes now, when tis so ill deservd.
Shakespeare: *H8* 3.2.40f.

D133.1 As dumb (silent, still) as DEATH (the grave [OW733a (Silent as the grave) 1829, 1889])
c1378 *Piers* B x 137: And as doumbe as deth [Wh D80]. a1400 *Meditations* 39.1466: And lay stille a(s) deth in swound. c1450 *Myroure of oure Ladye* 30 32: And lay styll as dede [Wh D83]. 1613 Beaumont *Knight of the Burning Pestle* 5.1.28: As mute and pale as death itself. 1679 [Leanerd] *Counterfeits* 1.1: All the House silent as Death [D135, with *Oth.*]. 1679 Dryden *Troilus and Cressida* 5.1 VI,375: These noisy streets . . . Shall be to-morrow silent as the grave.
Shakespeare: *Ham.* 2.2.486, *Oth.* 5.2.94

D136 As sure as DEATH (From *Tit.*; ditto OW789a)

Add: 1495 *Meditacyons of saynt Bernarde* B3 (10f.): For deth is sure and undowted. 1509 *Ship* I 154(23): The deth is sure [Wh D96]. 1590 Spenser *Faerie Queene* 1.11.12.3: Dead was it sure, as sure as death in deed.
Shakespeare: *Tit.* 1.1.487

D138.1 DEATH devours all things (*Varied*)
1557 Tottel P3^v: Set hym free From dark oblivion of devouryng death. 1596 C. Middleton *Historie of Heaven* C2: Hungrie death that all thinges doth devoure. 1604 T. Middleton *Father Hubburds Tale* VIII,65: The old devourer . . . death, had made our landlord dance after his pipe. c1605 (1630) Dekker *2 Honest Whore* 1.2.102−4: Deaths a good trencher-man, he can eat course homely meat, as well as the daintiest.
Shakespeare: *Jn.* 2.1.352−4, *Rom.* 2.6.7
Cf. D139: Death devours lambs as well as sheep [from 1620]; T326: Time devours all things.

D139.1 DEATH for death (Wh D91 *varied* from a 1420 [4])
Add: Sackville & Norton *Gorboduc* 4.2 F4^v: Blood asketh blood, and death must death requite [in B458]. 1598 (1601) Munday *Downfall Robert Earl of Huntington* v (MSR 732): Death asketh death you know.
Shakespeare: *MM* 5.1.409, *Tit.* 5.3.66

D140 DEATH has a thousand doors to let out life (*Varied* from 1587; OW225a Virgil, analogues from c1390)
Shakespeare: *MM* 3.1.39f., *TNK* 1.5.13f.

D142 DEATH is common to all (Erasmus' Latin, English *varied* from *Ham.*; OW173b *common* from 1597; Wh D97 *common* from a1400)
Shakespeare: *Ham.* 1.2.72−4

D142.1 DEATH is the end of all (every worldly sore) (*Varied*; OW173b *all* from 1584; Wh D94 from c1385)
Shakespeare: *MM* 3.1.40f., *1H6* 3.2.136f., *Rom.* 3.3.92

D142.2 Death is God's (a) sergeant[n]
1593 Nashe *Christs Teares* II,32: The Iudge deliver thee to Death, his Sariant. c1604 (1605) Chapman *All Fools* 1.2.81 (of Dame Nature): Her Sergeant Iohn Death. 1605 S. du Bartas (J. Sylvester) *Devine Weekes* 1.3 18^v: Death, dread Seriant of th'eternall Iudge, Comes very late to his sole-seated lodge. 1612 S. Hieron *Life and Death of Dorcas* (1624 *Sermons* I,391): Death it selfe is a Sergeant to arrest, and to bring to iudgement. 1617 J. Moore *Mappe of Mans Mortalitie* 46: Death continually waiteth for him [man] as a sergeant at his gates.
Shakespeare: *Ham.* 5.2.336f.

[n]Cf. S. Viswanathan, " 'This Fell Sergeant Death' Once More," *Shakespeare Quarterly*, 29 (1978), 84f.

D142.3 DEATH is a physician
1563 "Anthony, Lord Rivers" 363f. *Mirror for Magistrates* 258: That loathed leach, that never wellcum death, Through spasmous humours stopped up his breth. c1602 (1606) Chapman *Gentleman Usher* 4.1.4−6 (contemplating suicide): Hasten the cowardly protracted cure Of all diseases: King of Phisitians, death, Ile dig thee from this Mine of miserie.
Shakespeare: *Oth.* 1.3.309f., *Cym.* 5.4.7

D143 DEATH is the grand leveler (*Varied* from 1590; OW174a from 1578; Wh D101 from c1385)
Shakespeare: *Ham.* 4.3.23−5, *Cym.* 4.2.252f.

D148 DEATH pays all debts (*Varied*

from *1H4*; OW174a wrongly adds *R3* 4.4.21)[n]
E.g., Montaigne (Florio) *Essays* I I,37: The common saying is, that Death acquits us all of all our bonds. 1609 *Every Woman in Her Humour* H1[v]: Till death . . . cancels all bonds.
Shakespeare: *1H4* 3.2.157, *Mac.* 5.9.5, *Cym.* 5.4.157−9, *Tmp.* 3.2.131

[n]Cf. Introduction, p. xviii.

D158   To rhyme to DEATH, as they do rats in Ireland (*Varied* from c1581 [1595]; ditto OW674a)
Shakespeare: *AYL* 3.2.176f.

D158.1   To tickle to DEATH
c1610 (1613) Marston & Barksted *Insatiate Countess* 5.2 III,77: What saist thou to tickling to death with bodkins? ?1611 (1621) W. Mason *Handful of Essaies* 129: The Flatterer tickleth his friends to death. c1611 Tourneur *Atheist's Tragedy* 3.3.47−9: My passions are My subiects; and I can command them laugh; Whilst thou doest tickle 'em to death with miserie. 1612 Webster *White Devil* 5.3.196−9: O the rare trickes of a Machivillian . . . Hee tickles you to death; makes you die laughing.
Shakespeare: *Ado* 3.1.80

(?) D161   DEATH'S day is doomsday (1579, 1732)[n]
I.e., 1579 Lyly *Euphues* I,308: Every ones deathes daye is his domes daye. 1732 FUL., no. 1255.
Shakespeare: *3H6* 5.6.93, *R2* 3.2.188f., *1H4* 4.1.134, *Tit.* 2.3.42, *Rom.* 5.3.234

[n]See Introduction, p. xix.

D162   To be at DEATH'S door (Cf. Appendix B) (From 1550; Wh D107 from 1515)
Shakespeare: *3H6* 3.3.105

D165   I will not die in your DEBT (your debtor) (From 1508)

Shakespeare: *LLL* 5.2.43, 333, *AYL* 2.3.76, *Rom.* 1.1.238

D167.1   To be in DEBT to years (Cf. Appendix B)
c1618 (1647) Fletcher et al. *Knight of Malta* 3.2. VII,124: Nor would she imploy Her husband (though perhaps in debt to years As far as I am). c1624 (1639) Massinger *Unnatural Combat* 2.3.108−10: The praise . . . Must of necessity raise new desires In one indebted more to yeares. 1629 (1630) Massinger *Picture* 3.6.154f.: I am not yet so much In debt to yeares. 1636 (1655) Massinger *Bashful Lover* 3.1.111f.: You direct me sir As one indebted more to years.
Shakespeare: *1H4* 3.2.103

D168   To pay one's DEBT to nature (From c1500; Wh D116 from a1333)
Shakespeare: *R3* 2.2.94f., *Mac.* 5.9.5, *Son.* 126.11

D174   One   DECEIT   (falsehood) drives out another (*Deceit* from 1539 [Wh D121 c1520]; *falsehood Jn.*, *TNK*)
Shakespeare: *Jn.* 3.1.277, *TNK* 4.3.93f.

D179   He that DECEIVES (beguiles) another is oft deceived (beguiled) himself (*Varied* from 1484)
Shakespeare: *Oth.* 4.1.96f.
Cf W406: He has played WILY-BEGUILED with himself [OW891b from 1555; cf. Wh W280 c1475).

D180   He that once DECEIVES is ever suspected (*Varied* from 1576)
E.g., 1576 Pettie *Petite Pallace* 163: Can hee think to finde mee faithfull towards him, that am faithlesse to mine   owne   father?   1579   Lyly *Euphues* I,205: Well dothe he know . . . that she that hath bene faythlesse to one, will never be faythfull to any.
Shakespeare: *3H6* 4.4.30, *Oth.* 1.3.293, 3.3.206

D182 To deceive the DECEIVER is no deceit (From a1550; cf. Wh B213 [To defraud the beguiler is no fraud] from c1450)
Shakespeare: *AWW* 4.2.75f., *2H6* 3.1.264f.

D183.1 As good (a) DEED as drink (Cf. Introduction, p. xxiv) 1700 Congreve *Way of the World* 5.1.430−2: An it were not as good a deed as to drink . . . I would I might never take shipping.
Shakespeare: *TN* 2.3.126f., *1H4* 2.1.28−30, 2.2.22f.

D184.1 DEED(S) of darkness (1 murder; 2 fornication; 3 other) (Cf. Appendix B)
E.g., c1587 (c1592) Kyd *Spanish Tragedy* 2.5.25 (1): By day this deede of darknes had not beene. ?c1600 *Fatal Marriage* xvi (MSR 1834) (3): T'was a ded of darkenes. 1601 (1607) Marston *What You Will* Induction I,231 (2 mainly): O Fie some lights, sirs fie, let there be no deeds of darknesse done among us. c1605 (1612) Chapman *Widow's Tears* 1.3.161 (2): They . . . swallow downe the deedes of darknesse.
Shakespeare: *Lr.* 3.4.87, *Per.* 4.6.29

(?) D189 As the stricken DEER withdraws himself to die (*Varied* from 1557; OW780bf. supplements)
Shakespeare: *AYL* 2.1.33−5, *Tit.* 3.1.89f., *Ham.* 3.2.271

D195 DELAY breeds danger (is dangerous) (From 1548; Wh D157 from a1300)
Shakespeare: *1H6* 3.2.33, *1H4* 3.2.180

(?) D198.1 DELAYS are (not) denials (OW176b; as below, except *Ant.*)
1586 Warner *Albion's Eng.* IV.xxi M1: Delay, he sayeth, breedeth doubts, but sharpe denyall death. 1611 Cotgrave s.v. Vouloir: A delay imports a deniall. 1907 W. H. G.

Thomas *Comment.* on *Gen.* i-xxv: God's delays to Abraham were not denials.
Shakespeare: *Ant.* 2.1.3

D198.2 To feed with DELAYS
E.g., 1575 Gascoigne *Dan Bart. of Bathe* I,122: Feede them there with freshe delayes. 1580 Lyly *Euphues and his England* II,65: I wil not feede you with delayes. c1590 (1594) Greene & Lodge *Looking Glass* 128: Feed ye on delaies? c1593 (1598) Marlowe *Hero and Leander* I.425f.: She, wanting no excuse To feed him with delays, as women use.
Shakespeare: *Tit.* 4.3.43

D201 He that asks faintly begs a DENIAL (*Varied* from a1591; OW20b Seneca)
Shakespeare: *R2* 5.3.103

(?) D202.1 DENY it if you can
c1564 *Bugbears* 5.2.47: Say Naye if you can. c1590 (1595) Peele *Old Wives Tale* 709f.: Are not you the man sir, denie it if you can sir. Again 716.
Shakespeare: *2H6* 4.2.146, *2H4* 2.1.103

D211 DESIRE has no rest (1621, cf. 1582)
I.e., G. Harvey *Marginalia* 201: Desier sufferith no delay. 1621 Burton *Anatomy of Melancholy* I.ii.iii.11 I,324: A true saying it is, Desire hath no rest.
Shakespeare: *Son.* 147.10

D216 DESPAIR (Love) makes cowards courageous (*Varied*; *despair* from 1612 [OW178a 1579; Wh D168 c1420] ; *love* from 1576)
Shakespeare: *3H6* 1.4.40, *Oth.* 2.1.214−7, *Ven.* 1158, *Luc.* 272f.

(?) D216.1 In DESPITE of God (heaven, Christ) (Cf. Appendix B)
c1380 *Sir Ferumb.* 5807−9: He . . . afterward, in be dyspyt of crysst, Spet on be sant [*OED* 5a]. c1588 G.

Wither *View of the Marginal Notes* 2L1ᵛ: It may be you know the common Italian proverbe, In despite of God.

Shakespeare: *Cym.* 5.5.58f.

D221.1 As the DEVIL (luck) would have it (would)
1559 "Northumberland" 81 *Mirror for Magistrates* 135 (devell would). 1568 U. Fulwell *Like Will to Like* B1: When ye devil wil have it so it must needs so be. 1590 ?Nashe *Almond for a Parrat* III,344. c1602 (1607) Middleton *Family of Love* 4.4.112 (devil would). c1604 (1607) Middleton *Phoenix* 1.2.10f. 1606 Dekker *Seven deadlie Sinns* ed. Brett-Smith 42. 1673 Dryden *Assignation* 2.3.148 (ill luck will); 5.3.26.

Shakespeare: *Wiv.* 3.5.83, *1H4* 2.4.221

D225 The DEVIL and his dam (Cf. Appendix B) (From c1547; Wh D181 from c1350)
Shakespeare: *Err.* 4.3.51, *Shr.* 1.1.105, 3.2.156, *Wiv.* 1.1.149, 4.5.106, *1H6* 1.5.5, *Jn.* 2.1.127f., *Tit.* 4.2.64f., *Oth.* 4.1.148

D230 The DEVIL can cite Scripture for his purpose (*Varied* from 1579; OW180a from 1573; cf. Matt. 4.6)
Shakespeare: *MV* 1.3.98, *R3* 1.3.333−7

(?) D231 The DEVIL can transform himself into an angel of light (Cf. 2 Cor. 11.14; from c1577; Wh S61 c1450)
Shakespeare: *Err.* 4.3.55f., *LLL* 4.3.253, *Ham.* 2.2.599f., *Oth.* 2.3.351f.

D238.1 The DEVIL he (etc.) is (20b from 1589)
E.g., 1546 Heywood *Dialogue* II.i F3: One sayde, a well favourd olde woman she is. The devyll she is, said an other.
Shakespeare: *TN* 2.3.147

(?) D240.1 The DEVIL is a gentleman
Shakespeare: *H5* 4.7.137f., *Lr.* 3.4.143

(?) D241.1 The DEVIL is a liar and the father of lies (John 8.44; Wh D186 from c1000)
Shakespeare: *R3* 1.2.73, *1H4* 2.4.225

D243.1 The DEVIL is at one's elbow (Cf. Appendix B: To be at one's ELBOW) (Wh D211 [1])
I.e., 1534 More *Passion* 1315 C(2−6): We may well thyncke that the devyll is than even besy aboute us, and not as it is commenly sayde at our elbowe, but, even at our very harte.
Add: c1611 Dekker (1631) *Match Me in London* 5.2.101f.: Were thy case my case; I would set a Divell at her elbow in the very Church. 1621 (1658) Dekker et al. *Witch of Edmonton* 5.1.127−9: Thou never art so distant From an evil Spirit, but that thy Oaths, Curses and Blasphemies pull him to thine Elbow. 1666 TOR. *It. Prov.*, note 78, p. 134: The English say, Talk of the Devil, and he's presently at your elbow [in D294].
Shakespeare: *MV* 2.2.2f., *R3* 1.4.145−8, *Oth.* 5.1.3

(?)D263 The DEVIL rides on a fiddlestick (From *1H4*; ditto OW183b)ⁿ
Shakespeare: *1H4* 2.4.487f.

ⁿCf. Introduction, p. xx.

D266 The DEVIL sometimes speaks the truth (*Varied* from *R3*; OW183b supplements)
E.g., 1597 *Politeuphuia* 258ᵛ: The devils ofttimes spake truth in oracles, to the intent they might shadow theyr falshoods the more winningly.
Shakespeare: *R3* 1.2.73, *Mac.* 1.3.107, 123f.

D266.1   The DEVIL take all.
1589 Lyly *Pappe with an Hatchet* III,401: Marie the divell take al. 1596 (1598) Chapman *Blind Beggar of Alexandria* i.185: Now the great foole [cf. D242: The devil is an ass] take them all. 1609 W Est *Scourge of Securitie* E8ᵛ f.: God will have all or none. . . .He will . . . have the whole, or let the divel take al.
Shakespeare: *Wiv.* 1.3.76

D273   Give the DEVIL his due (From 1589)
Shakespeare: *TN* 1.5.250f., *1H4* 1.2.52f., 119, *H5* 3.7.116f.

D278   He must needs go that the DEVIL drives (From 1523)
Shakespeare: *AWW* 1.3.29f.

D288   Let the DEVIL pay the maltman (From c1536)
Shakespeare: *1H4* 1.2.52f.

D321   To move as does the DIAL hand, which is not seen to move (*Varied* from 1580; not in OW)
Add e.g.: 1580 Lyly *Euphues and his England* II,218f.: You were ignorant of the practises, thinking the diall to stand stil, bicause you cannot perceiue it to move. 1598 Meres *Palladis Tamia* 2L5ᵛ: Wee perceive the shadow of a diall passed, but perceyve it not passing.
Shakespeare: *Oth.* 4.2.54f., *Son.* 77.7f., 104.9f.

(?) D323.1 DIAMONDS cut glass (fig.)
1577 Grange *Golden Aphroditis* D4ᵛ (again F2ᵛ): The Dyamant cutteth the Glasse.
Shakespeare: *Per.* 2.3.36
Cf. Wh D227 (OW352b): As hard as a diamond; Wh G112: As frail as glass.

D326.1   He that DIES this year is excused for the next (OWa186b; 1578 only)

I.e., 1578 Thos. White *Sermon at Paul's Cross* 3 Nov. 1577, 81: That Heathen proverb . . . too common among Christians: He that dieth this yere is scused for the next.
Shakespeare: *2H4* 3.2.238

D335   There is no DIFFERENCE of bloods in a basin (*Varied* from 1562; OW187b from 1560)
Add: 1593 T. Churchyard *Challenge* N2ᵛ: Every mans blood in a bason lookes of one color.
Shakespeare: *AWW* 2.3.118–20

D336   There is small DIFFERENCE to the eye of the world in being nought and being thought so (1732 FUL., cf. 1581, *Son.*; cf. Introduction, p. xix)
I.e., 1581 Guazzo (Pettie) *Civile Conversation* III II, 31: She shall finde small difference (in respecte of the worlde) betweene beeing naughte, and beeing thoughte naughte.
Add: 1576 Pettie *Petite Pallace* 226: As good to bee naught for somewhat as to bee thought naught for nothing.
Shakespeare: *Son.* 121.1f.

D345   Cast no DIRT into the well that has given you water (1678 Ray, 1732 FUL., cf. *Tit.*, *Luc.*; OW189a adds 1707)
Add: 1595 R. Southwell *Saint Peters Complaint* 107f.: But I that dronke the drops of heavenly flood: Bemyred the giver with returning mud.
Shakespeare: *Tit.* 5.2.170, *Luc.* 577

D351.1   DISCORDS make harmony (*Varied*)ⁿ
1548 Elyot s.v. Concordia: Discors concordia, a unyon of thynges together, havynge contrarye natures and operations. 1565 Cooper s.v. Concordia: Discors concordia. Ovid. Joyning of thinges by nature contrarie. 1579 Spenser *Shepheardes Cal-*

ender Ded. Ep. 100f.: So oftentimes a dischorde in musick maketh a comely concordaunce. 1580 Lyly *Euphues and his England* II,151: In Musicke there are many discords, before there can be framed a Diapason. 1590 Spenser *Faerie Queene* 3.2.15.9: Dischord ofte in musicke makes the sweeter lay. 1599 Davies *Nosce Teipsum* 751f.: There's harmony in discords. 1601 (1603) Dekker et al. *Patient Griselda* 5.2.287f.: Discords mag good musicke.

Shakespeare: *MND* 4.1.117f., 5.1.60, *AWW* 1.1.172, *2H6* 2.1.55, *Tit.* 2.1.69f.

[n]Cf. e.g., Edgar Wind, *Pagan Mysteries in the Renaissance* (London, 1958), pp. 81–88 on *Harmonia est discordia concors.*

D354 DISCRETION is the better part of valor (Entry form based on *1H4*, idea from 1477; OW189b supplements, including *MND, Cor.*)

Shakespeare: *MND* 5.1.231f., *1H4* 5.4.119, *Cor.* 1.1.202f.

D357 A desperate DISEASE must have a desperate cure (*Varied* from 1539; OW178af. adds Latin [Extremis malis extrema remedia] and supplements)

Add e.g.: 1579 Lyly *Euphues* I,213f.: A desperate disease is to be committed to a desperate Doctor. 1593 Nashe *Christs Teares* II,20: To desperate diseases must desperate Medicines be applyde.

Shakespeare: *Ado* 4.1.252, *Rom.* 2 Chor. 13f. 4.1.68–70, *Ham.* 4.3.9f., *Mac.* 4.3.214f., *Cor.* 3.1.154f., 219–21

D363.1 A DISH for a king (Wh D258 [1])

I.e., c1495 *Arundel Vulgaria* 7.22: A disch for a kynge.

Shakespeare: *WT* 4.3.8

D380.1 Not worth a DISH-CLOUT (cloth) (*Varied*)

1594 Nashe *Unfortunate Traveller* II,301: He makes a dishcloth of his own Country in comparison of *Spaine*. 1596 Nashe *Saffron-Walden* III,54: Canonizing . . . the contemptiblest worlds dish-cloute for a Relique. 1601 A. Dent *Plaine Mans Path-way* L3[v]: You esteeme it no more then a dish-clout. 1636 (1655) Massinger *Bashful Lover* 5.1.32f.: I am gazing on This gorgeous House, our Cote's a dishclout to it.

Shakespeare: *Rom.* 3.5.219.

D381.1 To know one's DISTANCE (Cf. Appendix B)

1612 Jonson *Alchemist* 4.1.78: I pray you, know your distance. 1617 (1647) Fletcher *Mad Lover* 1.1 III, 5: I warrant you he knows his distance. 1624 (1640) Fletcher *Rule a Wife* 3.1. III, 193: He knows his distance Madam. 1629 Massinger *Roman Actor* 5.2.61: Know your distance.

Shakespeare: *AWW* 5.3.212

D398 Do well and have well (From 1480)

Shakespeare: *Shr.* 4.1.36f.

D402 It is better to DO well than to say well (Collections from 1596, variant 1567)

Shakespeare: *H8* 3.2.153.f.

D407 What we DO willingly is easy (*Varied* from a1593; ditto OW192b)

Add: 1560 T. Wilson *Rhetorique* 30: Goodwill makes great burthens light.

Shakespeare: *Mac.* 2.3.50, *Tmp.* 3.1.29f.

D426 That is but one DOCTOR'S opinion (From 1659; OW193b from c1552)

E.g., 1578 T. White *Sermon at Paul's Cross* 3 Nov. 1577 32: You will say . . . it is but one doctours opinion. 1592

Greene *Quip* XI,291: The Doctors doubt of that, quoth Cloth-breeches for I am of a different opinion.
Shakespeare: *Wiv.* 5.5.174

D430   Not worth a DODKIN (doit) (*Dodkin* from c1589 [1594]; *doit* 1607; OW193b supplements, adds *Tim.*)
Add: c1599 (1602) Marston *Antonio and Mellida* 2.1.89: A prince not worth a doit.
Shakespeare: *Cor.* 5.4.57, *Tim.* 1.1.211f.

(?) D441   As weary as a DOG (?c1515, *Shr.*, 1602) (Cf. *OED Dog-weary* from *Shr.*)
I.e., c1515 A. Barclay *Eclog.* II 18: On one dish dayly nedes shalt thou blowe, Till thou be all wary as dogge of the bowe [Wh D304 unique].
Shakespeare: *Shr.* 4.2.60

D443   Beat the DOG (whelp) before the lion (*Varied; whelp* from 1557 [Wh W211 from c1395], *dog* from *Oth.*; OW37a adds Latin, supplements)
Shakespeare: *Oth.* 2.3.274f.

D449   The DOG (wolf) barks in vain at the moon (*Varied; dog* from 1520, *wolf* from 1580)
Shakespeare: *AYL* 5.2.109f., *JC* 4.3.27

D453   A DOG (man, etc.) of wax (Cf. Appendix B) (*Man* from *Rom.*, *dog* from 1607; OW196a *dog* 1599)
Add e.g.: c1611 (1618) Field *Amends for Ladies* 3.3.99f.: When he is in his scarlet clothes, he looks like a man of wax, and I had as lief have a dog o' wax.
Shakespeare: *2H4* 1.2.158f., *Rom.* 1.3.76

D455   The DOG returns to his vomit (Cf. Prov. 26.11, 2 Peter 2.22) (From 1535; cf. Wh H567 from a900)
Shakespeare: *2H4* 1.3.97−9

D458   The DOG to his vomit and the swine (sow) to his (her) mire (Cf. 2 Peter 2.22) (From 1508; Wh H567 from a900)
Shakespeare: *H5* 3.7.64f.

D460   The DOG who hunts foulest hits at most faults (Collections from 1659, plus faint analogues in *TN*, 1637)
Shakespeare: *TN* 2.5.127f.

D464   Every (A) DOG has his (a) day (From c1527)
Shakespeare; *R2* 3.2.103, *Ham.* 5.1.292

D487   It is an ill DOG that deserves not a crust (Collections from 1580)
Shakespeare: *Cor.* 1.1.206

D488   It is an ill (poor) DOG that is not worth the whistling (Collections from 1546, *variant* 1602, *Lr.*)
I.e., 1602 Breton *Packet Letters* Pt. I: *Wks.* II,19: There are more maids then Maulkin [M39], and I count my selfe worth the whistling after.
Shakespeare: *Lr.* 4.2.29

(?) D497.1   No more trust than in a DOG'S TAIL (Wh D336 [1])
I.e., a1464 Capgrave *Chronicle* 281 11−2 : It was no more trost to the Pope writing than to a dogge tail (*var.* to a dogge's tail waggyng).
Shakespeare: *Lr.* 2.2.67

D506   To be (old) DOG at it (Cf. Appendix B) (From *TGV*; OW194b from 1590)
Shakespeare: *TGV* 4.4.12f., *AYL* 1.1.81, *TN* 2.3.60f.

D506.1   To beat one like a DOG a1533 *Arthur* 475 (19−20): They . . . bet them downe lyke dogges [in Wh D331]. c1560 (c1569) T. Ingelend *Disobedient Child* E4^v: Lyke a dogge, with a Cudgell I shalbe beaten. 1590 ?Nashe *Almond for a Parrat* III, 349: Your Bookes must bee lookt over, and you beaten lyke a dogge for your lying. 1607 Sharpham *Cupid's Whirligig* ed. Nicoll 58: Ladie, in your defence I would beate him like a Dog.

Shakespeare: *TN* 2.3.141f., *1H4* 3.3.86f., *Cor.* 4.5.51f.

D507 To blush like a black DOG (From 1579)

Shakespeare: *Tit.* 5.1.121f.

D509 To die like a DOG (a dog's death) (Cf. Appendix B) (From 1600; OW185bf. from 1529; Wh D321 from c1300)

E.g., 1481 Caxton *Godeffroy* 203.38−9: Dyeng and languysshyng for hongre lyke as other hundes. 1593 *Jack Straw* F1: In strangling cords die like dogs. 1600 (1659) Day & Chettle *Blind Beggar* H2^v: Let me dye like a Dog on a Pitchfork.

Shakespeare: *2H4* 2.4.174, *Tim.* 2.2.86f.

D510.1 To have as much pity as a DOG (Wh D326 a1500)

Shakespeare: *TGV* 2.3.10f.

D510.2 To lie (in field, etc.) like a DOG (hound) (Wh D329 *varied* from c1300)^n

Shakespeare: *Tmp.* 3.2.19

^{n}The dogs in Whiting's five examples are all dead.

D513.1 To toss like a DOG in a blanket

E.g., 1592 Nashe *Strange Newes* I,306: He tost his imagination like a dogge in a blanket. 1597 (1599) Chapman *Humorous Day's Mirth* 1.5.8−10: Ile have thee taken out in a blanket, tossed from forth our hearing. / In a blanket? what, do you make a puppie of me? c1599 (1602) Marston *Antonio and Mellida* 4.1.275: I'll toss love like a dog in a blanket. c1621 (1633) Massinger *New Way to Pay Old Debts* 4.1.36: Tossed like a dog still! 1626 (1631) Jonson *Staple of News* 4.3.80: You will be tost like

Block [margin: One of his Dogges], in a blanket else.

Shakespeare: *2H4* 2.4.222f.

D514 To use one like a DOG (From 1618; OW856b from 1530)

E.g., 1612 Brinsley *Ludus Literarius* (1627, ed. Campagnac) 291: To use them worse, then we would use a dogge, as they say.

Shakespeare: *MND* 2.1.210, *Lr.* 2.2.136f.

D519 The worst DOG that is wags his tail (Collections *varied* from 1578)

Shakespeare: *Lr.* 2.2.67

D526 All DOGS bark not (No dogs shall bark) at him (From 1540; OW197b supplements)

E.g., 1589 T. Cooper *Admon. People Eng.* E3: If he shall by any cunning bee able to pull away the reward of learning, hee right well seeth that hee shall have farre fewer dogges to barke at him.

Shakespeare: *MV* 1.1.94, *Lr.* 3.6.62f.

D528 Cowardly DOGS bark much (*Varied* from 1539)

Shakespeare: *H5* 2.4.69−71

D531 DOGS barking aloof bite not at hand (Collections from 1611, *variant* 1596 [OW197b 1592])

I.e., 1592 Delamothe 5: A dogge that barkes farre of, dares not come neare to bite.

Shakespeare: *H5* 2.4.69−71

(?) D533 DOGS must eat (*Cor.*)

Shakespeare: *Cor.* 1.1.206
Cf. D538: Hungry DOGS will eat (love) dirty puddings.

D538 Hungry DOGS will eat (love) dirty puddings (From 1546)

E.g., c1547 J. Bale *Three Laws* II B4^v: Where hungry dogges lacke meate, They wyll durty puddynges eate, For wante of befe and conye.

Shakespeare: *Cor.* 1.1.206

D539   Like DOGS, if one barks all
bark (Collections from 1639, *varied*
from 1612; OW198a adds Latin)
Shakespeare: *H8* 2.4.160f.

D556   Here is the DOOR and there is
the (lies your) way (From c1475)
Shakespeare: *Shr.* 3.2.210, *TN*
1.5.202, 3.1.134

D567   As dead (deaf, dumb) as a
DOORNAIL (*Dead* from *2H6*;
OW170b from c1350)
Shakespeare: *2H6* 4.10.40f., *2H4*
5.3.120f.

D568   As dull as (To sleep like) a
DORMOUSE (*Varied* from 1608;
Wh D353 from c1450)
E.g., c1450 Idley 95.866–7: Be
stronge in herte, bow not as a wande,
Or as a dormoyse that al day slepeth.
Shakespeare: *TN* 3.2.19f.

D570.1   To be stripped to one's
DOUBLET and hose (Cf. Appendix
B)
E.g.,1566 (1575) Gascoigne *Jocasta* 1
Dumb Show I,246: Drawne in by
foure Kinges in their Dublettes and
Hosen. 1566 (1575) Gascoigne *Supposes* 2.1.171–4: For revenge he had
sworne to . . . sende them home in
their dublet and their hose. 1605
Jonson et al. *Eastward Ho* 4.2.84–90:
They . . . are come dropping to
towne, like so many Masterlesse
men, i'their doublets and hose, without Hatte, or Cloake.
Shakespeare: *Wiv.* 3.1.46, *Ado*
5.1.199f.

D572   As innocent (harmless) as a
DOVE (Matt. 10.16) (From 1580)
Shakespeare: *Shr.* 3.2.157, *2H6*
3.1.69–71, *2H4* 3.2.159f.

D573   As loving (tame, meek, simple)
as a DOVE (pigeon) (*Loving* from
c1553, *tame* 1616; Wh D359 *meek*
from c1300; Wh D361 *simple* from
a1400)

Shakespeare: *Shr.* 2.1.293, *MND*
1.1.171, 1.2.82f., *PP* 7.2

D573.2   As white as a DOVE (Wh
D363 from c1440 [2])
Add: c1445 Lydgate *Miracles of St.
Edmund* 442.189; Ek whan a dowe
with snowych ffeherys whight [in
Wh S442: To be like snow].
Shakespeare: *Rom.* 1.5.48, 3.2.76,
Per. 4 Chorus 31–3, *WT* 4.4.363,
Ven. 10

D574   DOVES have no gall (*Varied*
from 1577; Wh D364 from c1000)
Shakespeare: *2H4* 3.2.159f., *Ham.*
2.2.577

D576.1   As soft as DOWN
c1587 (1590) Marlowe *2 Tamburlaine*
1.4.25: Their hair as white as milk
and soft as down. 1598 R. Tofte *Alba*
E2^v: As soft as Thistle down." 1606
Marston *Fawn* 4.1.474f.: A soule as
soft as spotless down upon the swan's
fair breast. 1607 Sharpham *Cupid's
Whirligig* ed. Nicoll 9: Was not my
behaviour unto thee as soft as
Downe?
Shakespeare: *1H4* 1.3.7, *WT*
4.4.363

(?) D587   DREAMS are lies (dotages,
etc.) (*Varied* from 1610–25; OW202a
from 1584, Wh D387 from a1376)
Shakespeare: *Rom.* 1.4.51

D592   He never DREAMED of it (Cf.
Appendix B) (1639 CL., cf. *Ham.*,
Oth.; not in OW)
Add (from *OED* Dream v^2. 5): 1538
Starkey *England* EETS I.ii.36: Yf a
man have helth and ryches, [he] ys
then of al men iugyd happy and fortunate . . . though he never dreme of
vertue. 1588 *Marprel. Epist.* ed.
Arber 27: They see themselves as-
sayled with such weapons, whereof
they never once drempt [in Wilson,
"Proverbial Wisdom of Shakespeare"].
Shakespeare: *Ham.* 2.2.10, *Oth.*
1.1.5

(?) D605.1 DRINK before you go c1589 (1592) Lyly *Midas* 1.2.139: Drinke before you goe. 1600 (1608) R. Armin *Nest of Ninnies* G4ᵛ: A worldling right, who as the word is, Drinck before you goe, sets the cart before the horse and sayes, goe before you drinke. 1614 (1631) Jonson *Bartholomew Fair* 1.4.96−9: Will't please you drinke, Master Waspe? / . . . you'ld ha' me gone, would you? Shakespeare: *Shr.* 5.1.11, *Ado* 3.5.53

D608.1 To DRINK more than will do one good ?1588 (1599) Porter *Two Angry Women of Abingdon* iv (MSR 1061f.) (Nicholas Proverbes): I know youle put a man over the shooes, and if you can, but he's a foole wil take more then wil do him good. x (2274) (Coomes): I have drunk more then wil do me good. Shakespeare: *2H4* 2.4.119f.

D612.1 To eat honey like a DRONE (in Wh D408 [To be like a drone]) I.e.,1408 Vegetius(1) 10b: Forsothe he is but as a drane in an hyve, and devoureth and etith out the hony. Add e.g.: 1578 T. Blenerhasset "Cadwallader" 145 *2 Mirror for Magistrates* 447: Like buzzing Drones they eate the hony of the Bee. 1583 Melbancke *Philotimus* D2: Neither would I have thee a drone to eate the swete that others sweat for, that ye eate ye hony, and they hould the hyve. Shakespeare: *Per.* 2 Chor. 18f., 2.1.46f., *Luc.* 836

D613 As lost as a DROP of water in the sea (*Varied* from 1567; OW204bf. from c1548) E.g., c1548 J. Bale *Imge of both Churches* Pt. 3 P.S. 623: Scarce is it in comparison . . . as one drop of water to the whole sea. Shakespeare: *Err.* 1.2.35−8, 2.2.125−7

D618 Constant DROPPING will wear the stone (*Varied* from 1530; cf. Job 14.19; OW141a Ovid, from c1200) Shakespeare: *Tro.* 3.2.186, *3H6* 3.1.38, 3.2.50, *Tit.* 2.3.140f, *Ven.* 200, *Luc.* 560, 959, *LC* 290f.

(?) D630.1 (As) dainty (as a) DUCK 1587 T. Churchyard "Wolsey" 194 *Mirror for Magistrates* 502: And I did swim, as dainty as a ducke. 1624 T. Heywood *Captives* 1.3 (MSR 622f.): Ffor see you, not too women, daynty ducks, woold they coold swime as [well]. Shakespeare: *MND* 5.1.281, *WT* 4.4.317

D634 Give everyone his DUE (Cf. Rom. 13.7; from c1588 [1599]; OW303a supplements) Shakespeare: *Tro.* 2.2.173f., *H5* 3.7.3f., *Tim.* 3.1.35

D637 To dine with DUKE HUMPHREY (From 1592; OW188a from 1591) Shakespeare: *R3* 4.4.174−7

D642 Draw DUN out of the mire (From *Rom.*; OW208b ditto, but combines with D643 [from c1386]) Shakespeare: *Rom.* 1.4.41 Cf. D643: Dun is in the mire.

D644 DUN is the mouse (From *Rom.*; OW208b ditto) Shakespeare: *Rom.* 1.4.40

D645.1 To foresee (despise) as DUNG (Wh D438 from 897) E.g., 1447 Bokenham 280.10299−300: I as dung now despyse Al temporal thingis. Shakespeare: *Ant.* 5.2.7

D648.1 Like DUST (powder) in the wind (Wh D443 from c900) E.g., c1395 WBible Ps. 1.4: Thei [the wicked] ben as dust, which the wynd

castith awei fro the face of erthe.
1447 Bokenham 178.6509−10: Yet
shul thei rote and a-wey pace As doth
dust beforn the whynds face?
Shakespeare: *Lr.* 4.2.30f.

D650   To cast DUST in a man's eyes
(fig.) (From 1612; OW209a *varied*
from c1450)
Shakespeare: *Per.* 1.1.97

(?) D650.1   To lay the DUST with
tears (blood) (Cf. Appendix B)
1598 A. Munday *Death Robert, Earl of
Huntingdon* xv (MSR 2057), of blood:
And with that purple shower the
dust alaid. c1606 G. Wilkins *Miseries
of Enforced Marriage* iv (MSR 740−2),
of tears: I . . . did with this water, this
very water, lay the dust.
Shakespeare: *TGV* 2.3.31f., *R2*
3.3.42f., *Lr.* 4.6.196f.

D651   To lick (kiss) the DUST
(ground) (fig.) (Cf. Ps. 72.9, Micah
7.17; *lick dust* from 1535 Ps.; *kiss
ground* from 1589)
Add e.g.: c1592 (1594) Marlowe
Edward II 1.4.100f.: I'll fire thy
crazed buildings and enforce The
papal towers to kiss the lowly
ground.
Shakespeare: *Mac.* 5.8.28

(?) D659.1   To DYE scarlet (Cf. Appendix B)
1600 (1608) R. Armin *Nest of Ninnies*
G4: They may carrowse freely,
though they die deepe in scarlet.
Shakespeare: *1H4* 2.4.15

E

E1   The EAGLE does not catch flies
(From 1573; OW211a from 1563)
Shakespeare: *Ant.* 2.2.181

E2   An EAGLE does not hatch a dove
(*Varied* from 1581; OW211a Hor-
ace, 1578)
E.g., 1583 Melbancke *Philotimus*

G2v: Tigres are not borne of lambes,
nor doves of ravens.
Shakespeare: *Tit.* 2.3.149

E3   Only the EAGLE can gaze at the
sun (*Varied* from 1579; Wh E1 from
a1398)
Shakespeare: *LLL* 4.3.331, *3H6*
2.1.91f., *R3* 1.3.263f., *Cym.*
1.4.11−3, *TNK* 2.2.34
Cf. E7.1: The EAGLE-SIGHTED
can gaze at the sun.

E4.1   The EAGLE'S eye pierces the
sun (Wh E1 *varied* from a1398)
E.g., a1449 *Cok* in *MP* II 815.81−3:
The royall egle . . . / Whoos eyen
been so cleer and so bryght, / Off
nature he perce may the sunne.
Shakespeare: *R2* 3.3.68f., *Rom.*
3.5.219f.

E5   An EAGLE'S old age (*Varied* from
1548; OW211a adds 1533−4)
Shakespeare: *Tim.* 4.3.224

E6   To have an EAGLE'S eye (From
Rom.; OW211a supplements)
Shakespeare: *Rom.* 3.5.219f.

E7   EAGLES fly alone (From 1590)
E.g., 1590 Sidney *Arcadia* I.ix I,56:
Eagles we see fly alone, and they are
but sheepe, which alwaies heard
together. c1613 (1623) [probably
from Sidney and *Tro.*] Webster
Duchess of Malfi 5.2.31f.: Eagles commonly fly alone: They are Crowes,
Dawes, and Sterlings that flocke together. 1639 CL. s.v. *Solitudo* 291.
Shakespeare: *Tro.* 1.2.243f.

E7.1   The EAGLE-SIGHTED can
gaze at the sun (*Varied*)
1589 Greene *Menaphon* VI,105: I
cannot chuse, being Eagle-sighted,
but gaze on the Sunne the first time I
see it. c1602 (1637) T. Heywood
Royal King 1.1 VI,7: I was borne
Eagle-sighted, and to gaze In the
Suns fore-head.
Shakespeare: *LLL* 4.3.222−4

Cf. E3: Only the EAGLE can gaze at the sun.

E11 He cannot hear on that EAR (side) (*Side* from 1533, *ear* from 1559)
Shakespeare: *JC* 1.2.213

E13 To turn (give) a deaf EAR (From 1540; E14 from a1396)
Shakespeare: *JC* 1.2.213

E14 When your EAR tingles (burns, glows) people are talking about (embarrassing) you (*Varied* from 1546; Wh E12 from c1385)
Shakespeare: *Ado* 3.1.107

E16 He may go shake his (Go shake your) EARS (From c1560; OW719a from 1537)
Shakespeare: *TN* 2.3.125, *JC* 4.1.26

E18 Lend (me) your EARS (awhile) (From *JC*; OW455b from 1581)
Shakespeare: *Shr.* 4.1.60, *JC* 3.2.73

E22.1 To hear with one's own EARS 1594 *Jack Straw* 2.3 (MSR 570): Trust me with my eares I heard him. c1618 (1661) Middleton *Hengist* 5.1.287: I heard them say it with my own ears. 1673 Dryden, *Assignation* 3.1.280: I heard her with these Eares.
Shakespeare: *2H4* 2.2.65f.

E23 To set (etc.) together by the EARS (From 1546)
Shakespeare: *AWW* 1.2.1, *Cor.* 1.1.233

(?) E27.1 As dead as EARTH 1616 W. Jackson *Celestial Husbandrie* 5 (of man): Living earth walkes upon dead earth, and shall, at the last be as dead, as his pavement, that he treads upon.
Shakespeare: *Lr.* 5.3.262

E27.1 As dull as EARTH c1611 (1631) Dekker *Match Me in London* 5.1.10f.: Thunder shakes Heaven first Before dull Earth can feele it. c1614 *Faithful Friends* 4.4 (MSR 2659): Dull as the earthe, more ignorant then fooles. 1635 H. Glapthorne *Lady Mother* 1.1 (MSR 146): He more Dull then earth.
Shakespeare: *TGV* 4.2.51f., *Rom.* 2.1.2

(?) E27.3 As far as EARTH from heaven (Wh E20 a1393)
Shakespeare: *TGV* 2.7.78

E28.1 EARTH is the (common) mother of us all (*OED Mother Earth* from 1586)
E.g., 1579 Lyly *Euphues* I,265: Is the earthe called the mother of all things onely bicause it bringeth foorth? No, but bicause it nourisheth those thinges that springe out of it. 1590 Spenser *Faerie Queene* 2.1.10.6: The earth, great mother of us all. c1590 (1605) *King Leir* 19 1628: I sweare by earth the mother of us all. c1592 (1594) Marlowe *Edward II* 3.2.128: By earth, the common mother of us all.
Shakespeare: *AYL* 1.2.201, *Rom.* 2.3.9, *Tim.* 4.3.177−9

E30 EARTH must go to earth (Dust to dust) (Cf. Gen. 3.19; *dust* from 1545; Wh E22 *dust* from c1000)
Shakespeare: *1H4* 5.4.85, *Rom.* 2.3.9, 3.2.59, *Cym.* 4.2.262ff., *Son.* 74.7
Cf. A119: ALL are of the same dust.

(?) E35.1 For my EASE (*of keeping off one's hat*)
1591 Florio *Second Fruits* 111: I do it for my ease. 1604 ?Webster Induction *Malcontent* 34: No, in good faith, for mine ease. 1607 Sharpham *Cupid's Whirligig* ed. Nicoll 56: I thanke ye heartily, tis for mine ease,

the weather is hot, hot, verie hot.
1633 Massinger *New Way to Pay Old Debts* 2.3.7f.: Is't for your ease You keep your hat off?
Shakespeare: *Ham.* 5.2.105

E42   You (etc.) take your EASE in your inn (From 1546; OW800a supplements)
Shakespeare: *1H4* 3.3.80f.

E43.1   As far as (From) the EAST from (to) the west (*Varied*; cf. Ps. 103.12, 107.3, Matt. 8.11)
E.g., c1485 *St. Paul* (Digby) 152–4: Ther is non suche living . . . Be est nor west, ferre nor nere. c1552 (c1567) Udall *Ralph Roister Doister* 3.3.25–8: He is . . . the . . . veriest lubber . . . Living in this worlde from the west to the east. 1580 Lyly *Euphues and his England* II,118: As far from trueth, as the East from the West. 1590 Spenser *Faerie Queene* 3.7.42.6f.: He . . . reeled to and fro from east to west. 1601 A. Dent *Plaine Mans Path-Way* Ee3: As farre as the East is from the West, so farre hath hee removed our sinnes from us.
Shakespeare: *AYL* 3.2.88, *Tro.* 2.3.263, *1H4* 1.3.195, *Oth.*4.2.143f., *Cym.* 4.2.372

E56   He that is at a low EBB at Newgate may soon be afloat at Tyburn (*Varied* from 1562 [1555 in OW495b])
Shakespeare: *1H4* 1.2.37f.

(?) E56.1   Neither EBB nor flow, but just standing water
1615 Webster "Fellow of a House" 14–6 Overbury *Characters* IV,34: His Religion lyes in wayte for the inclination of his Patron; neyther ebbes nor flowes, but just standing water, betweene *Protestant* and *Puritane*. 1633 T. Adams *Commentary . . . Saint Peter* 39, 68, 1390 (all borrowed from Webster).
Shakespeare: *Tmp.* 2.1.221–3

E56a   As black as EBONY (*LLL, TN,* 1607)
Add: 1598 (1601) A. Munday *Death Robert, Earl of Huntington* xviii (MSR 2746).
Shakespeare: *LLL*   1.1.243, 4.3.243, *TN* 4.2.38

(?) E56a.1   The EDGE of a feather-bed[n]
Shakespeare: *MV* 2.2.165

[n]Arden, following Warburton, calls "a cant phrase to signify the danger of marrying." I know of no supporting evidence. *OED Edge* I thinks *The Merchant of Venice* 2.2.165 and *Henry V* 3.6.47f. humorous variations on "the edge of the sword."

E57.1   To take off love's (someone's) EDGE
1598 Chapman *Hero and Leander* III.5: Love's edge is taken off. c1609 (1647) Beaumont & Fletcher *Coxcomb* 2.2.65f.: Coole your Codpiece, Rogue, or Ile cap a spell upon't, shall take your edge off. c1613 (1616) Beaumont & Fletcher *Scornful Lady* 5.1.63: You have ta'ne my edge off. c1614 *Faithful Friends* 1.1 (MSR 216): Take off the edge of Philadelphas greefe. 1635 H. Glapthorne *Lady Mother* 1.1: This country has tane my edge of quite.
Shakespeare: *Shr.* 1.2.72f., *MM* 1.4.58–61, *Ham.* 3.2.249f., *Tmp.* 4.1.28f.

E59   As nimble (quick) as an EEL (in a sandbag) (From c1611; OW567a from c1595, *quick* from *LLL*)
Shakespeare: *LLL* 1.2.28

E66   As like as one EGG is to another (*Varied* from 1542)
Shakespeare: *WT* 1.2.130

(?) E71.1   As good be an addled EGG as an idle bird (OW4a has *Euphues,* then *Tro.* 1617 *School of Defence* C3

Better an addle Egge than an ill Bird.
1732 Fuller no. 681.) See above, p.
xix.
Shakespeare: *Tro.* 1.2.133f.

E86   I have EGGS on the spit (From
1614; OW218b from 1598)
Shakespeare: *TNK* 2.3.73

E90   To take EGGS for money (From
1571; OW218a supplements)
Shakespeare: *WT* 1.2.161

E95   Not worth an EGGSHELL (egg)
(*Eggshell* from 1481; *egg* from c1500
[Wh A259 *ay* from a1300])
    Shakespeare: *Ham.* 4.4.53, *Lr.*
1.4.155−9, *Cor.*4.4.21

(?) E99.1   To pluck one by the
ELBOW (Cf. Appendix B)
1594 Nashe *Unfortunate Traveller*
II,266: My principall subiect pluckes
me by the elbowe.
Shakespeare: *2H4* 1.2.69f.

E100   To rub (scratch) the ELBOW
(fig.) (*Rub* from *LLL*, *scratch* from
1598; OW686b *scratch* from 1594)
Add: 1614 (1631) Jonson *Bartholomew Fair* 3.5.94−6: O rare! I would
faine rubbe mine elbow now, but I
dare not pull out my hand.
    Shakespeare: *LLL* 5.2.109, *1H4*
5.1.77

E102   To be out at ELBOWS (From
c1589; OW601b from 1586)
Shakespeare: *MM* 2.1.61

(?) E104   (Now he has) ELBOW-
ROOM (enough to turn him in) (Cf.
Appendix B) (*Varied* from c1540;
not in OW)
Shakespeare: *Jn.*5.7.28

(?) E105.1   The ELDER though fullest of pith is farthest from strength
1579 Lyly *Euphues* I,194: The Elder
tree thoughe hee bee fullest of pith,
is farthest from strength. 1589 Lyly
Pappe with an hatchet III,405:

Elders . . . being fullest of spungie
pith, prove ever the driest kixes.
Shakespeare: *Wiv.* 2.3.29

E107   He is (To be) out of his ELE-
MENT (From *Wiv., TN*; OW219a
ditto with 1599 analogue)
Add: 17 Sept. 1598 J. Chamberlain
I,45: Me thincks still I am out of my
element when I am among Lords.
    Shakespeare: *Wiv.* 4.2.177f., *TN*
3.1.57−9, 3.4.124, *Ham.* 2.2.141, *Lr.*
2.4.57f.

E112   The END justifies (does not
justify) the means (*Varied*; Shak.,
1620ff.; OW220b from 1583)
E.g., [1650 Jesuit Hermann Busen-
baum *Medulla theol.* Cum finis est
licitus, etiam media sunt licita.] 1583
G. Babington *Exposn. of the Commandments* PS 260: The ende good,
doeth not by and by make the
meanes good.
Add: c1604 (1605) Marston *Dutch
Courtesan* 4.2.46f.: Then let my
course be borne, though with side
wind, The end being good, the
means are well assigned.
    Shakespeare: *MV* 4.1.216, *MM*
3.1.257f., *Luc.* 528f.
    Cf. E203: Never do evil (ill) that
good may come of it.

E113.1   And there ('s) an END (*OED*
23 from *TGV*)
E.g., c1500 *Everyman* 850: Now farewell, and there an ende. 1575 Gascoigne *Dan Bart. of Bathe* I,102: One
word & there an end. 1596 Nashe
Saffron-Walden III,36: Nay, give the
divell his due, and there an ende.
1602 Jonson *Poetaster* 3.4.82f.: I love
good wordes, and good clothes, and
there's an end.
    Shakespeare: *Shr.* 5.2.98, *TGV*
1.3.65, 2.1.161, *Ado* 2.1.123f., *TN*
5.1.196f., *Tro.* 1.1.88, *R2* 5.1.69,
1H4 5.3.61, *2H4* 3.2.332, *H5* 2.1.10,
3.2.140f., *Rom.* 3.4.27f., *Mac.*
3.4.78f., *Cym.* 3.1.82

E116   The END crowns all (the work)
(From c1588 [c1592]; OW220b
Latin: Finis coronat opus, 1592;
both give early analogues without
crown)
E.g., 1592 Delamothe 29: The end
doth crowne 'the worke (La fin
couronne l'oeuvre).
Add: 1509 Watson *Ship* Ddl(25): For
the ende crowneth [Wh E75].
   Shakespeare: *Wiv.* 3.5.135f., *Tro.*
4.5.224, *AWW* 4.4.35, *2H6* 5.2.28

E116.1   The END tries (proves, etc.)
all (In E116, from c1550; Wh E81
from a1393)[n]
   Shakespeare: *Tro.* 4.5.225f., *2H4*
2.2.47, 2.4.280, *TNK* 1.2.113f.

[n]See Introduction, fn. 14.

E120   Everything has an END (From
c1475; Wh T87 from c1385)
   Shakespeare: *H5* 2.1.24

E122   He knows no END of his
good(s) (From 1562)
   Shakespeare: *AYL* 3.3.52f.

E124.1   Praise at the END (Wh E85
from a1300)
   Shakespeare: *Tro.* 3.2.90f.
   Cf. P83: Praise at parting.

E125   Remember (Mark) the END
(*Varied* from 1509; Wh E84 [from
c1280], 87 [from a1325]; Cf. Eccl.
7.36, etc.; OW843af. cites *Gesta Rom.*
ch. 103: Quidquid agas, prudenter
agas, et respice finem.)
E.g., 1550 Latimer *Serm.* 15 294:
Respice finem, mark the end; look
upon the end.
   Shakespeare: *Err.* 4.4.41, *2H4*
2.4.235, 280

E128.1   To draw to an END (i.e., to
conclude)
1566 *Answere for the Tyme* (STC
10388) B1: But to drawe to and [sic]
ende. 1589 Marprelate *Just censure*
D4: Well boy, to drawe to an ende.

1593 P. Stubbes *Motive to Good
Workes*180: But to drawe towards an
end. 1601 A. Dent *Plaine Mans Path-
Way* Ee7: Now then to conclude and
drawe to an end. 1604 Middleton
Father Hubburds Tale VIII,83: But to
draw to an end, as his patrimony did.
   Shakespeare: *Ham.* 3.4.216

E133.1   To make a good END (*OED*
8b 1667)
1583 A. Dent *Sermon of repentaunce*
D7[v]: It is merveilous to heare howe
the foolishe people of the world will
exalt them, and iustify them, saying:
he made a very good ende, as any
man could make, and died as quiet as
a Lamb, & set all things in good
order, before hee died. Hereupon
an other wicked & monstrous verlet
is encouraged to sinne. For thinketh
he, such a man lived as loosely as I, or
any man else, and yet hee made a
verie good ende. 1604 E. Grymeston
Miscelanea D2[v]: He that liveth well,
shall make a good end. 29 Oct. 1606
J. Chamberlain236: All the later part
of her sicknes she came to her self
and was well setled, and made a
goode end. 31 Dec.1612 400: Her
frends have the lesse cause to lament
her losse, specially seeing she made a
very goode and godly end.
   Shakespeare: *Ham.* 4.5.185f.

E136   He that ENDURES (suffers) is
not overcome (overcomes) (Collections from 1573; OW221b Virgil,
varied from c1374)
   Shakespeare: *Lr.* 3.4.18

E137   An ENEMY (adversity) makes
a man to know himself whereas a
friend (prosperity) flatters a man
and deceives him (*Varied; Adversity*
from 1573, *enemy* from *TN*, with
1508 analogue)
E.g., 1573 SANF. Ep. Ded. A3[v]: Adversitie is better than prosperity, for
the one maketh a man to know himself . . . the other engendreth pride
and forgetfulnesse of our humaine

condition. 1756 FRANKLIN 32: Love your Enemies, for they tell you your Faults.

Shakespeare: *TN* 5.1.12−20, *Lr.* 4.6.100−3

Cf. F410: It is better to have an open foe than a dissembling friend.

E137.1 A familiar ENEMY (foe) is the worst (Wh E97 *varied* from 897) E.g., a1500 Hill 130.14: In whom I trust most, sonnest me deseyvith.

Shakespeare: *Tmp.* 1.2.93−5

E140.1 Make your ENEMY your friend (OW222a 1639, cf. 1641) I.e., 1639 CL. 189. 1641 Fergusson 325: He is wise that can make a friend of a foe.

Shakespeare: *Mac.* 2.4.40f.

E146 ENGLAND is a good country but ill people (From 1659) Add: c1548 A. Borde *First Booke of the Introduction of Knowledge* C1: The Italyen and the Lombarde say. Anglia terra, bona terra, mala gent [sic]. That is to say, ye lande of England is a good land, but the people be yl.

Shakespeare: *2H6* 4.7.55f.

Cf. L49.1: A good land, a bad people.

(?) E155 One Englishman can beat three Frenchmen (Cf. *H5*, 1745; OW223b adds instances and analogues from 1748)

Shakespeare: *H5* 3.6.149f.

E157.1 X ENOUGH and (if) y enough (Cf. Appendix B) E.g., 1588 Greene *Pandosto* ed. Bullough VIII,181: We count our attire brave inough if warme inough. 1600 (1608) R. Armin *Nest of Ninnies* A3: One that was wise enough, and fond enough. 1600 (1602) Jonson *Poetaster* 4.1.31f.: Faith, impudently inough, mistries Chloe, and well inough. c1604 Marston *Malcontent* 3.1.108: Proud enough, and 'twill do

well enough. 1604 E. Grymeston *Miscelanea* H3^v: Death and misfortune come soone inough if slow inough. c1606 (1607) G. Wilkins *Miseries of Enforced Marriage* i (MSR 4): Tut, let us be Impudent enough, and good enough.

Shakespeare: *AWW* 4.1.20

E159 ENOUGH is enough (From 1546) Add: 1581 C. Thimelthorpe *Short Inventory* B4: Old lesson . . . quod satis est sufficit. 1590 Lodge *Rosalynde* ed. Bullough II,189: We have inough to satisfie: and Mistres I have so much Latin, Satis est quod sufficit.

Shakespeare: *LLL* 5.1.1

Cf. E158: Enough is as good as a feast [from 1546].

E175 ENVY (Calumny) shoots at the fairest mark (flowers, virtue) (*Varied; envy* from 1576, calumny from *MM*; not in OW)

Shakespeare: *MM* 3.2.186f., *Ham.* 1.3.38, *WT* 2.1.73f., *Son.* 70.2

E179 To ERR is human, (to repent is divine,) to persevere is diabolical (*Varied* from 1576; Wh S346 from c1390) E.g., 1487 *O thou most noble* 321(8f.): For the doctor saieth it is naturall to synne, But diabolike to persevere therein. 1576 Pettie *Petite Pallace* 7: Errare humanum est, in errore perseverare, bellvinum.

Shakespeare: *Per.* 1.3.43

E180 A sleeveless (bootless) ERRAND (Cf. Appendix B) (From 1546)

Shakespeare: *Tro.* 5.4.8f.

E186 To wash an ETHIOPE (blackamoor, Moor) white (From c1542; cf. Jer. 13.23; OW868a adds Lucian)

Shakespeare: *MND* 3.2.257

(?) E192.1 EVERYTHING must have its course (turn) (Wh E169 [2])

Shakespeare: *H5* 2.1.101f.
Cf. N48 (Nature), N81 (need), Y48 (youth), Wh F537 (Fortune) Wh K36 (kind), Wh L542 (love).

E194 He that is EVERYWHERE is nowhere (*Varied* from 1581)
E.g., Guazzo (Pettie) *Civile Conversation* II I,139: The Proverbe, That he is not any where, who is every where.
Add: 1592 ?Lyly *Quarrendon* I,462: But the harte that is everie where, is in deede no where.
Shakespeare: *TN* 2.4.75−8

E198 He sucked EVIL from the dug (*Varied* from 1531)
Shakespeare: *R3* 2.2.30, *Tit.* 2.3.145, *Rom.* 1.3.67f.

E200 He that helps the EVIL hurts the good (*Varied* from c1526; OW368a supplements)
E.g., 1539 Taverner *Publius* B2ᵛ: He hurteth the good, whosoever spareth the badde.
Shakespeare: *MM* 2.2.100−2

E203 Never do evil (ill) that good may come of it (From 1583; OW562af. from 1583 plus analogues; cf. Rom. 3.8)
E.g., 1582 G. Whetstone *Heptameron* I1: Men doo evill . . . that good may come of it, and it is allowed. And men doo good . . . that evill may come of it, and it is forbidden. 1583 G. Babington *Exposn. of the Commandments* 263: To doe evill that good may come of it, wee may not.
Shakespeare: *MV* 4.1.216, *R2* 2.3.145

(?)E212.1 To make one an EXAMPLE (Cf. Appendix B)
c1605 (1612) Chapman *Widow's Tears* 2.2.110f.: I beseech your good Honour . . . make him an example.
1609 (1616) Jonson *Epicoene* 4.2.118f.: I'll make thee an example.
1629 (1631) Jonson *New Inn* 5.2.64:

Ile make my selfe their booke, nay their example.
Shakespeare: *MM* 1.4.68, *Oth.* 2.3.251.

E215 To EXCUSE is to accuse (Collections, etc. from 1611, cf. *Jn.*; OW234a adds Latin [Hieronymus], French)
Shakespeare: *Jn.* 4.2.30f.

E222 No EXTREME will hold long (*Varied* from 1596 [1592]; OW235b supplements)
Shakespeare: *Ham.* 3.2.196f.

E231 The EYE is the window of the heart (mind) (*Mind* from 1545, *heart* from *R2*; ditto OW235b)
Add: 1586 Guazzo (B. Young) *Civile Conversation* IV II,179: The eies . . . are called the windowes of the heart, by the which love enters into the same, as many Poets both Greeke and Latine, have sufficiently declared.
Shakespeare: *LLL* 5.2.838, *R2* 1.3.208f.

(?) E231a The EYE sees not itself but by reflection (Analogue in Erasmus; *JC*, *Tro.*, 1600; not in OW)
I.e., 1600 Cawdray *Treas. Sim.* 428: As our eyes which do behold heaven and earth, and other innumearabl creatures of God, doo not see themselves, but looking in a Glasse . . . they perfectly see themselves.
Shakespeare: *Tro.* 3.3.105f., *JC* 1.2.52f.

E232 The EYE that sees all things else sees not itself (From 1594; OW236a from a1591)
Add: 1581 J. Bisse *Two Sermons* A8ᵛ: Many of them are like the eye, which seeth all thinges and cannot see it selfe.
Shakespeare: *AYL* 1.2.175, *Tro.* 3.3.105f., *JC* 1.2.52f.

E235 Have an EYE (Look) to the

main chance (From 1579)
Shakespeare: *2H6* 1.1.208–12

E236   He has an EYE behind (From
c1552; OW235b adds Plautus)
E.g., 1639 CL. s.v. Prudentia 266:
(behind him).
Shakespeare: *TN* 2.5.136, *Tim.*
1.2.163

E242.1   Let one's EYE be his (best)
cook
1583 P. Stubbes *Anatomie of Abuses*
ed. Furnivall II,34: According to the
old proverbe: Sit occulus ipsi coquus,
Let his eie be his best cooke.
Shakespeare: *H5* 5.2.148f.

E246   The sore EYE infects the sound
(*Varied* from 1561)
Shakespeare: *R3* 1.2.148

E248   To cry (look up) with one EYE
and laugh (down) with the other
(From c1520; Wh W538 [of women]
from 1369)[n]
Shakespeare: *Ham.* 1.2.11, *WT*
5.2.74–6

[n]This proverb is normally applied to
a hypocrite, or at least to someone
unsteadfast. But Claudius appears to
echo it without fear of such implications, and as Arden observes, there are
surely no such implications in the
gentleman's description of Paulina.
The sense, though not the language, is
more akin to L92a.

E248.1   To have an EYE (eyes) in
one's head[n]
1607 G. Wilkins *Miseries of Enforced
Marriage* x (MSR 2178): Are you
sure you ha eyes in your head.
Shakespeare: *1H4* 2.1.27f., *Cor.*
4.5.11f.
Cf. E259: He that has eyes in his
head will look about him [from
1616].

[n]OA *1H4* called "a common expression" (which it almost certainly was,

given the carrier's colloquial style);
except for 1616 Breton (E259),
however, OA's only evidence was an
irrelevant passage in Nashe.

E249.1   To love as one's own EYE
(eyesight) (Wh E221 *eye* from c1400
[2])
Add: 1562 A. Brooke *Romeus and
Juliet* 2149: Keepe it as thine eye.
1611 *Second Maiden's Tragedy* (MSR
771f.): Preserve more charily then
eyesight.
Shakespeare: *LLL* 5.2.444f., *Oth.*
3.4.66, *Lr.* 1.1.56
Cf. A290: As dear as the apple of
my eye.

E254   As many EYES as Argus (From
1538)
Shakespeare: *Tro.*1.2.29f.

E255   EYES as red as a ferret's (*Fierce*
1647, *red* a1700, cf. *JC*; OW236b *red*
1530)
Shakespeare: *JC* 1.2.186

E264.1   To believe one's (own) EYES
1519 Horman *Vulgaria* I2[v]: I can
scant byleue myn owne yies. 1607
Jonson *Volpone* 3.5.22: Pursue 'hem,
and beleeve your eyes. 1611 (1619)
Beaumont & Fletcher *King and No
King* 4.2.223–5: He . . . will ne'er
believe his eyes again. 1617 Middleton & Rowley *Fair Quarrel* 5.1.252:
Now, gentlemen, believe your eyes if
not my tongue. 1640 J. D. *Knave in
Grain* 3.2 (MSR 1376): Follow the
Doctor, believe your eyes.
Shakespeare: *Ham.* 1.1.56–8, *Oth.*
4.1.242f.

E264.2   To have one's EYES one's
own
22 Feb. 1600 J. Chamberlain 86:
Either theyre eyes were not theyre
owne, or els they had false spectacles
that made every thing that was don
seeme more then double. 1605 Jonson et al. *Eastward Ho* 4.1.149f.
(drunk): My braines, nor mine eyes

are not mine owne, yet. c1606 (1608) G Wilkins *Miseries of Enforced Marriage* iv (MSR 779): Oh: whats hear? Mine eyes are not mine own?
Shakespeare: *Ado* 4.1.71

E266.1   To see with one's own EYES (OW710a, from 1707)
c1553 (1575) Stevenson *Gammer Gurton's Needle* 4.4.21: I saw the needle, even with thes two eyes. 1596 Spenser *Faerie Queene* 6.12.18.4f.: For on her brest I with these eyes did vew The litle purple rose which thereon grew. c1615 (1657) Middleton *More Dissemblers besides Women* 3.1.114: Those things I saw with mine own eyes to-day. 1616 DR., s.v. Multitude, no. 1439: A man must see by his own eies. 1639 CL., s.v. Experientia, p. 110: I will trust mine own eyes better than report.
Shakespeare: *Rom.* 3.2.52, *Lr.* 4.6.141
Cf. E22.1: To hear with one's own ears.

(?) E273   To be an EYESORE (*OED* 2, 3 from 1530) (From 1546 Heywood)
Shakespeare: *Luc.* 205

F

F1   The FACE is the index of the heart (mind) (*Varied* from 1586; OW237a from a1575; *index* from c1593 [1598]; most examples reflect no proverbial formulation)
E.g., 1576 Lemnius (T. Newton) *Touchstone of Complexions* F1: The countenance . . . is the Image of the mynde. 1584 Withals I7: Your face doth testifie what you be inwardly.
Shakespeare: *TN* 1.2.50f., *Lr.* 3.6.53f., *WT* 1.2.447

F1.1   The FACE is no index to the heart (OW237a *varied* from 1567 [cf. on F1] ; no instance with *index*)
E.g., 1573 Sanford 98ᵛ: Iuvenal in his second Satyre sayeth: Fronti

nulla fides, that is, Trust not the face.
Shakespeare: *TN* 1.2.48−51, *Mac.* 1.4.11f.

F3   Fair FACE foul heart (*Varied* from 1584; cf. Wh F3−5, from a1400)[n]
Shakespeare: *Err.* 3.2.13, *H8* 3.1.145, *Rom.* 3.2.73, *Mac.* 1.7.82, 3.2.34f., *Luc.* 1530

[n]See Introduction, p. xxi, fn. 33.

F4   A fair FACE is half a portion (*Varied* from 1530)
E.g., 1591 FLOR. *Sec. F.* XII 191: But of all, the fayrest is the gretest treasure, For who borne is faire, is born an heir.
Shakespeare: *Lr.* 1.1.58

F5   A fair FACE must have good conditions (cannot have a crabbed heart [OW239a's entry form]) (*Varied* from c1572; OW239a supplements)
E.g., 1592 Delamothe 39: When the face is faire, the hart must be gentle. 1593 *Passionate Morrice* New Sh. S. 92: Building upon the proverbe . . .
Shakespeare: *Luc.* 1530

F7   A good FACE needs no paint (*Varied* from 1579)
E.g., 1579 Lyly *Euphues* Ep. Ded.I,181: Where the countenaunce is faire, ther neede no colours. 1608 J. Day *Law Tricks* 4.1 51: Good wine needs no bush [W462], nor a good face painting.
Shakespeare: *LLL* 2.1.13f.

F8   He has (To have) a brazen FACE (face of brass) (Cf. Appendix B) (From 1573)
Add: 1563 T. Churchyard "Shore's Wife" 297 *Mirror for Magistrates* 383: But he could set thereon a face of brasse.
Shakespeare: *LLL* 5.2.395, *Wiv.* 4.2.135, *Lr.* 2.2.28

F15.1   To die with one's FACE upward (*Varied*) (Cf. Appendix B) c1561 (1595) *Pedlar's Prophecy* (MSR 736f.): You are not like to live till you be old, Your fortune is to die upward. 1679 Dryden *Troilus and Cressida* 1.2 VI,299: Many a Grecian he has laid with his face upward.

Shakespeare: *Ado* 3.2.67−9, *JC* 5.3.93

F16 To laugh (smile) in one's FACE and cut one's throat (*Varied* from 1587; OW444b from 1390)

Shakespeare: *3H6* 3.2.182, *Ham.* 1.5.108, *Tim.* 1.2.46−9

F17 To set a good FACE on the matter (on a bad matter) (From 1562, *varied* from 1538)

E.g., 1538 Bale *K. Johan* 1978 100: Though it be a foul bye, set upon it a good face.

Shakespeare: *Son.* 137.12

F28 FAIR and foolish, black and proud, long and lazy, little and loud (From 1600)

E.g., 1600 W. Vaughan *Directions Health* V.iv 144: And the outward phisiognomy of the body, in the most part is verified by our ancient rimes: Faire and foolish, little and loud, Long and lazie, blacke and proud: Fat and merry, leane and sad, Pale and peevish, red and bad.

Shakespeare: *Oth.* 2.1.129ff.

F29 FAIR without but foul within (From c1550; OW240b *varied* from c1200)

Shakespeare: *Ado* 4.1.103, *Tro.* 5.8.1, *Mac.* 1.1.11, 1.3.38

Cf. F3: Fair face foul heart.

F32 He pins his FAITH (etc.) on another man's sleeve (*Faith* from 1660, *varied* from 1579)

E.g., 1604 (1607) Dekker *Westward Ho* 2.1.174: Who would pin their hearts to any Sleeve [?]

Shakespeare: *Oth.* 1.1.64

F33 No FAITH with heretics (From c1589 [1633]; OW241b from 1555)

Shakespeare: *Jn* 3.1.174f.

F34 There is no FAITH (trust, honesty) in man (*Trust* from 1586, *faith, honesty* from *Rom.*)

Add: 1601 A. Dent *Plaine Mans Path-Way* M5ᵛ: There is no truth, no honestie, no conscience, no simplicitie, no plaine dealing amongst men, in these most corrupt times. ?1621 Fletcher *Wild Goose Chase* 2.1.159f.: Is there no faith, No troth nor modesty in men?

Shakespeare: *1H4* 2.4.124f., *Rom.* 3.2.85f.

F34.1 As fresh as (the) FALCON (to the flight) (Wh F25)

E.g., c1300 *Beves* 36.735−6: Thanne was he ase fresch to fight, So was the faukoun to the flight.

Shakespeare: *R2* 1.3.61f.

F38.1 To FALL OUT and fall in (*Varied*)

1546 Heywood *Dialogue* I.xi D2: I came to fall in, and not fall out; II.i F4: Marke how they fell out, and how they fell in. 1600 (1603) Dekker et al. *Patient Grissil* 5.2.280: When lovers fall out is soone fall in. c1604 (1605) Marston *Dutch Courtesan* 4.1.83: Sometimes a falling out proves falling in.

Shakespeare: *Tro.* 3.1.103f.

F40 The FALLING-OUT of lovers is a renewing of love (*Varied* from 1520; OW242a Terence, supplements)

Shakespeare: *Son.* 119.11f.

Cf. F38.1: To fall out and fall in.

(?) F40.1 To fear FALSE FIRE

1606 W. Warner *Continuance of Albions England* K1: Who knowes false fire and feares? Who fat with painted meates they see? Who flies a

paper Giant? feares an Asse in Lyons skinne [A351]?
Shakespeare: *Ham.* 3.2.266

F47 (Too much) FAMILIARITY breeds contempt (From 1576; OW243b Pub. Syrus, Augustine, Alanus De Insulis, 1539)
Shakespeare: *Wiv.* 1.1.249f.

(?) F76 For FASHION'S sake, (as dogs go to the market [to church]) (1721, 1732; OW246a adds *AYL*)
Add: c1598 (1639) Deloney *2 Gentle Craft* 156: We must give our lovers an hundred denials for fashion sake. 1604 Marston *Malcontent* 4.5.108: Faith, as bawds go to church, for fashion sake.
Shakespeare: *AYL* 3.2.255

F79 The FAT (All the fat) is in the fire (From 1546)
Shakespeare: *TNK* 3.5.39

F83 It is impossible to avoid (undo) FATE (destiny) (*Varied* from 1573; Wh D169 from a1393)
Shakespeare: *R3* 4.4.218, *JC* 2.2.26f., *Oth.* 5.2.265

F92 Such a (Like) FATHER such a (like) son (*Varied* from 1509; Wh F80 from c1340)
Shakespeare: *AYL* 1.1.57−9, 61f., *1H4* 2.4.224

F97 You are your (To be one's) FATHER'S own son (From 1567)
Shakespeare: *Cor.* 1.3.57
Cf. F92: Such a (Like) father such a (like) son.

(?) F104.1 A FAULT unknown (unseen) is no fault (*Varied*)
c1606 (1607) Jonson *Volpone* 3.7.180−3: 'Tis no sinne, loves fruits to steale; But the sweet thefts to reveale: To be taken, to be seene, These have crimes accounted beene. c1610 (1613) Marston & Barksted

Insatiate Countess IV III,58: Her faults were none, untill thou madest 'em knowne. 1612 Webster *White Devil* 5.6.247: Shee hath no faults, who hath the art to hide them.
Shakespeare: *Luc.* 527
Cf. S472: A sin unseen is half pardoned.

F106 For FAULT (want) of a better (worse) (From c1570; *worse Rom.*, 1605)
Shakespeare: *Wiv.* 1.4.17, *2H4* 2.2.41f., *Rom.* 2.4.122f.

F107 He finds FAULT with others and does worse himself (He that will blame another must be blameless himself) (*Varied* from c1530; OW257b from c1425)
Shakespeare: *LLL* 4.3.130, *Ado* 1.1.288f., *AYL* 2.7.64f., *MM* 2.2.136−41, *Tim.* 5.1.39, *Luc.* 612f., *Son.* 152.5

F111 He that commits a FAULT thinks everyone speaks of it (from 1640 HERB., variant 1615; OW137b *varied* from 1509)
Shakespeare: *Luc.* 1342f.

F117 Who is in FAULT (guilty) suspects everybody (Literal from 1666 TOR., idea from *3H6*; OW249a adds *MV*)
Shakespeare: *MV* 1.3.160−2, *3H6* 5.6.11
Cf. C606: A guilty conscience is a self-accuser (feels continual fear).

F123 Wink at small FAULTS (*Varied* from 1579; OW896bf. from 1543)
Shakespeare: *H5* 2.2.54f.

F135 FEAR (Suspicion) is one part of prudence (*Varied* from 1604)
E.g. c1604 (1605) Chapman *All Fools* 2.1.273f.: Suspition is (they say) the first degree Of deepest wisedome. 1611 COT., s.v. Asseur: He that

feares, is assured; hee that feares false ground, treads surely.
Shakespeare: *Lr.* 1.4.328
Cf. T549: In trust is treason.

F141   Not too fast (Soft and fair) for FEAR of falling (breaking your shins) (From 1580; OW246b supplements)
Shakespeare: *Rom.* 2.3.94

F150   As light as a FEATHER (From c1535; Wh F94 from 1509)
Shakespeare: *MM* 4.2.30f., *2H6* 4.8.55, *3H6* 3.1.84−9, *Rom.* 1.1.180, *Lr.* 4.6.49

(?) F156   He is (To be) the best FEATHER of our wing (tail) (*Wing Cym.*, 1682; not in OW)
I.e., 1682 D'Urfey *Injured Princess* [Adapt. *Cym.*] 2.2 18: Your Lord [is] The best feather of our wing.
Add: 1595 J. Chardon *Fulfordo et Fulfordae* 50: Abbeylands . . . were unto some very sweete, and the best feather of their taile.
Shakespeare: *Cym.* 1.6.186

F158.1 Not worth (account at, grieve) a FEATHER (Wh F96−9 from 1378 [3])
Add: c1570 *Misogonus* 1.1.92: He settes me as light as a fether in the wynde [in F150].
Shakespeare: *MM* 2.4.11f.

F162   As wavering as FEATHERS in the wind (*Varied* from c1517)
Shakespeare: *2H6* 4.8.55, *3H6* 3.1.84−9, *WT* 2.3.154

F164   He would fain fly (flee) but he wants FEATHERS (From 1549; cf. Wh W363 from c1385)
E.g., 1509 Watson *Ship* C1ᵛ (14−5): Lustye galauntes that wolde flee without wynges. 1525 Berners *Froissart* IV 200(17): These calves that flye without wynges.
Shakespeare: *1H6* 1.1.75

F174   Better FED than taught (From 1546; Wh F107 from c1495)
Shakespeare: *AWW* 2.2.3f., 2.4.38

(?) F174.1   FEED and be fat (my fair Calipolis)
c1589 (1594) Peele *Battle of Alcazar* 2.3 (MSR 609, 617): Feede then and faint not faire Calypolis . . . Feede and be fat that we may meete the foe. 1599 (1600) Dekker *Shoemakers' Holiday* 5.2.187: Lets feede and be fat with my lordes bounty. 1601 (1602) Dekker *Satiromastix* 4.1.150: Feede and be fat my faire Calipolis. 1601 (1607) Marston *What You Will* 5.1 II,285: Feede and be fat my fayre Calipolis.
Shakespeare: *2H4* 2.4.179
Cf. L91: Laugh and be fat [from 1596].

F180   (A) white-livered (FELLOW) (Cf. Appendix B) (*White-livered* from 1546)
Shakespeare: *MV* 3.2.86, *Tro.* 2.2.50, *R3* 4.4.464, *2H4* 4.3.106, *H5* 3.2.32, *Lr.* 2.2.17, 4.2.50, *Mac.* 5.3.15

F181.1   X has no FELLOW (Cf. Appendix B)
E.g., 1584 Lyly *Campaspe* 5.3.11: A featherbed hath no fellow. 1599 (1600) Jonson *Every Man Out* 3.4.88: A frying pan, to the crest, had had no fellow. c1614 (1647) Fletcher *Valentinian* 5.5.5: A good Grace has no fellow. 1639 CL. s.v. Tempestiva, Tempus 307: Summer hath no fellow. 1659 HOW. *Eng. Prov.* 13: A fatt commodity hath no fellow [in F175].
Shakespeare: *MND* 4.1.33f., *H8* 1.3.41
Cf. S898 (Stone-dead, a1674 only); F175 (Feeling, from 1678)

F182   All FELLOWS at football (From 1600; OW9b *All fellows* from c1587)
E.g., 1639 CL. s.v. Aequalitas 14: To

be all fellowes at football, Never stand upon place.
   Shakespeare: *Lr.* 1.4.86–90

F210   A FIG for him (it) (From 1576; Wh F136 a1500)
   Add: 1601 (1607) Marston *What You Will* II II,252 (fico), c1605 (1606) Marston *Fawn* 1.2.299f. (fico). ?c1639 *Telltale* 3.2 (MSR 1477) (fico).
   Shakespeare: *Wiv.* 1.3.30, *2H6* 2.3.67, *H5* 3.6.57, 4.1.60, *Oth.* 1.3.319

F211   Not worth a FIG (From 1529; Wh F137 from a1450)
   Add: 1599 H. Buttes *Dyets Dry Dinner* B2: This was (as the latine proverbe speakes) *Ficulneum Auxilium*, a Figs-worth of help.
   Shakespeare: *Ant.* 5.2.235

F213   To give one a FIG (From 1600; OW255b from 1565–6)
   Shakespeare: *Jn.* 2.1.162

F215.1   To have one's FILL of fight-ing (Wh F143 from c1375 [4])
   Shakespeare: *Cym.* 2.1.20

F228   To have a FINGER (hand) in the pie (matter) (*Varied* from 1553; OW258b supplements)
   E.g. 1587 J. Bridges *Def. of Gvt. of C. of E.* 383: Have their finger in this pye.
   Shakespeare: *H8* 1.1.52f.

F229   To put (the) FINGER in the eye (From 1534)
   Shakespeare: *Err.* 2.2.204, *Shr.* 1.1.79

F230   To put one's FINGER in the fire (and need not) (From 1546; *and need not* from ?c1588 [1599])
   I.e., ?c1588 (1599) Porter *Two Angry Women of Abingdon* viii (MRS 1830f.; Nicholas Proverbes): I will not thrust my hand into the flame and neede not.
   Shakespeare: *Wiv.* 1.4.85f.

F236   His FINGERS are lime twigs (*Varied* from c1510; cf. Wh L293 [To be lime-fingered] from c1303)
   Shakespeare: *Tmp.* 4.1.245f.

F237   (His) FINGERS itch to (be at it) (1622 only; OW259a adds 1565)
   Add: c1591 (1592) *Arden of Fever-sham* 2.1.116: My fingers itches to be at the pesant. 1599 (1600) Drayton et al. *1 Sir John Oldcastle* 1.2.157f.: My fingers ends do itch To be upon those rudduks.
   Shakespeare: *Wiv.* 2.3.45f., *Tro.* 2.1.26, *Rom.* 3.5.164

F239   Lay thy FINGERS on thy lips (fig.) (From *Ham.*; OW259a adds 1509)
   Shakespeare: *Tro.*1.3.240, *Ham.* 1.5.187, *Oth.* 2.1.221

F244   I sucked (picked) not this (To suck, pick) out of my FINGERS' ends (fingers) (*Sucked* from 1546; OW784b supplements)
   Add: c1553 (1575) W. Stevenson *Gammer Gurton's Needle* 5.2.153: I picke not this geare, hearst thou, out of my fingers endes.
   Shakespeare: *Jn.* 3.4.167f.

F245   (To have it) at his (one's) FIN-GERS' ends (Cf. Appendix B) (From 1546)
   [Erasmus   *Adagia*   216E: Ad unguem.]
   Shakespeare: *LLL* 5.1.77f., *TN* 1.3.78

F246.1   As hasty as FIRE (Wh F169 from c1400 [2])
   Shakespeare: *R2* 1.1.19, *Oth.* 5.2.134

F247   As hot as FIRE (From c1535; Wh F170 from a1375)
   Shakespeare: *TNK* 5.4.65

F248   As red (bright) as FIRE (From c1480–1500)
   Shakespeare: *3H6*   3.2.51,   *Jn.*

4.2.163, *R2* 2.3.58, *JC* 3.2.115
Cf. C462.1: As red as coals.

F251   Do not blow the FIRE (coal)
thou wouldst quench (*Varied* from
1576)
E.g., 1580 Lyly *Euphues and his
England* II,55: Thus began to kindle
the flame which I shoulde rather
have quenched.
Shakespeare: *Cor.* 3.1.196, *Per.*
1.4.4

F254   FIRE and water have no mercy
(From 1585; Wh T183[Three things
are avoid of mercy] 1515)
Shakespeare: *Jn.* 4.1.119f.

F255   FIRE cannot be hidden in flax
(straw) (*Varied* from 1580; OW259b
adds 1557)
Shakespeare: *TNK* 5.3.97f.

(?) F261.1   FIRE is quenched in its
own smoke (Wh F184 a1475)
I.e., a1475 *Tree* 78.20f.: Lete it be
quenchid as fere in his own smoke.
Shakespeare: *Tim.* 4.3.143

F265   FIRE that's closest kept burns
most of all (*Varied* from 1565;
OW260b from Ovid, Chaucer)
E.g., 1577 J. Grange *Golden Aphroditis* G4ᵛ: Nothing she sayde of a long
time: but yet the smothering fire at
length breakes forth in flame. 1581
Guazzo (Pettie) *Civile Conversation*
I,18: And as hidden flames by force
kept downe are most ardent.
Shakespeare: *TGV* 1.2.30, *Ado*
3.1.77f.
Cf. O89.1: An OVEN damned up
bakes soonest.

F277   One FIRE (heat) drives out
another (*Varied; fire* from 1580, *heat*
from *TGV*)
Shakespeare: *TGV* 2.4.192, *Jn.*
3.1.277, 5.1.48, *Rom.* 1.2.45, *JC*
3.1.171, *Cor.* 4.7.54, *Son.* 144.14, *PP*
2.14

F278   Put not FIRE to tow (flax) (*Varied; tow* from 1530, *flax* from 1579)
Shakespeare: *2H6* 5.2.55

F283.1   To find (seek) FIRE in frost
1575 Gascoigne *Master F. J.* I,384: I
have found fire in frost. 1577 J.
Grange *Golden Aphroditis* D1ᵛ: Good
sir (quoth she) to find fire in frost. I
count it better lost. 1580 T. Churchyard *Chance* 13ᵛ: His hope is harde,
that seeks for fire from froste.
Shakespeare: *Ham.* 3.4.87

F284   To force FIRE from snow (ice)
(*Snow TGV*, 1636; OW260a *ice* 1611)
I.e., 1611 *Second Maiden's Tragedy* 2.2
(MSR 885): Would you have me
worke by wonders to strike fire out
of yce. 1636 W. Sampson *Vow
Breaker* 3.4.48: 'Tis impossible as to
force Fire from snow, Water from
flint.
Shakespeare: *TGV* 2.7.19, *MV*
3.2.30f.
Cf. W107: To fetch (wring) water
(blood) out of a stone (flint).

F285   To go (etc.) through FIRE and
water (From 1530; Wh F209 from
c900; cf. Ps. 66.12)
For *fire* only add: 1567 Pickering
Horestes v (MSR 586): Thou mayst,
have them through fire to go. 1607
?Heywood *Fair Maid of the Exchange*
xii (MSR 1982f.): You shall runne
through fire, Before you touch one
part of my desire. 1613 Marston
Insatiate Countess 2.1 III,29: Hee that
will runne through fire . . . will by
the heate of his love, grope in the
darke.
Shakespeare: *MND* 2.2.103, *Wiv.*
3.4.102−4, 3.5.126f.

F287.1   (To set) one's heart) on FIRE
(fig.) (Cf. Appendix B)
E.g., c1564 *Bugbears* 1.2.80: Wch
summe hathe so set me old master all
on fier. 1567 J. Pickering *Horestes* x
(MSR 1078−80): So fathers brother

in lyke sort, Revenge hath set on fyare. . . . So sore his hart is set on fyare, through raging rigorus heat. c1570 *Misogonus* 2.4.7: She hath sett him one fyer. 1575 Gascoigne *Fruites of Warr* I,162: To follow Hope which settes all hartes on fire. 1604 G. Abbot *Reasons* 88: His hart was on fire, to make himself by some worthy exploite, to become famous.
   Shakespeare: *Jn.* 2.1.351, *1H4* 3.1.264, 4.1.117, *H5* 2 Chorus 1, *Tim.* 3.3.33, *Cym.* 5.5.168

F295   I am not the FIRST (and shall not be the last) (*Varied* from 1576)
   Add: a1475 *Guy*[2] 34.1165g.: I am not the furste nodur the laste, That thorowe a woman downe ys caste. a1500 *Guy*[4] 52.1459f.: I ne am the fyrst ne the last, That women have in woe caste [in Wh W532: Women can deceive men (*varied*)].
   Shakespeare: *LLL* 4.3.48, *R2* 5.5.24f., *Lr.* 5.3.3, *Luc.* 1581f.

F300   As mute (dumb) as a FISH (From 1580; OW552b from c1450)
   Shakespeare: *MV* 1.1.97–102, *Tro.* 3.3.263

F301   As whole as a FISH (From a1563; Wh F228 from c1410)
   Shakespeare: *TGV* 2.5.19

F306   The FISH follow the hook (bait) (*Varied* from *Ado*; Wh F230 from c1000)
   Shakespeare: *Ado*   2.3.108f., 3.1.26–8

F311   The great FISH eat the small (*Varied* from 1509; Wh F232 from a1200)
   E.g., a1449 *Fabules* in *MP* II 575.239–30: Grete pykes, that swymme in large stewes, Smaller fysshe most felly they devour.
   Shakespeare: *2H4* 3.2.330f., *Per* 2.1.28f.

F319   Neither FISH nor flesh (nor good red herring) (From 1528, *herring* from 1546)
   Shakespeare: *1H4* 3.3.127

F327   To love it no more than (as well as) a FISH loves water (1581, *AWW*; ditto OW263b)
   Cf.   c1400   *Alexander   Buik*   III 333.7751–2: The folk that hardy was and gude, That better luffit fecht than fisch the flude [Wh F238].
   Shakespeare: *AWW* 3.6.85

F328   To swim like a FISH (duck) (*Fish* c1622 [OW794b from 1591], *duck Tmp.* [OW 1552])
   Shakespeare: *Tmp.* 2.2.128f.

F345   That is FLAT (Cf. Appendix B) (From *LLL*; OW266bf. from 1576)
   Shakespeare: *LLL* 3.1.101, *1H4* 1.3.218, 4.2.39

F349.1   FLATTERY is sweet poison (*Varied*)
   1576 G. Wapull *Tide Tarieth No Man* 990–2: As with the poison which is most delectable The heart of man is soonest infected, So the foe most hurteth who seemeth most amiable [cf. F410]. 1590 H. Swinburne *Briefe Treatise of Testaments* 2D4[v]: Flatteries . . . with whose sweete poison and pleasant sting manie men are so charmed. c1605 (1606) Marston *Fawn* 1.2.313: Thou grateful poison . . . flattery.
   Shakespeare: *Jn.* 1.1.213, *H5* 4.1.250f.
   Cf. P456.1: Love (Lust, A whore) is sweet poison.

(?) F361.1   By this FLESH and blood[n]
   1595 (1605) *Captain Thomas Stukeley* ii (MSR 209), xiii (1434). 1598 (1601) A. Munday *Downfall of Robert Earl of Huntington* xiv (MSR 303).
   Shakespeare: *2H4* 2.4.294f.

[n]I include only because Arden pre-

serves Delius's implication that in Falstaff's oath only "By this light" was current.

F363　FLESH is frail (Cf. Matt. 26.41; from 1575; Wh F272 from a1393)
Shakespeare: *Wiv.* 3.5.49f., *TN* 2.2.31f., *MM* 2.4.121, *1H4* 3.3.166−8, *H8* 5.2.45f.

F366　My (One's) own FLESH and blood (From 1565)
Shakespeare: *MV* 2.2.92f., 3.1.34, 37f., *AWW* 1.3.47f., *Tit.* 4.2.84, *Lr.* 2.4.221, 3.4.145, *WT* 4.4.689−95, *Tmp.* 5.1.74
Cf. Appendix B : FLESH AND BLOOD.

F367　To be FLESH and blood as others are (*Varied* from *JC*; OW268a from 1541)
Shakespeare: *Shr.* Ind. ii.127f., *LLL* 4.3.211, *Ado* 5.1.34, *TN* 5.1.32f., *AWW* 1.3.35f., *R2* 3.2.171, *JC* 3.1.67

F369　Young FLESH and old fish are best (From 1546; OW589af. from c1386)
Shakespeare: *AWW* 1.3.51f.

F371　In the coldest FLINT there is hot fire (*Varied* from 1579)
Shakespeare: *LLL* 4.2.88, *Tro.* 3.3.256f., *JC* 4.3.111−3, *Tim.* 1.1.22f., *Luc.* 181

F378　After a FLOOD (ebb) there comes an ebb (flood) (*Varied* from 1552)
E.g., 1552 TAV. 24: After a lowe ebbe commeth a floude.
Shakespeare: *1H4* 1.2.37f.

(?) F388.1　To pluck a FLOWER from among nettles (*Varied*)
a1439 Lydgate *Fall* I 111.4009−11: But offte tyme men may beholde and see That lelies growe among these netlis thikke [in Wh L280: A lily among thorns]. 1588 Wither *View* (STC 25889) 2K1ᵛ: It commeth as a rose among nettles, which a man can hardlie cul out, without stinging of his handes.
Shakespeare: *1H4* 2.3.9f.
Cf. M1344: A myrtle among nettles is a myrtle still [from 1640]; F384: A flower among thorns sends forth a very sweet smell [1616 DR.].

F389　As fresh as (any) FLOWER(S) (in May) (From 1500; Wh F306 from a1393)
Shakespeare: *Shr.* 2.1.246, *Ham.* 3.3.81, 4.5.158

F389.1　As sweet as any (the) FLOWER(S) (Wh F307 from a1300 [48])
Shakespeare: *Shr.* 2.1246

F390　As welcome as FLOWERS in May (Collections from 1591)
Shakespeare: *WT* 5.1.151f.

F394　The FLY (moth) that plays too long in the candle singes its wings at last (*Varied* from 1573; Wh B623 from 1340)
Shakespeare: *MV* 2.9.79

F410　It is better to have an open FOE than a dissembling friend (*Varied* from 1548; Wh F365 a1500)
E.g., a1500 *Thre Prestis* 49.1147f.: Now weil I se, and that I underta, Than feinyeit freind better is open fa.
Shakespeare: *3H6* 4.1.139

(?)F419　Fat FOLKS are faithful (good-natured) (*Varied* from JC; not in OW)
Shakespeare: *JC* 1.2.192
Cf.F28:Fair and Foolish. . . . .

F451.1　FOOL and his feather (fig.) (OW273b *varied* from c1553)
Shakespeare: *H8* 1.3.24f.
Cf. M218.1: Man borrows from the beasts (1609).

F480　He is a FOOL that forgets

himself (Collections from 1611, cf. *Jn*; OW275b adds c1374)

Shakespeare: *Jn* 3.4.48f, *Lr.* 4.6.281—4, *Cym.* 1.6.113

Cf. Appendix B: To FORGET oneself.

F496   Let him be begged (To beg one) for a FOOL (fig.) (From 1591; OW42b from 1584)

Shakespeare: *Err.* 2.1.41, *LLL* 5.2.490

F505.1   The more FOOL I (etc.)

1546 Heywood *Dialogue* F4ᵛ: Than prove I (quoth she) the more foole far awaie. c1599 (1610) Marston *Histriomastix* 1.1 III,250: The more fooles wee to follow them. c1604 (1605) Marston *Dutch Courtesan* 1.2.59: The more fool he. c1604 Middleton *Phoenix* 1.2.85: The more fool you. 1606 G. Wilkins *Miseries of Enforced Marriage* iv (MSR 1026): The more Foole he. c1611 (1631) Dekker *Match Me in London* 4.4.39: The more foole shee.

Shakespeare: *Shr.* 5.2.129, *AYL* 2.4.16

F506.1   To be both FOOL and knave E.g., c1539 J. Redford *Wit and Science* 749 (Wit having been called both "fool" and "knavish"): Yea, God's bones! "Fool" and "knave," too? Be ye there? c1589 (1592) Lyly *Midas* 1.2.108f.: Fooles you are, and therefore good game for wise men to hunt: but for knaves I leave you, for honest wenches to talke of. 1596 (1598) Chapman *Blind Beggar of Alexandria* vi.60—5: We are poore knaves. / Harke, you be even knaves still, and if you be poore long you're foolish knaves, and so ile leave you. / Nay swounes my Lord, no knaves neyther. 1597 (1599) Chapman *Humorous Day's Mirth* 3.1.37: You called me knave and foole, I thanke you small bones. c1605 (1606) Marston *Fawn* 5.1.287—9: Thy vice . . . now of a false knave hath

made thee a true fool. c1614 (1639) Fletcher *Wit without Money* 2.2.12—4: There be three kinds of fools . . . An innocent, a knave-fool, a fool politic.

Shakespeare: *AWW* 4.5.22—33, 5.2.53f., *Lr.* 1.4.42, 313, 2.4.84f., 3.2.72, *Tim.* 1.1.261

F509   To dote more on it than a FOOL on his bauble (*Varied* in collections from 1659; cf. Wh F394 [A Fool and his bauble] *varied* from a1400)

Shakespeare: *Tit.* 5.1.79

(?) F509.1   To play the knavish FOOL or the foolish knave. (*Varied*)

1562 Heywood *Epigrammes* Fifth Hundred 48.3f.: For man alive lyke thee franke choyse can have, To play the knavyshe foole, or the foolyshe knave. c1572 (1581) N. Woodes *Conflict of Conscience* 2.2 374: He can play two parts, the fool and the knave. 1604 (1607) Dekker & Webster 3.3.97—9: Though I have plaid the foole a little . . . I woulde not play the knave. 1624 Middleton *Game at Chess* 2.2.91f.: I have all my life-time played the fool till now. / And now he plays two parts, the fool and knave.

Shakespeare: *AWW* 4.5.22—33

Cf. F506.1: To be both fool and knave. Also Appendix B: To PLAY the fool (etc.).

F514   You have not (To think one has) a FOOL in hand (From 1592—c1600 [1615]; OW274a adds 1576)

E.g., 1576 *Common Conditions* F1ᵛ: Thinke not you have a foole in hand I waraunt yee.

Shakespeare: *TN* 1.3.64f.

F515   A FOOL'S bolt is soon shot (From a1500)

Shakespeare: *AYL* 5.4.64, *TN* 1.5.92f., *H5* 3.7.122

F519   A FOOL'S head of your own (From 1582)

Shakespeare: *Wiv.* 1.4.126f.
Cf. A388: An asshead of your own.

F523 To bring one into a FOOL'S paradise (*Varied* from 1477)
Shakespeare: *LLL* 4.3.70f., *Rom.* 2.4.165f., *PP* 3.13f.

(?) F526.1 FOOLS and children prophesy
1596 DEL. N7^v: Fooles and children often do prophesie [in C328].
Shakespeare: *JC* 1.3.65, *Lr.* 3.2.80, 5.3.71
Cf. C328: Children (Drunkards) and fools cannot lie (Children and fools speak truth [*varied* from 1537])

F531 FOOLS are wise as long as silent (when they hold their peace) (Cf. Prov. 17.28; *MV* analogue and collections from 1611; Wh F441 variants from c1390)
Add: 1557 ?Bryan "That few wordes shew wisdome, and work much quiet" *Tottel* 235.18−21: Who to this lore will take good hede, And spend no mo words then he nede, Though he be a fole and have no braine, Yet shall he a name of wisdome gaine. 1569 E. Elviden *Closet of Counsells* I6: By silence, the discretion of the silent, thou mayst deme, And silence used in a foole doth make him witty seeme.
Shakespeare: *MV* 1.1.95−7, 106

F535 FOOLS had never less wit in a year (From *Lr.* Q1, cf. 1594; not in OW)[n]
I.e., c1589 (1594) Lyly *Mother Bombie* 2.3.76f. (Silena responding to "there is nothing so fulsome as a shee foole"): Good God, I thinke Gentlemen had never lesse wit in a yeere.
Shakespeare: *Lr.* 1.4.166

[n]Cf. Appendix A, p. 43.

F537 FOOLS (Women) have wit enough to come in out of the rain

(*Women* from 1580, *fools* from 1599; ditto OW903b)
Add: 1589 J. Anger *Protection for Women* C1^v: It hath been affirmed by some of their sex, that to shun a shower of rain, & to know the way to our husbands bed is wisedome sufficient for us women.
E.g., 1599 H. Buttes *Diet's Dry Dinner* B4: For this is the height and depth of Fooles wisdome: they have the wit to keepe themselves out of the raine: Id est, Out of apparent danger.
Shakespeare: *TN* 1.3.74f., 5.1.389ff., *Lr.* 3.2.74−7

F543 FOOLS set stools for wise men (folks) to stumble at (to break their shins) (*Shins* from 1605)
Shakespeare: *AYL* 2.4.58f.

F546 FOOLS will be meddling (Prov. 20.3, collections from 1616, cf. *AYL*)
Shakespeare: *AYL* 3.2.115−8

F560 As softly as FOOT can fall (From 1530)
Shakespeare: *AYL* 3.2.328

F562 Do not make the FOOT the head (*Varied* from 1546; Wh F465 from a1393)
Add: 1563 Ferrers "Edmund, Duke of Somerset" 235−8 *Mirror for Magistrates* 398: A liege to lead his lord and soveraygne, What honest hart would not conceyve disdayne To see the foote appeare above the head, A monster is in spyte of nature bred.
Shakespeare: *Tim.* 1.1.93f., *Tmp.* 1.2.470

F565.1 Having wet his FOOT (feet), he cares not how deep he wades.
1573 J. Bridges *Supremacie of Christian Princes* 312: Like to one being out of his way, that after he is once over his shooes in the myre, careth not howe he bemyre himselfe. 1580 Lyly *Euphues and his England* II,6 (again 105): I resemble those that

having once wet their feete, care not how deepe they wade. 1589 Lyly *Pappe with an Hatchet* III, 412: Having once wet their feet in factions will not care how deep they wade in treason. 1591 C. Gibbon *A Work worth the Reading* F2: Common saying, that hee that is once wet, cares not how deepe he wade.

Shakespeare: *Mac.* 3.4.135−7

Cf. S379: Over shoes over boots.

F570 To set the best (better) FOOT (leg) forward (before) (*Varied* from c1495; OW47b supplements)

Shakespeare: *Jn.* 4.2.170, *Tit.* 2.3.192

F572 To thrust one's FEET (legs) under another man's table (*Feet* 1678 Ray, cf. *Shr.*; OW253a *legs* 1545, *feet* from 1573)

Shakespeare: *Shr.* 2.1.402

F579a To be (catch) cold on one's FEET (*Be*, 1607)

Add: c1589 (1594) Lyly *Mother Bombie* 5.3.88−90: Sing til we catch colde on our feet, and bee cald knave tyll our eares glowe [E14] on our heades!

Shakespeare: *Err.* 3.1.37

F582 Six FEET of earth make all men equal (Collections from 1659; OW738b *varied* from 1563, Wh F472 *seven* from a1325)

Shakespeare: *3H6* 5.2.25f., *Jn* 4.2.99f., *1H4* 5.4.88−92

F584 FORBEARANCE (Omittance, Sufferance) is no quittance (acquittance) (*Sufferance* from 1546, *forbearance* from 1592, *omittance AYL*)[n]

Shakespeare: *AYL* 3.5.133

[n]Given the speaker, we can be fairly sure that Phoebe's unique rhyming variant of a common proverb was not original.

F590.1 To have an impudent (etc.) forehead (Cf. Appendix B) (Cf. Jer. 3.3)

E.g., 1593 Harvey *Pierces Supererogation* II,236: Hee . . . most arrantly laboured, to shew himselfe the very brasen forhead of Impudency. 1595 M. Sutcliffe *Answere* (STC 23451) N3[v]: Penry saith, England hath an impudent forhead.

Shakespeare: *AYL* 2.3.50, *2H4* 1.3.8

F596 Long absent soon FORGOTTEN (Collections from 1616, *varied* from c1550; OW478b supplements)

Shakespeare: *Oth.* 3.3.17f.

F597 FORGIVE and forget (From 1526)

Shakespeare: *AWW* 5.3.9, *3H6* 3.3.200, *R2* 1.1.156, *Lr.* 4.7.83

F598.1 FORTUNE can both smile and frown (Wh F508 1516)

I.e., 1516 Skelton *Magnificence* 79.2524: Sodenly thus Fortune can bothe smyle and frowne.

Add: 1574 J. Higgins "Sabrine" 202f. *Mirror for Magistrates* 109: Farewell, and tell when Fortune most doth smile: Then will she frowne: she laughes but even a while.

Shakespeare: *Lr.* 2.2.173, *Per.* 1.4.108

F601 FORTUNE favors the bold (hardy, valiant) (From 1481; Wh F519 from c1385)

Shakespeare: *Cor.* 1.5.20−2

F603.1 FORTUNE is a strumpet (whore, huswife)

E.g., 1599 (1600) Jonson *Every Man Out* 1.3.11: See how the strumpet Fortune tickles him. 1610 W. Cornwallis *Essayes* "Of Fortune and her Children" ed. Allen 231: Shall man that is the Lord of the earth beg almes at the hande of a blinde strumpet. 1611 Jonson *Catiline*

V.600: O, the whore Fortune, and her bawds the fates. 1612 Webster *White Devil* 1.1.4: Fortun's a right whore. 1614 R. Tailor *Hog Hath Lost His Pearl* 1.1 (MSR 219f.): Undone by folly, fortune lend me more, Canst thou, and wilt not? pox on such a whore.
Shakespeare: *Jn.* 3.1.61, *H5* 5.1.80, *Ham.* 2.2.235f., 493, *Lr.* 2.4.52, *Mac.* 1.2.14f., *Ant.* 4.15.44, *Cym.* 3.1.31

F604 FORTUNE is blind (From 1588; OW282a from c1500)[n]
Shakespeare: *MV* 2.1.36, *H5* 3.6.28−32

[n]Cf. Introduction, fn. 14.

F606 FORTUNE is fickle (*Varied* from c1565; cf. Wh F523 [change-able] from a1338)
Shakespeare: *H5* 3.6.27, *Rom.* 3.5.60

F607.1 FORTUNE is (not) my foe (Wh F529 from c1378)
Shakespeare: *Wiv.* 3.3.65, *H5* 3.6.39

F611 He dances well to whom FOR-TUNE pipes (Collections from 1573)
Shakespeare: *Ham.* 3.2.70

F614 If FORTUNE me torments yet hope does me content (1659 HOW. *Fr. Prov.* 7, cf. *2H4*; OW282b supplements from 1592)
Shakespeare: *2H4* 2.4.181, 5.5.96

(?) F617 FORTUNE'S wheel is ever turning (*Varied* from c1517; cf. Wh F506 [Fortune and her wheel] from c1200)
Shakespeare: *H5* 3.6.27, *Lr.* 2.2.173

F617.1 He is (To be) FORTUNE'S FOOL
c1630 *Wasp* (MSR 663−71): Empty

Impertinent, one of fortunes fooles . . . she has flattered the wth gawds . . . and now . . . she hurles the Headlong to the Antipodes.
Shakespeare: *Rom.* 3.1.136, *Lr.* 4.6.190f., *Ant.* 5.2.3, *Tim.* 3.6.96

F621 FOUR make up a mess (fig.) (*Varied* from 1549)
Shakespeare: *LLL* 4.3.203

F626 The FOWLER is caught (taken) in his own net (snare) (*Varied* from 1576; OW561a from 1530)
Shakespeare: *Ham.* 3.4.206f., 5.2.306

(?) F628 As rank as a FOX (*TN*, 1693; not in OW)
Add: c1612 (1657) Middleton *No Wit No Help* 1.1.110: A mere sot for her suitor, a rank fox.
Shakespeare: *TN* 2.5.124

F629 As wily (subtle, crafty) as a FOX (From c1535; cf. Wh F585-91 from a1393)
Shakespeare: *MM* 3.2.8−10, *H8* 1.1.158−60, *Cor.* 1.1.172, *Cym.* 3.3.40

F642 The FOX when he cannot reach the grapes says that they are not ripe (are sour) (*Varied* from 1484 Aesop)
Shakespeare: *AWW* 2.1.69−72

F652.1 To smell a FOX (fig.) (Cf. Appendix B)
c1591 (1595) *Locrine* 2.5.93: But, oh, I smel a foxe [in R31]. 1608 R. Middleton *Time's Metamorphosis* ed. 1840 31: Beyond France transalpine You did not march; O I now smell a fox, France too hot, and there you caught the ———. 1611 Tourneur *Atheist's Tragedy* 4.3.273: A ghost? Where, my lord? I smell a fox.
Shakespeare: *2H4* 1.2.155
Cf. R31: To smell a rat.

F655 When the FOX (serpent) has

got in his head (nose) he will soon make the body follow (*Fox* from *3H6*; OW284b *serpent* 1578)

Add e.g.: 1556 J. Poynet *Shorte Treatise* E7: The nature of wicked Princes is muche like to the moldewarpes, which if they be suffred to have their snowtes in the grounde, and be not furthewith letted, will sodainly have in all the body: or to the weselles, that conveith in his hole body wher he hathe ones goten in his head. 1597 W. Hunnis *Seven Sobs* 23: Sinne may wel be comparde unto a serpent vile, Which with his bodie, head, and taile, doth manie one begile, For where the serpents head, to enter doth begin There al the bodie with the taile, apace comes sliding in. 1602 C. Sutton *Disce Vivere* 163: For the old serpent sayth Ierome is slipperie, and unlesse wee keepe out the head of suggestion, hee will get in his bodie of consent, and at last, taile and all, and so a habite and habitation of abode.

Shakespeare: *3H6* 4.7.25f

F663   He that will FRANCE (Scotland) win must with Scotland (France) first begin (From 1548; OW285b supplements)
Shakespeare: *H5* 1.2.167f.

F672.1   To FRET and fume (Cf. Appendix B: To STAMP and stare)
E.g., 1546 Heywood *Dialogue* II.v H4: Contrary to reason ye stampe and ye stare. Ye frete and ye fume, as mad as a marche hare. 1559 W. Baldwin "Clarence" 113f. *Mirror for Magistrates* 224: This made my father in lawe to fret and fume, To stampe and stare. 1574 J. Higgins "Madan" 25 *Mirror for Magistrates* 112: To freate and fume I did begin.
Shakespeare: *Shr.* 2.1.152, 3.2.228

F687   Better is a FRIEND in court than (A friend in court is worth) a penny in purse (From 1509)
Shakespeare: *2H4* 5.1.30f.

F693   A FRIEND in need is a friend in deed (indeed) (Collections from 1678, variants from 1581)
Shakespeare: *PP* 20.49f.

F694   A FRIEND is never known till a man have need (*Varied* from c1489; OW289b Enn. ap. Cic., c1190 French, c1300ff.)
Shakespeare: *R2* 2.2.85

F696   A FRIEND is one's second self (From 1539; OW289af. adds Aristotle)
Add e.g.: c1590 (c1592) ?Kyd *Soliman and Perseda* 2.1.99 (Erastus to his beloved): How fares Perseda, my sweete second selfe?
Shakespeare: *TGV* 3.1.172, *AYL* 1.3.97, *R3* 2.2.151, *R2* 2.1.275, *JC* 2.1.274, 282, *Ham.* 1.2.161, *Son.* 39.1ff., 42.13, 62.13, 133.6
Cf. B503.1: One soul (heart, mind) in bodies twain.

F716   One good FRIEND watches for another (Collections from 1611)
Shakespeare: *Son.* 61.10−3

F725   Who lends to a FRIEND loses double (French from 1594, English from *Ham.*; OW455b adds 1597)
Add: 1474 Caxton *Chesse* 112f.: And herof speketh Domas the philosopher and sayth that my frende borowed money of me And I have lost my frende and my money attones. [Wh F653]. 1586 M. Coignet (E. Hoby) *Politique Discourses* K7: And Seneca writeth, that often times he which lendeth money unto his friend, loseth both money and friend.
Shakespeare: *Ham.* 1.3.76

F738   FRIENDS (Men) may meet but mountains never (never greet) (*Varied* from 1530)
Shakespeare: *AYL* 3.2.184−6

F743.1   Here are none but FRIENDS
E.g., 1553 ?Udall *Respublica* 1669

(thy friends). c1592 ?Kyd *Soliman and Perseda* 2.1.39. 1597 (1599) Chapman *Humorous Day's Mirth* 1.2.64. 1599 (1600) Dekker *Shoemakers' Holiday* 1.1.74. c1605 (1608) Middleton *Trick to Catch the Old One* 4.2.75 (here's), c1618 (1656) Middleton et al. *Old Law* 1.1.87f.: Here's none but friends here, we may speak Our insides freely.
Shakespeare: *Ant.* 3.13.47

(?) F752 Keep well thy FRIENDS when thou hast gotten them (*Varied* from 1550)
E.g. 1597 [Bodenham] *Wit's Commonwealth* 62ᵛ: Be slow to fall in friendship, but when thou are in, continue firme and constant [scarcely a proverbial formulation].
Shakespeare: *Ham.* 1.3.62−5

F769 Farewell FROST (From 1564)
Shakespeare: *MV* 2.7.75

F784 Out of the FRYING PAN into the fire (From 1529)
Shakespeare: *TGV* 1.3.78f.

F785 Add FUEL to the fire (From 1586; OW293a adds 1566)
Shakespeare: *Tro.* 2.3.196, *2H6* 3.1.302f., *3H6* 5.4.70

G

G7 Light GAINS make heavy purses (From 1546)
Shakespeare: *MV* 5.1.130

G11 As bitter as GALL (From c1529; Wh G8 from c1225)
Shakespeare: *LLL* 5.2.237, *TN* 3.2.48f.

G11.1 GALL and honey (sugar) (Wh G12 *varied* from a1390)
E.g., a1420 Lydgate *Troy* I 18.218: Galle in his breste and sugre in his face.
Shakespeare: *H5* 2.2.30

G14.1 To run (etc.) a false GALLOP (*OED* 3a fig. from 1593 [1592])
1590 ?Nashe *Almond for a Parrat* III,366: I. a P. in those daies would have run a false gallop over his beades with anie man in England. 1592 Nashe *Strange Newes* I,275: I would trot a false gallop through the rest of his ragged Verses. 1594 Nashe *Terrors of the Night* III,368: I have rid a false gallop these three or foure pages. 1605 Jonson et al. *Eastward Ho* 1.2.62f.: Has the Court nere a trot? / No, but a false gallop, Ladie. c1612 (1657) Middleton *No Wit, No Help* 3.1.35f.: The least touch of a spur in this Will now put your desires to a false gallop.
Shakespeare: *Ado* 3.4.93f., *AYL* 3.2.113

G27 GAMING (Play), women, and wine, while they laugh they make men pine (1640, *varied* from c1576)
E.g.,1591 FLOR. *Sec. F.* V 73: Women, Wine, and Dice, will bring a man to Lice.
Shakespeare: *Lr.* 3.4.90−2

G42 He may go hang himself in his own GARTERS (*Varied* from *MND*; OW349b from 1591)
Shakespeare: *MND* 5.1.358f., *TN* 1.3.12f., *1H4* 2.2.43f.

G58.1 It takes three GENERATIONS to make a gentleman (OW298af., from 1598)
Shakespeare: *WT* 5.2.128−32

G63.1 As good a GENTLEMAN as the emperor[n]
1581 Guazzo (Pettie) *Civile Conversation* II I,184: Some Gentlemen, who having nothing but gentry by byrth to bragge of, are not ashamed to say, that they are as good Gentlemen as the Emperor, as if a Gentleman could not increase in gentry.
Shakespeare: *H5* 4.1.41−3, 4.7.137f.

[n]Since the Italian (at least in the only edition I've checked, that of Venice: Domenico Imbetti, 1589, P7[v]f.) reads "sono tanto nobili, quanto il Re," one suspects that Pettie's "Emperour" reflects an expression already current in England.

G66   A GENTLEMAN of the first head (From 1552; OW299a from 1509)
E.g., 1552 Huloet *Abced.* N5: Gentlemen of the first head. *To be applyed to such as would be esteemed a gentleman, having no poynt or qualitie of a gentleman, nor gentleman borne.
Shakespeare: *Rom.* 2.4.24f.

G97   A GIFT is valued by the mind of the giver (*Varied* from 1539)
Shakespeare: *Ham.* 3.1.97 – 100

G102   To get is the GIFT of fortune, to keep is the gift of wisdom (*Varied* from 1576)
Shakespeare: *Ado* 3.3.14f.

G116.1   Pray God (May) my GIRDLE break
1602 S. Rowlands *'Tis Merry When Gossips Meet* 41: If I make one, pray God my girdle break [in U10]. c1621 (1632) Massinger *Maid of Honour* 4.5.5: The king! breake gyrdle, breake! c1622 (1633) W. Rowley *Match at Midnight* 1.1 B2[v]: Wood my girdle may breake if I doe.
Shakespeare: *1H4* 3.3.151
Cf. U10: Ungirt, unblessed [from c1477].

G121   GIVE and take (Cf. Appendix B) (*Varied* from 1519; OW303a supplements)
Add: 1679 Dryden *Troilus and Cressida* 2.2: Give and take is square dealing.
Shakespeare: *R3* 5.3.6

G132.1   Flattering GLASS (*Varied*) (Cf. Appendix B)

E.g., c1590 (1596) *Edward III* 2.1.114 – 7: Her hair . . . Like to a flattering glas, doth make more faire The yelow Amber: *like a flattering glas* Comes in to soon. 1600 Lyly *Maid's Metamorphosis* 1.2.47f.: You care for nothing but a Glasse, that is, a flatterer. ?c1600 *Fatal Marriage* i (MSR 187): Those glasses flatter yee worse then Courtiers. 1612 Dekker *Troia-Nova Triumphans* 47: You thinke I set a flattering glasse before you. c1613 (1623) Webster *Duchess of Malfi* 1.1.208: Let all sweet Ladies break their flattering Glasses, And dresse themselves in her.
Shakespeare: *AYL* 3.5.54, *R2* 4.1.279

G134   As brittle as GLASS (From c1553; OW305b from c1412)
Shakespeare: *R3* 4.2.61, *R2* 4.1.288, *PP* 7.3, 13.4

G135   As clear (bright) as GLASS (*Clear* from 1526 [Wh G111 from c1350], *bright* from 1585 [Wh G108 from c1000])
Shakespeare: *PP* 7.3

G135.1   As frail as GLASS (Wh G112 [2])
E.g., 1436 *Libelle* 30.579 – 80: But wee be frayle as glasse And also bretyll.
Shakespeare: *MM* 2.4.124f.

G135.1   As gray as (any) GLASS (*of eyes only*) (OW337b; Wh G113)
Shakespeare: *TGV* 4.4.192

(?) G136.1   To stand on GLASS (Cf. Appendix B)
1584 Lyly *Sapho and Phao* 1.1.4: Who climeth, standeth on glasse, and falleth on thorne.
Shakespeare: *R3* 4.2.61

G142.1   To be like a GLOWWORM
E.g., 1590 Sidney *Arcadia* III 1,386: The nearer danger approched (like the light of a glow-worme) the lesse

still it seemed. 1598 Meres *Palladis Tamia* 174[v]: As the glow-worme shineth brightest when the night is darkest. 1607 W. Alexander *Alexandraean Tragedy* 5.3 3428f.: Some things afarre doe like the Glowworme shine, That lookt to neere have of that light no signe. 1609 G. Benson *Sermon* 49f.: The glorie of the world is a gliding pomp, of smal continuance, for all it seemes to have (like a gloworme) yet it hath neyther true warmth nor light. 1612 Webster *White Devil* 5.1.38f.: Glories, like glow-wormes, afarre off shine bright But lookt to neare, have neither heat nor light.

Shakespeare: *Per.* 2.2.43f.

G150.1 (An) X GO with thee
1578 G. Whetstone *1 Promos and Cassandra* 2.4 II,453: Goe, and a knave with thee. 1597 G. Harvey *Trimming of T. Nashe* E3[v]f.: Go to the place from whence you came, &c., with knaves name to you. c1606 (1607) Jonson *Volpone* 1.4.124: Rooke goe with you, raven. c1607 (1608) T. Heywood *Rape of Lucrece* 2199-201: Get thee to thy Tent and coward goe with thee, if thou has noe more spirit to a speedie encounter.

Shakespeare: *1H4* 5.3.22
Cf. K 137.1: Take the Knave (fool) with thee.

G156 They that cannot GO before must come behind (From 15th century, *2H6*, 1606; Wh G130[4])
Shakespeare: *2H6* 1.2.61

G157 To GO (stand) (a) high-lone (Cf. Appendix B) (*Stand* from 1581)
Shakespeare: *Rom. 1.3.36*

G158 To GO clean cam (Cf. Appendix B) (From 1579)
Shakespeare: *Cor.* 3.1.302

G165.1 There it GOES[n]
E.g., c1589 (1633) Marlowe *Jew of Malta* 4.1.4. c1590 (1596) *Edward III*

2.2.105. c1592 (1594) Marlowe *Edward II* 1.4.55. c1602 (1608) Middleton *Family of Love* 4.3.22. c1606 (1608) Middleton *Mad World, My Masters* 5.2.155. c1606 (?1607) ?Tourneur *Revenger's Tragedy* 4.2.199.

Shakespeare: *Tit. 4.3.77, Tmp.* 4.1.256; also Q1 *Ham.* D4[v]

[n]I include because often misglossed. Cf. Daniel J. Jacobson, "There it goes'—or Does It?" *English Language Notes*, 13 (1975-6), 6-10.

G167 As lecherous as a GOAT (1670 Ray, cf. *1H4* [excluded], *Oth.*; not in OW, Wh)
Add e.g.: 1553 J. Bale *Vocacyone of Johan Bale* F3 (of papist priests): They are lecherouse as gootes / the chastest amonge them. 1559 W. Baldwin "George, Duke of Clarence" 197-203 *Mirror for Magistrates* 227: But whom she doth forshewe shal rule by force, She termeth a Wulfe, a Dragon or a Beare: A wilful Prince, a raynles ranging horse. A bolde, a Lyon: a coward much in feare, a hare or hart: a crafy, pricked eare [sic]: A lecherous, a Bull, a Goote, a Foale: An underminer, a Moldwarp, or a mole.

Shakespeare: *H5* 4.4.19, *Oth.* 3.3.403, *Lr.* 1.2.127f., *Cym. 4.4.37*

G169 An (old) GOAT is no wiser (more reverend) for its beard (*Varied* from 1662; Wh G187 1484)
I.e., 1484 Caston *Aesop* 196 5f.: O mayster goote yf thow haddest be wel wyse with thy fayre berde.

Shakespeare: *Cor.* 3.1.176

G172 Above GOD there is no lord, above black there is no color, and above salt there is no savor (*Varied* in collections from 1573)
Shakespeare: *Tit.* 4.2.99f.

G173 As false as GOD is true (From

1546; OW243a from 1543)
Shakespeare: *R2* 4.1.64

(?) G173.1   As (So) GOD (shall) mend me[n]
E.g., c1552 (c1567) Udall *Ralph Roister Doister* 2.4.43: So God me mende. c1554 (1568) *Jacob and Esau* 1.3 (MSR 261): As God me mende. c1564 *Bugbears* 2.1.7: God mend this world with me. 1599 (1600) Jonson *Every Man Out* 5.6.6: For so god mend me.
Shakespeare: *AYL* 4.1.188f., *1H4* 3.1.249f., *Rom.* 1.5.79

[n]Cf. Introduction, p. xxvf.

G179.1   (GOD) bless (save) the mark (Cf. Appendix B) (OW311b *save* only: *Rom.*, 1761, 1815)[n]
c1602 (1608) Middleton *Family of Love* 3.2.7–9: I hope to hit the mark indeed. / God save it! c1609 (1647) Fletcher *Coxcomb* 5.1.94: God blesse the mark.
Shakespeare: *TGV* 4.4.19, *MV* 2.2.24, *1H4* 1.3.56, *Rom.* 3.2.53, *Oth.* 1.1.33

[n]Cf. Introduction, fn. 27.

(?) G179.2   GOD can do all save that he will not do (*Varied*)[n]
c1553 T. Becon *Displaying of the Popish Mass* PS 273: There are certain things which God cannot do . . . whatsoever is contrary to his word, that cannot God do. 1600 J. Bodenham *Bel-vedere* ed. 1875 3: God can doe all, save that he will not doe. 1601 A. Dent *Plaine Mans Path-Way* V3[v]: God can doo nothing against his wil and decree, because he will not. 1605 Saluste du Bartas (J. Sylvester) *Bartas Weekes & Workes* 2L3 [on God's justice]: God can doo all, save that he will not doo. 1608 T. Dodson *Sermon* B3[v]: GOD . . . can doe nothing, that is against his worde: not because that hee is not able to do it, but because his Power

doth never overtwharte [sic] and crosse his Will. . . . that which hee will not, that hee doth not. 1609 J. Wybarne *New Age of Old Names* 46 [vs. unwise clemency]: God is said, not to be able to doe that he will not, so we may say, Princes can not do that they should not.
Shakespeare: *MM* 2.2.52

[n]The 1600 Bodenham is probably from a lost (?) earlier edition of du Bartas's "The Fathers" rather than evidence of an actual proverb.

G185.1   GOD give you good night
E.g., c1470 *Mankind* 159–61: Here is the dore, here is the wey [D566]. Farwell jentyll Jaffrey [G81], I prey Gode gif yow goode night! c1554 (1568) *Jacob and Esau* 1.4 (MSR 387f.): And the eldest sonne is called the fathers might. / If yours rest in Esau, God give us good night; 2.3 (705f.): But Esau nowe that ye have solde your birthright, I commende me to you, and god geve you good night. c1572 (1581) N. Woodes *Conflict of Conscience* 2.3 589: Nay then, at the whole, God give you goodnight!
Shakespeare: *Shr.* 5.2.187, *Ham.* 1.1.16

G186   GOD gives his wrath by weight and without weight his mercy (Collections from 1596)
Shakespeare: *MM* 1.2.120f.

G188   GOD has done his part (From 1556)
Add e.g., 1553 ?Udall *Respublica* 1.2 76: Indeed, God and nature in me have done their part.
Shakespeare: *Per.* 4.2.70

G189   GOD has provided a remedy for every disease (1616 DR., analogues from 1576)
E.g., 1579 Lyly *Euphues* I,208: O yet gods have ye ordayned for every maladye a medicine, for every sore a

salve [S84], for every payne a plaister, leving only love remedilesse?

Shakespeare: *H8* 1.1.123–5

G189.1 GOD he knows, not I

E.g., 1553 ?Udall *Respublica* 4.3 1069: God above, He knoweth whose fault it is, and not I. 1575 Gascoigne *Dan Bart. of Bathe* I,101: And god he knoweth not I, who pluckt hir first sprong rose. Again "Fruits" I,175: God he knoes not I. 1583 Melbancke *Philotimus* Z1: But why? God knows, not I.

Shakespeare: *2H6* 3.2.131, *R3* 3.1.26, *Oth.* 3.3.297f.

G195 GOD is a good man (From a1519)

Shakespeare: *Ado* 3.5.36

(?) G198.1 GOD (Heaven) is my judge (Cf. Appendix B)

E.g., 1598 (1601) Jonson *Every Man In* 3.3.35 (God's), 4.1.35 (Gods). c1602 (1611) Chapman *May-Day* 3.3.76 (Gods). c1604 (1605) *London Prodigal* 5.1.115 (God), 201f. (Gods). 1604 (1606) Chapman *Monsieur D'Olive* 2.1.41 (Heaven). c1605 (1630) Dekker *2 Honest Whore* 5.2.322 (God).

Shakespeare: *MV* 5.1.157, *Oth* 1.1.59

(?) G211.1 GOD rewarde you for your kindness

1530 Palsgrave s.v. Guerdon 256 (3M4): God rewarde you for your kyndenesse.

Shakespeare: *Lr* 3.6.5

G217 GOD sends a curst (shrewd) cow short horns (From 1509)

Shakespeare: *Ado* 2.1.22f.

G220 GOD sends fortune to fools (From 1546)

Shakespeare: *AYL* 2.7.19

G224 GOD stays long but strikes at

last (1659 HOW., *varied* from *Tmp.*; OW312b adds 1591; cf. Wh G264 from a1300)

Shakespeare: *Tmp.* 3.3.72–5, *TNK* 1.4.4–6

Cf. V25: Vengeance (Divine vengeance) comes slowly but surely [*Varied* from 1560].

G227.1 GOD turn all to good

E.g., c1440 *Second Shepherds' Pageant* 375f.: Now God turne all to good, If it be his will. c1554 (1568) *Jacob and Esau* 2.4 (MSR 839): Tourne it all to good O Lorde, if it be thy wyll. 1566 (1575) Gasoigne *Jocasta* IV I,298: The gods turne all to good.

Shakespeare: *WT* 3.1.14f.

(?) G230 He is either a GOD or a painter, for he makes faces (*LLL*, 1609, 1732)[n]

I.e., 1609 Dekker *Gull's Horn Bk.* Proem: *Non-Dram. Wks.* II, 202: You Courtiers . . . will screw forth worse faces then those which God and the Painter has bestowed upon you. 1732 FUL. 1914.

Shakespeare: *LLL* 5.2.643

[n]Cf. on A95. OW311b retains, adding a couple of commonplace observations versus supplementing God's work with cosmetics, but I see no signs of anything proverbial. Even less relevant, I believe, is Arden's reference to a common Elizabethan jest about a painter who created handsome paintings but ugly children.

G236 Help thyself and GOD will help thee (*Varied* from 1552; OW310a supplements)

Shakespeare: *R2* 3.2.29f.

G237 I (To) owe GOD a death (From c1581; OW603b supplements)

Shakespeare: *R3* 2.2.94f., *1H4* 5.1.126, *2H4* 3.2.235

G251 Those that GOD loves (the gods love) do not live long (The good

die young) (*Varied* from 1546; OW314a Menander, Plautus)
E.g., 1576 Pettie *Petite Pallace* 50: The gods have had her up into heaven, as one to good to remaine on earth.
Add: c1595 A. Munday et al. *Sir Thomas More* 5.2.24–6: Well, he was too good a lord for us, and therefore, I feare, God himselfe will take him. c1613 (1616) Beaumont & Fletcher *Scornful Lady* 2.2.93f.: He was too good for us, And let God keepe him.
Shakespeare: *1H6* 1.1.6, *Rom.* 1.3.19f., *Per.* 4.1.9f.

(?) G252.1   To run as far as GOD has any ground[n]
Shakespeare: *MV* 2.2.110f.

[n]Arden call's Launce's speech proverbial, which it may well have been, but to date we have no verifying evidence.

G257   When God will punish he will first take away the understanding (Collections from 1640, *varied* from *Ant.*)
Add e.g.: 1588 L. Humphrey *View of the Romish hydra* Ilf.: Quem Deus punire decrevit, intellectam illi aufert. Whom God mindeth to punish, him he bereaveth of his wits.
Shakespeare: *Ant.* 3.13.111–3

G264.1   By this fire (etc.), that's (not) GOD'S angel (OW260b)[n]
E.g.,c1570 *Misogonus* 3.1.240: By this fier that bournez thats gods aungell.
Shakespeare: *1H4* 3.3.35

[n]Cf. Introduction, fn. 26.

G266   GOD'S blessing on your heart for it (From c1570)[n]
Shakespeare: *Wiv.* 2.2.107, 4.1.13, *2H4* 2.4.303

[n]Cf. Introduction, p. xxv.

G272   Out of GOD'S blessing into the warm sun (From 1540)
Shakespeare: *Ham.*   1.2.67, 2.2.184f., *Lr.* 2.2.161f.

G275.1   Kings (Princes) are GODS on earth (*Varied*; cf. Ps. 82.6)
E.g., c1580 (1593) H. B. *Moriemini* 8: The God of heaven is angrie with the gods on earth for want of dutie. 1581 Guazzo (Pettie) *Civile Conversation* II I,198: Princes . . . beeing Gods on earth; III II,112: The Prince being as we sayde yesterdaye, a God on earth. 1584 Lyly *Campaspe* 2.2.129 (of kings): They be Gods of the earth. c1587 (1590) Marlowe *1 Tamburiaine* 2.5.56: To be a king is half to be a god. c1589 (1592) Lyly *Midas* 4.1.67: To be a king is next being to a God. 1590 (1598) Greene *James the Fourth* 4.5.72: Seest thou not here thine onely God on earth? 1592 Nashe *Strange Newes* I, 286: Kings are Gods on earth. c1595 Munday et al. *Sir Thomas More* 2.4.126–8 (Add. II.103–5): He . . . Calls him a god on earth.
Shakespeare (cf. c1595 above): *LLL* 1.1.220f., *MM* 1.2.120, *R2* 5.3.136, *Per.* 1.1.103, *Luc.* 601f.

(?) G285a   GOLD speaks (1666, cf. 1594)
I.e., 1594 Barnfield *Affect. Shep.* 48: God is a deepe-perswading orator. 1666 TOR. *It. Prov.* 11 179: Man prates, but gold speaks.
Add: 1581 Guazzo (Pettie) *Civile Conversation* II I,187: It is said, that . . . the tongue hath no force where gold speaketh [in G295]. 1598 Marlowe *Hero and Leander* II.225f.: 'Tis wisdom to give much, a gift prevails, When deep persuading Oratory fails. 1673 Dryden *Assignation* 5.3.34: There's Rhetorique in Gold.
Shakespeare: *R3* 4.2.38

G286   He that has GOLD may buy land (Collections from a1598;

OW316a from a1628)[n]
Shakespeare: *Wiv.* 5.5.233

[n]OW dates Tilley's a1598 example c1641. Cf. on H475.

G298.1 The GOOD is not known until lost.
1608 D. Powell *Redemption of lost Time* A6: It is true which is spoken in the Castilian Proverb, El bien no es conocido hasta que es perdido, The good is not knowen untill it be lost. 1666 Tor. *It. Prov.* 22, p. 31: Good is not known till it be lost [in W924].
Shakespeare: *AWW* 5.3.60, *Ant.* 1.2.126, 1.4.43f.

G301 Evil-gotten (Ill-gotten) GOODS never prove well (prosper, endure) (From 1519; OW398b cf. Hesiod)
Shakespeare: *3H6* 2.2.46

G320.1 To do one (one's heart) GOOD (*OED Heart* 54g has *MND*)
E.g. 1537 (c1561) ?Udall *Thersites* A3: It would do my harte muche good. c1553 (1559) T. Becon *Displayeng of the popishe Masse* PS 282: It would do a woman good to see how cleanly sir John Sweetlips is. c1570 *Misogonus* 3.3.85: Twode do the good at hart rout. 1594 Nashe *Unfortunate Traveller* II,211: It would doa man good for to looke upon. 1596 (1599) Chapman *Blind Beggar of Alexandria* 2.2.251: It will do your hart good to see. c1597 (1609) Jonson *Case is Altered* 4.8.60: 'Twould do one good to looke on't. 1598 (1601) Jonson *Every Man In* 1.3.78f.: It wold do a man good to see.
Shakespeare: *MND* 1.2.70f., *Tro.* 1.2.204, 211f., *2H4* 3.2.48f., *Rom.* 2.4.212

(?) G324.1 That's not so good (now)
c1597 (1609) Jonson *Case is Altered* 2.2.35: That were not so good, me thinkes. 1599 (1600) Jonson *Every Man Out* 1.2.139: That's not so good,
me thinkes; 1.3.22: That's not so good now. 1601 (1607) Marston *What you Will* Induction II,232: Thats not so good. 1601 Jonson *Cynthia's Revels* 4.3.203: This was not so good, now.
Shakespeare: *Oth.* 4.1.23, 273

(?) G337 It is more your GOODNESS than my desert (From 1732 FUL.; analogues from 1583; not in OW)
E.g., 1583 Melbancke *Philotimus* B3[v]: If any man have tasted some extraordinary mercies, it was his free will, not their deserte.
Add: 1578 G. Whetstone, *1 Promos and Cassandra* 2.4 II,454: I thanke my good Lord Promos now, I am an officer made, In sooth more by hap then desart. c1609 (1655) T. Heywood & W. Rowley *Fortune by Land and Sea* 4.1 VI,424: This is more of your curtesie then our deserving.
Shakespeare: *2H4* 4.3.43f., *Per.* 2.3.12, 2.5.29f.

G342.1 To do one's GOOD WILL
1568 U. Fulwell *Like Will to Like* B1: I wil doo my diligence. 1596 (1605) *Captain Thomas Stukeley* ii (MSR 308f.): I have done my goodwill, but it will not doe. c1621 (1622) Middleton *Anything for a Quiet Life* 2.2.151: I'll tell her, at least, I did my goodwill.
Shakespeare: *2H4* 3.2.156f.

G347.1 As giddy as a GOOSE
1588 R. Some *Godly Treatise* Z4[v]: Hee that would saile after your compasse for Divinitie matters, should prove as giddie as a goose. 1681 E. Rawlins *Heraclitus Ridens* Mar. 1: I'll whirl her, till shees as giddy as a Goose [in G346 (dizzy)].
Shakespeare: *1H4* 3.1.228

G348 As wise as a GOOSE (gander, drake) (From 1509)
E.g., 1528 More *Wks.* (1557) 179b: And all as wise as wilde geese

[OW899a]. a1529 Skelton *Agst. Gar-nesche*: *Wks.* I,118: As wytles as a wylde goos.
Shakespeare: *MND* 5.1.232, *2H4* 5.1.70f., *Cor.* 1.1.172

G349   Good GOOSE (bear), bite not (*Goose* from ?c1588 [1599]: OW320a supplements)
E.g., ?c1588 (1599) Porter *Two Angry Women of Abingdon* x (MSR 2394; Nicholas Proverbes): Good Goose bite not.
Shakespeare: *Rom.* 2.4.78

G366   A Winchester GOOSE (Cf. Appendix B) (From 1559; OW892b from 1543)
Shakespeare: *Tro.* 5.10.54, *1H6* 1.3.53

G369   All his GEESE are swans (Collections from 1616, analogue c1517; OW298a supplements)
E.g., c1517 (1533) Skelton *Mag-nificence* A4ᵛ: In faythe els had I gone to longe to scole But yf I coulde knowe a gose from a swanne. 1589 *Pasquil's Ret.* C1: Every Goose . . . must goe for a Swan, and whatsoever he speakes, must be Canonicall.
Shakespeare: *Wiv.* 5.5.6–8
Cf. S1028.1: To make a swan a crow.

G375   To cut the GORDIAN KNOT (*Varied* from 1561; OW328bf. supplements)
Shakespeare: *H5* 1.1.46

G380.1   To be (Not to be) GOSPEL (Wh G401 from c1250)
Shakespeare: *TN* 5.1.287f.
Cf. G379: The gospel is in your mouth; A147: All is not gospel that comes out of his mouth [from 1546]

G380.2   As light as any GOSSAMER (Wh G402 c1435)
Shakespeare: *Lr.* 4.6.49

G387   The GOWN is his that wears it

and the world his that enjoys it (Collections from 1640, *variant* 1573)
I.e., 1573 SANF. 107: The gowne is not his that maketh it, but his that enjoyeth it.
Shakespeare: *Tim.* 1.1.21f.

G393   The GRACE of God is gear (great) enough (*MV*, collections from 1641; OW330a from 1377; cf. 2 Cor. 12.9)
Shakespeare: *MV* 2.2.149–51

G394   The GRACE of God is worth a fair (From 1546; Wh G230 from a1415)
Shakespeare: *Lr.*1.1.58
Cf. Wh G414: Grace passes gold [2 from c1425].

G395.1   In GRACE and virtue to proceed
1592 (1600) Nashe *Summer's Last Will* 439f. III,247: Go forward in grace and vertue to proceed. 1594 Nashe *Unfortunate Traveller* II,209: These are signes of good education. I must confesse, and arguments of In grace and vertue to proceed. 1597 T. Morley *Plaine and Easie Introduction* B3ᵛff.: Christes crosse be my speede, in all vertue to proceede. c1604 (1605) Marston *Dutch Courtesan* 3.2.43: On, in grace and virtue to proceed!
Shakespeare: *MM* 3.2.264

(?) G404   It goes (To go) against the GRAIN (fig.) (*Cor.*, 1670f.; OW65bf. adds 1650)
Shakespeare: *Cor.*2.3.233

(?) G422   To pluck the GRASS to know where the wind sits (fig.) (*MV*, a1670; ditto OW635b)
I.e., a1670 Hacket *Abp. Williams* II (1692) 16: No man could pluck the Grass better, to know where the Wind sat; no Man could spie sooner from whence a Mischief did rise.
Shakespeare: *MV* 1.1.17f.

G423 While the GRASS grows the horse (steed) starves (From a1537; Wh G437 from c1450)
Shakespeare: *Ham.* 3.2.343f.

G426 To be married rather to one's GRAVE (From ?c1588 [1599], analogue from c1583 [1590])
I.e., c1583 (1590) Sidney *Arcadia* I.v I,33: Shee . . . assured her mother, she would first be bedded in her grave, then wedded to Demagoras.
Shakespeare: *Rom.* 1.5.135, 3.5.140

G433 He fries (etc.) in his own GREASE (From 1540)
E.g.,1575 Gascoigne *Master F.J.* I,442: The sisters . . . began to melt in their owne grease.
Shakespeare: *Wiv.* 2.1.68, 3.5.113f.

G437 The GREATER embraces (includes, hides) the less (From *Luc.*; OW335b 1581 analogue)
Cf. 1413 *Pilg. Sowle* (Caxton) V.i (1859) 70: Nedes must the lesse be conteyned within the more [*OED Less* 6 with *TGV*].
Shakespeare: *TGV* 3.1.362, *Luc.* 663

G439 It is GREEK to me (From 1573; OW336b from c1566)
Shakespeare: *JC* 1.2.284

G446 The greater (One) GRIEF (sorrow) drives out the less (another) (*Greater* from 1598, *one* from *Rom.*; *varied*)
E.g., [ERAS, *Similia*, 572c: Major dolor obscurat minorem: 606b [in D174]: Ut amor pellat amorem, ceu clavus clavum, ira iram, et dolor dolorem.]
Shakespeare: *Rom.* 1.2.46, 48, *Oth.* 1.3.55−8, *Lr.* 3.4.8f., *Ant.* 2.1.43, *Cym.* 1.1.135f., 4.2.243

(?) G446.1 GRIEF has two tongues.
c1598 (1639) Deloney *2 Gentle Craft*

164: Griefe hath two tongues, to say and to unsay.
Shakespeare: *Ven.* 1007

G447 GRIEF is lessened when imparted to others (*Varied* from 1576)
Shakespeare: *R3* 4.4.130f., *Ham.* 3.2.338f., *PP* 20.53f.

G449 GRIEF pent up will break the heart (*Varied* from 1589)[n]
E.g., 1597 *Politeuphuia* 162[v]: Sorrowes concealed are the more sower, and smothered griefes, if they burst not out, will breake the hart. [OW338b].
Shakespeare: *Shr.* 4.3.77f., *Tro.* 4.4.16−20, *AWW* 3.4.42, *R3* 4.4.130f., *R2* 2.1.228f., *Ham.* 1.2.159, *Mac.* 4.3.209f.
Cf. O89.1: An oven dammed up bakes soonest.

[n]Cf. Introduction, p. xv.

G453 Never GRIEVE for that you cannot help (*Varied* from 1628; OW338bf. from *TGV*)
Add e.g.: 1590 Spenser *Faerie Queene* 1.4.49.5: Helpless hap it booteth not to mone; 2.3.3.3f.: Patience perforce [P111]; helplesse what may it boot To frett for anger, or for grief to mone?
Shakespeare: *TGV* 3.1.243, *R3* 2.2.103, *Ant.* 3.6.84f., *Cor.* 4.1.26, *WT* 3.2.222f.
Cf. e.g., C921: Past cure past care; Wh S514: Sorrow helps not [*varied* from a1325].

G456 As patient as GRISSEL (*Shr.* 1681; Wh G472 *Patient Grizel* from c1395)
Shakespeare: *Shr.* 2.1.295

G460.1 As x as ever trod (went) on (God's) GROUND (earth)
c1552 (c1567) Udall *Ralph Roister Doister* 4.4.11: The most loute and dastarde that ever on grounde trode.
c1559 (c1569) W. Wager *Longer*

Thou Livest 83f.: Fair, proper, small and gent, As ever upon the ground went. c1570 *Misogonus* 3.1.46: As verye a dingthrift as ere went one gods yer. ?c1588 (1599) H. Porter *Two Angry Women* x (MSR 2318–21) (Nicholas Proverbes): I know you are as good a man . . . as ere trode on Gods earth.
Shakespeare: *H5* 4.7.141f.
Cf. M66: As good a man as ever trod on shoe (neat's) leather (as ever went on legs)

G464 He that lies upon the GROUND can fall no lower (*Varied* from a1523; OW461a Alain de Lille Latin)
Shakespeare: *R2* 3.2.155, *Per.* 1.4.78

G468 To love (hate) the GROUND another treads on (From 1596; OW493b from c1529)
Shakespeare: *LLL* 1.2.167–9

G470 Who builds upon another's GROUND loses both mortar and stones (1666; cf. *Wiv.*, c1602)
I.e., c1602 (1611) Chapman 3.3.126: Yes, no doubt, for Aedificium cedit solo, says the lawyer. 1666 TOR. *It. Prov.* 24 p. 82.
Add: 1530 Palsgrave s.v. Edyfye 222ᵛ (3F6ᵛ): He is nat wyse yᵗ edyfyeth sumptuously upon an other mannes grounde.
Shakespeare: *Wiv.* 2.2.215f.

G473 To swallow (gape for) a GUDGEON (*Swallow* from 1579, *gape for* from 1659 [OW791a from 1577])
Shakespeare: *MV* 1.1.101f.

(?) G475 An unbidden GUEST is welcome when gone (*1H6*, cf. 1546; not in OW)
I.e., 1546 Heywood *Dialogue* II.viii I3ᵛ: Welcome when thou goest.
Shakespeare: *1H6* 2.2.55f.
Cf. W259: Welcome when you go.

G482 Out of (the) GUNSHOT (fig.) (From 1551)
Shakespeare: *Ham.* 1.3.35

H

H11 As thick as HAIL (From 1509; Wh H13 from a1200)
Shakespeare: *Mac.* 1.3.97

H18 (It goes) against the HAIR (From 1579; OW7a from 1387–8)
Shakespeare: *Wiv.* 2.3.40, *Tro.* 1.2.27, *Rom.* 2.4.95f.

H19 Not worth a HAIR (From 1509)
Shakespeare: *1H4* 3.1.138, 3.3.57f., *H8* 3.2.259

H24 There is but a HAIR between (1639 CL., *varied* from 1577)
E.g., 1577 H. I. *Decades* II.viii 359: Neither is there one hair's difference to choose, whether a man be killed with a sword or with a word.
Add e.g. 1596 Nashe *Saffron-Walden* III,9: Not a haire the worse; 39: Not a hairs difference.
Shakespeare: *2H4* 1.2.24, 2.4.253f.

H26 To hit (fit, know) it to a HAIR (From 1601 [1602])
Add e.g., 1600 (1601) Marston *Jack Drum's Entertainment* I III,191: Knowste thou him? / Oh, I to a haire. 1600 (1601) Jonson *Cynthia's Revels* 5.4.350f.: A court-Mistris, that . . . knowes the proportion of everie cut, to a haire. 1601 (1602) ?Middleton *Blurt, Master Constable* 2.2.43f.: You shall hit them to a hair.
Shakespeare: *Tro.* 3.1.144

H26.1 To hurt (lose) a HAIR (Cf. 1 Kings 1.52, 2 Sam. 14.11)
1553 ?N. Udall *Respublica* 1748: Not the proudest of them all can hurt me a hair! c1605 (1630) Dekker *2 Honest Whore* 4.1. 190f.: Doe but touch one haire of her, and Ile . . . quilt your

cap with old Iron. c1616 (1652) Middleton *Widow* 5.1.25: You shall not lose a hair.
Shakespeare: *MV* 3.2.302, *Tmp.* 1.2.30, 217

H29   Within (etc.) a HAIR'S breadth (From 1592; cf. Wh B526 from a1300)
Shakespeare: *Wiv.* 4.2.3
Cf. H28: Not to stir a hair's breadth [from 1533].

H30   As many as there are HAIRS on the head (*Oth., Mac., Cor.*, 1666 TOR.; not in OW; Wh H24 *more* 1465, as in Ps. 40.12)
Add e.g.: 1589 Nashe *Anatomie of Absurditie* I,16: How many hayres they have on their heads, so many snares they will find. c1589 (1592) Lyly *Midas* 1.1.11f.: Desirest thou . . . to have the yeres of thy life as many as the haires on thy head? 4.3.55f.: There be more phrases than thou hast haires!
Shakespeare: *Oth.* 5.2.74, *Mac.* 5.9.14, *Cor.* 4.6.133f.

H32   To cut (split) the HAIR[n] (i.e., to make fine or caviling distinctions) (*LLL, 1H4*, 1652ff.; ditto OW164a)
Shakespeare: *LLL* 5.2.258, *1H4* 3.1.138

[n]My entry form and definition follow OW164a. H32 (To split hairs), beginning with Erasmus, includes a very different kind of hair-splitter—in Bacon's words "A skinflint or niggard."

H47   He that has but HALF an eye (wit) may see it (*Varied*; *eye* from 1531)
Add: 1563 ?Cavell "Blacksmith" 190f. *Mirror for Magistrates* 409: For what is he that hath but halfe a wyt, But may well know that rebelles can not spede. c1613 (1616) Beaumont & Fletcher *Scornful Lady* 2.1.119−21: Who that had but halfe his wits about him would commit the

counsell of a serious sin to such a cruell nightcap?
Shakespeare: *Mac.* 3.1.81−3

H49   My better HALF (Cf. Appendix B; *OED Better* 3c) (From c1580 [1590])
Shakespeare: *Err.* 3.2.61, *LLL* 5.2.249, *MV* 3.2.248, *Ado* 2.3.170, *JC* 2.1.274, *Son.* 39.2, 74.8

H50.1   Not worth a HALFPENNY (Wh H44; *Galley-halfpenny* in *OED* from 1542)
1601 A. Dent *Plaine Mans Path-Way* K5: They thinke it is not worth a gally-halfe-penney.   1605 *London Prodigal* 3.3.87f.: Not worth a groat [G148], not worth a halfepenie, he.
Shakespeare: *Ham.* 2.2.274

H54   HALF-WARNED (Forewarned) is half-armed (fore-armed) (*Half* from 1530, *fore* from 1591; OW280b Latin, supplementary examples)
Shakespeare: *3H6* 4.1.113

H55   It is merry in HALL when beards wag all (From 1546)
Shakespeare: *2H4* 5.3.34

H60   It is hard (ill) HALTING before a cripple (From 1540)
Shakespeare: *PP* 18.10

H65   At HAND, quoth pickpurse (From 1575)
Shakespeare: *1H4* 2.1.48

H67   For one's HAND to be in (out) (Cf. Appendix B) (From *LLL*; OW346b *in* from c1460)
Shakespeare: *LLL* 4.1.133−5, *TNK* 4.1.139

H68   Give not your (right) HAND to every man (*Varied* from c1535)
Shakespeare: *Ham.* 1.3.64f.

(?) H68.1   The giving (bringing) HAND is fair (welcome)
a1400 *Cursor* III 1421 G 24819—20:

Welcum was his presand and he, Als bringand hand es wont to be [Wh H52]. 1636 (1655) Massinger *Bashful Lover* 1.1.87 : A giving hand is still fair to the receiver [in F24].
   Shakespeare: *LLL* 4.1.23
   Cf. F24: FAIR is not fair but that which pleases [from 1640].

H73   He is at his right HAND (Cf. Appendix B) (From *TGV*; OW677b ʼfrom c1528)
   Shakespeare: *TGV* 5.4.67, *Ado* 1.3.49

H74   He knows not (knows) his right HAND from his left (*Know* c1535, *knows not* 1672; OW677bf. supplements)
   Shakespeare: *Oth.* 2.3.114f.

H88   Put not your HAND between the bark and the tree (From 1546)
E.g., 1546 Heywood *Dialogue* II.ii Glf.: Howe saie you (saied he to me) by my wyfe. The divell hath caste a bone [D237] (sayd I) to set strife Betwene you. but it were a foly for me, To put my hande betweene the barke and the tre [i.e., cause dissension between husband and wife].
   Shakespeare: *LLL* 5.2.285

H94   To bear one in HAND (From c1495)
   Shakespeare: *Shr.* 4.2.3, *Ado* 4.1.303f., *MM* 1.4.51f., *2H4* 1.2.36f., *Ham.* 2.2.67, *Mac.* 3.1.80, *Cym.* 5.5.43

H95   To get (etc.) the upper HAND (Cf. Appendix B) (From a1470)
   Shakespeare: *R3* 4.4.37

H97   (To lend) a helping HAND (*Helping hand* from a1500 [Wh H81])
   Shakespeare: *R2* 4.1.161
   Cf. Appendix B: To lend a HAND.

H99   To make a HAND (fair hand) of a thing (*Fair hand* from 1592)
Add: 1576 Pettie *Petite Pallace* 183:

One harmefull hand made a hand of two harmelesse wightes.
   Shakespeare: *H8* 5.3.70, *Cor.* 4.6.117

(?) H109.1   Clap HANDS and a bargain (*Varied*) (Cf. Appendix B)
1580 *Euphues and his England* II,218: In matters of love . . . oftentimes they clap hands before they know the bargaine. 1598 (1601) *Death of Robert Earl of Huntington* xv (MSR 2269): Strike hands; a bargaine. 1601 (1602) Dekker *Satiromastix* 4.2.105: Clap handes, tis a bargaine. c1602 (1607) *Fair Maid of the Exhange* xii (MSR 2266): Give me thy hand, a bargaine.
   Shakespeare: *Jn.* 3.1.235, *H5* 5.2.129f., *WT* 4.4.383

H114   He has (To have) (both) his HANDS full (*Both* from c1470; *hands* from *Rom.*)
   Shakespeare: *Rom.* 4.3.11

H122   To wash one's HANDS of a thing (From 1554; Wh H87 1465; cf. Matt. 27.24)
   Shakespeare: *R3* 1.4.272, *R2* 3.1.5f., 4.1.239, 5.6.50, *Ham.* 3.3.45f.
   Cf. W85: All the water in the sea cannot wash out this stain.

H125   With unwashed HANDS (From 1540; OW348b supplements)
   Shakespeare: *1H4* 3.3.184, *Rom.* 1.5.4

(?) H130.1   Farewell (Come away) and be HANGED (F733 *Farewell* from 1573; OW245a *Farewell* from 1575)[n]
Add: c1579 F. Merbury *Marriage between Wit and Wisdom* vii (MSR 1179): Come a way & be hangd. 1594 Withals 08[v]: Away and be hanged. 1598 (1601) Jonson *Every Man In* 1.2.29f.: Let him go and hang. 1602 ?T. Heywood *How a Man May Choose* 947f.: My salutations are, Farewell

and be hangd, or in the divels name.
1639 *CL.* s.v. Execrandi 107: Go and
be hang'd.
  Shakespeare: *Shr.* 3.2.226, *TN*
3.4.123, *1H4* 2.1.22, 30f., *Ant.*
2.7.53, *Tmp.* 2.2.51, 54
  Cf. Appendix B : HANG.

[n]OW may have included an expansion of the common *and be hanged*
merely to indicate that Tilley had im-
properly combined two expressions
under F733: Farewell and be hanged,
friends must part. Cf. Introduction, fn.
27.

H147   As fearful as a HARE (1606,
cf. *TN*, 1666; OW250b adds c1591
[1592] analogue; cf. Wh H111 [As
dreadful as a hare (2)])
  E.g., 1666 TOR. *Prov. Phr.* s.v.
Poltrone 152: To be a greater
Coward than a hare, viz. which immediately at the least noise, makes
away, and betakes her self to her
heels.
  Shakespeare: *TN* 3.4.385f., *Tro.*
2.2.48, *Mac.* 1.2.35, *Cor.* 1.1.171,
Cym. 4.4.37

H148   As mad as a (March) HARE
(*Hare* from c1497, *March* from 1529)
  Shakespeare: *MV* 1.2.19f., *TNK*
3.5.73
  Cf. Appendix B: To be HARE-
BRAINED.

(?) H151   HARE is melancholy meat
(From 1558; ditto OW354a)
  E.g., 1558 Bulletin *Govt. Health* 64[v]:
The flesh of Hares bee hote and drie,
ingenderers of Melchancholie [more
a belief than a proverb].
  Shakespeare: *Ado* 2.1.214f., *1H4*
1.2.77

H165   So HARES may pull dead lions
by the beard (*Varied* from 1580;
OW354b supplements)
  Shakespeare: *Jn.* 2.1.137f.

H166   Better the HARM I know than

that I know not (From 1659 HOW.,
analogues from 1552 [1539];
OW55b adds 1576)
  E.g., 1576 Pettie *Petite Pallace* 246
(with context): The common saying
is, the chaunge is seldome made for
the better [B332], and your owne
sayinge is, that of your servauntes
you had rather keepe those whom
you know, though with some faultes,
then take those you knowe not, per-
chaunce with moe faultes.
  Shakespeare: *Ham.* 3.1.80f.

H169   He that drinks well sleeps well
and he that sleeps well thinks no
HARM (*Varied* from 1530)
  Shakespeare: *LLL* 1.1.44

H170   To be able to do HARM and
not to do it is noble (*Varied* from
c1583)
  E.g., c1583 (1590) Sidney *Arcadia*
II.xv I,246: But the more power he
hath to hurt, the more admirable is
his praise, that he will no hurt.
  Add: c1597 (1609) Jonson *Case is
Altered* 1.7.71–3: The property of
the wretch is, he would hurt and
cannot, of the man, he can hurt, and
will not.[n]
  Shakespeare: *LLL* 2.1.58, *AYL*
4.3.128, *MM* 2.2.107–9, *Cor.* 5.1.18,
Cym. 5.5.418f., *Tmp.* 5.1.27f., *Son.*
94.1

[n]Herford & Simpson trace to *Septem
Sapientum Sententiae*, once attributed to
Ausonius, I Bias, 6f.: Quid prudentis
opus? cum possis, nolle nocere. / Quid
stulti proprium? non posse et velle
nocere.

H175   As blind as a HARPER (1584
only; ditto OW67a)
  Add: 1533 More *Confutacion* 686
E(9f.): Like a blind harper that
harpeth all on one strynge [in Wh
S839]. c1600 *1 Return from Parnassus*
ed. Leishman 1.1 397: Goe fidlinge
thy pamphletes from doore to dore
like a blinde harper. c1606 (1607)

Jonson *Volpone* 1.5.38f.: Do'e he not perceive us? / No more then a blind harper.
Shakespeare: *LLL* 5.2.405

H176 Have among you, blind HARPERS (From 1546)
Shakespeare: *LLL* 5.2.405

H176.1 HARPIES have virgins faces and vulture's talons[n]
1579 Gosson *Schoole of Abuse* A2: The Harpies have Virgins faces, & vulturs Talents. 1595 R. Turner *Garland of a greene Witte* C1: The Harpies have virgines faces, the vultures talents. 1601 A. Dent *Plaine Mans Path-Way* M6: Like the Harpies, which have virgins faces, and Vultures talents.
Shakespeare: *Per.* 4.3.47−9

[n]Cf. Introduction, p. xxf.

H181.1 As swift as a HART (Wh H147 from a1375 [3])
1600 Dekker *Old Fortunatus* 4.1.27f.: You can runne swifter then a Hart.
Shakespeare: *Cym.* 2.4.27.

H196 Marry in HASTE and repent at leisure (*Varied* from 1566)
E.g., 1566 Tilney *Duties in Marriage* B4 Some have loved in post haste, that afterwards have repented them at leysure [OW515b].
Shakespeare: *Shr.* 3.2.11, *Ado* 2.1.73−80, *AWW* 1.3.36−8, *3H6* 4.1.18

H198 The more HASTE the less (worse) speed (*Varied* from a1521; Wh H168 *unvaried* from c1450)
Shakespeare: *H8* 1.1.141−3, *Rom.*2.3.94

(?) H203.1 Be neither too HASTY nor too slow (Wh H174 c1450)
Shakespeare: *Rom.* 2.6.15

H210 The greatest HATE proceeds from the greatest love (*Varied* from 1579)
Shakespeare: *R2* 3.2.135f.

(?) H215 HAVE is have (*Jn.*, *AYL*; ditto OW358b)
Shakespeare: *AYL* 5.1.40, *Jn.* 1.1.173
Cf. O100: OWN is own [from a1500; Wh O76 from c1250].

H218.1 HAVE after (as fast as I can) (*OED Have* 20 Ham.)
1553 ?Udall *Respublica* 978: Faith, and have after, as fast as I can, anon. 1563 Foxe *Actes and Monuments* ed. Pratt VII,548 (to Ridley on their way to the stake): "Yea," said master Latimer, "have after as fast as I can follow." 1601 (1607) Marston *What You Will* I II,242: Have after then a maine, the gam's a foote.
Shakespeare: *Ham.* 1.4.88f.

H226 He knows not a HAWK from a handsaw (Collections from 1672, cf. *Ham.* and 1600 analogue; OW434a instead deletes *not*, cites *Ham.*, 1850 only)
Shakespeare: *Ham.* 2.2.379

(?) H228.1 Gorged HAWKS do not esteem the lure (*Varied*)
1575 Gascoigne "Flowers" I,87: Too latte I found that gorged haukes, do not esteme the lure. I,94: And I fond foole with emptie hand must call, The gorged Hauke, which likes no lure at all. 1576 Pettie *Petite Pallace* 172: Gorged hawks will stoop to no lure.
Shakespeare: *Shr.* 4.1.191f.

H231.1 As dry as HAY (Wh H205 from c1000)
Shakespeare: *Mac.* 1.3.18

H235 Make HAY while the sun shines (From 1509)
Shakespeare: *3H6* 4.8.60f.

(?) H237.1   As any between this and his HEAD
1641 (1652) R. Brome *Jovial Crew* 5.1.160f.: There is not an honester gentleman between this and the head of him.
Shakespeare: *Wiv.* 1.4.25f.
Cf. H429: From hence to (Between this and)—[some distant place]. (Includes 1565 *K. Darius* B3: You are two as dronken knaves As are betweene this and your owne skins.)

H246   He dares not show his HEAD (himself) (for debt) (*Head for debt* from 1616 *DR.*, cf. *Tim.*, *Cym.* [excluded]; OW167b *head* 1551 [*OED* 54])
Shakespeare: *Son.* 26.13

H257.1   If the HEAD is off, no beast can live (*Varied*)
1570 T. Norton *Bull* (STC 18678) C1ᵛ: Remember noble Scanderbegs proverb, that no beast be it never so fierce, can live if the head be cut off. 1593 (?1594) Marlowe *Massacre at Paris* v. 23: The head being off, the members cannot stand.
Shakespeare: *3H6* 5.1.41

H259   It is better to be the HEAD of a pike than the tail of a sturgeon (Collections from 1659)
Shakespeare: *Oth.* 2.1.155

H268   To be over HEAD and ears (up to the ears) in a thing (love) (*Up to . . . in love* from c1552)
Shakespeare: *1H4* 4.1.117, *Rom.* 1.4.42f., *WT* 1.2.186, *Tmp.* 4.1.213f.

H270   To comb one's HEAD with a three-legged stool (From 1566–7; OW134a *varied* from c1525)
Shakespeare: *Shr.* 1.1.64

H272.1   To nip in the HEAD
1565 H. Osorius (R. Shacklock) *Pearl for a Prince* 31ᵛ: Princes doe unwisely which doo not nyp wickednes in the hed, So sone as it doth begin [OW567b, equating with B702, which fits only 1593 below]. 1593 Harvey *Pierces Supererogation* II,286: The weather was cold; his stile frostbitten; and his witt nipped in the head. c1602 Deloney *Thomas of Reading* 235: The London weavers were nipt in the head like birds, and had not a word to say.
Shakespeare: *MM* 3.1.90
Cf. B702: To nip (blast) in the bud (blossom).

H274   To thrust out (in) by the HEAD and shoulders (From 1595; OW360a from 1587)
Shakespeare: *Wiv.* 5.5.147f.

H278   As many HEADS as Hydra (From *1H4*; OW361a from 1575)
Shakespeare: *1H4* 5.4.25, *2H4* 4.2.38, *H5* 1.1.35, *Oth.* 2.3.304, *Cor.* 3.1.92f.

H280   They laid (To lay, cast) their HEADS together (From c1517)
Shakespeare: *Shr.* 1.2.139, *2H6* 3.1.165, 4.8.58f.

H282   To have a good HEADPIECE (1666 only)
I.e., 1666 TOR. *Prov. Phr.* s.v. Testa 215: A Man of Courage and spirit, and that can carry on a business bravely . . . A good Headpiece, saith the English.
Shakespeare: *Lr.* 3.2.25f.

H288   HEALTH is a jewel (great riches) (*Varied* from 1530)
Shakespeare: *Lr.* 1.1.58

H295   Who so deaf as he that will not HEAR (From 1546)
Shakespeare: *2H4* 1.2.66–9

H300   It is worth the HEARING (1616 Withals; OW922b from 1587)
Add: 1533 Udall *Floures* X7 (ne).

c1569 *Marriage of Wit and Science* 2.1 (MSR 284): If it be worth the hearing, say on.
Shakespeare: *1H4* 2.4.211, *Cym.* 1.1.57

H300.1   As HEART can think (wish) (or tongue can tell)
c1554 (1568) *Jacob and Esau* 4.6 (MSR 1188): As well as heart can wishe all thing is ready here. 1566 Erasmus *Diversoria* 427: They live as well as hearte can think. 1574 Higgins "Elstride" 316 *Mirror for Magistrates* 98: As ofte, as harte can thinke, or tonge can tell. c1587 (c1592) Kyd *Spanish Tragedy* 1.1.57f.: I saw more sights then thousand tongues can tell, Or pennes can write, or mortall harts can think. 1596 Nashe *Saffron-Walden* III,33: So rascally printed and ill interpreted as heart can thinke or tongue can tell.
Shakespeare: *2H6* 4.7.124f., *1H4* 4.1.84, *2H4* 1.1.13

H309   He is HEART of oak (*Wiv.*, 1605ff.; OW364b from 1582)
Shakespeare: *Wiv.* 2.3.29

H310.1   A HEART of (as hard as) iron (steel) (would melt) (Within Wh H277 [A heart of stone (iron, steel) would melt], *varied* from c1375)
Shakespeare: *Err.* 3.2.145, *3H6* 2.1.201f., *Jn.* 4.1.119f., *R2* 3.2.111, 5.2.34f., *H8* 3.2.424, *Tit.* 5.3.88, *Tim.* 3.4.82f., *WT* 5.3.37f., *Luc.* 593f.
Cf. S839: As hard as steel.

H311   A HEART of (as hard as a) stone (flint, marble) (*Varied* from c1489; *stone* Wh S763 from c1200, *marble* Wh M370 from a1500, *flint* Wh F284 from 1535)
Shakespeare: *TGV* 2.3.10f., *MV* 4.1.31, *TN* 1.5.286, 3.4.201, 5.1.124, *MM* 3.1.229, *2H6* 3.2.99, 5.2.50, *3H6* 2.1.201f., 3.1.38, *R3* 1.3.139, 4.4.228, *R2* 5.1.3, *1H4* 2.2.26, *2H4*

4.5.107, *Tit.* 2.3.140f., 5.3.88, *Oth.* 4.1.182f., *Lr.* 1.4.259, *Ant.* 4.9.15f., 5.2.240, *Tim.* 4.3.484, *WT* 5.2.89f., 5.3.37f., *TNK* 1.1.128f., *Ven.* 95, 199f., *Luc.* 593, 978, 1240−3
Cf. Appendix B: To STONE one's heart.

H317   I will not set at my HEART what I should set at my heel (what you [etc.] set at your heel) (*You* [etc.] from 1546; *my* 1659 HOW.)
Shakespeare: *Lr.* 3.2.31−3

H320a   A merry HEART lives long (*Varied* from 1553)
E.g., c1570 *Misogonus* 2.2.89f. (song): The merye man, with cupp and cann, Lives longer then doth twentye. 1600 *Weakest Goeth to the Wall* B2: Well up with my ware, and downe to my worke, and on to my song, for a merrie heart lives long.
Shakespeare: *LLL* 5.2.18, *2H4* 5.3.48, *WT* 4.3.125

H321.1   One's HEART is full high when his eye (?knee) is full low (Wh H292, 1546 Heywood only)
I.e., 1546 Heywood *Dialogue* I.x C4ᵛ: Of trouthe she is a wolfe in a lambes skyn [W614]. Her herte is full hye, whan her eie is full lowe. 1587 T. Churchyard "Wolsey" 47f. *Mirror for Magistrates* 497: Than downe I lookt, with sober countnaunce sad, But heart was up, as high as hope could go. 1636 Dekker *Wonder of a Kingdom* 5.2.120f.: I know your heart is up, tho your knees downe.
Shakespeare: *R2* 3.3.194f.

H323   Pluck up your HEART (from c1495)
Shakespeare: *Shr.* 4.3.38, *Ado* 5.1.203f.

H327   Set your HEART at rest (*MND*, collections from 1616; OW717b *MND*, 1670 Ray)
Add: 1576 G. Wapull *Tide Tarrieth*

No Man 898: Tush man, for that matter set thy heart at rest.
Shakespeare: *MND* 2.1.121

H328.1 TAKE a man's (good) HEART to thee (*OED* Heart 49 *Take heart*, from 14th century, includes *AYL*)
c1500 *Everyman* 352: Take good herte to you, and make no mone. c1569 *Marriage of Wit and Science* 4.3 (MSR 1106): But take your hart to you, and give attempte once more. 1575 Gascoigne *Glasse of Governement* 5.3 II, 77: What man stand up and take a mans harte unto you. 1605 Jonson et al. *Eastward Ho* 4.1.26f.: Take a good heart to thee. Tis a man, take a mans heart to thee. ?1621 (1652) Fletcher *Wild Goose Chase* 2.3.44: Take a man's heart to thee.
Shakespeare: *AYL* 4.3.173f., *H8* 5.1.104f., *WT* 3.2.231f.

(?) H329.1 To cleave a HEART in twain (Cf. Appendix B)
c1570 *Misogonus* 4.2.53: My harte now rents in twaine. c1576 *Common Conditions* 1452: I whose hart is cloven in twaine.
Shakespeare: *MM* 3.1.62, *Ham.* 3.4.156f.

(?) H330.1 To have a single HEART (Cf. Appendix B, Col. 3.22)
1598 (1616) W. Haughton *Englishmen for my Money* xii (MSR 2486f.): My love Comes from a single heart unfaynedly. 1601 A. Dent *Plaine Mans Path-Way* M5ᵛ: Men now a dayes studie the art of lying. . . . they have a heart and a heart. 1682 Sir T. Browne *Christian Morals* III.20 ed. Keynes I,148: To single Hearts doubling is discruciating: such tempers must sweat to dissemble.
Shakespeare: *Ado* 2.1.279f., *H8* 5.2.73
Cf. Appendix B: Double HEART.

H331.1 To have one's HEART dance (leap) for joy

c1395 Chaucer *Franklin's Tale* 1136: Anon for ioye his herte gan to daunce. 1557 *Tottel* I,253: My hart doth leape for ioy. 1600 (1603) Dekker et al. *Patient Grissil* 2.2.161: My heart shall leape for ioy, that her heart bleedes. c1602 (1606) Chapman *Sir Ciles Goosecap* 1.4.110f.: Now beshrew my heart, if my heart dance not for joy. 1639 CL s.v. Ominandi 236: My heart leaps for joy.
Shakespeare: *Cor.* 4.5.116f., *WT* 1.2.110f.

(?) H331.2 To have someone's HEART (leaping, panting) in one's hand
c1591 (1592) *Arden of Feversham* iii.105f.: Ne'er will I wash this bloody stain Till Arden's heart be panting in my hand. 1593 (?1594) Marlowe *Massacre at Paris* xx.6: O, that his heart were leaping in my hand. 1634 Dekker ?& Rowley *Noble Spanish Soldier* 4.2.160f.: I'le have their hearts, Panting in these two hands.
Shakespeare: *Oth.* 3.3.163.

H333 What is in the HEART of the sober man is in the tongue (mouth) of the drunkard (From 1539; Wh D425 [Where drunkenness reigns there is nothing secret (*varied*)] from c1000)
Shakespeare: *Ado* 3.3.104f.

H334 What the HEART thinks the tongue speaks (*Varied* from 1477; Wh M754 from a1393)
Shakespeare: *Ado* 3.2.13f., *AYL* 3.2.249f., *Rom.* 3.5.226, *Cor.* 2.1.53, 3.1.257

H338.1 (With) HEART and good will
1534 Heywood, *Play of Love* D2: I lykewyse myne with wyll and good harte. 1589 ?Nashe *Returne of . . . Pasquill* I,71 (With). 1592 Nashe *Foure Letters Confuted* I,301. 1599 Nashe *Lenten Stuffe* III,176. 1607 Gresham *A new almanack* (Crow, p.

259). 1610 Bretnor (Crow g273 Jan., June)

Shakespeare: *Err.* 4.4.85f.

Cf. R6.1: Not (Never) a rag of money.

H339   With HEART and hand (From 1616; *OED* 50 from a1547; OW363b *heart-hand* analogues from 1593)
Add: a1450 *Mortification* (York) 343f.: With hands and harte that I have, I thank the(e). E.g., 1600 (1659) Day & Chettle *Blind Beggar* V 13: Give me thy hand, and with thy hand thy heart.

Shakespeare: *3H6* 4.6.38f., *JC* 4.3.117f., *Oth.* 3.4.46, *Tmp.* 3.1.89f.

(?)   H341   HEARTS   may   agree though heads differ (1732 FUL., cf. *AWW*; ditto OW364b)[n]
Shakespeare: *AWW* 1.3.52−4

[n]See Introduction, p. xix.

(?)   H346.1   The   door   (gate)   to HEAVEN is low and one must stoop to enter (*Varied*)
E.g.: 1549 J. Proctor *Fal Late Arrian* C5: For although the Courte of Goddis woorde be veray large and ample, loftye and hyghe: yet the doore wherein ye must enter, is veray lowe: and none can enter into it, but such as are lowe, humble and meeke of spyrite. 1608 L. Wright *Pilgrimage to Paradise* 39f.: Saint Augustine (very aptly) compareth heaven, unto a faire stately Palace, with a little doore, whereat no man can enter except hee stoup very lowe. 1613 T. Adams *White Devil Wks.* (1862) II,252: But the gate hath two properties: it is low, strait, and requires of the enterers a stooping, a stripping. c1613 (1623) Webster *Duchess of Malfi* 4.2.239−41: Heaven gates are not so highly arch'd As Princes pallaces—they that enter there Must go upon their knees.

Shakespeare: *AWW*   4.5.50−2, *Cym.* 3.3.2−7

H347   He is well since he is in HEAVEN (From *Rom.*; ditto OW878b)
Shakespeare: *AWW*   2.4.1−11, *2H4* 5.2.2−5, *Rom.* 4.5.76, 5.1.17, *Mac.* 4.3.176−9, *Ant.* 2.5.32f., *WT* 5.1.29f.

H348   HEAVEN (God) is above all (Shak. only, from *R2*; OW365b adds c1599 [1602])
Add: c1570 *Misogonus* 2.3.55f.: Gods above all; thoughe you thinke him past whoo [cf. G264, H477], He may yet reduce him.

Shakespeare: *Tro.*   1.2.77,   *R2* 3.3.17, *H8* 3.1.100, *Oth.* 2.3.102

H349.1   A HEAVEN on earth (Cf. Appendix B)
E.g., 1599 (1600) Dekker *Old Fortunatus* 5.2.180: Who builds his heaven on earth, is sure of hell. 1601 (1607) Marston *What You Will* IV II,279 (of a beautiful woman):Who would distrust a supreame existence, Able to confound when it can create, Such heaven on earth. c1602 (1607) *Fair Maid of the Exchange* ix (MSR 1595f.): Such As thinke there is no heaven on earth but theirs. c1604 (1605) Chapman *All Fools* 1.1.111, of love: O tis the Paradice, the heaven of earth.

Shakespeare: *AWW* 4.2.66

H353   To go to HEAVEN in a string (From 1591; OW308a *variant* 1583)
I.e., 1583 Melbancke *Philotimus* K2[v]: He was gone to heaven in a halter. Cf. c1600 *Fatal Marriage* xviii (MSR 2219f.): A man may see heaven through a halter.

Shakespeare: *Oth.* 4.2.135f.

H355   To spit against HEAVEN (in heaven's face) (From 1583)
Shakespeare: *MV* 2.7.44f.

H356.1   Too HEAVY or (and) too hot (Wh H316 from a1393)
Shakespeare: *1H4* 5.3.33f.

Cf. N322: Nothing was too hot or too heavy for him [from 1542].

H361.1 To be (be made, born, etc.) under a HEDGE (Cf. Appendix B) 1550 Crowley *Epigr.* 10b: Two beggars that under an hedge sate. c1589 Lyly *Pappe with an hatchet* III,401: What care I to be found by a stile, when so many Martins have been taken under an hedge. 1591 S. Cottesford *Treatise Against Traitors* B5ᵛ: Their subtill decrees made (as we say) under a hedg. 1592 (1600) Nashe *Summer's Last Will* 1466f.: I was close under a hedge . . . playing at spanne Counter.
Shakespeare: *1H6* 4.1.43, *2H6* 4.2.51
Cf. S327: It is good sheltering under an old hedge [from 1678].

H374 Take HEED of a stepmother, the very name of her suffices (Collections from 1599)
Shakespeare: *Cym.* 1.1.71

H386.1 To have one's wit (mind) in his HEEL(S) (Wh W414 1406)
I.e., 1406 Hoccleve *Male Regle* 32.231−2: The soothe of the condicion in hem bred, No more than hir wit were in hire heele.
Add: 1585 de Serres (Stockwood) *Godlie and Learned Commentarie upon . . . Ecclesiastes* 113f.: So the Greekes do speake of a foole, that he hath his mind in his heeles. As we say in french. Il a l'entendement au talon.
Shakespeare: *Lr.* 1.5.8, *Tmp.* 2.1.276f.

H389 Out at HEELS (Cf. Appendix B) (From 1588; OW601b adds 1588)
Shakespeare: *Wiv.* 1.3.31, *Lr.* 2.2.157

H392 To kick up one's HEELS (From 1604; OW366b *turn* 1580 *kick* from 1592)
Shakespeare: *Ham.* 3.3.93

H393.1 To scorn with (at) one's HEELS (OW705a; *MV*, *Ado*, then 1611)
Add: c1600 (1602) *Thomas Lord Cromwell* 3.1.10: They scorned them with their heeles. 1606 Marston, *Fawn* 4.1.37f.: I scorn his letters and her leavings at my heel.
Shakespeare: *MV* 2.2.9, *Ado* 3.4.50f.

H397 As black (dark) as HELL (From 1511; Wh H329f. from a1400)
Shakespeare: *LLL* 4.3.250, *MND* 3.2.357, *MV* 5.1.87, *TN* 4.2.34f., 46, *H8* 1.2.123, *Ham.* 3.3.94f., *Lr.* 3.7.60

H397.1 As deep as HELL (OW 175bf.; from 1599 [1601] Jonson) H397 (dark) includes 1590 Spenser *Faerie Queene* 1.8.39.8: But all a deepe descent, as dark as hell.
Add: 1604 Marston, *Malcontent* "To the Reader" 14: With subtlety (as deep as hell).
Shakespeare: *Wiv.* 3.5.13, *MM* 3.1.93

H398 As false as HELL (From *Oth.*; ditto OW243a)
Add: ?c1608 (1662) ?W. Rowley *Birth of Merlin* 3.6.81. c1609 (1620) Beaumont & Fletcher *Philaster* 3.1.68.
Shakespeare: *Oth.* 4.2.39

H403 HELL is broke loose (From 1573)
Shakespeare: *Tmp.* 1.2.214f.

(??) H413.1 Cry HEM and have him (OW158a; only AYL and 1690 *Dict. Cant. Crew* F7: Hem. to call after one with an inarticulate Noise.)
Shakespeare: *AYL* 1.3.19f.

H436 HERCULES himself cannot deal with two (From 1539)
Shakespeare: *3H6* 2.1.53

H436.1   To be one of HERCULES' labors

E.g., 1548 Elyot s.v. Hercules: Herculei labores, where the laboures dooe seeme impossible to be atchieved. Again c1580 Conybeare 43. 1599 (1600) Jonson *Every Man Out* 4.6.7f.: It was almost one of Hercules labours for me. c1602 (1611) Chapman *May-Day* 3.2.8f.: For an old man to make a yong man cuckold, is one of Hercules labours. 1604 Dekker & Middleton *1 Honest Whore* 3.3.102: For a Harlot to turne honest, is one of Hercules labours. 1611 Dekker & Middleton *Roaring Girl* 3.2.192f.: 'Tis one of Hercules labours, to tread one of these Cittie hennes.
Shakespeare: *Ado* 2.1.365

H438   It (That) is neither HERE nor there (From *Wiv.*; OW561a from 1543)
Shakespeare: *Wiv.* 1.4.106, *Oth.* 4.3.59

H438.1   One cannot be HERE and there too (at once)
1604 Middleton *Father Hubberds Tale* VIII,93: Anon, anon, sir, I cannot be here and there too. c1604 (1607) Middleton *Phoenix* 2.3.196: The surgeons cannot be here and there too. 1672 WALK. 27, p.8: A man cannot be here and there and all at once [in M221: A man cannot be in two places at once].
Shakespeare: *Rom.* 1.5.14

H446   As dead as a HERRING (*Wiv.*, 1638ff.; OW170b adds 1603)
Shakespeare: *Wiv.* 2.3.12f.

H447   As lean (lank) as a shotten HERRING (*Varied* from 1590; OW450a from 1588)
Shakespeare: *1H4* 2.4.129f., *Rom.* 2.4.36f.

H474   To have one on the HIP (From 1546)

Shakespeare: *MV* 1.3.46, 4.1.334, *Oth.* 2.1.305

H474.1   To quit (give) one his HIRE (Wh H393 *varied* from a 1350 [3])
Add: a 1460 *Herod the Great* (Wakefield) 102: I shall gif him his hire [i.e. kill him]. c1597 (1637) Deloney *1 Gentle Craft* 100: We are come to give thee hire for thy pride.
Shakespeare: *2H6* 3.2.225

H475   HIT or miss (Cf. Appendix B) (From c1550)
Shakespeare: *Tro.* 1.3.383

H479   HOB nob (Hab nab, Hab or nab) (Cf. Appendix B) (From 1530)
Shakespeare: *TN* 3.4.240

H480.1   To turn into HOBNAILS (*Varied*)
1598 (1601) Jonson *Every Man In* 1.3.168−70: He ha's not so much as a good word in his bellie, all iron, iron, a good commoditie for a smith to make hobnailes on. 1607 *Puritan* 1.2.20−2: An old soldier and an olde Courtier have both one destinie, and in the end turne both into hobnayles.
Shakespeare: *2H6* 4.10.58f.

(?) H504.1   To pierce a HOGSHEAD (Cf. Appendix B)
1562 Heywood *Fifth hundred of Epigrams* 21: Of a wyne drawer. / Drawer, thy wyne is even with thee now I see: Thou persyste the wyne, and the wyne perseth thee. 1593 Harvey *Pierces Supererogation* II,91: She knew what she said, that intituled Pierce, the hoggeshead of witt: Penniles, the tospot of eloquence. 1640 *Witt's Recreations* repr. Hotter 239: On a Drawer Drunk / Drawer with thee now even is thy wine, For thou hast pierc'e his hogs-head, and he thine.[n]
Shakespeare: *LLL* 4.2.83−7

[n]Since the 1640 witticism derives directly or indirectly from Heywood's

epigram, there is apparently no reason to believe, with John Crow and the Arden editor, that "piercing a hogshead" was slang for getting drunk.

H522 To pick (find, make, etc.) a HOLE in a man's coat (From 1588; OW623a from c1533)
Shakespeare: *Wiv.* 3.5.141, *H5* 3.6.84

H524.1 To lay one up for HOLI-DAYS (OW378b from 1542; a predecessor of D20, *Holiday DAME*, 1678 Ray)
E.g., 1546 Heywood *Dialogue* II.x L4: In condicion they differd so many waies, That lyghtly he layde hir up for holy daies. 1580 Lyly *Euphues and his England* II,96: Thou goest about . . . to hang me up for holydayes, as one neither fitting thy head nor pleasing thy humor.
Shakespeare: *Ado* 2.1.326—9

H532 Court HOLY WATER (From 1519; OW148b adds 1562)
Shakespeare: *Lr.* 3.2.10

H533 He is gone to his long (last) HOME (Cf. Appendix B) (From 1580; Wh H422 from a800)
Shakespeare: *Tit.* 1.1.83, *Cym.* 4.2.261

H533.1 Between one and HOME
1599 Nashe *Lenten Stuffe* III,174: Little merchandise they beate their heades aboute, Queene Norwitch for that goeing betweene them and home. c1600 (1602) *Thomas Lord Cromwell* 1.2.108f.: Make hast, least some body get between thee and home, Tom. 1621 (1658) Dekker et al. *Witch of Edmonton* 4.1.19f.: I'll stand between thee and home for any danger.
Shakespeare: *3H6* 3.2.173

H535.1 To pay one HOME (Wh H423 1546 Heywood; OW379b

supplements, but muddles by combining with "With heave and ho" [as does H346])
Shakespeare: *1H4* 1.3.288, *WT* 5.3.4, *Tmp.* 5.1.70f.
Cf. H346: To pay one home with heave and ho [combined 1583 only].

H537.1 HOMO is a common name to all men (OW379b, from 1567)
Shakespeare: *1H4* 2.1.95

(?) H539.1 HONESTY is a fool(and trust his brother)
c1604 (1605) Chapman *All Fools* 4.1.183-5: Simple honesty, is my policy still. / The visible markes of folly, honesty, And quick Credulitie his yonger brother.
Shakespeare: *Oth.* 3.3.382f., *WT* 4.4.595f.

H544 As sweet as HONEY (From c1475; cf. Ps. 119.103)
Shakespeare: *LLL* 5.2.230f., 527f., *Tro.* 5.2.18, *1H4* 1.2.40f., *JC* 5.1.34f.

H544.1 HONEY-SWEET (Cf. Appendix B) (Wh H430a from c1000; ditto *OED*)
Shakespeare: *Tro.* 3.1.65, 141, *H5* 2.3.1

H547 He has HONEY in his mouth and the razor at his girdle (Collections from 1659 [cf. on H745]; OW381a adds 1581 Italian and English)
Shakespeare: *WT* 2.2.31
Cf. Appendix B : To be HONEY-TONGUED.

H551.1 HONEY and gall (poison, venom) (Wh H433 *varied* from a1325)
E.g., c1412 Hoccleve *Regement* 183.5085—7: Many a hony worde and many a kus Ther is; but wayte on the conclusion, And pryve galle all turnyth up-so-doun. c1450 Idley

87.403: That undir hony he hideth galle.

Shakespeare: *Tro.* 2.2.144, *H5* 2.2.30, *Rom.* 1.5.91f., *Luc.* 889

Cf. H556: No honey without gall [from *Tro.* above]; H561: Under honey ofttime lies bitter gall [from c1510]; T391: A honey tongue a heart of gall (poison) [from 1580].

H560   Too much HONEY cloys the stomach (*Varied* from 1576; Wh H437 from c1378; cf. Prov. 25.16,27)

E.g., 1584 Lyly *Campaspe* 2.2.73f.: There is no surfeit so dangerous as that of honney, nor anye poyson so deadly as that of love.

Shakespeare: *MND* 2.2.137f. *TN* 1.1.2f., *MM* 1.2.126, *1H4* 3.2.71f., *Rom.* 2.6.11−3, *Luc.* 698f., *Son.* 118.5−8

H561   Under HONEY ofttime lies bitter gall (poison) (*Varied* from c1510, *poison* from c1569; OW381b combines with T391: A honey tongue a heart of gall [poison])

Add e.g.: 1566 J. Securis *Detection and Querimonie* E6f.: Remember the proverbe that saith: Dulci sub melle saepe venena latent. Under sweet meats is many times a poyson hidde.

Shakespeare: *Ven.* 1143f.

H566   He is least worthy of HONOR that seeks it (1659, 1660, cf. *H5*; OW178a adds 1659 TOR., plus a 1539 version of L479)

Shakespeare: *H5* 4.3.28f.

H576   It is better to die with HONOR (grief, silence) than to live with shame (*Varied* from 1557; Wh D239 from a1200)

Shakespeare: *H5* 4.5.23, *Luc.* 1186f.

H583   HONORS change manners (From 1548)

E.g., 1564 Bullein *Dial. Fever* 70:

Honours do chaunge maners, yet pride will have a fall.

Shakespeare: *Jn.* 1.1.187

H586   The HOOD (habit, cowl) makes not the monk (From 1561; OW152a from c1200 with Latin, French)

Shakespeare: *TN* 1.5.56, *MM* 5.1.262, *H8* 3.1.23

H587   To beat it on the HOOF (i.e., to walk) (From 1620; OW383b from 1596 [1633])

Shakespeare: *Wiv.* 1.3.82

H589   Hold HOOK and line (From c1597; OW377b supplements)

Shakespeare: *2H4* 2.4.158

H604.1   HOPE leaves not a man (Wh H466 *varied* from a 1400 [4])

Shakespeare: *R3* 1.2.199f., *H8* 3.2.371f.

H605   If it were not for (Without) HOPE the heart would break (burst) (From a1536; OW384b from c1200)

Shakespeare: *R3* 1.2.199f.

H618   Wear a HORN and blow it not (From a1500; Wh H488 from a1393)

E.g., c1450 *Rylands MS.394* 93.29: He is wyse and well tawght, that berys a horn and blowes it nowght.

Shakespeare: *Jn.* 1.1.218f.

H620   Pluck (Pull) in your (one's) HORNS (From c1537; Wh H491 *varied* from a1300)

E.g., 1553 ?Udall *Respublica* 5.6 1604: I, Policy, have made him to pluck in his horns.

Shakespeare: *Cor.* 4.6.42−6

(?) H622   To wear a HORN (To be a cuckold) and not know it will do one no more harm than to eat a fly and not see it (*Horn* 1580 Lyly, 1732 Fuller; *cuckold* 1593)[n]

Cf. c1564 *Bugbears* 4.5.24−6: What daunger? of a pore horne inviseble. Tutte, no man shall see it, nor you your self shall fele it. That we see not nor fele not, cannot greve us a whitte.
Shakespeare: *Oth.* 3.3.338f.

[n]Cf. Introduction, p. xix.

H625   He wears the HORN(S) (*Varied* from c1510; cf. Wh H483 [Horns of cuckoldry] from a1400)
Shakespeare: *MND* 5.1.240f., *AYL* 4.2.13

H628   He is HORN-MAD (Cf. Appendix B) (From c1525)
Shakespeare: *Err.* 2.1.57, *Wiv.* 1.4.50, 3.5.152, *Ado* 1.1.270

H638   Do not spur a free (willing) HORSE (From 1477)
E.g., c1590 (1605) *King Leir* sc. 27 2309f.: My lege, tis needlesse to spur a willing horse, Thats apt enough to run himselfe to death. ?c1596 (1640) Jonson *Tale of a Tub* 3.7.24: Spurre a free horse, hee'll run himselfe to death.
Shakespeare: *LLL* 2.1.118f., *2H6* 1.3.150, *R2* 4.1.72

H642   A free HORSE will soon tire (*Varied* from c1588)
E.g., c1588 (1599) H. Porter *Two Angry Women of Abingdon* iii (MSR 881−3), to Nicholas Proverbes: A swift horse will tier, but he that trottes easilie will indure, you have most learnedly proverbde it.
Shakespeare: *LLL* 2.1.118f., *H8* 1.1.133f.

H657   He that has a white HORSE and a fair wife (woman) never wants trouble (*Varied*; *woman* from 1581, *wife* from 1591)
E.g., 1591 FLOR. *Sec. F.* XII 191: He that a white horse and a fayre wife keepeth, For feare, for care, for

ielousie scarce sleepeth.
Shakespeare: *Oth.* 1.1.21

(?) H665   A HORSE of that (another) color (fig.) (*That TN*, cf. *AYL*, slight analogue of a1563; OW387b adds *that* c1639, *another* 1867)
I.e., a1563 (1661) *Tom Tyler* 414: But I bridled a Colt of a contrarie hare [cf. 1606 Dekker *Seven deadlie Sinns* ed. Brett-Smith 52: In fitting your Coaches with horses, you are very curious to have them (so neere as you can) both of a colour]. c1639 *Telltale* (MSR 1145): I have never a horse of that Cullor. Cf. 1600 (1603) Dekker et al. *Patient Grissel* 5.1.35 (of epicures): I have seene monsters of that colour to.
Shakespeare: *AYL* 3.2.415, *TN* 2.3.167

H688   A running HORSE needs no spur (Collections from 1616)
1659 variant: HOW *Span. Prov.* 9: (A forward Horse).
Shakespeare: *R2* 4.1.72

H700   Touch (Rub) a galled HORSE on the back and he will wince (kick) (*Varied* from 1493; Wh H505 from c1382)
Shakespeare: *Ham.* 3.2.242f.

H711   Trust not a HORSE'S heel nor a dog's tooth (1678 Ray, cf. 1585, *Lr.*; OW842b *varied* from c1383 [c1450 in Wh H536])
E.g., c1450 John of Fordun *Scotichronicon* (1759) XIV.xxxii II,377: Till horsis fote thou never traist, Till hondis tooth, no womans faith. 1585 Robson *Choice Change* K2: Trust not 3 things. Dogs teeth, Horses feete. Womens protestations.
Shakespeare: *Lr.* 3.6.18f., *Tim.* 4.3.136

H713   From the HORSES to the asses (From 1540)
E.g., 1580 Baret A-25: *A proverbe

applyed to those which are fallen
from dignitie into a meaner estate: as
from a scholler to a Cartar.
Shakespeare: *Lr.* 1.5.32−4

H717.1 To be drawn with wild
HORSES (Wh H526 from c1380 [3])
Shakespeare: *TGV* 3.1.267

H741.1 One dies when his HOUR
comes (Wh H599 a1533)
Cf. 1574 J. Higgins "Albanact" 491f.
Mirror for Magistrates 66: Lo nowe I
fele my breath beginnes to fayle, My
time is come.
Shakespeare: *2H6* 5.2.13, *JC*
5.5.20, *Oth.* 3.3.275

H745 Better be (two HOURS) before
time than (three) behind it (too late)
(*Varied*; c1510, c1550, a1598, *Wiv.*)
I.e., c1510 Hickscorner C5ᵛ: Hyt is
better be tyme than to late. c1550
(1560) *Nice Wanton* A3ᵛ: Better in
time, than too late. a1598 FERG.
MS., no. 279.ⁿ Add: 1601 Pliny
(Holland) *Historie of the World*
XVIII.xxx 3F1ᵛ: And here, remember the old said Saw that may goe
well for an Oracle, Better two daies
too soone, then as many too late.
Shakespeare: *Wiv.* 2.2.312f.

ⁿTilley's a1598 for the Fergusson
manuscript collection is too early;
many entries are demonstrably at least
two decades later. Cf. John Crow's
review of Tilley, *Shakespeare Quarterly*, 3
(1953), 265. OW (which does not
include an equivalent of H745) uses
1641, the earliest known date of publication for any of the manuscript.

H747 HOURS of pleasure are short
(*Varied* from 1586)
E.g., 1586 Guazzo (B. Young) *Civile
Conversation* IV II,214: It is a true
sayinge, That the houres con-
secrated to pleasure, are but short.
Add: 1597 (1599) Chapman *Hu-
morous Day's Mirth* 2.1.14f.: Pleasure

be a thing that makes the time seeme
short.
Shakespeare: *Rom.* 1.1.164, *Oth.*
2.3.379, *Luc.* 990−92

(?) **H747.1** HOURS of sorrow are
long (*Varied*)
Shakespeare: *R2* 1.3.261, *Rom.*
1.1.161−3, *Luc.* 990−92
Cf. H747: HOURS of pleasure are
short.

H749 Before thou marry be sure of a
HOUSE wherein to tarry (Col-
lections *varied* from 1659, cf. *Lr.*)
Shakespeare: *Lr.* 3.2.27−30

H781 A smoking HOUSE and a
chiding wife make a man run out of
doors (Smoke, rain, and a cursed
wife drive a man out of his house)
(*Varied* from c1530; OW817b from
c1386)
Shakespeare: *1H4* 3.1.157−9

(?) **H782.1** To become the HOUSE
(Cf. Appendix B)
1588 R. Some *Godly Treatise* K1ᵛ: But
all these are wide of the Butte: onely
you do hit the white: you wil teach
them. *Sus Minervam.* It becommeth
not the house.
Shakespeare: *Lr.* 2.4.153

H784 To eat one out of HOUSE (and
home, harbor) (*House* from 1483,
and harbor [Wh H614 from a1460],
and home from c2H4)
Shakespeare: *2H4* 2.1.74

H784.1 To have a (no) HOUSE to
put (hide) one's head in
c1591 (1593) *Jack Straw* (MSR 95f.):
The Widdow . . . hath . . . scarse a
house to hide her head. 1604
(1606) Chapman *Monsieur D'Olive*
3.2.147f.: [He] creepes home againe
with lesse then a Snayle, not a House
to hide his head in. c1605 (1612)
Chapman *Widow's Tears* 1.2.50f.:
You speake as I had no house to hide

my head in. 1616 DR., s.v. Poore, or Povertie 1684: Hee hath not an house to put his head in.

Shakespeare: *Lr.* 3.2.25f., *Tim.* 3.4.63f.

Cf. Appendix B: To HIDE one's head.

(?) H805 In HUGGERMUGGER (Cf. Appendix B) (From c1517)

Shakespeare: *Ham.* 4.5.84

H806.1 To feed a HUMOR (Cf. Appendix B)

E.g., c1565 (1571) R. Edwards *Damon and Pithias* i.22: To feede the Kinges humour. 1579 Lyly *Euphues* I,181: I cannot feede their humors. ?1587 (1594) Marlowe *Dido* 3.1.50: I go to feed the humor of my love.

Shakespeare: *R3* 4.1.64, *Tit.* 4.3.29, 5.2.71

H811 HUNGER breaks (etc.) stone walls (From 1546; Wh H637 from c1420)

Shakespeare: *1H6* 1.2.38–40, *Cor.* 1.1.206

H819 HUNGER is the best sauce (*Varied* from 1542; Wh H642 from a1375)

Shakespeare: *Cym.* 3.6.32f., *TNK* 3.3.25

H833 Heigh-ho for a HUSBAND (From *Ado*; not in OW)

Shakespeare: *Ado* 2.1.320, 3.4.54f.

(?) H839 When the HUSBAND is sad (merry) the wife will be merry (sad) (*Varied* from c1553; not in OW)

E.g. 1557 Guevara (T. North) *Dial Princes* II.xv 225: Naturally women have in all things the spirite of contradiction, for so much as if the Husbands will speake, they will holde their peace. If he go forth, they will tarrie at home. If he will laugh, they will weepe. If hee will take pleasure they will vexe him.

Shakespeare: *AYL* 4.1.153–6, *Ant.* 1.3.3–5

(?) H844 To laugh like a HYENA (1594, *AYL*; OW445a adds 1837, 1857)

Shakespeare: *AYL* 4.1.155f.

I

I1 As chaste (pure) as ICE (snow) (From *Ham.*)

Add: 1590 Spenser *Faerie Queene* 2.2.9.7: For it is chaste and pure, as purest snow. c1605 (1606) Marston *Fawn* 4.1.389: More clearly chaste than ice or frozen rain; 416: She with child? untrodden snow is not so spotless.

Shakespeare: *AYL* 3.4.17, *Ham.* 3.1.135f., *Oth.* 5.2.275f., *Mac.* 4.3.53, *Cor.* 5.3.65, *Cym.* 2.5.13, *Tmp.* 4.1.55f., *TNK* 5.1.139f.

I3 To break the ICE (From c1535)

Shakespeare: *Shr.* 1.2.265

I7 Better to be IDLE than not well occupied (*Varied* from 1560)

E.g., 1576 Pettie *Petite Pallace* 63: It is better to bee idle, then ill imployed. c1590 Lyly *Love's Metamorphosis* 1.2.45f.: Better idle then ill employed.

Shakespeare: *AYL* 1.1.34f.

I9 IDLENESS begets lust (*Varied* from 1567)

Add e.g.: 1579 Lyly *Euphues* I,250: Idlenes is the onely nourse and nourisher of sensual appetite.

Shakespeare: *Tmp.* 2.1.155f., 167

Cf. L513.1: Love is the fruit of idleness

I13 IDLENESS is the mother (nurse, root) of all evil (vice, sin) (*Varied* from 1483; Wh I6 from a1050)

Shakespeare: *Ant.* 1.2.129f., *Tmp.* 2.1.155f., 167

I16   IF'S and and's (From 1513
[1543]; ditto OW396b)
    Shakespeare: *R3* 3.4.75

(?) I16.1   As dark as IGNORANCE
c1618 (1647) Fletcher et al. *Knight of
Malta* 4.2 VII,144: Far darker than
my jealous Ignorance.
    Shakespeare: *TN* 4.2.45

I27   He that speaks ILL of another let
him first think of himself (From
1573 SANF.)
    Shakespeare: *Wiv.* 2.2.185−8

I35   There is no ILL but may turn to
one's good (1659 HOW., *varied* from
1612)
    Shakespeare: *H5* 4.1.4

I41   ILL WILL (Evil will) never
speaks (said) well (From a1558;
OW401a from 1536)
    Shakespeare: *H5* 3.7.113

I49   Give an INCH and he will take an
ell (*Varied* from 1546)
    Shakespeare: *Rom.* 2.4.83f.

I52   He will not yield (budge, give
ground, stay) an INCH (foot) (Cf.
Appendix B) (From 1588)
Add: c1591 (1594) Greene *Orlando
Furioso* 2.1 785: Bouge not a foote to
aid Prince Rodamant. 1598 (1616)
W. Haughton *Englishmen for My
Money* iii (MSR 621): Ile not stay an
ynche maister.
    Shakespeare: *Shr.* Ind. i.14, *1H6*
1.3.38, *1H4* 2.3.114

I60.1   To die by INCHES (Cf. Appendix B) (OW186a from 1791;
OED 3b *by inches, inch by inch* has *Cor.,
Way of the World* 4.12)
    Shakespeare: *Cor.* 5.4.39, *Cym.*
5.5.50−2

I62   Better an INCONVENIENCE
than a mischief (1640, *varied* from
1580)
E.g., 1580 Lyly *Euphues and his*

England II,127: I though it good to
commit an inconvenience, that I
might prevent a mischiefe.
    Shakespeare: *Wiv.* 4.2.73f.

I66   INGRATITUDE comprehends
(is the worst of) all faults (vices)
(*Varied* from c1526; Wh I42 a1439)[n]
    Shakespeare: *TN* 3.4.354−7, *Rom.*
3.3.24, *Lr.* 1.4.259

[n]Cf. Introduction, p. xxviii.

(?) I66.1   INGRATITUDE is monstrous (a monster)
1603 R. Allen *Oderifferous Garden of
Charitie* 2I2^v: ... monstra natura
sint, quae creaturis omnibus grati-
tudinis sensum insevit. ... The
name of men is too good for them,
seeing they are monsters in nature
the which hath seeded a certain
sence of thankfulnesse in all creatures. 1616 Jonson *Every Man In*
3.6.56f.: And he to turne monster of
ingratitude, and strike his lawfull
host [1601 3.3.51f.: And yet to see an
ingratitude wretch: strike his host]!
    Shakespeare: *Tro.* 3.3.147, *Lr.*
1.2.94, 1.4.259−61, 1.5.39f., *Cor.*
2.3.9−11, *Tim.* 3.2.72f., 4.2.45f.

I70   To pocket up an INJURY
(wrong, etc.) (cf. Appendix B) (From
1589; OW636a supplements)
    Shakespeare: *Jn.* 3.1.200, *1H4*
3.3.162f., *H5* 3.2.50f., *Tmp.* 2.1.68

I71   INJURIES are written in brass
(etc.) (but benefits [etc.] in water
[etc.]) (*Brass* from 1623, *varied* from
Tit.; OW404a *brass* from 1591, *marble*
from c1513)
E.g., 1591 Ariosto (Harington)
Orlando Furioso xxiii.1: Men say it,
and we see it come to passe, Good
turns in sand, shrewd turns are writ
in brasse.
Add: 1607 J. de Serres, P. Matthieu
(E. Grimestone) *General Inventorie*
1016: It is the humor of the people
to write any good they have received

upon the Water, and to ingrave the wrongs are done them in brasse.
Shakespeare: *H8* 4.2.45, *Tit.* 4.1.102f., *JC* 3.2.75f.

I73　As black as INK (From c1515)
Shakespeare: *TGV* 3.1.288, *LLL* 5.2.41, *Cym.* 3.2.20

I81　INNOCENCE bears its defense with it (From 1573)
Shakespeare: *2H6* 3.2.232f.

I82　INNOCENCE is bold (From c1592)
Shakespeare: *MM* 3.1.208, *2H6* 4.4.59f., *Lr.* 2.1.54

I88　You (etc.) are IPSE (he, the man) (From 1579)
E.g., 1579 Lyly *Euphues* I,247: Though Curio bee olde huddle and twange, ipse, hee. c1579 C Merbury *Marriage between Wit and Wisdom* ii (MSR 287–90): In faith I am Ipse he even the very same a man of greate estimation in mine owne cuntry.
[Add: c1590 (1599) Greene *George a Greene* 1.4 229: He is the man, and she will none but him.] 1639 CL. s.v. Approbandi 30: That's hee!
Shakespeare: *LLL* 5.2.215, *AYL* 3.3.2f., 5.1.43f., *TN* 2.2.25, 5.1.326, *Tro.* 4.5.144, *AWW* 2.3.104, *2H4* 5.3.117, *Rom.* 1.5.83

I91　IRON not used soon rusts (fig.) (*Varied* from 1579; Wh I59 from a1200)
Shakespeare: *Cor.* 4.5.219, *PP* 7.4

I92　IRON (Silver, Gold) with often handling is worn to nothing (*varied; iron* and *silver* from 1579; *gold, Err.* and 1640)
Shakespeare: *Err.* 2.1.110–2

I94　(It is good to) strike while the IRON is hot (Literal from 1546; Wh I60 *varied* from c1385)
Shakespeare: *Wiv.* 4.2.223f., *3H6* 5.1.49, *H8* 5.1.176, *Lr.* 1.1.308

I97　To digest IRON (To have a stomach) like an ostrich (Simile from 1584; OW776a from ?1495)
Shakespeare: *2H6* 4.10.28

I109　As white as IVORY (From c1565; Wh I68 from c1380)
Shakespeare: *MV* 3.1.39f., *Tim.* 1.1.70, *Ven.* 230, 362–4, *Luc.* 407, 464, 1234

I110　He may go (To) pipe in an IVY LEAF (From a1550; OW626b from c1370)
Shakespeare: *Tit.* 4.3.24

J

J3　JACK would be a gentleman (From c1500)
Shakespeare: *R3* 1.3.71

J8　To play the JACK with one (From 1567)
Shakespeare: *Ado* 1.1.183f., *Tmp.* 4.1.197
Cf. Appendix B: To PLAY the fool (etc.).

(?) J9　A JACK-A-LENT (Cf. Appendix B) (From c1555; OW407a from 1553)
Shakespeare: *Wiv.* 3.3.27, 5.5.127

J12　JACK (Tom) DRUM'S entertainment (From 1579; OW407bf. *Tom* from 1577)
Shakespeare: *AWW* 3.6.38f., 5.3.321

J23　He is JACK-OUT-OF-OFFICE (Cf. Appendix B) (From 1546; OW409a supplements)
Shakespeare: *1H6* 1.1.175

J23.1　JACK-SAUCE (Cf. Appendix B)
E.g., 1553 ?Udall *Respublica* 122: What, ye saucy jack? c1565 (1571) R. Edwards *Damon and Pithias* xv (MSR

1378): What Iacke sauce, thinkst cham a foole? c1570 *Misogonus* 2.3.49: Yow Jack sauce. c1571 (1573) *New Custom* 1.2 B3: Marie avaunt Jackesauce, and pratling knave.

Shakespeare: *H5* 4.7.141

J29.1   A JADE'S trick (1c fig. has *Ado*) 1594 Nashe *Unfortunate Traveller* II,220: That which the Asse wants in wit, hee hath in honesty; who ever saw him kicke or winch, or use any iades tricks? 1598 (1601) Jonson *Every Man In* 3.1.148f.: Never ride me with your coller, and you doe, ile shew you a iades tricke. 1605 (1607) Dekker & Webster *Northward Ho* 2.2.97: Twas but a iades trike of him. 3 Sept. 1611 J. Chamberlain 304: I perceve yt was not Thomas . . . that plaide him that jades tricke.

Shakespeare: *Ado* 1.1.144, *Tro.* 2.1.19f., *AWW* 4.5.60f

(?) J29.2   To prove a JADE (2c has *Shr.*) c1564 *Bugbears* 4.2.65: They will prove them selfes iades.

Shakespeare: *Shr.* 1.2.247

J38.1   From JEALOUSY the good Lord deliver us 1616 DR. s.v. Iealousie, no. 1064: From Iealousie the good Lord deliver us. (Again s.v. Suspicion, no. 2092)

Shakespeare: *Oth.* 3.3.175f.

(?) J38.2   JEALOUSY is green-eyed Shakespeare: *MV* 3.2.110, *Oth.* 3.3.165f.

J41.1   That were a JEST (indeed) E.g., 1598 (1601) Jonson *Every Man In* 1.1.205: O Lord sir, that were a iest indeed. c1599 (1600) *Look About You* xiii (MSR 2056): Gods mary mother, heer's a iest indeed. 1602 ?T. Heywood *How a Man May Choose* 2196: That were a Ieast indeed. c1602 (1608) *Merry Devil of Edmonton* 1.1.100: Ha, ha, that were a iest.

1607 Sharpham *Cupid's Whirligig* ed. Nicoll 52: Marry there were a iest indeed.

Shakespeare: *Wiv.*   2.2.111f., 3.4.57f.

J45.1   It is ill JESTING with gods (*Varied*) 1603 J. Howson *Sermon* 17 Nov. 1602 Cf : Non est iocandum cum diis, It is ill iesting with Gods. Princes are the Gods of the Earth. c1613 (1623) Webster *Duchess of Malfi* 3.2.365: I do not like this jesting with religion. 1633 Ford *'Tis Pity* 1.1.4: But heaven admits no jest.

Shakespeare: *Jn.* 3.1.242

Cf. B583: Jest with boys and leave the saints (holy things) alone (last half from 1578).

J46   Leave JESTING while it pleases lest it turn to earnest (*Varied*; *Err.*, then 1622; OW452b from 1591) E.g., 1591 Ariosto (Harington) *Orl. Fur.* XII. *Moral*: We may see that things done in iest, oft turne to earnest.

Shakespeare: *Err.* 2.2.24

J49   As black as JET (From 1510) Shakespeare: *MV* 3.1.39f., *2H6* 2.1.110, *Tit.* 5.2.50

J49.1   I am a JEW (rogue, villain) (else) E.g., 1568 U. Fulwell *Like Will to Like* B3^v: Knaves are Christen men else you are a Iew. 1593 Nashe *Christs Teares* II,159: Let us leave of the Proverbe, which we use to a cruell dealer, saying, Goe thy waies, thou art a Iewe. 1598 (1601) Jonson *Every Man In* 3.1.40: I am a Iew [*knave* in 1616], if I know what to say; 5.2.384: I am the arrentst rogue that ever breathed else. 1599 (1600) Drayton et al. *1 Sir John Oldcastle* 2.1.122–5: If I do not make thee eate her peticote . . . I am a villaine. c1602 (1611) Chapman *May-Day* 1.2.84: I'me a villaine else.

Shakespeare: *MV* 2.2.112f., *Ado*, 2.3.262f., *1H4* 1.2.96, 101, 2.1.28–30, 2.2.22–4, 2.4.152, 179, 206, 3.3.160–2, *Oth.* 2.1.114, 4.1.125

(?) J50.1 It would make a JEW rue (Wh J40 a1508)
I.e., a1508 Skelton *Phyllyp* I 61.335–7: And it were a Iewe, It wolde make one rew, To se my sorow new.
Shakespeare: *TGV* 2.3.11f.

(?) J53 To be worth a JEW'S eye (1593, cf. *MV*; OW921b adds 1833 Marryat)
I.e., 1593 G. Harvey *Pierce's Supererogation* II, 146: As deare as a Iewes eye.
Shakespeare: *MV* 2.5.43
Cf. G96: As free of his gift as a blind man (poor man, Jew) of his eye [*poor man* from 1546; *Jew* from 1616 DR.; *blind man* 1670 Ray].

J55 None can guess the JEWEL by the casket (From 1639; OW411b from 1616, plus narrative base from a1450; both cite *MV*)
Shakespeare: *MV* 3.2

J57 JOAN is as good as my lady (in the dark) (*Varied*; OW412a supplements; *In the dark* without *Joan* from c1525; *Joan* without *in the dark* from 1598 [1601]; explicitly combined from 1611 DAV.)
E.g., c1525 J. Rastell *Gentleness and Nobility* C1ᵛ: Tote man for all sych venereall werk As good is the foule as the fayre in the derk. 1601 A. Dent *Plaine Mans Path-Way* E6: The olde Proverbe is verified, Every Iacke will be a Gentleman [J3], and Ione is as good as my Lady.
Shakespeare: *LLL* 3.1.205, *AYL* 3.5.39f., *Jn.* 1.1.184

J59 As patient as JOB (From 1586; Wh J45 from c1395)
Shakespeare: *2H4* 1.2.126f.

J60 As poor (bare) as JOB (From 1530; OW638a from c1300)
Shakespeare: *Wiv.* 5.5.156, *2H4* 1.2.126

J64 JOHN-A-DREAMS (John-a-nods) (Cf. Appendix B) (*Ham.*, 1608; OW412b *nods* from 1600)
Shakespeare: *Ham.* 2.2.568

J75 To be out of JOINT (fig.) (From c1591; OW414a from c1516; *OED* 2b from 1415:
Shakespeare: *Ham.* 1.5.188
Cf. Appendix B : Out of FRAME.

J82 JOVE laughs at lovers' perjuries (*Varied* from c1565; OW414a Tibullus, Ovid; cf. Wh G201, L527)
Shakespeare: *Rom.* 2.2.92f.

K

K10 He is wise enough that can KEEP himself warm (*Varied* from c1537)
Shakespeare: *Shr.* 2.1.265f., *Ado* 1.1.68, *TN* 2.3.136f.

K10.1 KEEP it (that) to yourself (Cf. Appendix B)
17 May 1598 (and passim) J. Chamberlain 37: I heare that Dr. Edes . . . was cleane out and could go no farther, but kepe that to yourself.
Shakespeare: *AWW* 1.3.122f., *R3* 3.2.102

(?) K24.1 To keep the KEY (fig.)ⁿ
c1608 (1638) W. Rowley *Shoemaker a Gentleman* 1.3.48: You have lockt the Closset and keepe the Key of it. 1617 Middleton & Rowley *Fair Quarrel* 2.2.65f. (of Anne): Here's your closet; put in What you please, you ever keep the key of it.
Shakespeare: *Ham.* 1.3.85f.

ⁿOn the basis of the above evidence the New Mermaid *Shoemaker*, perhaps rightly, calls "a stock expression."

K31   He is of the same (a strange) KIDNEY (Cf. Appendix B) (*My own* from c1531)
  Shakespeare: *Wiv.* 3.5.114f.

K38   The nearer in KIN the less in kindness (*Varied* from 1565)
Add: 1609 W. Symonds *Virginia* 19: The English Proverbe is true, The farther from kinne, the neerer to friends.
  Shakespeare: *Ham.* 1.2.65

K49   KINDNESS (Love, Kind) will creep where it cannot go (From 1481)
  Shakespeare: *TGV* 4.2.19f.

K51   To kill with KINDNESS (From c1558; OW423a supplements)
  Shakespeare: *Shr.* 4.1.208

K55   (Better) to be KING of a molehill (than a kaiser's slave) (Complete 1659 HOW., *varied* from 1583; OW426a from a1578)
  Shakespeare: *3H6* 2.5.14

K64   A KING (prince) loves the treason but hates the traitor (*Varied* from 1583; OW426a cf. Tacitus, supplementary examples)
  Shakespeare: *R3* 1.4.254f., *R2* 5.6.39f.

(?) K64.1   A KING may be above his laws in mercy (Wh K45 1515)
  Shakespeare: *Tit.* 1.1.117f.

(?) K65.1   The KING of courtesy (Cf. Appendix B, *OED* 6, 7c)
c1609 (1620) Beaumont & Fletcher *Philaster* 5.4.138: Go thy ways, thou art the king of courtesy!
  Shakespeare: *1H4* 2.4.10f.
  Cf. Appendix B: The FLOWER of courtesy.

K66   The KING of good fellows is appointed for the queen of beggars (Collections from 1636; OW426b *variant* c1565)
  Shakespeare: *H5* 5.2.242f.

K70   Like KING (prince) like people (From c1525; OW426a supplements; cf. Ecclus. 10.2)
  Shakespeare: *Luc.* 615f.

K71.1   An unwise KING is but an ape in the house roof (Wh K61 c1400)
1597 J. King *Lectures upon Jonas* (ed. 1611, p. 85): Ancient proverb . . . Rex fatuus in solio simia in tecto, a foolish king in a throne is an ape upon the house top, highly pearched, but absurdly conditioned. 1603 T. Carew *Certaine godly and necessarie Sermons* P7: One compares an evill officer to an Ape on the top of a house highlye pearched, but badly qualited.
  Shakespeare: *MM* 2.2.120

K72   What the KING wills, that the law wills (*Varied* from 1611; OW881b from 1539)
  Shakespeare: *3H6* 4.1.50, *Per.* 1.1.103

K80   The KING'S English (Cf. Appendix B) (From 1553; cf. Wh K44: The king is lord of this language)
  Shakespeare: *Wiv.* 1.4.5f.

K87   KINGS have long arms (ears, hands) (*Varied* from 1539; OW428b Greek, Latin, supplementary examples)
  Shakespeare: *2H6* 4.7.81, *R2* 4.1.11, *H8* 1.1.109–11, *Per.* 1.2.7f.

K89   Every KINGDOM divided soon falls (Cf. Matt. 12.25; *varied* from 1583; Wh K62 from c1000)
  Shakespeare: *Lr.* 1.1.37f.

K90   For a KINGDOM any law may be broken (*Varied* from 1565)
Add e.g. 1566 (1573) Gascoigne *Jocasta* 2.1 I,272: If lawe of right may any way be broke, Desire of rule within a climbing brest To breake a vow may beare the buckler best. 1588 Greene *Pandosto* ed. Bullough VIII,162: In love and kingdomes

neither faith, nor lawe is to bee respected. 1590 C. Viques *Letter* (STC 24767) B1ᵛf.: Si violandum est ius, regnandi causa violandum est [Cicero *De Off.* III.21]. If right is to bee violated, it is to bee violated for an Empire.
Shakespeare: *3H6* 1.2.16

K113   As kind as a KITE (1639 CL., 1670 Ray; OW424a from 1610)
Shakespeare: *Lr.* 1.4.262

K116   KITES of Cressid's kind (From 1573)
Shakespeare: *H5* 2.1.76, *Ant.* 3.13.89

K122   A crafty KNAVE needs no broker (From *2H6*, 1591; ditto OW153b)
Shakespeare: *2H6* 1.2.100

K129   More KNAVE than fool (From *Lr.*; OW543b from c1589 [1633])
Shakespeare: *Lr.*1.4.313
Cf. F506.1: To be both fool and knave.

K132   An old KNAVE is no babe (child) (*Child* from 1529, *babe* from 1562)
Shakespeare: *Lr.* 1.3.19
Cf. K131: No knave to the old knave [from 1571]; F506: There is no fool to the old fool [from 1546].

K137.1   Take the KNAVE (fool) with thee (*Varied*)
1565 *King Darius* 847: Take two knaves with you, by my faye. c1592 *Thomas of Woodstock* 3.3.43: Take a knave with ye. 1592 Nashe *Strange Newes* I,274: Go your wayes a dolt as you came. 1602 *Thomas Lord Cromwell* 3.2.168: Away with him! take hence the foole you came for.
Shakespeare: *Lr.* 1.4.315f.
Cf. G150.1 (An) x GO with thee.

K149   As full of KNAVERY (As full) as an egg is full of meat (*Full* from

c1552; OW293a supplements)
Shakespeare: *Rom.* 3.1.22f.

K157.1   To lay KNIFE aboard
c1598 (1639) Deloney *2 Gentle Craft* iii 155: I muse much (quoth Meg) where your Master layes his knife a boord now adayes. 1599 Nashe *Lenten Stuffe* III,189: Hydra herring will have every thing Sybarite dainty, where he lays knife aboord. c1608 (1611) L. Barry *Ram Alley* I1ᵛ: The truth is, I have laide my knife abord, The widdow sir is wedded.
Shakespeare: *Rom.* 2.4.201f.

(?) K157.2   To whet a KNIFE for one's own throat (OW882b; 1639 only)
Shakespeare: *R3* 1.3.243

K170.1   I KNOW him as well as he that made him.
1611 COT. s.v. Chauffer: Ie cognois bien de quel bois il se chauffe. I know him as well as he that made him.
Shakespeare: *1H4* 2.4.267f.

K171.1   I (etc.) KNOW thee (you) well enough (*to supposed knaves, villians*)
E.g., 1533 N. Udall *Floures* A4: Nihil me fallis. Thou canste not begyle me, or, I knowe the wel inoughe. 1597 (1599) Chapman *Humorous Day's Mirth* 1.5.110 (*I you*). 1599 (1600) Drayton et al. *1 Sir John Oldcastle* 1.3.64f. (*They thee*). c1600 (1602) *Thomas Lord Cromwell* 4.2.43 (*We you*). c1608 (1611) Dekker & Middleton *Roaring Girl* 3.3.203f. (*I you*). 1616 DR., s.v. Knowledge 1174 [with e.g., S558: I smell him out]: I kenne him well enough.
Shakespeare: *Ado* 2.1.133, *1H4* 3.3.64, *Tit.* 5.2.21, *Lr.* 4.6.177, *Cor.* 2.1.46, 65f., *WT* 4.4.638f.

K173   I KNOW (wot) what I know (wot) (*Wot* from 1546; OW435b *know* from 1570)
Shakespeare: *Err.* 3.1.11, *LLL* 5.2.490, *MM* 3.2.152, *Lr.* 1.5.16

K175   KNOW thyself (From 1481)
    Shakespeare: *MV*   1.1.7,   *AYL*
1.2.176,   3.5.57,   *TN*   5.1.19f.,   *Tro.*
2.1.66,   *MM*   3.2.232f.,   *3H6*   2.2.145,
H8   2.2.22,   3.2.378,   *Ham.*   5.2.139f.,
Lr. 1.1.293f., 1.4.251f., *Mac.* 2.2.70,
4.2.19,   *Ant.*   2.1.5,   2.2.90f.,   *Cor.*
2.1.67,   *Per.*   1.1.41f.,   2.1.71f.,   *Ven.*
525

K179.1   What one does not KNOW
does not hurt (*Varied*)
c1526 *Dicta Sap.* B4: It is no domage
that thou parceyvest nat. 1576 Pettie
Petite Pallace 204 (jealous wife soli-
loquizing): So long as I know it not, it
hurteth mee not. 1666 TOR. *It. Prov.*
5 195: He suffers not, who knows
not [all transferred from L461].
    Shakespeare: *Oth.* 3.3.338f.

K186   One KNOWS not where to
have you (*1H4*, 1671 CL.f.; OW438a
[with M228: A man cannot tell
where to have him] from a1576)
    Shakespeare: *1H4* 3.3.127f.

L

L1   He has his LABOR for his pains
(travail) (*Travail* from 1589, *pains*
from 1639; ditto OW438a)
Add: 1578 T. White *Sermon preached
at Pawles Crosse* 3 Nov. 1577 D5f.:
Many make them reape their labour
for theyr paynes.
    Shakespeare: *TGV* 1.1.116f., *Tro.*
1.1.70, *AWW* 2.1.125, *Oth.* 2.3.366f.,
Cym. 3.5.162

L9   You lose your (To lose one's)
LABOR (From *LLL*; OW485b from
c1515; Wh T442 from c1378)
    Shakespeare: *Err.*   5.1.97,   *LLL*
(title),   *MV*   2.7.74,   *Wiv.*   2.1.239,
AWW 3.5.7, *MM* 5.1.428, *3H6*
3.1.32, *Mac.* 5.8.8, *WT* 4.4.760

L25.1   To kick down the LADDER
(OW421b *varied* from *JC*[?], incor-
porating L26)

E.g., 1600 (1657) Dekker et al. *Lust's
Dominion* 4.3.54–6: That Philippo
Makes you his ladder, and being
climb'd so high As he may reach a
diadem, there you lie.
    Shakespeare: *JC* 2.1.22–7
    Cf. L26: To turn one's back on the
ladder (cut down the stairs) by which
one rose [*ladder JC, stairs* 1655].

(?) L30.1   My LADY'S eldest son (i.e.,
bastard?)
1606 (1607) *Puritan* 1.2.54–7: Then
was I turnde to my wittes, to shift in
the world, to towre among Sonnes
and Heyres, and Fooles, and Gulls,
and Ladyes eldest Sonnes.
    Shakespeare: *Ado*   2.1.9f.,   *Jn.*
1.1.158f.

L32.1   As white as (any) LAKE (*linen*)
(Wh L22 from c1300)
    Shakespeare: *Mac.* 5.3.16
    Cf. L306.1: As white as linen.

L34   As gentle (quiet, meek, mild,
etc.) as a LAMB (From 1520; Wh
25–36)
E.g., 1611 L. Barry *Ram-Alley* V H3^v:
As quiet as a sucking lambe.
    Shakespeare: *MND* 1.2.82f., *2H6*
3.1.69–71, *Jn.* 4.1.79, *Rom.* 2.5.44

L34.1   As   innocent   as   a   LAMB
(OW404b from 1589; L33 has 1590,
2H6)
    Shakespeare: *Shr.*   3.2.157,   *MM*
3.2.8–10, *2H6* 3.1.69–71, 4.2.79,
Mac. 4.3.16, 54, *WT* 1.2.67–9

L35.1   A LAMB (lion) here and a lion
(lamb) there (Wh L38 *varied* from
a1200)
E.g., a1420 Lydgate *Troy* I 18.216:
In porte a lambe, in herte a lyoun fel.
a1464 Capgrave *Chronicle* 145(12f.):
The Kyng of Frauns in face schewid
himself a lomb, and in work a leon.
    Shakespeare: *Ado* 1.1.14f.
    Cf. L311: A lion in the field, a lamb
in the town.

L36 The LAMB is more in dread of the wolf than of the lion (*Varied* from 1580)
Add: 1578 T. White *Sermon Preached at Pawles Crosse* 3 Nov. 1577 F4ᵛ: If a beast humble himselfe to a Lion he is the less cruell [cf. L316], but do it to a Wolfe and hee is the more fierce.
Shakespeare: *TN* 3.1.128f.

L49.1 A good LAND, a bad people
1550 O. Werdmuller (M. Coverdale) *Spiritual . . . perle* E6: And of this dyd these proverbes firste spring up: the more plentyful lande, the more folyshe and wycked people. 1607 H. Estienne (R. Carew) *World of Wonders* C3ᵛ: The old Greeke proverb, which hath bene found too true of other ages, A good land, a bad people.
Shakespeare: *2H6* 4.7.55f.
Cf. E146: England is a good country but ill people.

L54.1 No LAND there is that can this land subdue, if we agree within our selves, and to our realm are true.
1569 W. Seres *Aunswere to the Proclamation of the Rebels* A8ᵛ: A Proverbe olde, no land there is / that can this land subdue, If we agree within our selves, / And to our Realme be true.
Shakespeare: *Jn.* 5.7.117f.

L57 To water (dig, ear) another's LAND (1548, *AWW*, 1666)
I.e., 1548 Cooper s.v. Ager: Agros alienos irrigas, tuis sitientibus. A proverbe spoken of them that be diligente in other mens mattiers, and let theyr owne slepe: it is applied also to advouterers. 1666 TOR. *Prov. Phr.* s.v. Orto 124: To dig anothers garden . . . to Cuckold one, to do his work and drudgery, as they say for him.
Shakespeare: *AWW* 1.3.43–6, *2H4* 3.2.112f.

L68 The LAPWING cries most when farthest from her nest (*Varied* from 1580)

Add: 1573 J. Bridges *Supremacie of Christian Princes* 307: But herein ye play as the common people say the Lapwing or Pewet doeth, who when they seeke hir Neast, draweth them still further and further from it, wyth hir noyse and flittering about them, crying as the simple people imagine, here is it, here is it, when it is nothing neare it.
Shakespeare: *Err.* 4.2.27, *MM* 1.4.32

L69 Like a LAPWING that runs away with the shell on his head (*Varied* from 1598; ditto OW442a)
Shakespeare: *Ham.* 5.2.185f.

L82 LAST but not least (From 1589; ditto OW442b)
Shakespeare: *JC* 3.1.189, *Lr.* 1.1.83

L92 LAUGH and lie (lay) down (From c1522)
Shakespeare: *TNK* 2.2.150f.

L92a To LAUGH and cry at once (like rain in sunshine) From Shak.; OW444a from 1531)
Shakespeare: *R2* 3.2.10, *Lr.* 4.3.17–9, *Ven.* 413f.

L92a.1 To LAUGH and leap (leap and laugh) (Cf. Appendix B)
1566 (1575) Gascoigne *Supposes* 5.6.56–8: What the devill ayleth him to leap and laugh so like a foole in the high way? 1576 *Glasse of Governement* II,533: Fowle, and blacke, maie laughe & leape at large! 1599 (1600) Jonson *Every Man Out* 1.3.120f.: To sit and clap my hands, and laugh and leape, Knocking my head against my roofe with ioy.
Shakespeare: *LLL* 4.3.146, *MV* 1.1.49, *Son.* 98.4

L93 He LAUGHS that wins (From 1546)
Shakespeare: *1H4* 5.1.8, *Oth.* 4.1.122, *Tmp.* 2.1.32–7

L94　To be ready to burst with LAUGHING (From 1606; OW92b from c1565)
　　Shakespeare: *Tro.* 1.3.175−8

L94.1　To die LAUGHING (laugh oneself to death) (fig.) (*OED Die* 7c *Shr.*, *Tro.*, then 1778)
　　1609 W. Fiston *Schoole of good Manners* B7ᵛ: These are words of Fooles to say, I was like to bepisse myselfe with laughing: I had almost burst with laughing [L94]: I was like to have dyed with laughing. 1612 Webster *White Devil* 5.3.199: Hee tickles you to death; makes you die laughing. 1616 DR. s.v. Mirth 1401: A man laugheth ill, that laugheth himselfe to death. 1631 Adams *2 Peter* 432 (of flatterers): He is such a pleasing murtherer that he tickles thee to death; and like Salamons foole, thou dyest laughing.
　　Shakespeare: *Shr.* 3.2.241, *Tro.* 1.3.175−8, *MM* 2.2.122f., *Tit.* 5.1.112f., *Tmp.* 2.2.154

L119.1　As white as LAWN
　　1604 Dekker & Middleton *1 Honest Whore* 2.1.172: A skin, your satten is not more soft [Wh S62], nor lawne whiter.
　　Shakespeare: *Luc.* 259

L125　A LAWYER will not plead but for money (a fee) (1616 DR., *varied* from c1460 [Wh L110]; OW447b supplements)
　　E.g., 1584 R. Wilson *Three Ladies of London* C1ᵛ: Thou art akinne to the Lawyer, thou wilt doo nothing without a fee.
　　Shakespeare: *Lr. 1.4.128−30*

L131　I will LAY (set) it on, take it off who will (*Set* 1600 [1603], *lay* from *Tro.*)
　　Shakespeare: *Tro.* 1.2.206f.

L133.1　As dull as LEAD (Wh L121 a1500, a1522)
　　1599 (1600) Dekker *Old Fortunatus* 2.2.158f.: Thy soule is made of lead, too dull, too ponderous to mount up. 1599 (1600) Jonson *Every Man Out* Epilogue 24: Let forraine politie be dull as lead. 1600 Dekker et al. *Lust's Dominion* 1.1.20: I am now sick, heavie, and dull as lead.
　　Shakespeare: *LLL* 3.1.59, *2H4* 1.1.118

L134　As heavy as LEAD (From c1553; Wh L123 from a750)
　　E.g., a1325 *Maximion* in Boddeker 247.82: Myn herte is hevy so led.
　　Shakespeare: *LLL* 3.1.59, *1H4* 5.3.33f., *2H4* 1.1.118, *Rom.* 1.1.180, 2.5.17, *Ant.* 3.11.72, *TNK* 5.1.96f.

L135　As wan (pale) as LEAD (From 1503; Wh L126 *pale* from a1400; Wh L129 *wan* from c1325)
　　Shakespeare: *MV* 3.2.106, *Rom.* 2.5.17

L136　To have LEAD on one's heels (From c1475)
　　Shakespeare: *LLL* 3.1.59, *Cor.* 3.1.312

(?) L136.1　To weigh like any LEAD (Wh L135 c1475)
　　Shakespeare: *R3* 5.3.147f.

L140　He trembles (quakes, shakes) like an aspen LEAF (*Varied* from c1475; Wh A216 from c1385)
　　Shakespeare: *2H4* 2.4.105−9, *Tit.* 2.4.45

L153　Never too old (late) to LEARN (From c1620; OW563b from 1555)
　　E.g., 1572 J. Parinchef *Extract of Examples* 72−3: Salinus Julianus ... was woont to say that he would be glad to learne, albeit one of his feete were in the grave ... in these days we have an other sentence common in most mens mouthes, I am now too olde to learne. c1609 (1655) T. Heywood & W. Rowley *Fortune by Land and Sea* 1.1 VI,363: Nay school us

not old man, some of us are too old to learn.
Shakespeare: *Lr.* 2.2.127

(?) L153.1 Not too old to LEARN[n] (Wh O30 c1515)
I.e., c1515 Barclay *Eclogues* 71.538: Thou art not to olde for to lere.
Shakespeare: *MV* 3.2.160f.

[n]OW563b includes both passages above under L153, but the sense is quite different.

L165 Whom we love best to them we can say LEAST (*Varied* from 1576)
Add: 1576 Pettie *Petite Pallace* 202: Shee remembred it was one of the properties of love to bee silent. 1586 Guazzo (B. Young) *Civile Conversation* IV II,194: And to be short, In love matters whosoever holdeth his peace, speaketh. 1596 Marlowe *Hero and Leander* I.186: True love is mute. 1631 Jonson *New Inn* 1.6.115f.: O but I lov'd the more: and she might read it Best, in my silence.
Shakespeare: *TGV* 1.2.32, 2.2.17, *MND* 5.1.104f., *Ado* 2.1.306f., *Lr.* 1.1.62, *Ven.* 1146, Son. 23.13

L167.1 Give me (us) LEAVE (*A request for privacy*) (Cf. Appendix B)
1601 (1602) Dekker *Satiromastix* 2.1.101: I prethee give us leave. c1613 (1616) Beaumont & Fletcher *Scornful Lady* 3.1.142: And give me leave awhile Sir.
Shakespeare: *TGV* 3.1.1, *3H6* 3.2.33, *Jn.* 1.1.230, *1H4* 3.2.1

L173.1 LECHERY is no sin (Wh L167 *varied* from c1303)
E.g., c1378 *Piers B* iii 58: It is a synne of the sevene sonnest relessed.
Add: 1596 Lodge *Wits Miserie* G3[v] (Fornication speaking): Tut . . . lechery is no sinne, find me one Philosopher that held simple fornication for offensive. c1610 (1613)

Marston & Barksted *Insatiate Countess* III III,48: 'Tis custome, and not reason makes love sinne.
Shakespeare: *MM* 3.1.109f.

L176 As green as a LEEK (From 1573; Wh L180 from a1398)
Shakespeare: *MND* 5.2.335

(?) L191 How came you hither? On my LEGS (feet) (From *R3*; OW455a *feet* c1590)
Add: c1520 *Youth* 220f.: Who brought thee hither today? / That did my legs, I tell thee.
Shakespeare: *R3* 1.4.85f.

L192.1 To be lusty at LEGS (Cf. Appendix B)
c1601 (1602) ?Middleton *Blurt, Master Constable* 1.1.90−2: Talk of any subject but this jangling law at arms. / The law at legs then. / Will you be so lusty? 1606 Dekker *Seven Deadly Sinnes of London* ed. Brett-Smith 38: Tradesmen (as if they were dauncing Galliards) are lusty at legges and never stand still. 1620 (1622) Dekker & Massinger *Virgin Martyr* 4.2.10f.: Use the agility of your armes. / Or legs, I am lusty at them.
Shakespeare: *Lr.* 2.4.10

L195 Use LEGS and have legs (From 1582; OW856b *limbs* from c1576)
Shakespeare: *MV* 2.2.5f.

L202 To have (know) the LENGTH of one's foot (fig.) (From 1580)
Shakespeare: *LLL* 5.2.474

L206 A LEOPARD (panther) cannot change his spots (Jer. 13.23; from *R2*; OW456af. from 1546)
E.g., 1546 J. Bale *Exam[n] Anne Askewe* PS 177: Their old conditions will change when the blackamorian change his skin, and the cat a mountain her spots. 1579 Lyly *Euphues* I,191: Can the Aethiope chaunge or

alter his skinne? or the Leoparde his hewe?

Shakespeare: *MND* 3.2.260, *R2* 1.1.174f.

L225 Too much LIBERTY spoils all (*Varied* from 1611; OW831b from 1533, including *Err.*)
E.g.: 1533 Udall *Flowers for Latin Speaking* (1560) T4ᵛ: We be all the worse by havyng to much libertee. 1547 Baldwin *Moral Philosophy* Bk. III. D5: To muche libertie turneth into bondage.

Shakespeare: *Err.* 2.1.15, *MM* 1.2.124f.

L237 Tell a LIE and find (to know) a truth (From c1594; ditto OW806b with Spanish)
Shakespeare: *Ham.* 2.1.60, 63

L244 Anything for a quiet LIFE (From c1621; ditto OW15b)
Shakespeare: *Cym.* 3.3.30

L244.1 As dear as LIFE (Cf. Appendix B) (Wh L234 [2])
Add e.g.: a1564 *Bugbears* 1.1.5: My life is as dere to me as yours is to you. c1587 (1590) Marlowe *1 Tamburlaine* 5.2.263–76: Unspotted maids . . . Whose lives were dearer to Zenocrate Than her own life. 1590 Spenser *Faerie Queene* 1.1.54.2f.: For all so deare as life is to my hart, I deeme your love. 1596 Ibid. 4.1.6.6f.: Nathlesse her honor, dearer then her life, She sought to save.

Shakespeare: *MV* 4.1.283, *Tro.* 5.3.27, *AWW* 4.4.6, *R3* 3.2.78, *Lr.* 1.1.58

L248.1 LIFE is a flower (Wh L243 a1450)
I.e., a1450 *Gesta* 235(2–5): For the lyf of man is likenid nowe to a flour, nowe to hete or warmnes, and nowe to a fleinge shadowe . . . and nowe to an arowe shote to a marke.
Add: 1595 R. Southwell *Saint Peters*

Complaynt 95f. *Poems* 78 (of life): A flower, a play, a blast, a shade, a dream: A living death, a never turning streame.

Shakespeare: *AYL* 5.3.28
Cf. F386: It fades (withers) like a flower [Wh F317–20].

L249 LIFE is a pilgrimage (From 1576; Wh P201 from c1340; cf. Gen. 47.9)
Shakespeare: *AYL* 3.2.129f., *MM* 2.1.36, *1H6* 2.5.116, *R2* 2.1.154

L249.1 LIFE is a shadow (smoke) (OW461b: 1549 J. Calvin *Life and Conv. of a Christian Man* H1ᵛ: Mans lyfe, to be lyke a smoke or shadowe, is not onely knowen to learned men, but also the common people use no proverbe more in their mouthes.)
Add e.g., 1561 Job 8.9 (Geneva): For we are but of yesterday, and are ignorant: for our dayes upon earth are but a shadow. 1579 Lyly *Euphues* I,252: Our lyfe is but a shadowe.

Shakespeare: *Mac.* 5.5.24
Cf. on L248.1.

L251 LIFE is a span (From 1579; cf. Ps. 39.5)
Shakespeare: *AYL* 3.2.131f., *H8* 1.1.223, 3.2.140, *Oth.* 2.3.72, *Tim.* 5.3.3

(?) L251.1 LIFE is brittle
Cf. 1436 *Libelle* 30.579–80: But wee be frayle as glasse And also bretyll [Wh G112]. 1506 Hawes *Pastime* 204.5364: Of his wanton youthe brytle as the glasse [Wh G109]. 1566 (1575) Gascoigne *Jocasta* III I,290: This life of ours Is brittle.

Shakespeare: *1H4* 5.4.78

L260.1 My LIFE for (to) yours (i.e., I'm sure, Assuredly)
E.g., c1569 Marriage of *Wit and Science* 4.3 (MSR 1069): My life to yours it may be mended all. c1591 (1592) *Arden of Feversham* 1.1.387: My lyfe for yours, ye shall do well

enough. c1592 (1594) Marlowe *Edward II* 2.1.28: My life for thine she will have Gaveston! c1605 (1608) Middleton *Trick to Catch the Old One* 4.2.67: My life for yours, sir. c1606 (1607) Jonson *Volpone* 1.4.17: My life for his, 'tis but to make him sleepe.
Shakespeare: *MND* 3.1.41f.

L265   There is LIFE in it (*TN*, *Lr.*, *Ant.*, 1639)
I.e., 1639 CL., s.v. Spes pertinax 294: There's some life in't yet.
Add: 1606 (1607) *Puritan* 2.1.141: There's life int yet. 1616 Jonson *Devil is an Ass* 4.2.9: Yes, faith, there's life in't, now.
Shakespeare: *Ado* 2.2.19, *TN* 1.3.111, *Lr.* 4.6.202, *Ant.*3.13.176, 191
Cf. L269: While there's life there's hope [from 1539].

L277   A LIGHTENING (lightning) before death (From 1584)
Add: 1600 (1608) R. Armin *Nest of Ninnies* A3: Shee now begins to grow bucksome as a lightning before death, and gad shee will.
Shakespeare: *2H4* 4.2.81, *Rom.* 5.1.2−5, 5.3.88−90

L279   As swift as LIGHTNING (Shak., 1599ff.)
Add: c1300 *South English Legendary* II 473.300: Ac quic hi doth as light-inge thurf purgatorie gon [Wh L268]. c1410 Lovelich *Grail* II 290.451−2: As swift they weren In alle thing As to-forn the thondir is the lyhgtenyng [Wh L269]. c1587 (1590) Marlowe *l Tamburlaine* 2.3.57f.: These are the wings shall make it fly as swift As doth the light-ning. 1589 Greene *Menaphon* VI,76: Your loves are like lightning which no sooner flash on the eie, but they vanish.
Shakespeare: *MND* 1.1.145, *3H6* 2.1.129, *R2* 1.3.79, *Rom.* 2.2.119f., 3.1.172

L281   There is LIGHTNING lightly before thunder (Collections from 1616; OW464a *varied* from 1545; cf. Eccl. 32.11)
Shakespeare: *Jn.* 1.1.24−6, *Tmp.* 1.2.201f.

L282.1   LIKE for like (*Varied*)
1577 J. Grange *Golden Aphroditis* H2: So say I nowe, Render like for like. 1588 L. Humphrey *View of the Romish hydra* D5: I doe set downe this ground generally received by com-mon Law, Lex talionis: The Law of retaliation: That like will have like.
Shakespeare: *MM* 5.1.411
Cf. M800: Measure for measure.

L286   LIKE will to like (From 1509)
Shakespeare: *AWW* 1.1.223, *Lr.* 4.2.39

L287   LIKE will to like, quoth the devil to the collier (From 1568; OW465a from ?1559)
Shakespeare: *TN* 3.4.116f.

L290   They are so LIKE that they are the worse for it (From *WT*; ditto OW465a)
Shakespeare: *WT* 2.3.97f.

(?) L293.1   To show oneself in one's own LIKENESS
1616 DR. s.v. Shamelesse, no. 1955: He sheweth himselfe in his owne likenesse.
Shakespeare: *LLL* 4.3.44, *Rom.* 2.1.16−21, *Tmp.* 3.2.128f.

L295.1   As fair as the LILY (Wh L276 a1385)
Shakespeare: *Cym.* 4.2.201
Cf. L297: The lily is fair in show but foul in smell.

L295.2   As fresh as (the) LILY (lilies) (Wh L277 from a1420)
Shakespeare: *Cym.* 2.2.15

L295.3   As pure as a LILY (Wh L283
c1490 *lily-flower*)
   Shakespeare: *LLL* 5.2.351f.
   Cf. Wh L276−85 (clean, clear,
etc.)

L295.4   As sweet as LILY (Wh L278
a1400, 1501)
   Shakespeare: *Cym.* 4.2.201

L296   As white as a LILY (From
1485; Wh L279 from c1000)
   Shakespeare: *TGV* 2.3.20, *Tit.*
2.4.44, *Lr.* 2.2.17, *Mac.* 5.3.15, *Cym.*
2.2.15f., *Ven.* 228, 362−4, *Luc.* 71,
386, *Son.* 98.9

L296.1   LILY-WHITE (Cf. Appendix B) (Wh L279a from c1325 [*OED*
a1310])
   Shakespeare: *MND* 3.1.93, *Ven.*
1053

L297   The LILY is fair in show but
foul in smell (*Varied* from 1590)
   E.g., ?c1590 (1596) *Edward III*
2.1.451: Lillies that fester smel far
worse then weeds.
   Shakespeare: *Son.* 94.14[n]

[n]Actually, L297 is relevant to neither
of the cited passages. In turn, the 1618
citation under C668 made it tempting
to make a new entry, one on putrified
flowers. But cf. 1633 T. Adams, *Commentary . . . Saint Peter*, p. 173: "Putrified flowers stinke worse than
weeds," followed by p. 526: "festered
lillies smell farre worse then weeds."
The context of this last passage makes
almost certain that Adams simply borrowed from *Edward III*.

L304.1   To give one LINE (*OED sb.*[2]
2b from *2H4*)
1604 Dekker & Middleton *1 Honest
Whore* 2.1.55f.: So: give the fresh Salmon Lyne now: let him come
ashoare. c1604 (1605) Marston
Dutch Courtesan 5.3.46f.: Knowing
that the hook was deeply fast, I gave

her line at will. ?1621 (1652) Fletcher
Wild Goose Chase 2.2.42f.: Her
gravity will give me line still, And let
me lose myself. 1623 (1653) Middleton & Rowley *Spanish Gypsy*
3.2.176f.: Let the fish alone, Give
him line.
   Shakespeare: *2H4* 4.4.39 (F), *WT*
1.2.180f.

L305   To work by LINE and level
(measure) (*Varied* from 1587;
OW466a from c1420)
   Shakespeare: *Tmp.* 4.1.239

L305.1   Many LINES meet at the center (*Varied*)
E.g., 1600 (1601) Jonson *Cynthia's
Revels* 4.1.195−8: I would . . . wish
my selfe . . . the very center of
wealth, and beautie, wherein all lines
of love should meet. 1603 Montaigne (Florio) *Essaies* III.v 514: All
the worlds motions bend and yeelde
to this [sexual] coniunction: it is . . . a
Centre whereto all lines come. 1605
Marston *Dutch Courtesan* 2.1.121:
Love is the centre in which all lines
close. 1607 Matthieu (Grimeston)
General Inventorie 979: They were
drawne from one principle of truth,
as manie Lines are from one Center.
1612 T. Adams *Gallants Burden* Hl:
As many lines meete at the Center;
so all sinnes by a generall confluence
to this place.
   Shakespeare: *H5* 1.2.210

(?) L306.1   As white as LINEN
c1330 R. Brunne *Chron.* (1810) 334:
Alle thei fled on rowe, in lynen white
as milke (*OED* 3a).
   Shakespeare: *Mac.* 5.3.16
   Cf. L32.1: As white as lake (*linen*).

L307.1   As bold(ly) as (any, a) LION
(Wh L305 from a1325 [4])
   Shakespeare: *Jn.* 2.1.452, *Mac.*
1.2.35, *Cor.* 1.1.171

L308   As fierce (valiant) as a LION
(*Fierce* from c1485, *valiant* from *1H4*
[cf. Wh L305 (bold), 307 (courageous), etc.])
   Shakespeare: *Tro.* 1.2.20f., *1H4*
3.1.165

L311   A LION in the field, a lamb in
the town (*Varied* from 1557; Wh L38
[A lamb here and a lion there] *varied*
from a1200)
E.g., c1433 Lydgate *St. Edmund*
390.785: In pes lik lambes, in werre
lik leouns. a1439 *Fall* II 430.3650: In
werre a leoun, and a lamb in pes.
   Shakespeare: *R2* 2.1.173f., *Cor.*
2.1.12
   Cf. L35.1: A lamb (lion) here and a
lion (lamb) there.

L316   The LION spares the suppliant
(*Varied* from 1580; OW467a from
1554−7)
Add e.g.: 1559 "Lord Clifford" 18
Mirror for Magistrates 193: Poore selly
lambes the Lyon never teares.
   Shakespeare: *LLL* 4.1.88−91, *Tro.*
5.3.37f., *Tit.* 2.3.151f.
   Cf. L36: The lamb is more in
dread of the wolf than of the lion.

L316.1   A LION takes no lambs
(mice) (*Varied*)
1559 "Lord Clifford" 18f. *Mirror for
Magistrates* 193: Poore selly lambes
the Lyon never teares: The feble
mouse may lye among the beares.
1578 T. White *Sermon preached at
Pawles Crosse* 3 Nov. 1577 F4ᵛ: A
Lion takes no lambes, as an Eagle
takes no flies, Aquila non capit
Muscas [E1]. 1580 Lyly *Euphues and
his England* II,7: The Cat dare not
fetch the mouse out of the Lions den.
1588 Greene *Pandosto* ed. Bullough
VIII, 183: The Lyon never prayeth
on the mouse. ?c1600 *Fatal Marriage*
xii (MSR 1307f.): Who ever knew the
Eagles catch at fflees the lion seize
upon a silly Mouse.
   Shakespeare: *MM* 1.4.63f.

L316.2   To be like (a) LION(S) (Wh
L335 *varied* from c1000)
E.g., c1500 *Melusine* 113.10f.: Have
an herte as a fyers Lyon ayenst your
enemyes.
   Shakespeare: *TNK* 5.1.39

L316.3   To fare like (a) LION(S) (Wh
L344 *varied* from a1300)
E.g., a1450 *Partonope* 432.10577f.:
As a lyon that wode was he ferde,
That hongry was and lakked his
pray. a1470 Malory II 760.16f.: He
fared as hit had bene an hungry
lyon.
   Shakespeare: *1H6* 1.2.27f., 4.7.7.

L317   Wake not a sleeping LION
(From 1593; OW863b from ?c1586
[actually ?c1611])
   Shakespeare: *2H4* 1.2.153f.

L319   If the LION'S skin cannot the
fox's shall (*Varied* from 1573)
   Shakespeare: *MND* 5.1.231

L321.1   It is dangerous to play with
LIONS
1571 R. Edwards *Damon and Pithias*
xi (MSR 767): It is no safe playing
with Lyons, but when it please them.
c1576 *Common Conditions* 1581: Tis
not for the weake hart with the Lion
for to play. 1602 L. Lloyd *Briefe Con-
ference* P4ᵛ: It is an old saying, It is
dangerous to play with Lyons;
Leonem vellicare periculosum est.
   Shakespeare: *Ant.* 3.13.94f.

L367   Though he said LITTLE
(nought) he thought the more (*Varied*; *little* from c1475, *nought* from
c1509; cf. Wh M685 [To think more
than one says] *varied* from a1300)
   Shakespeare: *3H6* 4.1.83, *Mac.*
5.1.79

L374   As sure (true) as you (I) LIVE
(*Sure* from *TGV*; ditto OW789b)[n]
Add e.g.: 1554 T. Becon *Comfortable
Epistle* PS 209 (translating God's vow

in Ezek. 33.11): As surely as I live. /
1555 O. Werdmuller (M. Coverdale)
Spiritual . . . Perle 27 (ditto): As truly
as I live. c1591 (1592) *Arden of Feversham* 4.4.26f.: As surely as I live, Ile
banish pittie if thou use me thus.
  Shakespeare: *TGV* 4.4.15, *Ado*
5.4.64, *R2* 4.1.102, *1H4* 3.1.249,
Ham. 1.2.220f.

[n]Cf. Introduction, p. xxv.

L374.1   Do (Will) I LIVE?
1598 (1601) Jonson *Every Man In*
2.3.219f. But art thou sure he will
stay thy returne? / Do I live sir?
c1605 (c1608) Middleton *Your Five
Gallants* 2.1.197: Will I live? c1606
(1607) Jonson *Volpone* 5.12.20: Art'
sure he lives? / Doe I live, sir? c1606
(1607) G. Wilkins *Miseries of Enforced
Marriage* ix (MSR1796f.): Fail not. /
Will I live. 1620 (1622) Massinger
Virgin Martyr 1.1.2: Do I live? c1620
(1647) Fletcher & Massinger *Custom
of the Country* 5.2.1: Are you assur'd
the charm prevails? / Do I live?
  Shakespeare: *Shr.* 1.2.196, *2H4*
2.1.161
  Cf. L374.

L375−6.1   If (And) I LIVE[n] (Cf. Appendix B)
E.g., 1530 Palsgrave B4[v] (and). 1598
(1601) Jonson *Every Man In* 1.4.138
(and). c1598 (1639) Deloney *2 Gentle
Craft* 152, 166.
  Shakespeare: *Tit.*   1.1.410,
3.1.296, 4.1.112, 4.4.21f.

[n]Merely a variant of L374?

L378   It is not how long but how well
we   LIVE   (*Varied*   from   1605;
OW479b adds 1574)
I.e., 1574 Guevara (Hellowes) *Familiar Epistles* ed. 1584 192: The honest
care not to live long, but well. Add:
1579 Lyly *Euphues* I,310: The measure of lyfe is not length but honestie.
  Shakespeare: *Cor.* 3.1.152f.

L381   Live charily if not chastely
(*Varied* from 1561; OW116a from
1528, Wh C158 c1303)
  Shakespeare: *Oth.* 3.3.203f.

(?) L383.1   That I should LIVE to see
it (this day)
1586 in Hearne *R. Glouc.* (1724)
675/2: I am so unhappy to have
lyven to see this unhappy daye. 1596
Spenser *Faerie Queene* 6.11.29.1f.:
"Ah, well away!" sayd he then sigh-
ing sore, "That ever I did live, this
day to see." 1639 CL. s.v. Depre-
cantis 85: I wish I may never live to
see it. 1672 Dryden *2 Conquest of
Granada* 5.3.236: O Heav'n, that I
should live to see this day!
  Shakespeare: *Rom.* 3.2.63

L383.2   To LIVE to die, and die to
live (To die to live)
1557 "Of the ladie wentworthes
death" 1 *Tottel* x3[v]: To live to dye,
and dye to live againe. 1563 Dolman
"Hastings" 730 *Mirror for Magistrates*
295: He lived to dye, and dyed to
lyve. 1575 Gascoigne "Flowers" I,74:
Who lived to dye, and dyed againe to
live. 1579 Lyly *Euphues* I,308f.: So
shouldest thou lyue as thou mayst
dye, and then shalt thou dye to lyue.
c1592 (1594) Marlowe *Edward II*
3.3.58f.: The worst is death, and
better die to live Than live in infamy
under such a king. 1594 Kyd *Cornelia*
4.2.134f.: Nor labour I my vaine life
to assure; But so to die, as dying I
may live. 1601 A. Dent *Plaine Mans
Path-way* T7: Let us die while we are
alive, that we may live when we are
dead.
  Shakespeare: *Ado* 4.1.253.

L384   Too soon wise to LIVE long
(*Varied* from 1576)
  Shakespeare: *R3* 3.1.79

L395   Let the longer LIVER take all
(From 1605; OW481b from 1577)
  Shakespeare: *Rom.* 1.5.15

Cf. A192.1: He that wins shall take all.

L412 To chop LOGIC (From c1527)
Shakespeare: *Rom.* 3.5.149

L414 LOMBARDY is the garden of the world (Italy) (*World* from 1573; *Italy* from *Shr.*)
E.g., 1604 R. Dallington *View France* B2: As they say of Lombardy, that it is the garden of Italy: so may we truly say of France, that it is the Garden of Europe.
Shakespeare: *Shr.* 1.1.3f., *H5* 5.2.36, Epil. 7

L419 The LONG (short) and the short (long) of it (*Short and long* from 1571)
Shakespeare: *MND* 4.2.38f., *MV* 2.2.127, *Wiv.* 2.1.132f., 2.2.59f., *AWW* 2.3.28f., *H5* 3.2.117f.

L421.1 To have a woman's LONGING (fig.)
c1618 (1661) Middleton *Hengist, King of Kent* 3.3.244f.: I had such a woman's first and second longing in me To hear how she would bear her mock'd abuse. 1679 Dryden *Troilus and Cressida* 4.2 VI,361: I have a woman's longing to return.
Shakespeare: *Tro.* 3.3.237, *WT* 4.4.667

L422.1 To save one's LONGING (*OED Save* from 1593)[n]
Add e.g.: 1598 (1616) Haughton *Englishmen for My Money* viii (MSR 1453) (to a man): Well, I am content to save your longing. 1614 (1631) Jonson *Bartholomew Fair* 3.5.135f.: I'ld give halfe the Fayre . . . to save his longing. 1616 (1631) Jonson *Devil is an Ass* 1.2.33−5 (Fitz-dottrell speaking): Were hee a kinde divell . . . hee would come, but To save ones longing.
Shakespeare: *Tim.* 1.1.252f.

[n]The Arden *Timon of Athens,* accepting *OED*'s implication that the expression was elliptical for "To save a woman's longing" (as it appears to be in *OED*'s 1593 example), thinks Alcibiades's use "affected." However the phrase originated, the examples above show it was common enough in exclusively male contexts.

L423 LONG LOOKED FOR comes at last (From 1605, *Shr.*; OW480b from 1548)
Shakespeare: *Shr.* 2.1.333

(?) L426 Love not at the first LOOK (Love at first sight) (Marlowe, *AYL, Tmp.*, 1639; ditto OW493a)
I.e., a1593 (1598) Marlowe *Hero and Leander* I.175: Who ever lov'd, that lov'd not at first sight? 1639 CL., p. 28.
Add: 1596 (1598) Chapman *Blind Beggar of Alexandria* x.128: None ever lov'd but at first sight they lov'd. c1597 (1609) Jonson *Case is Altered* 4.7.3: Hay my love, O my love, at the first sight? c1604 (1605) Marston *Dutch Courtesan* 2.2.148: Did you ever hear of any that lov'd at the first sight?
Shakespeare: *AYL* 3.5.81f., *Tmp.* 1.2.441f.

L427.1 LOOK (well) about (you) (*OED* 11b includes *Shr.*)
E.g., 1553 ?Udall *Respublica* 5.8 1733: 'Twere more need to look about you. 1566 (1575) Gascoigne *Supposes* 1.1.25: Look well about you. 1597 (1599) Chapman *Humorous Day's Mirth* 2.1.23: Now I must looke about. c1599 (1600) *Look about You.* 1605 Jonson et al. *Eastward Ho* 5.4.205: Now London, looke about. 1609 Bretnor (Crow e 382 Aug.) 1639 CL. s.v. Ab initio, ad finem: Look well about you.
Shakespeare: *Shr.* 1.2.140, *AWW* 4.3.312, *2H4* 5.1.52f., *Rom.* 3.5.40, *JC* 2.3.7

L429 LOOK ere (before) you leap (From 1528)
Shakespeare: *2H4* 1.3.33

L431.1   LOOK up (*OED* 45c, Shak. only) (Cf. Appendix B)
c1559 (c1569) W. Wager *Longer Thou Livest* 1359−41: Look up lustily, use a gentleman's countenance. . . . / A feather would make me look aloft. c1599 (1610) Marston *Histriomastix* 5.1 III, 291: Looke up and play the Tamburlaine: you rogue you c1621 (1662) Middleton *Anything for a Quiet Life* 5.1.177: Look up, sir. 1700 Congreve *Way of the World* 5.1.394: Look up, man.
Shakespeare: *2H4* 4.4.113, *Ham.* 3.3.50, *WT* 5.1.215

L452   He wears a whole LORDSHIP on his back (1639, cf. *Jn.*, *H8*; OW874b *varied* from 1576)
Shakespeare: *2H6* 1.3.80, *Jn.* 2.1.70, *H8* 1.1.83f.

L454   As good (Better) LOST as (than) found (From 1546; OW54b supplements)
Shakespeare: *AWW* 2.3.205f., 5.1.42−5

L458   Give LOSERS leave to speak (talk) (*Varied* from 1533)
Shakespeare: *Wiv.* 1.4.121, *2H6* 3.1.182, 185, *Tit.* 3.1.232f.
Cf. P595.1: Anger (impatience) has its privilege [*Jn.*, *Lr.*]

(?) L461   He that is not sensible of his LOSS has lost nothing (1732 FUL., cf. *Oth.*; cf. K179.1)
Shakespeare: *Oth.* 3.3.342f.

L471   A LOUSE is a man's (beggar's) companion (*Gentleman's* from 1594, *beggar's* from 1616; OW488a supplements)
Add: 1586 R. Crowley *Fryer Iohn Frauncis* El[v]: This Epitheten lousie, hath bene thought meete for a Fryer ever since I could remember.
Shakespeare: *Wiv.* 1.1.19−21

L479   Follow LOVE (pleasure, glory) and it will flee, flee love (pleasure, glory) and it will follow thee (*Varied* from 1562; cf. Wh L487 a1400)
Shakespeare: *TGV* 5.2.49f.
Cf. L518: Love (Woman, Honor), like a shadow (crocodile, death), flies one following, and pursues one fleeing.

(?) L479.1   For LOVE or gold (Wh L480 a1300)
Shakespeare: *AYL* 2.4.71f.
Cf. OW493a: For love or money [from c1566].

L481   He that has LOVE in his breast has spurs in his sides (etc.) (Collections from 1640, cf. *Mac.*)
Shakespeare: *Mac.* 1.6.22−4

L498   LOVE, being jealous, makes a good eye look asquint (Collections from 1664, variants from 1591; ditto OW489b)
I.e., 1591 FLOR. *Sec. F.* VI 83: To much love makes a sound eye oftentimes to see a misse. 1640 HERB. 539: Love makes a good eye squint.
Shakespeare: *Lr.* 5.3.72

L500   LOVE cannot be hid (From 1599 [1600], analogue from 1596)
Add: c1593 (1598) Marlowe *Hero and Leander* II.131: O none but gods have power their love to hide.
Shakespeare: *TN* 3.1.147f.
Cf. L490: LOVE and a cough (smoke, itch) cannot be hid [from 1573; OW488a combines with L500, has Latin and supplementary examples].

L501   LOVE comes by looking (in at the eyes) (From 1539)
E.g., 1539 TAV. 12: Ex adspectu nascitur amor. Of syght is love gendred.
Shakespeare: *MV* 3.2.67, *TN* 1.5.296−8, *Rom.* 2.3.67f.

L505   LOVE has no respect of persons (*Varied* from 1576)
E.g., 1580 Lyly *Euphues and his*

England II,184: I but love regardeth no byrth . . . I but love knoweth no kindred.
Shakespeare: *TNK* 2.4.32

(?) L505.1 LOVE is a chameleon that feeds on air
1588 (1591) Lyly *Endymion* 3.4.129f.: Love is a Camelion, which draweth nothing into the mouth but ayre.
Shakespeare: *TGV* 2.1.172f.

L505.2 LOVE is a madness (lunacy)
1599 (1600) Dekker *Old Fortunatus* 3.1.7: Thou saiest love is a madnes, hate it then. 1599 (1600) Dekker *Shoemakers' Holiday* 3.4.18: Such is loves lunacie. 1604 Dekker & Middleton *1 Honest Whore* 4.4.104: All love is lunaticke. 1609 (1616) Jonson *Epicoene* 4.4.47f.: They say you are run mad, sir. / Not for love, I assure you, of you.
Shakespeare: *MND* 5.1.4−8, *AYL* 3.2.400−4, *H8* 1.4.27f., *Rom.* 1.1.190−3, 2.1.7
Cf. L517: Love is without reason; Wh L546: Mad love lasteth but a while [c1520].

L506 LOVE is blind (From c1475)
Shakespeare: *TGV* 2.1.70, 2.4.96, 4.2.46f., *MV* 2.6.36, *H5* 5.2.300f., *Rom.* 2.1.32f., 3.2.9, *Son.* 137.1

L507 LOVE is full of fear (*Full of* from 1594, *never without* from c1503; OW490b Ovid *full of dread* c1374, *fear* 1578)
Shakespeare: *Ham.* 3.2.167−72, *Ven.* 1021

L508 LOVE is lawless (*Varied* from 1576; OW491a from c1380)
Shakespeare: *TNK* 2.4.32

L509.1 LOVE is master (lord) (Wh L518 a1393 [1 each])
Shakespeare: *TGV* 2.4.136

L510 LOVE is never without jealousy (*Varied* from 1576)

E.g. c1590 (?1593) *Fair Em* 2.1.117: Ah, Em, faithfull love is full of ielosie.
Shakespeare: *TGV* 2.4.177, *Ven.* 1137

L513 LOVE is sweet in the beginning but sour in the ending (*Varied* from 1579; Wh L524 from a1393)
Shakespeare: *Ven.* 1137f.

L513.1 LOVE is the fruit of idleness (OW491a *varied* from 1540)
Add e.g.: 1585 W. Chub *True travaile* C7^v: The Poet sayth, Otia si tollas periere Cupidinis arcus, Take away Idleness, and thou dost break Cupid's bow.
Shakespeare: *Shr.* 1.1.151, *MND* 2.1.168
Cf. I9: Idleness begets lust.

L517 LOVE is without reason (*Varied* from 1509; Wh L533 from a1393)
E.g., 1582 Whetstone *Hept. Civil Disc.* F1^v: Reason and Love, are enemies. 1589 Greene *Tully's Love* VII,216: Womens reasons would seeme no reasons, especially in love, which is without reason.
Shakespeare: *MND* 3.1.143f., 5.1.4−8, *Cym.* 4.2.22

(?) L517.1 LOVE laughs at locksmiths (OW491b; *Ven.*, 1803, 1877)
Shakespeare: *Ven.* 575f.

L518 LOVE (Woman, Honor), like a shadow (crocodile, death), flies one following and pursues one fleeing (From 1586)
Shakespeare: *Wiv.* 2.2.207f.
Cf. L479: Follow love (pleasure, glory) and it will flee, flee love (pleasure, glory) and it will follow thee.

L522 LOVE makes men orators (*Varied* from 1593; OW488b supplements)
Add e.g.: c1593 (1598) Marlowe *Hero and Leander* II.72: Love always

makes those eloquent that have it.
1595 R. Parry *Moderatus* L4: It is
said, that love doeth make men
Oratours.
  Shakespeare: *Ven.* 1146
  Cf. L165: Whom we love best to
them we can say least.

L526   LOVE of lads and fire of chats is
soon in and soon out (1670 Ray, cf.
c1460, *Lr., Cym.*; ditto OW493a)
  I.e., c1460 *Good Wyfe wold a Pylgr.* in
Q. Eliz. Acad. EETS 41: A fyre of
sponys, and louve of gromis, Full
soun woll be att an ende [= Wh
F187].
  Shakespeare: *Lr.* 3.6.18f., *Cym.*
5.5.106f.

L531   LOVE will find a way (From
c1597; ditto OW493b)
  I.e., c1597 (1637) Deloney *1 Gentle
Craft* 136: Thus love, you see, can
finde a way, To make both Men and
Maids obey.
  Shakespeare: *Rom.* 1.1.171f.

(?) L534   Marry first and LOVE will
come after (From *Wiv.*; verbally
from 1714; OW515b adds 1699,
1780)
  E.g., 1600 (1601) Marston *Jack
Drum's Entertainment* III III,212:
Love should make mariage, and not
mariage Love. 1607 G. Wilkins *Miseries of Enforced Marriage* B1: You
stray from the steps of Gentility, the
fashion among them is to marry first,
and love afterwards by leisure.
  Shakespeare: *Wiv.* 1.1.245−7

(?) L539   A perfect LOVE does last
eternally (1596 DEL., analogues
from 1582; not in OW)
  Shakespeare: *Son.* 116.2ff.

L549   When LOVE puts in friendship
is gone (*Varied* from 1576)
  Shakespeare: *TGV* 2.4.203−6,
5.4.53f., *Ado* 2.1.175f.

L553   Your LOVE is (A friend worth)

a million (From 1H4; not in OW)
  Add c1600 *Fatal Marriage* vi (MSR
737f.): I did owe to him Millions of
Crownes, millions of my love.
  Shakespeare: *1H4* 3.3.136f.

(?) L555.1   LOVE'S Labour's Lost[n]
1609 Bretnor (Crow e 393 Dec.;
again Nov. 1611, May 1612)
  Shakespeare: *LLL* (title)

[n]Rather than merely reflecting the
expression "To lose one's labor,"
Shakespeare's title may itself have been
proverbial, like *Much Ado about Nothing,
All's Well that Ends Well, Measure for
Measure*, and at least twenty-five other
comedy titles of the decade following
1595. As indicated above, the only
strong evidence is a bit late, the recurrent appearance of "Loues labour's
lost" among the phrases of evil days in
Thomas Bretnor's almanacs. Although Wilson used Bretnor exten-
sively in revising *ODEP*, he excluded
this particular phrase from his revision. I do not know why.
  Except for Robert Tofte's well-
known allusion to the play—"LOVES
LABOR LOST, I once did see a Play,
Ycleped so" (1598 *Alba*, sig. G5)—
which treats the title as if it might be
proverbial, I have seen only suggestions of the phrase. The first stanza of
proverb-rich "A Warning for Wooers"
(c1565) concludes: "Buie not, with
cost, / The thing [love] that yeelds but
labour lost" (from *A Handefull of
Pleasant Delites* [1584], but included in
Bond's Lyly, III,465−7). Cf. also frus-
trated Balthazar of Kyd's *Spanish
Tragedy* 2.1.18: "all my labours lost,"
and 1600 ?Day ?Lyly *The Maid's Metamorphosis* 3.2.40f., of courtiers who
"sweare when they loose their labour in
love."

L556   He cannot LOVE me that is
afraid of me (1639 CL.; OW250a
adds 1621, 1624)
  I.e., 1621 Robinson 20. 1624 (1621)
Burton   *Anatomy   of   Melancholy*

III.ii.v.4 III,261 note in margin: The moral is, vehement fear expels love.
Shakespeare: *Ant.* 1.3.12

L558 It is impossible to LOVE and be wise (*Varied* from c1526; OW488b Publ. Syrus, supplementary examples)
E.g., 1539 Taverner *Publius* A5: To be in love and to be wyse is scase graunted to god. 1580 G. Harvey *Three Letters* (Oxford Spenser 627): To be wise, and eke to Love, Is graunted scarce to God above.
Shakespeare: *Tro.* 3.2.156f., *TNK* 1.1.230f.

L559 LOVE me little love me long (From 1546; Wh L568 from a1500)
Shakespeare: *MV* 3.2.111f., *Rom.* 2.6.14

L563 He LOVES to hear himself speak (talk) (From 1604; not in OW)
Add e.g.: 1581 Guazzo (Pettie) *Civile Conversation* I I,120: The ignorant man of weake understanding, which hath neede to keepe silence, is mervaylously delighted to heare him selfe speake. 1593 Nashe *Christs Teares* II,108: Hee . . . taketh a glory in hearing himselfe talke.
Shakespeare: *LLL* 1.1.166f., *Rom.* 2.4.147f.

L565 The LOVER is not where he lives but where he loves (*Varied* from 1577)
E.g., 1577 Grange *Golden Aphroditis* E4ᵛ: The hart being more where he loveth, than where he giveth life. Add: 1580 T. Salter *Contention betweene three Bretheren* C6: We commonly saye in these dayes, the minde and affection is rather where it loveth, then there where it liveth.
Shakespeare: *LLL* 5.2.816, *TN* 1.5.269, 4.1.59, *Tro.* 1.1.4f., *2H6* 3.2.408, *R3* 1.2.204, *Rom.* 1.1.197f., 2.1.1, 2.2.164, *Ven.* 580−2, *Son.* 22.6f., 109.3f.

(?) L571 A true LOVER'S (love's)−KNOT (Cf. Appendix B) (*TGV*, 1616; OW494a *love* from 1565)
Shakespeare: *TGV* 2.7.46

L572 As proud as LUCIFER (From 1616; OW651a from c1394)
Shakespeare: *TN* 1.5.250f.

(?) L582 There is LUCK in odd numbers (*Wiv.*, and a reference in Spenser to the superstition; OW496a adds Virgil and evidence *Wiv.*'s formulation was proverbial by the 19th century)
Shakespeare: *Wiv.* 5.1.2−4

L590 LYDFORD LAW (Halifax law): first hang and draw, then hear the cause (From 1565; Wh L593 c1405; OW345a supplements)
Shakespeare: *Oth.* 4.1.38f.

M

(?) M1.1 To set MACHIAVEL to school (Cf. Appendix B: To SET to school)
1610 G. Carleton *Jurisdiction* 99: Behold, Machiavel set to Schoole. 1612 T. James *Jesuits Downefall* C2ᵛ: They are able to set Aretin, Lucian, Matchiavel, yea and Don Lucifer in a sort to schoole.
Shakespeare: *3H6* 3.2.193

M2.1 As mad as a MAD DOG
1529 More *Supp. Soulys Wks.* 299/2: As mad not as a march hare, but as a madde dogge [OW497b (H148)]. c1620 (1647) Fletcher *Women Pleased* 4.3 VII,287: She is mad with Love, As mad as ever unworm'd dog was. ?1621 (1652) Fletcher *Wild Goose Chase* 4.3.96−8: I came from a world of mad Women . . . There's one that's mad; she seems well, but she is dog-mad.
Shakespeare: *Wiv.* 4.2.124f., *H8* 1.4.27f.

M2.2   A MAD DOG (hound) bites his master (fig.) (Wh H571 from 1340 [2]; OW498a from 1706)
   Shakespeare: *H8* 1.4.27−9, *Ant.* 2.5.80

(?) M14   As good a MAID as her mother (*Wiv.*, 1659 HOW.)
   Shakespeare: *Wiv.* 2.2.36−8

M14.1   As still as a (any) MAID (Wh M8 from c1395 [3])
   E.g., 1509 *Fyftene Joyes* E4 (*for* 3)(5): As styll he is and muet as a mayde.
   Shakespeare: *MV* 3.2.8

M26   She is neither MAID, wife, nor widow (From 1595; OW499a from 1591)
   Add: 1600 R. Armin *Quips upon Questions* D2ᵛ: Onely thus much I say, and talke no more, Nor mayde, wife, widdow, but a common whore.
   Shakespeare: *MM* 5.1.177−80

M34   MAIDS say nay and take it (From 1534)
   Shakespeare: *R3* 3.7.51

M37   (Old MAIDS) lead apes in hell (From c1560)
   Shakespeare: *Shr.* 2.1.34, *Ado* 2.1.41

M45   MAIDENS should be seen and not heard (From 1560; Wh M11 a1415)
   Shakespeare: *MV* 3.2.8

M45.1   By my MAIDENHEAD (Cf. Appendix B)ⁿ
   c1597 (1637) Deloney *1 Gentle Craft* 128: By my Maiden-Head, it is water indeed (quoth she). 1597 (1599) Chapman *Humorous Day's Mirth* 4.2.6: Nor I, by my maidenhead. 1600 (1601) Marston *Jack Drum's Entertainment* I III,189: Pish, by my maidenhead. c1602 (1606) Chapman *Sir Giles Goosecap* 5.2.168: And so say I, upon my maidenhead.

Shakespeare: *Rom.* 1.3.2, *H8* 2.3.23

ⁿIncluded only because used by Juliet's nurse.

M48   To MAKE or (and) mar (From c1527)
   Shakespeare: *Shr.* 4.3.94−7, *LLL* 4.3.189, *MND* 1.2.37, *AYL* 1.1.30f., *R3* 1.3.163−5, *2H4* Ep. 5f., *Rom.* 1.2.13, 2.4.115f., *Oth.* 5.1.4, *Mac.* 2.3.32, *Ant.* 3.11.65, 5.2.277

(?) M65   As a MAN must take a wife, for better or for worse (1738, *for better or for worse* from 1639, cf. *Ham.*; OW802a adds 1552 *Book of Common Prayer*)
   Shakespeare: *Ham.* 3.2.251f.

M66   As good a MAN as ever trod on shoe (neat's) leather (as ever went on legs) (*Varied* from c1570; OW725bf. *knave . . . two legs* 1545)
   Shakespeare: *H5* 4.7.161−3, *JC* 1.1.25, *Tmp.* 2.2.60f., 70, *TNK* 4.3.13f.

M68   As honest (good) a MAN (etc.) as ever broke bread (*Good* from c1588 [1599]; OW380a *honest* from 1585)
   Shakespeare: *Wiv.* 1.4.150f., *Ado* 3.5.38f.

M73.1   As soon dies a young MAN as an old (Wh M41 from c1430)
   Shakespeare: *Shr.* 2.1.390f.

M79   A black MAN is a pearl (jewel) in a fair woman's eye (From *Tit.*; ditto OW64b)
   Shakespeare: *TGV* 5.2.12, *Tit.* 5.1.42

M80   A blind MAN can (should) judge no colors (From 1530; Wh M50 from c1385)
   Shakespeare: *2H6* 2.1.124−8

M82 A blind MAN might see that (From 1562)
Add: 1582 J. Rivius (T. Rogers) *Foolishnes* (STC 21065) ed. 1586 37: But now a verie blind man (as the saying is) maie see.
Shakespeare: *1H6* 2.4.24

M96 An envious MAN grows lean (From a1500; OW225b supplements)
Shakespeare: *JC* 1.2.194, 208f.

(?) M104 Every MAN as his business lies (1678 Ray, cf. *1H4, Ham.*, 1682)[n]
I.e., 1682 A. Behn *False Count* 1.2 111: Every Man to his business, I say.
Shakespeare: *1H4* 2.2.77, *Ham.* 1.5.128–30

[n]Cf. Introduction, p. xxiii.

M107 Every MAN cannot be a master (Collections from 1596 [1592]; *varied* from 1546; OW229a from 1545)
Shakespeare: *Oth.* 1.1.43

M112 Every MAN for himself (for one) (From 1478)
Shakespeare: *Tmp.* 5.1.256f.

M116 Every MAN has (No man is without) his faults (*Varied* from 1583; Wh M235 from c1450)
Shakespeare: *Wiv.* 1.4.14f., *Ant.* 5.1.32f., *Tim.* 3.1.27, *Son.* 35.5

M125 Every MAN is either a fool or a physician to himself (From *Wiv.*; OW275a Tacitus, 1592ff.)
Shakespeare: *Wiv.* 3.4.96f.

M131 Every MAN likes his own thing best (From 1539; OW230a from 1525–40; both include *AYL*)
E.g., 1539 TAV. 6ᵛ: Every man thynketh hys owne thynge fayre. 1623 WOD. 480: Every one estimes, and praiseth what he hath.
Shakespeare: *AYL* 5.4.57f.

M158 Happy MAN happy dole (be his dole) (*Be his dole* from 1571)   .
Shakespeare: *Shr.* 1.1.139f., *Wiv.* 3.4.64f., *1H4* 2.2.76, *WT* 1.2.163

M161 He is a MAN, every inch of him (From 1595; OW403 from 1576)
Add: c1559 (1569) W. Wager *Longer Thou Livest* 1744: A man I am now, every inch of me. 1590 ?Nashe *Almond for a Parrat* III,351: [He] vauntes himselfe to bee, as hee is, as good a Gentleman everie inch of him as anie.
Shakespeare: *Lr.* 4.6.107

M162 He is (is not) a MAN of God's making (From c1591 [1593])
Add: ?c1588 (1599) Porter *Two Angry Women of Abingdon* iv (MSR 976): And thou beest a man of Gods making, stand to it.
Shakespeare: *LLL* 5.2.526, *MV* 1.2.56f., *AYL* 1.1.32f., 3.2.204f., *Rom.* 2.4.115f., *Ham.* 3.2.33–5

M163 He is a (tall) (good) MAN of his hands (*Good* from c1470, *tall* from 1530, *man* from a1588)
Shakespeare: *Wiv.* 1.4.25f., *2H4* 2.2.67f., *WT* 5.2.164–8

M170 He is now become a new MAN (Cf. 2 Cor. 5.17; *varied* from 1570)
Shakespeare: *R2* 5.3.146

M172 He that cannot be angry is no MAN (a fool) (1604 [misdated c1605], c1645)
I.e., 1604 Dekker & Middleton *1 Honest Whore* 1.2.63f.: I have heard it often said, that hee who cannot be angry, is no man.
Add: 1605 N. Breton *I Pray You Be not Angrie* ed. Grosart II,5: I have heard it spoken by a Wise man that he who cannot be Angry, is a Foole: but hee that will bee Angry, is more Foole.
Shakespeare: *Oth.* 3.4.134

M182   The healthful MAN can give good counsel to the sick (*Varied* from 1539)
E.g., c1585 (1592) Lyly *Gallathea* 1.1.92f.: In health it is easie to counsell the sicke, but it's hard for the sicke to followe wholesome counsaile.
Shakespeare: *Ado* 5.1.20–4

M183   An honest MAN and a good bowler (From *LLL*, 1635ff.)
E.g., 1635 F. Quarles *Emblems* ed. 1643 I.x *Wks.* III,53: The vulgar Proverb's crost: He hardly can Be a good bouler and an honest man.
Shakespeare: *LLL* 5.2.581–3

M187   A hungry MAN an angry man (Collections from 1641 [cf. on H745], cf. *TGV, Cor.*; OW393b supplements)
Shakespeare: *TGV* 1.2.67–9, *Cor.* 5.1.50–3

M194   If a man once fall all will tread on him (*Varied* from 1530; OW200b [He that is down, down with him] supplements)
Shakespeare: *Ven.* 707f.

M202   It is not given to every MAN to go to Corinth (From 1542; OW143bf. Greek, Horace)
E.g., 1542 Udall *Apoph.* 342: Lais an harlot of Corinthe . . . was for none but lordes and gentlemenne that might well paie for it. Whereof came up a proverbe that it was not for every manne to go unto Corinthe.
Shakespeare: *Tim.* 2.2.70

M209   Let every MAN have his own (From *Tit., MND*; ditto OW)
E.g., 1616 DR. 1844.
Shakespeare: *MND* 3.2.459, *Tit.* 1.1.280f.

M217   A MAN (one) among a thousand (From 1508)
Add: 1519 Horman *Vulgaria* E5: A goodly man amonge a thousand.
Shakespeare: *Ham.* 2.2.179

(?) M218.1   MAN borrows from the beasts (*Varied*)
E.g., 1592 T. Tymme *Plaine Discoverie* F3ᵛ: We rob and spoile all creatures of the world to cover our backes, and to adorne our bodies withal. From some we take their wooll: from many ther skins: from divers ther furres: from sundrie, their verie excrements as the silke [etc.]. 1603 Montaigne (Florio) *Essayes* II.xii 2B2ᵛ: We may be excused for borrowing those which nature had therein favored more then us . . . and under their spoiles of wooll, of haire, of fethers, and of silke to shroude us. 1609 W. Cowper *Three Heavenly Treatises* R8: Others . . . place their glory in their garments. This is a begd and vanishing glory; from the Wormes man borrowes silkes . . . from the Sheepe wool to be his garment; from the Oxen their skinne to be his shoes; from the Foules feathers, to dresse him like a foole. 1617 J. Boys *2 Exposition . . . Psalmes . . . English Liturgie* (STC 3467) Ps. 8 C3: As for apparell and ornament, wee borrow wool of the sheep, hayre of the Cammell, silke of the worme, muske of the mountaine Cat, furres of the beasts, and feathers of the foules.
Shakespeare: *Lr.* 3.4.103–5

M219   A MAN can die but once (From *2H4*; OW503b from c1425, Wh D242 from a1400)
Shakespeare: *2H4* 3.2.234f., *Ant.* 4.14.27

M226   A MAN cannot live on air like a chameleon (*Varied* from 1557)
Shakespeare: *TGV* 2.1.172–4, 2.4.25–8, *2H4* 1.3.28, *Ham.* 3.2.93f.

M238   MAN honors the place, not

the place the man (*Varied* from 1580)[n]
Add: 1590 M. Sutcliffe *Remonstrance* (STC 20881) 47: Non locus virum, sed vir locum honestat: The place giveth not credite to the man, but the man to the place.
Shakespeare: *AWW* 2.3.125f.

[n]Tilley's *Elizabethan Proverb Lore* (New York, 1926), p. 222, no. 423, traces through Erasmus to Plutarch.

M239 A MAN (thing, action) in print (Cf. Appendix B) (From 1576; OW648a supplements)
Shakespeare: *TGV* 2.1.169, *LLL* 3.1.172, *AYL* 5.4.90

(?) M240 The MAN in the moon (From c1517)[n]
Shakespeare: *LLL* 5.2.215, *MND* 5.1.245, *Tmp.* 2.1.249, 2.2.138f., 146

[n]I include only because Tilley, Wilson (OW504af.), and Whiting (Wh M138) follow some earlier collections—not of the Renaissance—in treating "the man in the moon" as proverbial. I would instead regard as proverbial only such expressions as "a tale of the man in the moon." Two instances are included under M240, and a third in OW; all, incidentally, precede Lyly's repeated use in the prologue for *Endymion*.

M246 MAN is but a bubble (From 1539; OW505a Greek)
Shakespeare: *R3* 4.4.90

M253 A MAN is nothing but worms' meat (*Varied* from 1523; Wh W675 from c1400)
Shakespeare: *AYL* 3.2.65, *1H4* 5.4.86, *Rom.* 3.1.107, *Per.* 4.2.24f.

M254 A MAN is weal or woe as he thinks himself so (*Varied* from 1549; OW873a from 1533)
E.g., 1533 Sir T. Elyot *Knowledge which maketh a Wise Man* M3[v]:

Nothing unto a man is miserable but if he so think it. 1591 Nashe *Pref.* Sidney's *Astrophil and Stella* III,332: So that our opinion (as Sextus Empiricus affirmeth) gives the name of good or ill to every thing.
Shakespeare: *Ham.* 2.2.249f., *Oth.* 2.3.270f.

M258 A MAN may cause his own dog to bite him (From 1562)
Shakespeare: *2H6* 5.1.151f., *Jn.* 4.1.115f., *H5* 2.2.82f.

M297 A MAN or a mouse (From 1542)
Shakespeare: *2H4* 3.2.159f.

M298 Man proposes, God disposes (From a1500; Wh M162 from c1378)
Shakespeare: *Ham.* 5.2.10f.

M299 A MAN should hear all parts ere he judge any (From 1546)
Shakespeare: *Ham.* 1.3.69

M321 No MAN can play the fool so well as the wise man (*Varied* from 1581; OW569af. from 1545)
E.g., 1581 Guazzo (Pettie) *Civile Conversation* II I,159: To plaie the foole well it behooveth a man first to be wise.
Shakespeare: *TN* 3.1.60
Cf. M428: A wise man may sometimes (He is not wise who cannot) play the fool.

M327 No MAN has (To have no) lease (letters) of his life (*Varied* from 1666, cf. *2H6*; OW570a 1377 *letter*)
E.g., 1377 Langland *Piers* B x 89: For we have no lettre of owre lyf, how longe it shal dure. 1629 *Oxinden Letters* 1607−42 ed. D. Gardiner 46: No man has a lease of his life for tearm of yeares.
Shakespeare: *2H6* 4.10.5f., *Mac* 4.1.98f., *Son.* 146.5

M328 No MAN (Nobody, None)

holds you (*Shr.*, 1631, 1738; OW570a adds c1595–6)
I.e., c1595–6 R. Carew *Excellency English Tongue* (*Eliz. Crit. Essays* ed. G. Smith II,292), with context: When wee would be rid of one, wee use to saye . . . by circumlocution, rather your roome then your companye [R168], Letts see your backe, com againe when I bid you, when you are called, sent for, intreated, willed, desiered, invited, spare us your place, another in your steede, a shipp of salte for you, save your credite, you are next the doore, the doore is open for you, theres noe bodye holdes you [M328], no bodie teares your sleeve, &c.
Shakespeare: *Shr.* 1.1.106, 3.2.210
Cf. D556: Here is the door and there is the way.

M333 No MAN is happy before his death (From 1552; OW352af. adds Aeschylus, Sophocles, Euripides, Herodotus, Ovid, and supplements)
Shakespeare: *Tit.* 1.1.176

M335 No MAN is wise at all times (*Varied* from 1539; OW571a from 1481)
Shakespeare: *Oth.* 2.3.241

M337 No MAN loses (wins) but another wins (loses) (*Varied* from c1526; ditto OW486b)
Shakespeare: *R3* 4.4.535f., *Mac.* 1.1.4, 1.2.67, *Ant.* 3.11.70

M341 No MAN ought to be judge in his own cause (From 1528; Wh M244 from c1449)
E.g., 1456 Hay *Law* 257.18f.: For the law civile sais, that na man suld be juge in his awin cause.
Shakespeare: *MV* 2.9.61f., *TN* 5.1.354f., *MM* 5.1.166f.

M357 The poor MAN pays for all (From c1561; OW639a adds c1630)
Shakespeare: *H5* 2.1.96

M366 The rich MAN walks to get a stomach to his meat, the poor man to get meat for his stomach (*Varied* from 1586)
E.g., 1586 W. Warner *Albion's England* V 27: *Poems* 571: The rich for meate seeke stomackes, and the poore for stomackes meate.
Shakespeare: *2H4* 4.4.105–8

M387 That which a MAN causes to be done he does himself (1692, 1732, cf. *H5*; OW112a supplements)
Shakespeare: *H5* 4.1.132ff.

M395.1 To be a MAN as other men are
1533 N. Udall *Floures* P5^v: *Homo sum* . . . I am a man, as other men be. 1581 I. B. *Dialogue* F4: As touching chastitie, I am a man as another man is. 1585 ?Munday *Fedele and Fortunio* IV (MSR 1433): Consider I am a man, subiect to ye same pressing yron of ye minde yt other men are. 1599 (1600) Drayton et al. *1 Sir John Oldcastle* 4.1.165f.: I confesse I am a frayle man, flesh and bloud as other are.
Shakespeare: *MND* 3.1.43f., *R3* 1.4.163f., *H5* 4.1.101f.
Cf. F367: To be flesh and blood as others are.

M395.2 To be a MAN of one's word
1594 Nashe *Christs Teares* II,180: The devill & he be no men of their words. c1605 (1630) Dekker *2 Honest Whore* 4.3.37f.: Th'art a man of thy word. c1606 (1608) Middleton *Mad World, My Masters* 5.2.168: They should be men of their words. 1637 Shirley *Hyde Park* 5.1.82f.: I would not have you a gentlewoman of your word Alone; they're deeds that crown all. 1666 TOR. *Prov. Phr.* s.v. Certosa 35: To be a man of ones word [in M184].
Shakespeare: *Lr.* 4.6.104

M399 To stagger (reel) like a drunken MAN (Ps. 107.27; from

1530; OW770a supplements)
Shakespeare: *Rom.* 2.3.3

M421 A wise MAN commonly has a fool to his heir (has foolish children) (*Varied* from 1552)
E.g., 1552 TAV. 58^v: Our common Englyshe proverbe sayeth, that the wysest men haue moost foles to their chyldren.
Shakespeare: *TN* 2.3.44

M426 A wise (valiant) MAN makes every country his own (*Varied*; *wise* from 1571 [OW900a from 1539], *valiant* from 1616 [cf. Wh L58 c1300])
Shakespeare: *R2* 1.3.275f.

M427.1 A wise MAN may sometimes overshoot himself (*Varied*)[n]
c1530 Palsgr. 649/2: I never wyste wyseman overshote himselfe thus sore [*OED overshoot* 3 *To overshoot oneself*]. c1585 (1592) Lyly *Gallathea* 4.1.44f. (to "cunning" Tyterus): You cannot over-reach me Tyterus, over-shoote your selfe you may. c1589 (1592) Lyly *Midas* 2.2.51f.: Your wisdome is overshotte in your comparison. c1604 (1605) Chapman *All Fools* 4.1.1f.: You see how too much wisdome evermore, Out-shootes the truth; 5.2.103f.: Did I not tell you you'd oreshoote your self With too much wisedome? 1616 (Cf. Introduction, p.000)
Shakespeare: *H5* 3.7.124
Cf. 091.1: To overshoot oneself (be overshot).

[n]See Introduction, p. xivf. on the need to distinguish between M427.1 and 091.1.

M428 A wise man may sometimes (He is not wise who cannot) play the fool (*Varied* from *TN*; OW900b from c1500)
E.g., 1557 Edgeworth *Sermons* OO3^v: Thys comon proverbe: Stultitiam simulare loco prudentia

summa est, To fayne foolishnesse in some case, is very highe wisedome.
Shakespeare: *TN* 3.1.67
Cf. M321: No man can play the fool so well as the wise man.

M458 An honest MAN's word is as good as his bond (*Varied* from 1616; OW380b from a1400)
E.g., c1500 *Lancelot* 1673: A kingis word shud be a kingis bonde.
Shakespeare: *TGV* 2.7.75, *MND* 3.2.266f., *TN* 3.1.21

M473 A MAN'S house is his castle (From 1581; OW389b another 1581)
Shakespeare: *Wiv.* 4.5.6

M476 A MAN'S praise in his own mouth does stink (*Varied* from 1484; cf. Wh P351 from a1387)
Shakespeare: *MV* 3.4.22f., *Tro.* 1.3.241f., 2.3.155−7, *Ant.* 2.6.42f.

M500 You set an old MAN's head on a young man's shoulders (*MV* [excluded], *Ado* 1639; OW589bf. adds 1591)
I.e., 1591 H. Smith *Preparative for Marriage* 14f.: It is not good grafting of an olde head uppon young shoulders. 1639 CL., s.v. Absurda 7.
Shakespeare: *Ado* 1.1.113f.

M502 All MEN are mortal (*Varied* from c1537; OW10a from c1386)
Add e.g.: c1589 (1592) Lyly *Midas* 5.2.158: Thou seest boy we are both mortall. 1606 *Puritan* 1.1.72f.: Wee are all mortall our selves.
Shakespeare: *MV* 1.3.22, *Ado* 1.1.59f.

M505 All MEN must die (*Varied* from 1578; Wh D243 from c735)
Shakespeare: *MM* 2.4.36, *3H6* 5.2.28, *2H4* 3.2.37f., *JC* 4.3.190

(?) M514 Dying MEN speak true[n] (*Speak true* varied from 1595; ditto OW210b)

Shakespeare: *Jn.* 5.4.26−9, *R2* 2.1.5−8, *Cym.* 5.5.41f.

ⁿSee Introduction, p. xvii.

M533 In young MEN to err is less shame (1666 TOR., cf. *1H4*, *JC* [excluded])
Shakespeare: *1H4* 5.2.16f.
Cf. Y48: Youth will have its course (swing).

M541 MEN are (but) men (From 1576)
Add e.g.: 1587 J. Bridges *Defence of the Government* X5ᵛ: Homines sumus, labi possumus: We are all but men, and may overslippe. 1590 ?Nashe *Almond for a Parrat* III,355: Men are but men and may erre.
Shakespeare: *MV* 1.3.22, *H8* 5.3.75, *Oth.* 2.3.241, *Mac.* 3.1.90

M544 MEN are not angels (*H8*, collections from 1616; OW524b from 1548)
E.g., 1548 Hall (1809 ed., 783): You knowe well that we be men frayle of condicion and no Angels.
Shakespeare: *H8* 5.2.45−7, *Oth.* 3.4.148

(?) M545 MEN are not made of steel (1631 only)ⁿ
I.e., 1631 Jonson *New Inn* 3.1.176: Your better man, the Geno-way Proverbe say's, Men are not made of steele.
Shakespeare: *Ant.* 4.4.33

ⁿJonson's speaker is responding to the condemnation "he has broken thrice."ˢ The "Geno-way Proverbe" may be T175 (all things thrive at thrice), or some variant.

M554 MEN must do as they may (can), not as they would (*Varied* from 1567; cf. Wh L410 1483)
Shakespeare: *AWW* 1.3.19, *R3* 5.3.91, *H5* 2.1.15f., 57−9, *Tit.* 2.1.106f., *Ven.* 564

M555 MEN (Men's love), not walls, make the city (prince) safe (*Varied* from 1489; OW525a Thucydides, supplements)
E.g., 1666 TOR. *It. Prov.* 115 no. 11: Walls make not a City, but men. 1732 FUL. 5121: 'Tis the Men, not the Houses, that make the city.
Shakespeare: *Cor.* 3.1.198f.

M567 Old MEN and far travelers may lie by authority (Collections from 1623, *varied* from 1509; OW591a supplements)
Shakespeare: *Son.* 17.10

(?) M568 Old MEN are covetous by nature (*Varied* from c1495; not in OW or Wh)
Shakespeare: *2H4* 1.2.228−30

M570 Old MEN are twice children (*Varied* from 1539; OW591a Aristophanes, 1527)
Shakespeare: *AYL* 2.7.165, *Ham.* 2.2.385, *Lr.* 1.3.19, *Cym.* 5.3.57, *Luc.* 954

M579 Rich MEN may do anything (*Varied* from 1639)
E.g., 1732 FUL. 4036: Rich Men Have no Faults.
Shakespeare: *Tim.* 1. 1.2.13

(?) M593 We are but MEN, not gods (1571, c1614, *Oth.*; not in OW)
I.e., 1571 R. Edwards *Damon and Pithias* xviii (MSR 1997): But sith he is no god, but a man, he must do as he may [cf. M554]. c1614 (1647) Fletcher *Valentinian* 2.3.42f.: Though I most strive to be without my passions, I am no god.
Shakespeare: *Oth.* 3.4.148
Cf. M544: Men are not angels.

(?) M599.1 When MEN are merriest death says "checkmate" (Wh M318 a1500)
Shakespeare: *2H4* 4.2.81, *Rom.* 5.3.88f.

M602 Wise MEN have their mouth (tongue) in their heart, fools their heart in their mouth (tongue) (Ecclus. 21.26; from 1477)
Add: 1609 Melton *Sixe-folde Politician* M8ᵛ: "That Italian proverb, La lingua del savio e ascosta nel suo cuore. The tongue of the Wiseman is hidden in his heart.
Shakespeare: *Ham.* 1.3.59, *Lr.* 1.1.91f., *Cor.* 3.1.256

M628 (Let him mend his MANNERS), it will be his own another day. (*Varied* from c1550)
E.g., c1550 (1560) *Nice Wanton* C2: Apply your lerning and your Elders obay, It wil be your proffit an other day. 1601 (1602) Dekker *Satiromastix* 4.3.200: The same hand still, it is your owne another day.
Shakespeare: *LLL* 4.1.107

M631.1 In MANNER and form following
1585 N. deNicholay (T. Washington) *Navigations . . . into Turkie* Q3: The endes . . . hang downe . . . over their shoulders in the fourme and maner as the picture following doth shew [*OED Form* 10]. c1589 (1592) Lyly *Midas* 5.2.168f.: You shall have the beard, in manner and forme following. 1594 Nashe *Unfortunate Traveller* II,248: I . . . offer up unto you the cities generall good will, which is a gilded Can, in manner and forme folowing.
Shakespeare: *LLL* 1.1.205

M633 To take one with the MANNER (From 1530)
Shakespeare: *LLL* 1.1.202f., *1H4* 2.4.315, *WT* 4.4.728

M638.1 As hard as MARBLE (Wh M370 from c1300)
Shakespeare: *Err.* 2.1.93, *Mac.* 3.4.21

M649 I will not go (run before my MARE to market (*R3*, 1678 Ray, 1709; ditto OW688b)
Shakespeare: *R3* 1.1.160

M655 To ride (shoe) the wild MARE (*Ride* from a1525, *shoe* from *2H4*; ditto OW725af.)
Shakespeare: *2H4* 2.4.246f.

M657 Whose MARE is dead? (From 1595; ditto OW886b)
Shakespeare: *2H4* 2.1.43

M670 As the MARKET goes (wives must) sell. (*Varied* until 1732; OW512b from 1545)
E.g., 1545 *Precepts of Cato* B3ᵛ: Accordynge to the proverbe and common saying, Take thy market whyle tyme is, least of thy pryce thou do mysse.
Shakespeare: *AYL* 3.5.60, *AWW* 1.1.154f.

M681 MARRIAGE is a lottery (From ?1596 [1640]; OW513a adds 1605)
Shakespeare: *AWW* 1.3.87f.

M682 MARRIAGE is destiny (From c1558−9; OW513b from 1548)
E.g., 1548 Hall *Chron.* ed. 1809 264: Bot now consider the old proverbe to be true yt saieth: that marriage is destinie.
Shakespeare: *Wiv.* 5.5.233, *TN* 1.5.310, *AWW* 1.3.62
Cf. C889: Cuckolds come by destiny.

M683 MARRIAGE is honorable (From 1576; cf. Heb. 13.4)
Shakespeare: *Ado* 3.4.30, 5.4.30

M688 MARRIAGES are made in heaven (From 1566)
Shakespeare: *H5* 5.2.359

M699.1 MARRY, and shall (Cf. Appendix B)
E.g., c1552 (c1567) Udall *Ralph Roister Doister* 1.4.109: Mary, and thou shalt. c1587 (c1592) Kyd

Spanish Tragedy 3.14.156: Ay marry my lord, and shall. 1598 (1616) W. Haughton *Englishmen for my Money* iii (MSR 627, 708). c1600 (1602) Marston *Antonio's Revenge* 5.3.55.
  Shakespeare: *2H6* 1.2.88, *3H6* 5.5.42, *R3* 3.4.34, *1H4* 5.2.33

M699.2 MARRY come up (Cf. Appendix B) (OW515a as in *OED int.* d): *Rom., Per.,* 1642 J. Eaton *Honey-c. Free Justif.* 14: Taunting and reproachfull terms, as, *Marry come up.*)[n]
  Shakespeare: *Rom.* 2.5.62, *Per.* 4.6.150

[n]Probably Wilson provided a separate entry for "Marry come up" in silent objection to Tilley's having included Shakespeare under a much later proverbial expression, "Marry come up, my dirty cousin" (C740). Only a few such exclamations are in Tilley, OW, or this appendix. "Marry come up" appears to have been interchangeable with the very common "Marry gup" (*int.* c). Cf., for example, 1604 Dekker and Middleton, *1 Honest Whore* 3.2.43: "Mary come up with a pox"; 3.2.67f. (same speaker): "Mary gup, are you growne so holy, so pure, so honest with a pox?"

M701 MARRYING is marring (*Varied* from 1546)
  Shakespeare: *Wiv.* 1.1.25f., *AWW* 2.3.298, *Rom.* 1.2.13

M723 Like (Such a) MASTER like (such a) man (servant) (From 1530)
  Shakespeare: *2H4* 2.1.189f., *Tmp.* 2.2.185

M727 (Most) MASTER wears no breech (*Most* from a1500; ditto Wh M406)
  Shakespeare: *2H6* 1.3.146

M754.1 No such MATTER (*OED* 22 from *Son.* 87)
  E.g., c1552 (c1567) Udall *Ralph Roister Doister* 4.5.41 (There was).

c1581 (1584) Peele *Arraignment of Paris* 1.1.48 (Theres). c1591 (1595) *Locrine* 2.2.85. 1610 Bretnor (Crow g 273 Jun.)
  Shakespeare: *Ado* 1.1.190, 2.3.216f., 5.4.82, *TN* 3.1.5., *Tro.* 3.1.88, *2H4* Ind. 15, *Ham.* 2.2.267, *Son.* 87.14

M755 To mince the MATTER (Cf. Appendix B) (From *Oth.*; OW533a adds 1533)
  Shakespeare: *Oth.* 2.3.247

M763 As fresh as MAY (From 1600; Wh M422 from c1385)
E.g., Chaucer *CT* V(F) 927–8: That fresher was and jolyer of array, As to my doom, than is the month of May. a1420 Lydgate *Troy* II 409.518–9: As fresche be-seyn as May is with his flouris, The ladies then ascended of the town.
  Shakespeare: *R2* 5.1.79, *1H4* 4.1.101, *Ham.* 3.3.81, *TNK* 3.1.5

(?) M768.1 The MAYMOON (?maymorn) of youth (Cf. Appendix B)
1576 Gascoigne *Steele Glas* II,136: I regarded not my comelynes in the Maymoone of my youth. 1576 Gascoigne *Grief of Joye* II,519: Of lustie youth, then lustily to treate, Yet is the very Mayemoone of delight. 1583 Melbancke *Philotimus* Ddl[v]: In pleasant *May* moone of mine age, I meane the lustie gallant prime.
  Shakespeare: *H5* 1.2.120

M778 As tall as a Maypole (Cf. Appendix B; *OED* lb from *MND*) (*MND*, 1607ff., but simile only in 1678 Ray)
Add e.g.: 1602 J. Manningham *Diary* Oct. 53: I cry you mercy, said the gent., I tooke you for a May pole [after he had danced around a tall man (in M897)].
  Shakespeare: *MND* 3.2.296

M800 MEASURE   for   measure

(From *3H6*; OW520b from 1530; cf. Matt. 7.2)

Add: 1588 L. Humphrey *View of the Romish hydra* D5ᵛ: It is a true proverb among the Hebrues, Middah Keneged middah, A measure for a measure: And our saviour useth the same.

Shakespeare: *MM* title, 5.1.411, *3H6* 2.6.55, *R3* 4.4.20f., *Tit.* 5.3.66

Cf. L282.1: LIKE for like.

M806   There is a MEASURE (mean) in all things (From c1500)

Shakespeare: *Ado* 2.1.71f.

(?) M828   MEAT was made for mouths (*Cor.*)

Shakespeare: *Cor.* 1.1.207

M834   Put not thy MEAT in an unclean dish (From c1535; *unclean dish AYL*)

E.g. 1539 TAV. 55: Put not meate into a pyspot. *Plutarche expouneth thys sayng thus. Cast not good sentencies in to the mynde of a wycked person, So that it is al one in effecte with that sayenge of Christ. Cast not perles afore swyne.

Add: 1579 Lyly *Euphues* I,281 (Pithagoras . . . sayinges): Not to put our meate in Scapio [i.e., a chamberpot]: That is wee shoulde not speake of manners or vertue, to those whose mindes are infected with vice.

Shakespeare: *AYL* 3.3.35–7

M837   She is MEAT for your master (From *2H4;* OW522a adds 1592)

I.e., 1592 Nashe *Pierce Penniless* I,195: As if they were no meate but his Maisterships mouth.

Shakespeare: *2H4* 2.4.125f.

M839   Sweet MEAT must have sour sauce (From 1562 [1549]; *varied* from c1500)

Shakespeare: *AYL* 3.3.30f., *Rom.* 2.4.80–2, *Son.* 118.5–8

M842   To be MEAT and drink to one (From 1533)

Shakespeare: *Wiv.* 1.1.294, *AYL* 5.1.10

M845   What they want in MEAT let them take in drink (From 1590; ditto OW865a)

Shakespeare: *2H4* 5.3.28

M846   When MEAT is in anger is out (1639 CL.)

Shakespeare: *TGV* 1.2.67–9

M850   All MEATS to be eaten, all maids to be wed (From 1546)

E.g., 1546 Heywood Dialogue II.ii F4ᵛ: That one loveth not, an other doth, which hath sped, All meates to be eaten, and all maydes to be wed.

Shakespeare: *Ado* 3.4.89f.

M852   I will neither (To) MEDDLE nor (or) make (From 1564)

Shakespeare: *Wiv.* 1.4.110, *Ado* 3.3.52, *Tro.* 1.1.14, 83

M863   MEDLARS are never good (ripe) till they be rotten (*Varied* from 1584)

Add e.g.: c1605 (1630) Dekker *2 Honest Whore* 1.1.98: Women are like Medlars (no sooner ripe but rotten.).

Shakespeare: *AYL* 3.2.118–20, *MM* 4.3.173f.

(?) M866   MELANCHOLY is the pathway to madness (1616 DR., cf. *Shr.*)[n]

Shakespeare: *Shr.* Ind. ii.133

[n]Cf. e.g., 1579 Lyly, *Euphues* (I, 256): "avoyde sollytarinesse, that breedes melancholy, melancholy, madnesse, madnesse mischiefe." But probably no proverb, in any strict sense, is involved.

(?) M868.1   A MEMBER of the commonwealth

1598 (1639) Deloney *2 Gentle Craft* 166: I . . . livd in London idly, like an unprofitable member of the common-wealth. c1609 (1620) Beaumont & Fletcher *Philaster* 1.1.55–9: She . . . has destroyed the worth of her own body by making experiment upon it, for the good of the commonwealth. / She's a profitable member.

Shakespeare: *LLL* 4.1.41, 4.2.76f., *MV* 3.5.34f.

Cf. Appendix B: PILLAR(S) of the state.

M872   The MENDS is in his own hands (From 1566–7)
Shakespeare: *Tro.* 1.1.68

M874   Either MEND or end (From *Tro.*; OW525b from 1578)
Shakespeare: *Tro.* 1.2.77f., *Mac.* 3.1.113, *WT* 2.3.183

M875   It is never too late to MEND (From 1594; OW563a from 1590 Greene *Never too Late* [title])
Shakespeare: *Shr.* 5.1.150, *Lr.* 2.4.229f.

M875.1 To MEND and to mar (*Varied*)
1559 T. Chaloner "King Richard the Second" 105 *Mirror for Magistrates* 117: Things hardly mende, but may be mard amayne. 1570 Ascham *Scholemaster* ed. Ryan 20: They rather break him than bow him [B636], rather mar him than mend him. 1640 J.D. *Knave in Graine* 2.4 (MSR 999f.): Wee seeke to mend so long, that we marre all.
Shakespeare: *Son.* 103.9f.
Cf. M48: To make or (and) mar.

M897   I cry you MERCY, I took you for a joint stool (From 1594)[n]
I.e., c1589 (1594) Lyly *Mother Bombie* 4.2.28 (Silena): I crie you mercy, I tooke you for a ioynd stoole.
Shakespeare: *Lr.* 3.6.52

[n]Cf. Appendix A, p. 43.

M898   It is in their MERCY that kings come closest to gods (*Varied* from *Tit.*)
Add: c1590 (1596) *Edward III* 5.1.39–42: Ah, be more milde unto these yeelding men! . . . Kings approch the nearest unto God By giving life and safety unto men.
Shakespeare: *MV* 4.1.188–97, *MM* 2.2.59–63, *R2* 5.3.118, 136, *Tit.* 1.1.117f.

(?) M899.1   To punish evil-doers is a great work of mercie
1566 T. Becon *New Postil* margins Dd4, Qq7v (both times on "Folyshe pitie marrethe the citie" [P366]): To punishe eveill doers, is a great work of mercie.
Shakespeare: *MM* 2.2.100–2

M901   A MERRY GREEK (Cf. Appendix B) (From c1553)
Shakespeare: *TN* 4.1.18, *Tro.* 1.2.109, 4.4.56

(?) M908.1   A lad (man) of METTLE (Cf. Appendix B, *OED* 3)
1614 'Overbury' *Characters* "Tinker" ed. Paylor 35: Some would take him to be a Coward; but beleeve it, he is a Ladde of mettle. 1616 (1631) Jonson *Devil is an Ass* 2.8.105: Make him a man of mettall. 1625 (1647) Fletcher *Chances* 5.3.69f.: This conjurer is a right good fellow too, A lad of mettle.
Shakespeare: *1H4* 2.4.12

M919.1   As still as MIDNIGHT (Wh M532 1532)
Add *varied*: 10 Oct. 1600 J. Chamberlain 106: As close and quiet as yf yt were midnight. 1609 (1616) Jonson *Epicoene* 4.7.19: The noise here is silence too't! a kinde of calme mid-night! 1672 Dryden *1 Conquest of Granada* 1.1.282: Hush'd as midnight silence.
Shakespeare: *H5* 3 Chorus 19, *Tmp.* 4.1.207

(?) M919.2 To have heard the chimes (seen the stars) at MIDNIGHT
1600 (1608) R. Armin *Nest of Ninnies* Ep. Ded. A2: I have seene the stars at midnight in your societies.
Shakespeare: *2H4* 3.2.214

M922 MIGHT overcomes right (From 1546; Wh M534 *varied* from c1330)
Shakespeare: *2H4* 5.4.24f.

(?) M924.1 To be too long by (half) a MILE (*OED* 1d fig. from *LLL*)
c1470 *Mankind* 582 (of evensong): It is to[o] longe, by on[e] mile.
Shakespeare: *LLL* 5.2.54

M927 I will go twenty MILES on your errand first (1670 Ray, cf. *MM*; OW308b Ray only)
Add: 1530 Palsgrave 387ᵛ (L3ᵛ): Tell hym yᵗ and I fetche hym he were better go fyve myle on myn errande.
Shakespeare: *MM* 3.2.37

M930.1 As sweet as MILK (Wh M544 from a1300)
Shakespeare: *LLL* 5.2.230f.

M931 As white as MILK (From c1495)
Shakespeare: *MND* 5.2.338, *MV* 3.2.86, *Ham.* 2.2.478, *Lr.* 4.2.50, *Per.* 4 Chorus 22

M931.1 MILK-WHITE (Cf. Appendix B) (Wh M545a from a1050 [= OED ?c1000])
Shakespeare: *TGV* 3.1.252, *MND* 2.1.167, *2H6* 1.1.254, *Tit.* 5.1.31, *Tim.* 1.2.183, *PP* 9.3

M967 He weeps MILLSTONES (*Varied* from *R3*; OW876b from c1400)
Shakespeare: *Tro.* 1.2.143f., *R3* 1.3.352, 1.4.239f.

M980 What is MINE is yours (and what is yours is mine [your own])
(*Your own* from 1576; OW533b adds 1591)
E.g., 1591 H. Smith *Prep. to Marriage* ed. 1657 31: He may not say as Husbands are wont to say, That which is thine is mine, and that which is mine is mine own: but that which is mine is thine, and my self too.
Shakespeare: *MV* 3.2.16−8, *MM* 5.1.537, *H5* 5.2.175f.

M985 New out of the MINT (*Varied*; *LLL, TN,* 1639ff.; OW564b from 1593)
I.e., 1593 Nashe *Christs Teares* II,15: Newe mynt my minde to the likenes of thy lowlines.
Add: 1597 G. Harvey *Trimming* A2ᵛ: I have founde out and fetcht from the mint some few new wordes to coulor him.
Shakespeare: *LLL* 1.1.178, *TN* 3.2.22, *R3* 1.3.255, *Lr.* 5.3.133

M987.1 MIRACLES (Wonders) are ceased (past)
1593 Nashe *Christs Teares* II,125: Since his Ascension into heaven, meanelesse miracles are ceased.
c1620 (1647) Fletcher & Massinger *Custom of the Country* 5.4.14f.: Wonders are ceased, sir; we must work by means.
Shakespeare: *AWW* 2.3.1, *H5* 1.1.67−9

M989 To leave (lie) in the MIRE (From c1522)
Shakespeare: *LLL* 2.1.120, *Lr.* 2.2.4f., *Tim.* 1.2.59

M999a One must not bemoan a MISCHIEF but find out a remedy for it (1666 TOR., cf. *3H6, R2*)
Add: 1562 A. Brooke *Romeus and Juliet* 1359f.: A wise man in the midst of troubles and distres, Still standes not wayling present harme, but seeks his harmes redres.
Shakespeare: *TGV* 3.1.243f., *3H6* 5.4.1f., *R2* 3.2.178f.

M1004 MISCHIEFS, like waves, never come alone (From c1591)
Add: 1613 R. Dallington *Aphorismes* K1ᵛ: One mischiefe or losse comes seldome alone, but followes like billowes, one in the necke of another.
Shakespeare: *R2* 2.2.98f.
Cf. M1013: One misfortune comes on the neck of another. Also S177.1: A sea of troubles (sorrows).

M1012 MISFORTUNE (Evil) never (seldom) comes alone (*Varied* from c1475; OW535b from c1300; cf. Ezek. 7.5)
Shakespeare: *R2* 3.4.28, *Rom.* 3.2.116, *Ham.* 4.5.78f., 4.7.163, *Per.* 1.4.63f.

M1013 One MISFORTUNE comes on the neck of another (From c1526)
Add: 1533 N. Udall *Floures* N7: Aliud ex alio malum. One myschiefe on anothers necke.
Shakespeare: *Ham.* 4.7.163, *Son.* 131.10f.

M1015 He will be MISSED when he is gone (*Varied* from 1576)
Shakespeare: *Ant.* 1.4.43f., *Cor.* 4.1.15

(?) M1017.1 To mistake one all this while
1602 ?T. Heywood *How a Man May Choose* 608: Insooth you have mistooke me all this while. c1616 (1652) Middleton *Widow* 5.1.317: I mistook you all this while.
Shakespeare: *R2* 3.2.174

M1030 To MOCK (mop) and mow (*Mock* from 1509)
Add: c1589 ?Lyly *Whip for an Ape* 13 III,418: The Ape delights with moppes and mowes.
Shakespeare: *Lr.* 4.1.61f., *Tmp.* 3.3.82.2, 4.1.47

M1031 He who MOCKS shall be mocked (*Varied* from 1484)

E.g., 1534 Heywood *Love* C1ᵛ (18): Wherewith I brought in moccum moccabitur; (21): To gyve mock for mock [Wh M612].
Shakespeare: *LLL* 5.2.140, *AYL* 1.2.208f.

M1034 As blind as a MOLE (From 1548)
Shakespeare: *WT* 4.4.836

(?) M1037.1 Bad MONEY drives out good (OW26a: 1902–4 Lean III,425 Bad money drives out good (money) [Gresham's Law]
Shakespeare: *Son.* 144.14, *PP* 2.14

(?) M1038.1 Have MONEY in one's purse (Wh M621 [1461])
I.e., 1461 Paston III 300(9–11): Withoute he have mony in hyse purse . . . ellys they wyll not sette by hem.
Shakespeare: *Oth.* 1.3.339ff.

M1040 (He) for my MONEY (Cf. Appendix B; *OED Go* 24b from 1549) (From 1598; OW538b from 1566)
Shakespeare: *Ado* 2.3.60, *Cor.* 4.5.232

(?) M1050 If MONEY go before all ways lie open (*Varied*; only *Wiv.* verbally close; from 1542)ⁿ
Shakespeare: *Wiv.* 2.2.168f., *Cym.* 2.3.67f.

ⁿCf. Introduction, fn. 15.

M1053 MONEY begets money (*Varied* from 1587; OW538a from 1572)
Shakespeare: *Ven.* 768

(?) M1090 Put MONEY in thy purse (*Oth.*, collections from 1654; OW538b supplements)
Shakespeare: *Oth.* 1.3.339ff.
Cf. M1038.1

M1102 What will not (cannot)

MONEY (gold) do? (*Varied* from 1578; OW315b [What cannot gold do?] supplements from 1592)
Shakespeare: *Cym.* 2.3.72f.

(?) M1105 MONMOUTH CAPS (Cf. Appendix B) (From 1585–1616; OW541a adds 1598)
Shakespeare: *H5* 4.7.100

M1109 To have a MONTH'S mind to a person (thing) (Cf. Appendix B) (From 1575)
Shakespeare: *TGV* 1.2.134

M1111 As changeful as the MOON (*Varied* from c1576; Wh M647 *changeable* from c1440, 650 *variant* from c1485, 655 *to change like* from c1395, 662 *to vary like* a1400)
Shakespeare: *Shr.* 4.5.20, *LLL* 5.2.212, *MM* 3.1.24f., *Rom.* 2.2.109, *Ant.* 5.2.240f.

M1114 He casts (To cast) beyond the MOON (From 1546; OW106a *beyond the moon* from c1516)
Add: 1601 Breton *No Whippinge* D3: No: this is not a world for simple wits, That can not looke a mile above the Moone.
Shakespeare: *Tit.* 4.3.66

M1117 It is midsummer MOON with you (From 1588)
Add: 1530 Palsgrave 404 (O2): He wyll waxe madde this mydsommer moone if you take nat good hede on hym.
Shakespeare: *TN* 3.4.56

(?) M1121.1 The pale-faced MOON (Cf. Appendix B)
1602 Addition to Kyd, *Spanish Tragedy* 3.12a.33: Yonder pale faced Hee-cat there, the Moone. 1622 Dekker & Massinger *Virgin Martyr* 2.2.45f.: Antoninus Playes the Endymion to this pale fac'd Moone.
Shakespeare: *R2* 2.4.10, *1H4* 1.3.202

M1128 (He strives for) the MOON-SHINE in the water (From 1530)
Shakespeare: *LLL* 5.2.208

M1134 As melancholy as MOOR-DITCH (From *1H4*)
Shakespeare: *1H4* 1.2.77f.

M1144 The MORE a man has the more he desires (*Varied* from c1523)
Shakespeare: *Mac.* 4.3.81f.
Cf. M1287: Much would have more.

M1154.1 No MORE of that if you love me
1611 COT. s.v. Oster: Ostez vous de là. Beware of that, no more of that if you love me. 1621 (1658) Dekker et al. *Witch of Edmonton* 2.2.34. c1621 (1662) Middleton *Anything for a Quiet Life* 2.2.66.
Shakespeare: *1H4* 2.4.283

M1155.1 That's MORE than I (etc.) know
?c1590 (1598) *Mucedorus* vi.15 (I). c1591 Peele *Edward I* ii (MSR 438) (you). 1592 (1594) *Knack to Know a Knave* x (MSR 1251): I assure thee tis more than I know. c1597 (1637) Deloney *1 Gentle Craft* 99 (in a series of proverbial expressions) (you do). 1598 (1601) Jonson *Every Man In* 3.5.34 (you). c1602 (1606) ?Chapman *Sir Giles Goosecap* 1.4.170 (I). c1602 ?T. Heywood *Fair Maid of the Exchange* v (MSR 539) (you).
Shakespeare: *Tro.* 4.2.51, *2H6* 5.1.215, *H5* 4.1.129

(?) M1158 There is MORE in it than you are ware of (*Varied*)
I.e., 1576 Gascoigne *Supposes* 4.4.18f.: Thou speakest truer than thou arte aware of. 1607 G. Wilkins *Miseries of Enforced Marriage* E2ᵛ: This foole speakes wiser then he is aware. 1639 CL., p. 194.
Shakespeare: *AYL* 2.4.57

(?) M1158.1 (There is) no MORE but so
?c1589 (1633) Marlowe *Jew of Malta* 4.1.130, 4.4.72. c1592 (1594) Marlowe *Edward II* 5.2.33. c1595 Munday et al. *Sir Thomas More* 4.1.252: Nay, and it be no more but so. c1602 (1607) Middleton *Family of Love* 2.4.147. 1604 (1606) Chapman *Monsieur D'Olive* 1.2.150 (There's).
Shakespeare: *R3* 4.2.80, *Ham.* 1.3.10

M1168.1 The grey-eyed MORN-(ING) (*OED Grey-eyed* b *Rom.*, then 1670)
E.g., 1592 (1600) Nashe *Summer's Last Will* 521. 1598 (1616) W. Haughton *Englishmen for My Money* i (MSR 3) (morning). 1599 (1600) Drayton et al. *1 Sir John Oldcastle* 4.1.156f. (morning). 1600 ?Lyly *Maid's Metamorphosis* 4.2.40. c1602 (1607) Middleton *Family of Love* 2.1.1 (morning). c1604 (1608) Chapman *Bussy D'Ambois* 5.3.147.
Shakespeare: *Rom.* 2.3.1, 3.5.19

(?) M1175 A red MORNING foretells a stormy day (*Varied* from 1551; OW741a retains most, but not *R2*, for "Sky red in the morning is a sailor's warning; sky red at night is the sailor's delight" [1893 Inwards 53]).
Shakespeare: *R2* 3.3.62−4, *1H4* 5.1.1f., *Ven.* 453f.

(?) M1182.1 To tread one into MORTAR
c1625 (1633) Massinger *New Way to Pay Old Debts* 1.1.87f.: I will helpe Your memory, and tread thee into mortar.
Shakespeare: *Lr.* 2.2.65f.
Cf. F447: Bray a fool in a mortar, you cannot make him leave his folly [Prov. 27.22].

M1183 Backare (, quoth MORTIMER to his sow) (Cf. Appendix B) (From 1546)
Shakespeare: *Shr.* 2.1.73

M1189 He is (To be) a MOTE in their (one's) eyes (From 1600; not in OW despite below)
Add: 1546 Bale *Exam. of Anne Askewe* PS 21ᵛ [in Wilson, "Proverbial Wisdom of Shakespeare"]: Johan Frith is a great moate in their eyes.
Shakespeare: *Ham.* 1.1.112

M1191 You can see a MOTE in another man's eye but cannot see a beam in your own (*Varied* from 1481; cf. Matt. 7.3)
Shakespeare: *LLL* 4.3.159f.

M1193 Ask the MOTHER if the child be like his father (*Varied* from 1562)
E.g., 1562 Heywood *Epig.* 50, p.208: Who is thy father childe, axt his mothers husband. Axe my mother (quoth he) that to understand.
Shakespeare: *Shr.* 5.1.32−4, *Ado* 1.1.105, *Jn.* 1.1.60−2, *1H4* 2.4.402f., *Tmp.* 1.2.55−7

(?) M1196 If your MOTHER had not lost her virginity you would not have been born (*idea only* from 1576; not in OW)
Shakespeare: *AWW* 1.1.136f., *Ven.* 203f.

M1201.1 To have had a MOTHER
1599 (1600) Drayton et al. *1 Sir John Oldcastle* 1.3.82: Well, you had a mother. c1621 (1657) Middleton *Women Beware Women* 4.2.183f.: I had a mother. I can dissemble too. 1626 (1631) Jonson *Staple of News* Ind. 17f.: Why, what should they thinke? but that they had Mothers, as we had. 1738 Swift *Pol. Conv.* I,423: I suppose the gentleman's a woman-hater; but, sir, I think you ought to remember, that you had a mother [in W637].
Shakespeare: *Tro.* 5.2.130, *TNK* 5.1.105−7
Cf. W637: To be born of woman.

M1202 Every MOTHER'S son (child) (From c1470)
Shapespeare: *MND* 1.2.78, 3.1.73

M1204 His MOTHER'S milk is not out of his nose (From 1607 [cf. on H745], cf. *TN*)
Shakespeare: *TN* 1.5.161f.

M1205 The MOTHER'S side is the surer side (From 1548)
🖚 Shakespeare: *Tit.* 4.2.126

M1208.1 (In one's) MOTHER-TONGUE (Cf. Appendix B) (Wh M722 from c1250)
Shakespeare: *LLL* 1.2.95f.

M1208.2 MOTHER-WIT (Cf. Appendix B) (Wh M723 from c1450 [3])
Shakespeare: *Shr.* 2.1.263, *LLL* 1.2.95f.

(?) M1214.1 A MOUNTAIN might be sooner (re)moved (Wh M726 1513)
I.e., 1513 Bradshaw *St. Werburge* 37.852−4: A mountayne or hyll soner, leve ye me, Myght be remoeved agaynst the course of nature. 1560 Ps. 125.1 (Geneva): Thei that trust in the Lord shalbe as mount Zion, which can not be removed, but remaineth for ever. 1596 (1605) *Captain Thomas Stukeley* xviii (MSR 2296): Thou movst a mountaine sooner then my mind.
Shakespeare: *1H6* 2.5.102f., *Jn.* 2.1.452f., *2H4* 4.1.186, *JC* 3.1.74
Cf. F738: Friends (Men) may meet but mountains never (never greet).

M1220.1 As fearful as a MOUSE (Wh M732 a1420)
Shakespeare: *2H4* 3.2.159f.
Cf. M297: A man or a mouse.

M1236.1 Not a MOUSE stirring (stirs)[n]
1622 Dekker & Massinger *Virgin Martyr* 3.3.131f.: Take heed no body listens. / Not a Mouse stirres. 1636 Dekker *Wonder of a Kingdom* 4.4.20: Ther's nothing stirring, the very mice are a sleepe.
Shakespeare: *MND* 5.1.387f., *Ham.* 1.1.10

[n]Cf. the familiar "Night before Christmas": "Not a creature was stirring, Not even a mouse."

M1237 To look like (As wet as) a drowned MOUSE (rat) (From c1500; *mouse* from *1H6*)
Shakespeare: *1H6* 1.2.12

M1240 Whist (Peace), and catch a MOUSE (Collections from 1639, *varied* from c1625)
E.g., 1632 Hausted *Rival Friends* 5.1 K4[v]: But peace and catch a mouse cry I.
Shakespeare: *Lr.* 4.6.89f.

M1243 MICE (Rats) quit a falling house (sinking ship) (fig.) (*Varied house* from 1612 [OW664bf. from 1579], *ship* cf. *Ant.*, *Tmp.* [excluded] [OW adds 1895]; examples in both are a mixture of literal and figurative)
Shakespeare: *Ant.* 3.13.63−5

M1248 A cool MOUTH and warm feet live long (Collections from 1611)
Shakespeare: *Tmp.* 1.1.53

M1259 Spit in his MOUTH and make him a mastiff (*Varied* from 1576)
Add: c1598 (1639) Deloney *2 Gentle Craft* 186: If I bewray your secrets call me dogs-nose and spit in my face like a young kitling.
Shakespeare: *1H4* 2.4.193f.

M1260.1 To be cold in the MOUTH (i.e., dead)
c1613 (1616) Beaumont & Fletcher *Scornful Lady* 2.2.18f.: Would I had been cold ith mouth before this day,

and nere have lived to see this disso-
lution. 1667 Quevedo (L'Estrange)
Visions ed. 1702 G4: Another, with
the Ephesian Matron, was solacing
her self with her Gallant, before her
Husband was thorough cold in the
mouth.
Shakespeare: *Tmp.* 1.1.53

M1264 To stop one's MOUTH
(From 1546)
Shakespeare: *TGV* 2.3.44f., *Jn.*
3.1.299, *H5* 5.2.271f., *H8* 2.2.8f.,
5.2.58, *Tit.* 2.3.185, 5.1.151, 161–7,
Oth. 2.3.304f., 5.2.71, *Lr.* 5.3.155
(Q), *Tim.* 2.2.147

M1264.1 To stop one's MOUTH
with a kiss (M1264 has *Ado*)
1602 ?Middleton *Blurt, Master Constable* 5.3.135: Mouth, I'll stop you
with a kiss. 1612 Webster *White Devil*
4.2.195: Stop her mouth, with a
sweet kisse, my Lord. c1613 (1623)
Webster *Duchess of Malfi* 3.2.26: I'll
stop your mouth. c1613 (1616)
Beaumont & Fletcher *Scornful Lady*
3.2.189: Stop her mouth. c1615
Middleton *Witch* 1.1.78f.: Not a
kiss? / I'll call aloud, i'faith. / I'll stop
your mouth. c1616 (1652) Middle-
ton *Widow* 1.2.136: What serve kisses
for but to stop all your mouths?
Shakespeare: *Ado*   2.1.310f.,
5.4.98, *Tro.* 3.2.133–7, *2H6* 3.2.396,
R2 5.1.95, *H5* 5.2.271–5

M1265 What is sweet in the MOUTH
is oft sour (bitter) in the maw (stomach) (*Varied* from *Luc.*; OW793a
adds 1592; cf. Rev. 10.9f.)
Shakespeare: *R2* 1.3.236, *Luc.*
698f.

M1277 Hear MUCH but speak little
(From 1586; OW362bf. *varied* from
c1420)
Shakespeare: *Ham.* 1.3.68

M1287 MUCH would have more
(From 1597, cf. *Luc.*; OW550a from
c1450, Wh M786 from a1400)
Shakespeare: *Luc.* 98

M1289.1 So MUCH for that (*OED So*
39h [*So much*] has 1707)
1600 (1657) Dekker et al. *Lust's Dominion*   1.2.221.   c1602   (1607)
?T. Heywood *Fair Maid of the Exchange* vii (MSR 1007), xii (1943).
Shakespeare: *R3* 5.3.85, *R2*
2.1.155, *TNK* 3.2.19

M1298 MUCK of the world (From
1530; Wh M798 from a1393)
Shakespeare: *Cor.* 2.2.126

M1308 A MULTITUDE of people is
a beast of many heads (From 1542;
OW509b Horace, 1531ff.)
Shakespeare: *2H4* Ind. 18f., *Cor.*
2.3.16f., 3.1.92f., 4.1.1f.

M1311 MUMBUDGET (Cf. Appendix B) (From 1571; OW551a *To play*
from 1559)
E.g., 1611 Cotgrave s.v. Court: To
play at Mum-budget, or be at a
Nonplus.
Shakespeare: *Wiv.*   5.2.5f.,
5.5.197f.

M1315 MURDER will out (cannot be
hid) (From 1481; Wh M806 *hid* from
c1325, *out* from c1390)
Shakespeare: *MV* 2.2.79, *TN*
3.1.147f., *R3* 1.4.283, *Tit.* 2.3.287,
Ham.   1.2.256f.,   2.2.593f.,   *Oth.*
5.1.109f.

M1319.1 MUSIC has a silver sound
(tongue) (*Varied*)
1576 Edwards *Paradise of Dainty De-
vices* ed. Rollins 206. 1590 Spenser
Faerie Queene 2.3.24.9: A silver
sounde, that heavenly musicke
seemd to make. 1599 (1600) Dekker
Old Fortunatus 1.1.330: Heres no
sweete Musicke with her silver
sound; 3.1.379: Musicke with her
silver tongue. 1602 Dekker *Satiromastix* 2.1.71f.: Musicke talke lowd-
er, that thy silver voice, May reach
my Soveraignes eares.
Shakespeare: *Rom.*   2.2.165f.,
4.5.128–32
Cf. S458.1: Silver is sweet.

M1330   MUST is for the king (From 1602, analogues from c1592)
E.g., c1592 (1594) Marlowe *Edward II* 4.6.81f.: Your majesty must go to Killingworth / Must! 'Tis somewhat hard, when kings must go.
Shakespeare: *R2* 3.3.143—6

M1330.1   I (etc.) MUST and will (Cf. Appendix B)
E.g., c1587 (1590) Marlowe *2 Tamburlaine* 4.3.53: I must and will be pleased. c1588 (1591) Lyly *Endymion* 1.2.54: I can doe it, I must, I will! ?c1589 Marlowe *Jew of Malta* 1.2.389: I must and will, sir; there's no remedy. c1600 *Fatal Marriage* xii (MSR 1277): Sir but I must and will. 1603 (1605) Jonson *Sejanus* III.141: You must, and will, sir. c1605 (1630) Dekker *2 Honest Whore* 4.1.128.
Shakespeare: *3H6* 1.1.85, *Jn.* 4.1.40, *Tit.* 1.1.357f., *Cor.* 3.2.97

M1331   What MUST (shall, will) be must (shall, will) be (From 1546; OW552a from 1519)
Shakespeare: *MV* 2.2.179f., *TN* 1.5.311, *Jn.* 4.1.55f., *R2* 3.3.207, *1H4* 2.3.105, *Rom.* 4.1.21

M1338   (He loves) laced MUTTON (Cf. Appendix B) (From 1578; OW552b from 1563)
Shakespeare: *TGV* 1.1.97; *MM* 3.2.181f.

N

N10.1   To blow (on) one's NAILS (fig.) (Wh N2 a1470)[n]
1566 Drant Horace *Sat.* ix E3: All the reaste might blow their nayles [*OED Blow* 16]. c1575 Churchyard *Challenge* Gg2: Neede blew his nailes. 1593 Bancroft *Survay* Aa4[v]: They maie shutte the dore: but for openinge of it they maie blowe their nailes.
Shakespeare: *Shr.* 1.1.107f.

[n]Whiting's single example appears to be literal, and hence no more proverbial than *LLL* 5.2.913 or *3H6* 2.5.3.

N12   To pare one's (the devil's) NAILS (fig.) (From 1548)
Shakespeare: *TN* 4.2.130, *H5* 4.4.71f.

N17   One NAIL drives out another (From 1539)
Shakespeare: *TGV* 2.4.193, *Cor.* 4.7.54

N22   A good NAME is better than riches (cf. Prov. 22.1; *varied* from 1477; Wh N12 from c1350)
E.g., a1500 *Eight Goodly Questions* 423(4): And remember, that good name is gold worth. a1500 *Good Wife* N212.96—7: For wise men and old Sayne good name is worth gold.
Shakespeare: *2H4* 2.4.31f., *Oth.* 3.3.157—61, *Lr.* 1.1.58

N36—7   To take one NAPPING (Cf. Appendix B) (From 1594; OW110b from 1562)
Shakespeare: *Shr.* 4.2.46, *LLL* 4.3.128

N42   N42   NATURE abhors a vacuum (From 1551; OW555a Plutarch, from c1550)
Shakespeare: *Ant.* 2.2.216—8

N43   NATURE does nothing in vain (From 1481; OW555a Aristotle)
Shakespeare: *Rom.* 2.3.17f.

N47   NATURE passes nurture (Collections from 1639 [cf. on H745], analogues from 1580; OW556a analogues from 1492)
E.g., 1492 *Dial. of Salomon & Marcolphus* ed. Duff 21: Nature goth afore lernyng.
Shakespeare: *Tmp.* 4.1.188f.

N51.1   Be NAUGHT a while (*OED* 1c *To be naught* from 1593)
1565 *King Darius* 747 (Iniquytie

speaking): Come away and be nought a whyle. 1606 Chapman *Gentleman Usher* 3.2.239f.: Kisse her; yfaith you must; get you togither and be naught awhile.
Shakespeare: *AYL* 1.1.35f.

N54 He that will not when he may, when he would he shall have NAY (shall not when he will) (Collections from 1546; Wh W275 *varied* from a1000)
Shakespeare: *Ham.* 4.7.118–21, *Ant.* 2.7.83f.

N56.1 To come NEAR one (now) (*OED* 12b from 1600)
E.g., c1585 (1592) Lyly *Gallathea* 3.1.75: What are you come so neere me? 1588 R. Some *Godly Treatise* 2A3: Nowe sir, to come a little neerer you. c1597 (1609) Jonson *Case is Altered* 2.2.16: Why now you come neere him. 1611 Dekker & Middleton *Roaring Girl* 3.2.232: Do I come neere you now sir?
Shakespeare: *TN* 3.4.64, *1H4* 1.2.13, *Rom.* 1.5.20

N57 I am NEAREST to myself (From c1570)
Add: 1533 N. Udall *Floures* C3: Proximus sum egomet mihi. I must be best frende unto my selfe, or I must serve myne owne selfe fyrste, or, I love you well, but I love my selfe better, or, every manne for hym selfe.
Shakespeare: *TGV* 2.6.23, *Tmp.* 1.1.20
Cf. M112: Every man for himself [from 1478]; M132: Every man loves himself best [from 1616].

N69 To slip (one's NECK out of) the collar (*Varied* from 1581; OW558b from 1563)
Shakespeare: *R3* 4.4.111f., *Rom.* 1.1.3–5

(?) N70.1 Extreme NEED best proves (*tests*) a valiant courage (Wh N44 c1523)

I.e., c1523 Barclay *Mirrour* 39(38): Extreme nede best proveth a courage valiaunt.
Shakespeare: *Jn.* 2.1.82

N95 Sharp as a NEEDLE (From 1552; Wh N66 a900)
Shakespeare: *Cym.* 1.3.19

N101 Two NEGATIVES make an affirmative (From 1593; OW851b from c1580 [1591])
Shakespeare: *TN* 5.1.21f.

N107 He that has an ill NEIGHBOR has oftentimes an ill morning (*Varied* from c1530; Wh N75 c1400)
Shakespeare: *H5* 4.1.6

N117 He dwells far from NEIGHBORS (has ill neighbors) that is fain to praise himself (*Varied* from 1509)
Add e.g.: 1592 Nashe *Strange Newes* I,294: A poore creature here is faine to commend himselfe for want of friendes to speake for him.
Shakespeare: *Ado* 5.2.73–7, *Tit.* 5.3.118
Cf. P545.1: He must praise himself since no man else will.

(?) N124.1 To climb a daw's (bird's) NEST
1556 Poynet *Politike Power* L1: [The priests] will sone . . . sende the commones to clymbe a dawes nest, and use them at their pleasur.
Shakespeare: *Rom.* 2.5.73f.

N130 You dance in a NET (and think nobody sees you) (*Varied* from 1534; OW166a from 1528)
Shakespeare: *H5* 1.2.93

N132 He has pissed (To piss) on a NETTLE (From 1546)
Shakespeare: *TNK* 3.5.57
Cf. N131: As angry (surly) as if he had pissed on a nettle [from 1670 Ray].

N135.1 To whip with NETTLES

1584 Lyly *Sapho and Phao* 5.2.73f.: You shal be . . . whipt with nettles, not roses. c1585 (1592) Lyly *Gallathea* 3.4.79: Venus' rods are made of Roses, Dianaes of Bryers. c1600 ?Nashe *Choise of Valentines* III,414: Thow wilt be whipt with nettles for this geare. 1602 Dekker *Satiromastix* 4.2.5: He . . . whipt them so with nettles.

Shakespeare: *1H4* 1.3.239f.

N135.2 To be NEVER the near (Cf. Appendix B)

E.g., 1533 N. Udall *Floures* C3ᵛ: You shalbe never the nere, or, it shal nothing avayle you. c1553 (1575) W. Stevenson *Gammer Gurton's Needle* 1.4.36: All was in vayne; my neele was never the nere. c1564 *Bugbears* 4.5.61: The truth shalbe smothered & youe never the nere. c1576 *Common Conditions* 1558: I . . . am never the near.

Shakespeare: *R2* 5.1.88

Cf. E27: Early up and never the near(er) [from 1546].

N160 In the NICK (nick of time) (Cf. Appendix B) (From 1565)

Shakespeare: *Oth.* 5.2.317, *TNK* 3.5.73

N164 After NIGHT comes the day (fig.) (From c1475; Wh N108 from c1385)

Shakespeare: *MND* 3.2.431f., *Mac.* 4.3.239f., *Son.* 145.10f.

N164.1 As dark as NIGHT (Wh N103 from a1393)

Shakespeare: *Son.* 147.14

N166 A blustering NIGHT a fair day (1640 HERB., cf. *Son.*; ditto OW71b)

Shakespeare: *Son.* 90.7

N167 Dark NIGHT is Cupid's day (From c1593 [1598])

Shakespeare: *TN* 3.1.148. *Ven.* 720

N167.1 Endless (eternal) NIGHT (darkness) (Cf. Appendix B)

1598 (1601) A. Munday *Death Robert Earl of Huntington* x (MSR 1760f.): A shambles of dead men about his feete, Sent by his sword unto eternall shade. 1600 (1601) Marston *Jack Drum's Entertainment* II III,202: Pasquill is sunk into eternal night. 1697 Dryden *Eneid* IV.992: Dido . . . clos'd her Lids at last, in endless Night [*OED Night* 2].

Shakespeare: *R3* 1.3.267f., 1.4.47, 5.3.61f., *R2* 1.3.177, 222

N173.1 Next the dark NIGHT the glad morrow (fig.) (Wh N108 *varied* from c1385)

Shakespeare: *Son.* 90.7

Cf. N164: After night comes the day.

N179 What is done by NIGHT appears by day (Collections *varied* from 1611, cf. *Luc.*; OW199a and Wh T163 add a1393)

I.e., a1393 Gower *CA* III 72.4597−600: Bot so prive mai be nothing, That it ne comth to knowleching; Thing don upon the derke nyht Is after knowe on daies liht.

Shakespeare: *Luc.* 747

N183 To sit (sing) like a NIGHTINGALE, with a thorn against one's breast (From *Luc.*; OW566b from 1576 [non-fig. from c1510; Wh N112 from a1449])

Shakespeare: *TNK* 3.4.25f., *Luc.* 1135f., *PP* 20.8−10

(?) N184 NIGHTWORK (Cf. Appendix B) (1639 CL., *2H4*; OW567a from 1594; ditto *OED*)

E.g., 1639 CL. s.v. Nox 227: Nightworks. Clandestina scelera.

Shakespeare: *2H4* 3.2.198f.

(?) N198.1 To give one the NOD (Cf. Appendix B)

1617 Moryson *Itin.* I.40: A Doc-

tor . . . commanded me to draw water for his horse, giving me no reward presently but only a nod [*OED* 1].
  Shakespeare: *Tro.* 1.2.196
  Cf. N198: A nod for a wise man and a rod for a fool [1678 Ray].

N206   He is put to (etc.) a NONPLUS (Cf. Appendix B) (From c1589 [1633]; OW576a *driven* from 1578)
  Shakespeare: *Ado* 3.5.62

N213   Out of the NORTH all ill comes forth (From 1598; Wh N124 from a1338; cf. Jer. 1.14)
  Shakespeare: *Per.* 4.1.51, *Cym.* 1.3.36

N215   As plain (seen) as the NOSE on a man's face (From *TGV*; OW629b from a1576)
  Shakespeare: *TGV* 2.1.135f., *TN* 4.1.8

N229   To bore one's NOSE (From c1570)
  Shakespeare: *H8* 1.1.128

N230   To follow one's NOSE (From c1590 [1599], variant c1508; OW272b supplements)
  Add e.g.: ?1580 G. Walker *Manifest detection . . . Diceplay* B8: Who so . . . but foloweth his nose (as they say alwais straight forward) may wel hold up y^e head for a yere or ii.
  Shakespeare: *Lr.* 2.4.69

N233   To lead one by the NOSE (like a bear, ass) (*Nose* from 1598, *ass Oth.*, *bear* from *WT*; OW449af. Lucian = L. *naribus trahere*, as was done with bears, from c1495)
  Add: 1590 ?Nashe *Almond for a Parrat* III,351: Must I ever leade you up and downe antiquitie by the nose lyke an Asse?
  Shakespeare: *Oth.* 1.3.401f., *WT* 4.4.801f.

N236   To play with the NOSE (From 1583)
  E.g., 1611 COT., s.v. Nasarder: To filip . . . also, to frumpe, or breake a ieast on; play with the nose of.
  Shakespeare: *MM* 1.3.29

N241   To snap (bite) off one's NOSE (From 1599; OW748a from *Ado*)
  Add: 1601 (1602) Dekker *Satiromastix* 5.2.199f.: But to bite every Motley-head vice by'th nose, you did it Ningle to play the Bug-beare Satyre.
  Shakespeare: *Ado* 5.1.115f., *MM* 1.3.29, 3.1.108, 5.1.339f.
  Cf. N236: To play with the NOSE.

N248   To change one's NOTE (From 1575)
  Add e.g.: c1560 (c1570) W. Wager *Enough Is as Good as a Feast* 1353: I will make you change your note.
  Shakespeare: *Tim.* 1.2.246

N256   He cares for NOTHING (*TN*, 1616, 1666)
  I.e., 1616 DR. 2296. 1666 TOR. *It. Prov.* 2 58: Who careth for nothing, liveth at a venture.
  Shakespeare: *TN* 3.1.26−30

N274   He who still keeps home knows NOTHING (*Varied* from 1611, cf. *TGV;* not in OW)
  Shakespeare: *Shr.* 1.2.50−2, *TGV* 1.1.2

N279   I will (etc.) say NOTHING (nought) but mum (From a1525)
  Shakespeare: *MM* 5.1.287, *Lr.* 1.4.196f., *Tmp.* 3.2.51

N282.1   Not for NOTHING (naught) (Cf. Appendix B)
  1533 N. Udall *Floures* Y7^v: Non est temere. It is nat for naught. 1599 (1600) Jonson *Every Man Out* 1.2.137f.: Those Mercuries . . . should remember they had not their fingers for nothing. ?c1600 *Fatal*

Marriage xvi (MSR 1857f.): Twas not for nothing my sonn soe slightly answer'd. 1604 (1606) Chapman *Monsieur D'Olive* 3.2.168f.: 'Tis not for nothing that this Pettie Broker followes me. c1605 (1612) Chapman *Widow's Tears* 2.4.91f.: Tis not for nothing your brother is asham'd on you.
Shakespeare: *MV* 2.5.24

N285 NOTHING can came of nothing (Entry form from *Lr.*; *varied* c1550; OW579a from c1380)
E.g., 1551 Cranmer *Ans. to Gardiner* 369: Sicut ex nihilo nihil fit, Ita nihil in nihilum redigitur. As nothyng can be made of nought, so nothynge can be tourned into nought.
Shakespeare: *Rom.* 1.1.177, *Lr.* 1.1.90, 1.4.132f.

N298.1 NOTHING is impossible
1599 (1600) Dekker *Old Fortunatus* 2.2.195f.: Well, there's nothing impossible: a dog has his day [D464], and so have you. ?c1600 *Fatal Marriage* xiii (MSR 1387): Nothing is impossible my love. 1602 ?T. Heywood *How a Man May Choose* 2262: As nothing is unpossible. c1606 (1607) Jonson *Volpone* 1.2.99–109: What thoughts he has ... And then concludes, there's nought impossible. 1616 DR. s.v. Impossibility 1100: A foole thinketh nothing impossible.
Shakespeare: *TGV* 3.1.369f.

N303 NOTHING is our own but time only (1639 CL., 1732 FUL.)
Cf. 1600 Bodenham *Bel-vedere* ed. 1875 231 [?from *R2*]: There's nothing we can call our owne, but death.
Shakespeare: *R2* 3.2.152

N309.1 NOTHING lasts ever (always) (Wh L87 c1380, Wh N158 1477, 1513)
I.e., c1380 Chaucer *HF* 1147: But men seyn, "What may ever laste?"

1477 Paston V 278(8): But no thyng lastyth evyr. 1513 More *Richard* 60 D(10): But nothing lasteth alway. Add: 1616 DR. 1429: What can last alwaies?
Shakespeare: *2H4* 1.2.214
Cf. W884: This world will not last aye.

N311 NOTHING more certain than death and nothing more uncertain than the time of its coming (*Varied* from a1500; Wh D96 from c735)
E.g., a1500 *Harley MS.2321* in *Rel. Ant.* I 208(10): Thou shalt departe, and knowest not what day. a1500 *Timor Mortis* in *MLR* 28 (1933) 236(25–8): There is no thyng that ever God made More certeyn to us than oure dethe is, But more uncerteyne thyng none is yhadd Than the ourre off dethe to us, ywysse.
Shakespeare: *R2* 3.2.103, *2H4* 3.2.37–40, *H5* 5.1.31–3, *JC* 2.2.36f., 3.1.99f.

N317 NOTHING so good but it (The best things, Everything) may be abused (*Nothing* from 1530; OW49a supplements)
Shakespeare: *Rom.* 2.3.19f.

N319 NOTHING (Nought) venture nothing (nought) have (From 1546)
Shakespeare: *Ven.* 567

N321 NOTHING violent can be permanent (*Varied* from 1565; OW581af. from 1562)
Shakespeare: *R2* 2.1.33f., *Rom.* 2.6.9, *Ham.* 3.2.196f., *Oth.* 1.3.344, *Luc.* 894

N327 There is NOTHING but is good for something (Collections from 1616, cf. *Rom.*; OW579 adds a1500, 1609)
Shakespeare: *Rom.* 2.3.17f.

N328 There is NOTHING so bad in which there is not something of good (1678 Ray *Adagia Hebr.*, cf. *H5*, 1623)

I.e., 1623 WOD. 505: No Evill without Good.
Shakespeare: *H5* 4.1.4

N331 They that have NOTHING need fear to lose nothing (From 1622; OW580a from c1557; cf. Wh N140, 142 from a1387)
Shakespeare: *3H6* 3.3.152

N351 NOW or never (Cf. Appendix B,) (From 1560; OW583a from c1380)
Shakespeare: *2H6* 3.1.331, *TNK* 3.6.185

N355 A NURSE'S tongue is privileged to talk (Collections from 1659)
Shakespeare: *Rom.* [Juliet's voluble nurse exemplifies the proverb.]

N360 Sweet is the NUT (kernel) but bitter (hard) is the shell (*Varied* from 1578; Wh N196 1475)
Shakespeare: *Shr.* 2.1.254f., *AYL* 3.2.109

O

(?) O1 As close as OAK (*Oth.* only, cf. Apperson; OW127b adds *hard* 1552, *close* 1763)
Shakespeare: *Oth.* 3.3.210

O3 OAKS may fall when reeds stand the storm (*Varied* from 1573; OW584b from c1374)
E.g., 1573 Tusser *500 Points Husb.* 64 149: Like as in tempests great, where wind doth beare the stroke, Much safer stands the bowing reede then doth the stubborne oke.
Shakespeare: *Cor.* 5.2.110f., *Cym.* 4.2.267

O7 An unlawful OATH is better broken than kept (*Varied* from 1481)
Shakespeare: *TGV* 2.6.11, *LLL* 2.1.105f., *Tro.* 5.3.15−24, *2H6* 5.1.182f., *3H6* 5.1.89−91, *Jn.* 3.1.270ff.

O9 To drink the OCEAN dry (From c1589 [1633]; OW203b cf. 1550)
Shakespeare: *R2* 2.2.145f.

O25 As smooth (etc.) as OIL (*1H4*, *glib* 1585; OW747a *soft* 1579, *smooth* a1637)
Add: 1579 Lyly *Euphues* I,224: They seeme smoothe as oyle. c1580 J. Conybeare 47: More mylde and quiet than oyle. 1598 Meres *Palladis Tamia* 2T1.
Shakespeare: *1H4* 1.3.7

O29 There is OIL (no oil) left in the lamp (fig.) (From *1H6*; OW587a from 1573)
Shakespeare: *AWW* 1.2.58f., *1H6* 2.5.8, *R2* 1.3.221

O30 To add OIL to (pour oil on) the fire (fig.) (From 1548; Wh O24 c1390)
Shakespeare: *AWW* 5.3.6−8, *2H6* 5.2.55, *Lr.* 2.2.77

O34.1 Not so OLD as true (*Varied*) (Cf. Appendix B)
c1560 (c1570) W. Wager *Enough is as Good as a Feast* 861: It is an old saying and a true. 1579 Lyly *Euphues* I,185: It hath bene an olde sayed sawe, and not of less truth then antiquitie. 1587 (Cf. on A167). c1588 (1599) Porter *Two Angry Women of Abingdon* x (MSR 2313f.; Nicholas Proverbes): Tis an olde Proverbe, & not so old as true.
Shakespeare: *Wiv.* 4.2.107

O37 OLDER and wiser (From 1632, e.g., 1639 CL.; ditto OW593b)
Shakespeare: *Lr.* 1.4.240, 1.5.41−5, *Luc.* 1550
Cf. Wh S60: Sapience is seen in old folk [c1475]; Old folks can much [c1395].

O38 The OLDER the worse (better) (*Worse* from 1639 [OW593b from 1621], *better* 1587 [OW])
I.e., 1587 Bridges *Defence* 126: Antiquitie of time makes a iolie claime.

Bonum quo antiquius, eo melius. A good thing the more auncient, the better.

Shakespeare: *Per.* 1 Chorus 10

(?) O40.1 As high as OLYMPUS
c1613 (1647) Fletcher *Bonduca* 5.1 VI,146: Raise his pile High as Olympus. 1679 *Troilus and Cressida* 4.2. VI,370: Be't so; and were it on some precipice, High as Olympus.

Shakespeare: *JC* 4.3.92, *Oth.* 2.1.187f.

(?) O40.2 Better ONCE than never
c1591 (1593) Peele *Edward I* xix (MSR 2417): Well saide Frier better once than never.

Shakespeare: *Shr.* 5.1.150

Cf. L85: Better late than never [from 1529; Wh L89 from c1330].

O50.1 Man (Life) is but a figure of ONE
1607 G. Meriton *Sermon of Nobilitie* B2^v: Every man in himselfe is but as a figure of 1. 1618 G. Strode *Anatomie of Mortalitie* D5: Our life is a poynt, and lesse then a poynt, a figure of one, to which we can adde no cipher, it is but the least peece of time, that may be measured out, a moment and lesse then a moment.

Shakespeare: *MND* 5.1.307−9, *Ham.* 5.2.74

O52 ONE and none is all one (One is as good as none, One is none) (From 1591)
E.g. 1591 H. Smith *Preparative Marriage: Wks.* I,12: We say that one is none.

Shakespeare: *Rom.* 1.2.32f., *Son.* 8.14, 136.8

O54 ONE is no number (From c1592 [1598]; OW597a Macrobius, 1561)
Shakespeare: *Rom.* 1.2.32f., *Son.* 8.14, 136.8

O62 That (If) ONE will not another will (*Varied* from 1546)

E.g., 1546 Heywood *Dialogue* I.iii A4: That that one maie not, an other maie.

Shakespeare: *LLL* 4.1.128

O62.1 To be ONE too many (too many by one) (*OED* 4e from *Err.*)
E.g., 1546 Heywood *Dialogue* II.v G4^v: We twayne are one to many (quoth I) for men saie, Three maie keepe a counsell, if two be awaie [T257]. 1575 Gascoigne "Flowers" I,64: If so thy wife be too too fayre of face: It drawes one gest too many to thine inne. c1577 (1578) T. Lupton *All for Money* 1045f.: I have two wives, I must needs confess. I have too many by one. 1580 Lyly *Euphues and his England* II,51: A banket where many Ladyes were and too many by one, as the end tryed.

Shakespeare: *Err.* 3.1.35, *TGV* 5.4.52, *Ado* 4.1.127−9, *Rom.* 1.1.128, 3.5.166

O62.2 To live ONE by another
1553 ?Udall *Respublica* 1797f.: Call yet it peace sirra, when brother and brother Cannot be content to live one by another? 1604 Marston *Malcontent* 4.4.4f.: Do not turn player; there's more of them than can well live one by another already.

Shakespeare: *MV* 3.5.22f.

O64 He is ONE-AND-THIRTY (fig.) (1678 Ray, cf. *Shr.*; OW595b from 1592)
Shakespeare: *Shr.* 1.2.32f.

O64.1 To not be (be) ONESELF (*OED Himself* 3b from 1690)
c1604 Chapman *All Fools* 1.1.140: Ile be my selfe, in spight of husbandry; 1.1.371: Fathers will be knowne to be them selves. c1604 (1605) Marston *Dutch Courtesan* 4.2.29: I am not now myself, no man; 5.3.61 (same speaker): I am myself. c1606 (1607) Jonson *Volpone* 5.2.39−41: I was A little in a mist; but not deiected: Never, but still my selfe. 1609 (1616)

Jonson *Epicoene* 3.5.15−8: I commend your resolution, that . . . would yet goe on, and bee your selfe. 1611 Jonson *Catiline* (four different speakers) II.348f.: Why, now my Fulvia lookes, like her bright name! And is her selfe! III.147: Be still your selfe [Again III.304]; IV.543: Friends, be your selves.

Shakespeare: *R2* 2.1.241, *1H4* 3.2.92f., *Ham.* 5.2.234f., *Lr.* 2.4.107−9, *Ant.* 1.1.42f., 3.10.25f.

Cf. Appendix B: To FORGET oneself.

O67   To weep (It may serve) with an ONION (*Varied* from 1548)
Shakespeare: *Shr.* Ind. i.125f., *AWW* 5.3.320, *Ant.* 1.2.169f., 4.2.35

O70   OPPORTUNITY (Night, Midnight) is whoredom's bawd (*Varied*; idea from 1539, but nothing verbal before *Luc.*; OW599b adds 1586)
I.e., 1586 Warner *Albion's Eng.* II.ix E2^v: Opportunitie can win the coyest She that is.
Add: 1580 Lyly *Euphues and his England* II,53: When I demaunded what was the first thing to winne my Lady, he aunswered Opportunitie, asking what was the second, he sayd Opportunitie: desirous to know what might be the thirde, he replyed Opportunitie. ?c1580 ?Lyly III,460: Oportunity will mate and winn the coyest she y^t is.
Shakespeare: *Tro.* 4.5.62, *Luc.* 886

(?) O74.1   To play the ORATOR
c1587 (1590) Marlowe *Tamburlaine* 1.2.128f.: Then shall we fight courageously with them, Or look you I should play the orator? 1593 G. Harvey *Pierces Supererogation* II,75: His constant zeal to play the Divels Oratour. 1611 Jonson *Catiline* III.687f.: You'have done most masculinely within, And plaid the orator.
Shakespeare: *1H6* 4.1.174f., *3H6* 1.2.2, 2.2.43, 3.2.188, *R3* 3.5.95

Cf. Appendix B: To PLAY the fool (etc.).

O81   To heap OSSA upon Pelion (From a1598; OW600b Virgil, from 1561)
Shakespeare: *Ham.* 5.1.251−3

O89.1   An OVEN dammed up bakes soonest (fig.) (*Varied*)
1579 Lyly *Euphues* I,210: Seeing the wound that bleedeth inwarde is most daungerous [W390], that the fire kepte close burneth most furious [F265], that the Ooven dammed up baketh soonest, that sores having no vent fester inwardly, it is high time to unfolde my secret love. 1598 Meres *Palladis Tamia* Z2^{v}f.: As the oven dampt up hath the greatest heate; fire supprest is most forcible; the streames stopt, either breake through or overflowe [S929]: so sorrowes concealed as they are most passionate, so they are most peremptorie.
Shakespeare: *Tit.* 2.4.36f., *Ven.* 331f.

O91.1   To OVERSHOOT oneself (be overshot)^n (Cf. Appendix B)
1530 Cf. M427.1. 1546 Heywood *Dialogue* II.iii G1^v: Overshoote not your selfe any syde to hyde. c1589 (1592) Lyly *Midas* 3.3.50: Indeed I was overshot in iudgement; 5.3.64f.: Is it possible that Mydas should be so overshot in iudgement? c1589 (1594) Lyly *Mother Bombie* 1.2.23f.: In this the overshooting of her selfe, she overweeneth of her selfe. 1605 Jonson et al. *Eastward Ho* 4.1.182: I knew you were overshot.
Shakespeare: *LLL* 1.1.142, 4.3.157f., *H5* 3.7.123, *JC* 3.2.150

^{n}See Introduction, p. xivf.

O94.1   To be like an OWL to wonder at
1566 (1575) Gascoigne *Supposes* 5.3.59f.: All the people wondring about me as it were at an owle. 1575 Gascoigne "Weedes" I,464: Lucius . . . Became . . . an owle, Well

woondred at in place where he did passe. 1599 (1600) Dekker *Old Fortunatus* 2.2.156: Let him live like an Owle for the world to wonder at. c1602 (1611) Chapman *May-Day* 1.2.103f.: Now will all these I say at your first entrance wonder at you, as at some strange Owle. 1616 DR. 2480: All men wonder at him like an owle in an Ivie-tree [in O96: To look like an owl in an ivy bush].
Shakespeare: *3H6* 5.4.56f.

O99 May we not do with our OWN what we list? (*Varied* from c1577; cf. Matt. 20.15)
Shakespeare: *MV* 1.3.113, 4.1.97f., *Cym.* 2.1.3–5

O105.1 OX and ass (*Varied*; supplementing O108.1)
E.g., c1589 (1592) Lyly *Midas* 4.1.148f.: It might bee hard to iudge whether he were more Ox or Asse. c1590 (1595) Peele *Old Wives Tale* 30: Be thou Oxe or Asse that appearest. 1598 (1616) W. Haughton *Englishmen for My Money* viii (MSR 1549f.): Yoo be an English Oxe to call a gentle moan Asse. ?1621 (1652) Fletcher *Wild Goose Chase* 1.2.66: They'll say you went out like an ox and returned like an ass else. 1658 Mennis & Smith *Musarum Deliciae* ed. 1874 I,94: He's an Oxe and an Asse, and a slubberdegullion, That wooes and does not bar Age.
Shakespeare: *Tro.* 5.1.59f.
Cf. O109: To plow (till) with an OX and an ass together [cf. Deut. 22.10].

O108.1 To make an OX of (*OED* 4a fig.)[n]
1566 Adlington *Apuleius* 89[v]: He by and by (being made a very oxe) lighted a candle. 1583 Melbancke *Philotimus* Ee2: But as I was a sottish Asse to beleeve a faithles trull: so she made me an horned Ox to harnish [?] my love. c1604 (1605) Marston *Dutch Courtesan* 3.3.142f.: And you

make an ass of me, I'll make an ox of you. 1640 H. Mill *Night Search* 126: At last he findes she made an Oxe of him.
Shakespeare: *Wiv.* 5.5.119f., *Tro.* 5.1.56–60
Cf. O105.1: OX and ass; A379.1: To make an ass of.

[n]OED says *to make an ox of* is an obsolete expression meaning *to make a fool of*, citing the Apuleius, Shakespeare, and Mill above. The two non-Shakespearean citations are both in cuckold stories, where horns have just been grafted on a husband's head, and the primary meaning of the phrase in each case is that the husband has been cuckolded, although—as is customary in such stories—he has been made an ass as well. (Perhaps for this reason, wholly unconnected with the juxtaposition of *ass* and *ox* in Deut. 22.10 [cf. O109], *ass-ox* combinations became common in contexts where *fool-cuckold* were wholly or partly irrelevant. Cf. O105.1) The meaning *to cuckold* appears to fit all instances I have seen.

P

P28 PAINTERS (Travelers) and poets have leave to lie (*Varied* from 1586; OW607af. Horace, from c1566)
Shakespeare: *Tim.* 1.1.220–2

P31 He shows (To show) a fair PAIR of heels (From 1546)
E.g., 1577 Grange *Golden Aphroditis* D3[v]: The valyaunt Souldiour hadde rather truste to the force of hys armes ... than in the fielde a fayre payre of heels to shew.
Shakespeare: *1H4* 2.4.48, *H5* 3.5.34

P34 One PAIR of heels (legs, feet) is worth two pair of hands (From c1553)
Shakespeare: *3H6* 2.2.104

P36   There went but a PAIR of shears between them (From 1579; OW607b adds 1604)
Shakespeare: *MM* 1.2.27f.

P37.1   To bear the PALM (*OED* 3 fig. c1611)
1548 Elyot s.v. Palm: Palmam ferre, to have the price or victorie, to be most excellent. c1572 (1581) N. Woodes *Conflict of Conscience* 3.1 723: He alone shall have the palm which to the end doth run. c1580 Conybeare 54: Palmam ferre: A proverbe signifieng to have the price and rewarde of a victorie, or to be most excellent, or to be crowned for a victorie. 1598 Chapman *Hero and Leander* VI.109–14: An empty gallant . . . much palm bears For his rare judgement in th'attire he wears. 1599 (1600) Jonson *Every Man Out* 3.9.9: To thinke what priviledge, and palme it beares. c1610 (1613) Marston & Barksted *Insatiate Countess* I III,17: The very heire of all her sexe, That beares the Palme of beauty from 'em all.
Shakespeare: *JC* 1.2.130f., *Cor.* 5.3.117f.

(?) P50   PARDON makes offenders (*Varied* from 1589; ditto OW609a)
E.g., 1589 *Triumphs Love and Fortune* 5.1 G2ᵛ: Sometime pardon breedes a second ill. 1596 *Knack to Know Hon. Man* G3ᵛ: Who spares the guyltie, anymates the bad.
Shakespeare: *MM* 2.1.284, *Tim.* 3.5.3, *Luc.* 1687

P57   Like a PARISH top (From *TN*)
Shakespeare: *TN* 1.3.41f.
Cf. T439: To be whipped like a TOP (From ?1596 [1640]; OW609b from c1580 [1590])

P60   To speak (prate) like a PARROT (From 1534; OW760b supplements from 1521)
E.g., 1534 Heywood *Play Love* E1: Speke parot I pray ye.
Shakespeare: *Oth.* 2.3.279

(?) P73   The big PART of her body is her bum (1546, *MM*; Wh P35 unique; not in OW)ⁿ
I.e., 1546 Heywood I.x C3: The bygge part of hir body is hir bumme. But littell tit all tayle [T355, and clearly proverbial].
Shakespeare: *MM* 2.1.217f.

ⁿCf. Introduction, fn. 26.

P75   He may his PART on Good Friday eat and fast never the worse for ought he shall get (1546, *Jn.*; ditto OW214af.)
I.e., 1546 Heywood *Dialogue* I.xi D4.
Shakespeare: *Jn.* 1.1.234f.

P80   The PARTHIANS fight flying away (fig.) (*Varied* from 1600; OW610b supplements)
Shakespeare: *Cym.* 1.6.20, *TNK* 2.2.50

P82.1   PARTING is mourning (pain) E.g., c1500 (c1520) *Everyman* A6ᵛ 302: I will remembre that partinge is mourninge [in P82, Wh D162]. a1500 *Eger P* 326.1341: Parting is a privye payne. c1515 Barclay *Eclogues* 139.823f.: Departing is a payne, But mirth reneweth when lovers mete againe [in Wh D162].
Shakespeare: *Rom.* 2.2.184
Cf. P82: It is tedious parting with a thing we love [1659, analogues c1500, c1535, *Rom.*])

P83   Praise at PARTING (From c1475; Wh P39 from a1450)
Shakespeare: *Tmp.* 3.3.39

P89   At an ill PASSAGE honor thy companion (Collections from 1659, *varied* from 1562)
E.g. 1666 TOR. *Prov. Phr.* s.v. Honore 81: To do honour to ones companyon at an ill passage, viz. to be willing that ones companion should lead the way, where the way is difficult and dangerous.
Shakespeare: *Jn.* 1.1.154–6, *Ven.* 888

(?) P101.1 The PATH is smooth that leads to danger.
c1597 (1637) Deloney *1 Gentle Craft* 81: But hereby we may see that the path is smooth that leadeth to danger.
Shakespeare: *Ven.* 788

P103 He that has no PATIENCE has nothing (Collections from 1611)
Shakespeare: *Oth.* 2.3.370

P107 PATIENCE is a plaster for all sores (*Varied* from 1553; Wh P55 from a1393)
E.g., a1500 MS. *Marginalia* in Hoccleve I 224 n.[6]: A sufficyent salve for eache disease ... Ys patyence. 1553 T. Wilson *Rhet.* 206: Pacience is a remedie for every disease.
Shakespeare: *H8* 1.1.123–5

P111 PATIENCE perforce (From 1504)
Shakespeare: *R3* 1.1.116, *Rom.* 1.5.89
Cf. Appendix B: Force PERFORCE.

P123 Fat PAUNCHES make (etc.) lean pates (From *LLL*; OW247b shows earlier currency of idea only)
Shakespeare: *LLL* 1.1.26

(?) P138.1 Not give two PEASCODS (Wh P93 a1475)
Shakespeare: *Lr.* 1.4.200
Cf. C501.1: Not worth a cod; P135: Not worth a pea (two peas) [from c1525; Wh P101 from a1300]).

P139 By PEACE plenty (*Varied* from 1589; Wh P68 from a1425)
Shakespeare: *H5* 5.2.34f.

P145 He is wise that can hold his PEACE (*Varied* from 1557)
E.g., 1557 "That few wordes shew wisdome" 9f. *Tottel* 234: A wise man can his tong make cease, A foole can never holde his peace.

Shakespeare: *AWW* 2.4.22f., *Rom.* 1.3.49

P153 To make PEACE with a sword in his hand (1639, cf. *2H6*; OW616af. adds 1594, 1609)
E.g., 1594 Lipsius (W. Jones) *6 Books of Politics* 2A3: The olde proverbe ... It is best treating of peace, with weapons in ones hand.
Shakespeare: *2H6* 2.1.35f.

P155 Blessed are the PEACEMAKERS (Matt. 5.9; c1588 [1599], *2H6*, 1732; not in OW)
E.g., c1588 [1599] Porter *Two Angry Women of Abingdon* viii (MSR 1836) (in a cluster of ten proverbs by Nicholas, 1830–7).
Shakespeare: *2H6* 2.1.34

P157 As proud as a PEACOCK (From c1495)
Shakespeare: *Err.* 4.3.80, *Tro.* 3.3.251, *1H6* 3.3.5f.

P165 Cast not PEARLS before swine (*Varied* from 1509; cf. Matt.7.6)
Shakespeare: *LLL* 4.2.89

(?) P166.1 Rich PEARLS are found in homely shells (*Varied*)
1591 (1601) ?Lyly *Ent. at Cowdray* I,429: Rich pearles are found in hard and homely shels. 1595 J. Chalkhill *Alcilia* ed. Bullen 340: In meanest show, the most affection dwells; And richest pearls are found in simplest shells.
Shakespeare: *AYL* 5.4.59–61

P181 I will take you a PEG (buttonhole, hole) lower (*Peg* from 1589, *buttonhole* from 1592)
Shakespeare: *LLL* 5.2.700f.

P189 A better PENNY (Cf. Appendix B) (From 1579)
Shakespeare: *Wiv.* 1.1.60f.

P215 Put two PENNIES (halfpennies) in a purse and they will

draw together (Collections from 1641 [cf. on H745]; OW657b adds 1628; both include *TN*)
Shakespeare: *TN* 3.1.49f.

P219.1 To have one's PENNY-WORTH (Cf. Appendix B)
c1552 (c1567) N. Udall *Ralph Roister Doister* 4.7.116: I will have some penyworth! c1564 (1571) R. Edwards *Damon and Pithias* xiii (MSR 1141): Ye slave I will have my penyworthes of thee. 1589 Marprelate *Hay* A2ᵛ: And I will have my penyworths of all of you. c1604 (1605) Chapman *All Fools* 2.1.301f.: I do not doubt, But t'have my pennyworths of these Rascals.
Shakespeare: *MV* 1.2.71f., *Ado* 2.3.42

P219.2 To take one's PENNY-WORTHS of the pillow
1611 COT. s.v. Pardormir: To sleepe soundly, to take a long, or full sleepe; to take his penniworthes of the pillow.
Shakespeare: *Rom.* 4.5.4

P238 Hate not the PERSON but the vice (*Varied* from 1533; Wh V30 supplements)
Shakespeare: *MM* 2.2.37

P243.1 Hoist with his own PETARD (OW376b; *Ham.*, 1885)
Shakespeare: *Ham.* 3.4.207

P256 As rare as the PHOENIX (From 1580; OW664b from 1568)
Shakespeare: *AYL* 4.3.17, *Cym.* 1.6.16f.

P263 He is purse-sick and lacks a PHYSICIAN (1546: *varied* thereafter)
Shakespeare: *2H4* 1.2.236−8

P267 PHYSICIAN, heal thyself (Luke 4.23; from 1511; cf. Wh L171 [Leech] from c1000)
Shakespeare: *2H6* 2.1.51

P271 They that are whole need not a PHYSICIAN, but they that are sick (Mark 2.17; from 1508)
Shakespeare: *AYL* 3.2.358f.

(?) P274.1 PHYSICIANS enriched give over their patients (*Varied*)
1567 W. Painter *Palace of Pleasure* II.xxvii 277ᵛ (of physicians): And therfore dispairing of his helth, with handes full of money they gave him over. c1613 (1623) Webster *Duchess of Malfi* 3.5.11−3: Physitians thus, With their hands full of money, use to give ore Their Patients.
Shakespeare: *Tim.* 3.3.11f.

P276 To be in a sad (etc.) PICKLE (Cf. Appendix B) (*Varied* from 1573; OW623b supplements)
Shakespeare: *Tmp.* 5.1.281

P289 A knotty PIECE of timber must have sharp wedges (*Varied* from 1539; OW433b supplements)
Add e.g.: 1588 R. Some *Godly Treatise* V4: Duro nodo, durus cuneus, &c. that is, A wedge of yron, is fittest for knottie wood.
Shakespeare: *Tro.* 1.3.316

(?) P289.1 A peerless PIECE (Cf. Appendix B)
1546 Heywood *Dialogue* I.iv Bl: This mayde, the peece peerelesse in myn eie.
Shakespeare: *WT* 5.1.94

(?) P290.1 A PIECE of earth
c1609 (1620) Beaumont & Fletcher *Philaster* 1.2.63f.: The gods prepared To trouble this poor piece of earth.
Shakespeare: *JC* 3.1.254, *WT* 5.1.94
Cf. Appendix B: A PIECE of flesh.

(?) P291.1 A PIECE of virtue
1658 T. Browne *Hydriotaphia* Ep. Ded. ed. Endicott 248: A compleat peece of vertue must be made up

from the Centos of all ages.
Shakespeare: *Ant.* 3.2.28f., *Per.* 4.6.111, *Tmp.* 1.2.56

(?) P310 Some cannot abide to see a PIG'S head gaping (*Varied* from 1592)
E.g., 1592 Nashe *Pierce Penilesse* I,188: Some will take on like a mad man, if they see a pigge come to the table. c1598 (1639) Deloney *Gentle Craft* 193: Some cannot abide to eate of a pig.
Shakespeare: *MV* 4.1.47

P327 Bitter PILLS (drink) may have wholesome effects (*Varied* from 1579; OW63a from c1374)
Shakespeare: *TGV* 2.4.149f., *MM* 4.6.7f.
Cf. P326: To swallow (digest) a bitter pill [*bitter* from 1623].

P328 (To be tossed) from PILLAR (post) to post (pillar, pillory) (From 1521, *pillory* from 1659 HOW.)
Shakespeare: *TNK* 3.5.115

P333 Not to care (pass) a PIN (From c1555)
Shakespeare: *LLL* 4.3.18, *Wiv.* 1.1.114, *R2* 3.3.26

P334 Not worth a PIN (From c1530)
Shakespeare: *TGV* 1.1.108, 2.7.55, *MM* 2.1.96, 2.2.45, 3.1.105, *2H4* 2.4.174, *Ham.* 1.4.65

P336 To hit (cleave) the PIN (fig.) (Cf. Appendix B) (From c1576 [OW126a from c1450]; *cleave* from c1587)
Shakespeare: *LLL* 4.1.136, *Rom.* 2.4.15

P336.1 As small (big) as a PIN'S HEAD (Wh P218 c1440)
I.e., c1440 Charles of Orleans 180.5385−6: For myn hool hert of yowre the quantite As of a pynns hed me yave or lasse. c1553 (1575) W. Stevenson *Gammer Gurton's Needle*

1.5.13: There is not one sparke so byg as a pyns head. 1605 Jonson et al. *Eastward Ho* 3.2.34: I have seene a little prick no bigger then a pins head. c1611 (1631) Dekker *Match Me in London* 1.2.55f.: Mine Eyes are no bigger then litle pinnes heads with staring.
Shakespeare: *1H4* 4.2.21f., *2H4* 4.3.51−3

P345 To put up one's PIPES (fig.) (From c1565; OW657a from 1556)
Shakespeare: *Rom.* 4.5.96, *Oth.* 3.1.19

P355 (To stay) a PISSING-WHILE (Cf. Appendix B) (From c1552)
Shakespeare: *TGV* 4.4.19

P356 He falls into the PIT he digs for another (Cf. Ps. 7.15, Eccl. 10.8, etc.; from 1580; Wh P232 from c900)
Shakespeare: *H8* 1.1.140f.

P357 As dark (black) as PITCH (From 1485)
Shakespeare: *LLL* 3.1.197, *Ven.* 821

P358 He that touches PITCH shall be defiled (*Varied* from 1521; Wh P236 from c1300; Ecclus. 13.1)
Shakespeare: *LLL* 4.3.3, *Ado* 3.3.57, *AWW* 4.4.24, *2H6* 2.1.192, *1H4* 2.4.412f.

P360 PITCH and pay (From c1500)
Shakespeare: *H5* 2.3.49

(?) P360.1 To smell of pitch and tar c1609 (1655) T. Heywood & W. Rowley *Fortune by Land and Sea* 4.1 VI,421 (of a mariner): He smels as they say of pitch and tar.
Shakespeare: *Tmp.* 2.2.52

P363 (Small) (Little) PITCHERS have (wide) ears (From 1546)
Shakespeare: *Shr.* 4.4.52, *R3* 2.4.37

P366 Foolish (Peevish) PITY mars a city (From 1556; OW277b supplements)
Shakespeare: *MM* 2.2.100–2

P368.1 It is PITY of his (etc.) life[n]
E.g.,1548 Udall etc. Erasm. *Par. Acts* 83b: Al the Iewes ... with great clamour cried, that it was pitie of his life [cf. Acts 22.22 OED Pity 3b.] c1561 (1569) T. Preston *Cambises* x.209f.: To murder his brother, and then his own wife—So help me God and halidom, it is pity of his life! c1570 *Misogonus* 2.5.32: So god shall iudge me pild Jacke its pittye of thy life. c1606 (1608) Middleton *Mad World, My Masters* 3.2.191–3: 'Twas e'en pity of your life ... if ever you should wrong such an innocent gentleman.
Shakespeare: *MND* 3.1.142f., 5.1.225f., *TN* 2.5.12, *MM* 2.1.76f.

[n]I have no idea why Shakespeare limited this expression to clowns and/or simpletons.

(?) P369.1 PITY destroys pity (*Varied*)
1604 (1607) W. Alexander *Alexandraean Tragedy* 4.2 2259f.: Pity shall barre pity, whil'st they all Waile for their friends, who through her pride were lost. c1613 (1623) Webster *Duchess of Malfi* 4.2.372f.: Alas! I dare not call: So, pitty would destroy pitty.
Shakespeare: *JC* 3.1.171

P370 PITY is akin to love (*Varied* from *TN*; ditto OW628b)
Add: c1593 (1598) Marlowe *Hero and Leander* II.287: Love is not full of pity (as men say). c1599 (1600) *Wisdom of Doctor Dodypoll* 3.3 (MSR 998): Pittie breeds love. 1622 (1647) Fletcher & Massinger *Spanish Curate* 5.1.82f.: Pity, some say, 's the parent Of future love.
Shakespeare: *TN* 3.1.123

(?) P372.1 A better PLACE (i.e., heaven) (*OED* World 1d *Better world* from 1715)
c1613 (1616) Beaumont & Fletcher *Scornful Lady* 2.2.90: Hee's in a better place my friend, I know't.
Shakespeare: *MM* 4.2.207f.

P373.1 In PLACE where (Cf. Appendix B)
c1589 (1594) Lyly *Mother Bombie* 1.3.25f.: Wert thou in place where, I would teach thee to cog. 1598 (1616) W. Haughton *Englishmen for My Money* iii (MSR 596f.): If I had you in place where, you would find me tough enough in digestion. 1604 (1607) Dekker *Westward Ho* 5.3.36f.: Were I in place where, Ide make thee prove thy wordes.
Shakespeare: *Shr.* 4.3.149f.

(?) P375.1 To be unworthy of one's PLACE (Cf. Appendix B)
1639 CL. s.v. Absurda, indecora, praepostera 4: Hee's unworthy of his place.
Shakespeare: *Oth* 2.3.101f.

P380 To graze on the PLAIN (common) (1546 HEY.; OW332b supplements)
E.g., 1546 Heywood *Dialogue* II.x L3[v]: He turnde hir out at durs, to grase on the playne.
Shakespeare: *Rom.* 3.5.188

P381 PLAIN DEALING is a jewel (From 1587)
E.g., 1587 Bridges *Def. Church Govt.* I 124: Plaine dealing (sayeth the Proverbe) is a Jewell.
Shakespeare: *Tim.* 1.1.210f.

P382 PLAIN DEALING is a jewel but they that use it die beggars (From 1583; frequently condensed)
Add e.g.: 1592 ?Lyly *Speeches Delivered to Her Maiestie* (STC 7600) I,477: Plaine dealinge, once counted a jewell, nowe beggery. 1605 T. Carew

Foure Godlie Sermons G2: Plain dealing is cald a Iewel of beggers.
Shakespeare: *Tim.* 1.1.210f.

P383 PLAIN DEALING is best (From 1575)
Cf. 1559 "Lord Clifford" 4 (variant) *Mirror for Magistrates* 192: Playnesse is best when truth is plainly tryde.
Shakespeare: *H8* 3.1.39

(?) P389 To be PLANET-STRUCK (struck with a planet) (From *Tit.*)
Add: 1599 (1600) Jonson *Every Man Out* 2.3.30: O, I am planet-strooke; 5.11.5: Some Planet strike me dead.
Shakespeare: *Tit.* 2.4.14, *Cor.* 2.2.113f.

P391 To water one's PLANTS (i.e., to weep) (From 1542)
Shakespeare: *Ant.* 1.2.169f.

P399 When PLAY (game, jest) is best it is time to leave (From a1500; Wh G26 from a1393)
Shakespeare: *Rom.* 1.4.39, 1.5.119

P401 To PLAY fast and (or) loose (From 1578; OW630b from 1557)
Shakespeare: *LLL* 1.2.157, 3.1.103, *Jn.* 3.1.242, *Ant.* 4.12.28

P407.1 It PLEASES you (is your pleasure) to say so
1584 Lyly *Campaspe* 5.4.104: It pleaseth your maiestie to say so. 1598 (1601) Jonson *Every Man In* 3.4.90: Oh God sir, its your pleasure to say so sir. 1599 (1600) Jonson *Every Man Out* 3.1.24f.: Nothing but *Salutation*; and, *O god, sir*; and, *It pleases you to say so, Sir*; cf. 3.4.12, 5.2.69. 1600 (1601) Jonson *Cynthia's Revels* 1.4.123: O, tis your pleasure to say so, sir. 1604 (1606) Chapman *Monsieur D'Olive* 2.2.55: It pleaseth your good excellence to say so. 1609 (1616) Jonson *Epicoene* 5.1.90: O, it pleases him to say so, sir.
Shakespeare: *Ado* 3.5.19 *AYL* 4.1.66, *Per.* 2.5.29f.

P417 PLEASURE the rarer used the more commendable (Collections *varied* from 1616, cf. 1539)
I.e., 1539 TAV. 24: A seldom use of pleasures maketh the same the more pleasaunt.
Shakespeare: *Son.* 52.3

P420 There is no PLEASURE without pain (*Varied* from c1526; OW633bf. supplements)
E.g., 1576 Pettie *Petite Pallace* 107: Pleasure must bee purchased with the price of paine.
Shakespeare: *TN* 2.4.70f.

(?) P435.1 Who holds the PLOW reaps no corn
1580 T. Churchyard *Chance* C3 (warning a courtier): He reaps no Corne, that helps to holde the Plowe; E4: Thou were as good goe holde the Plowe, As in the Court seeke Fortune now.
Shakespeare: *LLL* 5.2.883f.
Cf. P431: He that by the plow would thrive himself must either hold or drive [from 1678].

P441.1 To pull (pluck) one's PLUMES
E.g., 1584 Lyly *Sapho and Phao* 5.2.79f.: I will pull those plumes, and cause you to cast your eyes on your feet, not your feathers. c1587 (1590) Marlowe *1 Tamburlaine* 1.1.30–3: Tamburlaine . . . doth mean to pull my plumes. 1587 (1591) Greene *Farewell to Follie* IX,260: Cresus was proude of his pelfe, but Solon pulde downe his plumes. c1590 (1596) *Edward III* 1.1.85f.: I'll take away those borrowed plumes of his, And send him naked to the wildernes. c1592 (1594) ?Greene *Selimus* xxviii (MSR 2400): Selimus hath pluckt your haughtie plumes.
Shakespeare: *1H6* 3.3.7, *R2* 4.1.108, *Ant.* 3.12.3
Cf. P158: The peacock has fair feathers but foul feet [OW616b from 1532].

P456.1   Love (Lust, A whore) is sweet POISON (*Varied*)
E.g., 1506 Hawes *Pastime* 178.4751f.: For the blynde love dooth perceyve ryght nought That under hony the poyson is wrought [in Wh H433 (H55.1)] 1547 W. Baldwin *Treatise of Morall Phylosophie* 05ᵛ: A fayre whore is a swete poyson. 1562 A. Brooke *Romeus and Juliet* 219: He swalloweth downe loves sweete empoysonde baite. 1580 Baret W−209: A faire harlot is aptlie compared unto sweete wine mingled with deadlie poyson. 1584 Lyly *Campaspe* 2.2.73−5: There is no surfeit so dangerous as that of honney [cf. H560], nor anye poyson so deadly as that of love. c1588 (1591) Lyly *Endymion* 5.2.14f.: Which proveth love to bee, as it was saide of in olde yeares, Dulce venenum.
Shakespeare: *Rom.* 1.2.49f., *Ant.* 1.5.26f.
Cf. F349.1: Flattery is sweet poison; R32.1: Like rats, men swallow sweet poison until they die.

P457   One POISON expels another (*Varied* from 1567; cf. Wh V21 [venom] from c1378)
Shakespeare: *2H4* 1.1.137, *Rom.* 1.2.49f., *Cym.* 1.6.125f.

(?) P457.1   POISON disperses itself into every vein[n]
1579 Lyly *Euphues* I,218: As one droppe of poyson disperseth it selfe into everye vaine. 1580 Lyly *Euphues and his England* II,73: We know by Phisick that poyson wil disperse it selfe into every veyne, before it part the hart. c1592 ?Kyd *Soliman and Perseda* 5.4.145: The poison is disperst through everie vaine.
Shakespeare: *Rom.* 5.1.59−61

[n]When used literally, as in all but the *Euphues* example above, I suppose this merely reflects a common wording of a medical fact, not anything proverbial.

P458.1   POISON under sugar (Wh P289 from a1420 [2])
Add: 1592 (1600) Nashe *Summer's Last Will* III,278: All bookes, divinitie except, Are . . . Poyson wrapt vp in sugred words.
Shakespeare: *2H6* 3.2.45, *R3* 3.1.13f.
Cf. H561: Under honey ofttime lies bitter gall (poison) [from c1510].

(?) P464.1   POMP and circumstance (*OED Circumstance* 7 Oth., 1805+)
1631 Massinger *Believe as you List* 1.1.21f.: With all pompe and circumstance of glorie.
Shakespeare: *Oth.* 3.3.354

P465   Standing FOOLS gather filth (Collections from 1639, analogues in *MV, Lr*; OW771a adds 1579)
I.e., 1579 Gosson *Schoole of Abuse* 52: Standing streames geather filth; flowing rivers, are ever sweet.
Add: 1601 A. Dent *Plaine Mans Path-way* I7ᵛ: Standing ponds . . . gather skum and filth.
Shakespeare: *MV* 1.1.89, *Lr.* 3.4.133f.

P474   POOR and proud (fie, fie) (From 1581; cf. Wh M267 from a900, Ecclus. 25.2)
Shakespeare: *TN* 3.1.127

P490   As deaf (dumb) as a POST (Both from 1575)
Shakespeare: *AYL* 4.1.8f., *Cor.* 5.6.49

P497   A little POT is soon hot (From 1546)
Shakespeare: *Shr.* 4.1.6

P504   To go to (the) POT (Cf. Appendix B) (From 1530)
Shakespeare: *Cor.* 1.4.47

P516.1   I would not for twenty POUND
c1554 (1568) *Jacob and Esau* 4.5 (MSR 1180f.): I would not for

twenty pounde I tell ye, That any pointe of default should be found in me. c1560 (c1570) W. Wager *Enough is as Good as a Feast*. 1042: I would not for twenty pound it should come to his ear.
Shakespeare: *Shr.* Ind. 1.21

P529 POVERTY parts fellowship (good company, friends) (From c1475; OW642b from 1350; both include *AYL*)
Shakespeare: *AYL* 2.1.51f.

(?) P537 A POX on these true jests (*LLL*, 1659 Howell)[n]
Add: 1626 (1631) Jonson *Staple of News* 5.5.20: Pox o'these true ieasts, I say.
Shakespeare: *LLL* 5.2.46

[n]See Introduction, pp. xv, xix

P537a PRACTICE what you preach (Literal from 1678, idea from 1579)
Cf. c1378 *Piers* B xiii 79: That he precheth he preveth nought [Wh P358]. a1400 *Song against the Friars* in Wright *Political Poems* I 268(1−2): Ful wysely can thai preche and say; Bot as thai preche no thing do thai [Wh P359]. a1450 Audelay 29.530−1: A prechur schuld lyve parfytly And do as he techys truly [Wh P361]. 1533 Heywood *Pardoner* B3[v] (34−5): For that except the precher hym selfe lyve well, his predycacyon wyll helpe never a dell.
Shakespeare: *MV* 1.2.14f., *Ham.* 1.3.47−51

P540 PRAISE by evil men is dispraise (*Varied* from c1526; OW643bf. supplements)
Shakespeare: *Tim.* 4.3.172−4

P545.1 He must PRAISE himself since no man else will (Wh P349 [2])
Add: 1549 Erasmus (T. Chaloner) *Pr. Folly* A2: The common proverbe, which saieth, that he maie

rightly praise hym selfe, whom none other bodie will [in N117].
Shakespeare: *Ham.* 5.2.183f.

P546 He PRAISES who wishes to sell (*Varied* from *LLL*; OW644b supplements)
Shakespeare: *LLL* 4.3.236, *Tro.* 4.1.78f., *Son.* 21.14, 102.3f.
Cf. B445: He that blames would buy.

P547 He that PRAISES himself spatters himself (1640; analogues from c1523; cf. Wh P351 [To praise oneself is wrong] *varied* from a1387)
Shakespeare: *Ado* 5.2.73−5, *Tro.* 1.3.241f., 2.3.155−7, *Ant.* 2.6.42f.

P550.1 More PRATTLE than practise
1611 Bretnor (Crow g 396): More prattle then practise.
Shakespeare: *Oth.* 1.1.26

P570 The PREY entices the thief (From 1576)
Add: 1563 T. Churchyard "Shore's Wife" 98: A pleasaunt pray entiseth many a thiefe. 1594 Nashe *Unfortunate Traveller* II, 276: The rich pray makes the theefe. c1597 (1637) Deloney *1 Gentle Craft* 98: Rich preys do make true men theeves.
Shakespeare: *Ven.* 724, *Son.* 48.14

(?) P571.1 The PRICKING of thy finger is the piercing of his heart
1579 Lyly *Euphues* I,197: A friend . . . will accompt . . . the pricking of thy finger, the percing of his heart. 1591 Lyly *Endymion* 3.1.22f.: Whatsoever seemeth a needle to pricke his finger, is a dagger to wound my heart.
Shakespeare: *3H6* 1.4.54f.

P576 PRIDE goes before and shame (ambition) comes after (From a1500; Wh P385 a1400; *ambition* only *2H6*, including bad Q)
Shakespeare: *2H6*1.1.180

P581   PRIDE will have a fall (From 1529; Wh P393 *varied* from c1340)
Shakespeare: *R3* 5.3.176, *R2* 5.5.88

P587   To be one's PRIEST (i.e., to kill) (From c1510; Wh P400 from a1300)
Shakespeare: *2H6* 3.1.272

P587.1   To play (be) both PRIEST and clerk (witness)
c1560 (c1569) T. Ingeland *Disobedient Child* D2ᵛ: Many a tyme and oft, I am fayne To play the Priest, Clarke and all. 1584 Lyly *Campaspe* 5.4.117f.: Beleeve me, Hephestion, these parties are agreed, they would have me both priest and witnesse. 1611 COT. s.v. Faire: Faire le prestre Martin. To answer himselfe; to play both Priest, and Clarke. Again Martin.
Shakespeare: *R2* 4.1.173

P595   To break PRISCIAN'S head (From c1517)
Shakespeare: *LLL* 5.1.28f.

(?) P595.1   Anger (impatience) has its PRIVILEGE
Shakespeare: *Jn.* 4.3.32, *Lr.* 2.2.70
Cf. L458: Give losers leave to speak.

P595.2   To be a PRIVILEGED MAN
a1548 Hall *Chron., Edw. V* 10: He nether is nor can bee a sanctuarye or privileged man (*OED Privileged* b). 1588 R. Some *Godly Treatise* S4: You are a priviledged man: you may say what you list. The best is, I can receive no disgrace by any speeches of such as you are.
Shakespeare: *Tro.* 2.3.57
Cf. T389: His tongue is no slander.

P602   Great PROMISE small performance (*Varied* from 1562; OW640b from 1548)

Shakespeare: *H8* 4.2.41f., *Oth.* 4.2.182f., *Tim.* 5.1.27−30

P603   PROMISE is debt (From c1500)
Shakespeare: *Ham.* 3.2.193

P611   PROSPERITY gets friends but adversity tries them (*Varied* from 1597; OW650b from a1500)
Shakespeare: *WT* 4.4.573−5

P614   Too much PROTESTING makes the truth suspected (*Varied* from *Ham.*; not in OW)
E.g., c1620 (1647) Fletcher & Massinger *Custom of the Country* 5.3.5−7: Nay, no more protestations; Too many of them will call that in question Which now I doubt not.
Shakespeare: *Ham.* 3.2.230

P614.1   The PROUDEST of you (them) all
1553 ?Udall *Respublica* 5.8 1748: Not the proudest of them all can hurt me a hair! 1578 T. Lupset *All for Money* 1171: The proudest of them all shall not make me now to shrink! c1587 (1599) Greene *Alphonsus* 4.3 1512−4: How now, sir boy? let Amurack himselfe, Or any he, the proudest of you all, But offer once for to unsheath his sword. c1589 (1594) Greene *Friar Bacon and Friar Bungay* 2.2 552f.: A companie of scabbes! the proudest of you all drawe your weapon if he can. 1600 Dekker *Shoemakers' Holiday* 5.2.132f.: The prowdest of you that laies hands on her first, Ile lay my crutch crosse his pate. c1618 (1661) *Hengist, King of Kent* 5.1.100f.: I scorn as much to live by my wits as the proudest of you all.
Shakespeare: *Shr.* 4.1.87f., *Wiv.* 2.2.76, *1H6* 4.7.84, *3H6* 2.2.96f., *R3* 2.1.129

P614.2   PROVE (Assay, Try) ere you purpose (plain, trust, trow, take, love, praise) (Wh P429 from a1400)

E.g., a1500 *Against Hasty Marriage* I in Robbins 37.1: Prove or thow preyse yt.
Shakespeare: *Tro.* 3.2.90f., *Oth.* 5.1.66
Cf. T595: TRY (Try your friend) before you trust [from a1536]

P615.1 To hit a PROVERB in the head (neck) (*Varied*)
c1589 (1594) Lyly *Mother Bombie* 4.2.11: There was an auncient proverbe knockt in the head. 1597 (1599) Chapman *Humorous Day's Mirth* 3.1.178: There's a proverbe hit dead in the necke like a Cony. 1606 (1607) E. Sharpham *Fleer* 2.1.35f.: They are no proverb breakers: beware the buyer say they. 1620 (1622) Dekker & Massinger *Virgin Martyr* 2.3.66f.: She sav'd us from the Gallowes, and only to keepe one Proverbe from breaking his necke, weele hang her [in T109: Save a thief from the gallows and he will cut your throat (hang thee if he can)]. 1624 (1661) R. Davenport *City Nightcap* 1.2: So you break one Proverbs pate, and give the other a plaister.
Shakespeare: *1H4* 1.2.118f.

P620 As fit as a PUDDING for a friar's mouth (From 1568)
Shakespeare: *AWW* 2.2.26f., *Oth.* 2.1.253

P655 A heavy PURSE makes a light heart (*Varied* from 1521)
Shakespeare: *Lr.* 4.6.146f.

P664 To line one's PURSE (Cf. Appendix B) (1521, 1604; cf. OW466b; *OED Line v.*[1] 3 adds 1550)
Shakespeare: *Oth.* 1.1.53.

P669 Ill PUTTING (Put not) a naked sword in a madman's hand (*Varied* from 1539; Wh M90 from a1400)
Shakespeare: *2H6* 3.1.347

Q

Q3 To pick a QUARREL (Cf. Appendix B) (From c1510)
Shakespeare: *1H4* 3.3.67

Q11.1 What (kind of) a QUESTION is that
c1576 *Common Conditions* 600f.: If I can do it, quoth you? What kinde of question is that? c1602 (1611) Chapman *May-Day* 2.4.338: What a question's that? c1606 (1607) Middleton *Michaelmas Term* 1.1.28: What a question's that!
Shakespeare: *MV* 3.4.79, *TNK* 2.3.61

Q13 He touches him (To touch one) to (on) the QUICK (Cf. Appendix B) (From c1517)
Shakespeare: *Err.* 2.2.130, *Tit.* 4.2.28, 4.4.36, *Ham.* 2.2.597, *Tmp.* 5.1.25

Q14.1 To run like (be quick as) QUICKSILVER (Cf. *OED* 2 from 1562)
a1420 Lydgate *Troy* I 2.5.2457–8: And the water, as I reherse can, Like quik-silver in his stremys ran [Wh Q18]. 1593 Harvey *Pierces Supererogation* II,41: A fine-witted man, as quicke as quick-silver; 323f.: Looke for a quill, as quicke, as quicksilver. 1599 (1600) Jonson *Every Man Out* 1.3.197: As humorous as quicksilver. c1605 (c1608) Middleton *Your Five Gallants* 3.2.106f.: It runs like quicksilver from one to another.
Shakespeare: *2H4* 2.4.228f., *Ham.* 1.5.66

Q15 QUIETNESS is a great treasure (1664 COD., cf. a1521; OW660b adds 1587, 1590)
I.e., c1587 (1599) Greene *Alphonsus* 1.1.146: A quiet life doth passe an Emperie. c1590 (1599) ?Greene *George a Green* 5.1.1050: Quietnes is best.
Shakespeare: *Cym.* 3.3.30

Q16   To get (have) one's QUIETUS (quietus est) (Cf. Appendix B) (*Quietus est* from 1530, *quietus* from *Ham.*; ditto OW660b, *OED* 3)
  Shakespeare: *Ham.* 3.1.74, *Son.* 126.12

R

R1   R is the dog's letter (From 1509; OW661a Persius)
  Shakespeare: *Rom.* 2.4.208f.

R6.1   Not (Never) a RAG of money (OW661b from 1592)
  E.g., 1592 Nashe *Foure Letters Confuted* I,301: Valete humanae artes, heart and good will, but never a ragge of money.
  Add: 1592 Lodge *Euphues shadow (Deaf Man's Dialogue)* M1^v: Oh it is a proper man: but never a rag of money. 1600 *Wisdom of Doctor Dodypoll* 2.2 (MSR 543): But not a rag of money.
  Shakespeare: *Err.* 4.4.85f.
  Cf. H338.1: (With) heart and good will.

R6.2   Out of RAGS into robes
  1639 CL. s.v. Proficientium in melius 261.
  Shakespeare: *LLL* 4.1.82f.

R8   After RAIN (showers) comes fair weather (the sun) (From 1484, *sunshine* from 1576)
  Shakespeare: *Ven.* 799

R16   Small (little) RAIN lays (allays) great winds (*Varied* from c1500; Wh R15 from a1200)
  E.g., 1586 Guazzo (Young) IV II,183: With one onlie teare proceeding from you, our hot bloud is cooled . . . and to signifie this, that Proverbe tooke his beginning, and grew in use, That a little rain alaieth a great wind.
  Shakespeare: *Tro.* 4.4.53, *Mac.* 1.7.25, *Ven.* 458, *Luc.* 1788–90

Cf. T275: After thunder (wind) comes rain.

R22   As lean as a RAKE (From c1485)
  Shakespeare: *Cor.* 1.1.23

R30.1   The RAT betrayed herself with her own noise
  1533 N. Udall *Floures* N8^vf.: Suo ipsius iudicio periit sorex, The ratte betrayed hir selfe with her owne noyse, and so was taken, is a proverbiall spekynge of any bodye that are betrayed by theyr owne wordes. Again c1580 Conybeare 54.
  Shakespeare: *Ham.* 3.4.24, 4.1.9f.

R31   I smell a RAT (From 1553)
  Shakespeare: *Ham.* 3.4.24

R32.1   Like RATS, men swallow sweet poison until they die (*Varied*)
  1600 (1657) Dekker et al. *Lust's Dominion* 5.2.92–4: These dignities Like poyson make men swell, this Ratsbane honour O 'tis so sweet, they'le lick it till all burst. 1605 J. Hall *Meditations and Vowes* no. 95 Fl (of ambition): It affordes as much discontent in inioying, as in want, making men like poysoned Rats, which when they have tasted of their bane, cannot rest till they drinke, and then can much lesse rest, till their death. c1640 (1654) Glapthorne ?& Chapman *Revenge for Honour* 2.1.110–3: As pride or lust does minds unstaid and wanton: 'T makes men like poison'd rats, which when they've swallow'd The pleasing bane, rest not until they drink, And can rest then much less, until they burst with't.
  Shakespeare: *MM* 1.2.128–30, *Cor.* 3.1.155–7
  Cf. P456.1: Love (Lust, A whore) is sweet poison.

R32.2   As black as a RAVEN('s feather) (Wh R42 from a1300 [3])
  Add: 1678 Ray 281: As black as a

coal [C458]; as a crow or raven [in C844].
Shakespeare: *Tit.* 2.3.83, *Rom.* 3.2.19, 76, *TNK* 4.2.83f., *Son.* 127.9

(?) R33 The croaking RAVEN (screeching owl) bodes misfortune (death) (From c1589 [1633]; OW665af. from 1578)[n]
E.g., 1584 Lyly *Sappho and Phao* 3.3.59f.: I mistruste her not: for that the owle bath not shrikte at the window, or the night Raven croked, both being fatall.
Shakespeare: *MND* 5.1.376−8, *Ado* 2.3.81−3, *Tro.* 5.2.190f., *1H6* 4.2.15, *2H6* 3.2.40, *3H6* 2.6.56f., 5.6.44f., *R3* 4.4.507, *Tit.* 2.3.97, *JC* 1.3.26−8, *Ham.* 3.2.254, *Oth.* 4.1.20−2, *Mac.* 1.5.38−40, 2.2.3f., *TNK* 1.1.20, *Ven.* 531, *Luc.* 165

[n]Cf. Introduction, fn. 13.

(?) R34 The RAVEN chides blackness (*Tro.*, 1612, 1732; not in OW)[n]
I.e., 1612 Webster *White Devil* 5.3.88f.: Did you ever heare the duskie raven Chide blacknesse? 1732 FUL. 4729: The Raven said to the Rook; stand away, black-Coat.
Shakespeare: *Tro.* 2.3.211

[n]The example from Webster is almost surely a borrowing. Cf. E7.

R36 As sharp as a RAZOR (From 1519)
E.g., c1554 (1568) ?N. Udall *Jacob and Esau* 5.4 (MSR 1514): That worde is to me sharper than a rasers blade.
Shakespeare: *Tit.* 1.1.314
Cf. T401.1: To have a TONGUE like a razor.

R38 READ not before you learn to spell (1639 CL., cf. *Rom.*, 1600)
I.e., 1600 Breton *Pasquil's Foolscap*: *Wks.* I, 22: He that will Reade, before he learne to Spell . . . Let him be

sure . . . Such madhead fellowes are but Fooles indeede.
Shakespeare: *Rom.* 2.3.88

R63 RELIGION a stalking-horse to shoot other fowl (From 1604; OW670a adds 1579 analogue)
Add: 1605 W. Wilkes *Obedience* F4: Waitlesse youthes . . . make religion their stalking horse, under whose bellie they shoote at what their appetites doe most affect.
Shakespeare: *AYL* 5.4.106
Cf. S816: To make one a stalking-horse [from 1612].

R71 There is no REMEDY but patience (From a1555; OW670b from 1530)
Shakespeare: *TGV* 2.2.1f.
Cf. C922: What cannot be cured must be endured. Also Appendix B: (There's) no REMEDY.

R71.1 Where there is no REMEDY it is folly to chide (Wh R81 *varied* from c1390)
E.g., 1509 Barclay *Ship* II 179 lf.: He is a Fole: and voyde of wyt certayne That mourneth for that which is past remedy.
Add: 1530 Palsgrave 405 (O3): To waxe sorowfull for the thing that is paste remedye it is but a folye. 1593 Greene *Mamillia* II,154: Rather remember the olde proverbe, not so common as true, past cure, past care, without remedie, without remembrance [in C921]. 1616 DR. 1604: We must not care for that, which cannot be remedied.
Shakespeare: *1H6* 3.3.3f., *Oth.* 1.3.202, *Mac.* 3.2.11, *Cym.* 1.6.96f.
Cf. G453: Never grieve for that you cannot help.

(?) R72.1 We should REMEMBER ourselves
c1580 *Conversion of a Sinner* (STC 5648) 60[v]: A man ought to remember himselfe, and that he is a Chris-

tian. 1588 J. Carpenter *Remember Lots wife* D7ᵛ: Thus must we remember our selves. God graunt we forget not our selves. When man forgetteth himselfe and his condition, there is none evill which he will feare to commit.
Shakespeare: *Ham.* 1.2.6f., *Lr.* 4.6.229

R73   The REMEMBRANCE of past sorrow (dangers) is joyful (*Varied* from 1539; OW671af. Seneca, from c1375)
Shakespeare: *Rom.* 3.5.52f.

R80   REPENTANCE   [religious] never comes too late (From a1591; OW563b adds c1230)
E.g., c1230 *Ancrene Wisse* ed. Tolkien EETS no. 249 173: Nunquam sera penitentia si tamen vera. Nis neaver to leete penitence that is godliche imaket.
Shakespeare: *Oth.* 5.2.83.

R83   A false REPORT rides post (1659 HOW. only)
Shakespeare: *2H4* Ind. 4
Cf. P489: The lame post brings the truest news [from 1640 HERB.].

R84   (REPORT has) a blister on her tongue (*Varied* from 1580; OW68a: A blister will rise upon one's tongue that tells a lie.)
E.g., 1580 Lyly *Euphues and his England* II,21: My tonge would blyster if I should utter them. 1584 Lyly *Sapho and Phao* 1.2.36f.: You have no reason for it but an old reporte. / Reporte hath not alwaies a blister on her tongue.
Shakespeare: *LLL* 5.2.335, *MM* 2.3.12, *Rom.* 3.2.90, *Mac.* 4.3.12, *Tim.* 5.1.132, *WT* 2.2.31

R86.1   To set (up) one's REST (fig.) (*OED* sb.² 7a–6, from 1587)ⁿ
Shakespeare: *Err.* 4.3.27, *MV*

2.2.102f., *AWW* 2.1.135, *Rom.* 4.5.6, 5.3.110, *Lr.* 1.1.123f.

ⁿOW717b briefly discusses this common expression, but for some reason allows it no entry. Cf. on *Romeo and Juliet* 5.3.110.

R90   REVENGE is sweet (*Varied* from 1566; OW673a supplements)
Shakespeare: *Cor.* 5.3.45

R92   To pardon is a divine REVENGE (1666 TOR., varied from 1580; OW858b [The noblest vengeance is to forgive] varied from 1547)
E.g., 1573 Sanford 10: The divine Petrach sayde . . . Nobilissimum vindictae genus est parcere. The noblest kind of revengement is to forgive.
Shakespeare: *AYL* 4.3.128, *Cor.* 5.1.18f., 5.3.154f.

R93   Saving your (Sir) REVERENCE (Cf. Appendix B) (From *Rom.*; Wh R100, OW701a from c1400)
Shakespeare: *Err.* 3.2.91, *MV* 2.2.26, 130f., *Ado* 3.4.32, *MM* 2.1.90, *1H4* 2.4.469, *Rom.* 1.4.42, *Cym.* 4.1.5

R98   Neither RHYME nor reason (*Varied* from a1529)
Shakespeare: *Err.* 2.2.48, *Wiv.* 5.5.125f., *AYL* 3.2.398

R98.1   RHYME and reason (Variously contrasted) (Wh R103 from c1303)
Shakespeare: *TGV* 2.1.141–4, *LLL* 1.1.99, 1.2.107f., *H5* 5.2.155–8
Cf. R99: It may rhyme but it accords not [from 1546].

R103   The RICH have many friends (Cf. Prov. 19.4; varied from pre-1546)
Shakespeare: *PP* 20.33f.

R117.1 To RIDE and run (and go) (Cf. Appendix B)
c1560 (c1570) W. Wager *Enough is as Good as a Feast* 176f.: If I should not take pains, ride, run and go For my living, what thereof would ensue? c1569 *Marriage of Wit and Science* (MSR 85): Both ryde and runne and travayle too and froe If thou intend that famous Dame to wed; 487f.: My master would be glad to runne ryde or goe, At your commaundement. 1576 G. Wapull *Tide Tarieth No Man* 1061: To hear of such days I would ride and run. 1601 A. Dent *Plaine Mans Path-Way* R7ᵛ: When Potentates are offended ... against a man ... then he must runne and ride, send presents, use his friends. 1605 (1607) Dekker & Webster *Northward Ho* 4.1.177–9: Ile follow thee, run, ryde, doe what thou canst, ile run and ride over the world after thee.
Shakespeare: *Lr.* 1.4.32

R119 Good RIDING at two anchors men have told, for if the one fail the other may hold (From 1562; OW323b adds Propertius)
Shakespeare: *TN* 1.5.22–4

R130 He that hops best gets the RING (From 1540)
Shakespeare: *Shr.* 1.1.140

R130.1 To be cracked in the RING
1592 Nashe *Strange Newes* I,269: Thou hast crackt thy credit through the ring. c1593 (1597) Lyly *Woman in the Moon* 3.2.265f.: I would not refuse her, provided alwayes she be not clipt within the ringe. 1604 Dekker & Middleton *1 Honest Whore* 3.1.25f.: I hope you wil not let my othes be crackt in the ring. c1612 (1647) Fletcher *Captain* 2.1.77–9: At length Come to be married to my Ladies Woman, After she's crackt i'th' Ring. c1613 (1647) Fletcher *Bonduca* 1.2 VI,93: The devil's dam, Bonduca's daughter, her youngest,

crackt i'th' ring. 1632 (1641) Jonson *Magnetic Lady* 3.7.19f.: In a most strange discovery. / Of light gold. / And crack't within the Ring.
Shakespeare: *Ham.* 2.2.427f.

R133 Soon RIPE soon rotten (From 1546)
Shakespeare: *AYL* 3.2.118–20

R133.1 He must RISE early (betimes) that will go beyond (etc.) me (Varied)
E.g., c1564 *Bugbears* 4.5.63f.: If they thinke to beguyle or geve me such a gleke, they must aryse earlye. 1577 Grange *Golden Aphroditis* K2: You had neede to rise very early, if that flatteryng face of yours coulde goe beyonde me herein. 1580 Munday *Zelauto* P2ᵛ: You must rise somewhat more early, if you goe beyond me [in OW175a (F645)]. ?1581–90 (now dated 1611) *Timon* 4.2 62: Hee that will cheate mee must arise betimes [in D279].
Shakespeare: *TNK* 5.2.59f.
Cf. D279: He must rise betimes that will cozen the devil [from 1630]; F645: He that will deceive the fox must rise betimes [from 1616].

R136 The RISING of one man is the falling of another (Varied from 1571)
Shakespeare: *R2* 4.1.318, *Lr.* 3.3.25

R140 ALL RIVERS (waters) run into the sea (fig.) (Varied from c1515; cf. Eccl. 1.7)
E.g., 1583 Melbancke *Philotimus* B1ᵛ: All waters runne in to the sea and it no bigger. c1616 (1623) Webster *Devil's Law-Case* 2.1.344f.: The greatest Rivers i'th world Are lost in the Sea.
Shakespeare: *MV* 5.1.95–7, *H5* 1.2.209, *Luc.* 649-51

R144 To rule the ROAST (roost) (From c1500)
Shakespeare: *2H6* 1.1.109

R151   As fixed (firm) as a ROCK
(*Varied* from 1558; OW261a from
1541)
  Shakespeare: *Jn.* 2.1.452f., *2H4*
4.1.186, *Mac.* 3.4.21, *Cor.* 5.2.110f.

R153   He has made a ROD (staff) for
his own tail (head) (*Varied* from
c1489)
  Shakespeare: *Lr.* 1.4.173f.

R156   To kiss the ROD (From *TGV*;
OW430a from 1528)
  Shakespeare: *TGV* 1.2.59, *R2*
5.1.32

R158   As swift as a ROE (From 1585;
Wh R170 from c1330)
  Shakespeare: *Shr.* Ind. ii.48, *LLL*
5.2.309

R172.1   A ROPE for parrot
c1589 (1592) Lyly *Midas* 1.2.45: A
rope for Parrot. c1589 (1594) Lyly
Mother Bombie 3.4.56f.: The goose
does hisse; the duck cries quack; A
Rope the Parrot, that holds tack.
1598 (1616) W. Haughton *Englishmen for my Money* ix (MSR 1773): An
Almonde for Parret, a Rope for Parret. 1604 Dekker & Middleton *1
Honest Whore* 5.2.281: Heres a roape
for Parrat. 1615 Bretnor (Crow e
549): A rope for Parrat.
  Shakespeare: *Err.* 4.4.42f., *1H6*
1.3.53

R177   As red (ruddy) as a ROSE
(From 1477)
  Shakespeare: *2H4* 2.4.25, *Rom.*
4.1.99, *Ven.* 10, *Luc.* 71, 258, *Son.*
98.10

R178   As sweet as a ROSE (From
c1460; Wh R201 from a1400)
  Shakespeare: *Rom.* 2.2.43f., *WT*
4.4.220, *Son.* 54.3ff., 98.10f.

R182   No ROSE without a thorn
(prickle) (fig.) (From 1576; cf. Wh
R204 [Roses and thorns] from a900)

E.g., 1579 Lyly *Euphues* I,184: The
sweetest Rose hath his prickel.
  Shakespeare: *AYL* 3.2.111f.,
AWW 1.3.129f., 4.2.18f., *1H6*
2.4.69, *Per* 4.6.35f., *Ven.* 574, *Luc.*
492, *Son.* 35.2

(?) R196   There is the RUB (*Ham.*,
and metaphorical uses of *rub* from
1614; OW686af., *Ham.* and 1712ff.,
plus metaphorical use of *rub* in
1577−8)
  Add: c1612 (1617) Middleton *No
Wit, No Help* 1.1.11: There's another
rub too.
  Shakespeare: *Ham.* 3.1.64

R198   RUE and thyme grow both in
one garden (fig.) (Collections from
1641 [cf. on H745]; OW687a
supplements)
  Shakespeare: *Jn.* 3.1.324f.
  Cf. P116: Let patience grow in
your garden [from 1562; Wh P53
varied includes *thyme, rue*].

R208   He may ill RUN that cannot go
(From 1546)
  Shakespeare: *Tmp.* 3.2.18f.

(?) R211.1   He that RUNS fast may
stumble on stones (Wh R238 c1450)
I.e., c1450 Idley 91.621: He that
renneth fast may stomble on stonys.
  Shakespeare: *Rom.* 2.3.94,
5.3.121f.

R213   Strew green RUSHES for the
stranger (*Varied* from 1546)
  Shakespeare: *Ham.* 1.5.165
  Cf. S914.1: Give the stranger
welcome.

S

S6   It is a bad SACK that will abide no
clouting (Collections from 1546)
  Shakespeare: *2H4* 4.1.159

S12   More SACKS to the mill (From
1590; ditto OW690a)
  Shakespeare: *LLL* 4.3.79

S13 To mourn in SACK and claret (1666 TOR., *sack* from 1589)
Shakespeare; *2H4* 1.2.197f.

(?) S14 I am SAD because I cannot be glad (c1553, *TGV*, *MV*; OW690af. ditto without ?)
I.e.,c1553 (c1567) Udall *Ralph Roister Doister* 3.3.11f.: But why speake ye so faintly? or why are ye so sad? / Thou knowest the proverbe—bycause I can not be had [glad?].[n]
Shakespeare: *TGV* 4.2.26–9, *MV* 1.1.47f.

[n]*Roister Doister* editors, so far as I know, reject (or are unaware of) the suggested emendation.

S21.1 SAFE and sound (Cf. Appendix B) (OW691a from 1529, Wh S10 from a1325)
Shakespeare: *Err.* 4.4.150

S24.1 (To) bear (a) low SAIL (fig.) (Wh S14 from a1393 [2])
Add e.g.: 1575 Gascoigne *Fruites of Warre* I,158: How much were better ... To beare low sayle. 1578 G. Ferrers "Humphrey Duke of Gloucester" 452f. *Mirror for Magistrates* 459: I advise, forewarned by my case, To beare low sayle. 1579 Gosson *Schoole of Abuse* 24: I will beare a lowe sayle, and rowe neere the shore. 1598 (1601) Jonson *Every Man In* 1.1.79: Beare a low saile.
Shakespeare: *3H6* 5.1.52

S24.2 To hoist up SAIL (fig.) (Wh S15 1546 Heywood)
Shakespeare: *TN* 1.5.202
Cf. S23: Hoist your sail when the wind is fair [from 1583].

S24.3 To strike (the) SAIL(S) (fig.)
1559 "Thomas Earl of Salisbury" 192f. *Mirror for Magistrates* 150: Whan fortune fayles, it is the best advice To strike the sayle, least al lie in the mire. c1605 (1606) Marston

Fawn 4.1.535: Thus few strike sail until they run on shelf. 1611 Dekker & Middleton *Roaring Girl* 4.2.119: Yes wife strike saile, for stormes are in thine eyes. c1621 (1662) Middleton *Anything for a Quiet Life* Epilogue: I am sent t'enquire ... whether we ... must strike Our Sails (though full of hope) to your dislike.
Shakespeare: *3H6* 3.3.4f., *R2* 2.1.265f., *2H4* 5.2.17f.

S25 To set up his SAIL to (To sail with) every wind (*Varied* from 1598; OW692b from c1515)
E.g., c1515 (c1530) Barclay *Eclog.* II 1145: In court must a man sayle after every winde, Himselfe conforming to every mans minde.
Shakespeare: *Lr.* 1.4.100f.

S28 Enough to make a SAINT swear (to anger, vex a saint) (1619; OW696a from c1560)
Shakespeare: *Shr.* 3.2.28

S42 Like SAINT GEORGE, who is ever on horseback yet never rides (*Varied* from 1579; OW693bf. supplements)
Shakespeare: *Jn.* 2.1.288f.

S54 SAINT NICHOLAS'S clerks (Cf. Appendix B) (From 1553; OW695a supplements)
Shakespeare: *1H4* 2.1.61f.

(?) S66 On SAINT VALENTINE'S DAY all the birds in couples do join (From 1477; Wh S26 and OW696b from c1380)[n]
Shakespeare: *MND* 4.1.139f.

[n]Although called "an old proverb" in an example of c1673, and included in all three collections, this appears to be more folklore than proverb. Cf. Introduction, fn. 13.

S68 Would I were young (etc.) for your SAKE (*Young Wiv.*, 1607; *a handsome young lord* 1738)

Add: c1597 (1619) Deloney *Jacke of Newberie* 61f.: O that I were a yongue wench for thy sake. 1579 Dryden *Troilus and Cressida* 1.2 VI,297: Would I were a lady for his sake.
Shakespeare: *Wiv.* 1.1.260

S84 There is a SALVE for every sore (From c1550)
Shakespeare: *3H6* 4.6.87f.

S88 To build on SAND (Matt. 7.26; from 1585; OW698bf. from 1548−9)
Shakespeare: *Tro.* 3.2.191f.

S90.1 As many (thick) as the SANDS (gravel) of the sea (Wh S55 from 897; cf. e.g., Ps. 139.18)
Shakespeare: *TGV* 4.3.33

S91 As difficult as to number the SANDS in the sea (From 1552; cf. Rev. 20.8)
Shakespeare: *R2* 2.2.145f.

(?) S96.1 Sour SAUCE is served before dainteous meat (fig.) (Wh S64 c1523)
Shakespeare: *JC* 1.2.300−2
Cf. M839: Sweet meat must have sour sauce.

(?) S97 Sweet SAUCE begins to wax sour (1546; ditto OW793b, Wh S65)[n]
I.e., 1546 Heywood *Dialogue* II.i F3[v]: Whan she sawe swete sauce begyn to waxe sowre, She waxt as sowre as he.
Shakespeare: *Son.* 118.5−8

[n]Unique in each. Cf. Introduction, fn. 26.

(?) S111 SAY I told you so (*MM*, 1612, 1640; OW828a [I told you so] adds 1827, 1872)
I.e., 1612 N. Field *Woman Is Weathercock* 1.2.329: Remember a scorn'd Souldier tolde thee so. 1640 (?1596) Jonson *Tale of a Tub* 2.2.167: Take heed . . . zay I told you so.

Shakespeare: *AWW* 4.3.227, *MM* 2.1.243, 3.2.184

S114 Though I SAY it (that should not say it) (From c1570; OW814b from a1400)
Shakespeare: *MV* 2.2.52, 139, *H5* 4.1.101, *WT* 4.4.177f.

S116 It is sooner (easier, better) SAID than done (*Sooner* from 1546, *easier* [Wh S73 1483], *better* [Wh S73 a1500])
Shakespeare: *3H6* 3.2.90

S117 No sooner SAID than (So said so) done (From c1592; OW574a varied from 1566)
E.g., 1566 P. Beverley *Ariodanto and Genevra* ed. Prouty 98: So thought, so don. 1577 J. Fitjohn *Diamond most Precious* H2[v]: So sayd, and so done, is a thread well spone.
Shakespeare: *Shr.* 1.2.185, *TGV* 2.4.29f., *Mac.* 4.1.149

S118.1 You (I) have SAID (sir)
E.g., 1578 T. Blenerhasset "Carassus" Ind. 7 *2 Mirror for Magistrates*: You have said (quoth Inquisition). 1581 W. Haddon (J. Bell) *Against Ierome Osorius* B9[v]: You have sayd Syr. You have said in deede, or rather . . . you have spurled out . . . slaunderous reproches. c1587 (1592) Kyd *Spanish Tragedy* 3.14.93: Lorenzo thou hast said, it shall be so. c1588 (1591) Lyly *Endymion* 2.2.91: I have saide,—let thy wits worke. 1598 (1616) W. Haughton *Englishmen for my Money* iii (MSR 595): You have sayd sir.
Shakespeare: *TGV* 2.4.29, *AYL* 3.2.121, *TN* 3.1.11, *H8* 5.1.86, *Oth.* 4.2.201, *Mac.* 4.3.213, *Ant.* 1.2.57, 2.6.107, 3.2.34

S119 SAYING and doing are two things (From 1562; Wh S83 variant 1525)
Cf. 31 Dec. 1611 J. Chamberlain

325: This is well saide yf yt be as well don.

Shakespeare: *H8* 3.2.149−52, *Ham.* 1.3.25−7

(?) S128.1 To treat like a SCARE-CROW
1602 W. Burton *Works* 493: We deale with the Lord . . . as birds play with a skar-crow standing in a corne field with a bow and arrow in his hands, as though he would shoote, but doth not: and therefore they even waxe bold by little and little, and at last even flie to him, and sit downe upon him, and picke upon him. 1616 C. Richardson *Sermon concerning . . . Malefactors* 12f.: The Magistrate . . . must not be like a Scarre-Crowe to let the birds picke strawes out of his nose.

Shakespeare: *MM* 2.1.1−4

S152.1 The SCORPION flatters with its head when it will sting with its tail (Wh S96 *varied* from a1200; cf. Rev. 10.10)

Shakespeare: *Cym.* 4.2.144f.
Cf. S858: The sting is in the tail.

S159 To pay SCOT AND LOT (From *1H4*; Wh S97 from c1100)
Shakespeare: *1H4* 5.4.114

S160 Out of all SCOTCH AND NOTCH (1589, 1598, cf. *Cor.*; not in OW)
Add: c1589 (1594) Lyly *Mother Bombie* 2.3.77f. (Silena): We gird them and flout them out of all scotch and notch. 1596 Nashe *Saffron-walden* III,10: Thou wilt be as ready as any catchpoule, out of all scotch & notch to torment him.

Shakespeare: *Cor.* 4.5.186f.

S169 Between SCYLLA and Charybdis (*Varied* from 1576; Wh S101 from c1449)
Shakespeare: *MV* 3.5.16f.

S169.1 As boundless as the SEA
1601 (1602) Marston *What You Will* V II,294: No sea so boundless vast but hath a shore. 1612 Dekker *If It Be Not Good* 1.2.239: Ile be a Sea, (boundles).

Shakespeare: *Rom.* 2.2.133, *Ven.* 389

S169.2 As deaf as the SEA
1583 D. Ortuñez de Calahorra (R. P.) *2 Myrror of Knighthood* 17: O Heart more hard than Hircan Tiger fell! and are more deafe then senselesse troubled seas.

Shakespeare: *Jn.* 2.1.451, *R2* 1.1.19

S169.3 As deep as the SEA (Wh S103 from a1000 [2])
Add: 1592 Lyly *Midas* 4.3.9: A curres mouth is no deeper than the sea.

Shakespeare: *Rom.* 2.2.133f.

S170 As mad as the (troubled) SEA (*Ham., Lr.,* c1623; not in OW)
I.e., c1623 Dekker *Welsh Ambassador* 4.3.3: Her braines are wilder then a trobled sea.
Add: a1393 Gower *CA* II.228.86: I wode as doth the wylde Se [Wh S113]. c1600 (1657) Dekker et. al. *Lust's Dominion* 5.1.284f.: My desire Is raging as the Sea, and mad as fire.

Shakespeare: *Tit.* 3.1.222, *Ham.* 4.1.7, *Lr.* 4.4.2, *Tmp.* 1.1.15f.

S170.1 As salt as any (the) SEA (Wh S106 from c1380 [2])
Shakespeare: *2H6* 3.2.96

S174 In a calm SEA every man may be a pilot (*Varied* from c1590 [1598]; OW99b c1594 Bacon *Promus* 431: Tranquilo quilibet gubernator [from Seneca, *Ep. Mor.* 85.34, ut aiunt])
Add: 1592 ?Lyly *Ent. Quarrendon* I, 466: A good sayler was better seene in a storme than in a calme.

Shakespeare: *Tro.* 1.3.34−45, *Cor.* 4.1.6f.

S177.1   A SEA of troubles (sorrows)[n]
E.g., 1557 *Tottel* R2: A sea of wofull
sorowes. ?1580 *Conversion of a Sinner*
(STC 5648) 51f.: What is this world I
say, other than . . . a durtie dunghill,
a sea of stormy troubles. 1582 Guevara (North) *Dial of Princes* IV.20
3L2^v: They will plunge themselves so
deepe into a sea of troubles, that it
cannot be chosen, but they must
needes at last drown. 1588 in Lyly
III,471: Farewell false love . . . A sea
of sorows. 1617 J. Moore *Mappe of
Mans Mortalitie* 48: Wee live here as
in an Ocean Sea of troubles.
   Shakespeare: *Ham* 3.1.58, *Luc.*
1100
   Cf. M1004: Mischiefs, like waves,
never come alone.

[n] For additional instances cf. F. P.
Wilson, "Shakespeare and the Diction
of Common Life" (1941) in *Shakespearian and Other Studies* (Oxford Univ.
Press, 1969), p. 102[n]5. Although he
did not see fit to include the phrase in
OW, he here notes that the Latin
equivalent (*Mare malorum*) is in Erasmus' *Adagia*.

S181   The SEA refuses no river (is
   never full) (*Varied* from c1590
   [1601]; cf. Wh S928 c1400)
   Add: 1583 J. Jewel *Exposition upon
   . . . Thessalonians* I3^v: As the Sea is
   never filled with water, though al the
   streames of the world runne into it:
   so the greedinesse of an Usurer is
   never satisfied. c1597 (1637) Deloney *1 Gentle Craft* 86: My greedy
   eye . . . did feed upon thy beauty,
   and yet like the Sea was never
   satisfied.
   Shakespeare: *TN*   1.1.10f.,
   2.4.100f., *Son.* 135.9f.

S182.1   To ebb and flow like the SEA
   (Wh S111 from 1404)
   E.g., 1509 Barclay *Ship* II 319(8f.):
   This worlde all hole goeth up and
   downe It ebbes and flowes lyke to the
   se.

Add: 1553 ?Udall *Respublica* 433f.:
But as the waving seas do flow and
ebb by course, So all things else do
change to better and to worse. 1587
T. Churchyard "Cardinal Wolsey"
490 *Mirror for Magistrates* 511: This
weltring world, both flowes and ebs
like seas.
   Shakespeare: *LLL* 4.3.212, *AYL*
2.7.72f., *1H4* 1.2.31f.
   Cf. e.g., F378: After a flood (ebb)
there comes an ebb (flood).

S191.1   SECOND to none (*OED* 2 has
   Chaucer analogue, then *Err.*)
   1559 G. Ferrers "Thomas of Woodstock" 14 *Mirror for Magistrates* 92:
   Seconde to none in glory and fame.
   c1590 (1596) *Edward III* 3.3.224:
   Your manage may be second unto
   none. 1591 ?Lyly *Ent. at Cowdray*
   I,423: He would be second to none.
   1596 Spenser *Faerie Queene* 5.3.5.3f.:
   The second had to name Sir Belli-
   sont, But second unto none is prow-
   esse prayse. 1601 Jonson *Cynthia's
   Revels* 5.2.71f.: A man rarely parted,
   second to none in this court.
   Shakespeare: *Err.* 5.1.7, *2H4*
   2.3.33f.

S196   Trust no SECRET with a woman (1639 CL., *varied* from 1584)
   Shakespeare: *1H4* 2.3.109f., *JC*
   2.1.291−7
   Cf. W706.1: Women can keep no
   counsel.

S214   Be what thou would SEEM to
   be (*Varied* from 1539)
   Shakespeare: *Oth.* 3.3.126, 128,
   Lr. 1.4.13, *Cor.* 3.1.217, *Luc.* 600f.

(?) S228.1   To take (hold) a SER-
   PENT by the tongue (fig.)
   Shakespeare: *Ado* 5.1.90, *Jn.*
   3.1.258
   Cf. W603: He holds a WOLF by
   the ears [from 1538].

S246   He that has not SERVED
   knows not how to command (*Varied*
   from 1539)

E.g., 1539 Taverner 2: Nemo bene imperat, nisi qui parverit imperio. No man can be a good ruler, onles he hath bene fyrste ruled.
Shakespeare: *2H6* 5.1.6

S253 SERVICE is no inheritance (heritage) (*Heritage* from 15th century; Wh S169 from c1412)
Shakespeare: *AWW* 1.3.23f.

S255 An old SERVINGMAN a young beggar (From 1598; ditto OW592b)
Shakespeare: *Wiv.* 1.3.17f.

S261 To be afraid of his own (a) SHADOW (From 1550)
Shakespeare: *Luc.* 997

S262 To fight with (one's own) SHADOW (From 1570; OW256a from 1565)
E.g., 1659 Fuller *Appeal* III 592: To fight with a shadow, (whether one's own or another's), passeth for the proverbial expression of a vain and useless act.
Shakespeare: *MV* 1.2.61f.

S262.1 To flee like a SHADOW (Wh S180 from a1200)
Shakespeare: *MND* 1.1.144

S263 To follow one like his SHADOW (From 1551; Wh S181 c1422)
Shakespeare: *TNK* 2.6.34f.

S264 To make a SHAFT (bolt) or a bolt (shaft) of it (From 1594)
Shakespeare: *Wiv.* 3.4.24

S277 SHAME take (Evil to) him that shame (evil) thinks (From 1484; OW397af. from c1460)
E.g., W. Segar *Bk. Honor and Arms* V.vii II,15: Hony soyt qui mal y pence [motto of the Order of the Garter]. Which may bee thus in English: Evill come to him, that evill thinketh.
Shakespeare: *Wiv.* 5.5.69

S284 To lick into SHAPE (From *3H6*; OW458b Donatus, 1413ff.)
Shakespeare: *3H6* 3.2.161f.

S285 As many SHAPES as Proteus (From 1589; OW720b adds c1550)
Shakespeare: *3H6* 3.2.192

S292 As savage as a SHE-BEAR when she is robbed of her whelps (From c1569; Wh B103 from c1395; cf. 2 Sam. 17.8, Prov. 17.12, Hos. 13.8)
Shakespeare: *MV* 2.1.29, *Tit.* 4.1.96f.

S295.1 As simple as a SHEEP
Cf. c1500 *Lyfe of Roberte* 242.596: Ye be as wyse as a shepe newe shorne [Wh S213]. 1579 Spenser *Shepheardes Calender* "July" 130: Simple as simple sheepe. c1593 (1597) Lyly *Woman in the Moon* 4.1.108: As simple as a sheepe.
Shakespeare: *Ham.* 5.1.116f.

S300 He that makes himself a SHEEP shall be eaten by the wolf (*Varied; fox* from 1583, *wolf* from 1593)
Add: 1580 M. Cope *Exposition uppon the Proverbes of Solomon* 571: Divelishe proverbe, Hee that becommeth a sheepe, maketh him selfe a praye for the Wolfe.[n]
Shakespeare: *JC* 1.3.104f.

[n]A common objection. Cf. e.g., 1613 S. Egerton *Indecorum* F7, vs. marrying for money: "And (as though the corruption of nature were not sufficient to draw us to sinne against God in this behalfe) Satan hath his proverbs (as well as *Salomon*, though not so holy as *Salomons*) which hee bloweth into our ears to harden us in this sin. As for example, Fat sorrow (saith one) is better than leane [S650, from 1662; ditto OW247b]—and another (as very a worldling as hee) saith, It is better to weepe upon carpets, then upon rushes [unique]: insinuating thereby, that

marriage . . . is a heavie and miserable yoake." One encounters similar objections to C305, P382, Y36, Y48, and a great many proverbs Shakespeare did not use.

S308 One scabbed SHEEP mars (infests) a whole flock (*Varied* from 1520; OW702b Juvenal, from c1350)
Shakespeare: *MV* 4.1.114f.

S312 A SHEEP often strays if the shepherd is away (1539, *TGV*, 1596) I.e., 1539 TAV. 45ᵛ: Ovium nullus usus, si pastor absit. There is no goodnes of shepe, yf the shepherde be awaye. 1596 DEL. 05ᵛ: An ill shepheard doth often feede the woolfe.
Shakespeare: *TGV* 1.1.74f.

S334.1 To (make) SHIFT for one (*OED* sb. 6 *To make (a) shift* from c1460; v. 7 *To shift for oneself* from a1513)
1530 Palsgrave 350ᵛ (E2ᵛ): Let me alone I shal shyft for one of us I trowe. 1559 "Jack Cade" 122f. *Mirror for Magistrates* 175: The rest within an houre Shranke all awaye, eche man to shift for one. c1572 (1581) N. Woodes *Conflict of Conscience* 2.2 337: Put me before, and I will shift for one. 1578 G. Whetstone *1 Promos and Cassandra* 2.4 II,454: Each shyft for one; 4.6 II,472: Every man shyft for one. 1592 (1594) *Knack to Know a Knave* ii (MSR 313): While we live, let each man shift for one.
Shakespeare: *2H6* 4.8.31, *Tmp.* 5.1.256
Cf. M112: Every man for himself.

S337 He is put to his SHIFTS (1616 DR., cf. *Tit.*; OW723a from 1542)
Shakespeare: *Tit.* 4.2.176

S342.1 To break (burst) one's SHINS (fig.)
E.g., c1553 (1575) W. Stevenson *Gammer Gurton's Needle* 1.5.25:

Hodge he hied him after till broke were both his shinnes. 1580 Baret C−59: As we say, not to fast for breaking your shinnes [in F141: Not too fast for fear of falling (OW246b adds 1616, 1624)]. c1590 (c1592) ?Kyd *Soliman and Perseda* 1.4.53: Have you burst your shin? 1597 (1599) Chapman *Humorous Day's Mirth* 5.2.4f.: Ile bring you there where you shall honor win, But I can tell you, you must breake your shinne. 1598 (1601) Jonson *Every Man In* 1.2.55−7: Here is a style indeed . . . why, it is able to breake the shinnes of any old mans patience in the world.
Shakespeare: *LLL* 3.1.70ff., *Wiv.* 1.1.282f., *AYL* 2.4.58f.

S346 A great SHIP asks deep waters (Collections from 1640)
Shakespeare: *Tro.* 2.3.266

S366 A great (Hercules') SHOE will not fit a little (a child's) foot (*Hercules* from 1548)
E.g., 1548 Cooper s.v. Herculis Cothurnos: Herculis cothurnos, was used for a proverbe, wherein a thynge of lyttelle importaunce was set foorthe with great eloquence or other thynge, solemne, more apte for a greater mattier. 1579 Gosson *Schoole of Abuse* 21 You will smile . . . to see how this morall Philosopher toyles too draw the Lyons skin upon Aesops Asse [A351]. Hercules shoes on a childes feete.
Shakespeare: *Jn.* 2.1.143f.

S379 Over SHOES over boots (fig.) (*TGV*, 1607ff.; ditto OW603a)
E.g., 1648 Sanderson *Serm.* (1681) II,248: Over shoes, over boots; I know God will never forgive me, and therefore I will never trouble to seek His favour . . . this is properly the sin of despair.
Add e.g.: 1588 R. Some *Godly Treatise* Aal: Seeing you are over shoes, adventure over bootes too.

1606 T. Fitzherbert *Treatise Concerning Policy* 382: He that is once over the shooes in sinne, and iniquity, must for his saufty, goe over head and eares.
Shakespeare: *TGV* 1.1.24f., *MND* 3.2.48f., *Mac.* 3.4.135–7

S380 To be over SHOES (fig.) (Cf. Appendix B) (From 1578)
Shakespeare: *Err.* 3.2.103f.

S396 SHORT and sweet (From 1552)
Shakespeare: *R2* 5.3.117

S397 She is SHORT-HEELED (From a1521)
E.g., c1588 (1599) H. Porter *Two Angry Women of Abingdon* iii (MSR 739f.): Mistresse flurt, you foule strumpet, Light alove, shorte heeles.
Shakespeare: *Ado* 3.4.47

S398.1 This is as it SHOULD be
c1552 (c1567) Udall *Ralph Roister Doister* 3.3.129: Now is it even as it shoulde bee; 4.1.8: Such newes will please him well; this is as it should be. 1597 (1599) Chapman *Humorous Day's Mirth* 4.3.31: O did he so! why that was right even as it should be. 1600 (1657) Dekker et al. *Lust's Dominion* 2.3.132: Why this is as it should bee. c1609 (1655) T. Heywood & W. Rowley *Fortune by Land and Sea* 1.2 VI,371: So things are as they should be.
Shakespeare: *Rom.* 4.2.29

S408 More SHOW than substance (*Varied* from *Rom.*; OW729b from 1594)
Add e.g.: 1594 C. Gibbon *Praise of a good name* A2: Many like the floud Tagus in Spaine . . . carry a show without substance, as that doth a gravel like gold.
Shakespeare: *Rom.* 3.2.77, *Son.* 5.14

S411 April SHOWERS bring May flowers (*Varied* from c1555; OW17b from c1430)
Shakespeare: *Tro.* 1.2.173–6; *Ant.* 3.2.43f.

S431.1 To turn the wrong SIDE out (fig.)
c1605 (1606) Marston *Fawn* 4.1.120: Women are but men turn'd the wrong side outward. c1610 (1631) T. Heywood *1 Fair Maid of the West* 4.1.42 (of parchment): The three sheep-skins with the wrong side outward.
Shakespeare: *Ado* 3.1.68, *TN* 3.1.12f., *Oth.* 2.3.52, *Lr.*4.2.9

S443 ECCE SIGNUM (From c1588 [1599]; OW217a from c1475)
Shakespeare: *1H4* 2.4.169

S446 SILENCE is (gives) consent (*Varied* from c1475; OW733a from c1380)
Shakespeare: *R3* 3.7.144–6, *Cym.* 2.3.94

S447 SILENCE is the best ornament of a woman (*Varied* from 1539; OW733a Sophocles, supplements)
Shakespeare: *Cor.* 2.1.175

S449 As soft as SILK (From c1495)
Shakespeare: *Cor.* 1.9.45

S451 SILK and satin (Fine clothes) make not a gentleman (Collections *varied* from 1616, cf. *WT*; OW129bf. adds 1615)
I.e., 1615 W. Goddard *Nest of Wasps* 57: Nowe tis cloathes the gentleman doth make.
Shakespeare: *WT* 5.2.128–32

S453 As bright (white) as SILVER (*Bright* from c1552 [Wh S320 from c1300], *white* from 1589 [Wh S323 c1440])
Shakespeare: *LLL* 5.2.895, *Luc.* 1405

S453.1 SILVER-BRIGHT (Cf. Ap-

pendix B) (Wh S320a from a1420)
Shakespeare: *Jn.* 2.1.315

(?) S458.1   SILVER is sweet (Wh S324
a1376)
Shakespeare: *Rom.*   2.2.165,
4.5.128–32

S462.1   (As) SIMPLE as (though) I
stand here
E.g., 1590 Sidney *Arcadia* II.14
I,237: I, simple though I sit here,
thought once my pennie as good silver [P194], as some of you do. c1592
?Kyd *Soliman and Perseda* 2.2.11f.: I
was one of the mummers my selfe,
simple as I stand here. 1598 (1601)
Jonson *Every Man In* 1.1.84: I am his
next heire, as simple as I stand here.
1598 (1601) Munday *Downfall of
Robert Earl of Huntington* vi (MSR
792f.): Well, there be on us, simple
though wee stand here, have as
much love in hem as . . . Iohn. c1603
(1606) *2 Return from Parnassus* 2.4
685f.: I am Stercutio his father Sir,
simple as I stand here.
Shakespeare: *Wiv.* 1.1.219
Cf. S818: As true as you stand
there [in *Fulgens and Lucrece* only].

S467.1   (Every) SIN brings in another
(*Varied*; Wh S333 from c1400 [2];
OW735b Seneca, supplements)
Add: c1609 (1655) T. Heywood &
W. Rowley *Fortune by Land and Sea*
1.3 VI,378: Murderers once being in
Wade further till they drown: sin
pulls on sin.
Shakespeare: *R3* 4.2.64, *Per.*
1.1.137
Cf. C826: Crimes (Mischiefs) are
made secure by greater crimes (mis-
chiefs).

(?) S475   Compelled SINS are no sins
(*Varied* from 1578; not in OW)
Shakespeare: *MM* 2.4.57f.

(?)   S476.1 Seven   deadly   SINS
(OW717b, from 1340)
Shakespeare: *MM* 3.1.109f.

S477   SINS are not known till they be
acted (1640 HERB., 1659 N.R., cf.
Luc.; ditto OW737a)
Shakespeare: *Luc.* 527

S485   SINK or swim (From c1517)
Shakespeare: *1H4* 1.3.194

(?) S490   The three SISTERS (From
c1566; OW817a and Wh S353 from
c1449, with allusions earlier)[n]
Shakespeare: *MND* 5.1.336, *MV*
2.2.63, *2H4* 2.4.199

[n]Cf. Introduction, fn. 13.

S506   As true (honest) as the SKIN
between your (his) brows (From
c1552)
Shakespeare: *Ado* 3.5.12

S507   (He is ready) to leap out of his
SKIN (for joy) (From 1584; cf. Wh
S363 *be* c1300, *fly* a1425)
Shakespeare: *WT* 5.2.49f.

(?) S515   A red SKY in the evening is a
sign of a fair day (Cf. Matt. 16.2;
from 1584; OW741a from 1555)
Shakespeare: *R3* 5.3.19–21

S520   It may be a SLANDER but it is
no lie (From 1546; cf. OW741af. [To
slander one with a matter of truth],
from 1578)
E.g., 1583 Melbancke *Philotimus* N3:
But I had better slaunder them
trulye, which is no Slaunder indeede, then flatter them falsely as
thou doest.
Shakespeare: *H8* 2.1.153f., *Rom.*
4.1.33

(?) S521.1   SLANDER is sharper than
a sword.
1613 (1647) Fletcher *Honest Man's
Fortune* 2.1 X,222: Slander is sharper
than the sword.
Shakespeare: *Cym.* 3.4.33f., *WT*
2.3.86f.
Cf. S522: Slander leaves a scar
[from 1616].

(?) S523   Base is the SLAVE that pays (is commanded) (From *H5*; not in OW)
I.e., c1619 (1647) Fletcher & Massinger *Little French Lawyer* 4.6.115f.: Come hither, little gentleman. / Base is the slave commanded: come to me. 1631 T. Heywood *2 Fair Maid of the West* V (MSR 416): My Motto shall be, Base is the man that paies.
Shakespeare: *H5* 2.1.96

S525.1   Morning SLEEP is golden (Golden sleep) (Wh S375 from a1449 [3])
Add: 1540 Palsgrave *Acolastus* 1.1 25: I myght take my golden slepe in the mornynge and tourne me on the other syde to rounde with my pyllowe [in C696: Take counsel of your pillow].
Shakespeare: *R3* 4.1.82f., *1H4* 2.3.40f., *Rom.* 2.3.37f., *Per.* 3.2.22f.

S527   SLEEP is the image of death (From *MND*; OW741b from 1577)
1519 Horman *Vulgaria* 48(18): Slepe is a counterfette dethe. 1522 More *Treatyce* 80 F(10−2): Among al wise men of old, it is agreed that slepe is the very ymage of death [Wh S376].
Shakespeare: *Shr.* Ind. i.35, *MND* 3.2.364, *Mac.* 2.3.76, *Cym.* 2.2.31, *WT* 5.3.20

S530   It is good SLEEPING in a whole skin (From 1543)
Shakespeare: *Wiv.* 3.1.109

S534   To have (pin) in (on) one's SLEEVE (*Have* from 1581; Wh S381 from c1440)
Add: 1588 R. Some *Godly Treatise* I4: They will not bee satisfied, you say, before every one of your reasons bee answered. A peremptorie resolution. They are pinned belike on your sleeve.
Shakespeare: *LLL* 5.2.321
Cf. F32: He pins his faith [etc.] on another man's sleeve [from 1548].

S548   With SLUGGARDS every day is holiday (*Varied* from 1539)
E.g., 1542 Udall *Apoph.* 155: With the slouthfull and idle lubbers that love not to dooe any werke, every daye is a holydaye.
Shakespeare: *1H4* 1.2.204

S558   I (To) SMELL him out (Cf. Appendix B) (From 1546)
Add: 1604 (1607) Dekker & Webster *Westward Ho* 5.4.236: Have we smelt you out foxes.
Shakespeare: *Ado* 3.2.51, *Lr.* 1.5.23, 4.6.103, *WT* 4.4.642f.

S569   No SMOKE without some fire (From 1576; cf. OW573bf. from c1375)
Shakespeare: *Tim.* 4.3.143, *Per.* 1.1.138

S570   Shunning the SMOKE he fell into the fire (*Varied* from 1576; OW747a from c1530)
Shakespeare: *AYL* 1.2.44, 287

S577   I will SMOKE you (Cf. Appendix B) (From *AWW*; OW747a from c1552)
E.g., 1553 *Manifest Detection Dice Play* ed. Halliwell 39: When the money is lost, the cousin begins to smoke.
Shakespeare: *AWW* 4.1.27

S579   As slow as a SNAIL (From 1565; Wh S415 from c1440; Wh S424 *a snail's pace* from a1400)
Shakespeare: *Err.* 2.2.194, *MV* 2.5.47, *AYL* 2.7.146, 4.1.54, *Tro.* 5.5.18, *R3* 4.3.53, *TNK* 5.1.42

S580   Like a SNAIL, he keeps his house on his back (head) (*Varied* from a1535)
Add e.g.: 1579 Lyly *Euphues* I,224: They shoulde be ever lyke to y^t Snaile, which hath ever his house on his head.
Shakespeare: *AYL* 4.1.54f., *Lr.* 1.5.27−31

S585 SNAKE in the grass (*Varied* from a1529; Wh S153 from c1395)
E.g., c1408 Lydgate *Reson* 106.4022–4: But lowh under the freshe flours Ful covertly, who kan declare, Many serpent ther doth dare. a1420 *Troy* I 17.185–6: Lyche an addre undre flouris fayre, For to his herte his tongue was contrarie.
Shakespeare: *2H6* 3.1.228, *R2* 3.2.19f., *Rom.* 3.2.73, *Mac.* 1.5.65f.

S587 A SNATCH and away (to go) (Cf. Appendix B) (*Away* from c1584; OW748af. from 1581)
E.g., 1585 Higgins *Nomenclator* I(79): A standing dinner eaten in haste: a snatch and away. c1604 (1605) T. Heywood *2 If You Know Not Me* xii (MSR 1864f.): Bones a me, cannot a snatch and away serve your turne, but you must lie at racke and manger?
Shakespeare: *LLL* 3.1.22, *Tit.* 2.1.95f.

S590 As seasonable (etc.) as SNOW in summer (harvest) (Prov. 25.13, 26.1; from c1565 [1595]; OW748b supplements)
Shakespeare: *R3* 1.4.242

S591 As white as (the driven) SNOW (From c1534)
Shakespeare: *MND* 3.2.141f., *Rom.* 3.2.19, *Ham.* 3.3.46, 4.5.36, 195, *Oth.* 5.2.4, *WT* 4.4.218, 363f., *TNK* 5.1.139f., *Ven.* 362–4, *Scn.* 130.3

S591.1 SNOW-WHITE (Cf. Appendix B) (Wh S437a from a900 [*OED* from c1000])
Shakespeare: *LLL* 1.1.242, 4.2.132, *Tit.* 2.3.76, *Luc.* 196, 419f., 1011

S593.1 To melt like SNOW (before the sun) (Wh S445 from c1303, 896 from c1450)
Add e.g.: 1557 *Tottel* Q2ᵛ: All con-

sume: as snow against the sunne. 1562 A. Brooke *Romeus and Juliet* 98: He languisheth and melts awaye, as snow against the sonne.
Shakespeare: *MND* 4.1.165f., *2H6* 3.1.223, *Ven.* 750

S595 Like a SNOWBALL, that rolling becomes bigger (1666 *TOR.*, *varied* from 1643)
Add e.g.: c1605 (1606 Marston *Sophonisba* 5.2 II,62: And as you see a snow ball being rolde At first a handfull, yet, long bould about, Insensibly acquires a mighty globe, So his cold griefe through agitation growes. 1607 de Serres-Matthieu (Grimestone) *General Inventorie* (STC 22244) 849: This great desseine of the League (like unto a Ball of Snowe) did increase in manie Townes whereas the Kings obedience was growne cold. 1612 Webster *White Devil* 4.2.189f.: I, I, your good heart gathers like a snow-ball Now your affection's cold.
Shakespeare: *Jn.* 3.4.176f.

S598 To take in SNUFF (Cf. Appendix B) (From 1560)
Shakespeare: *LLL* 5.2.22, *MND* 5.1.249f., *1H4* 1.3.41

S601 SOFT and fair (goes far) (From 1542; Wh F17 from c1385)
Shakespeare: *Ado* 5.4.72

(?) S601.1 SOFT (and) swift (Cf. Appendix B)
c1589 (1594) Lyly *Mother Bombie* 3.4.154: Soft, swift; the place if it be there now, will bee there tomorrowe. 1589 Lyly *Pappe with an Hatchet* III,408: We hope to see him ... looke over all the Citie at London Bridge. Soft swift, he is no traytor.
Shakespeare: *Shr.* 5.1.1
Cf. S601, P3: Soft pace goes far.

(?) S620.1 SOMETHING nothing
c1588 (1599) Porter *Two Angry Wom-*

en of Abingdon iii (MSR 698): Come let me heare, that somthing nothing then. 1603 T. Powell *Welch Bayte* C2ᵛ: Before this newes was stale come a taile of fresh sammon to countermand it with other newes of a something nothing.
Shakespeare: *Oth.* 3.3.157

S621 There is SOMETHING (somewhat) in the wind (From 1571)
Shakespeare: *Err.* 3.1.69

S623 SOMEWHAT (Something) is better than nothing (*Somewhat* from 1546, *something* from 1562 [1555])
Shakespeare: *Err.* 2.2.51, *Lr.* 1.4.193f., 2.3.21

S636 To sell (etc.) it for a SONG (Cf. Appendix B) (From *AWW*; OW712b adds 1609)
Add: 1605 Jonson et al. *Eastward Ho* 5.5.142f.: If youle be wonne with a Song, heare my lamentable tune, too. 1614 (1631) Jonson *Bartholomew Fair* 1.5.166f.: She is not a wise wilfull widdow for nothing, nor a sanctified sister for a song.
Shakespeare: *AWW* 3.2.9

S637 To sing another SONG (fig.) (From c1500; Wh S478 from a1393)
Shakespeare: *Tim.* 1.2.246

S639.1 SOON at night (i.e., tonight) (Cf. Appendix B)
E.g., 1585 ?Munday *Fedele and Fortunio* (MSR 114, 126, 274). 1596 (1605) *Captain Thomas Stukeley* viib, viii (MSR 958, 1017).
Shakespeare: *Wiv.* 1.4.8f., 2.2.283, 286, *MM* 1.4.88, *2H4* 5.5.90, *Rom.* 2.5.76, *Oth.* 3.4.198

S641 The SOONER the better (From c1572 [1581]; Wh R38 1477)
Shakespeare: *2H6* 1.4.14

S649 To rip up (rub) old SORES (*Varied* from 1559)

Shakespeare: *2H4* 1.2.147f., *Tmp.* 2.1.139

S656 SORROW is dry (From 1538)
Shakespeare: *Rom.* 3.5.59

S665.1 I would (should) be SORRY else
c1597 (1637) Deloney *1 Gentle Craft* 128: Else we should be sorry. 1601 (1602) Jonson *Poetaster* 2.2.79. 1609 (1616) Jonson *Epicoene* 2.5.6, 63 (should). 1610 (1612) Jonson *Alchemist* 3.4.14 (I'lld). c1616 (1652) Middleton Widow 5.1.147 (should). c1618 (1661) Middleton *Hengist* 5.1.28 (should). 1623 (1653) Middleton & Rowley *Spanish Gypsy* 3.2.82 (should). c1630 *Wasp* (*MSR* 769f.) (shold).
Shakespeare: *TNK* 3.5.77

S666.1 As SOUL(S) from body(ies) part (or vice versa)
c1600 (1602) Marston *Antonio's Revenge* 2.2.125: Thus heat from blood, thus souls from bodies part. c1602 (1611) Chapman *May-Day* 4.2.67f.: So parts the dying body from the soule, As I depart from my Aemilia. c1610 (1613) Marston & Barksted *Insatiate Countess* III III,38: As we part, so bodies part from soules. c1612 (1633) Donne "Valediction Forbidding Mourning" 1–5: As virtuous men pase mildly away, And whisper to their soules, to goe . . . So let us melt.
Shakespeare: *H8* 2.3.15f.

S666.2 A prophetic (presaging) SOUL (Cf. Appendix B)
c1602 *Thomas Lord Cromwell* 1.2.49: I speake with a presaging soule. c1604 (1607) Dekker & Webster *Sir Thomas Wyatt* 1.2.62f.; We are led with pompe to prison. O propheticke soule. 1606 J. Hind *Eliosto Libidinoso* E2ᵛ: His propheticke soule layd downe before him, both the enormitie of the fact and the condigne punishment. c1614 *Faithful Friends* (MSR

724f.): My prophetick Soule tels me my absence, gives too free a scoape to them that hate mee. 1618 (1632) T. Goffe *Courageous Turk* 4.4 (MSR 1378f.): Why should not a propheticke soule attend On great mens persons, and forewarne their ils? 1622 (1653) Middleton & Rowley *Changeling* 5.1.109: Oh my presaging soul!
Shakespeare: *Ham.* 1.5.40, *Son.* 107.1

S668.1 To love as one's (own) SOUL (Wh S526 from c1400 [2])
Shakespeare: *TGV* 5.4.36f., *Tit.* 3.1.102

S672 As meet as a SOW to bear a saddle (*Varied* from 1546)
Shakespeare: *H5* 3.7.62f.

S681 The still SOW eats up all the draff (From 1546; Wh S535 from c1450)
Shakespeare: *Wiv.* 4.2.107

S691 One SOWS, another reaps (John 4.37; from 1577; ditto OW597b)
Shakespeare: *2H6* 3.1.380f.

S699 To call a SPADE a spade[n] (From 1539)
E.g., 1539 TAV. 14[v]: Plaine and homely men call a fygge, a fygge, and a spade a spade.
Shakespeare: *Cor.* 2.1.190
Cf. D508: To call a dog a dog [from 1589].

[n] Variant nouns were common, such as ape, atheist, bread, Coridon, daw, gull, hog, jade, papist, tree, and whore. Wh H531 adds *horse*.

S704 As flattering (fawning) as a SPANIEL (*Flattering* collections from 1616, *fawning* from c1589; Wh S549 *fawning* a1470)
Shakespeare: *H8* 5.2.161f., *JC* 3.1.42f., *Ant.* 4.12.21

S705 The SPANIEL, that fawns when he is beaten, will never forsake his master (*Varied* from 1579)
E.g., 1579 Lyly *Euphues* I,249: The kinde Spaniell, which the more he is beaten the fonder he is.
Shakespeare: *TGV* 4.2.14f., *MND* 2.1.203f.

S714 Of a little SPARK a great fire (From 1509; cf. Ecclus. 11.32)
Shakespeare: *2H6* 3.1.302f., *3H6* 4.8.7f.

S714.1 SPARK of hope
1546 Heywood *Dialogue* II.xi L4: This sparke of hope have I. 1605 Jonson *Sejanus* IV.147f.: Still puffing in the darke, at one poore coale, Held on by hope, till the last sparke is out.
Shakespeare: *R2* 5.3.21
Cf. Appendix B: SPARK of life.

S715 As lustful as SPARROWS (From *MM*; OW497a *lecherous* from c1390)
Shakespeare: *MM* 3.2.175f., *Tmp.* 4.1.100

S724 To SPEAK as one finds (*Shr.*, 1666 Torriano; Wh S579 1546 Heywood)
Shakespeare: *Shr.* 2.1.66

S725 To SPEAK (Not to speak) as one thinks (From 1559; OW760a Terence, c1500ff.)
Shakespeare: *MND* 3.2.191, *1H6* 5.3.141, *2H6* 3.1.247, *Oth.* 5.2.251

S731 The SPEAR of Achilles could both wound and heal (*Varied* from 1580; Wh S596 c1395; Wh A30 adds a1449)
Shakespeare: *2H6* 5.1.100f.

S733.1 To need no SPECTACLES (*Varied*)
1582 R. Browne *Booke* (STC 3910) E3[v]: A man needeth not spectakles to see the Sunne shine. 1596 ?J. Har-

ington *Ulysses upon Aiax* A2f.: You . . . are seene for a spectacle of follie, to those that cannot see without their spectacles. c1609 (1647) Fletcher *Coxcomb* 5.1.40f.: Well, there's Knavery in't, I see that without spectacles. 1615 E. Hoby *Curry-Combe for a Coxe-Combe* 33: Any curious eye without the helpe of Spectacles might easily discerne.
    Shakespeare: *Ado* 1.1.189, *Lr.* 1.2.35

(?) S749.1   To digest (see) a SPIDER[n] 1594 Nashe *Christs Teares* To the Reader II,179: I . . . determined with my selfe to disgest a Spider, that is, swallow all iniuries, to my credit how banefull soever. c1612 (1657) Middleton *No Wit, No Help* 2.1.390−3: Have I so happily found What many a widow has with sorrow tasted, Even when my lip touch'd the contracting cup, Even then to see the spider?
    Shakespeare: *WT* 2.1.45
    Cf. S749: He has swallowed a spider [i.e., played the bankrupt; from 1659].

[n]Very possibly no more than a superstition is involved in the Middleton and Shakespeare passages. Cf. Introduction, p. xvi.

S764   In SPITE of one's teeth (etc.) (*Teeth* from c1489, *heart* from 1627) Add: 1601 A. Dent *Plaine Mans Path-way* P4[v]: You shall spite of your hearts, ill ye, nill ye, be brought forth unto judgement.
    Shakespeare: *Wiv.* 5.5.125, *Ado* 5.2.68

S771   He must have a long SPOON that will eat with the devil (*Varied* from 1546)
    Shakespeare: *Err.* 4.3.63f., *Tmp.* 2.2.98f.

S788   A SPRINGE to catch a woodcock (*Varied* from 1579)

Add: 1596 Copley *Fig for Fortune* Spenser Society 17: Caught . . . like woodcocks in a springe.
    Shakespeare: *TN* 2.5.83, *Ham.* 1.3.115, 5.2.306

S794   Untimeous SPURRING spills the steed (From a1585 [OW]; OW855b, cf. 1581) I.e., 1581 Guazzo (Pettie) *Civile Conversation* I I,134: By too much spurring, the horse is made dull.
    Shakespeare: *R2* 2.1.36
    Cf. H638: Do not spur a free (willing) horse.

S803.1   To be the STAFF of one's age a1489 Caxton *Blanchardyn* 213: And is she gon, the comfort of my youth, the staffe of my age [*OED* 4 fig.]. 1581 Guazzo (Pettie) *Civile Conversation* III II,68: Children, whiche are growne to perfection . . . hee may well terme the lyght of his eyes and the staffe of his age. 1602 ?T. Heywood *How a Man May Choose* 428f.: Have I with care and trouble brought thee up, To be a staffe and comfort to my age? 1623 (1653) Middleton & Rowley *Spanish Gypsy* 4.3.31f.: I am unbless'd to have but one son only, One staff to bear my age up.
    Shakespeare: *MV* 2.2.66f.

S804   To set up (down, in) one's STAFF (*Down* from 1573, *up* from 1594, *in Err.* only; ditto OW717b) Add e.g., 1602 ?Middleton *Blurt, Master Constable* 5.3.37: Here he calls and sets in his staff. 1604 (1607) Dekker & Webster *Westward Ho* 5.4.230f.: That leane gentleman set in his staffe there.
    Shakespeare: *Err.* 3.1.51

S807   To hold one at STAFF'S (stave's) end (From 1596; Wh S653 from c1375) E.g., 1601 A. Dent *Plaine Mans Path-Way* O8: So shall we both keepe

Sathan at the staves ende, and also much sinne out of our soules.
    Shakespeare: *TN* 5.1.284f.

S813.1   To be bound to a STAKE (OW770a only *Mac.* and a a1500 version of B354; cf. Wh S657)
    Add: 1513 Douglas *Aeneid* II 11.297f.: Quha is attachit ontill a staik, we se, May go na ferthir bot wreil about that tre [Wh S664]. 1579 Lyly *Euphues* I,201: Euphues being thus tyed to the stake by their importunate intreatie, began as followeth. 1590 ?R. Armin *Tarltons newes out of Purgatorie* G2 (of marriage) The poor wench was bound to the stake.
    Shakespeare: *JC* 4.1.48, *Lr.* 3.7.54, *Mac.* 5.7.1f.

S813.2   To have one's honor (reputation, fame) at the STAKE[n]
    c1606 (1607) Jonson *Volpone* 5.10.44: My life, my fame . . . Are at the stake. c1620 (1647) Fletcher & Massinger *Custom of the Country* 3.4 I,345: My honour's at the stake now. 1623 (1647) Fletcher *Wandering Lovers* 5.1 V,145: O best friend, my honour's at the stake too.
    Shakespeare: *TN* 3.1.118–20, *Tro.* 3.3.227f., *AWW* 2.3.149, *Ham.* 4.4.55f.

[n]*OED* regards the *Twelfth Night* and *All's Well* passages above as instances of *stake* in the sense of "that which is placed at hazard" (sb.[2] 2a). But the *Twelfth Night* and *Troilus* passages suggest rather "The post to which a bull or bear was fastened to be baited" (sb.[1] 1c).

S816   (To make one) a STALKING-HORSE (Cf. Appendix B) (1670 Ray; varied from *AYL*; not in OW)
    E.g. 1639 CL. s.v. Hypocrisis 140: The other's but his stalking horse. Add s.v. Fraus 126: You shall not make me your stalking horse.
    Shakespeare: *AYL* 5.4.106
    Cf. R63: Religion a stalking-horse to shoot other fowl.

S818   As true as you STAND there (c1497 [Wh S667], *Mac.*; not in OW)
    Shakespeare: *Mac.* 3.4.73
    Cf. S462.1: (As) simple as I stand here.

S823   The higher STANDING (up) the lower (greater) fall (Collections from 1639; *varied* from 1509)
    Add e.g.: 1557 *Tottel* T4: The higher hall the greater fall such chance have proude and lofty mindes. 1576 Pettie *Petite Pallace* 77: Boystrous windes do most of all shake the highest towers [T509], the higher the place is the sooner and sorer is the fall.
    Shakespeare: *R3* 1.3.258f.

S825   One may point (look) at a STAR but not pull (reach) at it (*Varied* from 1580)
    Add: 1580 Lyly *Euphues and his England* II,204: In thinges above reach, it was easie to catch a straine, but impossible to touch a Star.
    Shakespeare: *TGV* 3.1.156, *AWW* 1.1.85–7, *2H6* 3.1.158

S825.1   As many as the STARS (Wh S675 *varied* from c875, including many Biblical)
    Shakespeare: *Tro.* 4.4.44

S826   STARS are not seen by sunshine (at midday) (fig.) (*Varied* from 1576)
    Add e.g.: 1557 *Tottel* Q1: She shewes her self as sonne among ye starres.
    Shakespeare: *Per.* 2.1.37–42

S826.1   STARS shine brightest (clearest) in the darkest night
    1610 T. Collins *Penitent Publican* F2[v] (of mercy): Starres shine clearest in the darksome night. 1614 A. Roberts *Sacred Septenarie* 43 (of faith): The stars shine brightest in the darkest night.
    Shakespeare: *Ham.* 5.2.256f.
    Cf. Wh S683: To glitter like stars. E.g., a1422 Lydgate *Life* 353.604–6:

With fyre of love, brynnyng also bryght . . . As done the sterres, in the frosty nyght.

S826.2: To be like STARS to the moon (*or vice versa*)
c1569 Ingeland *Disobedient Child* B2ᵛ: For this my Beautie, As the Moone, the starres, I do farre excell. 1605 Jonson *Sejanus* II.35f.: To shine Bright, as the Moone, among the lesser lights. c1610 (1613) Marston & Barksted *Insatiate Countess* I III,17: Others compar'd to her, shew like faint Starres To the full Moone of wonder in her face.
Shakespeare: *LLL* 4.3.226f., 5.2.205, *MV* 5.1.92f., *2H4* 4.3.51–3
Cf. M1120: The moon is not seen where the sun shines.

S828 He has gotten (To get, have) the START of him (Cf. Appendix B) (From 1580)
Shakespeare: *Wiv.* 5.5.161, *JC* 1.2.130

S834 As mute as a STATUE (*Varied* from 1607)
Add: c1617 (1621) Fletcher et al. *Thierry and Theodoret* 1.1.147: Now you stand still like Statues.
Shakespeare: *R3* 3.7.25

S839 As hard (stiff, strong, tough) as STEEL (*Hard* 1509, *3H6*; Wh S699 from c1175)
Shakespeare: *TGV* 1.1.140f., *Cor.* 1.9.45, *Ven.* 199
Cf. H310.1: A heart of (as hard as) iron (steel).

S839.1 As sharp as STEEL (Wh S700 from 1509 [2])
Shakespeare: *TN* 3.3.5

S840 As true (trusty, sure) as STEEL (*True* from c1480)
Shakespeare: *MND* 2.1.197, *Tro.* 3.2.177, *Rom.* 2.4.198

S842 He is (To be) STEEL (metal) to the back (From 1579)
Shakespeare: *Tit.* 4.3.48, *Ant.* 4.4.33

S844.1 To be hooped with (have ribs of) STEEL
c1599 (1602) Marston *Antonio and Mellida* 5.1.196: And twere not hoopt with steele, my brest would break. c1600 (1602) Marston *Antonio's Revenge* 4.1.67–9: Now patience hoope my sides, With steeled ribs, least I doe burst my breast With struggling passions. 1623 (1653) Middleton & Rowley *Spanish Gypsy* 5.1.151f.: Are you all marble-breasted? are your bosoms Hoop'd round with steel? 1679 *Troilus and Cressida* 3.1 VI, 325: O give me ribs of steel, or I shall split with pleasure.
Shakespeare: *Ado* 4.1.150f., *Tro.* 1.3.177, *2H4* 2.3.54

S848 STEP after step the ladder is ascended (Collections from 1640, cf. *Tro.*)
Add: c1592 *Thomas of Woodstock* 1.1.183f.: We must use ladders & by stepps assend Till by degrees we reach the Altitude.
Shakespeare: *Tro.* 1.3.101f.

S848.1 To be a STEPMOTHER (Wh S720 *varied* from c1300)
Shakespeare: *Tro.* 3.2.194, *Cym.* 1.1.71

S861 I would I might never STIR (else) (From *Jn.*)
Add: 1599 (1600) Jonson *EMO* 2.3.223f.: By this good aire, as I am an honest man, would I might never stirre, sir.
Shakespeare: *Wiv.* 5.5.187, *Jn.* 1.1.145

S866.1 As senseless (etc.) as STOCK(S) and stone(s)
c1407 Lydgate *Reson & Sens.* 6411:

As deffe as stok or ston [*OED* 1c]. c1587 (1599) Greene *Alphonsus, King of Aragon* 4.2 1258: Some lay as dead as either stock or stone. 1598 (1616) W. Haughton *Englishmen for my Money* iv (MSR 772): What Stocks, what stones, what senceles Truncks be these? 1599 (1600) Dekker *Old Fortunatus* 5.2.55: You Stocke, you stone, you logs end.
Shakespeare: *JC* 1.1.35, *Ven.* 211

S867   To beat one like a STOCK-FISH (From 1552)
Shakespeare: *Tmp.* 3.2.70f.

S868   To wear yellow STOCKINGS (hose) (and cross garters) (Only *TN* and 1666 have *garters, TN* earliest for *stockings* or *hose*; OW925 [To wear yellow stockings] has *hose* from c1590, *weare the yellow* from 1600, *stockings* in 1606)
Shakespeare: *TN* 2.5.171

S872   My STOMACH (belly) has struck twelve (rung noon) (*Varied* from 1571)
E.g., 1571 R. Edwards *Damon and Pithias* vii (MSR 418): It is high dinner time, I know by my belly.
Shakespeare: *Err.* 1.2.66
Cf. B287a: The belly is the truest clock [From 1590 for part of idea; nothing verbally like entry form until 1594 French, 1611 English].

S874   To go against one's STOMACH (Cf. Appendix B) (From 1581)
Shakespeare: *AYL* 3.2.21, *H5* 3.2.52f.

S876   As cold as a (any) STONE (From c1503; Wh S758 from a1300)
E.g., c1300 *South English Legendary* I 21.80: This child ligge ded so cold so eny ston.
Shakespeare: *H5* 2.3.24, *Ven.* 211, *Son.* 94.3

S877   As deaf as a STONE (From 1520–40; Wh S760 from c1408)
Shakespeare: *JC* 3.2.142f.

S878   As hard as a STONE (flint, rock) (*Flint* from 1521 [Wh F284 from a750], *stone* from 1566 [Wh S763 from a800], *rock* from 1566)
Shakespeare: *2H4* 4.4.33, *Tit.* 3.1.45, *Rom.* 2.6.17, *JC* 1.1.35, 3.2.142f., *Lr.* 3.2.64

S878.1   As mute as a (any) STONE (Wh S765 from c1408)
Shakespeare: *R3* 3.7.25, *Ant.* 2.2.110

S878.2   As steadfast as (the, any, a) STONE(S) (Wh S770 from c1200)
E.g., a1500 Richardoune in *Lapidaries* 60.7: Nat variable ne movyng, but as a stidefast stone.
Shakespeare: *Son.* 94.3f.

S879   As still as a STONE (From c1475; Wh S772 from c1200)
Shakespeare: *Tit.* 3.1.46, *Ant.* 2.2.110

S879.1   STONE-STILL (Cf. Appendix B) (Wh S772a from a1200)
Shakespeare: *Jn.* 4.1.76, *Luc.* 1730

S880   He has not a STONE (etc.) to cast (throw) at a dog (*Varied* from 1594, *stone* from *Wiv.*)
Add: 1575 Gascoigne *Posies* Ep. Ded. I,6: He who will throw a stone at everie Dogge which barketh, had neede of a great satchell or pocket. 1589 L. Wright *Hunting of Antichrist* A3ᵛ:Wisdome do will me, not to cast a stone at every barking dog.
Shakespeare: *Wiv.* 1.4.112f.
Cf. W762: He has not a word to cast at a dog [OW915a combines with S880].

S889   The STONE you throw will fall on your own head (cf. Ecclus. 27.25;

varied from 1548; Wh S777 c1395; not in OW)
Shakespeare: *H8* 5.2.138−40

(?) S893.1 To turn STONE with wonder
c1606 (1607) Jonson *Volpone* 4.5.154f. These things, they strike, with wonder! / I am turn'd a stone. 1609 (1616) Jonson *Epicoene* 1.2.2: Strooke into stone, almost . . . with tales o' thine uncle! 1616 Jonson *Poetaster* To the Reader 68: Then turne stone with wonder! 1622 (1647) Fletcher & Massinger *Spanish Curate* 4.4.40: I am turn'd a stone with wonder. 1627 (1636) Massinger *Great Duke of Florence* 2.3.156f.: It was your beauty That turn'd me statue.
Shakespeare: *WT* 5.3.39−42

(?) S895.1 The STONES would speak (Cf. Luke 19.40; *varied*)
1573 (1575) Gascoigne *Posies* I,75: When men crye mumme and keepe such silence long, Then stones must speake, els dead men shall have wrong. 1583 J. Jewel *Exposition . . . Thessalonians* I5: If the stones coulde speake, they would say as much. 1594 (1605) J. Radford *Directorie* A3: Which trueth to speake and teach, if man shoulde cease; the very rockes, and stones might crie out.
Shakespeare: *Mac.* 2.1.57f.

S908 After a STORM comes a calm (fair weather) (*Calm* from c1538)
Shakespeare: *Oth.* 2.1.185

S914 It is (no) more STRANGE than true (*Varied* from *MND*; OW779a from a1534)
E.g., a1534 J. Heywood *Love* A3: The case as ye put it I thynke more straunge Then true.
Add: 1574 J. Higgins "Madan" 13 *2 Mirror for Magistrates* 111: Thou shalt perceive, not halfe so straunge as true.
Shakespeare: *MND* 5.1.2, *MM* 5.1.37, 44, *Ham.* 1.2.220f.

(?) S914.1 Give the STRANGER welcome (*Varied*)
1546 Heywood *Dialogue* II.iii G2: She bad us welcome and merily toward me, Greene rushes for this straunger, strawe here (quoth she) [in R213]. c1597 (1637) Deloney *1 Gentle Craft* 116: To strangers common courtesie doth teach us to shew the greatest favour. 1598 T. James To the Reader A. Brucioli *Commentary . . .canticles* *6ᵛ: Intreat him as a stranger, that is, gently & kindly. ?c1612 (1657) Middleton *No Wit No Help* 4.1.157f.: You're a stranger, sir; Your welcome will be best. c1613 (1616) Beaumont & Fletcher *Scornful Lady* 2.1.11f.: Sir as a stranger you have had all my welcome. c1622 (1657) Middleton *Women Beware Women* 2.2.219f.: She's a stranger, madam. / The more should be her welcome.
Shakespeare: *MV* 3.2.237, *Ham.* 1.5.165
Cf. R213: Strew green rushes for the stranger [from 1546].

S917 Not to care (give) a STRAW (rush) (*Straw* from c1500 [Wh S810 from c1300], *rush* from 1562 [Wh R245−9 from a1376])
Shakespeare: *WT* 3.2.110

S918 Not worth a STRAW (From c1489)
Shakespeare: *H5* 2.3.51, *Ham.* 4.4.26, 55, *Luc.* 1021

(?) S925.1 How runs the STREAM? (To see how the stream runs)
1610 (1612) Jonson *Alchemist* Pro. 20−2: If there be any, that will sit so nigh Unto the streame, to looke what it doth run, They shall find things, they'ld thinke, or wish, were done.
Shakespeare: *TN* 4.1.60, *2H4* 4.1.70
Cf. W144: To know which way the wind blows [from 1546]; W884.1: Thus (How) goes (fares) the world.

S927   It is hard (folly, in vain) to strive against the STREAM (From 1509)
Shakespeare: *Tim.* 4.1.27, *Ven.* 772

S929   The STREAM (current, tide) stopped swells the higher (*Varied* from 1576; OW780 from 1563)
Shakespeare: *TGV* 2.7.25f., *MM* 3.1.242f., *Jn.* 2.1.335–40, *Cor.* 3.1.247f., *Ven.* 331f., *Luc.* 645f., 1118f.

S930   To go (swim, run) with the STREAM (tide) (*Go* from 1579, *run* from 1593, *swim TNK*; not in OW)
Add: 1594 Nashe *Unfortunate Traveller* II,245: He decreed with himselfe to swim with the stream, and write a booke forthwith in commendation of follie.
Shakespeare: *TNK* 1.2.7–11

S930.1   To   swim   against   the STREAM (with the crab, trout)
1569 T. Norton *Treatises* G2ᵛ: An other sort there is, like kestrelles or troutes, they ever flye agaynst the wynde, or swimme agaynst the streame. 1583 H. Howard *Defensative*¶. 3ᵛf.: A kind of habite, of swimming alwaies with the Trout against the stream. 1584 Lyly *Campaspe* 3.5.34f.: Thou   maist   swimme against the streame with the Crab. 1586 Withals B2ᵛ: It is hard swimming against the streame [in S927]. 1604 E. Grymeston *Miscelanea* H3: A perverse man is like a sea crab that alwaies   swimmes   against   the streame. c1604 (c1607) Chapman *Bussy D'Ambois* 3.2.332: Why, this swims quite against the stream of greatness.
Shakespeare: *2H4* 5.2.34

S934   Harp   no   more   on   that STRING (From 1543)
Shakespeare: *MM* 5.1.64, *R3* 4.4.364

S936   To harp upon one (the same) STRING (From c1538; Wh S839 from c1385)
Shakespeare: *Ham.* 2.2.187, *Ant.* 3.13.142, *Cor.* 2.3.252

S941   Many (Little) STROKES fell great oaks (*Varied; many* from 1539; OW782a supplements)
E.g., 1579 Lyly *Euphues* I,225: Many strokes overthrow the tallest Oke. 1587 T. Hughes *Misfortunes of Arthur* 2.3 103: The smallest axe may fell the hugest oake.
Shakespeare: *3H6* 2.1.54f.

S945.1   To be STUFFED with virtues (good parts) (Cf. Appendix B)
?1552 T. Becon *Principles of Christian Religion* A3ᵛ: Your father is learned, and hath a brest stuffed with al godlye vertues.
Shakespeare: *Ado* 1.1.56f., *Rom.* 3.5.181

S951   Lose not the SUBSTANCE for the   shadow   (*Varied*   from   1579; OW110a from 1551)
Shakespeare: *Tit.* 3.2.80

S955   Of SUFFERANCE comes ease (From   1546;   cf.   Wh   S859   from a1393)
Shakespeare: *2H4* 5.4.25

S957.1   As sweet as SUGAR (Wh S870 from c1378)
Add: 1553 ?Udall *Respublica* 256: Sweeter than sugar. 1557 *Tottel* N3: Sweeter than sugar sweet.
Shakespeare: *LLL* 5.2.230f., *MV* 3.2.119, *R2* 2.3.6f.

(?) S960.1   To have one's SUIT (i.e., courtship) be cold (Cf. Appendix B)
c1589 A. Munday *John a Kent* III ed. Collier 30: Shee's gon from Courte, and no man can tell whether, and colde their sute should they pursue them hether. c1602 (1607) *Fair Maid of the Exchange* xi (MSR 1908): For well I wote his sute is cold, 't must die.

c1606 (c1607) ?Tourneur *Revenger's Tragedy* 1.1. 26−9: Oh, she was able to ha' made a usurer's son Melt all his patrimony . . . and yet his suit been cold.
Shakespeare: *TGV* 4.4.181, *MV* 2.7.73

(?) S962 SUITS hang half a year in Westminster Hall, at Tyburn half an hour's hanging ends all (1562 Heywood *Epig.*, Cf. *1H4*)
Shakespeare: *1H4* 1.2.69−73

S964 To be sick of the SULLENS (From 1580; OW731a supplements)
Shakespeare: *Ant.* 1.3.13

(?) S965.1 Next to SUMMER is winter (fig.) (Wh S876 a1513)
Add: 1563 Sackville "Induction" 56 *Mirror for Magistrates* 300: The sommers beauty yeeldes to winters blast.
Shakespeare: *2H6* 2.4.2f.
Cf. W506.1: After winter follows summer (May).

S966.1 As fair as the SUMMER'S DAY(S) (Wh S878 a1500)
Wh S877 (bright) adds c1390 *Castel of Love* 374.737−8: And feirore of liht Then the someresday whon hee ·is briht. c1400 *Emaré* 7.191−2: After the mayde fayr and gent, That was bryght as someres day.
Shakespeare: *Per.* 2.5.35f.

S967 As good (etc.) as one shall see in a SUMMER'S day (From c1589 [1594]; Wh S880 1528)
Add: c1588 (1599) Porter *Two Angry Women of Abingdon* x (MSR 2318−20; Nicholas Proverbes): I know you are as good a man as ever drew sword, or as was ere girt in a girdle, or as ere went on Neats leather, or as one shall see upon a summers day, or. . . .
Shakespeare: *MND* 1.2.86f., *H5* 3.6.63f., 4.8.22, *Son.* 18.1

S968 Although the SUN shines leave not your cloak at home (Collections from 1640; OW12b [Wh H305] cf. c1390)
I.e., c1390 Chaucer *Proverbs* i: What shul thise clothes thus manyfold, Lo! this hote somers day? After greet hete cometh cold; no man caste his pilche [cloak] away.
Shakespeare: *Son.* 34.1−4

S968.1 As bright as the SUN (Wh S881 *varied* from a800)
Shakespeare: *TGV* 3.1.88

S969 As clear as the SUN (From 1539; Wh S882 from c1300, *summer sun* a1420)
Shakespeare: *H5* 1.2.86

S971.1 He that gazes upon the SUN shall at last be blind (fig.) (OW298a *varied* from 1528)
Shakespeare: *LLL* 1.1.84f., 5.2.374−6

S979 The rising, not the setting, SUN is worshipped by most men (*Varied* from 1553)
Add e.g.: I. Gentillet (G. Harte) *Declaration* (STC 11266) B5ᵛ: For as Pompei said unto Scilla, there be more that doe worship yᵉ sunne rising, than yᵉ sunne setting.
Shakespeare: *R2* 2.4.21−3, 3.2.217f., *Tim.* 1.2.145, *Son.* 7.1−12

S981.1 The SUN is brighter than all other stars (fig.) (Wh S889 *varied* from c1300)
Shakespeare: *2H4* 4.3.51−3
Cf. S826.2: To be like stars to the moon.

S982 The SUN is never the worse for shining on a dunghill (*Varied* from 1578; Wh S891 from c1303)
Shakespeare: *Wiv.* 1.3.63

S985 The SUN shines upon all alike (From 1552; cf. Matt. 5.45, Wh S893 from c1000)

E.g., 1553 Latimer *Serm.* 19 363: He letteth his sun shine as well over the wicked as over the good. 1553 T. Wilson *Rhet.* 32: The Sunne shineth indifferently over all.
Shakespeare: *TN* 3.1.38f., *Tro.* 1.3.89−94, *R3* 5.3.281−7, *R2* 1.3.145, *H5* 4 Chorus 43, *Cym.* 3.4.136, *WT* 4.4.444−6

(?) S987 To get the SUN of one (fig.?) (From *LLL*; OW787b literal from 1548)
Shakespeare: *LLL* 4.3.365f.

S988 To set forth the SUN with a candle (lantern, taper) (*Varied* from 1540)
Shakespeare: *Jn.* 4.2.14f., *Rom.* 2.2.19f.

S992 Two SUNS cannot shine in one sphere (c1612, *varied* from *Tit.* ; OW851af. from 1542)
E.g., 1542 Erasmus (Udall) *Apoph.* (1877) 209: Unto Darius he [Alexander] made aunswere in this maner, that neither the yearth might endure or abyde two sonnes, nor the countree of Asia, two kinges.
Shakespeare: *1H4* 5.4.65, *Tit.* 5.3.17

(?) S992.1 To flee like the SUN-BEAM (Wh S904 1513)
Shakespeare: *Rom.* 2.5.5

S993 He that hangs himself on SUN-DAY shall hang still uncut down on Monday (1546 Heywood)
Shakespeare: *Shr.* 2.1.299
Cf. Appendix B: I'll see you HANG'D first.

(?) S995.1 As swift as the SUN-GLEAM (Wh S909 a1200)
Shakespeare: *Rom.* 2.5.5

(?) S1011 Every SURFEIT foreruns a fast (1583, *1H4* [transferred to H560], *MM*; not in OW)
I.e., 1583 Melbancke *Philotimus* Q4^v.

Shakespeare: *TN* 1.1.2f., *MM* 1.2.126
Cf. H560: Too much honey cloys the stomach.

S1017 SUSPICION has double eyes (c1680, 1719, cf. *1H4*; OW790b adds 1605)
I.e., 1604 (1605) Daniel *Philotas* 3.3 Chorus 1150: Suspition full of eyes, and full of eares.
Add: c1623 Dekker *Welsh Ambassador* 4.3.54: Suspition sealinge upp her hundred eyes.
Shakespeare: *1H4* 5.2.8

S1019 SUSPICION (Accusation) is no proof (*Suspicion varied* from 1546, *accusation* 1629)
Add e.g.: 1588 Greene *Pandosto* ed. Bullough VIII,169: The Oracle. / Suspition is no proofe.
Shakespeare: *Oth.* 1.3.106

S1021.1 To be out of (in) one's SWADDLING CLOUTS (fig.)
1580 W. Charcke (J. Stockwood) in R. Cawdrey *Shorte and fruitefull treatise* D4: They . . . as it were in their swadling clouts have any time tasted the most sweet meate of milke. 1580 Lyly *Euphues and his England* II,4: The other . . . being but yet in his swathe cloutes, I commit most humbly to your Lordships protection. c1585 (1592) Lyly *Gallathea* 3.1.96−8: He . . . being yet scarce out of his swath-clowtes, cannot understand these deepe conceits. 1589 R. Some *Godly Treatise* A2^v: It is high time . . . to meete with this mischiefe. It is out of the swadling cloutes.
Shakespeare: *1H4* 3.2.112, *Ham.* 2.2.382f.

S1023 As swift as a SWALLOW (From 1553; Wh S923 from a1300)
Shakespeare: *R3* 5.2.23, *2H4* 4.3.32f., *Tit.* 2.2.24, 4.2.172

S1026 SWALLOWS, like false friends, fly away upon the approach

of winter (*Varied* from 1539)
Shakespeare: *Tim.* 1.1.100f.,
3.6.29–32
Cf. B393: Birds of a feather will
flock (fly) together.

S1028   Like a SWAN, he sings before
his death (*Varied* from c1489)
Shakespeare: *MV* 3.2.44f., *Jn.*
5.7.21f., *Oth.* 5.2.247f., *Luc.* 1611f.,
PhT 15

S1028.1   To make a SWAN a crow
1573 Gascoigne *Dan B. of Bathe*
I,132: To make a Swan of that which
was a Crowe [in OW298a (G369)].
c1600 *Fatal Marriage* xvi (MSR
1847–9): Thus must I . . . confes
against all reason truth and right the
swannes a crow and say the Crow is
white [C853]. 1612 Dekker *If It Be
Not Good* 1.2.213: Our swan turnes
crow. c1614 *Faithful Friends* (MSR
1252): Compare the Crowe to the
unspotted Swann.
Shakespeare: *Rom.* 1.2.87
Cf. G369: All his Geese are swans.

(?) S1030.1   To SWEAR and for-
swear (Cf. Appendix B)
1626 (1631) Jonson *Staple of News*
1.3.50: Haste to be rich, swear, and
forsweare wealthily.
Shakespeare: *AYL* 5.4.55f.

S1031   To live by the SWEAT of
one's brows (Cf. Gen. 3.19; *varied*
from 1553; Wh S940 from a1023)
Shakespeare: *Tmp.* 2.1.160f.

S1034.1   After SWEET the sour
comes (Wh S942 *varied* from a1393)
E.g., a1393 Gower *CA* II 68.1190f.:
Fulofte and thus the swete soureth,
Whan it is knowe to the tast.
Shakespeare: *Luc.* 867f.

(?) S1037.1   SWEET is sweeter after
bitterness (Wh S944 1420)
Shakespeare: *AWW* 5.3.334

(?) S1038.1   SWEET-AND-TWENTY
(Cf. Appendix B)

1608 (1631) T. Brewer *The Life and
Death of the merry Devill of Edmonton*
C4[v]: In like manner, loved hee
(sometime) to be mad merry,
amongst a mad company of his bare-
chind boone companions, his little
wanton wagtailes: his sweet and
twenties: his pretty pinckineyd pigs-
nies &c. as hee himselfe vsed commonly to call them.
Shakespeare: *TN* 2.3.51, *TNK*
5.2.109

(?) S1040.1   SWEETNESS shall turn
to gall (Wh S948 c1412)
Shakespeare: *Rom.* 1.5.91f.

S1042   As drunk as a SWINE (sow,
David's sow) (From c1500)
Shakespeare: *Shr.* Ind. i.34, *AWW*
4.3.255f., *Ham.* 1.4.19, *Mac.* 1.7.67

S1046   SWITCH (Swits) and spur(s)
(From *Rom.*; ditto *OED spur* 2)
Shakespeare: *Rom.* 2.4.69

(?) S1046.1   At one (fell) SWOOP
(Cf. Appendix B) (OW796a; *Mac.*,
1612 Webster without *fell*, Byron;
OED eb has more late instances)
Shakespeare: *Mac.* 4.3.219

S1048   A leaden (wooden) SWORD
(dagger) in an ivory (golden,
painted) sheath (scabbard) (*Varied*
from 1542)
E.g., 1550 TAV. *Flowers Sent.* B1: A
goodlye person that speaketh un-
goodlye wordes, draweth forth a
leaden swerde out of an Ivery
skaberd.
Shakespeare: *LLL* 5.2.480f.

(?) S1052   The SWORD is tried on
the anvil (*Varied* from *Cor.*; not in
OW)[n]
I.e., 1627 (1636) Massinger *Great
Duke of Florence* 2.3.129-32: Allea-
geance Tempted too farre, is like the
triall of A good sword on an An-
vill . . . that often flies in peeces without service to the owner. 1664
S. Butler *Hudibras* II.249 135: The

beaten Soldier proves most manful,
That, like his Sword, endures the
Anvil.
Shakespeare: *Cor.* 4.5.109f.

[n]Edwards and Gibson note on the
Massinger (V, 194): "Stochholm points
out the source of this comparison in
Whitney's *Choice of Emblems* (ed. Green,
p. 192). Tilley cites the passage under
S1052, but it is not properly speaking
proverbial."

S1054   To slay (cut one's throat) with
a leaden SWORD (From 1559;
OW796b from 1533)
E.g., 1580 BARET P-527: Plumbeo
iugulare gladio . . . A Proverbe aptlie to be used to those which are overcome with an easie argument. Add:
1587 Holinshed *Chronicles* ed. Bullough III, 395: He thought it the
part of a wise man . . . to leave the
following of such an unadvised capteine, as with a leden sword would
cut his owne throat.
Shakespeare: *LLL* 5.2.480f.

T

T7   To stand to one's TACKLING
(tackle) (Cf. Appendix B) (From
1562; OW770b from 1534)
Shakespeare: *TNK* 2.3.55

T8   He frets like gummed TAF-
FETY (grogram, velvet) (From *1H4*;
ditto OW287b)
Shakespeare: *1H4* 2.2.2

T10   TAG, rag, and bobtail (Tag and
rag) (Cf. Appendix B) (*And bobtail*
from 1659, *tag and rag* from 1553)
Shakespeare: *JC* 1.2.258, *Cor.*
3.1.246f.

T17   The TAILOR makes the man
(From *AWW*; OW797b adds Latin
for A283)
Shakespeare: *AWW* 2.5.16, *Lr.*
2.2.54f., *Cym.* 4.2.81–3
Cf.   A283:   Apparel   makes
(Clothes make) the man.

T18   The TAILOR must cut three
sleeves for every woman's gown
(*Varied* from 1612; OW797b from
1583)
Shakespeare: *Shr.* 4.3.142

T27   TAKE it as you will (list, please)
(From 1580; OW799a from c1530)
Shakespeare: *TN* 2.3.188f., *Rom.*
1.1.26, 40f., *Tim.* 5.1.178, *Tmp.*
3.2.129
Cf. T221.1: Think what you will.

T28   TAKE it or leave it (From 1603;
OW799b cf. 1576; Wh T14 1519)
Shakespeare: *Lr.* 1.1.205

T28.1   TAKE me with you (*OED* 59b
only *Rom.*, then Congreve)[n]
E.g., c1585 (1592) Lyly *Gallathea*
5.3.149. 1588 (1591) Lyly *Endymion*
4.2.91. c1589 (1592) Lyly *Midas*
4.2.18. c1589 (1594) Lyly *Mother
Bombie* 1.3.153, 5.3.357. 1598 (1616)
W. Haughton *Englishmen for My
Money* xii (MSR 2431). 1599 (1600)
Jonson *Every Man Out* 5.4.16. c1602
(1608) *Merry Devil of Edmonton* 2.1.1.
c1605 (1608) Middleton *Trick to
Catch the Old One* 2.1.53. 1627 (1636)
Massinger *Great Duke of Florence*
4.2.37 (us).
Shakespeare: *1H4* 2.4.460, *Rom.*
3.5.141

[n]*OED* provides only a simple definition: "to speak so that (he) can 'follow'
or apprehend one's meaning." Contexts often imply resentment or hostil-
ity on the part of the speaker, however,
and sometimes imply no difficulty
whatever in understanding literally
what has been said. Edwards & Gibson
find three distinct meanings in Massinger (V, 344).

T34   It is safe TAKING a shive of a
cut loaf (Collections from 1639, cf.
Tit.; ditto OW724b)
Shakespeare: *Tit.* 2.1.86f.

T38   A good TALE ill told is marred
in the telling (Collections from 1562

[1549]; OW802b Latin, *spyllt* c1532)
Shakespeare: *Lr.* 1.4.32f.

T48 Thereby hangs (lies) a TALE
(*Lies* from a1523; *hangs* from *Shr.*)
Add: 1579 T. Churchyard *Choise*
(STC 5235) Y4ᵛ: Thereby hangs a
tale.
Shakespeare: *Shr* 4.1.58, *Wiv.*
1.4.149, *AYL* 2.7.28, *Oth.* 3.1.8, *TNK*
3.3.41

T49 To (make one) tell another
TALE (From 1481)
Shakespeare: *Wiv.* 1.1.77, *Tro.*
1.2.84f., *Oth.* 5.1.125

T50 To take the TALE (word) out of
one's mouth (*Word* from 1530, *tale*
from c1570)
Shakespeare: *H5* 4.7.42f.

T51 You (To) tell a TALE to a deaf
man (*Varied* from c1538; OW803a
from 1533−4)
Shakespeare: *Tmp* 1.2.106

T53 TALES of Robin Hood are
good for fools (*Varied* from 1509)
Shakespeare: *TNK* Prologue 20f.

(?) T53.1 TALES twice told are
ungrateful
1586 ?J. Case *Praise of Musicke* (STC
20184) 24: Colworts twise sodde are
harmeful [C511], and tales twise
tolde ungratefull.
Shakespeare: *Jn.* 3.4.108f.,
4.2.18f.
Cf. T39: A good tale is none the
worse to be twice told (OW802b
from 1577).

T64 The greatest TALKERS (crack-
ers, boasters) are the least (not the
greatest) doers (*Varied* from c1523;
OW803af. from 1509)
Shakespeare: *R3* 1.3.350, *H8*
2.2.78

(?) T64.1 You (He) will be
TALKING

1602 ?T. Heywood *How a Man May
Choose* 758f. (to garrulous old
Lusam): You are such another
[A250], You will be talking.
Shakespeare: *Ado* 3.5.33, *Tmp.*
2.1.27

(?) T66 He has pissed his TALLOW
(fig.) (1678 Ray, 1694; *OED Piss* 2b
literal fromc1450 [of a hart in rut-
ting time], fig. *MWW*, then 1694)
Shakespeare: *Wiv.* 5.5.14f.

(?) T66.1 With a TANG[n]
1618 J. Barlow *Good Mans Refuge* C2:
Immoderate mourning, is a meanes
to draw downe a heavier iudgement.
When boys will pule, and cry out for
a little lash, the Master many times
sets it on with a tang.
Shakespeare: *Tmp.* 2.2.50

[n]With no instance of the phrase
except for *The Tempest OED* debates
whether the image involves odor (sb¹
5c) or sound (sb²).

T82.1 An ocean (sea) of TEARS (Cf.
Appendix B)
c1587 (c1592) Kyd *Spanish Tragedy*
2.5.23: To drown thee with an ocean
of my tears. c1588 (1590) Marlowe *2
Tamburlaine* 3.2.47: I had wept a sea
of tears for her.
Shakespeare: *TGV* 2.7.69, *2H6*
3.2.143, *3H6* 2.5.106
Cf. S177.1: A sea of troubles.

(?) T82.2 TEARS are women's
weapons
1576 Pettie *Petite Pallace* 48: But having no other weapon but weepyng to
defende her selfe, by pitiful excle-
mations and cries shee kept him
from satisfying his insaciable desire.
1621 P. Camerarius (J. Molle) *Living
Librarie* K4: (As Ulpian the lawyer
saith) Teares are womens weapons.
Shakespeare: *Lr* 2.4.277f.

(?) T85.1 I cannot TELL (i.e., I
don't know what to think or say) (Cf.

OED 7b *Can tell* from c1370; cf. Appendix B)
E.g., 1598 (1601) Jonson *Every Man In* 4.2.124. 1601 (1607) Marston *What You Will* II II,250. 1601 (1602) Jonson *Poetaster* 3.1.50, 3.4.37. c1602 (1608) Middleton *Family of Love* 5.3.101. 1605 Jonson et al. *Eastward Ho* 1.1.42. c1605 (1606) Marston *Fawn* 3.1.160. 1606 (1607) *Puritan* 1.2.15.

Shakespeare: *R3* 1.3.69, *2H4* 1.2.168, *H5* 2.1.20, 25

T88   When? Can you TELL? (From ?c1588; OW882b from 1590)
Cf. c1552 (c1567) Udall *Ralph Roister Doister* 1.2.72: We shall then get you a wyfe I can not tell whan! c1570 *Misogonus* 3.2.5: I had not worse lucke of a day, I can not tell whan.

Shakespeare: *Err* 3.1.39, 52, *1H4* 2.1.39, *Tit.* 1.1.202

T89   So you TOLD me (I heard you say) (From *LLL*, 1606; OW828a *heard you say* from 1497)
Shakespeare: *LLL* 1.2.142

T90a   He can tell TEN (the fingers in his hand) (*Ten* c1609, *fingers* 1666 TOR.; not in OW)
Add: 1622 Fletcher & Massinger *Spanish Curate* 4.7.58f.: This silly thing knows nothing, Cannot tell ten.

Shakespeare: *TNK* 3.5.79

(?) T91.1   To be the TENTH worthy (muse)[n]
c1552 (c1567) Udall *Ralph Roister Doister* 1.2.126: No, it is the tenth Worthie. 1594 Drayton "Amour. 8" 13f. *Ideas Mirrour*; My Muse, my Worthy, and my Angel then, Makes every one of these three nines a ten.

Shakespeare: *Son.* 38.9

[n]Cf. Janet Scott, *Les sonnets élisabethains* (1929), pp. 146f.

T98.1   THEN was then and now is now (OW582bf., from 1530)
Shakespeare: *AYL* 3.4.30

T112   The THIEF does fear each bush an officer (*Varied* from 1583; OW810a adds 1563; entry form *3H6*)
Shakespeare: *3H6* 5.6.12, *1H4* 2.2.105−7, *Luc.* 997

T119   The great THIEVES hang the little ones (punish the less) (Shak., then from 1611; Wh T68 *varied* from a1387)
E.g., c1523 Barclay *Mirrour* 34(8−14): What difference betwene a great thiefe and a small. . . . The small thiefe is judged, oft time the great is Judge.

Shakespeare: *MM* 2.1.19−23, 2.2.175f., *1H4* 1.2.62−5, *Lr.*4.6.151ff.

T119.1   One true man is too hard for two THIEVES
1589 Lyly *Pappe with an Hatchet* III,407: Three honest men shall bee able to beate six theeves. 1592 Nashe *Strange Newes* I,298: One true man is stronger than two theeves. 1602 F. Marbury *Sermon* 13 June E7[v]: Usuall saying . . . one true man is too hard for two theeves.

Shakespeare: *1H4* 2.2.93

(?) T121a   THIEVES are never rogues among themselves (c1703, with *1H4*, c1629 analogues; OW382a takes all but *1H4* to begin "There is honour among thieves")
E.g. c1629 ?J. Clavell *Soddered Citizen* 1.4 16: I doe believe thee. . . . Theeves have betweene themselves, a truth, And faith which they keepe firme.

Shakespeare: *1H4* 2.2.27f.

T127   For a lost THING care not (*Varied* from 1484; Wh T160 from 1438)
Add e.g.: 1579 Petrarch (T. Twyne) *Phisicke against Fortune* 2K3[v]: Admit

death be evyll, whiche the learned denye, truely no man wyl denie but that weepyng is in vayne, for that whiche cannot be recovered.
Shakespeare: *R3* 2.2.11
Cf. G453: Never grieve for that you cannot help.

T138 It is an easy THING to find a staff to beat a dog (*Varied* from 1564; OW769b supplements)
Shakespeare: *2H6* 3.1.171

T141.1 Merry it is to look on (one's) own THING (Wh T139 *varied* from c1350)
E.g., c1350 *Good Wife E* 162.63: Mirie is oune thing to loke (*H* kepe).
Shakespeare: *AYL* 5.4.57f.

T142 The more common a good THING is the better (From 1576; OW137b supplements)
Shakespeare: *AYL* 4.1.123f., *2H4* 1.2.214−6
Cf. T158: Too much of one THING is good for nothing.

T145 That THING which is rare is dear (From 1606; OW812a from 1597)
Add: 1578 J. Keltridge *Exposition, and Readynges* A4: It is a speech received commonly among men, that rare things, should be deare thinges.
c1609 (1647) ?Fletcher *Wit at Several Weapons* 2.1 IX,91: Rare things are pleasing.
Shakespeare: *1H4* 1.2.207, *Lr.* 1.1.57

(?) T147 There is no new THING under the sun (Eccl. 1.9; 1596, 1662 [According to Solomon], cf. *Son.*; Wh T146 c1395 WBible; OW580b adds Chaucer analogue [Wh G494 (3)])
Shakespeare: *Son.* 59.1

T149 The THING done has an end (is not to do) (*To do* 1641 FERG., *end* 1666 TOR., cf. *Mac.*; ditto OW811b)

Add: c1380 Chaucer *HF* 361: But that is don, is not to done [in Wh D287].
Shakespeare: *Mac.* 1.7.1

T158 Too much of one THING is good for nothing (is naught) (From c1500; Wh M793 from a1440)
Add: 1611 COT. s.v. Manger: A man may take too much of a good thing [in T142].
Shakespeare: *AYL* 4.1.123f., *2H4* 1.2.214−6

T165 All THINGS are (To be) turned topsy-turvy (upside down) (From 1528, 1523)
Shakespeare: *1H4* 2.1.10, 4.1.82

T188 Little THINGS are pretty (From 1539)
Shakespeare: *LLL* 1.2.21, *R3* 4.1.100

T199 THINGS are not as they seem (*Varied* from 1573)
Shakespeare: *Luc.* 600f.

T200 THINGS done cannot be un-done (From 1539; Wh D287 *varied* from a1300)
Shakespeare: *Wiv.* (Q) 5.5.144, *R3* 4.4.291, *Tit.* 4.2.73f., *JC* 4.2.8f., *Mac.* 1.7.1, 3.2.12, 5.1.68, *Per.* 4.3.1

T202 THINGS must be as they may (From c1590 [1595])
Shakespeare: *H5* 2.1.6f., 20, 22f., 125f.; *Per.* 2.1.113
Cf. B65: Be as be may (is no banning).

T216 When THINGS are at the worst they will mend (*Varied* from 1582)
Shakespeare: *Lr.* 4.1.6, *Mac.* 4.2.24f.

T220 One may THINK that dares not speak (Collections from 1616, cf. *Mac.*; ditto OW812b)
Shakespeare: *Mac.* 5.1.79

T221   They that THINK none ill are soonest beguiled (They that do no harm suspect none) (1546, *varied* from 1590)
  Shakespeare: *Ham.* 4.7.134−6, *Oth.* 1.3.399f., *Lr.* 1.2.179−81

(?) T221.1   THINK what you will
a1456 *Passe forth* clxxii(3): Thenke what thou wilt, but speke ay with the leeste [Wh T205]. 1611: Speak fair and think what you will [S720; proverb collections from 1611].
  Shakespeare: *MND* 5.1.195, *R2* 2.1.209
  Cf. T27: Take it as you will (list, please) [from 1580; OW799a from a1530].

T225   I had THOUGHT to (have) ask(ed) you (*Err.*, c1589 [1594])[n]
I.e., c1589 (1594) Lyly *Mother Bombie* 2.3.64 (Silena): I had thought to aske you.
  Shakespeare: *Err.* 3.1.55

[n]Cf. Appendix A, p. 43.

T230   As sharp as a THORN (From c1485; Wh T221 from c1350)
  Shakespeare: *R2* 4.1.323

T232   It early pricks (It pricks betimes) that will be a THORN (From 1523)
  Shakespeare: *3H6* 5.5.13, *Rom.* 1.4.25f.

T239   To sit (stand) upon THORNS (*Sit* from 1529, *stand* from 1540)
  Shakespeare: *WT* 4.4.585, *Son.* 99.8

T240   As swift as THOUGHT (From 1594; Wh T233 from c1200)
  Shakespeare: *LLL* 4.3.327, 5.2.261, *MV* 3.4.52, *AYL* 4.1.142, *Tro.* 4.2.14, *Jn.* 4.2.175, *2H4* 4.3.34, *H5* 3 Chorus 1−3, 5 Chorus 15, *Rom.* 2.5.4f., *Ant.* 4.6.34, *WT* 4.4.544, *Luc.* 1216, *Son.* 44.7f. *Upon a thought*: *Mac.* 3.4.54. *With a thought*: *1H4*

2.4.217, *JC* 5.3.19, *Ant.* 4.14.9, *Tmp.* 4.1.164

T244   THOUGHT is free (From c1475)
  Shakespeare: *TN* 1.3.69, *MM* 5.1.453, *R3* 2.1.105f., *Oth.* 3.3.135f., *Tmp.* 3.2.123

(?) T248.1   A THOUSAND POUND (hyperbolically)
E.g., 1537 (c1561) ?N. Udall *Thersites* D2: Styre not ones for a thousande pounde. c1570 *Misogonus* 2.1.3: A thousand pounde I had rather have lost by this day. 1599 (1600) Dekker *Shoemakers' Holiday* 3.3.19f.: I had rather then a thousand pound, I had an heart but halfe so light as yours. 1599 (1600) Drayton et al. *1 Sir John Oldcastle* 4.4.52: No, not to hurt you for a thousand pound.
  Shakespeare: *Wiv.* 3.3.123f., *Ado* 1.1.90, 3.5.24f., *2H6* 3.3.13, *1H4* 2.4.147f., *Ham.* 3.2.286f.

T249   His THREAD is spun (From 1590; OW815b from 1584)
  Shakespeare: *2H6* 4.2.29
  Cf. Appendix B: The THREAD of life.

T250   It hangs (To hang) by a THREAD (hair) (*Hair* from 1581; *thread* Wh T244 from a1396; OW343b supplements, including *Jn.*)
  Shakespeare: *Jn.* 5.7.53f.

T257   THREE (two) may keep counsel if two (one) be away (*Three* from 1546, *two* from 1579)
  Shakespeare: *Rom.* 2.4.197
  Cf. T642.1: TWO may keep counsel if the third be away.

T259   To stumble at the THRESHOLD (fig.)[n] (From *3H6*)
  Shakespeare: *LLL* 3.1.117, *3H6* 4.7.11f.

[n]Cf. Introduction, p. xvif.

T264 First THRIVE and then wive (1639 Clarke, *Shr.*; OW263a *varied* from 1577)
Shakespeare: *Shr.* 1.2.56, *Per.* 5.2.9f.

T267.1 To cut one's own THROAT (with one's own knife) (fig.) (OW163b *varied* from 1583)
Add: 1587 Holinshed ed. Bullough III,395: Such an unadvised capteine, as with a leden sword would cut his owne throat.
Shakespeare: *R3* 1.3.243

T268 To lie in one's THROAT (From 1590; OW460a from 1576)
Cf. 1533 J. Heywood *Johan Johan* 657: Thou liest . . . evyn to thy face. 1553 ?Udall *Respublica* 651: You liest valsely in your heart!
Shakespeare: *Shr.* 4.3.132, *LLL* 4.3.11f., *TN* 3.4.156f., *R3* 1.2.93, *R2* 1.1.125, *2H4* 1.2.82, 85, *H5* 2.1.47−9, 4.8.16, *Ham.* 2.2.574, *Oth.* 3.4.13, 5.2.156, *Mac.* 2.3.37f., *Per.* 2.5.55f.

(?) T268.1 To roar (etc.) with a wide THROAT (Cf. Appendix B)
1553 ?Udall *Respublica* 845: And against us all four with a wide throat doth he roar; 1194: Doth it become thee to bark with such a wide throat? c1554 (1568) *Jacob and Esau* 1.2 (MSR 130f.): Then maketh he . . . with his wyde throate such shouting and hallowing.
Shakespeare: *MM* 2.4.153

T275 After THUNDER (wind) comes rain (*Wind* from 1548, *thunder* from c1550 [Wh T267 from c1395])
Shakespeare: *1H6* 3.2.59, *3H6* 1.4.145f., 2.5.85f., *Luc.* 1788−90

T275.1 As dreadful as THUNDER
c1408 Lydgate *Reson* 144.5486: More dredful than stroke of thunder [in Wh T266]. c1604 (1607) Dekker & Webster *Sir Thomas Wyatt* 4.1.69: As loud though not so full of dread

as thunder. c1610 (1613) Marston & Barksted *Insatiate Countess* III III,51: Revenge in woman fals like dreadful thunder.
Shakespeare: *Mac.* 4.1.85f.

(?) T276.1 THUNDER looses beds of eels (*Varied*)
1598 Marston *Scourge of Villanie* VII.78−80: They are naught but Eeles, that never will appeare, Till that tempestuous winds or thunder teare Their slimie beds. 1613 G. Wither *Abuses* ed. 1863 168: Let loose, like beds of eels by thunder. c1620 (1647) Fletcher & Massinger, *False One* 4.2.200f.: I'll break like thunder Amongst these beds of slimy Eeeles.
Shakespeare: *Per.* 4.2.142f.

T276.2 To din (etc.) like THUNDER (Wh T271 from a1300)
E.g., c1400 *Sowdone* 35.1207: He smote as doth the dinte of thondir.
Shakespeare: *R2* 1.3.80f.

(?) T281.1 To play TICK-TACK (fig.) (Cf. Appendix B)
c1550 (c1565) R. Wever *Lusty Juventus* 827: You will to tick tack. c1589 (1594) Lyly *Mother Bombie* 5.3.64−6: At laugh and lie downe [L92], if they play, What Asse against the sport can bray? Such Tick-tacke has held many a day.
Shakespeare: *MM* 1.2.189−91

T283 The TIDE must be taken when it comes (1559, cf. *JC*; ditto OW821b)
I.e., 1559 Cooper s.v. Occasio: Occasio praemenda, a proverbe, when the sunne shinneth make hay: the tide muste be taken when it commeth.
Shakespeare: *JC* 4.3.218−24

T287.1 As fierce as TIGER(S) (Wh T287 from a1449 [2])
Shakespeare: *Rom.* 5.3.38f., *TNK* 5.1.40

T287.2   As swift as a TIGER (Wh T288 c1408)
   Shakespeare: *Cor.* 3.1.310f., *TNK* 5.1.40f.

T287.3   To be like a TIGER (Wh T292 from a1420)[n]
   Shakespeare: *H5* 3.1.6

[n]Whiting's 14 entries for the cruel, eager, fell, fierce (etc.) tiger contrast with the total silence in both Tilley and OW.

T289   To wash a TILE (wall of loam) (From 1548, *loam* a1600; OW822a supplements)
   Shakespeare: *TNK* 3.5.40

(?) T290   He does not desire to die before his TIME (Cf. *1H4*, 1640) I.e., [ERAS. Adagia 104C: Qui mori nolit ante tempus.] ?1596 (1640) Jonson *Tale of a Tub* 4.6.50–2: Come, goe with me: Ile lead. Why stand'st thou man? / Cocks pretious Master, you are not mad indeed? You will not goe to hell before your time?
   Shakespeare: *1H4* 5.1.127f.
   Cf. H741.1: One dies when his hour comes.

T291   He is wise that is ware (wary) (in TIME) (*Varied* from a1536; OW902 from 1303)
   E.g., 1303 R. Brunne *Handl. Synne* 8085: He wys is, that ware ys.
   Shakespeare: *Wiv.* 2.3.10f.

T301   In TIME of prosperity friends will be plenty, in time of adversity not one among twenty (From 1659; analogues from c1500; OW650b supplements)
   Shakespeare: *Ham.* 3.2.207–9, *WT* 4.4.573–5

T303   In TIME the ox (bull) will bear the yoke (*Varied* from 1557; OW402b adds Ovid)
   E.g., 1582 T. Watson *Hekatompathia*

47: In time the Bull is brought to weare the yoake. c1587 (c1592) Kyd *Spanish Tragedy* 2.1.3: In time the savage Bull sustaines the yoake.
   Shakespeare: *Ado* 1.1.261

T305.1   It is TIME to look about
   E.g., c1560 (c1570) W. Wager *Enough is as Good as a Feast* 883: Passion of me, it was time to look about. 1575 Gascoigne "Flowers" I,67: I thought highe time about me for to looke. c1593 (?1594) Marlowe *Massacre at Paris* xx.72: Nay, then 'tis time to look about. 1616 DR. s.v. Warning 2352: It is time to looke about him.
   Shakespeare: *Lr.* 4.7.91f.
   Cf. L427.1: Look (well) about you.

T307.1   It is TIME to trudge (Cf. Appendix B)
   c1560 (c1570) W. Wager *Enough is as Good as a Feast* 329: By gis (quoth Saint Stephen) it was time to trudge. 1623 (1647) Fletcher & Massinger *Lovers' Progress* I V,86: Nay, if you fall to fainting, 'Tis time for me to trudge.
   Shakespeare: *Err.* 3.2.153

(?) T308.1   Keep TIME in all[n]
   1599 (1600) Jonson *Every Man Out* 4.3.107f.: Tut, a man must keepe time in all.
   Shakespeare: *Oth.* 4.1.92

[n]*OED Time* 50 *To keep time: Mus.* begins with Jonson's *Cynthia's Revels* but records no figurative use until the 19th century.

T308.2   Let TIME try
   1546 Heywood *Dialogue* II.v H4 (followed by T338): Let tyme trie.
   Shakespeare: *AYL* 4.1.200
   Cf. T338: Time tries the truth.

T311   Take TIME (occasion) by the forelock, for she is bald behind (*Varied* from 1539)
   Shakespeare: *Err.* 2.2.69f., 106,

Ado 1.2.14f., *AWW* 5.3.39, *Jn.* 3.1.324, *Oth.* 3.1.49

T312 Take TIME when time comes (while time serves) (*Varied* from c1535; OW825a supplements)
Shakespeare: *AYL* 5.3.30, *3H6* 5.1.48, *Ant.* 2.6.23, *Tmp.* 2.1.301f.

T314 There is a TIME for all things (Everything has its time) (Cf. Eccl. 3.1; from 1508)
Shakespeare: *Err.* 2.2.65

T319 The third TIME pays for all (pays home, throws best) (From 1574; OW813b from 1350)
Shakespeare: *Wiv.* 5.1.2, *TN* 5.1.37

T322 TIME (and thought) tame the strongest grief (*Varied* from 1539; OW824b Terence, Chaucer)
E.g., 1539 TAV. 38: Tyme taketh away grevaunce.
Shakespeare: *TGV* 3.2.14f.

T323 TIME and tide (The tide) (Wind and tide) tarries (stays for) no man (*Tide* from c1500; *Time and tide* OW822b from 1592, *Wind and tide* OW821b from 1589)
Shakespeare: *Err.* 4.1.46, *TGV* 2.2.14, 2.3.35f., *JC* 4.3.218–24

T324 TIME brings the truth to light (*Varied* from 1530)
Shakespeare: *MM* 5.1.116f., *2H6* 3.1.65, *Oth.* 3.3.245, *Lr.* 1.1.280, *Cym.* 4.3.45, *Luc.* 939f.
Cf. T333: Time reveals (discloses) all things [OW823a combines].

T326 TIME devours (consumes, wears out) all things (*Devour* from *LLL*; OW823a from 1559)
Add: 1559 "Thomas, Earl of Salisbury" 1-3 *Mirror for Magistrates* 143: What fooles be we to trust unto our strength, Our wit, our courage, or our noble fame, Which time it selfe must nedes devour at length.

Shakespeare: *LLL* 1.1.4, *TNK* 1.1.69f., *Son.* 19.1
Cf. D138.1: Death devours all things.

T327 TIME flees away without delay (has wings) (*Varied* from 1589; OW823b from c1386)
E.g., 1613 Drayton *Poly-Olb.* X.322 209: Wing-footed Time them farther off doth beare.
Shakespeare: *AYL* 3.2.306, *Son.* 19.6

T332 TIME lost (past) we cannot win (recall) (*Varied* from c1509; Wh T307 from c1380)
E.g., a1449 Lydgate *Evil Marriage* in *MP* II 456 (var.): Take hede and lerne, thou lytell chylde, and se That tyme passed wyl not agayne retourne.
Shakespeare: *R2* 3.2.69

(?) T332.1 The TIME of life is short c1595 Munday et al. *Sir Thomas More* 5.4.89: You see, my lord, the time of life is short.
Shakespeare: *1H4* 5.2.81, *H5* 4.5.23

T332.2 TIME out of mind (OW824b, from 1414)
Shakespeare: *MM* 4.2.15f., *Rom.* 1.4.61

T334.1 TIME steals (passes, goes, flies) (Cf. Appendix B) (Wh T325; *steal* from c1390)
Shakespeare: *Err.* 4.2.60
Cf. A70: Old AGE comes stealing on.

T336 TIME tries all things (From 1553)
Shakespeare: *Ado* 1.1.260, *AYL* 4.1.199f., *Tro.* 4.5.225f., *3H6* 3.3.77, *WT* 4.1.1

T340 TIME wears away love (fancies) (*Varied* from 1580)

Shakespeare: *Ham.* 4.7.111−3, *Cym.* 2.3.42−4

T340.1 To beguile the TIME (Cf. *OED Beguile* 5)
c1589 (1592) Lyly *Midas* 2.1.126: With talk we may beguyle the time.
Shakespeare: *MND* 5.1.40f., *.TN* 3.3.41, *AWW* 4.1.22, *Mac.* 1.5.63

T340.2 To obey the TIME (Cf. Appendix B)
1623 (1624) Massinger *Bondman* 1.3.19f. We must obey the time, and our occasions. 1626 (1629) Massinger, *Roman Actor* 1.1.113f.: I will obey the time, it is in vaine To strive against the torrent.
Shakespeare: *Oth.* 1.3.300, *Lr.* 5.3.324

T340.3 To redeem the TIME (*OED Redeem* 8 from 1526)[n]
c1550 (c1565) R. Wever *Lusty Juventus* (MSR 98f.): Walke circumspectly, redemyng the tyme, That is to spend it well. c1570 *Misogonus* 1.1.139f. (of worse-than-Hal Misogonus): But what . . . If yet I can make him the tyme to redeme? 1587 J. Chardon *Second Sermon* B7f.: If wee knewe when Death . . . woulde come, we would redeeme the time. We would amend all that is amisse. c1590 (1596) *Edward III* 3.2.16−9: I, so the Grashopper doth spend the time In mirthfull iollitie, till winter come; And then too late he would redeeme his time, When frozen cold hath nipt his carelesse head. c1602 *Fair Maid of the Exchange* xiii (MSR 2489f.): So I my time ill spent Meane to redeeme with frugall industry.
Shakespeare: *1H4* 1.2.216f.

[n]Since *OED* includes, prior to the 18th century, only Tyndale's translation of Col. 4.5 and Prince Hal's famous promise, and since Hal's meaning has been debated, I did not relegate this phrase to Appendix B. But I have included only a few examples where

the sense appears tolerablv clear. Cf. Paul Jorgensen, " 'Redeeming Time' in Shakespeare's *Henry IV*" *Tennessee Studies in Literature*, 5 (1960), 101−9.

(?) T340.4 When TIME and place serve (Cf. Appendix B)
1581 Guazzo (Pettie) *Civile Conversation* I I,31: You can not name mee any Philosopher . . . who, when time and place served, had not conversation.
Shakespeare: *Ado* 5.1.255f.

T341.1 When TIME was (i.e., once upon a time) (Cf. Appendix B)
a1598 (1639) Deloney *2 Gentle Craft* 148: Might I have had my owne hearts desire when time was, I would rather have chosen to lye with a man. c1613 (1616) Beaumont & Fletcher *Scornful Lady* 3.2.151f.: I was cosen'd when time was, we are quit Sir.
Shakespeare: *Tmp.* 2.2.139

T343 TIMES change and we with them (1666 TOR., Latin 1598; OW825b *varied* from 1579; Wh T299 1484)
E.g., 1484 Caxton *Esope* II.viii f6: Men say comynly[n] that after that the tyme goth so must folke go. 1579 Lyly *Euphues* I,276: The tymes are chaunged as Ovid sayeth, and wee are chaunged in the times.
Shakespeare: *Lr.* 5.3.30f., *Mac.* 4.3.235

[n]The 1889 reprint used by Whiting mistakenly reads *conynly*.

T343.1 Were he ten TIMES my father (etc.)
c1570 *Misogonus* 2.5.10: And he were my father ten tymes, heist have as good as a bringe [G122]. ?1596 (1640) Jonson *Tale of a Tub* 4.6.34f.: Sir, an' you were my Master ten times over . . . you shall pardon me [for disobeying]. 1602 ?T. Heywood *How a Man May Choose* 479f.: Then if you were my Father twentie times,

You shall not chuse but let me be my selfe. c1604 (c1607) Chapman *Bussy D'Ambois* 4.1.225f.: I will defy him, Were he ten times the brother of the King.
Shakespeare: *Ham.* 3.2.333f.
Cf. Appendix B: TEN times.

T347 A TINKER stops one hole and makes two (three) (*Varied* from c1576; OW826a adds 1564)
Shakespeare: *TNK* 3.5.82f.

T352a Tip for tap (From 1575; cf. OW826b)
Shakespeare: *2H4* 2.1.193
Cf. T356: Tit for tat [from 1546].

T361 To hate one like a TOAD (*Varied* from 1550; OW827a from 1548)
Shakespeare: *Tit.* 4.2.67, *Rom.* 2.4.203, 3.5.31

T363 As hot as a TOAST (fig.) (From a1529)
E.g., 1573 G. Harvey *Let. Bk.* 51: He that not ful two howers before, in the hale, had bene as whot as a tost against me.
Shakespeare: *2H4* 2.4.56f.

T384 He has lost his TONGUE (From 1639, cf. 1616)
I.e., 1616 Withals 562: He hath left his tongue at home. 1639 CL. s.v. Taciturnitas 302.
Shakespeare: *TN* 2.2.20

T389 His TONGUE is no slander (From c1599; OW829b supplements, including *TN*)
Shakespeare: *TN* 1.5.94
Cf. P595.2: To be a privileged man.

T400.1 To bite one's TONGUE (fig.) (*OED Bite* 16 *2H6* only)
c1593 (1597) Lyly *Woman in the Moon* 4.1.129: Ile make them bite their tongues and eate their wordes.
Shakespeare: *2H6* 1.1.230, *3H6* 1.4.47

T400.2 To file one's TONGUE (Cf. Appendix B) (Wh T378 from c1385)
Shakespeare: *LLL* 5.1.10

T401.1 To have a TONGUE like a razor (*Varied*)
1340 Ayenbite 66 (10f.): The tonge more kervinde thanne rasour [in Wh R51]. c1400 *Vices and Virtues* 64.2f.: Than ben here tonges scharper than any rasours [in Wh R53]. 1484 Caxton *Royal Book* F7^v (23f.): Tongues more cuttyng than a rasour [in Wh R51]. 1598 Meres *Palladis Tamia* Z5^v: An il tongue is compared to a sharp rasor.
Shakespeare: *LLL* 5.2.256f.
Cf. R36: As sharp as a razor; W839: Words hurt (cut) more than swords.

T402 To keep a good TONGUE in one's head (From *MV*; OW829b from 1542)
Add: 1595 O. Oat-meale *Quest of Enquirie* A3: Keep a good tung in your head, least it hurt your teeth.
Shakespeare: *MV* 2.2.156f., *Tmp.* 3.2.35, 112

T402.1 TONGUE and heart (Variously contrasted) (Wh T383 from a900)
Shakespeare: *MM* 1.4.33

T413 To have it at one's TONGUE'S end (From 1607; OW830b from 1539)
Shakespeare: *LLL* 3.1.11f.

T414.1 To have two TONGUES (Wh T381 from c1395; cf. 1 Tim. 3.8)
Add: c1598 (1639) Deloney *2 Gentle Craft* 164: Griefe hath two tongues, to say and to unsay.
Shakespeare: *Ado* 5.1.169f., *MM* 2.4.139, 172–4
Cf. Appendix B: DOUBLE-TONGUE.

(?) T416 To be TONGUE-TIED
(Cf. Appendix B; *OED* from 1529)
(From 1546 Heywood)
  Shakespeare: *MND* 5.1.104, *Tro.*
3.2.210, *1H6* 2.4.25, *3H6* 3.3.22, *R3*
3.7.145, 4.4.132, *JC* 1.1.62, *WT*
1.2.27, *Son.* 66.9, 85.1, 140.2

T420 To have a sweet TOOTH
(*Varied* from 1580; Wh T409 a1393)
  Shakespeare: *TGV* 3.1.327 *Tro.*
4.5.293, *AWW* 2.3.41f., *Jn.* 1.1.213

T423 From the TEETH outwards
(From c1550; OW806af. supple-
ments)
  Shakespeare: *Ant.* 3.4.10

T424 Good that the TEETH guard
the tongue (*Varied* from 1578;
OW806b from 1572)
  Shakespeare: *MM* 3.2.134f., *R2*
1.3.166f.

T424.1 I will pick your TEETH (A
threat)
  1578 G. Whetstone *1 Promos and Cassandra* 5.5: I'fayth Barber, I wyll
pyck your teeth straight [as he hap-
pens literally to do later in the scene].
1596 (1605) *Captain Thomas Stukeley*
x (MSR 1165−8) (duelling): Sir your
teeth bleeds this picktooth is to
keene, *Drum soundeth and a Bag-
pipe.* / Hark the enemies charges we
must to the walles, another time ile
pick your teeth as well.
  Shakespeare: *Lr.* 4.6.244

T429 To cast (hit) in the TEETH
(fig.) (From 1540)
  Shakespeare: *Err.* 2.2.22, *2H4*
5.3.92, *H5* 2.1.47−9, *JC* 4.3.99,
5.1.64, *Oth.* 3.4.184
  Cf. Appendix B: To the (one's)
TEETH.

T430.1 To laugh (smile) to show
one's TEETH (*Varied*)
  1581 Guazzo (Pettie) *Civile Conversation* II I,158: Some . . . by their
continuall girning and shewing of

their teethe make men doubt
whether they honour them, or laugh
at them. c1589 (1594) Lyly *Mother
Bombie* 2.3.58f.: Why laugh
you? / [*Silena*] Because you should
see my teeth. 1609 W. Fiston *Schoole
of good Manners* B7ᵛ: Some laugh so
unreasonably, that therewith they
set out their Teeth like grinning
Dogges. 1612 Webster *White Devil*
3.3.81−3: What a strange creature is
a laughing foole, As if man were
created to no use But onely to shew
his teeth. 1615 (1622) J. Abernethy
Christian and Heavenly Treatise 2C8
(among the "Signes and Symptoms"
of pride): He will laugh of purpose
with Ignatius, to show his white
teeth. 1735 Franklin 10: Sal laughs at
every thing you say. Why? Because
she has fine teeth [With *LLL* this con-
stitutes T428: She smiles on everyone to show her fine teeth].
  Shakespeare: *LLL* 5.2.331f.

T431 To set one's TEETH on edge
(From 1532; cf. Jer. 31.29, Ezek.
18.2)
  Shakespeare: *1H4* 3.1.131, *WT*
4.3.7

T436 From TOP (head) to toe (heel)
(*Top* from 1489 [Wh T421 from
c1200]; *head* from 1562 [Wh H215
from c1400])
  Shakespeare: *Tro.* 2.1.27, *R3*
3.1.156, *Cor.* 2.2.108, *WT* 4.4.227

T436.1 To be armed from TOP to
toe (cap-à-pie) (From 1489 [in
T436]; *cap-à-pie OED* from 1523)
  Shakespeare: *Ham.* 1.2.200, 227f.,
Cym. 1.6.19

T439 To be whipped like a TOP
(From ?1596 [1640]; OW609b from
c1580 [1590])
  Shakespeare: *TNK* 5.2.50
  Cf. P57: Like a parish top.

T440 To sleep like a TOP (*TNK*,

1693, *Town-Top* 1666 TOR.; ditto
OW741b)
Shakespeare: *TNK* 3.4.26

T443 A TORCH turned downward
is extinguished by its own wax (*Varied* from 1580)
Add:1607 de Serres-Matthieu
(Grimeston) *General Inventorie* 969:
These two Noblemen were like unto
two Torches, which beeing held
downward are quenched with the
Waxe which did nourish and give
them light.
Shakespeare: *Per.* 2.2.32f.

T455.1 The TOWN'S no grange
1639 CL., s.v. Solitudo 291: The
town's no Grange.
Shakespeare: *Oth.* 1.1.105f.

T456.1 To have a TOY(S) in one's
head
E.g., 1546 Heywood *Dialogue* II.vi
11: she hath founde suche knakx In
her bouget [K118], and such toies in
hir hed. c1560 (c1569) T. Ingeland
Disobedient Child C3: Such toyes in my
heade do ever swym; F3ᵛ (Satan): I
have such fetches, such toyes in this
head. 1585 ?Munday *Fedele and Fortunio* 71 (like 70's "some strawes were
in the pad" for "pads in the straw"):
But now have at her again, with a
fresh hed in my toy. c1604 (1605)
Chapman *All Fools* 3.1.78f.: Ile tell
you what a sudden toy Comes in my
head; 202f.: These will put such idle
toyes out of their heads into yours;
228f.: What are they, but meere
imaginary toyes, bred out of your
owne heads?
Shakespeare: *WT* 4.4.319

T476 A TRAVELER may lie with
authority (*Varied* from a1521;
OW836b from c1362)
E.g., c1592 (1594) Marlowe *Edward
II* 1.1.28–31: What art thou? / A
traveler. / Let me see—thou wouldst
do well To wait at my trencher and
tell me lies at dinner time.

Shakespeare: *AWW* 2.5.28–31,
Tmp. 3.3.26f.

T497 The TREE (fruit) is known by
the fruit (tree) (fig.) (Cf. Matt. 12.33;
from c1561; Wh T465, 472 from
c1000)
Shakespeare: *1H4* 2.4.428f.

T509 The highest TREES abide the
sharpest storms (winds) (fig.) (*Varied*
from 1557)
Add e.g.: 1588 M. Kyffin *Blessednes
of Brytaine* B3: As Highest Hils, bide
fiercest force of Weather And Tall
Trees tops, beare greatest stresse of
Winde.
Shakespeare: *R3* 1.3.258

T515 A good (etc.) TRENCHER-
MAN (Cf. Appendix B) (From *Ado*;
OW838b from 1590)
E.g., 1629 Shirley *Wedding* 1.1 368:
Oh, he is reported a good trencher-
man, he has a tall stomach. 1673
D'Avenant *Law agst. Lovers* I 119: He
is a valiant trencher-man, and has a
good stomach.
Shakespeare: *Ado* 1.1.51f.

T517 In a TRICE (Cf. Appendix B)
(From 1503; Wh T479 from a1425;
OW excludes)
Shakespeare: *TN* 4.2.123, *Lr.*
1.1.216, *Cym.* 5.4.167, *Tmp.* 5.1.238,
TNK 3.4.17

T518 I know a TRICK worth two
(etc.) of that (From *1H4*; ditto
OW839a)
Cf. a1400 *King Edward* 964.420: I
con a game worthe thei twoo [Wh
G24].
Shakespeare: *1H4* 2.1.36f.

T518.1 To teach one a TRICK
c1589 (1594) Lyly *Mother Bombie*
2.3.5f.: Ile teach him one schoole
trick in love. 1598 (1601) Jonson
Every Man In 5.3.121f.: Sirha away
with him to the iayle, ile teach you a

tricke for your must. 1598 (1616) W. Haughton *Englishmen for my Money* ix (MSR 1714f.): We may chaunce teach him a strange tricke for his learning. 1607 G. Wilkins *Miseries of Enforced Marriage* xi (MSR 2542): Ile teach you tricks for this.
Shakespeare: *Shr.* 4.2.55–7

T521   Do not put TRICKS upon travelers (From 1709; both Tilley and OW657b cite *Tmp.*)
Shakespeare: *Tmp.* 2.2.57f.
Cf. Appendix B: To PUT a trick upon one.

T527.1   TROILUS   the   true   (Wh T483 from a1400)
Shakespeare: *Tro.* 3.2.182

T537   To catch one like a TROUT with tickling (Literal 1584, fig. from *TN*)
Add: c1599 (1602) Marston *Antonio and Mellida* 2.1.107: Fut, how he tickles yon trout under the gills! c1604 (1605) Chapman *All Fools* 3.1.119: A man may grope and tickle um like a Trowt.
Shakespeare: *TN* 2.5.22

T539   To lay it on with a TROWEL (From *AYL*; ditto OW448a)[n]
Shakespeare: *AYL* 1.2.106

[n]Cf. F. P. Wilson, "The Proverbial Wisdom of Shakespeare" (in *Shakespearian and Other Studies*, p. 154f.): "In the same dictionary [Richard Huloet's *Abcedarium* of 1552] I find (under 'Trowell') '*thrullisco,as,ang.* to laye on wyth a trowell'. Here is a phrase which, as I have always thought, Shakespeare himself made proverbial. I still think so; for whereas Huloet is strictly literal, Shakespeare's Celia applies the expression ironically and metaphorically to Touchstone's fine language, so making it possible for us to apply it to any excess whether of style or manners."

T546   To sound one's own TRUMPET (*Varied* from 1576; OW70a from 1560)
E.g., A. Fleming *Panopl. Epist.* 59: I will . . . sound the trumpet of my own merits.
Shakespeare: *Ado* 5.2.85f., *Tro.* 2.3.155

T549   In TRUST is treason (From c1475; Wh T492 from 1460, cf. Wh E97 from c1300)
Shakespeare: *Lr.* 1.4.328, *Tmp.* 1.2.93–5

T555   TRUST is the mother of deceit (From 1636 CAM., cf. *Tmp.*; OW842af. adds nonfigurative analogues from c1400; cf. T549)
Shakespeare: *Tmp.* 1.2.93–5

(?) T558.1   Never TRUST me if X.
E.g., c1520 Heywood *Four P's* 605: If ever ye be hanged, never trust me. c1570 *Misogonus* 3.1.200: And thast not for this tauk, ner trust me ill kivinge. 1578 T. Lupset *All for Money* 860: Never trust me again if I tell you not true. c1589 (1594) Lyly *Mother Bombie* 1.2.47: If I come not about you never trust mee. 1596 (1598) Chapman *Blind Beggar of Alexandria* vii.86: Oh excellent or never trust mee. 1598 (1601) Jonson *Every Man In* 1.4.37: Ne're trust me, if I was not proud.
Shakespeare: *Shr.*   5.2.17,   *MV* 2.2.197,   *Wiv.*   4.2.196f.,   *TN* 2.3.72–4, 188, 3.2.58, *Tro.* 5.2.59, *AWW*   3.6.32f.,   *1H6*   2.2.48,   *R2* 2.2.108–11, *WT* 5.2.170–2
Cf. Appendix B: HANG me if X.

(?) T559.1   (Welcome all but) trust none (*Varied*)
1579 Lyly *Euphues* I,186: Hee welcommed all, but trusted none. 1594 Nashe *Unfortunate Traveller* II,220: Hee must be familliar with all but trust none. 1604 Marston *Malcontent* 4.3.144: 'Tis good trust few: but, O, 'tis best trust none!

Shakespeare: *AWW* 1.1.64

Cf. T559: He who trusts not is not deceived [OW843a from 1597]; F741: Have but few friends though much acquaintance [collections from 1659, plus slight analogues].

T562   As TRUTH gets hatred so flattery wins love (friends) (From 1539)

Add: 1578 T. White *Sermon at Pawles Crosse* 3 Nov. 1577 3: An olde proverbe of proofe . . . Veritas odium parit, That Flatterie breedeth frendship, & Truthe bringeth hatred.
Shakespeare: *H5* 3.7.114f.

T565   It is as true as TRUTH itself (From c1565)
Shakespeare: *LLL* 4.1.63, *Tro.* 3.2.169f.

T566   Speak (etc.) the TRUTH and shame the devil (From 1548)
Shakespeare: *Wiv.* 4.2.114–9, *1H4* 3.1.58, 61

(?)   T567 They have neither TRUTH nor honesty in them (Cf. *1H4*, 1639 CL.)

I.e., 1639 CL. 128: He hath neither truth, nor honestie. Ibid. 248.
Shakespeare: *1H4* 3.3.153f.
Cf. F34: There is no faith (trust, honesty) in man.

T575   TRUTH (Plain dealing) has no need of rhetoric (figures) (*Varied* from a1597; OW843b from 1535)
Shakespeare: *LLL* 4.3.235
Cf. T585: Truth needs no colors.

T581   TRUTH is truth (From 1576)
Shakespeare: *LLL* 4.1.48, *AWW* 4.3.156, *MM* 5.1.45, *Jn.* 1.1.105, *1H4* 2.4.229f.

T583   TRUTH loves (fears no) trial (*Loves* 1639 CL., *fears no* 1732 FUL., cf. *R2*; OW844b *feareth no* 1581)
Shakespeare: *R2* 1.3.96

T585   TRUTH needs no colors (*Varied* from 1519)
Shakespeare: *LLL* 4.2.149f., *Son.* 101.6

T587   TRUTH seeks no corners (From 1564; Wh T512 1483)
Shakespeare: *H8* 3.1.30f., 39

T589   The TRUTH shows best being naked (*Varied* from 1579)

E.g., 1579 Lyly *Euphues* Ep. Ded. I,181: A naked tale doth most truely set foorth the naked truth. 1582 Lyly to Burleigh I, 28: He yᵗ is wis shall iudg trueth, whos nakednes shal manifest her noblenes. 1590 Lodge *Rosalynde* ed. Bullough II,236: In manie words lies mistrust, and . . . trueth is ever naked.
Shakespeare: *LLL* 5.2.710, *1H6* 2.4.20, *Tim.* 5.1.67, *Son.* 103.3f.
Cf. T561: As naked as truth [from 1601].

T590   The TRUTH, the whole truth, and nothing but the truth (From 1640, analogues from 1580; OW845a supplements)

E.g., 1580 Lyly *Euphues and his England* II,101: Speake no more then the trueth, utter no lesse. Add: 1601 A. Dent *Plaine Mans Path-Way* M5: For it is hard to finde a man that will speake the truth, the whole truth, and nothing but the truth.
Shakespeare: *1H4* 2.4.171, *Oth.* 2.3.219

T591   TRUTH will come to light (break out) (*Varied* from *MND*; Wh S491 from c1025, Wh T509 from a1393)

E.g., 1439 *St. Albon* 160.1915–7: Trouthe wyll out, magre fals envie, Ryghtwysenes may not be hyd, it is certayne, As for a tyme it may be overlayne.
Shakespeare: *MND* 5.2.128, *MV* 2.2.79f., *Oth.* 5.2.219

T593 TRUTH'S tale is simple (Truth is plain) (From 1539)
Add e.g.: 1590 M. Sutcliffe *Remonstrance* (STC 20881) A2ᵛ: Veritas est simplex, mendacium est multiplex, there is but one trueth.
Shakespeare: *Tro.* 3.2.169f., *R3* 4.4.358

T594 All TRUTHS must not be told (*Varied* from c1485; OW11b from c1350)
E.g., c1350 *Douce MS, 52* no. 57: Alle the Sothe is not to be sayde. 1509 Barclay *Ship Fools* II 325: At eche season: trouth ought nat to be sayde.
Shakespeare: *Ant.* 2.2.108

T595 Try (Try your friend) before you trust (From a1536, *friend varied* from 1580 [Wh F658 1450])
Shakespeare: *Ham.* 1.3.62−5

T598.1 Out of TUNE (fig.) (*OED* 3b 1579 below)
c1564 *Bugbears* 1.3.25: Your braines are owt of tune. 1579 Tomson *Calvin's Serm. Tim.* 280/2: How many occasions are there to bring us out of tune? 1588 R. Some *Godly Treatise* L1: Your note must be poena perfidiae, that is, that you are justly met with. Otherwise you sing out of tune.
Shakespeare: *TN* 2.3.113, *Ham.* 3.1.158 (F1), *Oth.* 5.2.115f.

T609 To turn TURK (Cf. Appendix B) (From *Ado*; OW848a from 1592)
Shakespeare: *Ado* 3.4.57, *Ham.* 3.2.276, *Oth.* 2.3.170

T612 He swells like a TURKEY COCK (*Varied* from *H5*; OW846a adds 1601)
Shakespeare: *TN* 2.5.30f., *H5* 5.1.14

T616 One good TURN asks (requires, deserves) another (From 1562; OW325b from c1400)
Shakespeare: *TN* 3.3.15−8, *MM*

4.2.58f., *Ham.* 4.6.20−2, *Ant.* 2.5.58, *Tim.* 3.2.60, *Son.* 24.9, 47.2

T624 As true as a TURTLE to her mate (*Varied* from c1520; Wh T542f. from c1000)
E.g., 1481 Caxton *Mirror* 102(25−8): Whan the Turtle hath lost her make whom she hath first knowen, never after wyl she have make, ne sytte upon grene tree, but fleeth emonge the [*for* dry] trees contynuelly bewayllyng her love. a1500 *Sen that Eine* 103.18−21: Evin as men may the turtill trew persaif Once having loist hir feir On the dry brainche ay faytfull to the graif Bewayling perseveir.
Shakespeare: *Tro.* 3.2.177f., *1H6* 2.2.30f., *WT* 4.4.154f., 5.3.132−5, *PP* 7.2

T632 Best to bend while it is a TWIG (fig.) (*Varied* from 1530)
Shakespeare: *Per.* 4.2.87f.

T635 In the TWINKLING (twink) (of an eye) (Cf. Appendix B) (1 Cor. 15.52; *twinkling* from 1549; Wh T547 *twink* from a1471)
Shakespeare: *Shr.* 2.1.310, *MV* 2.2.168, *Tmp.* 4.1.43

T638 If TWO ride upon a horse one must sit behind (c1640, cf. *Ado*)
I.e.,c1640 SMYTH 67 p. 32: (an horse). *That in each contention one must take the foile.
Shakespeare: *Ado* 3.5.36f.

T642.1 TWO may keep counsel if the third be away (but the third never) (T257 includes 1616 BRET., *Tit.*)
Add: 1558 W. Wedlocke *Image of Idlenesse* F1ᵛ: Common proverbe . . . two maye chaunce to kepe counsell, but yᵉ thred never. 1605 *Life and Death of Gamaliel Ratsey* B1: Two may keepe counsaile, if the third be away.
Shakespeare: *Tit.* 4.2.144

U

U15 Better be UNMANNERLY than troublesome (etc.) (*Disobedient* 1591, *ceremonious* 1599, *troublesome Wiv.*, collections from 1659)
Shakespeare: *Wiv.* 1.1.312f.

U22 Once a USE and ever a custom (*Varied* from 1565)
E.g., 1591 STEP. 152: Use bringeth a continuall custome.
Shakespeare: *TGV* 5.4.1

U24 USE (Usage, Practice) makes mastery (perfectness) (*Usage* from 1487 [Wh U8 from a1387], *use* from 1546 [Wh U8 from c1400], *practice* from 1611)
Shakespeare: *Mac.* 3.4.141f.

U25.1 To USE as one is used (*Varied*) (Cf. Appendix B)
c1597 (1609) Jonson *Case is Altered* 1.3.13: Your friend as you may use him. 1599 (1600) Dekker *Old Fortunatus* 5.2.18f.: As you use me, marke those words well, as you use me.
Shakespeare: *AWW* 1.1.214f., *2H4* 2.2.131f.

V

V16 He turns like a VANE on the housetop (with the wind) (c1475, *Ado*, 1616; Wh V5f. from c1385)
Shakespeare: *Ado* 3.1.66

V18 VARIETY takes away satiety (1639 CL., 1664 COD., cf. *Ant.*; OW858a analogues from 1539)
E.g., 1539 TAV. 12^v: Man is much delyted wyth varietie. 1599 Minsheu *Span. Dial.* 10: Others say varietie breedes delight. Add e.g.: 1542 T. Becon Preface to Bullinger (Coverdale) *Golden boke of christen matrimonye* A7^v: Shyft of meates is good [cf. M831]. Iucundum nihil est, nisi quod reficit varietas. 1592 ?Lyly *Ent. Quarrendon* I,460: Nature is delighted in nothing so muche as in varietie.
Shakespeare: *Ant.* 2.2.234f.

(?) V22 I will VEASE thee (Cf. Appendix B) (*Shr.*, 1678 Ray; OW858b from c890)
Shakespeare: *Shr.* Ind. i.1

(?) V25.1 May the stored VENGEANCES of heaven fall on one's head
c1609 (1647) Beaumont & Fletcher *Coxcomb* 1.1.22: Let all the stor'd vengeance of heaven's justice—.
Shakespeare: *Lr.* 2.4.162f.
Cf. V25: Vengeance (Divine vengeance) comes slowly but surely [*varied* from 1560]. Also Appendix B: A VENGEANCE on him.

V26 VENICE, he that does not see thee does not esteem thee (*Varied* from 1573)
Shakespeare: *LLL* 4.2.97–100

V28 He has spit his (To spit one's) VENOM (From 1546: OW766af. from c1200)
Shakespeare: *R3* 1.2.144f., *Per.* 3.1.7f.

V36 Empty VESSELS sound most (*Varied* from 1547)
Shakespeare: *2H4* 1.3.74f., 2.4.60f., *H5* 4.4.69, *Lr.* 1.1.153f.

V50 Do not triumph before the VICTORY (*Varied* from 1552)
Shakespeare: *AYL* 1.2.208f., *H5* 3.7

V52 It is a great VICTORY that comes without blood (Varied from *Ado*; OW860a from 1591)
E.g., c1593 Ovid (Marlowe) *Amores* II.xii.5f.: That victory doth chiefly triumph merit, Which without bloodshed doth the prey inherit.
Shakespeare: *Ado* 1.1.8f.

V60   The VINE brings forth three grapes: the first of pleasure, the second of drunkenness, the third of sorrow (From 1585; OW860b from 1539)
Shakespeare: *TN* 1.5.130−3

V61   The VINE embraces the elm (*Varied* from 1569)
Shakespeare: *Err.* 2.2.174, *MND* 4.1.43f.

V68   To nourish a VIPER (snake) in one's bosom (*Varied* from c1570; Wh A42 [Adder] from c1395)
Shakespeare: *2H6* 3.1.343f., *R2* 3.2.131, 5.3.57f., *Cor.* 3.1.262−4, 285

V73   Make a VIRTUE of necessity (From 1571; OW861b Quintilian, St. Jerome, Chaucer)
Shakespeare: *TGV* 4.1.60, *R2* 1.3.278

V74   Only VIRTUE (True fame) never dies (*Varied*; *true fame* from 1573; *virtue* from 1616)
Add: 1574 J. Higgins *Mirror for Magistrates* 204 (Finis): Vivit post funera virtus. 1580 A. Munday *Zelauto* I4ᵛ (ditto). 1587 "Sir Nicholas Burdet" 608 *Mirror for Magistrates* 482: Vivit (quoth I) post funera virtus.
Shakespeare: *LLL* 1.1.1−3, *Tit.* 1.1.390

V80   VIRTUE is found in the middle (mean) (From 1591; Wh V45 from c1400)
E.g., 1484 Caxton *Ordre of Chyvalry* 56.16−57.1: Vertue and mesure abyde in the myddel of two extremytees.
Shakespeare: *Tim.* 4.3.300f.

V81   VIRTUE is its own reward (*Varied* from 1596; OW861af. adds 1509 variant: "Vertue hath no rewarde")

Add e.g.: 1604 R. Eedes *Six ... Sermons* 13ᵛ: Vertue hath no reward better, vice no punishment greater, than it selfe.
Shakespeare: *Mac.* 1.4.22f., *Cor.* 2.2.127f., *Tim.* 1.1.130

V92   A well-favored VISOR will hide her ill-favored face (1546, Shak.)
I.e., 1546 Heywood *Dialogue* II.i F2ᵛ: Many men wishte, for beautifying that bryde ... Some well favour'd visor, on hir yll favour'd face.
Shakespeare: *LLL* 5.2.387f., *Rom.* 1.4.29f.

W

W1.1   As a weak as a WAFER (*Varied*) 1577 J. Grange *Golden Aphroditis* P1ᵛ: She treades so nice, she would not wafers breake. c1605 (1612) Chapman *Widow's Tears* 2.3.83−5: For all these solemn vows, if I do not make her prove in the handling as weak as a wafer, say I lost my time in travel. 1619 Drayton *Idea* 8.10 II, 314: Thy Lips, with age, as any Wafer thinne. c1625 Fletcher *Chances* 2.1.118: A womans oaths are wafers, break with making. 1636 Dekker *Wonder of a Kingdom* 1.2.61: Walls of chastitie? walls of wafer-cakes.
Shakespeare: *H5* 2.3.51
Cf. P605: Promises, like pie-crust, are made to be broken [from 1681].

W3.1   To pay one his (take one's) WAGES (fig.) (Wh W3 *To pay one* from c1421)
E.g., c1422 Hoccleve *Jereslau's Wife* 165.725f.: God qwyte yow wole and your wages paye In swich(e) wyse that it yow shal affraye. Add: 1604 E. Grymeston *Miscelanea* C3ᵛ (of facing death): Feare not now to goe take thy wages.
Shakespeare: *Cym.* 4.2.261

W5   To be angry at (laugh at, be afraid of) the WAGGING of a straw

(From c1517; OW863a from c1374)
Shakespeare: *R3* 3.5.7
Cf. W5.1: To fear the wagging of a
feather.

W5.1   To fear the WAGGING of a
feather (*Varied*)
c1552 (c1567) Udall *Ralph Roister
Doister* 4.7.47: Thus will ye be turned
with waggyng of a fether?
Shakespeare: *AWW* 5.3.232, *Ven.*
302

W7   It is evil (ill, not good) WAKING
of a sleeping dog (From 1546;
Wh H569 [hound] from c1385)
Shakespeare: *2H4* 1.2.153f., *H8*
1.1.121f.

W19   WALLS (hedges, etc.) have ears
(eyes) (From 1573)
Shakespeare: *MND* 5.1.208f.

W20   We see not what is in the WAL-
LET behind (*Varied* from 1552;
OW709b supplements)
Shakespeare: *Tro.* 3.3.145

W23   As small as a WAND (From
1550)
Shakespeare: *TGV* 2.3.20f.

W23.1   As straight as a WAND
c1589 (1594) Lyly *Mother Bombie*
1.3.106f.: They studie twentie
yeeres together to make us grow as
straight as a wande. 1598 Marlowe
Hero and Leander I.61: His body was
as straight as Circe's wand.
Shakespeare: *Per.* 5.1.109

W38.1   As WANTON as a whelp
(calf, kid) (W291 *whelp* from c1535;
OW866a *calf* from 1576)
1565 Cooper *Thesaurus* s.v. Lascivus
Wantoner then a yonge kidde [*OED*
adj. 3b]. 1590 Spenser *Faerie Queene*
1.6.14.4: Leaping like wanton kids in
pleasant spring.
Shakespeare: *1H4* 4.1.103, *WT*
1.2.126

W43.1   In WAR some win and some
lose (Wh W39 *varied* from a1338)[n]
Shakespeare: *R3* 4.4.535, *Mac.*
1.1.4, *Ant.* 3.11.70

[n]Many citations are simply early versions of C223, but several are
pertinent.

W47   WAR is death's feast (Collections from 1623, 1611 analogue;
ditto OW866a)
Shakespeare: *Jn.* 2.1.352−4,
5.2.176−8

W61   All his WARDROBE is on his
back (From 1591; OW104a *wealth*
1578)
Shakespeare: *Shr.* Ind. ii.9f., *Jn.*
2.1.70

W76   As angry as a WASP (From
1526)
Shakespeare: *Shr.* 2.1.209

W81.1   To WASTE one's wind
(breath, words) (Wh W329 *words,
wind* from a1400; cf. Wh B525 *breath*
c1300)
E.g., 1546 Heywood *Dialogue* II.iii
G2f.: I will . . . Spend som wind at
nede, though I wast wind in vayn.
1557 Wyatt *Tottel* F1: What nedes
these threatnyng woordes, and
wasted wynd? c1576 *Common Conditions* 1844: In vaine you wast your
breath.
Shakespeare: *MND* 3.2.168, *MM*
2.2.72
Cf. B642: You but spend your
breath (wind) in vain.

W85   All the WATER in the sea cannot wash out this stain (*Varied* from
Ado)[n]
Shakespeare: *Ado* 4.1.140f., *R2*
4.1.242, *Ham.* 3.3.45f., *Mac.* 2.2.57f.
Cf. H122: To wash one's hands of
a thing.

[n]Nothing really proverbial may be
involved, especially in *Richard II* and

Macbeth. More relevant than the usually cited *Hippolytus* 715–8 or *Hercules Furens* 1323-9 are the meditations on Christ's passion once attributed to St. Bernard. Cf. *Saint Bernard His Meditations,* Med. XII (ed. 1614 ["The third edition"], sig. L10), addressed to Pilate: "Well might a little water cleare the *spots* of thy *hands,* but all the water in the *Ocean* could not wash away the blots of thy soule."

W86.1 As unstable (false) as WATER (*Unstable* W86 from 1526, OW855a from c1380 [cf. Gen. 49.4]; *false* from *Tro.*)
Shakespeare: *Tro.* 3.2.191f., *Oth.* 5.2.134, *WT* 1.2.131f.
Cf. W86: As good (false, unstable) as ever water wet [*false* 1591].

W88 As weak as WATER (Ezek. 7.17; from 1545)
Shakespeare: *R2* 3.3.58

W99 Much WATER goes by the mill that the miller knows not of (From 1546)
Shakespeare: *Tit.* 2.1.85f.

W106 To cast (etc.) WATER into the sea (Thames) (From 1509)
Shakespeare: *3H6* 5.4.8, *Tit.* 3.1.68, *TNK* 1.3.7

W107 To fetch (wring) WATER (blood) out of a stone (flint) (*Varied* from a1542, *water flint* from 1589)
Shakespeare: *Tim.* 4.3.484, *WT* 3.2.192f.

W109 To look to (etc.) one's WATER (fig.) (From 1546; OW483b from 1377)
E.g., 1593 Peele *Edward I* 1.8 F2ᵛ: I have cast your water, and see as deepe into your desire, as he that hadde dived everie day into your bosome.
Shakespeare: *Mac.* 5.3.50f.

W111 To pour WATER into a sieve

(*Varied* from 1477; Wh W86 from c1450)
Shakespeare: *Ado* 5.1.4f., *AWW* 1.3.202f.

W114 To write in WATER (sand) (*Water* from 1580, *sand* 1623 WOD.)
Shakespeare: *H8* 4.2.45f.

W123 WATER runs smoothest where it is deepest (*Varied* from 1580; Wh W70 [Still waters run deep (ditto OW774b)] *varied* from c1390)
Shakespeare: *2H6* 3.1.53

W130 Shallow WATERS make the greatest sound (*Varied* from *Luc.*; OW719b from 1576)
Shakespeare: *Luc.* 1329
Cf. Wh W70 (OW774b, W123): Still waters run deep [*varied* from c1390].

W135.1 As soft as WAX (Cf. Appendix B)
E.g., 1474 Caxton *Chesse* III.v (1883) 123: For the women be likened unto softe waxe or softe ayer. [*OED soft* 23].
Shakespeare: *Tit.* 3.1.45, *PP* 7.4

W136 Soft WAX will take any impression (From 1579; OW750af. from a1500)
E.g., a1500 *15c. School-Bk.* ed. W. Nelson 20: Then [in childhood] the myn of a yong mann is as waxe, apte to take all thynge. c1550 *Nice Wanton* C2: Chyldren in theyr tender age, ye may worke them like waxe, to your own entent.
Add e.g., 1579 Lyly *Euphues* I,185: Euphues, whose witte beeinge lyke waxe apte to receiue any impression.
Shakespeare: *MND* 1.1.49, *TN* 2.2.29f., *Rom.* 3.3.126, *Ven.* 565f., *Luc.* 1240–3

W137.1 To melt (etc.) like WAX against the fire
E.g., c1300 *South English Legendary* II 585.412: Ac bigonne al to multe

awey ase wex deth ayen fure. c1375
St. Thomas in Horstmann *Legenden
1881* 23.232−4: The devyll and all
that he in stode Was wastid all unto
muk and myre, Right als wax wastes
ogayns the fire [in Wh W102, 105].
1580 Baret M-68: [Goods] which will
soone vanish and decrease as waxe
against the fire [in W137].
  Shakespeare: *3H6* 3.2.51, *Jn.*
5.4.24f.

W138 To work (upon one) (anything) like WAX (From 1546)
  Shakespeare: *3H6* 2.1.171

(?) W142.1 The shortest WAY is
commonly the foulest, the fairer way
not much about.
  1609 D. Tuvil *Essayes, Morall and
Theologicall* 26f.: But it is in life, as it is
in wayes; the shortest is commonly
the foulest, & surely the fairest is not
much about [margin: Sir. Fran.
Bacon]. 1609 J. Boys *Exposition . . .
Principall Scriptures* ed. 1610 K4ᵛ:
The shortest way commonly, the
foulest, the fairer way not much
about.
  Shakespeare: *Mac.* 1.5.17f.

W144.1 To see which WAY the
game goes (fig.)
  1601 A. Dent *Plaine Mans Path-Way*
T3ᵛ: Oh now I see which way the
game goeth: you would faine make
Christ a cloake for your sinnes.
  Shakespeare: *MND* 3.2.289

W148 There is no WAY but one (i.e.,
death) (From 1542)
  Shakespeare: *TN* 3.2.39, *H5*
2.3.15f., *Oth.* 5.2.358f.

W149 This is the WAY (trick) to
catch the old one (From 1606;
OW838a adds 1598 variant)
  I.e., 1598 (1616) W. Haughton *En-
glishmen for my Money* ix (MSR 2000):
Now for a tricke to overreach the
Divell.
  Shakespeare: *LLL* 4.3.284

W150 To go another WAY to work
(From 1581)
  Shakespeare: *TN* 4.1.33f.

W152 The WAY to be safe is never
to be secure (He that is secure is not
safe) (*Varied* from *R2*; OW872a supplements from 1585)
  Shakespeare: *R2* 2.1.265f., *Lr.*
4.1.20, *Mac.* 3.5.32f.

W155 (Yours to command) in the
WAY of honesty (1616 DR., 1639
CL., cf. Shak.)
  Add: 1594 Nashe *Unfortunate
Traveller* II,217: Yours to use in the
way of honestie. 1596 Nashe *Saffron-
Walden* III,16: Nay then, a spirit in
the way of honestie too. ?1596 (1640)
Jonson *Tale of a Tub* 4.4.12−4:
She . . . care not What man can doe
unto her, in the way Of honesty, and
good manners. 1599 Nashe *Lenten
Stuffe* III,213: I will deale more
boldly, & yet it shall be securelie and
in the way of honestie. c1604 (1607)
Middleton *Phoenix* 5.1.251−3: I will
not . . . come near a man in the way
of honesty. 1605 (1607) Dekker &
Webster *Northward Ho* 2.1.76: Sir
you are welcome in the way of
honesty.
  Shakespeare: *Wiv.* 2.2.73f., *Jn.*
1.1.181, *TNK* 5.2.71

W165.1 To be clean out of the WAY
(*OED* 37 fig. *Out of the way* from
a1225)
  1548 Elyot s.v. Erro: Thou arte
cleane out of the waie, thou art
utterly deceyved. Again 1565
Cooper, c1580 Conybeare 24.1573
Gascoigne *Master F. J.* I,491: I have
wandred somewhat beside the path,
and yet not clean out of the way.
c1589 (1633) Marlowe *Jew of Malta*
4.4.45: Now am I clean—or rather,
foully—out of the way.
  Shakespeare: *Oth.* 1.3.358f.

W166 To go the WAY of all flesh
(Cf. Josh. 23.14; from 1607;

OW871b from 1337−8)
E.g. c1604 (1605) Marston *Dutch Courtesan* 1.1.76−8: I am now going the way of all flesh. / Not to a courtesan? 1604 (1606) Chapman *Monsieur D'Olive* 1.2.148f.: Give her but six pence to buye her a handbasket, and sende her the way of all fleshe [i.e., to become a whore].
Shakespeare: *2H4* 5.2.4, *TNK* 5.2.35

(?) W176   Many WAYS meet in one town (city) (*H5*, *TNK* only; not in OW)
Add: 1613 (ded. 5 Nov. 1612) T. Tuke *Discourse of Death* C3: As into a great Citie, or into the maine Sea, so unto death there are many waies. It is as the center, wherein all the lines doe meete; a towne of Mart, wherein many waies from contrarie coasts doe end.
Shakespeare: *H5* 1.2.208, *TNK* 1.5.15f.
Cf. L305.1: Many lines meet at the center.

W185   The WEAKEST goes to the wall (*Varied* from a1550; Wh W130 from a1500)
Shakespeare: *Rom.* 1.1.13−6

W204   To beat one at his own WEAPON (From c1600; OW36b from 1591)
Shakespeare: *Ham.* 3.4.206f.

W209   It is better to WEAR out than rust out (a1718, cf. *2H4*; OW56b supplements, analogue 1557)
I.e., 1557 Edgeworth *Serm.* Preface: Better it is to shine with labour, then to rouste with idlenes.
Shakespeare: *2H4* 1.2.218−20
Cf. I91: Iron not used soon rusts; I92: Iron (gold) with often handling is worn to nothing.

W211.1   As angry (etc.) as a WEASEL a1500 in Thomas Wright *Songs and Carols* (PS 23, 1847) 4−5: Ther wer 3 angry, 3 angry ther wer: A wasp, a wesyll, and a woman. a1500 in Smith *Common-place Book* 12−3: Take iii schrewys: a waspe, a wesill, a woman [in Wh T247].
Shakespeare: *1H4* 2.3.78, *Cym.* 3.4.159

W217   Fair WEATHER after you (From 1540)
E.g., c1588 (1598) H. Porter *Two Angry Women of Abingdon* iii (MSR 927; Nicholas Proverbes): You should say God send faire weather after me.
Shakespeare: *LLL* 1.2.144, *Ado* 1.3.24

W220   There is no WEATHER ill when the wind is still (*LLL*, collections from 1623)
Shakespeare: *LLL* 4.2.33

W221   To make fair WEATHER (From 1546)
Shakespeare: *Ado* 1.3.24, *2H6* 5.1.30, *Jn* 5.1.21, *H8* 1.4.22

W232   WEDDING and hanging go by destiny (*Varied* from 1546)
Shakespeare: *MV* 2.9.83, *TN* 1.5.19f. *2H6* 4.2.123

W238   An ill WEED grows apace (fast, well) (fig.) (*Varied* from a1500)
Shakespeare: *R3* 2.4.13−5, 3.1.103

W241   WEEDS come forth on the fattest soil if it is untilled (fig.) (*Varied* from 1579; OW247a adds 1393)
Shakespeare: *2H4* 4.4.54, *Ham.* 1.2.135−7, *Ant.* 1.2.109f.

W242   The WEEDS overgrow the corn (fig.) (From c1470)
Shakespeare: *LLL* 1.1.96, *Luc.* 281

W244   He is in by the WEEK (From 1546)
Shakespeare: *LLL* 5.2.61

W248.1   The WEEPING of an heir is laughter under a vizor (mask) [Publilius Syrus *Heredis fletus sub persona risus est* (Aulus Gellius *Noctes Atticae* XVII.xiv)].
E.g., c1526 *Dicta Sap.* C4: The wepyng of an heire is dissembled laughyng, yea he reioyceth though he wepe [in E248]. 1576 G. Cardano (T. Bedingfield) *Cardanus Comforte* 16ᵛ: The wepyng of yᵉ heire is the weepynge of one that laugheth under a vizar. c1605 (1612) Chapman *Widow's Tears* 1.1.125f.: Their weeping is in truth but laughing under a Maske. c1606 (1607) Jonson *Volpone* 1.5.22f.: The weeping of an heire should still be laughter, Under a visor.
Shakespeare: *2H4* 2.2.52−5
Cf. E248: To cry with one eye and laugh with the other.

(?) W257   To bid one WELCOME to the fieldsⁿ (1546, *LLL*)
I.e., 1546 Heywood *Dialogue* I.xi E2: Byddyng me welcome straungely over the feelds.
Shakespeare: *LLL* 2.1.93

ⁿWhiting retains the Heywood-based entry (Wh W187); OW does not. Very possibly Heywood intended nothing proverbial by the line. Cf. Introduction, fn. 26. And cf. c1597 (1637) Deloney, *1 Gentle Craft* 126: "you . . . made me a fool to come over the fields to you."

W258   WELCOME is the best cheer (*Varied* from 1611; OW877b from c1430)
E.g., c1430 Lydgate *Isopes* 434: As men seyen & reporte, at the leste, Nat many deyntees, but good chere maketh a feste. c1550 Heywood's poem in J. O. Halliwell's ed. *Wit & Science* 112: Welcum is the best dysh.
Shakespeare: *Err.* 3.1.21−6, *Mac.* 3.4.32−6
Cf. G338: GOOD WILL and welcome is your best cheer (*varied*, from c1477)

W259   WELCOME when you go (From 1546)
Shakespeare: *LLL* 2.1.213f., *1H6* 2.2.55f.

(?) W259.1   The WELKIN roars (Cf. Appendix B)
1604 Dekker & Middleton *1 Honest Whore* 1.2.129: By this welkin that heere roares. 1605 Jonson et al. *Eastward Ho* 1.1.107f.: Turne good fellow, turne swaggering gallant, and *let the Welkin roare, and Erebus also.* 1617 Middleton & Rowley *Fair Quarrel* 4.1.29f.: O, sir, does not the wind roar, the sea roar, the welkin roar? 1635 Quarles *Embl.* viii.33: One frisks and sings . . . and makes the Welkin rore [*OED* 2c].
Shakespeare: *2H4* 2.4.168

W260   Let WELL alone (Erasmus's *Adagia*, Lr., Son.; OW453b from c1396)
Add: c1580 J. Conybeare 25: Manum de tabula: Leave whiles it is well. 1600 Bodenham *Bel-vedere* ed. 1875 54: Some men so strive in cunning to excell, That oft they marre the worke before was well.
Shakespeare: *Jn.* 4.2.28f., *Lr.* 1.4.346, *Son.* 103.9f.
Cf. M875.1: To mend and to mar.

(?) W260.1   As deep as a WELL (OW175b; *Rom.*, Heywood)
I.e., 1606 T. Heywood *2 If you Know not Me* (MSR 2501).
Shakespeare: *Rom.* 3.1.96

(?) W269   WELL, WELL is a word of malice (1670 Ray, 1721 KEL., and 4 instances of *Well, well* in Shak.; OW879a *R2*, 1670 Ray)
Add e.g. (merely because as relevant as Shak.): 1546 Heywood *Dialogue* I.xi E3ᵛ: Well well (quoth he); II.v H2ᵛ: Well well . . . (said shee).
Shakespeare: *AYL* 4.3.19, *Tro.* 1.2.250f., *1H6* 2.4.55, *R3* 3.5.33, *R2* 2.3.152, 3.3.170, *1H4* 1.2.69, *Oth.* 3.4.183, *Ant.* 3.7.66, *Cor.* 2.1.27,

4.2.43, *Per.* 4.2.110, 4.3.19, *TNK* 5.3.34

(?) W274.1 To be mad WENCHES (Cf. Appendix B)
1584 Lyly *Sapho and Phao* 1.4.43: Wee are madde wenches, if men marke our wordes. c1589 (1594) Lyly *Mother Bombie* 2.3.77 (Silena): Wee maides are madde wenches. 1599 (1600) Dekker *Shoemakers' Holiday* 2.2.22: Th'art a mad wench; 4.1.40: How dost thou madde wench? c1605 (1612) Chapman *Widow's Tears* 1.1.92f.: Are not we mad Wenches, that can lead our blind husbands thus by the noses?
Shakespeare: *LLL* 2.1.257, 5.2.264

W276 Who goes to WESTMIN-STER for a wife, to Paul's for a man, and to Smithfield for a horse may meet with a whore, a knave, and a jade (*Varied* from 1585)
Shakespeare: *2H4* 1.2.52–4

W279 As white as WHALES'S-BONE (From 15th century; Wh W203 from c1325)
Shakespeare: *LLL* 5.2.332

W280.1 I'll (I) tell you (thee) WHAT (*OED* 20 *2H4*, then 1877)
E.g.,[c1598 (1639) Deloney *2 Gentle Craft* 144 (thee), 196 (you), 180.] 1599 (1600) Dekker *Shoemakers' Holiday* 1.1.18, 4.4.79f.
Shakespeare: *Shr.* 1.2.112, *Ado* 5.4.100, *2H4* 1.1.51, 5.4.7f, 18

W280.2 What (Whom) have we here? (Cf. Appendix B)
E.g., 1553 ?Udall *Republica* 3.6.850. c1570 *Misogonus* 1.3.1 (What monster). c1576 *Common Conditions* 1700 (Whom). 1584 Lyly *Sapho and Phao* 5.2.70. c1592 ?Kyd *Soliman and Perseda* 5.2.48. 1596 (1598) Chapman *Blind Beggar of Alexandria* ix.128 (Who). 1596 (1605) *Captain Thomas Stukeley* i (MSR 49).
Shakespeare: *AWW* 3.2.17, *2H6*

1.4.58, 5.1.12, *1H4* 5.4.131, *Tit.* 2.3.55, *WT* 3.3.69, 4.4.623, *TNK* 3.5.96

W280.3 WHAT is that to the purpose? (*OED* 12a *To the purpose* from 1384) (Cf. Appendix B)
1579 F. Merbury *Marriage between Wit and Wisdom* ii (MSR 205): But what is that to the purpose. 1605 Jonson et al. *Eastward Ho* 3.3.142: A Porcpisce? whats that to th' purpose? 1640 J. D. *Knave in Grain* 4.1 (MSR 1999): What's this to the purpose?
Shakespeare: *TN* 1.3.21

W280.4 WHAT is that to you (thee)? (Usually *What's*)
E.g., c1593 (1597) Lyly *Woman in the Moon* 1.1.164 (thee), 3.2.113. ?1596 (1640) Jonson *Tale of a Tub* 2.6.9. c1602 (1607) ?T. Heywood *Fair Maid of the Exchange* vi (MSR 645). 1611 Dekker & Middleton *Roaring Girl* 2.1.140. 1614 (1631) Jonson *Bartholomew Fair* 1.4.121f., 4.6.53.
Shakespeare: *Shr.* 2.1.303, *TN* 3.4.364, *Jn.* 5.6.4, *R2* 5.2.100, *Oth.* 3.3.315
Cf. Appendix B: What have you to DO?

W280.5 (Anything,) WHAT you will (*OED* C4 *TN*, then 1908)[n]
E.g., c1593 (1597) Lyly *Woman in the Moon* 5.1.34 (Any thing). 1599 (1600) Jonson *Every Man Out* 5.6.56f. (Anything). 1601 (1607) Marston *What You Will* (and passim). 1609 Bretnor (Crow g643 May): What thou wilt.
Shakespeare: *MND* 1.2.92, *AYL* 2.5.20, *TN* subtitle, 1.5.109, *Oth.* 4.1.34

[n] I include because a play title. Cf. on L555.1.

W295.1 I know WHERE you are (he, she is)
1552 (c1567) Udall *Ralph Roister Doister* 3.2.12: I know where she is; Dobinet hath wrought some wile.

1576 G. Wapull *Tide Tarrieth No Man* 1463: I cry you mercy! I know where you are now.
Shakespeare: *Shr.* 1.1.222f., *AYL* 5.2.29, *Lr.* 4.6.145

W298.1　X is the WHETSTONE of wit
1557 R. Recorde *The Whetstone of witte, whiche is the seconde parte of arithmetike.* 1579 S. Gosson *Schoole of Abuse* A2: Poets are the whetstones of wit. 1580 Lyly *Euphues and his England* II,55: Wine is such a whetstone for wit. 1602 F. Davison *Poetical Rhapsody* To the Reader A4: Love, being virtuously intended, & worthily placed, is the Whetstone of witt. c1605 (1630) Dekker *2 Honest Whore* 3.1.61: Lust can set a double edge on wit.
Shakespeare: *AYL* 1.2.54f.

W299　A WHETSTONE cannot itself cut but yet it makes tools cut (*Varied* from 1578; OW883a from Horace, Chaucer)
Shakespeare: *AYL* 1.2.54f.

(?) W306.1　Things called WHIPS
1600 (1608) R. Armin *Nest of Ninnies* G3^v: There are as Hamlet sayes things cald whips in store. c1600 (1602) Marston *Antonio's Revenge* 4.1.249: There is a thing call'd scourging Nemesis. 1602 *Spanish Tragedy* 3.11.42f. (3d addition): And there is Nemesis, and Furies, And things called whippes.
Shakespeare: *2H6* 2.1.133f.

W311　Not worth a WHISTLE (From a1525)
Shakespeare: *Lr.* 4.2.29

W313　You may (To) WHISTLE (go whistle) for it (From 1548; OW884a from 1513)
Shakespeare: *WT* 4.4.698, *TNK* 3.5.39

W314.1　To hit the WHITE (OW375a from 1586)

Shakespeare: Shr. 5.2.186, *Oth.* 2.1.132f.

(?) W316.1　WHITHER away so fast? (Cf. Appendix B)
c1560 (c1570) W. Wager *Enough is as Good as a Feast* 353: What, brother Covetous? whither away so fast? c1590 (1605) *King Leir* sc. 12 991: My honest friend, whither away so fast?
Shakespeare: *TGV* 3.1.51, *LLL* 4.3.184, *R3* 2.3.1, *H8* 2.1.1

(?) W318.1　WHO am I?
E.g., c1559 (c1569) W. Wager *Longer Thou Livest* 1039f.: No cap off? no knee bowed? no homage? Who am I? is there no more good manner? c1604 (1607) Middleton *Phoenix* 2.3.38 (Q2): Pray, who am I, niece? 1610 (1612) Jonson *Alchemist* 1.1.12f.: Why! who Am I, my mungrill? Who am I?
Shakespeare: *H8* 2.2.66, *Lr.* 1.4.78

W318.2　WHO would have thought it?
E.g., c1589 (1594) Lyly *Mother Bombie* 4.2.38 (Silena). c1604 (1608) J. Day *Law Tricks, or Who Would Have Thought It.* c1610 (1613) Marston & Barksted *Insatiate Countess* II III,34. 1639 CL. s.v. Vincere & vinci 320.
Shakespeare: *Rom.* 3.2.42

W321　Once a WHORE and ever a whore (Collections from 1659; OW594b adds 1613)
Shakespeare: *Tim.* 4.3.84f.

W331　There is never a WHY but there is a wherefore (*Varied* from 1573)
Shakespeare: *Err.* 2.2.43f.

W332　The WHY and (or) the wherefore (Cf. Appendix B) (From 1481)
Shakespeare: *Err.* 2.2.48, *H5* 5.1.3f., *Ham.* 1.4.57

(?) W333.1　To be one of the WICKED
c1604 (1605) Marston *Dutch Courte-*

san 1.2.19: I am none of the wicked that eat fish o' Fridays. c1606 (1607) *Puritan* 1.3.66f.: But, if hee bee one of the wicked, hee shall perish. c1621 (1657) Middleton *Women Beware Women* 4.2.80−3: I'm damn'd, I'm damn'd! . . . One of the wicked; dost not see't? a cuckold, a plain reprobate cuckold!
  Shakespeare: *1H4* 1.2.93−5, *2H4* 2.4.327f.

W351 A good WIFE makes a good husband (From 1546)
  Shakespeare: *MV* 5.1.130

W390 To run the WILD-GOOSE chase (From *Rom.*; OW889b supplements)
  Add e.g., 1595 M. Sutcliffe *Answere unto . . . Throkmorton* R3: [Throckmorton had described Hacket's prayer as] like the wilde-goose chase, and without either rime or reason.
  Shakespeare: *Rom.* 2.4.71

W392 To be wedded to one's WILL (From 1546)
  Shakespeare: *LLL* 2.1.211f., *Son.* 135.1

W393 To take the WILL for the deed (From c1460; Wh W267 *varied* from a1400)
  Shakespeare: *Ant.* 2.5.8f.

(?) W395.1 WILL is no law (Wh W272 c1440 [1])
  1611 (1619) Beaumont & Fletcher *King and No King* 2.1.105: Your own will is your law.
  Shakespeare: *TGV* 5.4.14
  Cf. K72: What the king wills, that the law wills.

W397 WILL will have will (wilt) though will woe win (Collections from 1546)
  Shakespeare: *Son.* 135f.

W398 With as good a WILL as ever I came from school (From 1573)
  Shakespeare: *Shr.* 3.2.150

W400.1 Whether one WILL or no c1340 Rolle *Psalter* 227 (65.10): Whedire we wild or we wild not [in Wh W277: Will he nill he].
  Add e.g.: c1460 *Harrowing* (Wakefield) 196: Wheder ye will or none. c1576 *Common Conditions* 1027: Wil you have me a shipboard whether I wil or no? 1410: You wilbe medling with maids whether they will or no. 1585 ?Munday *Fedele and Fortunio* V (MSR 1765): I must I perceive whither I will or no.
  Shakespeare: *MND* 3.1.153, *1H6* 4.7.25, *2H6* 3.2.265, 3.3.10, *Tmp.* 3.1.86
  Cf. W401: Will he nill he.

W401 WILL he nill he (From 1553; Wh W277 from c1200)
  Shakespeare: *Shr.* 2.1.271, *Ham.* 5.1.17

W403 To wear the WILLOW (willow garland) (From 1578; OW874af. from c1550)
  Shakespeare: *Ado* 2.1.187−9, 218, *3H6* 3.3.228, 4.1.100, *Oth.* 4.3.51

W408 WIN it (etc.) and wear it (From c1570; OW892a from c1552)
  Shakespeare: *Ado* 5.1.82, *2H4* 4.5.221

(?) W408.1 The battle (field) is WON and lost (lost and won) c1591 (1593) Peele *Edward I* xvi (MSR 2360): Sweete brother flie the field is wonne and lost.
  Shakespeare: *Mac.* 1.1.4, *Ant.* 3.11.70

W411 As swift as the WIND (From c1535; Wh W294 from c1300)
  Shakespeare: *LLL* 5.2.261, *MND* 3.2.94, *2H4* Ind. 4, *Rom.* 2.5.8, *TNK* 2.3.77

W412 As wavering (unstable, changeable, etc.) as the WIND (From 1509; cf. Wh W289ff.)
  Shakespeare: *Tro.* 3.2.192,

5.3.110, *3H6* 5.1.57, *Rom.* 1.4.100, *WT* 1.2.131f.
Cf. W698: Women are as wavering (etc.) as the wind [from 1546].

W419 Is the WIND in that door (corner) (fig.) (From c1470)
Shakespeare: *Ado* 2.3.98, *1H4* 3.3.88

W421 It is an ill (evil) WIND that blows no man good (fig.) (From 1546)
Shakespeare: *3H6* 2.5.55, *2H4* 5.3.86

W424 A little WIND kindles, much puts out the fire (fig.) (*Varied* from 1586)
Shakespeare: *Shr.* 2.1.134f., *Jn.* 5.2.83−7

W429 Sail with the WIND and tide (fig.) (*Varied* from 1546)
E.g., 1591 FLOR. *Sec. F.* VI 97: For wisdome sailes with winde and tide.
Shakespeare: *3H6* 5.1.53, *Oth.* 2.3.63

W432 To go down the WIND (fig.) (From c1597 [1609]; OW201a supplements)
E.g., 1604 Breton *Grimellos Fort.*: *Wks.* II, 8: My purse grew so bare . . . two or three yeares brought me so downe the winde that I could never look up more.
Shakespeare: *Oth.* 3.3.262

W434 To have one in the WIND (fig.) (From 1540)
Shakespeare: *AWW* 3.6.114

W435.1 To sail against WIND and tide (stream) (fig.)
E.g., c1523 Barclay *Mirrour* 66(27f.): It is not lesse folly to strive agaynst kinde Then a shipman to strive agaynst both streme and winde [in Wh S830]. 1563 G. Ferrers "Edmund Duke of Somerset" 13f. *Mirror for Magistrates* 388: Who so

wyth force wil worke agaynst kynde, Sayleth as who sayeth, agaynst the stream & wynde. c1564 (1571) R. Edwards *Damon and Pithias* xviii (MSR 1885): Against the wind and striving stream I sayle. 1574 J. Higgins "Albanact" 505f. *2 Mirror for Magistrates* 66: But what avayles to strive against the tyde? Or els to sayle, against the streame and winde. 1583 H. Howard *Defensative* G1: If God be [not] with us . . . we saile both against wynde and tyde. 1590 Spenser *Faerie Queene* 3.4.9.6−8: Love . . . And Fortune . . . saile withouten starres gainst tyde and winde.
Shakespeare: *3H6* 4.3.59
Cf. W429: Sail with the wind and tide.

(?) W435.2 To shoot against the WIND (fig.)
1588 Greene *Pandosto* ed. Bullough VIII,179: He that striveth against Love, shooteth with them of Scyrum against the wind.
Shakespeare: *Tit.* 4.3.58

W439 To turn with (as) the WIND (fig.) (*As* c1576 [Wh W337 from a 1400], *with* 1670 Ray [OW848a from 1565; cf. Ecclus. 5.9])
Shakespeare: *Lr.* 2.2.78f.

W441 What WIND blows (brings, drives) you hither? (fig.) (From c1489)
Shakespeare: *Shr.* 1.2.48f., *2H4* 5.3.85

W448a The WIND puts out small lights but enrages great fires (fig.) (*Varied* from *Luc.*; Wh F191 from a1200)
Shakespeare: *Luc.* 647f.

W450 Huge (High) WINDS blow on high hills (courts, towers) (*Varied* from 1484)
Shakespeare: *R3* 1.3.258
Cf. on T509: The highest trees abide the sharpest storms.

(?) W452.1 To live in a WINDMILL
Cf. 1601 A. Dent *Plaine Mans Path-
Way* G5^v: Even as a wind-mill beateth
it selfe, maketh a great noise, whirl-
eth and whisketh about from day to
day, all the yeare long: yet at the
yeares end, standeth still where it be-
gunne. 1609 (1616) Jonson *Epicoene*
5.3.61–3: My very house turnes
round with the tumult! I dwell in a
windmill!
Shakespeare: *1H4* 3.1.159f.

W456 To come in at the WINDOW
(o'er the hatch) *Window* from 1551
[OW134bf. supplements], *hatch Jn.*,
1634 [OW deletes *o'er the hatch*])
I.e., R. Brome & T. Heywood *Lanc.
Witches* I IV, 174: It appears then by
your discourse, that you came in at
the window. / I would have you
thinke I scorne like my Granams Cat
to leape over the Hatch. / He hath
confest himselfe to be a Bastard.
Add: 1583 Melbancke *Philotimus*
2A2: This is like Gentlemen in our
daies, who will be cozins to all of any
port or great report in the whole
shire, though their gransires dog
scarse leapt over their grandames
hatch.
Shakespeare: *Jn.* 1.1.171

W460 Good WINE makes a merry
heart (*Varied* from 1593; cf. Eccl.
10.19, Ps. 104.15)
Shakespeare: *H5* 5.2.41

W461 Good WINE (drink) makes
good blood (*Varied* from c1570)
E.g., 1584 Lyly *Campaspe* 5.3.11:
Good drinke makes good bloud.
1586 Guazzo (Young) *Civile Conversation* IV II,161: Drinke neverthe-
lesse, saide Ladie Fraunces, for it will
engender bloud in you in dispight of
love [more an allusion to a belief
than an example of a proverb].
    Shakespeare: *Ado* 1.1.250–2,
AWW 2.3.99f., *2H4* 4.3.89–92, *TNK*
· 3.3.17

W462 Good WINE needs no bush
(ivy bush, sign) (fig.) (From 1539)
Shakespeare: *AYL* Epilogue 3

W466 No WINE without lees (Collections from 1600; *varied* from
1580)
E.g., 1580 Lyly *Euphues and his England* II,100 (with context): Ther
is . . . no wine made of grapes but
hath leese, no woeman created of
flesh but hath faultes. (Repeated
1598 Meres *Palladis Tamia* G2^v.)
Shakespeare: *Oth.* 2.1.251f.

(?) W470.1 To drink neater WINE
than is made of grapes[n]
1591 ?Lyly *Ent. at Theobalds* I,419:
She would eat fairer bread than is
made of wheat [B622], wear finer
cloth than is made of wool, drink
neater wine than is made of grapes.
Shakespeare: *Oth.* 2.1.251f.

[n]B622 is in 1546 Heywood. For the
second clause cf. 1579 Lyly, *Euphues* (I,
181): "to eate finer bread then is made
of wheat, to wear finer cloth then is
wrought of Woll."

W471 When WINE (ale) is in wit is
out (*Ale* from 1562)
Shakespeare: *Ado* 3.5.34

W500 Although I WINK I am not
blind (*Varied* from 1566)
Shakespeare: *TGV* 1.2.136

W506.1 After WINTER follows
summer (May) (fig.) (Wh W372 *varied* from c1385)
Shakespeare: *2H6* 2.4.2f.

W510 WINTER eats that summer
gets (From c1460; Wh W373 from
c1450; cf. Prov. 6.6–8)
Shakespeare: *Lr.* 2.4.68

W513.1 A WINTER('S) tale[n]
?1557 J. Olde *Short Description of Antichrist* A7: According to olde wives
Fables and winter tales [*OED* 5].

c1587 (1594) Marlowe & Nashe *Dido* 3.3.58f.: Who would not undergo all kind of toil To be well stored with such a winter's tale? c1589 (1633) Marlowe *Jew of Malta* 2.1.24f.: Now I remember those old women's words, Who, in my wealth, would tell me winter's tales. c1590 (1595) Peele *Old Wives Tale* 83: A merry winters tale would drive away the time trimly.

Shakespeare: *R2* 5.1.40f., *WT* (title), 2.1.25

[n]Cf. on W280.5.

(?) W520 There is no WISDOM (law) below the girdle (*Wisdom* a1734, *law* 1691, analogues from *Lr.*)
Shakespeare: *Lr.* 4.6.126f.
Cf. Wh L553: To be full (true) of love beneath the girdle but not above [from a1500 (2)].

(?) W522 Who weens himself wise, WISDOM wots him a fool
(1562; all examples but 1562 better fit C582)
I.e., 1562 Heywood *Epigrammes* Fifth hundred 1: Wise men in olde time, wold weene them selves fooles. Fooles now in new time, wil weene them selves wise. . . . Who weenth him selfe wise, wisdome wotth him a foole.
Add: First hundred 87: Among fooles thou art taken a wise man, And among wyse men, thou art knowne a foole.
Shakespeare: *AYL* 5.1.31f., *TN* 1.5.33f.
Cf. C582: He that is wise in his own conceit is a fool.

W532 He is not WISE that is not wise for himself (From 1539; OW902a Greek, Cicero, from c1532)
Shakespeare: *Ham.* 1.2.6f.
Cf. F480: He is a fool that forgets himself.

(?) W534.1 To be none of the WISEST
1566 (1575) Gascoigne *Supposes*

2.1.104f.: Me thought by his habite and his lookes, he should be none of the wisest. 1598 (1616) W. Haughton *Englishmen for My Money* viii (MSR 1689–91): I was drinking . . . and therefore no maruaile though I be none of the wisest at this present.
Shakespeare: *Tmp.* 2.2.73f.

W547 Do not set your WIT against a fool's (a child) (From 1551)
Shakespeare: *MND* 3.1.134, *Tro.* 2.1.86

(?) W550 He has no more WIT than a stone (*TN*, 1672)
I.e., 1672 WALK. 61 11: He hath no more wit than a stone; no more brains than a burbout [B598]. He is a very Cods-head.
Shakespeare: *TN* 1.5.85

W553 He has WIT (wisdom) at will that with angry heart can hold him still (From c1450)
Shakespeare: *Tim.* 1.1.234

W555 His WIT is in the wane (1562 [c1549] Heywood, 1616 DR.)
Add: 1562 Heywood *Epigrammes* Fifth Hundred 69: Thy will shall showe thy witte in the wane.
Shakespeare: *MND* 5.1.253f.

W560 Little WIT serves unto whom fortune pipes (*Varied* from 1573)
Add: 1589 Negri de Bassano *Freewyl* M1: Smal wit sufficeth a fortunate man.
Shakespeare: *AYL* 1.2.104, *Ham.* 3.2.70

W563.1 To have a green WIT (Cf. *OED Green headed* from 1569, *Green head* from 1589) (Cf. Appendix B)
1583 Greene *Mamillia* II,46: Your talk . . . sheweth surely but a green wit [also 49, 79]. 1590 Greene *Never Too Late* VIII,44: His grave widome exceedes thy greene wit. c1595 R. Turner *Garland of a greene Wit.*
Shakespeare: *LLL* 1.2.89

W570 WIT, whither wilt thou?
(From *AYL*; OW904a from 1539)
  Shakespeare: *AYL* 1.2.56, 4.1.166

(?) W575.1 Bless thy five WITS
?1621 (1652) Fletcher *Wild Goose
Chase* 5.6.98: 'Bless your five wits!
  Shakespeare: *Lr.* 3.4.58, 3.6.57

W576 The finest WITS are soonest
subject to love (*Varied* from 1576)
Add: 1563 T. Churchyard "Shore's
Wife" 147 *Mirror for Magistrates* 378:
The rypest wittes are soonest thralles
to love.
  Shakespeare: *TGV* 1.1.43f.

W578 Good WITS jump (From
1618, *Shr.*; ditto OW326bf.)
  Shakespeare: *Shr.* 1.1.190

W579 Great WITS (Poets) to madness sure are near allied (*Varied* from
1592 [1600])
Add: c1604 Marston *Malcontent* To
the Reader 38: Sine aliqua dementia
nullus Phoebus.
  Shakespeare: *MND* 5.1.7f.

W583 (To be frightened, scared) out
of one's WITS (From c1534)
  Shakespeare: *MND* 1.2.79f., *Wiv.*
2.1.138f., 2.2.279

W584 Aroint thee, WITCH, quoth
Besse Locket to her mother (1678
Ray, cf. *Mac.*; OW690b [Rynt you
witch] adds *Lr.*, supplements)
  Shakespeare: *Lr.* 3.4.124, *Mac.*
1.3.6

W585 I think you are a WITCH
(From 1618, *varied* from 1616;
OW904b supplements)
  Shakespeare: *Ant.* 1.2.40

W591 With a WITNESS (Cf. Appendix B) (From 1592; OW905a
from 1578)
  Shakespeare: *Shr.* 5.1.118

W600 WOE to the land (kingdom)
whose king is a child (Eccl. 10.16;

from 1543; Wh W436 *varied* from
a1200)
  Shakespeare: *1H6* 4.1.192, *R3*
2.3.11

W601 As hungry as a WOLF (From
1540)
  Shakespeare: *H8* 1.1.159

W601.1 As lecherous as a she WOLF
1639 CL., s.v. Similitudinis 286.
  Shakespeare: *Oth.* 3.3.404

(?) W601.2 As ravenous as a WOLF
(Wh W440 a1450)
  Shakespeare: *H8* 1.1.159

W602 Give not the WOLF (fox) the
wether (sheep) to keep (Make not the
wolf your shepherd) (*Varied* from
1576; OW907af., 1513ff.; *fox* peculiar to Shak.)
  Shakespeare: *TGV* 4.4.91f., *Tro.*
3.2.193, *MM* 5.1.298f., *2H6*
3.1.252f.

W606 One WOLF (etc.) will not eat
(bite, prey upon) another (*Wolf* from
1576, *bear* from *Ado*; OW194af. *dog*
from 1543)
  Shakespeare: *Ado* 3.2.78, *Tro.*
5.7.18f.

W614 A WOLF in a lamb's (sheep's)
skin (Cf. Matt. 7.15; from c1460)
  Shakespeare: *1H6* 1.3.55, *2H6*
3.1.77f., *Rom.* 3.2.76, *Son.* 96.9f.

(?) W631 If she (he) were the only
WOMAN (man) (in the world)
(1584, c1600, *Ant.*; not in OW)
I.e., 1584 Lyly *Sapho and Phao* 4.4.61:
My mother will make muche of you,
when there are no more men than
Vulcan. c1598 (1639) Deloney *2
Gentle Craft* 163: This were enough if
there were no more men in the
world but one.
  Shakespeare: *Ant.* 1.2.165f.
  Cf. M39: There are more maids
than Malkin [from 1546].

W637 To be born of WOMAN (*Varied* from 1584)
Add: ?1585 J. Deacon *Nobody is my name* C5: I perceive . . . you came of a woman: you must have your minde in this matter whosoever saieth nay.
Shakespeare: *Wiv.* 2.3.48, *H5* 2.1.117, *Tim.* 4.3.414, 493f., *Ven.* 201f.
Cf. M1201.1: To have had a MOTHER.

W637.1 To be a WOMAN
E.g., 1584 Lyly *Campaspe* 2.2.47: I, but she is wise, yea, but she is a woman! 1584 Lyly *Sapho and Phao* 4.4.56–8: Wel, I can say no more, but this which is enoughe, and as much as any can say: Venus is a woman. c1591 (1594) Greene *Orlando Furioso* 2.1.627–30: I thinke Angelica is a woman. / And what of that? Therefore unconstant, mutable, having their loves hanging in their ey-lids. c1598 (1601) Jonson *Every Man In* 3.5.27f.: You are a woman; you have flesh and blood enough in you. c1604 (1605) Marston *Dutch Courtesan* 5.2.133: She is a woman—that is she can lie [cf. W707.1]. c1605 (1612) Chapman *Widow's Tears* 2.1.13f.: In briefe Brother, I know her to be a woman; 4.1.124 Ile not despaire but shee may prove a woman. 1611 ?Middleton *Second Maiden's Tragedy* 68f.: O shees a woman, and her eye will stande upon advauncement.
Shakespeare: *1H4* 3.3.61

W637.2 To play the WOMAN (Cf. Appendix B: To PLAY the fool, etc.)
1598 (1601) Jonson *Every Man In* 5.2.405-8: Do not you play the woman with me? / Whats that sweete hart? / Dissemble? 1604 (1607) Dekker & Webster *Westward Ho* 4.2.151f.: Awake sweete Moll, th'ast played The woman rarely, counterfetted well. 1613 (1630) Middleton *Chaste Maid in Cheapside* 2.1.152:

Thou'lt make me play the woman and weep too.
Shakespeare: *H8* 3.2.429–31, *Mac.* 4.3.230

W637.3 To be a WOMAN of good carriage (*bawdy*)
1599 (1600) Jonson *Every Man Out* 3.3.33–5: If there be any lady, or gentlewoman of good carriage, that is desirous to entertaine (to her private uses) a yong, straight, and upright gentleman. 1602 ?T. Heywood *How a Man May Choose* 957f.: You have bene often tried To be a woman of good carriage. c1605 (1606) Marston *Fawn* 4.1.50f. (Puttotta): I am a woman of a known, sound, and upright carriage. c1606 (1608) Middleton *Mad World, My Master* 1.2.31f.: A woman of an excellent carriage all her lifetime, in court, city, and country.
Shakespeare: *Rom.* 1.4.94

W637.4 To be a WOMAN of the world
c1602 (1608) *Merry Devil of Edmonton* 3.1.12f. (of one entered into a nunnery): The wench . . . is no more a woman of this world. c1605 (1606) Marston *Fawn* 5.1.253–5: In most lamentable form complaineth to your blind celsitude your distressed orators the women of the world.
Shakespeare: *AYL* 5.3.4f.
Cf. Appendix B: MAN OF THE WORLD.

W638 Trust not a WOMAN when she weeps (From 1604; OW842b from 1597)
Shakespeare: *Tim.* 1.2.65f.
Cf. C318.1: Trust no child (etc.) [a1500].

W640 Who has a WOMAN has an eel by the tail (*Varied* from 1579; OW908a adds a1576)
Shakespeare: *TNK* 3.5.48–50
Cf. E61: He holds a wet eel by the

tail [from 1576; Wh E48 from c1395].

W646   A WOMAN and a glass are ever in danger (Collections from 1640; analogues from 1535) Shakespeare: *MM* 2.4.124–30, *Per.* 4.6.142, *PP* 13.4, 10f.

W649   A WOMAN conceals what she knows not (*Varied* from 1589; Wh W485 1519; OW908a c1386) Shakespeare: *1H4* 2.3.111

W651   A WOMAN either loves or hates to extremes (*Varied* from 1576; OW908a from c1526) E.g., c1526 *Dicta Sap.* B1: Aut amat aut odit mulier, nihil est tertium. A woman to eyther part is inclined over vehemently. Shakespeare: *Ado* 5.1.177f.

W655   A WOMAN is the weaker vessel (From 1576; OW908b from c1548; cf. 1 Peter 3.7) Shakespeare: *LLL* 1.1.272f., *AYL* 2.4.6, *2H4* 2.4.60, *Rom.* 1.1.15f.

W658   A WOMAN, like a German clock, is still repairing (never goes true) (*Varied* from *LLL*) Shakespeare: *LLL* 3.1.190f.

W660   A WOMAN says nay (no) and means aye (*Varied* from 1509) Shakespeare: *TGV* 1.2.55f., *PP* 18.42

W670   A WOMAN'S answer is never to seek (*Varied* from a1558; Wh B148 *verbatim* from a1500) Shakespeare: *AYL* 4.1.172

(?) W671.1   A WOMAN'S fault 1585 Greene *Planetomachia* V,133: She rose up railing with bitter terms against his folly, whereas God knowes, it was the onely thing shee desired: a womans faulte, to thrust away that with our little finger, which they pull to them with both theyr

handes. 1588 Greene *Pandosto* ed. Bullough VIII,183: Thou hast deniall at thy tongues end, and desire at thy hearts bottome; a womans fault, to spurne at that with her foote, which she greedily catcheth at with her hand. c1608 (1662) W. Rowley *Birth of Merlin* 2.1.126f.: Her name is Joan Go-too't. I am her elder, but she has been at it before me; 187f.: A womans fault, we are all subject to go to't, sir. c1613 (1623) Webster *Duchess of Malfi* 4.2.232f.: I would faine put off my last womans-fault, I'ld not be tedious to you. Shakespeare: *1H4* 3.1.240

W673   A WOMAN'S mind and winter wind (Winter weather and women's thoughts) change oft (*Varied* from c1500) E.g., 1590 Greene *Royal Exchange* VII,292: Whereunto alludeth our old English proverbe. Wynters wether, and womens thought. And gentlemens purposes chaungeth oft. Shakespeare: *2H4* 4.4.34

W675   A WOMAN'S strength is in (A woman's weapon is) her tongue (*Varied* from 1546, *weapon* from 1560) Add e.g.: 1582 G. Whetstone *Heptameron* L4: Women ... have no weapons but their tongues. Shakespeare: *R2* 1.1.48f. Cf. T82.2: Tears are women's weapons.

W681   All WOMEN may be won (*Varied* from 1579; OW911a adds 1589) E.g., 1588 Greene *Perimedes* VII,68: Melissa was a woman and therefore to be woone. Shakespeare: *1H6* 5.3.78f., *R3* 1.2.228, *Tit.* 2.1.82f.

W700.1   WOMEN are frail (*Varied*) a1400 Wyclif *Sermons* II 139 15f.: For wymmen ben freel as water [in Wh W61]. 1575 Baldwin & Palfreyman *Treatise of Morall Philosophie*

2D1^v: Weoman are so fraile y^t with keepers w^t great pain, they can kepe them selves. 1591 Ariosto (Harington) *Orlando Furioso* II.71 R4^v: Damsell leave of dispaire, Nature humane, and womens sex is fraile. c1605 (1606) Marston *Fawn* 4.1.296: Pity the frailty of my sex.

Shakespeare: *TN* 2.2.29–32, *MM* 2.4.124–30, *Ham.* 1.2.146, *Ant.* 5.2.122–4, *Cym.* 1.4.91

W702 WOMEN are in church saints, abroad angels, at home devils (*Varied* from c1550)
E.g., c1601 (1602) ?Middleton *Blurt, Master Constable* 3.3.154f.: [Women] be saints in the church, angels in the street, devils in the kitchen, and apes in your bed.

Shakespeare: *Oth.* 2.1.109–12

W703.1 WOMEN are oft unstable (Wh W526 *varied* from a1300)
E.g., c1489 *Blanchardyn* 130.7–9: For it is sayde of a custume, that the herte of a woman is mutable and inconstaunt, and not in purpos stedfast.

Shakespeare: *JC* 2.4.39f.

(?) W704 WOMEN are tempted by gifts (*Varied* from 1575; not in OW)[n]
E.g., 1590 R. Wilson *Three Lords and Three Ladies of London* E2^v: Women weake are tempted soone with giftes. 1600 Thynne *Embl. and Epig.* 58: Trust Ovid then, whoe spake what he did knowe: it shewes great witt, large giftes for to bestowe. 1659 HOW. *Br. Prov.* 26: All gifts plead during pleasure.

Shakespeare: *TGV* 3.1.89, *Ham.* 1.5.43–5

[n]Although variously worded echoes of Ovid's *Artis Amatoriae* ii.275–8 are fairly frequent, OW was probably right to exclude any equivalent entry.

W706.1 WOMEN can keep no counsel (Wh W534 *varied* from c1378)

E.g., 1474 Caxton *Chesse* 27 (19–20): Wherfore it is a comyn proverb that women can kepe no counceyle. 1617 Middleton & Rowley *Fair Quarrel* 2.2.98f.: I will revive a reputation That women long has lost: I'll keep counsel.

Shakespeare: *JC* 2.4.9

W707.1 WOMEN can weep (and lie) at will (Wh W537 *varied* from c1375 [4])
Add: c1604 (1605) Marston *Dutch Courtesan* 5.2.133: She is a woman—that is, she can lie.

Shakespeare: *1H4* 3.3.61

W707.2 WOMEN desire to have sovereignty (Wh W539 from c1395 [2])
Add: 1576 Pettie *Petite Pallace* 266: Wee say women are alwayes desirous of soveraintie [in W697 (Women are ambitious), a very dubious entry].

Shakespeare: *H8* 2.3.28f.

W709 WOMEN have no souls (From 1566)[n]
Shakespeare: *TGV* 2.3.15–7

[n]Cf. Herford and Simpson's note (X, 464) on an instance of this proverb in Jonson's *Masque of Beauty.*

W718 WOMEN receive perfection by men (*Varied* from 1576)
Shakespeare: *Jn.* 2.1.439f., *Rom.* 1.3.95

W723 WOMEN will have their wills (*Varied* from 1552; Wh W519 from a1450)
Shakespeare: *Err.* 4.2.18, *Jn.* 2.1.194, *JC* 2.2.71, *Cym.* 2.5.34, *Son.* 135f.. 143.13

(?) W724.1 To fear is WOMANISH c1613 (1623) Webster *Duchess of Malfi* 5.5.125f. (altering Sidney's *wormish*): In what a shadow, or deepe pit of darknesse, Doth (womanish and fearefull) mankind live!

Shakespeare: *Tro.* 1.1.107, *R3* 1.4.261, *H8* 2.1.37f., *Rom.* 4.1.119

W728 A WONDER lasts but nine days (From 1525)
Shakespeare: *AYL* 3.2.174, *2H6* 2.4.69, *3H6* 3.2.113f.

W731 (WOO,) wed, and bed (wear) her (From 1580)
Shakespeare: *Shr.* 1.1.144, *AWW* 3.2.21

W732 He has lost himself (To be) in a WOOD (fig.) (*MND*, 1608ff.; OW913a supplements)
Shakespeare: *MND* 3.1.149f.

(?) W750 The WOOING was a day after the wedding (1732 FUL., cf. from 1579)[n]
I.e., 1579 Lyly *Euphues* I,228: I cannot but smile to heare, that . . . the woeing should bee a day after the weddinge. 1632 Hausted *Rival Friends* 5.6 M1[v]: But father, if I marry her to day, When must the wooing be? to morrow sir? 1732 FUL., no. 4840.
Shakespeare: *Rom.* 3.5.118f.

[n]See Introduction, p. xix.

W757.1 To go WOOLWARD (Cf. Appendix B) (OW914a from c1315)
Shakespeare: *LLL* 5.2.711

W762 He has not a WORD to cast (throw) at a dog (From 1593; OW915a from c1590 [1598])
Add: ?1590 J. Greenwood (?J. Throckmorton) M. *Some laid open* 42: Scarse a good argument betwixte us to throw at a dog's heade.
Shakespeare: *AYL* 1.3.2f.
Cf. S880: He has not a STONE (etc.) to cast (throw) at a dog.

W763 (He is but) a WORD and a blow (From c1569; OW914b from 1563)
Shakespeare: *Rom.* 3.1.40

W767 No WORD but mum (From 1523)
Shakespeare: *2H6* 1.2.89, *R3* 3.7.3

W772 There is many a true WORD spoken in jest (From 1665, cf. *Lr.*, 1598 [cf. on H745]; cf. Wh S488 from c1390 [2])
E.g., 1533 More *Apologye* 194 (23f.): For as Horace sayeth, a man maye somtyme saye full soth in game. [Horace *Satire* I.i.24f.]
Shakespeare: *Lr.* 5.3.71

W773.1 To be as good as one's WORD (OW317b, from 1577)
Shakespeare: *Wiv.* 3.4.108, *TN* 3.4.323, *1H4* 3.3.143f., *2H4* 5.5.85, *H5* 4.8.31f.
Cf. M395.2: To be a MAN of one's word.

W776 While the WORD is in your mouth it is your own, when it is once spoken it is another's (1672 WALK., cf. *Ham.*, 1646; cf. Wh W626 1509)
E.g., 1509 Barclay *Ship* I 110(21f.): So whan thy worde is spokyn and out at large, Thou arte nat mayster, but he that hath it harde.
Shakespeare: *Ham* 3.2.97f.

W777 A WORD (and a stone) let go (A word spoken) cannot be called back (*Word* from 1509; OW914b Horace, cf. c1386ff.)
E.g., 1548 W. Patten *Exped. into Scotland* (Tudor Tracts 154): The word thus uttered cannot be called again.
Shakespeare: *MM* 2.2.57f.

W778.1 A WORD (or two) in your ear
c1560 (c1570) W. Wager *Enough is as Good as a Feast* 684f.: Might I be so bold As to have a word or two with you in your ear? c1561 (1595) *Pedlar's Prophecy* (MSR 180): Let me have a word or two in your eare; 191: But mayd a word or two in your eare againe. c1595 Munday et al. *Sir Thomas More* 4.1.219: A woord in

your eare. c1611 (1631) Dekker *Match Me in London* 3.2.60: A word in your Highnesse eare—.
Shakespeare: *Ado* 4.2.27, 5.1.143
Cf. Appendix B: To speak in the EAR.

W794   Fair WORDS (promises) make fools fain (From c1485)
Shakespeare: *JC* 3.1.42

W796   Few WORDS among friends are best (*Varied* from 1568)
E.g., 1580 Munday *Zelauto* K1: Fewe woords among freendes (they say) is fittest. 1602 *Poet. Rhap.* 128 I,186: The firmest faith is in the fewest wordes.
Shakespeare: *Shr.* 1.2.65f., *Tro.* 3.2.95

W797   Few WORDS and many deeds (Collections from 1596, plus analogues)
Shakespeare: *Tro.* 4.5.98
Cf. W820: Not words but deeds.

W798   Few WORDS are best (*Varied* from 1500)
Shakespeare: *LLL* 4.2.165, *Wiv.* 1.1.120, *H5* 3.2.36f.
Cf. W813.1: I love few (not many) words.

W799   Few WORDS show men wise (From 1562, *varied* from c1475)
E.g., [ERAS. *Similia* 570F: Ita sapit, qui pauca loquitur, sed ad rem.] 1562 Heywood *Epigrammes* 95: Few woords shew men wise, wise men doe devise.
Shakespeare: *LLL* 4.2.80, *Wiv.* 1.1.120, *H5* 3.2.36f., *Lr.* 1.4.15f.

W813.1   I love few (not many) WORDS (*OED* 22 *Of few words* from c1450)
1596 (1598) Chapman *Blind Beggar of Alexandria* ii.65: Sweet nimph I loue few wordes. 1598 (1601) Jonson *Every Man In* 2.3.75: I loue few words: you haue wit: imagine. c1602

(1606) Chapman *Gentleman Usher* 3.2.88–90: Well, take my iewell, you shall not be strange, I loue not manie words. / My lord, I thanke you, I am of few words too. c1639 *Telltale* 1.3 (MSR 489): I am a man of few words.
Shakespeare: *AWW* 3.6.84, *H8* 3.2.270
Cf. W796-9.

W820   Not WORDS but deeds (*Varied* from c1527; W642 from c735)
Shakespeare: *TGV* 2.2.18, *Tro.* 3.2.55, *1H6* 3.2.49, *H8* 3.2.153f.

W825   To eat one's WORD(S) (From 1571; OW214b from 1551)
Shakespeare: *Ado* 4.1.278, *AYL* 5.4.149, *Tro.* 2.3.217, *2H4* 2.2.137f., *Tit.* 2.1.55

W832   WORDS are but sands (words), it is money buys lands (*Sands* from 1659, *words* 1666; OW915b *Words are but words* from c1595)
E.g., c1595 Munday et al. *Sir Thomas More* 4.4.1: Woords are but wordes and payes not what men owe.
Shakespeare: *Oth.* 1.3.218
Cf. W840.1: Words pay no debts.

W833   WORDS are but wind (Cf. Job 6.26) (From c1486)
Shakespeare: *Err.* 3.1.75, *LLL* 4.3.66, *Ado* 5.2.52, *Tro.* 5.3.108–10, *PP* 3.9, 20.31

W839   WORDS hurt (cut) more than swords (*Varied* from 1523; Wh W640 *slay* from a1200)
Shakespeare: *Tit.* 1.1.314, *Cym.* 3.4.33f., *WT* 2.3.86f.
Cf. T401.1: To have a tongue like a razor; D8.1: To speak daggers.

W840.1   WORDS pay no debts
c1595 Munday et al. *Sir Thomas More* 3.1.109: Woords are but wordes, and paies not what men owe. 5 Jan. 1608 J. Chamberlain 250: The Italians say parole non pagano debiti, and so they replied.

Shakespeare: *Tro.* 3.2.55
Cf. P518 (Pound of care), S660
(Sorrow).

(?) W865.1   All the WORLD to nothing (*OED* 21 *All the world* from c1175)
    1598 (1601) Jonson *Every Man In*
1.4.200: She heard me, all the world
to nothing.
    Shakespeare: *R3* 1.2.237, *Rom.*
3.5.213f.

(?) W870   He that is giddy thinks the
WORLD turns round (*Shr.*, 1621;
ditto OW300b)
I.e., R. Burton *Anat. M.* III.iv.i.3
III,418 : Though ... the whole
world contradict it, they care not ...
and as Gregory well notes of such as
are vertiginous, they think all turns
round and moves.
    Shakespeare: *Shr.* 5.2.20

W876.1   In the universal (versal, var-
sal) WORLD (Cf. Appendix B) (*OED
Universal* 8a from 1649; *Versal* 1 begins with *Rom.*) c1595 Munday et al.
Sir Thomas More 5.2.15f.: I thinke
there lives not a more harmelesse
gentleman in the universall worlde.
    Shakespeare: *H5* 4.1.66, 4.8.9f.,
Rom. 2.4.206

W877.1   It is a hard WORLD (As
hard as the WORLD goes)
c1561 (1595) *Pedlar's Prophecy* (MSR
111): Yet as hard as the world went
there, To fill up my packe I brought
more geare. c1561 (c1569) Preston
Cambises ii.38: The world shall go
hard if I do not shift. c1590 (1595)
Peele *Old Wives Tale* 327f.: Here is a
peece of Cake for you, as harde as
the world goes. 1599 (1600) Drayton
et al. *1 Sir John Oldcastle* 1.3.14: It is a
hard world the while. 1601 A. Dent
Plaine Mans Path-Way H4: For it is an
harde world, and goods are not easie
to come by.
    Shakespeare: *3H6* 2.6.77, *R2*
5.5.20f.

W878   It is a WORLD to see (From
c1525)
    Shakespeare: *Shr.* 2.1.311, *Ado*
3.5.35

W878.1   It was never merry WORLD
since x
c1550 (c1565) R. Wever *Lusty Juventus* (MSR 655f.): The world was
never mery, Since children were so
bolde. 1581 I. B. *Dialogue* (STC
1039) B8^v: You are one of these new
men y^t would have nothing but
preaching, it was never merry world
since y^t sect came first amongst us.
1581 J. Field *Caveat for Parsons
Howlet* E1 (parodying a papist): It
was never merry world since there
was so much talke of the scripture.
?1589 ?J. Throckmorton *Dialogue*
(STC 6805) D2: *Papist.* It was never
merry worlde since there was so
many puritans. 1594 W. Burton *Exposition of the Lords Prayer* (in 1602
Works 143): Many say now adaies: it
was never merry world since we had
so much preaching. 1599 (1600)
Dekker *Old Fortunatus* 1.2.75f.:
Twas never merie world with us,
since purses and bags were invented.
    Shakespeare: *TN* 3.1.98f., *MM*
3.2.5f., *2H6* 4.2.8f.

W879   Let the WORLD wag (slide,
pass) (From c1525; OW919b from
c1425)
    Shakespeare: *Shr.* Ind. i.5f., ii.143,
AYL 2.7.23, *1H4* 4.1.96f.

W882   This WORLD is a stage and
every man plays his part (*Varied* from
1549; OW918b from c1530)
    Shakespeare: *MV* 1.1.77f., *AYL*
2.7.139f., *2H4* 1.1.155-9, *Lr.*
4.6.183, *Mac.* 5.5.24f., *Son.* 15.3

W884.1   Thus (How) goes (fares) the
WORLD (Wh W665 from c1385)
E.g., a1393 Gower *CA* II20.570:
Now up now down, this world goth
so; III 433.1738: So goth the world,
now wo, now wel. 1481 Caxton *Rey-*

nard 97(4–5): Thus fareth the world that one goth up and another goth doun.
Add: 1530 Palsgrave 250b: Howe goth the worlde. c1553 (1575) W. Stevenson *Gammer Gurton's Needle* 2.1.66: As the world now gose.
Shakespeare: *Shr.* 4.1.33f., *R3* 3.2.96, *JC* 5.5.22, *Ham.* 2.2.178, *Lr.* 4.6.147f., *Cor.* 1.10.31f., *Tim.* 1.1.2, 2.2.36, *WT* 2.3.72f.

W885.1 (To drink until) the WORLD goes round (*OED* 7c 1788) c1597 (1619) Deloney *Jacke of Newberie* 61: First one drunke to her, and then another . . . so that . . . she thought the world ran round.
Shakespeare: *Ant.* 2.7.117f., *Cym.* 5.5.232

W889 We weeping come into the WORLD and weeping hence we go (*Varied* from 1576)
E.g., 1601 P. Holland (Pliny) *Hist. World* VII Proem 152: Man alone, poore wretch, she nature hath layed all naked upon the bare earth, even on his birth day, to cry and wraule presently from the very first houre that hee is borne in such sort.
Add e.g.: 1617 J. Boys *2 Exposition . . . Psalmes . . . English Liturgie* (STC 3467) Ps. 8 C2^v: Therefore [margin: Cyprian ser: de bono patientiae, idem Plato in Axiocho & August: ser: 31 ad fratres in eremo.] the first voyce that is uttered by the new borne infant is crying, hereby Prophecying that hee is come into a world full of care and calamities.
Shakespeare: *Lr.* 4.6.178–82

W889.1 What a WORLD is this c1595 A. Munday et al. *Sir Thomas More* 1.2.172. 1599 (1600) Drayton et al. *1 Sir John Oldcastle* 2.2.26f., 64f., 3.2.11f., 4.2.31, 140. c1604 (1605) Chapman *All Fools* 4.1.45. 1617 Middleton & Rowley *Fair Quarrel*

3.1.157. ?1621 (1652) Fletcher *Wild Goose Chase* 5.6.84.
Shakespeare: *AYL* 2.3.14, 2.7.9, *2H6* 3.2.380, *R3* 2.1.83

W892.1 The WORLD changes every day (is changed)
1533 N. Udall *Floures* G2^v: Omnium rerum vicissitudo est. The worlde chaungeth every day. 1548 Elyot s.v. Vicissitudo: The worlde chaungeth every day. Again 1565 Cooper, c1580 Conybeare 23. 1578 G. Whetstone *1 Promos and Cassandra* 4.1.1: With my Mistresse the worlde is chaunged well. c1605 (?1608) Middleton *Your Five Gallants* 1.1.85: Tut, the world's changed.
Shakespeare: *Err.* 2.2.152, *MM* 3.2.50

W893 The WORLD goes (runs) on wheels (From 1546)
Shakespeare: *TGV* 3.1.315, *Ant.* 2.7.90–2

(?) W893.1 The WORLD grows honest (wise)
c1589 (1594) Lyly *Mother Bombie* 3.4.169f.: I have nothing to live by but knavery, and if the world grow honest, welcome beggerie. 1598 (1616) W. Haughton *Englishmen for My Money* xii (MSR 2650f.): I thinke the world's growne wise, Plaine folkes (as I) shall not know how to live.
Shakespeare: *Ham.* 2.2.237

W895 The WORLD is (a) wide (parish, place) (*Parish* from 1659, *place* 1738; OW918b adds 1581)
I.e., 1581 W. Fulke *Brief Confutation* 17^v: The worlde is wide.
Add: 1591 Spenser *Prosopopoia* 90: Wide is the world.
Shakespeare: *Rom* 3.3.16

W896 The WORLD is full of fools (knaves) (From 1596; OW918b Cicero, 1591 without *world*)
E.g., 1596 Harington *Metam. Ajax*

55: And for the foole, the olde proverbe may serve us, Stultorum plena
sunt omnia, the world is full of
fooles.
    Shakespeare: *AYL* 2.7.13, *TN*
3.1.38f., *Lr.* 4.6.183

W909   Tread on a WORM (on the
tail) and it will turn (From 1546)
    Shakespeare: *3H6* 2.2.17

W910   There cannot lightly come a
WORSE except the devil come himself (1616 DR.; analogues from *2H6*)
    Shakespeare: *MV* 3.1.77f., *2H6*
3.2.303

W911   If the WORST come to the
worst (From 1597, *MV* analogue)
1596 Nashe *Saffron-walden* III,39: If
the worst come to the worst, a good
swimmer may doo much.
    Shakespeare: *MV* 1.2.89f.

W912   It is good to fear the WORST
(*Varied* from c1495)
    Shakespeare: *MND* 1.1.62f., *MV*
1.2.95, *Tro.* 3.2.73, *3H6* 4.6.96, *R3*
2.3.31, *Jn* 4.2.135f., *1H4* 4.4.34f.,
H8 3.1.25, *JC* 5.1.95f., *Mac.*
3.4.133f.

W914   Let him do his WORST (Collections 1616, 1639)
E.g., 1616 DR., s.v. Contempt 336.
Add e.g.: 1567 J. Pickering *Horestes*
iii (MSR 456f.): Drawe thy sword
vylyne, yf thou be a man, And then
do the worst, that ever thou can.
c1570 *Misogonus* 2.4.200: But let
them doe their worst. c1576 *Common
Conditions* 1322: Do thy worst. 1578
T. Lupton *All for Money* 958f.: Nay,
let them do to her the worst that they
can. c1587 (1590) Marlowe *2 Tamburlaine* 5.1.112: Do all thy worst.
c1605 (1608) Middleton *Trick to
Catch the Old One* 4.4.176: Why, do
your worst for that, I defy you.
c1610 (1616) Jonson *Every Man In*
4.11.85: Why, then, let him doe his
worst, I am resolute.

Shakespeare: *H5* 3.3.5, *Oth.*
1.2.17, 5.2.159, *Lr.* 4.6.137, *Mac.*
3.2.24, *Cor.* 5.2.105f., *Son.* 19.13

W914.1   None of (Not) the WORST
c1569 T. Preston *Cambises* ii.130:
Gramercy, Snuf, thou art not the
worst. c1590 (1595) Peele *Old Wives
Tale* 618f.: I shall have a husband
and none of the worst. 1601 A. Dent
Plaine Mans Path-Way X1ᵛ: I am sure
if I be badde, I am not the worst in
the worlde. 1639 CL., s.v. Modestia
212: None of the worst.
    Shakespeare: *Lr.* 2.4.257f.

W915   To know the WORST is good
(Shak., 1639 CL.)
Add: c1570 *Misogonus* 2.4.210: I
know the worst. c1613 (1630) Middleton *Chaste Maid in Cheapside*
3.3.37: You know the worst.
    Shakespeare: *MND* 1.1.62f., *Jn.*
4.3.27, *Mac.* 3.4.133f.

W918   The WORST is behind (From
1546)
    Shakespeare: *Ham.* 3.4.179
    Cf. B318: The best is behind.

W923   The WORTH of a thing is as it
is esteemed (*Varied* from *Tro.*; collections from 1611)
Add: 1575 T. Churchyard "In
prayse of Gascoignes Posies" 9 in
Gascoigne I,21: Fame shewes the
value first, of everie precious thing.
    Shakespeare: *Tro.* 2.2.52, *MM*
2.2.150f.

W924   The WORTH of a thing is
best known by the want (*Varied* from
Rom.; OW922a from 1586)
    Shakespeare: *Ado* 4.1.218–20,
AWW 5.2.52–60, *R2* 5.6.40. *Rom.*
1.1.232f., *Ant.* 1.2.126, 1.4.43f., *Cor.*
4.1.15

W927   A green WOUND is soon
healed (fig.) (Collections from 1639;
varied from 1578; OW337af. from
c1532)
    Shakespeare: *2H6* 3.1.285–7

(?) W928.1 It is hard to heal a WOUND that is oft broken (fig.) (Wh W696 *varied* from a 1400 [3], but all literal)
Shakespeare: *2H4* 1.2.147f.
Cf. e.g., H283: It is ill healing of an old sore [fig., from 1509].

W929 Though the WOUND be healed yet the scar remains (fig.) (*Varied* from 1573; OW923a adds a 1542)
Shakespeare: *Luc.* 731f.

W947 WRONG has no warrant (Collections from 1641 [cf. on H745]; OW924a from a 1628)
Shakespeare: *H8* 3.2.244

W946 To forget a WRONG is best revenge (remedy) (Collections *varied* from 1639, cf. *Cor.*)
Shakespeare: *Cor.* 5.3.154f.

X

X1.0 X me no x
E.g., 1553 ?Udall *Respublica* 146: Founder me no foundering. c1553 (1575) W. Stevenson *Gammer Gurton's Needle* 5.2.92: Swear me no swearing. c1564 *Bugbears* 1.1.52: Diner me no diners. c1576 *Common Conditions* 430: Tinke mee no tinks. c1590 Peele *Old Wives Tale* 461: Parish me no parishes.
Shakespeare: *R2* 2.3.87, *Rom.* 3.5.152

Y

Y25 This seven YEAR(S) (From c1475; Wh Y11 from a893, a sampling from 410 examples)
Shakespeare: *Shr.* Ind. i.122, *Ado*

3.3.126, *AYL* 3.2.317, *TN* 1.1.25, *Tro.* 1.3.12, *1H6* 4.3.37, *2H6* 2.1.2, *1H4* 2.4.312, *Lr.* 3.4.139, *Cor.* 2.1.114f., 4.1.55, *Per.* 4.6.171, *WT* 4.4.578

(?) Y29.1 To be sick of the YELLOWS (fig.) (Cf. Appendix B) (OW926a 1596 [1605], *Wiv.* Q: *OED* 2 fig. adds 1598 [1601], 1638)
Shakespeare: *Wiv.* 1.3.101f.(Q)

Y31 (It is too late) to call again YESTERDAY (From c1517; cf. 2 Esdras 4.5)
Shakespeare: *R2* 3.2.69

Y36 You shall never be (labor) YOUNGER (*Be* from 1566)
Shakespeare: *Shr.* Ind. ii.143f.

Y43 YOUTH and age will never agree (*Varied* from *LLL*; OW929a from c1390)
E.g., 1556 Heywood *Epigrammes* First Hundred 33: Age and youth together can seeld agree.
Shakespeare: *PP* 12.1

(?) Y44.1 YOUTH hardly can obey an old decree.
1600 J. Bodenham *Bel-vedere* ed. 1875 220: Yowth hardly can obey an old decree [in Y43].
Shakespeare: *LLL* 4.3.213

Y48 YOUTH will have its course (swing) (From 1579)
E.g., 1585 E. Sandys *Serm.* 8 152: Youth, they say, must have his swing: let old age wax holy.
Shakespeare: *1H4* 5.2.16f.

Y51 YOUTH in a basket (*Wiv.*, 1606, c1625 [1632]; ditto OW929a)
Shakespeare: *Wiv.* 4.2.116f.

APPENDIX B

Marginal Exclusions

This appendix lists phrases that can be called proverbial as legitimately, or illegitimately, as those in Appendix A labeled "cf. Appendix B" (cf. p. 43 and Introduction, fn. 28). Because they do not appear in Tilley, they are not included in the index. But it would be foolish wholly to ignore them. This appendix, and the terminal footnote under each work, represent a compromise. Obviously, one could include more phrases than appear below. I have probably missed some that indisputably should be here, although many may feel I have included too many.

Entries are numbered according to the capitalized word under which *OED*'s citation appears. Each entry lists the *OED* location, the *OED* earliest date or example, and pertinent passages in Shakespeare. Footnotes are kept at a minimum, but if I can prove *OED* in error when it begins with Shakespeare, I so indicate.

AA1   To cry AIM (2c from 1589) *Wiv.* 3.2.44, *Jn.* 2.1.196

AA2   To give AIM (2c from 1545) *TGV* 5.4.101, *Tit.* 5.3.149

AA3   ALACK the day (b. from *Rom.*; *Alas* from c1394 with modifier) *MV* 2.2.70, *Wiv.* 3.5.38, 4.2.69, AYL 3.2.219, *TN* 2.1.24, 2.2.38, *Tro.* 3.2.47, *R2* 4.1.257, *2H4* 2.1.13, *Rom.* 3.2.39, 72, *Oth.* 3.4.158, 4.2.42, 124, *Mac.* 2.4.23

AA4   ALL in all (8d from 1539; cf. A133) *Shr.* 2.1.129, *2H6* 2.4.51, *R3* 3.1.168, *H5* 1.1.42, *Ham.* 1.2.187, *Oth.* 4.1.88, 265

AA5   ALL to naught (12 from c1175) *Ven.* 993

AA6   (What) ALL AMORT? (From c1590; *Alamort* 2 from 1592)[n] *Shr.* 4.3.36, *1H6* 3.2.124

[n]See 1578 Whetstone, *1 Promos & Cassandra* 2.7 (ed. Bullough, II, 457): "All a mort knave, for want of company?"

AA7   Let me ALONE (for that) (i.e., Leave it to me; often to do evil) (Included in 4 from 1366?) Passim

AA8   Ever and ANON (*LLL*, then 1647)[n] *LLL* 5.2.101, *1H4* 1.3.38

[n]See 1590 Spenser, *Faerie Queene* 3.9.28.1, 3.10.58.4

BB1   BAG and baggage (19 from 1422) *AYL* 3.2.161, *WT* 1.2.206

BB2   To bid (a, the) BASE (sb.²b from 1548) *TGV* 1.2.94, *Ven.* 303

BB3   To be at a BECK (2 from a1470; cf. B182: To be at beck and bay) *Son.* 58.5

BB4   To have a BEETLE brow (be beetle-browed) (a. 1 from 1362, including 1546 [1562] Heywood) *Rom.* 1.4.32

BB5 To have a BEETLE-head (be beetle-headed) (sb. 3 from 1553–87) *Shr.* 4.1.157

BB6 BELIEVE it[n] Passim

[n]Cf. c1602 (1606) Chapman, *Gentleman Usher* 3.2.416–9: "Out upon't, that phrase is so runne out of breath in trifles, that we shall have no beleefe at all in earnest shortly. Beleeve it tis a prettie feather; beleeve it a daintie Rush; beleeve it an excellent Cockscombe.

BB7 The heart in one's BELLY (8 from 1491) *1H4* 4.2.21f.

BB8 To be BESIDE one's wit, one-self (5a from 1490) *Err.* 3.2.77f., *Ado* 5.1.128, *TN* 4.2.86, *JC* 3.1.180

BB9 (To do all) for the BEST (10b from c1386) *Rom.* 3.1.104, *Cor.* 4.6.143

BB10 To look (talk) BIG (8b from *Shr.*)[n] *Shr.* 3.2.228, *R2* 3.2.114, *1H4* 4.1.58, *2H4* 1.3.8, *WT* 4.3.106

[n]E.g., c1569 Wager, *The Longer Thou Livest* 820: "I would look big like a man." c1570 *Misogonus* 1.1.72: "He shall learne to looke bigge, stand stoute and go brave."

BB11 BLACK-MOUTHED (From 1595) *H8* 1.3.58

BB12 To have one's heart BLEED (1c from c1374) or WEEP (3b from 14th century) *2H4* 2.2.48, 4.4.58, *H8* 3.2.335., *Tim.* 1.2.205, *WT* 3.3.51f., 5.2.88f., *Tmp.* 1.2.63f.

BB13 The BLOOD of the grape (2 fig. from 1382 [Gen. 49.11]) *Tim.* 4.3. 429

BB14 To be blithe and BONNY (3 from *Ado*) *Ado* 2.3.67

BB15 By the BOOK (14 from *Rom.*) *Rom.* 1.5.110

BB16 (From) the BOTTOM of one's heart (stomach) (5b from 1549, 1557)[n] *H5* 2.2.97

[n]1546 Heywood, *Dialogue* I.x, C3: "whan the meale mouth hath won the bottome Of your stomake, than wil the pikthanke it tell To your most enmies."

BB17 Fire and BRIMSTONE (1 from a1300; 1b *TN*, *Oth.*) *TN* 2.5.50, *Oth.* 4.1.234

BB18 BY AND BY (3 from 1407) Passim

CC1 The CANDLE [of life] (3b from 1535; Job 21.17) *3H6* 2.6.1, *R2* 1.3.223, *Oth.* 5.2.7ff., *Lr.* 1.4.217, *Mac.* 5.5.23, *Ant.* 4.14.46, 4.15.85 (Tilley includes in C41; cf. Appendix C)

CC2 With CAP and knee (4g from 1581; common earlier) *1H4* 4.3.68, *Tim.* 3.6.97

CC3 With CAP in hand (4g from 1565) *Ant.* 2.7.57

CC4 To make a CARBONADO of one (From c1587 [1590]) *1H4* 5.3.58

CC5 All on (upon, at) a (one) CAST (3b fig. from a1300) *1H4* 4.1.45–7

CC6 To CATCH one's death (30 from 1297) *Rom.* 2.5.52

CC7 CATERPILLARS of the commonwealth (2 fig., 1579, 1631) *R2* 2.3.165f.

CC8 Out of all CESS (sb.[1] 3 from 1588) *1H4* 2.1.7

CC9 To CHARM the tongue (4 from 1547) *Shr.* 1.1.209, 4.2.58, *2H6* 4.1.64, *3H6* 5.5.31, *Oth.* 5.2.183f.

CC10   CHERRY lip(s) (8 from 1570; common earlier) *MND* 3.2.140, 5.1.190, *R3* 1.1.94

CC11   Cannot CHOOSE (but) (5 from 1522); *but* 5b from 1542) *Shr.* Ind. i.42, 5.1.11 (shall), *MV* 3.1.114f., *Wiv.* 1.1.303, 5.3.17, *TN* 2.5.174f., 4.1.57, *Tro.* 1.2.135, *AWW* 1.3.214f., *R3* 4.4.289, *1H4* 3.1.146, *2H4* 3.2.207f., *Rom.* 1.3.50, *Ham.* 4.5.69, 4.7.65 (shall), *Cor.* 4.3.37, *Tim.* 5.1.177, *Cym.* 2.3.34, *Tmp.* 1.2.186, *Ven.* 79

CC12   At a CLAP (7 from 1519) *Lr.* 1.4.294

CC13   Man (etc.) of CLOUTS (4c from 1467; cf. OW128b) *Jn.* 3.4.58

CC14   COAL-BLACK (From a1250; Wh C324a) *2H6* 2.1.110, *Tit.* 4.2.99, 5.1.32, *Luc.* 1009

CC15   (By) COCK-AND-PIE (From 1550) *Wiv.* 1.1.303, *2H4* 5.1.1f.

CC16   To COME and go (i.e., appear and disappear) (26b from c1340) *Jn.* 4.2.76

CC17   To CONTAIN oneself (14a from 1590) *Shr.* Ind. i.100, *Tro.* 5.2.180, *Ant.* 2.5.75

CC18   To have a COPPER-NOSE (be copper-nosed) (1, 2 from 1579–80) *Tro.* 1.2.104–6

CC19   To keep a CORNER (6c from *Oth.*, but fairly common earlier) *Oth.* 3.3.272

CC20   Under CORRECTION (1b from 1374) *LLL* 5.2.489, 493, *MM* 2.2.10, *H5* 3.2.120f., 5.2.138f.

CC21   To set a COUNTENANCE (1d 1600; cf. c1590 [1595] Peele *Old Wives Tale* 659f.: Ile nowe set my countenance and to hir in prose.) *Shr.* 4.4.18

CC22   To hunt COUNTER (1 from 1575) *Err.* 4.2.39, *2H4* 1.2.90, *Ham.* 4.5.110f.

CC23   To strain COURTESY (1c from 1528) *Rom.* 2.4.50f., *Ven.* 888

CC24   To bear one's CROSS (10 from 1550) *AYL* 2.4.12, *2H4* 1.2.225f.

DD1   To make DAINTY (sb. 7 from 1579) *Rom.* 1.5.19f.

DD2   I'll see you DAMNED first (not in *OED*; cf. HANG) *TN* 3.4.284f., *1H4* 2.4.146f., *2H4* 2.4.156

DD3   The prince of DARKNESS (4 fig. a. from 1526) *AWW* 4.5.42f., *Lr.* 3.4.143

DD4   DART of death (lb fig. from 1509) *Cym.* 4.2.211, *Ven.* 948

DD5   By DAY and night (lb from 1386) *H8* 1.2.213, *Tit.* 4.3.28, *Lr.* 1.3.3

DD6   DAY and night (lb from c1250) *TN* 5.1.96, *AWW* 5.1.1, *1H4* 1.3.184, 5.1.35, *2H4* 5.5.21, (?) *Ham.* 1.5.164, 3.2.217, *Ven.* 1186

DD7   From DAY to day (19 from 1297) *Mac.* 5.5.20

DD8   One of these DAYS (7b 1535 [1 Sam. 27.1], 1586) *H5* 2.1.87f.

DD9   DEAD and gone (32a from 1482) *1H6* 1.4.93, *2H6* 2.3.37, *Jn.* 4.2.84, *Tit.* 5.3.166, *Ham.* 4.5.29f.

DD10   To be the DEATH of x (7 from *1H4*) *Ado* 2.2.19f., *1H4* 2.1.12f., *TNK* 5.2.67

DD11   The DEVIL take him (etc.) (17

from 1548) *Wiv.* 4.5.106, *AYL* 3.2.214, *Tro.* 4.2.74f., 5.2.195f., 5.7.23, *R2* 5.5.101, *1H4* 1.3.255, *H5* 4.5.22, *Ham.* 5.1.259, *Tmp.* 3.2.80f.

DD12 What (etc.) the DEVIL (20 from c1385) Passim

DD13 To DEW with tears (2 from a1325) *2H6* 3.2.339f.

DD14 What have you to DO? (33c from 1530) *Shr.* 1.2.224, 3.2.216, *Wiv.* 3.3.154f.

DD15 Till DOOMSDAY (lb from c1200; ditto Wh D346) *Err.* 3.2.99, *LLL* 4.3.270, *Ham.* 5.1.59, *Ant.* 5.2.231f.

DD16 DOUBLE-TONGUE (1 from c1386) *LLL* 5.2.245, *Ado* 5.1.169

DD17 To deal DOUBLE (3 from *Rom.*; *Double-dealing* from a1529, *Double-dealer* from 1547) *Rom.* 2.4.168f.

DD18 To DRINK deep (10b from a1300) *1H4* 2.4.15, *H5* 1.1.20, *Ham.* 1.2.175

DD19 To DRIVE away the time (21 from 1484) *1H4* 2.4.28

EE1 To speak in the EAR (i.e., confidentially) (3 from a1300) *Wiv.* 1.4.102f., 2.2.96f. Cf. W778.1

EE2 (Both) EARLY and late (1c from 1330) *2H6* 1.1.90f.

EE3 About one's EARS (fig.) (1c from 1652 but common earlier) *3H6* 5.1.108, *H5* 3.7.83f., *Cor.* 3.2.1, 4.6.98f.

EE4 To have EGRESS and regress (1 from 1538) *Wiv.* 2.1.217f.

EE5 To be at one's ELBOW (4 from a1548) *Ado* 3.3.98, *R3* 1.4.145, *2H4* 2.1.20, *Oth.* 5.1.3

EE6 EVEN or odd (15c from c1460; Wh O18) *Rom.* 1.3.16f.

EE7 EVER and anon (2b from 1590) *LLL* 5.2.101, *1H4* 1.3.38

FF1 By my FAITH and TROTH (Separately, *Faith* 11c from c1350, *Troth* from 1374; in combination, e.g., c1561 [1595] *Pedlar's Prophecy* 1285) *Ado* 1.1.226

FF2 To look (etc.) one's FILL (1b from c1300; *weep* 1f from a1290) *Shr.* 1.1.73, *Tro.* 4.5.236, *3H6* 2.5.113, *Ham.* 4.5.130

FF3 FIRST and last (i.e., "one and all") (5e 1589) *Mac.* 3.4.1f.

FF4 FLESH AND BLOOD (1 from 1340; cf. F366f.) *LLL* 1.1.185, *2H6* 1.1.233, *Ham.* 1.5.22, *Per.* 4.6.34, 5.1.152, *Tmp.* 5.1.114

FF5 FLESH and fell (1c from c1000; cf. a1475 *Death of Herod* [Coventry] [Death speaking of worms]: They shul etyn both flesch and felle.) *Lr.* 5.3.24

FF6 The FLOWER of chivalry (7 from ?1370), of courtesy (9 from 1297; Wh F311) *1H4* 2.4.10f., *Rom.* 2.4.57f., 2.5.43, *Cor.* 1.6.32

FF7 FOOT to foot (26b from 1553) *Ant.* 3.7.66

FF8 To tread under FOOT (cf. 33 from c1205; *2H6* earliest for *tread*, but cf. 1590 Spenser *Faerie Queene* 3.1.50.3f.) *2H6* 5.1.208f.

FF9 To FORGET oneself (5a To omit care for oneself, from a1200; b To lose remembrance of one's own station . . . to behave unbecomingly, from *R2* [but common earlier]; c To lose one's way, from 1582; d To lose consciousness, from c1390) *Shr.* Ind. i.41, *2H6* 2.4.27, *R3* 4.4.420, *Jn.* 3.1.134, 4.3.83, *R2* 3.2.83, *JC*

4.3.29f., 35, *Ham.* 5.2.76, *Cym.* 1.6.112f.

FF10 Out of FRAME (5 from 1581) *LLL* 3.1.191, *Ham.* 1.2.20

GG1 Upon the GAD (sb.[n] 4b *Lr.* only) *Lr.* 1.2.26

[n]Cf. OW769a: Upon the spur (a variant of S789: He is all on the spur). E.g., 1613 T. Adams *White Devil* (1862) III, 224: Either he must be unmerciful or over-merciful; either wholly for the reins, or all upon the spur. Add: 1617 Middleton & Rowley *Fair Quarrel* 5.1.59: He's upon the spur. OW769a's "On the spur of the moment" begins with 1806.

GG2 The earth (etc.) GAPES (1b transf. *earth* from c1375, *hell* from c1460) *3H6* 1.1.161, *R3* 1.2.65, 4.4.75, *2H4* 5.5.53f., *H5* 2.1.61, 3.6.42

GG3 (One's) last (latter) GASP (1b from 1577) *AYL* 2.3.70, *1H6* 1.2.127, 2.5.38, *3H6* 2.1.108, *Cym.* 1.5.53

GG4 GATE of mercy (5 fig. a1300) *H5* 3.3.10

GG5 To give up (yield) the GHOST (From a900; ditto Wh G55) *1H6* 1.1.67, *3H6* 2.3.22, *R3* 1.4.37, *JC* 5.1.88

GG6 (Let it) GO BY (77b from 1450) *Shr.* Ind. i.9f., 1.2.254 Cf. PASS

GG7 GO to! (91b from 1513) Passim

GG8 (And) GOD before (9c from a1450) *H5* 1.2.307, 3.6.156

GG9 GOOD NIGHT (1 fig. from 1553) *R3* 4.3.39, *1H4* 1.3.194, *Ant.* 3.10.29, *WT* 1.2.410f., *TNK* 3.4.11

GG10 GOOD words (used ellipt. [= L. *bona verba*]) (7b from c1592) *Wiv.* 1.1.120, *Tro.* 2.1.88

GG11 What a (the) GOODYEAR (a from c1555) *Wiv.* 1.4.121f., *Ado* 1.3.1, *2H4* 2.4.58f., 177

GG12 (To dye) in GRAIN (fig.) (10b fig. from 1567) *Err.* 3.2.106f., *TN* 1.5.237

GG13 GRANDAM earth (4 fig. from 1602, *Grandmother* 1c fig. from 1626; both common in 17th century. ?1597 [1602] *Spanish Tragedy* 3.12A.19) (cf. E28.1) *1H4* 3.1.33

GG14 GRANDMOTHER Eve (2 from 1526) *LLL* 1.1.263f., *Wiv.* 4.2.24

GG15 A soused GURNET (lb from *1H4*) *1H4* 4.2.11f.

HH1 Out of HAND (i.e., at once) (33 from 14th century; 3 times in 1546 Heywood) *1H6* 3.2.102, *3H6* 4.7.63, *Tit.* 5.2.77

HH2 Under HAND (35b from 1611)[n] *AYL* 1.1.140

[n]1584 Lyly, *Campaspe* 5.4.99f.: "But *Apelles*, forsooth, loveth under hand, yea & under *Alexanders* nose."

HH3 To go HAND IN HAND with (1b fig. from 1576) *Err.* 5.1.426, *R3* 5.3.313, *Ham.* 1.5.49, *Cym.* 1.4.70

HH4 HANG me if, And be HANGED, I'll be HANGED if, I'll see you HANGED first (etc.) (3c *variously*, sometimes late, but all were current) Passim

HH5 To HANG in a (the) balance (17 from 1430−40) *AWW* 1.3.124

HH6 To HANG the lip (4b from 1568) *Tro.* 3.1.139

HH7 To go HARD but (2c from 1530) *Shr.* 4.4.108, *TGV* 1.1.85, *MV* 3.1.72, *2H4* 3.2.329

HH8 To be HARE-BRAINED (From 1548) *1H6* 1.2.37, *1H4* 5.2.19

HH9 Under (the) HATCHES (4 fig. from c1550) *Wiv.* 2.1.92f.

HH10 HAVE with you (i.e., I'll go with you, Let's go) (20 from 1575, but misleadingly defined) *LLL* 4.2.146, *Wiv.* 2.1.156, 221, 231, 3.2.92, *AYL* 1.2.256. *Tro.* 5.2.185, *1H6* 2.4.114, *Oth.* 1.2.53, *Cor.* 2.1.270, *Cym.* 4.4.50

HH11 To hop HEADLESS (1b from c1330) *2H6* 1.3.137

HH12 Double HEART (6b from 1382; 1 Chron. 12.33) *Ado* 2.1.279

HH13 HEART(S) of gold (14 from 1553) *1H4* 2.4.278, *H5* 4.1.44

HH14 To find in one's HEART (40 from c1440) *Err.* 4.4.155, *Wiv.* 4.2.216f., *Ado* 1.1.126f., 3.5.21f., *AYL* 2.4.4f., *1H4* 2.4.49f., *Tmp.* 2.2.155f.

HH15 To take it to (at) HEART (44 from a1300) *MV* 5.1.145, *TN* 3.4.100f., *Ham.* 1.2.100f., *Tim.* 1.2.218f.

HH16 With all my HEART (Common for at least two centuries) Passim

HH17 HERE, there, and everywhere (11 from c1590; cf. c1576 *Common Conditions* 310: Here and there and every where) *Tro.* 5.5.26, *1H6* 1.1.124, *Oth.* 1.1.136

HH18 To HIDE one's head (1d from c1400) *LLL* 5.2.86, 632, *MND* 3.2.406, *Tro.* 4.4.137, *1H6* 1.5.39, *2H6* 5.1.85, *R2* 3.3.6, *JC* 4.3.16

HH19 It is HIGH time to x (11 from 1581, but common much earlier) *Err.* 3.2.157

HH20 To be HONEY-TONGUED (From *LLL*) *LLL* 5.2.334, *Ven.* 452 (Cf. H547)

HH21 By my HOOD (1c from c1374, including 1546 Heywood) *MV* 2.6.51

II1 Devil INCARNATE (1 from 1395) *H5* 2.3.31f., *Tit.* 5.1.40

II2 At an INCH (3a from 1583; I58 from 1581; OW666a from c1560) *2H6* 1.4.42

II3 ITCHING palm (Ppl. a 2 fig. *itching* from a1225, *palm* from *JC*) *JC* 4.3.10, 12

JJ1 Not a JOT (From 1538) *Shr.* 1.1.236, *TN* 3.4.329, *MM* 3.2.61, *Ham.* 5.1.113, 207, *Oth.* 3.3.215, *Lr.* 1.4.8

JJ2 (God) give you JOY (9e from a1440, but with no examples of conventional blessing for newlyweds, actual or prospective) *Shr.* 2.1.319, 4.2.52, *LLL* 5.2.448, *Wiv.* 5.5.236, *Ado* 2.1.301, 336, 3.4.24, *AYL* 3.3.47, *Tit.* 1.1.400, 4.3.77, ?*Ant.* 5.2.260, 279, *Cor.* 2.3.111, 134f., *Per.* 2.5.87

KK1 To be KEY-COLD (From 1529 [= Wh K16a]; cf. K23: As cold as a key) *R3* 1.2.5, *Luc.* 1774

KK2 To KILL one's heart (7c from c1470) *LLL* 5.2.149f., *AYL* 3.2.246, *1H6* 5.4.2, *3H6* 2.5.87, *R2* 5.1.98, *H5* 2.1.88, *Tit.* 3.2.54, *Ant.* 4.6.33, *WT* 4.3.82f.

KK3 To do one's KIND (3c from c1230) *Ant.* 5.2.262f.

KK4 To KNIT one's brows (From c1386) *2H6* 1.2.3

LL1 To LAUGH to scorn (3 from c1340) *Err.* 2.2.205, *AYL* 4.2.18, *1H6* 4.7.18, *Mac.* 4.1.79, 5.5.3, 5.7.12

LL2   The LAUREL crown of war (2a from 1387) *3H6* 4.6.33−5, *Tit.* 1.1.74

LL3   To make a LEG (4 from 1589) *AWW* 2.2.9f.

LL4   To LEND a hand (2e from 1598) *AWW* Ep. 6, *1H4* 2.4.2

LL5   Man is a LITTLE WORLD (From c1200) *Lr.* 3.1.10

LL6   To   be   LONG-TONGUED (From 1553) *3H6* 2.2.102

LL7   To LOSE oneself (10a from 1581) *Err.* 1.2.30, 40, *Rom.* 1.1.197, *Ant.* 1.2.117

MM1   To be MADE (a made man) (forever) (7 from c1590)[n] *MND* 4.2.17f., *1H4* 2.2.58, *Oth.* 1.2.51, *WT* 3.3.120, *TNK* 3.5.74, 76, 158

[n]Add e.g.: 1576 Pettie, *Petite Pallace*, p. 100: "weath sufficient to make a man (as they say)"; c1585 (1592) Lyly, *Gallathea* 2.3.44f.: "thou art then made for ever."

MM2   To MAKE one (15b from 1542) *Shr.* 1.2.247, *LLL* 5.1.153, *Wiv.* 2.3.46, *TN* 1.5.201, 2.5.207, *1H4* 1.2.100, 137, *Per.* 2.1.111f.

MM3   To MAKE one's hair stand on end (53c from 1534) *2H6* 3.2.318, *R3* 1.3.303, *Ham.* 1.5.16−9, *Mac.* 1.3.135

MM4   A MAN of men (6b 1594, then *Ant.*)[n] *Ant.* 1.5.72

[n]Cf. 1589 Nashe, Preface to *Menaphon* (III, 317): "sir Iohn Cheeke, a man of men". McKerrow questions the legitimacy of OED's 1594 citation and adds a legitimate example from 1593.

MM5   To be one's own MAN (41a

sane from 1556; b *one's own master* from 1608) a *Tmp.* 5.1.213; b *2H6* 4.2.83

MM6   MAN   OF   THE   WORLD (From c1200) *2H4* 5.3.97f. Cf. To go to the WORLD.

MM7   Night's (black) MANTLE (in 2a fig. from c1386) *1H6* 2.2.1f., *3H6* 4.2.22, *Rom.* 3.2.15

MM8   MAP of woe (etc.) (2b *misery* etc. from 1591) *2H6* 3.1.203, *R2* 5.1.12, *Tit.* 3.2.12

MM9   To hit the MARK (7e from 1655 but common earlier; cf. M669 [*miss*] from 1530, 7e from c1350) *2H6* 1.1.243, *H8* 2.1.165, *Rom.* 1.1.207, 2.1.33, *Per.* 1.1.162

MM10   (It makes) (It is) no MATTER (18a from 1478) Passim

MM11   There is (a) MATTER in it (11c from 1549) *Oth.* 3.4.139, *WT* 4.4.841f.

MM12   To MEASURE one's length (2f from *MND*) *MND* 3.2.428f., *AYL* 2.6.2, *Lr.* 1.4.90f., *Cym.* 1.2.23f.

MM13   To cry one MERCY (3 from 1578) Passim

MM14   A MISCHIEF on it (9b from 1519) *1H6* 5.3.39. Cf. MURRAIN, PESTILENCE,   PLAGUE,   VENGEANCE

MM15   MORE and less (i.e., high and low) (B1a from a1300) *1H4* 4.3.68, *2H4* 1.1.209, *Mac.* 5.4.12, *Son.* 96.3

MM16   The MORE is the pity (1g from 1562) *MND* 3.1.145, *AYL* 1.2.86f., *1H4* 2.4.467f.

MM17   A man of MOULD (sb.[1] 4b from c1320) *H5* 3.2.22

MM18   MOUNTING mind (1 from 1577) *LLL* 4.1.4

MM19   To be in every man's MOUTH (3g from 1513) *Jn* 4.2.161, 187

MM20   To make a MOUTH (4b from 1551) *MND* 3.2.238, *Ham.* 2.2.364, 4.4.50

MM21   With full MOUTH (3H from c1290) *H5* 1.2.230f.

MM22   MUCH good do it (may it do) you (2f, ironically from 1542 [but frequently nonironic]; in 1546 Heywood *Dialogue* II.vii I3ᵛ) *H5* 5.1.53

MM23   MUCH good do it your good heart (A nonironic later variant of the above) *Shr.* 4.3.51, *Wiv.* 1.1.81f., *Tim.* 1.2.72

MM24   A MURRAIN on (take) him (1b from c1560) *Tro.* 2.1.19f., *Cor.* 1.5.3, *Tmp.* 3.2.80 Cf. MISCHIEF, PESTILENCE, PLAGUE, VENGEANCE.

MM25   To be MUSIC to one (to one's ear) (2c fig. from c1586) *Err.* 2.2.114, *Rom.* 2.2.165f., *WT* 4.4.518f.

NN1   NEITHER of both (of either) (B2b *both* from 1537, *either* from *LLL*) *LLL* 5.2.459

NN2   By NIGHT and day (8b from c1220) *Err.* 4.2.60

NN3   NIGHT and day (6a from c950) *Tro.* 3.2.114

NN4   A thing of NOTHING (3b from 1583) *Ham.* 4.2.28–30

NN5   A thing of NOUGHT (4c from c1425) *MND* 4.2.13f.

NN6   NUT-BROWN (From a1300 [Wh N189]) *Shr.* 2.1.254f.

OO1   The OLIVE (branch) of peace (3 from c1400; Wh O32 from c1380) *TN* 1.5.209f., *3H6* 4.6.33–5, *2H4* 4.4.87, *Ant.* 4.6.5f.

OO2   It is all ONE (for that) (to me) (13b from c1380) Passim

OO3   OUT upon (on) it (etc.) (Int. 2b from 1413) *Err.* 2.1.68, 3.1.77, 4.4.126, *MV* 3.1.35, *Wiv.* 1.4.165, 3.3.103f., *Ado* 4.1.56, *AWW* 5.2.48, *R3* 4.4.507, *Jn.* 1.1.64, *1H4* 1.3.208, *H8* 3.1.99, *Tit.* 3.2.54, *Rom.* 2.4.114, 3.5.168, *TNK* 2.4.5

PP1   To send (set) one PACKING (*Pack* 10b from 1594; common earlier) *R3* 3.2.61, *1H4* 2.4.297, *Ham.* 3.4.211

PP2   PAPER-white (11b c1385 [Wh P24]) *2H4* 5.4.10, *H5* 2.2.74

PP3   For my (own) PART (25 from c1440) Passim

PP4   (But) let that PASS (23 *Let pass* from 1530) *LLL* 5.1.101, *Wiv.* 1.4.15, *R3* 4.2.85 (Q). Cf. GO

PP5   To PAY home (3b from 1567; Wh H423 has 1546 Heywood) *1H4* 1.3.288

PP6   Force PERFORCE (5b, no examples; cf. e.g., c1587 [c1592] Kyd *Spanish Tragedy* 3.9.12f.) *2H6* 1.1.258, *Jn.* 3.1.142, *2H4* 4.1.114, 4.4.46

PP7   A PESTILENCE on (take) him (4 from c1386) *Tro.* 4.2.21, *Ham.* 5.1.179, *Ant.* 2.5.61. Cf. MISCHIEF, MURRAIN, PLAGUE, VENGEANCE

PP8   A PIECE of flesh (3d from 1593)[n] *LLL* 3.1.135, *Ado* 4.2.82, *AYL* 3.2.66, *TN* 1.5.27f., *1H4* 2.4.243, *Rom.* 1.1.29, *Cym.* 4.2.127

[n]c1587 (c1592) Kyd, *Spanish Tragedy* 3.6.79f.: "thou art even the merriest piece of man's flesh that e'er groaned at my office door."

PP9   PIECE of work (7 from c1540) *Ham.* 2.2.303

PP10   PILLAR(S) of the state (etc.) (3b from c1385) *MV* 4.1.238f., *Tro.* 4.5.211f., *2H6* 1.1.75

PP11   A PLAGUE on (take) him (3d from 1566) Passim. Cf. MISCHIEF, MURRAIN, PESTILENCE, VENGEANCE

PP12   To PLAY (it) off (6d from *1H4*; cf. D649 Play off your dust 1639 CL. s.v. Bibacitas 46) *1H4* 2.4.17

PP13   To PLAY the fool (etc.) (34 *fool* from 1426, *man* from c1530, *devil* from c1790 [but cf. e.g., D302 (To play the devil in the horologue) from 1519])[n] *1H6* 1.6.16, *Jn.* 2.1.135, *2H4* 2.2.142f., *Ham.* 3.1.131f., *Cor.* 3.2.15f., *WT* 1.2.257, *Tmp.* 1.1.10

[n]Cf. 1546 Heywood *Dialogue* I.xi, E3: "You plaied the man, for ye made thrift ren away"; II.ix, L2[v]: "God gyve grace, I playe not the foole this daie."

PP14   No POINT (6b from 1542) LLL 2.1.190, 5.2.277

PP15   (To come) to the POINT (22b from c1533) *MM* 2.1.97, *1H4* 4.3.89, *WT* 3.3.89f.

PP16   To stand (up) on (one's) POINTS (5b from c1590) *MND* 5.1.118

PP17   Haste POST-HASTE (From 1538) *3H6* 2.1.139, *Oth.* 1.2.37, 1.3.46

PP18   To PUT a trick upon one (23d from *AWW*) *AWW* 4.5.60, *Tmp.* 2.2.57f.

RR1   On the RACK (fig.) (sb.[3] 1c begins with *MV*) *MV* 3.2.25f., 32, *Oth.* 3.3.335

RR2   No REMEDY but x (2b from c1386) *Wiv.* 1.3.33, *AWW* 4.3.303, *MM* 3.1.61f., 3.2.1f., *1H6*, 2.2.57, *Jn.* 4.1.90f., *Cor.* 3.2.26, *WT* 5.1.77

RR3   (There's) no REMEDY (2c from 1538) *MND* 5.1.208, *Wiv.* 1.3.33, 2.2.122, 5.5.231, *TN* 3.4.305, 333, *Tro.* 4.4.55, *MM* 2.1.285, 2.2.48, *Oth.* 1.1.35, *Cor.* 3.2.26, *Cym.* 3.4.162, *WT* 4.4.656, *Son.* 62.3

RR4   (God) REST you merry (3b from 1548) *AYL* 5.1.59, *Rom.* 1.2.62, 81

RR5   RUBY lips (Cf. 5 1592, *ruby-red* 1591) *JC* 3.1.260, *Cym.* 2.2.17, *Ven.* 451

SS1   In (good) SADNESS (2b from 1544) *Shr.* 5.2.63, *Wiv.* 3.5.123, 4.2.91, *AWW* 4.3.203, *Rom.* 1.1.199–204

SS2   To pick a SALAD (2c from 1520; Wh S28 [1520]) *AWW* 4.5.13–5

SS3   To SAY the truth (11 from 1484) *MND* 3.1.143, *Tro.* 1.2.96f., *MM* 1.2.132f., *1H6* 4.1.30, 5.4.159, *3H6* 5.7.33, *R3* 4.3.30, *1H4* 4.2.45, *H5* 3.6.142, *Cor.* 4.6.142 Cf. TELL

SS4   To SET to school (26 from c1290) *Lr.* 2.4.67, *Luc.* 1819f.

SS5   SHADOW (Shade) of death (*Shadow* 1b from a900, *shade* 1c from *1H6*) *1H6* 5.4.89, *2H6* 3.2.54, *R3* 1.3.266

SS6 To SHAKE hands with (as greeting, 9a fig. from 1565; as farewell, 9b fig. from 1577) *3H6* 1.4.102, *Jn.* 4.2.82; *Mac.* 1.2.21, *Ant.* 4.12.19f.

SS7 God send you good SHIPPING (3b from c1580) *Shr.* 5.1.42

SS8 SHORT tale to make (8 from 1575; common earlier) *3H6* 2.1.120, *Ham.* 2.2.146f.

SS9 To make SHORT work (5c from 1577) *Rom.* 2.6.35

SS10 SHORTER (Shorten) by the head (*Short* 2a from 1548) *2H6* 3.1.80f., 4.4.12, *R2* 3.3.13f.

SS11 To do one a SHREWD turn (5 from 1464) *AWW* 3.5.67f., *H8* 5.2.210f.

SS12 To give someone the SLIP (sb.³ 8 from 1567) *Rom.* 2.4.45–8

SS13 SO SO (from 1530) Passim

SS14 SPARK of life (3 from c1440) *3H6* 5.6.66, *JC* 1.3.57

SS15 (Not) to SPEAK of (11 from 1485, *not* from 1582) *H8* 2.2.82

SS16 To SPEAK (one) fair (33 from c1375) *Err.* 4.2.16, 4.4.152, *Shr.* 1.2.179, *MND* 2.1.199, *MV* 4.1.275, *TN* 5.1.189, *2H6* 4.1.120, *3H6* 5.4.24, *R3* 1.3.47(Q), *R2* 3.3.128, *2H4* 5.2.33, *Tit.* 5.2.140, *Rom.* 3.1.153, *Cor.* 3.1.262, 3.2.70

SS17 X be your (etc.) SPEED (4b from c1375) *TGV* 3.1.300, *AYL* 1.2.210, *1H4* 3.1.188, *H5* 5.2.183, *Rom.* 5.3.121

SS18 (In) SPITE of spite (5c from 1592; 5b has *in spight of their despight* 1576) *3H6* 2.3.5, *Jn.* 5.4.4f

SS19 To STAMP and stare (2a from c1375; cf. F672.1) *Shr.* 3.2.228, *Jn.* 3.1.122

SS20 To STAND one upon (It stands me upon) (78q from 1549) *R3* 4.2.58f., *R2* 2.3.138, *Ham.* 5.2.63, *Ant.* 2.1.50f., *Cor.* 2.2.150

SS21 Swearing and STARING (From c1515) *Wiv.* 5.5.160

SS22 To thank one's STARS (3b from 1599 [actually 1600]) *TN* 2.5.170

SS23 (You are) an early STIRRER (3a from *2H4*) *R3* 3.2.36, *2H4* 3.2.2, *H5* 4.1.6, *JC* 2.2.110, *Per.* 3.2.12

SS24 To STONE one's heart (2 from *Oth.*) *Oth.* 5.2.63

SS25 To make oneself (it) STRANGE (11d from 1390) *TGV* 1.2.99, *Tit.* 2.1.81

SS26 SUCH as one (it) is (9b from a1240, including 1546 Heywood) *MV* 3.2.150, *AWW* 1.3.32f., *R2* 2.3.42, *Ham.* 1.5.131, *Ant.* 3.12.7

SS27 SUGARED words (2e from 1387) *2H6* 3.2.45

SS28 From SUN to sun (5 from 15th century) *R2* 4.1.55, *Cym.* 3.2.68

SS29 To make one SURE (i.e., dead) (3 from *Tit.*) *Tit.* 2.3.187, *1H4* 5.3.46f., 5.4.124f., *Per.* 1.1.166f.

TT1 To TAKE (it on) one's death (40b from 1553) *2H6* 2.3.88, *Jn.* 1.1.110, *1H4* 5.4.150f.

TT2 To tell tales (1c from c1450; cf. T54: To tell tales out of school) *Lr.* 2.4.228

TT3   To be a TALL man (fellow) (cf. M163) (3 from a1518) *Shr.* 4.4.17, *TN* 1.3.20, *R3* 1.4.152

TT4   To the (one's) TEETH (6b from 1542; Wh T415 from 1532) *H8* 1.2.36, *Ham.* 4.7.56

TT5   To TELL on someone (16 from 1539 [1 Sam. 27.11]) *Oth.* 5.2.147 (F1)

TT6   To TELL (you) the truth (18 from c1350) *Ado* 2.1.116 Cf. SAY

TT7   By these TEN bones (1e from c1485) *2H6* 1.3.190

TT8   TEN times (1c hyperbolically from 1388) Passim

TT9   THIS many a day (II 1f from 1578–1600; current by c1550) *H8* 5.2.21, *Ham.* 3.1.90

TT10   The THREAD of life (6 fig. b from 1447) *1H6* 1.1.34, *H5* 3.6.47f., *Oth.* 5.2.205f., *Per.* 1.2.108 (Tilley put all four under T249)

TT11   Three   times   THRICE (Thrice three) (2 c1460 only)[n] *LLL* 5.2.488, *MV* 1.3.159, *2H6* 3.2.358

[n]Add e.g.: 1574 Higgins, "Induction" 114, *2 Mirror for Magistrates*, p. 44: "And three times thrice I wishte my selfe away."

TT12   THROUGH   and   through (4e, 5 from 15th century) *Ado* 5.1.68, *AYL* 2.7.59, *Tro.* 5.10.26, *1H4* 2.4.167f., *WT* 4.4.112

TT13   THUS and thus (1e from a1325) *MM* 3.2.53, *Lr.*1.2.104f., *Cym.* 5.5.203

TT14   To stand on a TICKLE point (7 from 1569) *2H6* 1.1.215f.

TT15   (God) (give you) the (good, fair, etc.) TIME of day (28b from *R3*, but common earlier) *LLL* 5.2.339, *2H6* 3.1.14, *R3* 1.1.122, 1.3.18, 2.1.48, 4.1.5f., *2H4* 1.2.93f., *H5* 5.2.3, *Tim.* 3.6.1, *Per.* 4.3.35

TT16   In good (happy) TIME (42c c At the right or a seasonable moment, luckily, from 1586; d As an expression of ironical acquiescence, incredulity, amazement, from *Tmp.*, but common earlier) Passim

TT17   Many a TIME and oft(en) (18 has 1560; common earlier) *MV* 1.3.106 *2H6* 2.1.91, *JC* 1.1.37, *Tim.* 3.1.23

TT18   The TIME hath been (49 from 1509) *Err.* 2.2.113, *Mac.* 3.4.77

TT19   To trifle (the) TIME (5 from 1586; common earlier) *MV* 4.1.298

TT20   To stand on TIPTOES (1b fig. from 1579) *H5* 4.3.41f.

TT21   By the same TOKEN (15 from 1463) *Tro.* 1.2.281

TT22   To bide the TOUCH (5 from 1587; common) *1H4* 4.4.9f.

TT23   To keep TOUCH (24 from a1529) *TNK* 2.3.41, 3.3.53

TT24   TRIP and go (3 from 1579; common earlier) *LLL* 4.2.140

TT25   To serve one's TURN (30b from 1540) *Shr.* 4.2.62, *TGV* 3.1.131, 134, 379, 3.2.92, *LLL* 1.1.298f., 1.2.178, *Wiv.* 5.5.103, *AYL* 5.2.48f., *Tro.* 3.1.74, *AWW* 4.1.47, *R2* 3.2.90, *Tit.* 2.1.96, 3.1.164, *Ham.* 3.3.52, *Oth.* 1.1.42, *Cor.* 4.5.88, *Tim.* 2.1.20, *WT.* 4.4.509

TT26   To be TWAIN (3a from *Son.*) *Tro.* 3.1.101, *Son.* 36.1

TT27 TWICE or thrice (1d from c1400) *TGV* 1.2.114, 3.1.356, *Ado* 3.2.10, *H5* 5.1.74f., *WT* 5.2.105

TT28 TWO-LEGGED ass (etc.) (From 1561) *1H4* 2.4.187f.

UU1 UP AND DOWN (i.e., entirely) (6 from 1542) *Shr.* 4.3.89, *TGV* 2.3.28f., *Ado* 2.1.118f., *Jn.* 1.1.223, *Tit.* 5.2.107

VV1 VALE of years (2d from *Oth.*) *Oth.* 3.3.265f.

VV2 A VENGEANCE on (take) him (2b from a1500) *Shr.* 2.1.404, *TGV* 2.3.19, *Wiv.* 4.1.62, *Tro.* 2.3.17f., *2H6* 3.2.304, *Lr.* 2.4.162f. Cf. MIS-CHIEF, MURRAIN, PESTI-LENCE, PLAGUE

WW1 To give (take) the WALL (16 from 1537) *Rom.* 1.1.12

WW2 Pale and WAN (4 from 1542) *Err.* 4.4.108, *Tit.* 2.3.90

WW3 With a WANION (a from 1567) *Per.* 2.1.17

WW4 To WASH one's brains, head (etc.) (with drink) (5c from 1589) *Ant.* 2.7.99

WW5 In (the) WAY of marriage (35h from 1482) *MV* 2.1.42, 2.9.13, *Wiv.* 1.4.84

WW6 To bring one on the WAY (2 from c1450; Gen. 18.16) *LLL* 5.2.873, *MM* 1.1.61, *R2* 1.3.304, *Oth.* 3.4.197, *WT* 4.3.114

WW7 Go (Come) thy WAY(S) (7b, 23b) Passim

WW8 To WEEP out one's eyes (8 from c1290; OW158a from 1611) *TGV* 2.3.12f., *Tro.* 5.10.48, *R3* 1.2.166, *JC* 4.3.99f.

WW9 To WEIGH one's words (12b from 1340) *Oth.* 3.3.118f.

WW10 WELL said (3d from 1590)[n] Passim

[n]OED apparently includes merely as a version of "You say well," with "the implied object being some particular saying." But the phrase was often used, both by Shakespeare and his predecessors, to commend an action or an attitude rather than anything spoken. Cf. e.g., c1552 (c1567) Udall, *Ralph Roister Doister* 4.7.19 (to a silent but courageous servant): "Wel sayd, Truepeny!" or *1 Henry IV* 5.4.75 (to a silent but courageous Prince Hal): "Well said, Hal! to it, Hal!" Sometimes both senses are implied.

WW11 WELL TO LIVE (From 1579) *MV* 2.2.53, *WT* 3.3.121

WW12 I know (wot) not WHAT (8b from c1560) *AWW* 5.3.261, *R2* 2.1.250, *2H4* 2.4.315

WW13 WHAT else? (5 from 1591; common earlier) *Shr.* 4.4.2, *2H6* 1.4.5, *3H6* 4.6.56, *Ant.* 3.7.28, 3.11.27, *Cor.* 4.6.148 Also 4d, from 1579, for *3H6* 3.1.51

WW14 WHAT-DO-YOU-CALL-EM (*Varied* from 1593; current earlier) *AYL* 3.3.73f., *AWW* 2.3.22

WW15 To spit WHITE (15b from 1594) *2H4* 1.2.211f.

WW16 To turn up the WHITE of the eye (2 from 1448) *Cor.* 4.5.194−6

WW17 Far and WIDE (adv. 1b from a900) *Rom.* 2.4.86

WW18 WIDE-MOUTH(ED) (From 1593) *1H4* 1.3.153

WW19 If (And) it be thy (your)

WILL (8 from c1225) *TN* 1.5.32, *Cor.* 4.4.7, *WT* 3.3.68f.

WW20(?)   To be on the WINDY side of (1d *Ado TN*, 1814 . . .) *Ado* 2.1.315, *TN* 3.4.164

WW21   (Not) to sleep a (one) WINK (1b from 1303) *Cym.* 3.4.99

WW22   To be WITH (i.e., be even with) (22d from MND but cf. c1561 *Cambises* ii.62, iii.5f.) *Shr.* 4.1.167, *MND* 3.2.403, *TN* 3.4.320. *2H6* 2.1.47, *Rom.* 2.4.74

WW23   At (in) a (one) WORD (13 from 1300, 14 from *TGV*) *TGV* 2.4.71, *Ado* 2.1.114, 120, *2H4* 3.2.297, *Cor.* 1.3.109, *Cym.* 3.5.82

WW24   By WORD of mouth (19 from a1553) *TN* 2.3.130f., 3.4.191f., *JC* 3.1.279f.

WW25   X is the WORD (12e from *MV*) *MV* 3.5.51f., *H5* 2.1.71f., *Ant.* 1.2.135, *Cym.* 5.4.153

WW26   A WORD or two (2c from 1581) *Oth.* 5.2.338

WW27   For (all) the WORLD (i.e., exactly, in every respect) (21e from c1386) *Shr.* 3.2.65f., *Wiv.* 1.1.49, *1H4* 3.2.93f.

WW28   (Not) for (all) the WORLD (7f

[b] from *LLL*) *TGV* 2.4.168, *LLL* 2.1.99, *Wiv.* 1.4.64, *Ado* 4.1.290, *H8* 2.3.45f., *Rom.* 2.2.74, 97, *JC* 5.5.6, *Oth.* 4.3.64, 68, *Per.* 4.1.84, *Tmp.* 5.1.173

WW29   To go to the WORLD (4c from 1565) *Ado* 2.1.318f., AWW 1.3.17−9

WW30   WORLD without end (6b from a1225) *LLL* 5.2.789, *Son.* 57.5

WW31   Loving WORM (10c from a1553) *LLL* 4.3.151f., ?*Ant.* 5.2.243ff., *Tmp.* 3.1.31

WW32   WORM of conscience (11 from c1386) *Ado* 5.2.84, *R3* 1.3.221

WW33   Man is a WORM (10b from c825) *Lr.* 4.1.33

WW34   WORSE and worse (2e from a1154; in 1546 Heywood) *Shr.* 5.2.93, *MV* 3.2.247, *Mac.* 3.4.116, *Per.* 4.6.132, *Ven.* 774

WW35   To WRITE (oneself) man (8b, c from *1H4*) *2H4* 1.2.26f., *AWW* 2.3.198f.

YY1   YEA and nay (no) (3a from 1387) *Wiv.* 1.4.93, *Cor.* 3.1.145

YY2   By YEA and nay (no) (3b from *LLL*) *LLL* 1.1.54, *Wiv.* 1.1.87, 4.2.192, *2H4* 2.2.131, 3.2.9

APPENDIX C

Tilley's "Shakespeare Index" Exclusions

About one-fifth of my exclusions from Tilley's "Shakespeare Index" are cited legitimately elsewhere in that index, and accordingly appear in the present index and in Appendix A. The remainder appear below. Parenthetical numbers after each entry indicate cryptically my bases for exclusion.

 (1) Not a proverb; cf. Introduction, especially pp. xii−xvi.

 (1b) A proverb only when figurative; cf. Introduction, pp. xxii and fns. 13, 22

 (2) Too little evidence to warrant calling a proverb, at least in Shakespeare's day.

 (3) Too little verbal similarity to warrant citing Shakespeare; Introduction, fn. 32.

 (4) Irrelevant, or insufficiently relevant, to the cited passage.

 (5) Less worth citing than the entry cited.

Some exclusions, especially among those labeled (1) or (1b), nevertheless contain useful and pertinent matter for the passage cited. These are italicized.

I have tried to keep these exclusions to a minimum, and have frequently retained with a question-mark entries I would not have included had they not been in Tilley's "Shakespeare Index." Judgments may differ, however, especially on those labeled (4). Where the legitimacy of an exclusion appears questionable, the user must examine Tilley's evidence in full.

A26 Neither praise nor dispraise thyself, thy ACTIONS serve the turn (2, 3, 5)

A56 AFRICA is always producing something new (monsters, serpents) (1b)

A67 AGE should be housed (2, 3)

A93 *Fresh AIR is ill for the diseased or wounded man* (1; cf. Introduction, p. xvi)

A159 All lies and bleeds (lies a bleeding) (1b)

A206 To make ALL sure (3, 4)

A228 Never less ALONE than when alone (He is never alone who is accompanied with noble thoughts) (4)

A235 AMBITION loses many a man (2, 3)

A284 Handsome APPAREL makes fools pass for wise men (hides much deformity) (3, 4?)

A285 APPEARANCES are deceitful (?1, 3)

A300 Sodom APPLES outwardly fair, ashes at the core (3, 4)

A369 The dull ASS's trot lasts not long (5)

A406 Without AWL (all) the cobbler's nobody (2, 4)

B93 As broad as a BARN DOOR (2, 3)

B99 The BASILISK'S eye is fatal (1; cf. B99.1)

B137 As naked as they were BORN (4)

B143 A red BEARD and a black head, catch him with a trick and take him dead (2, 3, 4)

B168 BEAUTY is a blessing (2, 3, 4)

B177 Where BEAUTY is there needs no other plea (2, ?3)

B221 The BEETLE flies over many a sweet flower and lights in a cowshard (4)

B365 A BIRD is known by its note and a man by his talk (4)

B389 Ye are my BIRD for as black as ye are (2 [cf. on H745], 3)

B456 BLOOD is inherited but virtue is achieved (?1, 2, 4)

B486 At the BOARD be a maid but a clown in bed (3, 5)

B549 What are you good for? to stop BOTTLES? (2, 3, 4)

B569 He that will play at BOWLS must expect to meet with rubs (2; *LLL* 4.1.138f., *R2* 3.4.3f. only)

B637 The BREAKING OPEN of letters is the basest kind of burglary (2; cf. Introduction, p. xix)

B682 A new BROOM (besome) sweeps clean (3; *new* is essential)

C41 His CANDLE burns within the socket (3)

C141 A CAT may look on a king (3, 4)

C211 Without CERES and Bacchus Venus grows cold (3, 4)

C312 Many kiss (love) the CHILD for the nurse's sake (3, 4)

C331 CHILDREN are poor men's (parents') riches (3, 5)

C412 He that never CLIMBED never fell (4)

C460 Let them that be acold blow at the COAL (1b, 4)

C495 The COCKATRICE slays by sight only (1; not in OW or WH; cf. C496.2)

C581 COMPLIMENTING is lying (2)

C597 A clear CONSCIENCE laughs at (fears not) false accusations (4)

C609 A quiet CONSCIENCE sleeps in thunder (2)

C696 Take COUNSEL of your pillow (4)

C732 Full of COURTESY full of craft (3)

C740 Marry come up, my dirty COUSIN (4; cf. M699.2)

C828 If one dwell by (next door to) a CRIPPLE he will learn to halt (3, 4)

C918 Two CURS shall tame (bite) each other (*Tame* ?1, *bite* 2; cf. Introduction, fn. 15)

C924 CURSES return upon the heads of those that curse (3,4)

D12 Dear bought and far fetched are DAINTIES for ladies (4)

D28 DANGER and delight grow both upon one stalk (stock) (2, 3; cf. Introduction, p. xix)

D42 He is out at first DASH (3, 4)

D60 The better DAY the better deed (3)

D79 He that fights and runs away may live to fight another day (?2, 4)

D82 I wept when I was born and every DAY shows why (3, 5)

D129 One seldom loses by DEALING with honest men (3, 4)

D135 As silent as DEATH (2, 5)

D206 DESERT and reward be ever far odd (seldom keep company) (3)

D252 The DEVIL is known by his claws (cloven feet, horns) (1b; cf. Introduction, fn. 22)

D362 He is DISGUISED (1; merely *OED* 6) *Ant.* 2.7.122−5

D383 DISPRAISE by evil men is praise (3, 4)

D410 He is handsome that handsome DOES (3)

D418 Everything is easy after it has been DONE (2, 3,?4)

D554 Every DOOR may be shut but death's door (2, 3, 4)

D555 He must stoop that has a low DOOR (2, 5)

D571 He that casts all DOUBTS shall never be resolved (2, 3; cf. Introduction, p. xix)

D616 Fat DROPS fall from fat flesh (2, 3)

D643 DUN is in the mire (3, 5)

E31 The EARTH produces all things and receives all again (2, 3)

E32 The EARTH that yields food yields also poison (1)

E98 My ELBOW itches, I must change my bedfellow (1b, 2, 4)

E172 ENVY never dies (3, 4)

E196 Do EVIL and evil will come of it (3, 4, 5)

E217 One ought to make the EXPENSE according to the income (means) (2, 3)

E220 EXPERIENCE is the mistress of fools (3)

E223 Run not from one EXTREME to another (2, 3)

F24 FAIR is not fair but that which pleases (4, 5)

F41 There is FALSEHOOD in fellowship (5; cf. Introduction, fn. 10)

F116 Where no FAULT is there needs no pardon (3, 4)

F134 FEAR has a quick ear (3, 4)

F138 Foolish FEAR doubles danger (2, 3, 4)

F219 To the FILTHY all things taste filthy (2, 3, 4, 5)

F224 Here I FOUND you and here (As I found you) I leave you (3, ?4)

F351   Keep FLAX from fire and youth from gaming (2, 3, 4)

F391   The fairest FLOWERS (freshest colors) soonest fade (4)

F422   Little FOLKS are fond of talking about what great folks do (2)

F488   He that sends a FOOL expects one (4)

F585   What is FORBIDDEN (baneful) is desired (*Forbidden* 4, *baneful* cf. R32.1)

F711   Make not thy FRIEND too cheap to thee nor thyself too dear to him (2, 4)

F732   Drink and be FRIENDS (3)

F741   Have but few FRIENDS though much acquaintance (4, 5)

F762   Trencher FRIENDSHIP (3)

F766   When the FROG has hair thou wilt be good (2, 3)

F774   Sharp FROSTS bite forward springs (2, 4)

G19   To be hanged on a fair GALLOWS (with a silken halter) (3)

G58   It is good GEAR that lasts aye (2 [cf. on H745; cf. OW319bf., Wh L87, Wh N158], 3)

G91   Soon GOTTEN soon spent (3)

G132   His GLASS is run (1b)

G152   GO forward and fall, go backward and mar all (3, 5)

G212   GOD send me a friend that may tell me my faults; if not, an enemy, and to be sure he will (2, 3)

G318   Set GOOD against evil (Do good for evil) (2; cf. 1 Thess. 5.15)

H31   Gray HAIRS are death's blossoms (2, 3)

H86   A moist HAND argues an amorous nature (fruitfulness) (1)

H128   As idle as one may HANG together (?1, 2)

H130   Better be half HANGED than ill wed (2, 3)

H161   Set the HARE'S head (foot) against the goose giblets (3, 5)

H285   Better in HEALTH than in good conditions (2, 3)

H292   To drink HEALTH is to drink sickness (1; cf. Introduction, p. xvii, in Dekker's *2 Honest Whore* 4.3.99 the noun is *healths*)

H302   Faint HEART ne'er won fair lady (3)

H305   A good HEART conquers ill fortune (3, 4; cf. Introduction, fn. 6)

H312   The HEART of a fool is in his tongue (mouth) (5)

H565   Either live or die with HONOR (4)

H602   HOPE is the last thing that man has to flee unto (3, 4)

H646   A good HORSE cannot be of a bad color (2, 3)

I55   An INCH in a man's nose is much (2; 1732 Fuller; cf. Introduction, p. xix)

I72   INJURIES slighted become none at all (2)

J37   Like JANUS, two faced (3, 4)

J42   Who is nettled at a JEST seems to be touched in earnest (2, 3, 4)

J50   Invite not a JEW either to pig or pork (2, 3)

J87   To weep for JOY is a kind of manna (2, 3)

J92   To give one a JUDAS KISS (3)

J101   To drink the JUICE of mandrake (mandragora) (1)

L65   There were no ill LANGUAGE if it were not ill taken (2, 4)

L70   To sing like a LARK (4)

L85   Better LATE than never (5)

L111   To have the LAW in one's own hand (3)

L250   LIFE is a shuttle (2; cf. Introduction, fn. 11)

L329   You licked not your LIPS since you lied last (2, 3, 4)

L386   He LIVES long that lives well (5)

L407   To keep under LOCK and key (3)

L499   LOVE cannot be compelled (forced) (3, 4)

L505a   LOVE is a sweet torment (?1, 3)

L514   LOVE is the loadstone of love (2, 3, 4)

L568   LOVERS ever run before the clock (?1, 2; cf. Introduction, fn. 15)

L570   LOVERS' vows are not to be trusted (1)

M20   A MAID oft seen, a gown oft worn, are disesteemed and held in scorn (3, 4)

M44   MAIDENS should be meek till they be married (?1, 2 [cf. on H745], 3)

M49   You MAKE me scratch (claw) where it does not itch (3, 4; *not* essential)

M71   As long lives a merry MAN as a sad (4)

M100   Every MAN (one) after his fashion (3, ?4)

M148   A good honest MAN nowadays is but a better word for a fool (2, 3)

M184   An honest MAN is as good as his word (5: cf. W773.1)

M211   Like a MAN in a dropsy, the more he drinks the more he may (3, 4)

M243   A MAN is a man (4)

M283   A MAN must not shape an answer before that he know the question (errand) (3)

M326   No MAN ever lost his credit (honor) but he that had it not (4)

M360   The properer (honester) MAN the worse luck (3, 4)

M425   The wise MAN knows himself to be a fool, the fool thinks he is wise (?1, 2, 5)

M471   MAN'S extremity is God's opportunity (3)

M472   A MAN'S gift makes room for him (2, 3)

M475   A MAN'S mind often gives him warning of evil to come (1; cf.

Introduction, p. xvi; cf. also *R2* 2.2.9ff., 142)

M536 Keep not ill MEN company lest you increase the number (3, 4)

M553 MEN (Women) may blush to hear what they were not ashamed to act (do) (3)

M562 MEN will talk on it when we be dead, do what we can (2, 3, 4)

M609 Young MEN may die, old men must die (4, 5)

M738 He is like the MASTER BEE that leads forth the swarm (2, 3)

M777 The MAYOR OF NORTH-AMPTON opens oysters with his dagger (2, 3, 4)

M785 To leave the MEAL and take the bran (4)

M875 It is never too late to MEND (repent) (5)

M895 He shall find MERCY that merciful is (2, ?4)

M905 MESSENGERS should neither be headed nor hanged (3, like most of the non-Shakespearean examples)

M1130 As tawny (black) as a MOOR (4)

M1160 To be MORE than he can answer (2, 3)

M1231 It is a bold (wily) MOUSE that breeds (nestles) in the cat's ear (3)

M1235 A MOUSE in time may bite in two a cable (3, 4)

M1316 He that lives with the MUSES shall die in the straw (Learning ever dies in beggary) (?1, 2, 3)

M1319 A MUSHROOM grows in a night (1b)

M1333 He looks as if he lived on Tewkesbury MUSTARD (4; cf. OW809a: Tewkesbury mustard [1])

N41 He that follows Nature is never out of his way (2 [cf. Introduction, p. xix], 3, 4)

N124 N124 Destroy the NEST and the rooks will flee away (1b, 2, 3)

N199 To play at NODDY (2, 4)

N210 To ring NOON on one's head (4)

N276 I know NOTHING except that I know not (4)

N299 NOTHING is impossible (hard, difficult) to a willing heart (mind) (3, 5)

N307 NOTHING is well said or done in a passion (in anger) (1; cf. Wh W707: Wrath said never well [3 from 1393]. Cf. Introduction, p. xvif.)

N363 It is NUTS to him (2, 3)

O9a To ask what it is O'CLOCK (?1, 4)

O40 Sweet OLIVER (1)

P24 Without (No) PAINS no gains (profit) (4)

P166 PEARLS are restorative (2, 3, 4)

P186 PENELOPE'S web (3)

P252 To appeal from PHILIP drunk to Philip sober (3)

P462 POLICY goes beyond strength (3, 4)

P468 The POOR have few friends (3)

P483 The PORPOISE (dolphin) plays before a storm (1b)

P548 He that PRAISES publicly will slander privately (2, 3)

P557 PRAYERS like petards break open heaven gate (2, 3)

P559 To say his PRAYERS backward (1b, 4)

P571 To shoot nigh the PRICK (3)

P613 With PROSPERITY be thou not lifted up and with adversity be not cast down (2, 3)

P619 Great PUDDER to small purpose (2, 3)

Q1 To be in a QUANDARY (?1, 3)

R43 Let REASON rule all your actions (3, 4)

R89 The REVEALING of griefs is a renewing of sorrow (3)

R100 To be so lean that one's RIBS may be counted (2, 4)

R147 ROBIN GOODFELLOW (1; cf. Introduction, fn. 13)

S47 SAINT LUKE was a saint and a physician and yet he died (3)

S80 SALT seasons all things (3, 4)

S85 As strong as SAMSON (3)

S121 SAYING is one thing and doing another (4; cf. S119)

S150 SCORN at first makes afterlove the more (?1, 2; cf. Introduction, fn. 6)

S184 To plow the SEA (1b)

S206 Who so blind as he that will not SEE? (4)

S212 SEEING is believing (3, 4, 5)

S225 Whited SEPULCHERS (Women are whited sepulchers) (4)

S244 He that SERVES everybody is paid by nobody (3, 4)

S458 SILVER has a silver sound (3, 4)

S482 All good SINGERS have colds (2, 3, 4)

S574 SMOKE, rain, and a very curst wife make a man weary of house and life (5; cf. Introduction, fn. 14)

S616 Give SOMETHING of thine own to the devil and turn him away (2, 3, 4)

S647 SORE upon sore is not a salve (3)

S662 When SORROW is asleep wake it not (2, 3, 4)

S713 Any small SPARK shines in the dark (2, 3, 4)

S742 What we SPENT we had, what we gave we have, what we lent we lost (3, 4; cf. OW764b)

S858 The STING [of scorpions] is in the tail (4, 5)

S903 STORE is no sore (3)

S978 The morning SUN never lasts a day (2, 3, 4?)

S989 When the SUN is highest he casts the least shadow (4)

S1038 Take (Mingle) the SWEET with the sour (4)

T129   Give a THING and take again and you shall ride in hell's wain (2, 3)

T140   It is an ill THING to be wicked (wretched) but a worse to be known so (to boast of it) (3, 4, 5)

T183   He lives unsafely that looks too near on THINGS (2, 3)

T219   First THINK and then speak (4, 5)

T228   He that sows THISTLES shall reap thorns (prickles) (3)

T234   The THORN comes forth with his point forwards (3,4)

T273   To bite his THUMBS (1b)

T298   In TIME all haggard hawks will stoop to lure (3, 4)

T313   Take TIME when time comes lest time steal away (3)

T325   TIME cures every disease (3)

T333   TIME reveals (discloses) all things (4)

T360   Full as a TOAD of poison (3; and only 1678 Ray outside Shakespeare)

T405   The TONGUE is not steel yet it cuts (5)

T446   As true as TOUCH (3)

T448   As the TOUCHSTONE tries gold, so gold tries men (4)

T532   He that seeks TROUBLE never misses it (4)

T534   Search not too curiously lest you find TROUBLE (2, 3, 5)

T551   No TRUST is to be given to a woman's word (a woman) (2, 3, 5)

T560   As innocent as TRUTH (silence, grace) (?1, 2)

T619   Ten good TURNS lie dead and one ill deed report abroad does spread (3, 5)

T640   To be TWO (twain) (1; cf. Appendix B: To be TWAIN)

U8   To be utterly UNDONE (3; *utterly* essential)

U12   UNITY (Union) is the strongest building (bulwark) of cities (3, 4)

U13   UNKISSED unkind (2, 3)

U28   An USURER is one that puts his money to the unnatural act of generation, and the scrivener is his bawd (2; cf. Introduction, fn. 19)

V24   VENGEANCE belongs only to God (2; cf. Introduction, p. xvi)

V63   As sharp (keen) as VINEGAR (3)

V79   VIRTUE is a jewel of great price (3)

V85   VIRTUE is the true nobility (4)

W83   Good WATCH prevents misfortune (2, 3)

W91   Fair WATER makes all clean (2, 3, 4)

W134   As pliable as WAX (3, 5)

W160   He tells me my WAY and does not know it himself (2, 4, 5)

W194   The greatest WEALTH is contentment with a little (2, 5)

W240   One ill WEED (turd) mars a whole pot of pottage (porridge) (3)

W377 Who has a fair WIFE needs more than two eyes (2, 3)

W418 If there be any WIND stirring it is most evident about the church (1b, 2)

W539 WISHERS and woulders are never good householders (3, 4)

W446 WIND and weather, do your worst (2, 3)

W545 Bought WIT is best (4)

W548 He has more WIT in his head than you in both your shoulders (2, 4)

W588 There is WITCHCRAFT in fair words (2, 3)

W603 He holds a WOLF by the ears (3)

W674 A WOMAN's mind (A woman) is always mutable (5)

W683 Discreet WOMEN have neither eyes nor ears (4)

W692 Without WOMEN we men cannot be (3, 4)

W705 WOMEN are wasps if angered (2, 5)

W758 After WORD comes weird (2, 3, ?4; cf. on H745)

W761 He has his saying WORD and his denaying word (2, 3)

W828 Where many WORDS are, the truth goes by (4)

W866 As good be out of the WORLD (Better be dead) as out of fashion (2, 3)

W873 I hate no one but love all the WORLD (?1, 3)

W930 The WOUND that bleeds inwardly is most dangerous (4)

BIBLIOGRAPHY

The following bibliography is mainly to identify modern editions cited in Appendix A. It does not include Renaissance editions employed, or plays in the Malone Society Reprint series (all identified in Appendix A by MSR prior to line number). Except in the initial section of dictionaries and collections, it does not include works whose examples in Appendix A are merely transcribed from Whiting, OW, or even Tilley.

DICTIONARIES AND PROVERB COLLECTIONS

1519. Horman, William. *Vulgaria.*

1530. Palsgrave, John. *Lesclarcissement de la Langue Francoyse.*

1533. Udall, Nicholas. *Floures for Latine Spekynge Selected and Gathered Oute of Terence.*

1539. Taverner, Richard. *Proverbes or Adagies with Newe Addicions Gathered Out of the Chiliades of Erasmus by Richard Taverner. Hereunto be Also Added Mimi Publiani.*

1542. Udall, Nicholas. *Apophthegmes, That Is to Saie, Prompte, Quicke, Wittie and Sentencious Saiynges . . . First Gathered . . . by . . . Erasmus . . . And Now Translated . . . by Nicolas Udall.*

1546. Heywood, John. *A Dialogue of Proverbs,* ed. Rudolph E. Habenicht. Berkeley and Los Angeles: University of California Press, 1963. Also 1549.

1548. Elyot, Sir Thomas. *Bibliotheca Eliotae,* ed. Thomas Cooper.

1552. Huloet, Richard. *Abcdarium Anglico Latinum.*

1552. Taverner, Richard. Cf. 1539.

1565. Cooper, Thomas. *Thesaurus Linguae Romanae & Britannicae.*

1573. Sanford, James. *The Garden of Pleasure. . . . Wherein Are Also Set Forth Divers Verses and Sentences in Italian, with the Englishe to the Same.*

1578. Florio, John. *Florio His firste Fruites,* ed. A. del Re. Taihoku, 1936.

c1580. Conybeare, John. *Letters and Exercises of the Elizabethan Schoolmaster John Conybeare,* ed. W. D. Conybeare. London: Henry Frowde, 1905. (Adagia: pp. 23-56).

1580. Baret, John. *An Alveary or Triple Dictionary, in Englishe, Latin, and French.*

1584. Withals, John. *A Short Dictionarie in Latine and English.* Also later editions.

1591. Florio, John. *Florios Second Frutes.*

1591.————. *Giardino di Recreatione.*

1591. Stepney, William. *The Spanish Schoole-master.*

1596, ?1592. Delamothe, G. *The French Alphabeth . . . Together With the Treasure of the French Tung.* [Ded. Ep. "De Londres ce 11. d'Aoust. 1592"; OW dates 1592] 1595, 1596.

1599. Minsheu, John. *A Dictionarie in Spanish and English.*

1609ff. Bretnor, Thomas. Yearly almanacs (unexamined). See John Crow, below.

1611. Cotgrave, Randle. *A Dictionarie of the French and English Tongues.*

1616. Draxe, Thomas. *Bibliotheca Scholastica Instructissima. Or, A Treasurie of Ancient Adagies, and Sententious Proverbes, Selected Out of the English, Greeke, Latine, French, Italian and Spanish.* Enumeration follows the reprinting of the English proverbs in *Das Elisabethanische Sprichwort,* ed. M. Förster, *Anglia,* XLII (1918).

1639. Clarke, John. *Paroemiologia*

Anglo-Latina. Also 1671.

1640. Herbert, George. *Outlandish Proverbs*, in *Works*, ed. F. E. Hutchinson (Oxford: Clarendon Press, 1941), pp. 321–362.

1641. Fergusson, David. *Fergusson's Scottish Proverbs From the Original Print of 1641 Together With a Larger Manuscript Collection of About the Same Period. . . .* ed. Erskine Beveridge. S.T.S., n.s., no. 15 (1924).

1659. Howell, James. ΠAPOIMIO-ΓPAϕIA. *Proverbs . . . in English . . . Italian, French and Spanish . . . British.*

1664. Codrington, Robert. *A Collection of Many Select, and Excellent Proverbs out of Severall Languages.*

1666. Torriano, Giovanni. *Piazza Universale di Proverbi Italiani, Or, A Common Place of Italian Proverbs and Proverbial Phrases.*

1670. Ray, John. *A Collection of English Proverbs.* Also 1678.

1672. Walker, William. *Paroemiologia Anglo-Latina.*

1732. Fuller, Thomas, M.D. *Gnomologia: Adagies and Proverbs; Wise Sentences and Witty Sayings, Ancient and Modern, Foreign and British.*

ANTHOLOGIES AND SERIES

Adams: *Chief Pre-Shakespearean Dramas*, ed. Joseph Quincy Adams. Cambridge, Mass.: Houghton Mifflin, 1924.

Bang: *Materialien zur Kunde des Alteren Englischen Dramas*, ed. W. Bang, Louvain, 1902–1914.

Bevington: *Medieval Drama*, ed. David Bevington. Boston: Houghton Mifflin, 1975.

Bond: *Early Plays from the Italian*, ed. R. W. Bond. Oxford: Clarendon Press, 1911.

Brandl: *Quellen des Weltlichen Dramas in England vor Shakespeare*, ed. Alois Brandle. Strassburg: Karl J. Trübner, 1898.

Brooke: *The Shakespeare Apocrypha*, ed. C. F. Tucker Brooke. Oxford: Clarendon Press, 1908.

Bullough: *Narrative and Dramatic Sources of Shakespeare*, ed. Geoffrey Bullough. 8 vols, London: Routledge and Kegan Paul, 1957–1975.

MSR: *Malone Society Reprints.* Oxford: Oxford University Press, 1906 (not listed individually below).

Nettleton: *British Dramatists from Dryden to Sheridan*, ed. George H. Nettleton and Arthur E. Case. Boston: Houghton Mifflin, 1939.

Schell: *English Morality Plays and Moral Interludes*, ed. Edgar T. Schell and J. D. Shuchter. New York: Holt, Rinehart and Winston, 1969.

Revels: *The Revels Plays*, ed. Clifford Leech, later David Hoeniger. London: Methuen, 1958–.

Regents: *Regents Renaissance Drama*, ed. Cyrus Hoy. Lincoln: University of Nebraska Press, 1963–.

Arden of Feversham (Brooke).

The Birth of Merlin (Brooke).

Bugbears (Bond).

Common Conditions, ed. C. F. Tucker Brooke. Elizabethan Club Reprints no. 1. New Haven: Yale University Press, 1915.

Corpus Christi Cycles (Bevington).

Edward III (Brooke).

Fair Em (Brooke).

Jack Juggler, ed. W. H. Williams. Cambridge: Cambridge University Press, 1914.

King Darius (Brandl).

King Leir (Bullough, VII).

Locrine (Brooke).

The London Prodigal (Brooke).

Mankind (Bevington).

The Merry Devil of Edmonton (Brooke).

Misogonus (Brandl).

Mucedorus (Brooke).
The Puritan (Brooke).
Thomas Lord Cromwell (Brooke).
The World and the Child (Schell).
Woodstock, ed. A. P. Rossiter. London: Chatto and Windus, 1946.
A Yorkshire Tragedy (Brooke).
The Interlude of Youth (Schell).

Adams, Thomas. *The Works of Thomas Adams*. Nichol's Series of Standard Divines. 3 vols. Edinburgh, 1861–1862.

Alexander, Sir William. *The Poetical Works of Sir William Alexander Earl of Stirling*. ed. L. E. Kastner and H. B. Charlton. Manchester: Manchester University Press, 1921.

Baldwin, William, et al. *The Mirror for Magistrates*, ed. Lily B. Campbell. Cambridge: Cambridge University Press, 1938.

"Beaumont, Francis and John Fletcher." Where possible: *The Dramatic Works in the Beaumont and Fletcher Canon*, ed. Fredson Bowers et al. Cambridge: Cambridge University Press, 1966–1979 (vols. 1–4). Next: *The Works of Francis Beaumont and John Fletcher*. Variorum edition, ed. A. H. Bullen et al. London: G. Bell and Sons, 1904–1912 (vols. 1–4). Unlineated: *The Works of Francis Beaumont and John Fletcher*, ed. Arnold Glover and A. R. Waller. 10 vols. Cambridge: Cambridge University Press, 1905–1912.

Becon, Thomas. *The Early Works of Thomas Becon*, *The Catechism of Thomas Becon*, ed. John Ayre. Parker Society (vols. 2, 3). Cambridge: Cambridge University Press, 1843–1844.

Blenerhasset, Thomas. *The Seconde Part of the Mirrour for Magistrates*. In Parts Added to *The Mirror for Magistrates* ed. Lily B. Campbell. Cambridge: Cambridge University Press, 1946.

Bodenham, John. *Bel-vedere, or the Garden of the Muses*. Spenser Society, 1875.

Brome, Richard. *A Jovial Crew*, ed. Ann Haaker (Regents, 1968)

Brooke, Arthur. *The Tragicall Historye of Romeus and Juliet* (Bullough, I).

Burton, Robert. *The Anatomy of Melancholy*. Bohn's Popular Library. 3 vols. London: G. Bell and Sons, 1926–1927.

Chamberlain, John. *The Letters of John Chamberlain*, ed. Norman E. McClure. Vol. 1. 1598–1616. Philadelphia: The American Philosophical Society, 1939.

Chapman, George. *The Plays of George Chapman: The Comedies*, ed. Allan Holaday et al. Urbana: University of Illinois Press, 1970. *The Plays and Poems of George Chapman*, ed. T. M. Parrott. Vol. 1. *The Tragedies*. London: Routledge and Kegan Paul, 1910.

Congreve, William. *The Way of the World* (Nettleton)

Cornwallis, Sir William. *Essayes*, ed. Don Cameron Allen. Baltimore: The Johns Hopkins Press, 1946.

Crow, John. "Some Jacobean Catch-Phrases and Some Light on Thomas Bretnor." In *Elizabethan and Jacobean Studies Presented to Frank Percy Wilson in Honour of his Seventieth Birthday*, ed. Herbert Davis and Helen Gardner. Oxford: Clarendon Press, 1959, pp. 250–278. (All Bretnor data is from Crow's enumerated listing of almanac phrases for "good" and "evil" days. *CB e300 His credite is crackt* signifies that this phrase is #300 "evil" in Crow's Bretnor article.)

Daniel, Samuel. *The Complete Works in Verse and Prose*, ed. Alexander B. Grosart. Vol. 3. *The Dramatic Works*. 1885.

Dekker, Thomas. *The Dramatic Works of Thomas Dekker*, ed. Fredson Bowers. 4 vols. Cambridge: Cambridge University Press, 1953–1961.

Deloney, Thomas. *The Works of Thomas Deloney*, ed. Francis Oscar

Mann. Oxford: Clarendon Press, 1912.

Donne, John. *The Poems of John Donne,* ed. H. J. C. Grierson. 2 vols. Oxford: Clarendon Press, 1912.

Drayton, Michael. *The Works of Michael Drayton,* ed. J. W. Hebel (with K. Tillotson and B. H. Newdigate). 5 vols. Oxford: Basil Blackwell, 1931–1941.

—— et al. *1 Sir John Oldcastle* (Brooke).

Dryden, John. *The Works of John Dryden,* ed. Edward Niles Hooker, H. T. Swedenberg, Jr., et al. Berkeley and Los Angeles: University of California Press, 1956–. Where unlineated: *The Works of John Dryden,* ed. Sir Walter Scott. Rev. and cor. by George Saintsbury. 18 vols. Edinburgh: W. Paterson, 1882–1893.

Field, Nathan. *Plays,* ed. William Peery. Austin: University of Texas Press, 1950.

Ford, John. *'Tis Pity She's a Whore,* ed. Derek Roper (Revels, 1975).

Gascoigne, George. *The Complete Works of George Gascoigne,* ed. J. W. Cunliffe. 2 vols. Cambridge: Cambridge University Press, 1907–1910. *Supposes* (Adams).

Greene, Robert. *The Plays and Poems of Robert Greene,* ed. John Churton Collins. 2 vols. Oxford: Clarendon Press, 1905. For prose (unless otherwise indicated): *The Life and Complete Works in Prose and Verse of Robert Greene,* ed. A. B. Grosart. 15 vols. London: The Huth Library, 1881–1886. *Pandosto* (Bullough, VIII).

Guazzo, Stephen. *The Civile Conversation of M. Steeven Guazzo.* Tudor Translations, 2d ser., no. 7. 2 vols. New York: Alfred A. Knopf, 1925.

Harvey, Gabriel. *The Works of Gabriel Harvey,* ed. A. B. Grosart. 3 vols. London, 1884–1885.

Herrick, Robert. *The Poetical Works of Robert Herrick,* ed. F. W. Moorman. Oxford: Clarendon Press, 1915.

Heywood, John. John Heywood's *Works* and Miscellaneous Short Poems, ed. Burton A. Milligan. Illinois Studies in Language and Literature, no. 41. Urbana: The University of Illinois Press, 1956. *Johan Johan* (Bevington).

Heywood, Thomas. *The Dramatic Works of Thomas Heywood,* ed. R. H. Shepherd. 6 vols. London: John Pearson, 1874. *How a Man May Choose a Good Wife from a Bad,* ed. A. E. H. Swaen (Bang, 1912).

Higgins, John. *The First Parte of the Mirour for Magistrates.* In Parts Added to *The Mirror for Magistrates,* ed. Lily B. Campbell. Cambridge: Cambridge University Press, 1946.

Hulme, Hilda M. *Explorations in Shakespeare's Language.* London: Longmans, 1962.

Jonson, Ben. *Ben Jonson,* ed. C. H. Herford, Percy and Evelyn Simpson. 11 vols. Oxford: Clarendon Press, 1925–1952.

Kyd, Thomas. *The Works of Thomas Kyd,* ed. F. S. Boas. Oxford: Clarendon Press, 1901.

Lodge, Thomas. *Rosalynde* (Bullough, 2).

Lupset, Thomas. *All for Money* (Schell).

Lyly, John. *The Complete Works of John Lyly,* ed. R. Warwick Bond. Oxford: Clarendon Press, 1902.

Marlowe, Christopher. *The Complete Plays of Christopher Marlowe,* ed. Irving Ribner. New York: The Odyssey Press, 1963. *Marlowe's Poems,* ed. L. C. Martin. New York: The Dial Press, 1931.

Marston, John. *Antonio and Mellida, Antonio's Revenge,* ed. G. K. Hunter (Regents, 1965). *The Dutch Courtesan,* ed. M. L. Wine (Regents, 1965). *The Fawn,* ed. Gerald A. Smith (Regents, 1965). *The Malcontent,* ed. George K. Hunter (Revels, 1975). All other: *The Plays of John Marston,* ed. H. Harvey Wood. 3 vols. Edinburgh: Oliver and Boyd, 1934–1938. *The Poems of John Marston,* ed. Arnold Davenport. Liverpool: Liverpool University Press, 1961.

Massinger, Philip. *The Plays and Poems of Philip Massinger*, ed. Philip Edwards and Colin Gibson. 5 vols. Oxford: Clarendon Press, 1976.

Middleton, Thomas, *The Works of Thomas Middleton*, ed. A. H. Bullen. 8 vols. London: John C. Nimmo, 1885–1886.

Munday, Anthony et al. *Sir Thomas More* (Brooke),

Nashe, Thomas. *The Works of Thomas Nashe*, ed. Ronald B. McKerrow. 5 vols. Oxford: Clarendon Press, 1904–1910. Rpt., with corrections and supplementary notes by F. P. Wilson, 1958.

Parnassus. The Three Parnassus Plays (1598–1601), ed. J. B. Leishman. London: Ivor Nicholson and Watson, 1949.

Peele, George. *The Life and Works of George Peele*, ed. C. T. Prouty et al. 3 vols. New Haven: Yale University Press, 1952–1970.

Pettie, George. *A Petite Pallace of Pettie his Pleasure*, ed. Herbert Hartman. London: Oxford University Press, 1938. Preston, Thomas. *Cambises* (Adams).

Puttenham, George. *The Arte of English Poesie*, ed. Gladys D. Willcock and Alice Walker. Cambridge: Cambridge University Press, 1936.

Redford, John. *Wit and Science* (Bevington).

Sackville, Thomas and Thomas Norton. *Gorboduc* (Adams).

Sampson, William. *The Vow Breaker* (Bang, 1914).

Sharpham, Edward. *Cupid's Whirligig*, ed. Allardyce Nicoll. London: The Golden Cockerell Press, 1926.

Sidney, Sir Philip. *The Complete Works of Sir Philip Sidney*, ed. Albert Feuillerat. 4 vols. Cambridge: Cambridge University Press, 1912–1926.

Southwell, Robert. *The Poems of Robert Southwell*, ed. James H. McDonald and Nancy Pollard Brown. Oxford: Clarendon Press, 1967.

Spenser, Edward. *The Complete Poetical Works of Edmund Spenser*, ed. R. E. Neil Dodge. Boston: Houghton Mifflin, 1908.

?Stevenson, William. *Gammer Gurton's Needle* (Adams).

Stubbes, Philip. *Philip Stubbes's Anatomy of the Abuses in England in Shakspere's Youth*, ed. Frederick J. Furnivall. New Shakspere Society, ser. 6, no. 12. London: N. Trübner, 1882.

Tottel. Tottel's Miscellany (1557–1587), ed. Hyder Edward Rollins. 2 vols. Cambridge, Mass.: Harvard University Press, 1929.

Tourneur, Cyril. *The Atheist's Tragedy*, ed. Irving Ribner (Revels, 1964).

———. *The Revenger's Tragedy*, ed. R. A. Foakes (Revels, 1966).

Udall, Nicholas. *Ralph Roister Doister* (Adams).

———. *Respublica* (Schell),

Wager, William. *Enough Is as Good as a Feast, The Longer Thou Livest the More Fool Thou Art*, ed. R. Mark Benbow (Regents, 1967).

Wapull, George. *The Tide Tarrieth No Man* (Schell).

Webster, John. *The Complete Works of John Webster*, ed. F. L. Lucas. 4 vols. London: Chatto and Windus, 1927.

Whetstone, George. *Promos and Cassandra* (Bullough, 2).

Wilson, F.P. "The Proverbial Wisdom of Shakespeare" (MHRA 1961, expanded), in *Shakespearian and Other Studies*, ed. Helen Gardner. Oxford: Clarendon Press, 1969, pp. 143–175.

Woodes, Nathaniel. *The Conflict of Conscience* (Schell).